Pitching to the Pennant

Memorable Teams in Baseball History

Pitching to the Pennant
The 1954 Cleveland Indians

Edited by **Joseph Wancho**

Associate Editors: **Rick Huhn, Leonard Levin, Bill Nowlin, and Steve Johnson**

Published by the **University of Nebraska Press, Lincoln and London,** and the **Society for American Baseball Research**

Library of Congress Cataloging-in-Publication Data
Pitching to the pennant : the 1954 Cleveland Indians / edited by
Joseph Wancho ; associate editors, Rick Huhn, Leonard Levin, Bill
Nowlin, and Steve Johnson.
pages   cm.   —(Memorable teams in baseball history)
ISBN 978-0-8032-4587-7 (pbk.)—ISBN 978-0-8032-5472-5 (epub)—
ISBN 978-0-8032-5473-2 (mobi)
1. Cleveland Indians (Baseball team)—History—20th century. 2.
World Series (Baseball) (1954) I. Wancho, Joseph.
GV875.C7P568 2014
796.357'64097713209045—dc23
2013041972

Set in Sabon by Laura Wellington.

Contents

Acknowledgments . . *vii*

Introduction . . *ix*
Joseph Wancho

1. Hank Greenberg . . *1*
Ralph Berger

2. Al Lopez . . *11*
Maxwell Kates

3. Tony Cuccinello . . *18*
Barb Mantegani

4. Mel Harder . . *21*
Mark Stewart

5. Red Kress . . *29*
Chris Rainey

6. Bill Lobe . . *35*
Joseph Wancho

7. A Seven-Year-Old's Perspective on the 1954 Indians . . *37*
David Bohmer

8. Timeline, April 13–April 30 . . *39*
Joseph Wancho

9. Bob Feller . . *41*
C. Paul Rogers III

10. Dave Hoskins . . *51*
John Watkins

11. Don Mossi . . *55*
Mark Stewart

12. Hank Majeski . . *62*
Mark Hodermarsky

13. Dale Mitchell . . *65*
Scott Longert

14. Mike Garcia . . *71*
Warren Corbett

15. Timeline, May 1–May 16 . . *76*
Joseph Wancho

16. Larry Doby . . *78*
John McMurray

17. George Strickland . . *83*
Mel Marmer

18. Cleveland Stadium (1932–96) . . *88*
Tom Wancho

19. Jim Hegan . . *92*
Rick Balazs

20. Timeline, May 17–May 31 . . *97*
Joseph Wancho

21. Dave Philley . . *99*
Cort Vitty

22. Bob Lemon . . *103*
Jon Barnes

23. Rudy Regalado . . *110*
Steve Johnson

24. Ray Narleski . . *116*
Joseph Wancho

25. Timeline, June 1–June 15 . . *121*
Joseph Wancho

26. Sam Dente . . *123*
Jack Morris

27. 1954 Cleveland Indians by the Numbers . . *130*
Dan Fields

28. Jim Dyck . . *134*
Greg Erion

29. Bob Chakales . . *141*
Bill Nowlin

30. Timeline, June 16–June 30 . . *152*
Joseph Wancho

31. Al Rosen . . *154*
Ralph Berger

32. Wally Westlake . . *159*
Bob Hurte

33. Dick Tomanek . . *166*
   Thomas Ayers
34. Dave Pope . . *170*
   Tom Heinlein
35. Timeline, July 1–July 13 . . *175*
   Joseph Wancho
36. Luke Easter . . *177*
   Justin Murphy
37. Early Wynn . . *185*
   David L. Fleitz
38. Hal Naragon . . *189*
   Tracy J. R. Collins
39. 1954 All-Star Game . . *194*
   Rick Huhn
40. Timeline, July 15–July 31 . . *200*
   Joseph Wancho
41. Al Smith . . *202*
   Gary Livacari
42. Vic Wertz . . *206*
   Mark Armour
43. Hal Newhouser . . *211*
   Mark Stewart
44. Bill Glynn . . *221*
   Richard Marsh
45. Timeline, August 1–August 15 . . *225*
   Joseph Wancho
46. José G. Santiago Guzmán . . *227*
   Edwin Fernández
47. Bob Kennedy . . *230*
   Philip A. Cola
48. Mickey Grasso . . *234*
   Cort Vitty

49. Bobby Avila . . *239*
   John Stahl
50. Joe Ginsberg . . *244*
   Mel Marmer
51. Timeline, August 17–August 31 . . *248*
   Joseph Wancho
52. Cleveland Indians World Championships, 1920 and 1948 . . *250*
   Joseph Wancho
53. Rocky Nelson . . *257*
   David L. Fleitz
54. Art Houtteman . . *262*
   Warren Corbett
55. Bob Hooper . . *267*
   Joseph Wancho
56. Timeline, September 1–September 14 . . *270*
   Joseph Wancho
57. Ken Coleman . . *272*
   Curt Smith
58. Jim Britt . . *279*
   Mort Bloomberg
59. Jimmy Dudley . . *283*
   Joseph Wancho
60. Timeline, September 17–September 26 . . *286*
   Joseph Wancho
61. 1954 World Series . . *287*
   Jeanne M. Mallett
62. A Day in the Grandstand . . *297*
   Matthew Silverman
   Notes and References . . *303*
   Contributors . . *335*

Acknowledgments

Pitching to the Pennant was created as the result of a discussion between Steve Johnson, Rick Huhn, and me at the Seymour Medal Conference in April 2009. It was my good fortune that Steve and Rick joined me in this project, because their willingness to share the workload made the task so much easier. Not only did they each contribute an article to the book, but they also undertook some of the editing responsibilities. Steve also assisted with photo identification and selection. They both helped fact-check, with Rick undertaking the majority of the bios and articles.

Bill Nowlin and Len Levin proofread every article in the book, each offering sound editing critique. Bill, who has been at the helm of many SABR Bio Project books, was kind enough to draw from those experiences and share his ideas with me. He was always willing to help whenever I asked. Len is the most prolific editor for the Bio Project, with more than 600 bios to his credit. His patience and willingness to help at a moment's notice was appreciated.

It was good timing that the project was far enough along when SABR and University of Nebraska Press (UNP) announced their partnership to create the Memorable Teams in Baseball History series. Mark Armour and Bill Nowlin worked with UNP on which books were to be included, and *Pitching to the Pennant* was accepted as one of the original six books for the series. Rob Taylor and Courtney Ochsner of UNP made this first-time editor's experience a reasonably enjoyable one.

A big thanks goes to the respective photo departments of the Cleveland Public Library and Cleveland State University Library. They were both very helpful in the search for photos, pulling endless photo files of every player and coach. The Photo Duplication Department at CPL was very efficient placing the photos onto CDs and explaining the billing and crediting process. Special thanks to both Greg Crouse and Patricia Rzonca. Greg jumped in and lent a hand with the fact-checking when we needed an extra eye. Patricia provided a pair of fresh eyes, proofreading the manuscript as it made a final pass. Finally, a tip of the Chief Wahoo cap goes to Mark Armour, Chairman of SABR's Bio Project Committee. His advice and general support of the project was of great value.

Last but not least, as the phrase goes, my thanks to the many SABR members who contributed to the project by writing a bio or an article. It is their work that makes this book such a wonderful final product. To have so many talented authors come together between the covers of one book is truly amazing. They volunteered their time, and I am indebted to them. It was my pleasure to work with each individual.

Introduction

Joseph Wancho

In Cleveland, Ohio, we have suffered mightily because of our sports teams. If one were to combine the city's losing seasons from the last world championship (the Browns football team in 1964), the total would be 138 seasons. That's a lot of ineptness, bad luck, embarrassment, and just plain losing. It always makes me wince when I hear Cubs fans bemoaning their team's misfortune. Try a whole city losing and get back to me.

Because of this, we Clevelanders have taken to naming the failures of our sports teams. Most Cleveland sports fans can tell you where they were or whom they were with when "The Drive," "The Fumble," "The Shot," "Red Right 88," "The Sweep," and "The Meltdown" occurred. That last reference is to Game Seven of the 1997 World Series. When asked how long it has taken him to get over that loss, former Indians manager Mike Hargrove still replies, "I will let you know."

Before all of these heartbreaks occurred, a different generation of fans suffered from the result of the 1954 World Series. Quick, which team held the record for most regular-season wins in the American League until 1998 and currently holds the highest winning percentage? That's right: the 1954 Cleveland Indians, with 111 wins that enabled the Tribe to win at a clip of .721. As the ball club departed by train for New York, from track 13 no less, they were considered the favorites to win the fall classic over their counterparts from the senior circuit, the New York Giants.

However, their hopes were dashed in Game One by Willie Mays and his back-to-the-plate catch at the Polo Grounds. Oh sure, they played three more games, but after the lid-lifter, the Giants washed the starch out of Cleveland.

The Indians fielded a handful of competitive teams—a child's handful—over the next three decades, and it would be forty-one years before a pennant-winning flag fluttered in the wind above the ballpark. They were forty-one long and almost laughable years. "Stressful" would not even be a proper adjective when describing these four decades, since after sellout crowds in cavernous Cleveland Stadium for Opening Day, crowds rarely approached twenty thousand unless there was a promotion like Farmer's Night or fireworks on the Fourth of July.

Cleveland is a football town. Ohio is a football state. That's just the way things are. From high school football games on crisp, cool Friday nights to "Script Ohio" and the Ohio State Buckeyes on Saturday afternoons, to the Cleveland Browns on Sundays. In 1954, while the Indians' hopes were squashed by the Giants, the Browns claimed the NFL championship with a 56–10 victory over Detroit. Ohio State shared a national championship with UCLA after posting a perfect 10-0 season, including a Rose Bowl win over Southern Cal. As the Indians struggled while the NFL was becoming popular, fans clung to the team that was winning more consistently. And that was the Browns.

Even as the Indians were setting records on the diamond in the summer of '54, news of one of the country's most sensational murders came to light. On July 4, Marilyn Sheppard, the pregnant wife of Dr. Sam Sheppard, was beaten to death in suburban Bay Village. The controversial murder case, which was never solved, pushed any news of the

Indians to the "bottom of the fold" in the Cleveland dailies.

And yet, the story of this great team deserves to be told. *Pitching to the Pennant* is a biographical sketch of the entire 1954 Indians team. Included are biographies ranging from Hall of Fame players Bob Feller, Bob Lemon, and Larry Doby to MVP Al Rosen, to bench players Rudy Regalado and Bob Chakales. There are also stories about Cleveland Stadium, the 1954 All Star Game and the World Series, as well as some personal perspectives on the 1954 Indians.

The 1954 edition of the Tribe goes largely forgotten because the team did not win a world championship. But in truth, the 1954 Indians, with two twenty-game winners; a third pitcher who won nineteen and the ERA title; the league leaders in home runs, RBIS, and batting average; the *Sporting News* MVP; and six future members of Cooperstown, including the manager, might have been the best Indians team ever.

Please accept my invitation to get to know these men, relive an important part of baseball history, and acquaint yourself with many untold stories of the 1954 Cleveland Indians. This book is written entirely by members of the Society for American Baseball Research (SABR). It is their superb research and writing that make it a must in any baseball fan's library.

Pitching to the Pennant

Chapter 1. **Hank Greenberg**

Ralph Berger

Hank Greenberg— Greenberg was a two-time Most Valuable Player with Detroit. He was the home run king of his era, leading the American League four times. After his playing days, he served as the Indians' general manager until 1957.

Tall, awkward, and lumbering—that's how many baseball scouts saw Hank Greenberg. What they didn't see was a man determined to become the best person he could be. Through hard work and faith in himself, Greenberg became a star baseball player and a success in all other aspects of his life.

Henry Benjamin Greenberg was born to Romanian Jewish immigrants on New Year's Day 1911 in Greenwich Village, New York. His father and mother met in America and were married in New York. Initially, the family lived in tenements on Barrow Street and then Perry Street. Hank had two brothers, Benjamin, four years older, and Joseph, five years younger, and a sister, Lillian, two years older. By the time Hank was six, his father's busi-

ness had grown enough to enable them to move to the Crotona Park section of the Bronx. His father, David, owned a small textile mill where material was shrunk in order to make suits, and his mother, Sarah (née Schwartz), was a housewife. The family's life in Crotona Park was peaceful and uneventful. Since it was a predominantly Jewish section, Greenberg knew practically nothing of anti-Semitism. Hank attended PS 44. His parents wanted him to be a professional man, a doctor or lawyer, but he loved baseball and became a professional baseball player. All of his siblings graduated from college and became professional people. The neighbors called him a bum because of his baseball playing and clucked their tongues when they spoke of

Mrs. Greenberg and her son Henry. Hank was six foot three by the time he was a teenager, but he was skinny and awkward.

He took to sports with a vengeance. Nicknamed "Big Bruggy" while a student at James Monroe High School, Greenberg became an outstanding athlete in baseball, basketball (he led his basketball team to a New York City title in 1929), and soccer.

Baseball was his passion, though. To find Hank, all one had to do was to go to the Crotona Park recreation field to watch him swing at pitch after pitch until his hands blistered.

After graduation from high school in 1929, Hank played semipro baseball for the Red Bank (New Jersey) Towners and later with Brooklyn's Bay Parkways. The scouts were after Greenberg. The Giants gave him a tryout, but John McGraw thought he was too awkward. Paul Krichell, of the Yankees, took Hank to a Yankees game. As they watched batting practice, Krichell turned to Greenberg and said, pointing to Lou Gehrig, "He's all washed up. In a few years you'll be the Yankees' first baseman."[1] Greenberg knew better and decided not to go with the Yankees. Instead, he signed with Detroit in September of 1929 for $9,000, feeling he would have a better chance of becoming their first baseman. Part of the deal was that he would attend New York University. After only one semester, he dropped out to concentrate fully on baseball.

Hank played in 1930 for Hartford, then at Raleigh, North Carolina; he even got into one game for Detroit, pinch-hitting on September 14. In 1931 he was at Evansville in the Three I League. While at Raleigh, one of his teammates walked slowly around Hank, staring at him. Greenberg asked him what he was looking at. The fellow said he was just looking, as he'd never seen a Jew before. "The way he said it," noted Greenberg, "he might as well have said, 'I've never seen a giraffe before. I let him keep looking for a while."[2] The befuddled teammate admitted that he'd seen nothing, that Greenberg looked like anyone else.

In 1932 at Beaumont, in the highly regarded Texas League, he became a feared slugger, hitting thirty-nine homers and leading Beaumont to the Texas League title. On his way to Detroit while playing in the Minors, Hank stuck to his work ethic and steadily improved his batting and fielding. As he saw it, with so little to do in small towns, he passed the time working on his skills. In Beaumont, Greenberg was not an oddity as he was in other southern towns. Beaumont had a strong Jewish presence, and one congregant of the local synagogue remembers Greenberg attending services there.

In an interview with Mike Ross of the Society for American Baseball Research, Greenberg recounted the life of a rookie: "No one would talk to me. Waite Hoyt's locker was next to mine and he never even said hello to me. Of course the veteran players always looked upon rookies as someone who could take your job away. But I tried to be kind to rookies and would at times take them out to dinner. I guess it kind of made me feel like a big shot. Heck, I could afford it."[3]

When Greenberg joined the Tigers in 1933, he immediately ran into tough times. Bucky Harris, the manager, refused to play Greenberg because he favored Harry Davis, a slick-fielding but light-hitting first baseman. The Tigers had paid $75,000 for Davis. Harris was determined that Davis was going to be the first baseman. Harris placed Greenberg at third base with disastrous results. Greenberg, unhappy with the situation, went to Frank Navin, the fair and popular owner of the Tigers. Listening quietly, Navin told Hank that he would bat against left-handed pitching and Davis would bat against right-handed pitching. When Harris refused to do this, Navin phoned down to Harris and told him in no uncertain terms that Greenberg was to bat against left-handed pitching. Harris complied. Hank, playing in 117 games, batted .301, hit 12 homers, and drove in 87 runs.

The next season, 1934, Harris was gone and Mickey Cochrane took over as manager. Greenberg and Cochrane hit it off immediately, and Hank began to blossom as a hitter and a better-fielding first baseman. Greenberg showed that he had a great ability to learn and applied himself assiduously to the tasks of batting and fielding. Cochrane showed his confidence in Greenberg by selling Harry Davis. Hank now had first base all to himself.

At the age of twenty-three, Greenberg was adept at negotiating, and when contract season came around, Greenberg wanted a raise from $3,300 to $5,500. Owner Frank Navin refused to give in to the player's demand. Finally, in February, Navin called Greenberg and read him the riot act, but at the end he gave Hank $5,000 and added a $500 bonus if the Tigers finished third or higher in the standings. Detroit, with Mickey Cochrane as manager, won their first pennant since 1909. Greenberg took home his bonus of $500.

During the 1934 season, Rosh Hashanah, the Jewish New Year, took place in September when the Tigers were chasing the pennant. Greenberg was in a quandary whether or not to play on that religious day. He consulted a rabbi, who told him it was permissible to play. He pounded out two homers that day to win the game 2–1. However, Hank observed Yom Kippur and did not play.

The 1934 Tigers team would send four players to the Hall of Fame: Goose Goslin, Mickey Cochrane, Charlie Gehringer, and Hank Greenberg. The Tigers' infield, known as the Battalion of Death, drove in an amazing 462 runs in 1934, and the Tigers as a team scored 957 runs, with only one team coming within 150 runs of that total. Greenberg batted .339 and drove in 139 runs, with 63 doubles and 26 homers. The Battalion of Death infield was awesome in its hitting. Collectively, Greenberg, second baseman Charley Gehringer, shortstop Billy Rogell, and third baseman Marv Owen combined to also hit .327 with 48 homers. Everyone in the infield drove in 100 runs or more except Owen, who batted in 96. Charley Gehringer said that with men on base, Greenberg was a tough man to get out.

They played the St. Louis Cardinals in the 1934 World Series and lost to them in a wild seven-game series. Greenberg batted .321 in the series but struck out nine times, seven coming with men on base.

In 1935 Greenberg slugged 36 homers, drove in 170 runs, and helped the Tigers return to the Fall Classic against the Chicago Cubs. He was named the Most Valuable Player in the American League that season.

In the second game of the series, Fabian Kowalik broke Greenberg's wrist with a pitch. Greenberg stayed in the game and even tried to score from first on a two-out single the same inning. But he could not continue to play in the series because his wrist swelled up. Without Greenberg in the lineup, the Tigers still managed to win the Series from the Cubs when Goose Goslin singled in Mickey Cochrane in the bottom of the ninth of Game Six with the winning run.

Twelve games into the 1936 season, Greenberg was off to a sizzling start with sixteen runs batted in. But the furies struck again. He broke the same wrist when he had a collision with Washington outfielder Jake Powell. Many felt then that Hank's baseball career was over. Others felt that Powell had intentionally tried to injure Greenberg. Stoically, Greenberg kept his feelings to himself. The Tigers would not repeat as winners that year. Greenberg's injury, along with manager Mickey Cochrane's nervous breakdown, took the heart out of the team.

In 1937 Greenberg stroked 49 doubles and 40 homers and batted in 183 runs, one shy of the AL record held by Lou Gehrig. Hank regretted not breaking Gehrig's RBI record more than his failure in chasing Ruth's home run record. To Greenberg, driving in runs was the greater accomplishment. There was no more talk of his career ending.

During the 1938 season, Greenberg was in pursuit of Babe Ruth's home run record of sixty. During his chase, he had multiple homers in one game eleven times, a record. With five games left in the season, Greenberg had fifty-eight homers, but he failed to hit another one. On the last day of the season, the Tigers played a doubleheader in Cleveland. The Indians moved those games to the more spacious Cleveland Municipal Stadium. Bob Feller pitched the first game and struck out a record eighteen batters, fanning Greenberg twice. Even with his many strikeouts, Feller lost the game. In the second game, Greenberg managed a double that clattered off the distant fence in left-center field, but he had no homers. With twilight settling over the field, umpire George Moriarty reluctantly called the game because of darkness. Turning to Hank, he said, "I'm sorry, Hank, this is as far as I can go." Greenberg, downcast and tired, replied, "That's all right, George, this is as far as I can go too."[4] Hank said he didn't feel tired or tense the last week but admitted, when it was all over, that he felt a bit depressed and very fatigued. In 1961, when Roger Maris was chasing the homer record, Greenberg understood the terrible pressure Maris was under. "It's a feeling that time is running out and you become impatient. You get paralyzed at the plate. You are afraid to swing at a bad pitch and you end up taking good ones."[5]

Greenberg felt the pressure while chasing Ruth's home run record and became increasingly aware that he was a hero to the Jewish population, who identified with him and saw themselves as not helpless. He was a Jew, tall, strong, with his head held high, proving to be one of the best ballplayers and refuting the idea that Jews were weak. Moreover, Greenberg was now closely reading the accounts of the crisis in Europe and becoming more cognizant of his role as a Jewish hero.

Greenberg never used his being Jewish as an excuse for moments when the going was rough. When Harry Eisenstat, a young Jewish pitcher, came to the Tigers, Greenberg warned him never to use the alibi of being Jewish. He simply told Eisenstat to behave himself and work and play hard.

In 1939 the Tigers slipped to fifth place, despite thirty-three homers by Greenberg. The same year,

questions about Greenberg's first baseman's glove came up. Some said it was too big and had too many laces in which to snare the ball. To a lot of people, it was akin to a catcher's glove. This prompted one scribe to write, "The glove has 3 lengths of barbed wire, 4 corners, 2 side pockets, a fish net, rod and trowel, a small sled, a library of classics, a compact anti-aircraft gun, a change of clothes and a pocket comb."[6] After due consideration, the Commissioner's Office declared Hank's glove illegal. The prescribed measurements were officially declared to be eight inches wide at the palm and twelve inches high. Hank's glove exceeded those measurements.

But more important was the geopolitical climate of the world. Hitler was on the march, Mussolini had conquered Ethiopia, and the Japanese were ravaging China. On September 1, 1939, Hitler invaded Poland, and World War II was on. The lights went out all over Europe and cast a pall over America.

At the end of the 1939 season, the Tigers asked Greenberg to take his big bat to left field and take a $5,000 cut from his $40,000 salary. The idea was to get Rudy York's bat into the lineup on a regular basis by putting him at first base, where they felt his fielding woes would cause the least damage. Greenberg had worked hard to become a more than adequate first baseman. Now, after all that work, he was asked to play a totally unfamiliar position as well as to take a salary cut. Hank thought it over carefully and came up with a counterproposal: "I want the same salary as last year. I would go down to spring training and work out in left field and work to try to learn the position real hard. You can decide after spring training is over, whether you want me to play the outfield. If you want me to stay in the outfield, you will have to give me a $10,000 bonus."[7] Greenberg felt he was taking all the risks in this experiment and had the most to lose. Greenberg's work ethic kicked into high gear. In fact, he went to many spring training camps, at his own expense, to question the best left fielders of that time on how to play the position.

The experiment of 1940 paid off. The Tigers took the AL pennant, and Greenberg got his $10,000 bonus. He also slugged 41 homers and drove in 150 runs. During September, he carried the team on his back by blasting out 15 homers, which enabled the Tigers to make up a four-game deficit on their way to the pennant. Hank won the September Player of the Month award. The Tigers lost the World Series to the Cincinnati Reds. The series went the full seven games. But the Reds prevailed by overcoming a 3–2 deficit in games with superb pitching by Bucky Walters, who shut out the Tigers in Game Six, and another gem by Paul Derringer, who outpitched Bobo Newsom in a 2–1 win. Greenberg batted .357 in the series, driving in six runs. Greenberg, again, won the Most Valuable Player Award in the American League and is one of only three players to win MVPs at two different positions.

Meanwhile, the war in Europe took a nasty turn for the British and French. The Nazi blitzkrieg, faced with the French Maginot Line, took an end run around it and overran the Lowlands, smashing into northeastern France. The French capitulated in June 1940. The British army was trapped against the English Channel at Dunkerque; only a daring and valiant effort by the British navy and civilians saved most of the men trapped. Britain was now left alone to face the might of the German military. Greenberg was well aware of these events, following news reports closely.

The year 1941 was chaotic for Greenberg. The United States instituted a draft to strengthen its military, and Greenberg's number, 321, was low, meaning he would probably be called for duty sometime early in 1941. The press, eager to get his opinion on his potential call-up, pursued Greenberg relentlessly. His first statement was one he would repeat over and over again. He would not seek deferment on any grounds, and when his time came he would willingly go. But the rumors surrounding his status would not go away. Some speculated he would seek deferment based on his position as a "necessary employee." Again, he said he would not. Some said he would be rejected because of flat feet. To escape all this, he took a trip to Hawaii. On his return to the mainland on a bitterly cold February night, reporters besieged him at La Guardia Airport. They asked the same questions about his draft status. Greenberg wondered what the fuss was all about, noting that he wasn't the only person who might be going into the army. The press persisted. Finally, Hank, who was usually a genial fellow in answering questions, became agitated. He refused to answer any more questions and got into a car with his father and his brother Joe, and headed home.

At spring training, Greenberg underwent his army physical and was pronounced unfit for military duty because of flat feet. The press jumped all over this, and one wag said, "What is he going to do, fire a gun with his feet?" Others said he had bribed someone in the army or the Selective Service System. Stung by all this, Greenberg asked for another physical, and this time he passed and was classified 1-A.

He was told that he would be inducted on May 7. The turmoil surrounding his status had not sat well with Greenberg, and he started off the season poorly. On his last day, he did belt two homers. Glad that it was all over, Greenberg went into the army, away from the press and their tiresome questions. Hank took his basic training at Fort Custer, Michigan. Greenberg served several months, before being released in early December 1941 because he was over the age of twenty-eight. He had risen to the rank of sergeant in the tank corps.

A few days later, the Japanese bombed the U.S. Navy base at Pearl Harbor, Hawaii. Shortly thereafter, Greenberg enlisted in the air force and was sent to Officers Training School. Upon graduation, he was commissioned a first lieutenant. At first, he did inspection work at air bases, and then he requested a transfer to a war zone. He was sent to the China-Burma-India Theater and was part of the first B-29 unit to go overseas, and he flew on missions over the Himalayas, affectionately known as the "Hump."

Greenberg was recalled from China in the middle of 1944. Sicily had been liberated and the Italians had surrendered. The Nazis were being driven back on all fronts, and the Japanese were giving up, island after island. Greenberg was reassigned to an outfit in New York at 44 Broad Street. The war was coming to an end in Europe, and the Nazis surrendered on May 7, 1945. Halfway through the 1945 season, Greenberg was released from the air force with the rank of captain, four battle stars, and a Presidential Unit Citation. Hank had hardly swung a bat for four and a half years.

Everybody welcomed Greenberg's return to baseball. Hank was now more than a great ballplayer returning to play; he was also a hero, having served his country for four and a half years. The ethnic tag of Jewish ballplayer also disappeared. It appeared he had been fully assimilated.

He worked out tirelessly and returned to the Tiger lineup in July. He felt pretty good but thought that his legs were not what they used to be. He homered in his first game. The Tigers were in a tight pennant race with the Washington Senators in 1945, one that came down to the end of the season. It was personal to Greenberg, who had some bad memories about the Senators. He recalled the time Jake Powell ran into him for no reason, breaking his wrist, and the Senators catcher who gave Jimmie Foxx the signs so he could tie him for the homer title in 1935. He remembered the fight with Joe Kuhel, the White Sox player who slid into him and ripped off his shoes while trying to spike him. Kuhel was now the Senators' first baseman.

On the last day of the season, the Tigers played the St. Louis Browns in a doubleheader. In the first game, Greenberg nearly cost the Tigers the game when he was caught off third base. But redemption came in the top of the ninth with the Browns leading the Tigers, 4–3. Hub Walker led off with a single. Skeeter Webb bunted him over. The throw to second base hit Walker, and Webb was safe at first. Now there were men on first and third. Eddie

Mayo laid down a bunt, sacrificing Webb to second. With men on second and third, the Browns decided to walk Doc Cramer, a left-handed hitter. Because Nellie Potter was a right-hander, they decided they had a better chance with Hank as a right-handed batter, and were hoping he would hit a grounder for a double play that would win the game for the Browns. The first pitch from Potter was a ball. Hank watched Potter's grip on the ball carefully and saw that on the next pitch Potter was going to throw a screwball. Greenberg connected and sent a long, low line drive down the left-field foul line. Greenberg's fear was that it would go foul, but it did not, and the Tigers won the game when the Browns were set down in the bottom of the ninth. Greenberg recalled, "There were hardly any people in the stands when I hit the homer and not many newspapermen either. But it was no big deal; my teammates gave me a big welcome. The best part of that homer was hearing how the Washington Senators players responded: 'Goddam that dirty Jew bastard, he beat us again.'"[8]

In the 1945 World Series, the Tigers defeated the Chicago Cubs in seven games. Greenberg hit .304, drove in seven runs, and homered twice.

On February 19, 1946, Hank Greenberg married Caral Lasker Gimbel, heiress to department store millions, in the living room of County Ordinary Edwin W. Dart in Brunswick, Georgia. They had eloped to avoid a big wedding because the Gimbel and Greenberg families, coming from vastly different levels of society, did not mix well.

In 1946 the star players returned to baseball. Now that the war was over, the fans hungrily filled the stadiums. The question in the minds of fans, managers, and the ballplayers themselves was how they would perform after missing two, three, or four years of playing time. Ted Williams, who had served as a fighter pilot for the marines, picked up right where he left off and helped the Red Sox to a pennant. Many of the returning stars regained their form and were productive players, while others suffered a drop in their former abilities. Greenberg's average fell to .277, but with a blistering September, he ended leading the league in homers with 44 and in runs batted in with 127.

The 1946 season was Greenberg's last for Detroit. While driving, he heard on his car radio that he had been waived out of the American League and claimed by the Pittsburgh Pirates for $75,000. Dan Daniel of the *New York World Telegram* suggested that it was a photograph of Hank in a Yankee uniform that led to the Tigers waiving him. The story goes that Greenberg was ordered by the air force, in August 1943, to play in an All-Star War Bond Game. He flew into New York without any equipment. The day before the game, the stars had a workout at Yankee stadium. The Yankees could not find a Detroit uniform for him, so they put him in a Yankee uniform. A photographer had him pose for a photo in the Yankee pinstripes. Three years later, the photo emerged and Hank was waived by Detroit. Daniel offered yet more speculation as to why Greenberg was immediately sent packing after the photo was released:

> Another possible reason for Greenberg's being put on the waiver list was his applying for the position of General Manager of the Tigers. Greenberg was turned down by owner Walter O. Briggs Sr., who felt that Greenberg did not have the qualifications for the job. Shortly afterwards he was put on the waiver list and no one picked him up. Was the reason for putting him on the waiver list due to his applying for the General Manager's job?

At first, Hank decided it was time to retire. But John Galbreath, owner of the Pirates, lured him into one more season by offering him a contract for $100,000. He was the first player to reach that plateau; for good measure Galbreath threw in a racehorse.

The Pirates hoped to help the pull-hitting Greenberg by shortening the left-field wall by about twenty-five feet. The area became known as Greenberg's

Gardens and later as Kiner's Korner. Bone chips in his elbow as well as other ailments during the 1947 season bothered Greenberg. His average dipped to a career-low .249, and he managed just twenty-five homers and seventy-four RBIs.

Greenberg's contributions in his year in Pittsburgh transcended his modest numbers. Always willing to help others, he set about helping Ralph Kiner to become a prodigious home run hitter. Kiner was having difficulties during the first part of the season. The Pirates were on the verge of sending him down to the Minors. Greenberg interceded and told the front office they had a potentially terrific hitter in Kiner. They listened to Hank, and with Greenberg's help, Kiner fulfilled his potential. Kiner and Greenberg were roommates on the road. Hank told Kiner that when he was chasing Ruth's home run record in 1938, he received some hate mail and death threats. But Greenberg never said that he was cheated out of his attempt to break Ruth's record. Greenberg also had words of encouragement for Jackie Robinson when he broke into baseball as the first black player.

Greenberg retired at the end of the 1947 season. Old injuries were affecting his play. The bone chips in his elbow were extremely bothersome. After his retirement, he had them removed. His career totals for nine and a half years were impressive: 1,628 hits, 1,276 runs batted in, a .313 lifetime batting average, 331 homers, 1,051 runs scored, 379 doubles, and an amazing .605 slugging average. But the most awesome statistic is his .92 runs batted in per game, tying him for the all-time lead with Lou Gehrig and Sam Thompson. Only Babe Ruth, Ted Williams, Gehrig, and Jimmie Foxx were ahead of him in the all-time slugging percentage department. One year he was out with an injury; for four and a half years he was in the military. One can only speculate what numbers he would have put up had he not missed those years. Five times Greenberg was voted into the All-Star Game, and in 1956 he was inducted into the Hall of Fame. In 1983, just thirty-seven years after his leaving Detroit, the Tigers retired his No. 5 uniform. Greenberg observed that Lefty Grove, Bob Feller, and Dizzy Dean were the toughest pitchers he had to face.

A little-known record that Hank shares with Babe Ruth was his 96 extra-base hits or more in four different seasons: 96 in 1934, 98 in 1935, 103 in 1937, and 99 in 1940. Ruth is the only other player to have 96 or more extra-base hits in four different seasons. Gehrig had two, Joe DiMaggio had one, Jimmie Foxx had one, and Rogers Hornsby did it two times. Sluggers like Ted Williams, Willie Mays, and Hank Aaron never had 96 or more extra-base hits in any season.

Hank was not through with baseball. He became an assistant to Bill Veeck, who owned the Cleveland Indians. He later became the Indians' general manager. Greenberg was instrumental in bringing success to the Indians, especially when they won the pennant in 1954. But things turned sour, and he was relieved of his duties after the 1957 season.

Despite the Indians' general success, Greenberg's tenure in the front office was often stormy, due in large part to his own personality. A highly intelligent man, Greenberg had his own idea of how things should be done and was as stubborn as he was intelligent. He was ambivalent toward Larry Doby, the first African American player in the American League, believing that Doby thought "he wasn't getting the publicity that Jackie Robinson was getting."[9] In a subtly structured sentence, he seemed to damn Doby with faint praise: "But as far as being a ballplayer, he sure could play."[10] He fired the popular Lou Boudreau because Boudreau didn't fit his notion of the manager as company man. He couldn't wait to get rid of Ken Keltner to bring in Al Rosen, who had been held back because of the war and the popular Keltner. Ultimately, he and Rosen had a falling-out over money. He made his dissatisfaction with Al Lopez so well known that Lopez resigned after the 1956 season to become manager of the White Sox. Lopez turned the Sox into pennant winners in short order while the Indians began to move down in the standings. Along with Lopez he lost Luis Aparicio, who became the spark plug of the White Sox. According to Bill James, Aparicio made a handshake agreement to sign with the Indians for $10,000, but Greenberg balked at paying the bonus and offended Aparicio during the subsequent negotiations, and Aparicio signed with the White Sox for $6,000. Four Hall of Fame members and two high-quality players—Hank Greenberg managed to alienate a lot of talent over a few years.

Bill Veeck and Greenberg had become close friends. When Hank was released from his Cleveland duties as general manager, he was appointed vice president of the Chicago White Sox and became part owner, along with Veeck, in 1959. Greenberg, an astute person, also became an investor in Wall Street and made millions in the 1960s bull market.

During his tenure as a baseball administrator, Greenberg was partially responsible for the creation of the player pension plan and organized the split of World Series and All-Star Game receipts on the basis of 65 percent for the owners and 35 percent for the players. He also testified on behalf of Curt Flood in Flood's unsuccessful anti-trust suit against Major League Baseball. Bill Veeck felt that Greenberg would have made a fine commissioner of baseball.

Meanwhile, Hank's marriage to Caral had disintegrated. Caral had a life of her own. She was fond of show horses, art, and music. Hank was always busy with his administrative duties in baseball. Caral felt she was bringing cultural awareness into Hank's life; unfortunately, her efforts drove them apart. Eventually, Caral asked for and got a divorce because of their differing lifestyles. They were the proud parents of three fine children. Hank gained custody of them and moved to New York so they could be near their mother. Hank's older son, Glenn, took to football rather than baseball and was an outstanding defensive lineman at Yale. Their daughter, Alva, owns a newspaper and successfully runs its advertising department. Steve, their younger son, was an English major and a fine athlete at

Yale. Steve had a five-year Minor League Baseball career. He went on to become a lawyer and a baseball player's agent. Bill Madlock was his first client.

After selling his share in the White Sox at a tidy profit, Greenberg retired to Beverly Hills, California. There, he lived the good life and became a star amateur tennis player, winning many titles. He married Mary Jo Tarola, a minor movie actress (known on screen as Linda Douglas) in Beverly Hills on November 18, 1966. Mary Jo appeared in three movies but did not relish being a movie actress. She was content with being Hank's wife.

In 1985 Greenberg was having physical problems, and doctors were having a hard time in coming up with the true diagnosis. One doctor suggested he go to a urologist for X-rays. Greenberg went to Dr. Norman Nemoy; after a battery of tests, the doctor discovered a tumor in one of his kidneys. Hank was told that it was cancer and that an immediate operation was needed. Greenberg's cancer-ridden kidney and tumor were removed, but the cancer had spread. Determined to lick the illness, Greenberg fought for thirteen months before succumbing on September 4, 1986. He was survived by Mary Jo, his children, two brothers, a sister, and eight grandchildren. Greenberg is buried in Hillside Memorial Park in Los Angeles.

In the 1930s, baseball's ethnic characteristics were changing. The Irish and Germans that had dominated the baseball scene were declining. Now Italians, Poles, and Jews were entering the game. Two of the marquee players who fit those ethnic groups were Hank Greenberg and Joe DiMaggio. Ethnicity was overtly cited in newspapers as well as on the field. Players called Greenberg and other Jewish players "Christ Killers" and DiMaggio and fellow Italians "Dago."

Greenberg followed DiMaggio's career closely and set his sights on outdoing him. Greenberg and DiMaggio were the first of their ethnic groups to become great stars in the Majors. The similarity ends there. DiMaggio, a taciturn, dour person, remained solely a great baseball player. Poorly educated, he did very little in his life after baseball to further his education or advance himself. Greenberg, on the other hand, was articulate, intelligent, and outspoken, a man of ideas with ambition beyond being merely a baseball player. Greenberg transcended his life as a star baseball player and went on to other careers. DiMaggio was content to be called "the greatest living baseball player." DiMaggio kept himself in the limelight by doing ads for Mr. Coffee and the Bowery Bank and being the husband, albeit briefly, of Marilyn Monroe. DiMaggio seemingly remained a humble man, and the fans accepted this. Greenberg, on the other hand, was intelligent, aggressive, contentious, outspoken, and made some enemies. Greenberg did not shun the limelight, but neither did he care if he was in it.

As a ballplayer, Greenberg's ethnic background was irrelevant only as long as he was hitting. But on the broader level of society, Greenberg still found doors that were closed to him. In spite of his status as a star baseball player, he was not permitted into certain areas of American life.

Hank Greenberg was a complex individual. His sterling career as a baseball player was only a stepping-stone to a life full of ambition, risk taking, and success. Never afraid to speak his own mind, he hammered away at life as he hammered a baseball. Through hard work, he achieved a victory over bigotry and left this life as an example to be followed. Reluctant at first, Greenberg bravely took on the mantle of hero for the Jewish population in their fight against ethnic hatred and the forces of Fascism and Nazism. Greenberg was a "superstar" baseball player, a wealthy, self-made man, but most of all, he lived life to the fullest and never backed off from anyone or anything.

Greenberg's journey began in the Bronx with stops along the way in Hartford, Evansville, Beaumont, Detroit, the war (China-Burma-India), Pittsburgh, Cleveland, and Chicago. It ended in Beverly Hills. The real journey started and ended in the mind of a human being who sought a career in baseball and, having achieved it through hard work, moved on to other endeavors. He triumphed over bigotry. Instead of letting the ethnic hatred deter him, he used it to motivate himself in becoming better as a player and as a person. Henry Benjamin Greenberg was a self-made man.

Chapter 2. **Al Lopez**

Maxwell Kates

He was equally as adept at coordinating pitchers and throwing out base runners as he was as a leader and strategist in the dugout. However, Alfonso Ramon Lopez chose to credit his supporting cast of players for his successes rather than himself. Much like his mentor Casey Stengel, Lopez knew that he could not have won the American League pennants in 1954 or 1959 without his players. Although disappointed that he never played or managed for a world champion, he received countless honors from his peers on the diamond, his community, the Baseball Hall of Fame, and fans spanning four generations.

Lopez was the son of Spanish immigrants. His father, Modesto, was attracted to employment offers in the cigar trade in Cuba. After convincing his bride to abandon their Castilian roots, they spent "eight or nine years" in Cuba; they migrated yet again to the United States in 1906, settling in the Ybor City section of Tampa.[1] The Lopez family settled in a modest four-bedroom house that lacked running water.[2] It was here that their seventh of nine children, Alfonso, was born on August 20, 1908. At the time, Ybor City was hardly the popular nightclub district that it is today. Lopez encapsulated his neighborhood living conditions with the following anecdote told to Tom McEwen: "'Tough place, Ybor City was, once. I went to work one day and had to step around a couple of guys who had been murdered in the streets.'[3] Among Lopez' earliest memories was the stench of his father's cigar-stained clothing upon returning from the factory where he worked as a tobacco selector. He vowed to work diligently to avoid having to follow in his father's footsteps."[4]

Al Lopez—A catcher with Brooklyn and Boston in the 1930s, Lopez served as the Indians' manager from 1951 to 1956. The Indians won the pennant once, and finished second the other five years.

In the days before the ubiquity of the automobile, Lopez remembered no traffic in the unpaved streets of Ybor City.[5] The beach was a source of leisure for Lopez and his friends for crabbing, fishing, and swimming.[6] It was an older brother who introduced him to a second childhood pastime, baseball. Throughout his youth, Lopez played the game with friends on weekends at local sandlots. Dominoes and gin rummy were two additional lifelong hobbies. A member of the Catholic faith, Lopez attended the Jesuit High School of Tampa, but dropped out after his freshman year to support his family.[7]

Lopez accepted a job working for La Joven Francesca Bakery. Nearly nine decades later, he still remembered delivering bread by horse and buggy for the factory workers: "We would hang it in a paper bag, on a nail, by their front door!"[8] Lopez's introduction to professional baseball was nothing short of unorthodox.

In 1925, still five years short of the age of majority, he was hired by the Washington Senators to catch batting practice in spring training. "For some reason," he told Bill Madden, "they didn't want to use their regular catchers, Muddy Ruel and Pinky Hargrave, and I was playing sandlot ball when they called and offered me $45 a week. Heck, I'd have done it for nothing, but that was my start in professional baseball."[9] The young catcher impressed a veteran right-hander fresh from recording six shutouts among twenty-three victories for the defending World Series champions. After practice had concluded, Walter Johnson congratulated Lopez, offering, "Nice game, kid. You're going to be a great catcher someday."[10] Lopez never forgot the experience of catching the Big Train: "Johnson threw hard, maybe the hardest of all, but he was easy to catch because he was always around the plate."[11]

Lopez took his experience catching the Washington Senators to a tryout with the Tampa Smokers of the Florida State League. He made the team, adding an extra $150 every month toward his family's budget throughout the 1925 season.[12] Lopez was later promoted to Jacksonville, and on August 26, 1927, his contract was purchased by the Brooklyn Robins for $10,000.[13] He spent most of the 1928 season playing for Macon, where he earned a spot on the South Atlantic Association All-Star team.[14] Brooklyn manager Wilbert Robinson was sufficiently impressed with reports on his catching prospect to recall him to "the show" in September. Lopez made his debut at Ebbets Field against the Pittsburgh Pirates in the first game of a doubleheader on September 27, 1928.[15]

The first pitcher Lopez faced in the Majors was legendary spitball artist Burleigh Grimes. Although the pull-hitting rookie made contact with Grimes, none of the balls he hit evaded the glove work of third baseman Pie Traynor or shortstop Glen Wright.[16] The Robins beat the Pirates 7–6 in an extra-inning victory for Jesse Petty.[17] Although Lopez failed to hit safely in a dozen official at bats during his National League initiation, he remembered the experience as "my greatest thrill as a player."[18]

After another year of seasoning in the Minors, Lopez had returned to Brooklyn in 1930. He established an offensive personal best for himself as a rookie, batting .309 and driving in 57 runs; meanwhile, his fielding average was .983 in 126 games behind the plate.[19] Compared to other catchers around the league, Lopez was considered small, standing five feet eleven and weighing a mere 180 pounds.[20] As Arthur Daley chronicled in the *New York Times*, "What he lacked in bulk, he compensated for in agility, speed, intelligence, and class."[21] As a rookie, Lopez was responsible for a change in the rulebook. A fly ball out of Bob Meusel's reach bounced over the Cincinnati outfielder's head and into the stands and was ruled a home run. After the season, this type of play was reclassified as a ground-rule double.[22]

After five consecutive sixth-place finishes, the Robins leapt to challenge the St. Louis Cardinals and the New York Giants for the National League pennant.[23] Although the Robins fell to fourth place by September, they won eighty-six games and set a franchise attendance record by drawing more than a million for the first time.[24] As one of the catalysts in the Robins' turnaround, Lopez was offered a raise, no questions asked.[25] The man Daley called "Happy Hidalgo" enhanced his reputation as a dependable catcher, fielding .977 in 1931 and .976 a year later for the rechristened Brooklyn Dodgers.[26]

As a young player, Lopez carried a reputation of an umpire baiter. On one instance, he found himself ejected from a game at the Baker Bowl in Philadelphia. En route to the visitors' clubhouse in center field, Lopez paused at the pitcher's mound to drop his glove, mask, and chest protector. Infuriated, the umpire ordered him to leave the field. Lopez ignored him, continuing his mock burlesque act by removing one shin guard, then another, and tossing them gingerly beside him. At that point, he collected his belongings and moved toward center field slower than a Studebaker with a flat tire.[27]

In 1933 Lopez tested the patience of another authority figure, Dodgers general manager Robert Quinn. When training camp opened, Lopez was nowhere to be found—he was holding out for a better contract. Manager Max Carey called him, urging him to reconsider, as his job was threatened by "a young catcher who looks pretty good."[28] That "young catcher" was actually a year older than Lopez, but the two backstops would emerge as lifelong friends. Ray Berres later served as Lopez's pitching coach for more than a decade with the Chicago White Sox. In 1932 the Dodgers had acquired another of Lopez's future coaches, shortstop Tony Cuccinello.

On the heels of batting .301 in 1933, Lopez was assigned to represent the Dodgers at the 1934 All-Star Game at the Polo Grounds. Among the thousands of spectators who "happened to be at that game" was Evelyn Kearney.[29] Known to all as "Connie," the Broadway chorus girl met Lopez after the game.[30] Five years later, on October 7, 1939, the pair was wed.[31] They welcomed a son, Al Jr., in 1942.[32] Over the years, the Lopez family would expand to include three grandchildren and nine great-grandchildren.[33]

The 1934 season also introduced Lopez to new Brooklyn manager Casey Stengel. Despite his later successes with the Yankees, Stengel led the Dodgers to pedestrian records of 71-81 in 1934 and 70-83 in 1935.[34] Rumors began to circulate that several star players would soon be traded. Stengel attempted to placate any apprehension Lopez might have by assuring him that "it's going to be to a good club."[35] Instead, on December 12, 1935, Lopez and Cuccinello were traded to the Boston Braves. Lopez was

understandably offended at Stengel's false reassurance. In 1935 the Braves won 38 and lost 115, establishing themselves as the worst team in baseball.[36] As Lopez recalled, "Then [in 1938], he comes over to Boston to manage and trades me to Pittsburgh."[37]

Lopez played for the Pirates through the 1946 season, when he was traded to Cleveland for outfielder Gene Woodling on December 7.[38] He was well respected enough in the latter stages of his career that even superstars from opposing teams asked him for advice. In March 1939, when legendary Yankee Lou Gehrig suddenly stopped hitting with alacrity, he turned to Lopez for advice on his swing.

"So I told him, 'the only thing I can think is that you're not slapping the ball, you're pushing at it."[39] At the time, Gehrig's diagnosis of ALS was undetected.

Lopez's arrival in Cleveland coincided with the inception of the Indians' golden age. Bill Veeck was the owner, Lou Boudreau the manager, Bob Feller and Bob Lemon anchored the rotation, and on July 5, 1947, the trailblazing Indians integrated the American League with the emergence of Larry Doby. Lopez caught for one season for the Indians as Jim Hegan's backup and then retired. Nineteen seasons in the Major Leagues yielded 1,547 hits, 206 doubles, 43 triples, 51 home runs, 652 runs batted in, and a lifetime average of .261. Catching 1,918 games, a Major League record until 1987, he produced a sterling .985 fielding percentage.[40] In 1941 he caught 114 games with the Pirates without as much as a passed ball.[41] Lopez knew his career as a catcher would not last forever, so as a member of the Bees, he invested in Texas land options prior to a real estate boom.[42] Lopez enjoyed the financial freedom to concentrate on his career ambition: managing in the Major Leagues.

"I always wanted to manage when my playing career was finished, but if that was part of Veeck's plan when he got me, he never told me about it."[43] Not offered a position with the Indians, Lopez was assigned in 1948 to manage the Indianapolis Indians of the American Association. The baby Indians flourished under Lopez's tutelage, winning twelve of their first fifteen.[44] Led by Les Fleming's .323 batting average and Bob Malloy's record of 21-7, they finished with a record of 100-54.[45] Lopez even caught in forty-two games for the Indians.[46] They finished ahead of the Milwaukee Brewers by eleven games to garner the American Association pennant. Was this a sign of big league accomplishments for Lopez?

After two more years at Indianapolis, Lopez was hired on November 10, 1950, to manage the Cleveland Indians.[47] One of the keys to his success in Cleveland was his rapport with chief operating officer Hank Greenberg.

"We worked well together. Hank picked up some good players, guys who were especially important to us in 1954 when we had a lot of injuries. The club in those days didn't spend a lot of money . . . but Hank was able to do some things that didn't cost a lot because we did so well."[48]

The Indians were consistent if not spectacular under Lopez, winning ninety-three games in 1951, ninety-three in 1952, and ninety-two in 1953. Yet it was not enough to unseat the New York Yankees from the apex of the American League. Managed by Lopez's nemesis Casey Stengel, the Bronx Bombers were completing their sweep of five successive World Series titles. Without the financial wealth or the farm system resources of the Yankees, the Indians left their fans frustrated.[49] Lopez retained a personal respect for Stengel, describing him as "a great guy and a fine manager [who] loved to teach." He added, "I learned a lot from Stengel—but apparently not enough."[50]

Fate would be kinder to the Cleveland Indians in 1954. Although the Yankees won 103 games, their highest total under Stengel, they were relegated to listening to the World Series on the radio. The Indians, meanwhile, played evenly against the Yankees and the White Sox while posting a torrid 89-21 record against the other five clubs.[51] Posting an overall record of 111-43, the Tribe vaulted to the American League pennant. As Lopez later reported to veteran sportswriter Russell Schneider, the Indians "had a lot of leaders, which is one of the reasons we did so well. I've got to say that (Al) Rosen was the number one guy. I had great respect for the way he played the game and the way he demanded that others play the game."[52]

The Indians were leaders on the mound. Bob Lemon and Early Wynn earned league titles with twenty-three wins apiece, while the club converted nineteen victories from Mike Garcia, fifteen from Art Houtteman, and thirteen from Bob Feller.[53] Lopez described his pitching staff as "the greatest ever assembled."[54]

The Indians were leaders at the plate as well. Second baseman Bobby Avila captured a batting crown hitting .341, while Larry Doby led the American League with 32 home runs and 126 runs batted in. The Indians were tops in the American League with 156 dingers.[55]

Lopez credited the Indians' bench and bullpen as integral components in the team's success. Without contributions from acquisitions Sam Dente, Hank Majeski, Vic Wertz, and Wally Westlake, he maintained that the Tribe "probably could not have won."[56] Credit should also be given for converting pitchers Don Mossi and Ray Narleski into relievers—"a big factor in beating the Yankees."[57]

They fell into a slump against the New York Giants during the World Series.[58] In the eighth inning of Game One, Vic Wertz hit a line drive that traveled 460 feet deep into the Polo Grounds before landing in Willie Mays's glove.[59] After Dusty Rhodes delivered a pinch home run for a tenth-inning Giants victory, momentum remained on their side. The Giants swept the Indians in four straight. Lopez insisted that the Indians would have fared better had they opened the series at Municipal Stadium, where Wertz's line drive would have been a home run.

Losing the 1954 World Series did not prevent the City of Tampa from dedicating its new spring training facility in Lopez's honor.[60] For better than three decades, Al Lopez Field was the winter home of the Cincinnati Reds. It did not take long for Lopez to make history in "his" stadium. On the very first play of the 1955 spring opener, he argued the call with umpire John Stevens.[61] The arbiter warned the manager that "one more word and you're gone." Lopez protested, "You can't throw me out of this ballpark. This is my ballpark—Al Lopez Field." Stevens said, "Get out of here." Years later, Lopez reflected with perplexity that anyone would throw him "out of [his] own ballpark."[62] Lopez also had the distinction of outliving the use of his stadium, which was destroyed in 1989.

After two more second-place finishes in Cleveland, Lopez resigned as the Indians' manager in 1956. Chronic stomach ailments brought forth by years of anxiety suggested it was time for a change in scenery.[63] He took his managerial acumen to Chicago, where he replaced Marty Marion as the manager of the White Sox. Though he assumed control of a talented roster, the White Sox were notorious for their "June swoon" and as "hitless wonders." Marion advised Lopez that "he better bring his pitchers with him."[64]

Playing in spacious Comiskey Park, the White Sox under Lopez's stewardship focused their game around pitching, speed, and defense. Importing his philosophy from another cavernous ballpark, Cleveland, Lopez stressed the stolen base, the hit and run, and run manufacturing to get ahead of the opposition.[65] A player and coach for Lopez in Indianapolis, Gutteridge was El Señor's second in command for better than a decade in Chicago. Gutteridge remembers, "As an organization, the White Sox were trying everything they could to win."[66] He also recalls Lopez advising his players, "If you don't let them score that run and you score that run—you *win*."[67] Lopez inherited an outfield of Minnie Minoso, Larry Doby, and Jim Rivera. His middle infielders, Nellie Fox and Luis Aparicio, were both defensive stalwarts destined for Cooperstown. Doby was not the only Cleveland personality with whom Lopez reunited in Chicago. Bill Veeck and Hank Greenberg joined the club as executives a year later.

The White Sox opened the 1957 season by winning eleven of their first thirteen games.[68] On June 8, the Sox enjoyed a six-game lead in the junior circuit, their largest advantage since Buck Weaver was permitted to play third base. But when the dust cleared on 1957, Lopez found his White Sox in a familiar position, in second place behind the Yankees. However, true to his word, Lopez relied upon pitching, speed, and defense to win ninety games. The Sox led the American League with 109 stolen bases.[69] On the mound, Billy Pierce (20-12, 3.26) and Dick Donovan (16-6, 2.77) led the rotation, which was coordinated by veteran receiver Sherm Lollar. Observed Don Gutteridge from his view in the dugout, "Of course, Al Lopez was excellent with pitchers, too. He was a great catcher for so many years that he really knew what was going on with his pitchers. Between Lopez and Berres, they really knew pitching and always got the most out of our staff."[70]

The city and the uniform had changed for Lopez, but after managing in the American League since 1951, his club still finished second to the New York Yankees. The 1958 season marked the seventh year out of eight that a Lopez club played bridesmaid to the Bronx Bombers. Although the White Sox won ninety games in 1957 and eighty-two in 1958, it was not enough to stop Casey Stengel's juggernaut from adding to their surplus of American League titles. Lopez's critics, particularly those in the New York media, accused him of being anti-Yankee. Defending himself, he argued, "I'm anti any club that wins all the time.[71]

Jim Rivera has fond memories of playing for Al Lopez. The outfielder described his manager as "very fair," adding, "If you did something good, he would compliment you. If you struck out or made an error, he wouldn't say a word as long as you hustled and worked hard."[72] However, broadcaster Milo Hamilton insisted that Lopez was a disciplinarian as the situation warranted. If a player made a mental mistake, he reprimanded the poor soul behind closed doors rather than before his teammates or the media.[73] Hamilton also remembered Lopez for his sense of fashion. Always dressed in a suit and tie when not in uniform, the manager "had a presence you couldn't forget."[74] Hamilton added that when Lopez traveled, "he just looked the part of somebody *important*."[75]

And important he was. In 1959 Al Lopez accomplished something no White Sox manager had done in four decades. He led his club to an American League pennant. Despite hitting only 97 aggregate home runs, fewest of any team, the "Go-Go Sox" led the American League with 113 stolen bases, 46 triples, and a 3.29 earned run average.[76] Early Wynn won twenty-two games and the Cy Young Award while Nellie Fox batted .306 as the league's Most Valuable Player.[77] Fastest on the base paths was Aparicio, who led the league with 56 steals.[78] The Sox won 35 of 50 one-run decisions, winning their first season series over the Yankees since 1925 by posting a 13-9 record against New York.[79]

White Sox fans knew that 1959 would be an unusual season on April 22, when they scored eleven runs in one inning on ten walks, a hit batsman, three errors, and only one hit.[80] The Sox battled the Indians for control of first place for most of the summer when in July, Chicago raced ahead by winning eleven games of a twelve-game homestand.[81] Although Cleveland recovered to within a game in the standings by late August, the Sox reaffirmed their dominance over the Indians with a four-game sweep at Cleveland.[82] When the Sox clinched the pennant on September 22, Mayor Richard J. Daley activated air raid sirens throughout Chicago. A White Sox fan, Hizzoner had no idea of the extent of the terror he instilled in the citizenry. As Harold Rosenthal later reported, "Everyone wanted to know how far up Michigan Avenue the Russians had advanced."[83]

In contrast to the 1954 World Series, the White Sox opened the 1959 Fall Classic with an 11–0 victory at home. Early Wynn threw seven scoreless innings against the Los Angeles Dodgers as Ted Kluszewski drove in five runs on two homers and a single.[84] Although they led 2–1 in the sixth inning of Game Two, the Sox lost the game and ultimately the Series, four games to two.[85]

Although the White Sox remained competitive in the early 1960s, they did not return to the World Series under Lopez's tutelage. Managing pennant races for fifteen consecutive summers took their toll on his well-being. Managing was no longer fun for a man in his fifties who spent many late nights pacing the clubhouse floor due to an insomniac condition.[86] Not even Lopez's gin rummy marathons with broadcaster Bob Elson were enough to lift his spirits. As was reported in *Time*, the insecurity of having never won a World Series "kept him melancholy."[87] Few were aware of his stomach condition, let alone its severity, which prevented him from digesting fruit or vegetables and forced him to drink milk—a beverage he detested.[88] After leading the Sox to a 95-67 record in 1965, good for another second-place finish, Lopez's illness forced him to step down as manager in favor of Eddie Stanky.

While the White Sox initially prospered under Stanky, they floundered in 1968. Mired in eighth place on July 11, the Sox fired Stanky; as Lopez was healthy enough to return to work, he was hired to his second tour of duty with the Sox. Although the Pale Hose won twenty-one and lost twenty-six under Lopez, it was not enough to salvage the season.[89] The 1968 Chicago White Sox went 67-95, finishing thirty-six games behind Detroit tied for eighth place.

The White Sox began the 1969 season with promise as Carlos May belted two home runs in a 5–2 victory in the home opener against the expansion Kansas City Royals.[90] However, the early-season heroics were a false hope. A respectable record of 8-9 through May 2 was not enough to prevent Lopez's insomnia from returning. As he told Hal Bodley decades later, "That's when I knew it was time to get out."[91] Announcing his retirement to coaches Berres, Gutteridge, Kerby Farrell, and Johnny Cooney, Lopez told them he wanted "one of you four to take over from me."[92] Gutteridge reluctantly accepted. Dressed in one of his trademark suits, Lopez returned to Comiskey Park in 1970 to watch an Opening Day loss to Minnesota before departing the Chicago sports scene for good.[93]

Lopez returned to Tampa, where he enjoyed his retirement. He played cards regularly with lifelong friends, watched *The Price is Right* religiously, and golfed his age well into his seventies. In 1977 he was inducted into the Baseball Hall of Fame. His baseball interest peaked during the 1990 World Series between clubs managed by Tony LaRussa and Lou Piniella, both Tampa natives.

Even in his nineties, Lopez showed few signs of slowing down. He was one of four Hall of Famers invited to throw the ceremonial first pitch to welcome the Tampa Bay Devil Rays into the American League on March 31, 1998.[94] At his ninety-fifth birthday party, a gala event at Tampa's Columbia Restaurant, Lopez was awarded an honorary doctorate from the University of South Florida.[95] Then on October 26, 2005, he "stayed up past his bedtime" to watch the Chicago White Sox finally win the World Series.[96]

"They have a darn good ball club," he told sportswriter Hal Bodley. "I was so happy to see it. Chicago's a real fine city, and that manager [Ozzie Guillen] is doing a great job."[97]

Four days after watching the White Sox sweep the Houston Astros for the 2005 World Championship, Al Lopez was gone. Hospitalized after suffering a massive heart attack, Lopez died on October 30, age ninety-seven.[98] He was buried beside his wife, Connie, who had died in 1983. As Tom McEwen wrote in his obituary of El Señor, his heart "would have to be massive" because "he had given so much of his heart away."[99]

Lopez may have been a humble man in life, but after his death he continued to receive honors and accolades. In 2006 he was enshrined into the Cleveland Indians Hall of Fame.[100] The Devil Rays now offer the Al Lopez Award to the organization's top rookie in spring training. Meanwhile, the Rays invited his son, grandson, and great-grandson to throw the ceremonial first pitch in 2006—each of them named Alfonso Ramon Lopez.[101]

As a catcher and as a manager, Al Lopez was undoubtedly a baseball legend. He earned the respect and acclaim of teammates and adversaries alike, and became an inspiration to thousands of athletes and spectators in Tampa. Lopez returned to his hometown each winter, watching his community expand over the course of the twentieth century. Though modest about his accomplishments, he left an indelible mark in the minds of fans from Ybor City to Brooklyn, from Cleveland to Chicago, and all points in between.

Chapter 3. **Tony Cuccinello**

Barb Mantegani

A diminutive Italian from Astoria, New York, on Long Island, who was introduced to baseball on the local sandlots, Tony Cuccinello was involved in what remains the closest batting race in Major League history, when, as a member of the Chicago White Sox, he lost the 1945 American League batting title to George "Snuffy" Stirnweiss of the Yankees by a margin of .000087.

Cuccinello had a fast start in 1945, keeping his average in the .380–.390 range for the first few months. The heat of the Chicago summer eventually wore Tony down, however, and at what was then the advanced age (for a ballplayer) of thirty-seven, Cuccinello did not play every day, and in fact had to play more in September to achieve sufficient at bats to qualify for the batting title. Stirnweiss edged out Cuccinello on the final day of the season, when a White Sox doubleheader was rained out and Stirnweiss went 3 for 5 against the Boston Red Sox. One of those hits, however, was scored an error initially, and then changed to a hit by the official scorer, who just happened to be a writer for the *Bronx Home News*. According to Cuccinello, he was told at the time that the official scorer only changed the call after he was informed that the White Sox had been rained out and Cuccinello's season was over. Ironically, Cuccinello later coached Stirnweiss with the Cleveland Indians, and Snuffy confirmed the shenanigan.

Anthony Francis ("Tony" or "Cootch") Cuccinello was born November 8, 1907, in Long Island City, New York. Tony played in a semipro league in New York City and eventually signed a contract to play for the Syracuse Stars of the International League in 1926, while still a teenager. After two

Tony Cuccinello—An infielder, Cuccinello spent most of his career in the National League, with Brooklyn and Cincinnati and Boston. His coaching career spanned three decades, and he was part of three pennant-winning teams: Cleveland (1954), Chicago (1959), and Detroit (1968).

months Cuccinello was sent to the Class B Lawrence (Massachusetts) Merry Macks, where he spent the rest of 1926 and 1927, when he hit .310. In 1928 he was assigned to the Danville Veterans of the Three I League. After another season hitting .310, Cuccinello caught the attention of Branch Rickey, who saw him play and bought him for the Columbus Senators in the American Association. Cuccinello's performance at Columbus (.358 batting average with 20 home runs and 111 runs batted in, and a league-leading 227 hits and 56 doubles) earned him a quick promotion to the Major Leagues, when the Reds purchased his contract after the 1929 season. Tony made his debut on Opening Day, April 15, 1930, playing third base in a losing effort against the Pittsburgh Pirates.

Cuccinello had a solid rookie season, batting .312 with ten home runs and seventy-eight RBIs. In 1931 the Reds shifted Tony to second base and he responded with a .315 average and ninety-three RBIs, a club record for second basemen until broken by Joe Morgan in 1975. In his best offensive performance that year, he got hits in six consecutive at bats, including two doubles and a triple. He led the league's second basemen in put-outs, assists, errors, and double plays.

Despite Cuccinello's performances on the field, he refused to sign the contract the Reds tendered to him and found himself shipped to the Brooklyn Dodgers to begin the 1932 season. Tony played in all 154 games that year, turning in respectable offensive numbers for a second baseman (.281, 12 homers, 32 doubles, and 77 RBIs) but, more important, becoming a teammate of future Hall of Fame manager Al Lopez, with whom he would begin a lifelong friendship. That same year Cuccinello married Clara Caroselli (after the season, on October 29), and they produced three children: Anthony Jr. in 1936, Darlene Ann in 1938, and Alan Joseph on their thirteenth wedding anniversary in 1945. Cuccinello's performance in '32 earned him a spot on the roster of the first All-Star Game in 1933 (the so-called Game of the Century), where he had the dubious distinction of pinch-hitting for Carl Hubbell in the top of the ninth and striking out to end the game.

In 1935 Cuccinello's younger brother, Al, made his Major League debut and played in fifty-four games with the New York Giants, the only Major League experience Al would have. The brothers played against each other several times that year, and both homered in the same game on July 5. Tony's homer was a solo shot in the top of the eighth and Al's a two-run blast in the bottom of the ninth of a game Brooklyn won 14–4. After four years with the Dodgers, Cuccinello was on the move again when Brooklyn traded him to the Boston Braves. In Boston in 1936, Cuccinello had one of his best offensive seasons, batting .308 and driving in eighty-six runs. Tony's excellent defensive performances continued in Boston as well, and he teamed with a player he later described as the finest of the shortstops he played with in his career, Eddie Miller.

In 1939 Cuccinello suffered a knee injury after Dick Bartell of the Chicago Cubs slid into him at second base, and surgery sidelined him for two months. His first game back after the surgery, Cuccinello had ten assists in a twenty-two-inning game. The knee never really improved despite the surgery, and Cuccinello was traded to the Giants midway through the 1940 season. At the end of that season, Cuccinello retired for the first time so that he could manage the Jersey City Giants in the International League. Jersey City finished fifth in the eight-team league in 1941, and Cuccinello was prepared to manage again in 1942, but instead was called by his former Brooklyn manager, Casey Stengel, then with the Braves, who asked Cuccinello to join his staff as a player-coach. In 1942 Cuccinello threw batting practice, coached third base, and pinch-hit for Stengel, and in mid-season 1943 he was released so that he could sign with the Chicago White Sox, a team desperately in need of players to replace those who enlisted in the military. Cuccinello, who suffered from chronic laryngitis, was not drafted into military service, and therefore was able to continue his career.

From mid-1943 through the 1944 season, Cuccinello was a reserve infielder who appeared in fewer than fifty games each year, and he later said that but for the war, he likely would have retired before the 1945 season. But in 1945 Cuccinello went to a northern spring training in French Lick, Indiana, where he had a mineral bath every day, followed by a rubdown and a nap, and entered the season feeling the best he had ever felt. Perhaps it was the mineral baths or the naps, but nevertheless, after the Indiana spring training, Cuccinello embarked on his near title-winning year, and he retired from playing for good at the end of that campaign.

Cuccinello was out of baseball in 1946, but he managed the Tampa Smokers in the Florida International League to 104 wins and a second-place finish in 1947. The following year he reunited with Al Lopez in Indianapolis, where they coached the Indianapolis Indians of the American Association to a 100-win season and an online ranking among the 100 best Minor League teams of the twentieth century. In 1949 Cuccinello began a three-year stint as a coach with his first Major League team, the Reds, and in 1952 he joined Al Lopez's coaching staff on the Cleveland Indians, the first of several such positions he would hold. Coincidentally, 1952 was also the last year of former nemesis Snuffy Stirnweiss's career, also with the Indians.

Cuccinello's first postseason experience came as a coach with the Indians in the 1954 World Series, which the heavily favored Indians lost to the New York Giants. In 1957 Cuccinello followed Lopez to the Chicago White Sox, and in 1959, as third base coach, he was involved in a controversial play that some said at the time led to the White Sox's demise at the hands of the Los Angeles Dodgers in the 1959 World Series. In Game Two of the Series, Sherm Lollar, the White Sox catcher, was on first base in the bottom of the eighth with nobody out, a man on second, and the score 4–2 in favor of the Dodgers. The next batter, Al Smith, doubled to left-center. The runner at second (Earl Torgeson, running for Ted Kluszewski) scored easily. Cuccinello waved Lollar home, where he was thrown out—by a good margin, by all accounts. When the Sox went on to lose the Series four games to two, Cuccinello immediately was awarded goat horns and tagged with the blame for the Series loss.

Lopez defended his friend and fellow coach, telling a Chicago Daily News reporter that in his opinion the play itself was fine, and, more important, that the play was not the turning point of the Series, that the Sox's inability to run in the Coliseum was what led to their demise.

Lopez repeated that opinion in an interview with *The Sporting News*, noting that it took a perfect play by the Dodgers' defense to nail Lollar at the plate. One of the Dodgers involved in the play, outfielder Wally Moon, expressed the same opinion during the off-season after the World Series when he said that he also might have sent Lollar if he were in Cuccinello's shoes, because the odds were against the Dodgers' making the play.

In any event, Cuccinello survived the controversy and continued coaching in Chicago into Eddie Stanky's managerial tenure, which started in 1966. In 1967 Cuccinello joined the staff of new Tigers manager Mayo Smith, and at the beginning of the season Cuccinello took on Dick McAuliffe as a private project, to help McAuliffe make the switch from shortstop to second base. At the time, Cuccinello said McAuliffe had to work on slowing himself down, and in 1968 the work seemed to bear fruit, as McAuliffe's defensive improvement was cited by both opposing manager Alvin Dark of the Cleveland Indians and Tigers coach Hal Naragon as a key factor in the Tigers' success. Cuccinello enjoyed his first and only World Series championship in 1968 when the Tigers defeated the St. Louis Cardinals in seven games.

Cuccinello left the Tigers in 1969 to reunite with Al Lopez, who managed the White Sox for seventeen games that season. Cuccinello then retired to Tampa, Florida, where he worked as a Yankees scout in the area until retiring from baseball completely in 1985. Cuccinello passed away of congestive heart failure on September 21, 1995, at a hospital in Tampa.

Chapter 4. **Mel Harder**

Mark Stewart

When Mel Harder guided thirteen Indian arms through an astonishing 111-win season, there was no "how- to" book for pitching coaches. That's because he was still writing it. During Harder's two-decade stint as an active hurler, pitchers were often treated like zoo animals—objects of curiosity, the care and feeding of whom was left to whichever coach claimed a modicum of mound expertise. Or whoever drew the short straw. Harder took a more enlightened approach when it came to conveying the fine points of his craft, making minor technical adjustments and gently nudging his pupils toward self-discovery. It was his pleasure and his nature to do so.

Melvin Leroy Harder was born on his family's farm, near Beemer, Nebraska, on October 15, 1909. He grew up in Omaha. Harder was an athletic boy, but because he was nearsighted, he did not compete in many sports. Eventually, the bespectacled teen found his way to the pitcher's mound and discovered he could make a baseball do fantastic things. He had a smooth overhand delivery that produced a natural sink. Harder used a traditional curve as an off-speed pitch, but this would not become his "money pitch" until later in his career. By his late teens he could change speeds and locations well enough to ruin the timing of opposing hitters, and was considered enough of a prospect to warrant a contract offer from the Minor League Omaha Buffaloes.

Harder was a sinewy six-footer when he made the transition from high school hurler to seventeen-year-old pro in 1927. He started the year with the Buffaloes, but he did not work in any games. The team decided to stash him in the Class D Mississippi Valley League with Dubuque. Harder went 13-

Mel Harder—Mel Harder had 223 wins in a career that spanned twenty years in a Cleveland uniform. He served an additional seventeen years as a pitching coach for the Tribe. He started the first game at Cleveland Stadium on July 31, 1932.

6 for the Dubs, helping them open up a big lead in the standings. There was just one problem. Teams in this league were technically independent, and by the rules of the day they had to own their players. The Dubs had to return Harder to Omaha and forfeit his thirteen victories.

In Omaha, Harder won four of eleven decisions against Class A competition. He nonetheless caught the eye of several big league teams, including the St.

Louis Cardinals, the Chicago White Sox, and the Indians. All three made offers, but Cleveland's was the best and they took possession of Harder prior to the 1928 season. Despite a glowing evaluation from scout Cy Slapnicka, the Indians had no illusions about the type of player Harder might one day become: a dependable but decidedly unflashy innings-eater whose success would hinge on his ability to entice batters into getting themselves out.

That is precisely what Mel Harder became. During the 1930s he enjoyed as much success as any pitcher of this kind. In an era marked by lusty hitting, Harder stood out as a pitcher who was especially stingy when it came to giving up the long ball. He didn't hurt himself with walks and was adept at getting opponents to pound balls into the dirt.

In February 1928 Harder arrived at the Indians' new spring-training facility in New Orleans. The team would continue to train there through the 1930s. Harder was the only teenager in camp with a realistic shot at making the Opening Day roster. New manager Roger Peckinpaugh saw enough from the eighteen-year-old to take him north when the team broke camp; he was the youngest player in the league that season.

Harder spent 1928 in the Cleveland bullpen, until the second game of a September 27 doubleheader against the Boston Red Sox. In Harder's first Major League start, Boston peppered him with ten hits in seven innings, handing him his second loss of the year against no victories. In all, Harder made twenty-three appearances, mostly in mop-up duty. His earned run average was 6.61 in forty-nine innings.

Harder played all but six weeks with the Indians in 1929. They sent him down to their farm club in New Orleans to pitch in a pennant race, then brought him back up in September. Harder finally worked his way into the starting rotation in 1930. He functioned as a swingman, starting nineteen times and relieving in seventeen games. In all, Harder threw 175⅓ innings and went 11-10.

Harder was part of a promising young rotation that included Wes Ferrell, Willis Hudlin, and Clint Brown. He spent another season as the Tribe's swingman in 1931. During this time, he improved his ability to pitch to spots, a skill that would ultimately define him through his long career. Without a blazing fastball, this is how he survived and ultimately thrived in the big leagues.

Using his sinking fastball, fast-improving curve, and change of pace, Harder upped his victory total to thirteen against fourteen losses in 1931. His ERA of 4.36 was actually lower than the team average (1931 was not a kind year for AL pitchers in general). Harder started twenty-four times and completed nine games. He also made sixteen relief appearances. Even as a full-fledged member of the starting four, he would often pitch in relief and move his starts around to accommodate teammates. His flexibility only added to his worth.

In 1932 it didn't take much to understand the value of Mel Harder, now entering his prime years at age twenty-two. He went 15-13 with a 3.75 ERA, placing him in the top ten in that category. Harder completed more than half of his thirty-two starts and was among the stingiest pitchers in the American League when it came to yielding homers and issuing bases on balls.

That season, on the last day of July, Harder had the honor of throwing the first pitch at the new Cleveland Stadium, the largest ballpark in the country. More than seventy-six thousand fans filled the place. Harder and his teammates were awestruck when they took the field. None had ever played baseball before that many fans before. In fact, no one ever had. Harder lost to Lefty Grove and the Philadelphia A's, 1–0. The deciding hit was a grounder up the middle by Mickey Cochrane that Harder nearly speared with his glove. Harder was never considered a great fielding pitcher, but he would have plenty of practice scooping up come-backers and covering first on dribblers to the right side. He led the league in pitchers' put-outs in four seasons.

Harder took another important step forward in 1933. He had mastered all of his pitches at this point, and he toughened up with runners on base. His 2.95 ERA was the best in the league among pitchers with 200 innings or more pitched, and contributed to the team's AL-best 3.71 ERA. Run support was still a big problem, as witnessed by Harder's 15-17 record. Despite ranking among the leaders in several important pitching categories, he found himself on the losing end of many games he might have won with a better lineup behind him. That was true both offensively and defensively. In fact, throughout his career it was Cleveland's defensive inadequacy more than a lack of hitting that hampered the club's chances. For a man who pitched to contact, this was especially harmful to Harder.

No pitcher wants to feel that he has to throw a shutout in order to win, but in 1934 Harder often took the mound with that mind-set. The result was his best year to date. He blanked opponents six times, tying Lefty Gomez for the AL crown. He won twenty games and lowered his ERA to 2.61. Harder was a man who finished what he started, logging seventeen complete games in twenty-nine starts. He also finished what others started, closing out a dozen games as a reliever and being credited retroactively with four saves.

Harder was the winning pitcher in the 1934 All-Star Game. After Yankees Lefty Gomez and Red Ruffing had been cuffed around by the National League, Mel pitched the final five innings, relieving Ruffing with no one out in the bottom of the fifth with the AL leading 8–6. Pie Traynor scored from third on a double steal to make the score 8–7, but the NL did no more damage against Harder, who allowed one hit during his appearance. The Americans won, 9–7. The next day the headlines trumpeted the strikeout skill of Carl Hubbell (Babe Ruth, Lou Gehrig, Jimmie Foxx, Al Simmons, and Joe Cronin in succession) and barely mentioned Harder's performance. In three innings, Hubbell had allowed four base runners. In five in-

nings, Harder had allowed but two—and picked up the victory to boot.

Harder continued to flourish in 1935. He won a career-best twenty-two times, finishing second in victories to former teammate Wes Ferrell, now with the Red Sox. Harder did lead the league in fewest walks (1.7) and home runs (0.2) per nine innings pitched. He sparkled again in the All-Star Game. This time he pitched three scoreless innings in relief of Gomez in a 4–1 victory, picking up the save.

The 1936 Indians figured to make some noise in the pennant race. The emergence of Hal Trosky as a middle-of-the-lineup force—along with the development of hitters Joe Vosmik and Odell Hale—gave the Tribe a formidable lineup. Along with Harder and Hudlin, the pitching staff featured hot-tempered journeyman Johnny Allen and Oral Hildebrand, who threw a 90 mph fastball and 75 mph change-up with an identical motion.

Alas, it was not to be. Trosky and Allen were sensational, but injuries and underperformance elsewhere on the club limited Cleveland to just eighty wins. Even the midseason addition of seventeen-year-old Bob Feller failed to elevate the Indians from the second division.

Harder was among the casualties. In the second half, he attempted to pitch through shoulder bursitis that sucked the life out of his fastball. He was able to go 15-15, but his ERA told the true story—it ballooned to an almost inconceivable 5.16. The injury occurred at the end of July, shortly after Harder pitched two more scoreless innings in the All-Star Game. At the time, his record stood at 14-6 with an ERA just under 4.00. Harder went 1-9 the rest of the way and gave up six or more runs nine times. In his lone victory, he was shelled for twelve hits.

Another player might have incurred the wrath of his teammates, but Harder was a particularly popular Indian. He had taken one for the team more times than anyone could remember. He was also a generous, thoughtful player who loved to share his baseball knowledge. The nickname bestowed upon Harder by the players was Wimpy—not because he was a moocher, but because of his fondness for hamburgers.

Harder was never the same pitcher after July of 1936, but the pitcher he became still helped the team. The curve and changeup he had developed since coming to the Indians were now better than average. No longer able to muster his good fastball, Harder fiddled with his grip and developed a slider that, when delivered with his straight overhand delivery, was extremely difficult to hit. Seeing as he never had a real put-away pitch, this proved just as effective as his old fastball.

Over the next few seasons, Harder would have good luck with some of the league's best hitters. Notably, Joe DiMaggio batted under .200 against him and once struck out three times in a game.[1] For his part, Harder often listed DiMaggio among the toughest batters he faced. Right-handed Joltin' Joe would sit on Harder's curve and either pull it down the line or smash it to right. Their battles were endlessly entertaining.

Harder tended to have the most trouble with lefties who hit the ball hard to all fields. Lou Gehrig, Bill Dickey, and Charlie Gehringer were particularly tough on him. They knew that trying to pull Harder was likely to result in a weak grounder to second, so they concentrated on taking him the other way. He had much better luck against sluggers who aimed for the fences all the time, like Babe Ruth.

In 1937 Harder went 15-12 with a 4.28 ERA and led the Indians in innings pitched. It says a lot about his recovery that he was named to his fourth straight All-Star squad. And for the fourth year in a row, he was handed the ball with the game on the line and asked to close out the NL. He took over from Tommy Bridges in the seventh inning and did not allow a run, picking up his second All-Star save. Of the nine outs he recorded, eight were on grounders.

Harder continued to shine in 1938, going 17-10 and turning in a staff-best 3.83 ERA. With Feller improving and rising stars Jeff Heath and Ken Kelt-ner bolstering the offense, the Indians were starting to look like a contender. To get past the Yankees and Red Sox, however, they would need more pitching. In 1939 Feller blossomed into a twenty-four-game winner and Harder chipped in fifteen despite an aching elbow, yet the Tribe was still desperately short of quality starters. Cleveland finished third for the second year in a row.

During the 1939 season, Harder could add to his growing list of credits "movie star." He was one of several players featured in a film produced to celebrate the centennial of baseball. The concept was to trace the evolution of the game from Abner Doubleday to the present day, while underscoring the idea that baseball players have always embodied homespun American values. Harder was shown hunting in the off-season with Joe Vosmik, who had been traded to the Browns in 1937. This segment was meant to illustrate that the bonds of friendship among ballplayers could not be severed by a trade.

Coming out of spring training in 1940, the Indians appeared to have solved their starting pitching woes. Feller and Harder were followed in the rotation by young Al Milnar and veteran Al Smith, who combined for thirty-three victories. The Indians had a shot at their first pennant in two decades until a rift developed between the players and manager Ossie Vitt. Vitt inspired the hatred of his players by bad-mouthing them in the press, criticizing them loudly from the dugout while they were on the field, and benching regulars without warning or reason. His wife was rumored to help him make personnel decisions by consulting the stars.

Things went from bad to worse in June after Vitt removed Harder from a game in Boston after he had given up several early runs, and asked him when he planned on earning his salary. Picking on an Indian whose leadership had earned him a second nickname, "The Chief," was a huge mistake. On the train ride back to Cleveland, the players met secretly and formed a twelve-man delegation to have it out with the Bradleys, the owners of the team.

MARK STEWART

Harder volunteered to head up this group, along with Hal Trosky, who also had a bone to pick with the manager. The Indians' best run-producer had been dropped to sixth in the lineup because Vitt subscribed to a theory that this was where a team should bat its top hitter. The group went into the front office and reported that the manager had lost control of his team. Harder made it clear that the players believed they could not win the pennant with Vitt at the helm.

The team's position was that Vitt would stay and the players would simply have to deal with it. From that point on, they ignored Vitt. They held players-only meetings and occasionally consulted with coach Johnny Bassler on strategy. They developed their own signals. Vitt, angry and paranoid, lashed out at his players through the press. The fans, egged on by sportswriters who painted the situation as the inmates running the asylum, joined their manager in branding the Indians Boo-Hoo Boys and Crybabies.

The Indians were still a talented bunch, and they opened up a five-and-a-half-game lead during the summer. However, they played uninspired ball thereafter. Cleveland lost the lead and couldn't catch the Tigers down the stretch. Vitt panicked and overused Feller, and the Indians finished one game behind Detroit. It was one of the uglier baseball stories of the pre–World War II era. Years later Harder expressed regrets about 1940—not for his role in the player revolt, but for his lackluster 12-11 record. Suffering once again from a sore elbow, he never pitched at 100 percent. In a season where one or two more wins could have made a difference, Harder felt that he had let the club down.

Harder turned thirty over the winter, and his arm woes returned during 1941. For the first time since becoming a starter, he failed to win in double digits, finishing 5-4. Four of those victories came in his first four starts, at which point his ERA stood at 2.27. The season from that point on was a lesson in agony. The team finally shut him down in July and

cut him after the season. For a time, it looked as if the Mel Harder era in Cleveland had come to an end.

Surgery, rest, rehab, and the talent drain of World War II enabled Harder to return to the mound in 1942. He accepted an invitation from Cleveland's new player-manager, twenty-four-year-old Lou Boudreau, to pitch in spring camp. Harder not only made the team, he won a spot in the starting rotation. He took the mound twenty-nine times that year and, for the first time in his career, did not make a single relief appearance. Harder won thirteen of twenty-seven decisions and completed thirteen of his starts in 1942. Four of those games were shutouts, the second most in the American League.

Harder looked as though he would have another strong year in 1943, but he cracked his wrist in May and did not pitch again until mid-July. He finished with an 8-7 record and a sparkling 3.06 ERA in eighteen starts. As the war continued to deplete Cleveland's pitching, the club depended on the aging right-hander more and more. Harder was their top winner in 1944, posting a 12-10 record and 3.71 ERA. His 5–4 win at Fenway Park on May 10 was his 200th career victory.

The cumulative effect of age and injuries finally took Harder down in 1945. He did not throw a pitch in a game that counted until July, and his season ended one week into September. He won just three of ten decisions despite a respectable 3.67 ERA. The Indians were shut out in three of his seven losses and scored just one run in a fourth. Harder pitched his way into the mix again during the spring of 1946. He twirled a shutout in his first start of the season, but a hand injury kept him off the mound for a month and limited his effectiveness the rest of the way. At the age of thirty-six, he went 5-4 with a 3.41 ERA.

Mel Harder's last hurrah as an active player came in 1947. In the second half he had difficulty pitching deep into his starts, and manager Boudreau benched him in favor of Bob Lemon. Harder's final appearance on the mound as a Major Leaguer came on September 7 at Comiskey Park against the White

Sox. (He started the game, a 3–2 Indians victory, but didn't get the win.)

Mel Harder won 223 games in twenty seasons for the Indians and lost 186. His ERA of 3.80 was better than average for the time he pitched. Harder struck out 100 batters only once in his career, in 1938, but he never came close to walking 100. He gave up 161 home runs in 3,426⅓ innings, most of which he logged during the homer-happy 1930s. (During that decade, he was the only right-hander in baseball to win in double figures every year.) From 1932 to 1939, he was the only Major Leaguer to win at least fifteen games a season. His .545 winning percentage was .28 better than the teams he played for—a wider margin than AL contemporaries Lefty Gomez and Red Ruffing, both of whom were later inducted into the Hall of Fame. Only Ted Lyons and Harder's ex-manager Walter Johnson pitched more seasons with one club than Harder.[2]

The 1947 season may have closed the door on Harder's career as a pitcher, but it opened a window on a brand-new opportunity. As he became less helpful to Boudreau as a pitcher, he became more helpful as a pitching coach. Harder's résumé as a teacher actually dated back to the 1930s, when he shared pitching tips with Bob Feller. First he helped the young fireballer find the strike zone. Then Harder gave him some helpful hints on his curve. These two improvements accelerated the transformation of Feller into the staff ace.

Bob Lemon was another Harder success story. Before the war he was an outfielder/third baseman with a natural sink on his throws. When he returned to Cleveland from the service in 1946, Harder helped convert him to a pitcher, explaining how to harness the sinker and, to give him a second pitch, teaching him how to throw a breaking ball. Lemon caught on so quickly that by mid-1947 he was the guy who replaced Harder in the rotation.

Bill Veeck, who had purchased the Indians in 1946, was an astute baseball man. He coupled Harder's demotion with an offer to become the team's pitching oracle—not just for the Indians but, going forward, for the entire organization. He already had the look of a pitching professor with the eyeglasses; all he lacked was the title. Harder accepted, and soon he would become one of baseball's greatest proponents and best teachers of the slider, a pitch that forever altered the balance of power between pitcher and hitter.

To get his charges to think as he did, Harder had a teaching method that went against the grain of contemporary baseball thinking. Rather than dictate orders to pitchers, he framed suggestions in ways that made sense to each man. That way they would incorporate his ideas into their repertoire as their own. This worked for the young guys, the old guys, and the reclamation projects.

In 1948 the Indians opened the season without old No. 18 on the roster for the first time since the 1920s. However, a few weeks later there was a familiar face wearing uniform No. 43. It was Mel Harder. He had started the year working with youngsters in Oklahoma City, but he came back to join a staff of astute baseball minds surrounding Boudreau, including Bill McKechnie and Muddy Ruel. Harder functioned as the Indians' first base coach for most of 1948 and became the full-time pitching coach the following season.

Many sources incorrectly state that Harder was out of baseball in 1948, noting the sad irony that the team won its one and only World Series since 1920 without the Chief. They could not have been more wrong. Indeed, Harder and Ruel cobbled together a rotation that began with Feller, Lemon, and Gene Bearden and then dropped off a cliff. The job Harder, as a first-year coach, and Ruel did with the back end of the team's pitching staff was nothing short of fantastic. They coaxed unusually productive years out of Steve Gromek, Eddie Klieman, Russ Christopher, and Sam Zoldak. They are answers to trivia questions today, but in 1948 this group combined for two wins, twenty-three saves, and a cumulative ERA of well under 3.00. Even Satchel Paige got into the act, twirling a pair of shutouts and going 6-1 as a forty-something-year-old rookie.

The Indians, Red Sox, and Yankees went down to the wire, with Cleveland and Boston tying for first with identical 96-58 records. Boudreau, the soon-to-be MVP, slugged two homers in the one-game playoff at Fenway Park to win the pennant. Harder's bullpen faltered in the World Series against the Boston Braves, imploding in Game Five. But by then the Indians held a three-games-to-one lead. Lemon and Bearden combined to win the next game, 4–3, and take the Series.

Harder got two more talented pitchers to work with in 1949, Mike Garcia and Early Wynn. Garcia had been in the Cleveland system since the early 1940s; second baseman Joe Gordon nicknamed him the Big Bear when he joined the team in 1949. Garcia already had a good sinking fastball as a rookie. Harder's job was to refine his slider and teach him a usable curve. When he finally mastered these off-speed pitches in 1951, he went from an 11-11 record in 1950 to 20-13 in '51. Like Harder, Garcia enjoyed pitching out of the pen; he picked up six saves in '51.

Harder had a huge impact on Wynn's career. When the Indians acquired him from the Senators, Wynn was twenty-nine. He had been pitching in the Majors since the early 1940s, mixing a fastball with the knuckleball he had learned from the other Washington pitchers, walking as many batters as he struck out. Upon his arrival in Cleveland, Wynn proved a willing student. Harder showed him how to change the speed on his heater and tutored him in the art of the breaking ball. His curve went from below average to above average, and he eventually developed a dependable slider. More important, he could vary the speed on all of his pitchers, driving hitters crazy. Wynn went on to win 20 games five times and finished with 300 victories.

From 1948 to 1953, Harder produced eleven twenty-game winners. He had three on the staff in 1951 and 1952. His crowning achievement came in 1954. Al Lopez, a catcher on the team in Harder's last season as a player, had become the club's manager in 1951. The Indians had finished as runner-up to the Yankees every year since, but in 1954 they ran away with the AL flag, winning a then-record 111 games. The Tribe had quality hitters, but it was the team's pitching that elevated the club to record-setting status. Indeed, the team ERA of 2.78 was the best for a ball club since the Deadball Era. Lemon, Wynn, and Garcia were dominant as usual, but it was Harder's influence on the rest of the staff that helped the club make history.

After 1954 Harder continued to develop and occasionally reclaim pitchers for the Indians. In 1955 Herb Score arrived in camp with a blinding fastball and little else. Harder taught him a curve, and Score went out and won sixteen games on the way to setting a new rookie record for strikeouts. He followed that triumph with a twenty-win season, and seemed destined for Feller-like immortality before Gil McDougald's liner derailed his career. Score later said that if Mel Harder couldn't teach you a curveball, no one could.

Among Harder's other post-1954 success stories were the resurrection of Cal McLish and the burnishing of Mudcat Grant, Jim Perry, Gary Bell, Tommy John, and Luis Tiant—each of whom became an All-Star. The only pitcher he encountered who had nothing to learn from him was a teenager named Sam McDowell. Of Sudden Sam, Harder said that he could throw any pitch he wanted already. All he needed was some seasoning.

Mel Harder's thirty-sixth and final season in the Cleveland organization was 1963. He sought work elsewhere after that, a casualty of the Gabe Paul regime. The Indians had made some ill-advised moves in the years prior, and there was a general house-cleaning after several sub-.500 seasons. Harder's replacement was Early Wynn, who said simply that "Mel Harder made me a pitcher."[3]

It didn't take long for Harder to catch on with another club. Viewed as baseball's ultimate Mr. Fix-It, he was hired to work with horrendous pitching staffs on the Mets in 1964 and the Cubs in 1965. He had a little more to work with on the Reds from 1966 to 1968. During his time in Cincinnati, Harder helped develop Gary Nolan into a quality starter and Clay Carroll into a quality closer. Harder's first year with the Reds marked his twentieth as a coach. Thus he became the first (and, as of 2011, the only) person to play twenty years in the Majors and coach twenty years in the Majors.[4]

Harder's last baseball job was a reunion with Joe Gordon, who was tabbed to manage the expansion Kansas City Royals in 1969. In 1970 Harder retired from the game and moved to his winter home in Arizona.

During the 1960s there was a groundswell of support for Mel Harder's enshrinement in Cooperstown. Statistically and anecdotally, he might be characterized as a borderline Hall of Famer, with as much to recommend him as to deny him entry. What set Harder apart from all other candidates was his remarkable record as a pitching coach. When he began his second career, there was really no official position of "pitching coach." By the time he left the game, every team had one.

One other piece of information that made Harder unusual is that he actually *did* earn enough votes from the Veterans Committee for enshrinement. One year he garnered the required 75 percent, but two other players got more. By the rules of the day, he would have to wait.

And wait he did. When he died at the age of ninety-three in Chardon, Ohio, in 2002, he was still on the outside looking in.

Chapter 5. **Red Kress**

Chris Rainey

On July 27, 1955, the players and staff of the Cleveland Indians presented a brand-new $3,000 Oldsmobile to coach Red Kress for his untiring work with the team. The Indians' third baseman, Al Rosen, summed it up by saying that the team wanted to do something for Red to pay him back for all he had done for the team. Casey Stengel, his boss on the 1962 New York Mets, called Kress "the hardest-working man I ever knew," adding that he never asked anything of the players that he didn't demand of himself. Kress's ability to throw long sessions of batting practice every day was legendary. An infielder by trade, Kress was no slouch on the mound. A speed meter used in 1939 recorded him throwing at 139 feet per second (about 96 miles per hour). Kress professed to having never had a sore arm. He even quipped that "Satchel Paige couldn't make that claim."[1] Kress's pitching notoriety was such that during spring training of 1953, *The Sporting News* mentioned that "the Tribe's human pitching machine needed oiling after he tore some skin off his forefinger."

According to some baseball records, Ralph Kress was born on January 2, 1905, in Columbia, California. But a search of the *Oakland Tribune* showed him playing high school basketball in February of 1925 and on the football team in September 1925, which could explain why the 1968 Macmillan Encyclopedia listed the year of his birth as 1907. His parents, Edward and Dora (Meuses) Kress, were born in California in 1865 and 1871, respectively, and married in 1888. The Kress name is German/Irish, but there are indications in census records that the family was originally from France and may have emigrated to Canada and then to

Red Kress—Kress was a former infielder with St. Louis, Washington, and Chicago in the American League. He served as a coach for many Minor and Major League teams, including the Cleveland Indians, the Los Angeles Angels, the New York Giants, and the New York Mets. (The Cleveland Press Collection, Cleveland State University Library)

the us. This may allude to Dora's father, who was born in Canada and moved to California. Red was one of nine children and grew up in Columbia, Tuolumne, and finally Oakland as the family slowly moved west across California after Edward Kress died in a quarry accident.

Kress made a name for himself playing on the Oakland sandlots and at Berkeley High School.

He was "discovered" playing for the Barrel House team in the Standard Oil Twilight League by a scout named C. C. Chapman and signed with the St. Louis Browns on December 28, 1926, beginning a life-long career in professional baseball that ended only with his death on November 29, 1962. In a 1956 interview in *The Sporting News*, Kress mentioned that "I never laid off a single winter. If I wasn't playing or managing winter ball in South America, I'd play, manage, or coach some team in California."[2]

The Browns farmed Kress out to Tulsa in the Western League for the 1927 season. The Western League was pretty fast company for a rookie, and Red found himself on a team loaded with talent. He was installed as the shortstop and played every game, hitting .330. When Tulsa's season concluded, the Browns called him up for a quick look. Kress made an inauspicious debut, in Washington on September 24. The first ball hit to him was a slow roller, and he threw wildly to second base trying for a force. He flied out his first time at bat, but he later singled. The Browns were impressed with Kress and took him to spring training in West Palm Beach, Florida, in 1928. Kress hurt his ankle in an exhibition that kept him on the bench until the fifth game of the season, the Browns' home opener against Detroit. He went 2 for 2 with a double in the loss. He didn't miss a game for the rest of the season. At bat he hit .273 and drove in eighty-one runs for the third-place Browns.

Kress improved in nearly every category in 1929. He was third among shortstops in chances per game and led the league with a .946 fielding average and ninety-four double plays. At the plate his average jumped to .305, and he led the team with nine home runs and 107 RBIS. Over the winter, management allowed him to name his price and he signed for $7,000. In 1930 Kress upped his batting average to .313 with sixteen home runs and increased his RBIS to 112. He led the league playing in 154 games, but his fielding fell off from 1929; he led the league in errors at shortstop. (Kress played thirty-one games

at third base as the Browns looked at Jim Levey as a shortstop.) Despite the growing Depression, the Browns raised his pay for 1931 to $9,000, with some bonus clauses. Red picked up some extra cash in the fall of 1930 touring with the Lefty Grove All-Stars. On October 29 the Major Leaguers played the Royal Giants, a team of black players in the California winter league featuring Mule Suttles, Biz Mackey, and Willie Wells. Grove's team won 6–3, after Kress lashed a bases-loaded single in the first to help the All-Stars jump out to a lead they never relinquished.

In 1931 the Browns turned shortstop over to Levey. That marked the beginning of Kress's life as a jack-of-all-trades. He saw action in eighty-four games at third base, but he also played shortstop, first base, and the outfield. The unsettled job situation did not seem to affect his hitting; he batted .311 and drove in 114 runs while hitting sixteen home runs again. After the season ended, he married Lucille Baker in Tulsa in a double wedding with Lin Storti, a former teammate at Tulsa. Kress departed after the ceremony for a cross-country barnstorming trip with Earle Mack of the Philadelphia Athletics. Then he and Lucille set up residence in the San Francisco Bay area. The couple had one child, a daughter, Lila.

The Depression was worsening, the Browns had finished in the second division again, and the team sent Kress and other players contracts calling for pay cuts; they wanted to cut Kress from $9,000 to $7,000. Kress became a holdout. He proposed that the two sides compromise at $8,000. The team agreed on an $8,000 offer, but said it was good for just one day and would then drop by $500 a day. Kress's reply was printed in the *St. Louis Post-Dispatch* on March 25: "I sure have lots to be swell-headed about working for the Browns for a measly $8,000. . . . Will leave here Saturday, need expense money for wife and myself."[3] Owner Phil Ball was not amused and made sure his final telegram was printed in the paper, saying in essence that Kress had an inflated opinion of his ability and that the club

CHRIS RAINEY

did not need his as much as he might think. Kress signed for $8,000, reported to spring training, and won the starting job at third base, but his days in St. Louis were numbered. On April 25 he was traded to the Chicago White Sox for pitcher Bump Hadley and outfielder Bruce Campbell. The 1932 White Sox were a weaker squad than the Browns and welcomed Kress's bat, but because of young shortstop Luke Appling, Red saw most of his action in the outfield. He did lead the Sox in homers with nine.

The 1933 White Sox underwent a major overhaul. Kress took over at first base and the entire outfield was replaced. Kress struggled at the plate, hitting only.248. The 1934 team was worse. Kress was benched and then swapped to Washington for infielder Bob Boken. The Senators' shortstop was manager Joe Cronin, so Kress was assured of being a utility player. He saw action at five positions until mid-August, when he broke his thumb in a practice session pitching to Heinie Manush for a movie, *Batter Up.* Kress was done for the season. His average with Washington was a dismal .228.

Kress's fortunes improved somewhat in 1935, which included a remarkable reprieve from demotion to the Minors. He spent the first half of the season as a pinch hitter and occasional outfielder or first baseman. (He even came in as a mop-up pitcher in three games.) In late July, Kress was hitting .140 and was about to be sent to the Minors, but suddenly injuries struck the Senators and Kress was given a start on July 24. The Senators lost but he smacked four hits and found himself back in the lineup for good, even working his way into the cleanup spot. He ended the season with a .298 average. After the season Kress joined Earle Mack on a barnstorming trip to North Dakota, Montana, and British Columbia.

The 1936 Senators had Cecil Travis and Buddy Lewis in the infield, so Kress served as a backup. He was in the lineup on July 19 in Washington when the Indians were visiting. Kress played in 109 games and hit .284. Over the winter there was

speculation that he would become the manager at Chattanooga, a Senators farm club in the Southern Association. Instead, on January 29, 1937, he was sent to Minneapolis in the American Association along with another player and cash for first baseman/outfielder Jimmy Wasdell. Given the starting shortstop job, the thirty-two-year-old Kress had a strong season. Minneapolis was in the pennant chase the whole season. Kress hit .334, clubbed twenty-seven homers, and had 157 RBIs. In the field he led the league in errors, but also in chances per game. Correspondents for *The Sporting News* who covered the American Association named him the league's most valuable player.

Minneapolis sold off its veteran players after the season. Kress and pitcher Charley Wagner were sent to the Boston Red Sox for about $50,000 and four players. Then the Red Sox sent him to the Browns with outfielder Buster Mills and pitcher Bobo Newsom for outfielder Joe Vosmik. While these deals were being made, Kress was in California playing for the Pasadena Merchants in the California Winter League. In March he served as a coach and player for the Bellingham, Washington, squad. Bellingham was a farm club of the Hollywood Stars, and Kress had been asked to help with exhibition games.

At St. Louis, Kress became the everyday shortstop and had a fine season. He hit .302 and led the league shortstops with a .965 fielding average. In March 1939 he staged a brief holdout before joining the team for spring training. He started the season at shortstop but on May 13 was traded to the Detroit Tigers in a ten-player deal precipitated by a fiery confrontation between Bobo Newsom and manager Fred Haney. Kress stepped into the shortstop position for the Tigers and had early success, but he slumped at bat, finishing with a .242 average. That winter he played for Hollywood in the California Winter League. For 1940 the Tigers signed him to a player's contract with the agreement that he would also coach at first base. The 1940 Tigers were a veteran crew and Kress saw limited action, batting ninety-nine times with a .222 average before becoming a full-time coach on August 1. After a spirited stretch drive, the Tigers won the pennant, then lost the World Series to Cincinnati in seven games. The day after the Series ended, the Tigers released Kress, who was surprised because, he asserted, general manager Jack Zeller had talked him out of taking the manager's job with Hollywood the previous off-season and had told him the team had plans for him after he was through playing.

After his release, Kress was named player-manager of the St. Paul Saints in the American Association. He saw action in 118 games and hit .293 with ten homers, but the Saints finished seventh and he was fired. He then signed to play and coach for league rival Louisville. He played in 119 games, including six as a relief pitcher, and hit .249. After the season, the Colonels traded him to Toronto of the International League, where in 1943 he served as a utilityman and coach. He pitched in fifteen games, with a 3-2 record, and hit .266 in 169 at bats as the Maple Leafs won the pennant but fell to Syracuse in the final round of the playoffs. Kress returned to Toronto in 1944 and played in seventy games, twelve as a pitcher. He batted .259 and had a 2-6 record. Manager Burleigh Grimes and Kress were fired at the end of the season.

In 1945 the well-traveled Kress joined the Baltimore Orioles as a player/coach. With the ranks of ballplayers depleted by World War II, he played in eighty-five games, including nineteen as a pitcher (nine starts, eight of them complete games). He played every position except catcher. On April 22 he was in the outfield for a doubleheader against Buffalo, made a sparkling catch, and threw a runner out at second. At bat he collected two home runs, two doubles, a triple, and a single with four RBIs. In the Governor's Cup playoffs, he started a game against Montreal and lost 1-0 on a ninth-inning error. In 1946 he was a coach for the New York Giants. With the team's pitching staff beset by injuries, Kress even pitched in relief, on July 17, giving

up five runs in three and two-thirds innings. It was his final appearance in a Major League game. At the plate he ended with a .286 average in 5,087 at bats. Red settled in as the first base coach for the Giants, until he was released after the 1949 season.

In October, Kress was hired to manage the Sacramento Solons in 1950. That winter he managed Rosabell in the California Winter League. The Solons met in Anaheim for spring training. Sacramento was short on talent and the scribes picked them to finish in the second division. Red was tough on the squad from the opening bell. He told the players that no one was guaranteed a job. The first day's practice lasted four hours. When play began, the Solons sank to the bottom of the league. The team's board of directors gave Red a vote of confidence on May 9, but their confidence ended on June 1. On July 1 Kress was back in the dugout as the manager of Superior in the Northern League. He took over a third-place club and kept it in contention for the rest of the season, finishing five games out. He even put himself into the game as a pitcher on four occasions, tossing twenty-seven innings and going 2-1. In the playoffs Superior beat Eau Claire four games to one, but lost in the finals to Sioux Falls.

Kress was hired to manage El Centro in the Southwest International League in 1951. Pitching trouble started early in the season, and Red pressed himself into service as a pitcher. His mound work was so impressive that he was named to the all-star game and came out the winner of an 8–7 game when he tossed five innings and gave up only one run. El Centro fired Kress on July 6 in a cost-cutting move, but he was immediately hired to manage first-place Juarez. Between the two teams, Kress played in thirty-five games, thirty of them as a pitcher. He hit a robust .373 and had a record of 8-6 on the mound. He made eight starts and tossed three complete games. Kress ended his Minor League pitching career with a record of 20-23 and an earned run average of 4.07.

In 1952 Kress was hired by the Indians to manage the Daytona Beach Islanders in the Florida State

League. He took on the job with his usual zeal. Sportswriters wrote that he tossed ninety minutes of batting practice the first day of training camp. The team started slowly at 10-14 but finished the first half of the season above .500; and when two franchises folded, the team picked up players to help in the second half. A 77-59 record earned the Islanders a spot in the playoffs. They swept first-place DeLand in round one, but fell to Palatka in the finals. That December, Kress was hired as an Indians coach. Tony Cuccinello handled third base and Kress was the first base coach in a partnership that lasted until 1957. Red tossed lots of batting practice and worked with Ray Boone at shortstop. Cleveland won ninety-two games in 1953, but finished eight and a half games behind the Yankees. That winter Kress managed the Gavilanes team in Venezuela to a third-place finish.

The Indians went to spring training in 1954 with a strong veteran cast. When the wins began to pile up and the pennant was assured, Cuccinello was sent to scout the Giants, and Kress shifted to the third base box for a short time. After pocketing his $3,356.25 losers' share of the World Series money, Kress was hired on to manage Santa Marta in the Venezuelan League. With a squad made mostly of native players from Class C and D leagues, the team got off to a bad start, and Kress was fired in early November when its record was 4-9.

The 1955 Indians started to show their age, finishing in second place, three games behind the Yankees. That winter Kress went to Venezuela again to manage Gavilanes. He had a strong group of Indians farmhands, plus Luis Aparicio at shortstop. The team got off to a 7-0 start and fought for the pennant. On January 17 first-place Gavilanes was facing second-place Pastora in Maracaibo. Kress was coaching at third base and reports were that he was riding the Pastora players to the point of being insulting. In the sixth inning, Pastora manager Jim Atkins rushed from the dugout and socked Red in the nose, breaking it. A bench-clearing brawl ensued, and it took police fifteen minutes to get peace restored. Eventually the umpires declared a forfeit and gave the win to Gavilanes. The rest of the pennant race was spirited, but Gavilanes wrapped it up with one game to go. The players had been promised an extra two weeks' salary if they won the pennant, but the ownership announced that it could not pay the bonus. Kress and the American players on the team sat out the last game of the season; he said in an article in *The Sporting News* on March 21, 1956, that the owners had benched the players and he sat out the game too in support of them.

In 1956 Kress was back as a coach with the Indians, who again finished second to the Yankees. That November the Estrellas Orientales squad in the Dominican League, which was stocked with Cleveland farmhands including Roger Maris, got off to a bad start, and Kress was named manager on November 17. But he was fired a month later after little success.

Manager Al Lopez left Cleveland for the White Sox in 1957. Eddie Stanky replaced Cuccinello as a coach but Kress stayed on. He started collecting his pension that year, getting $265 a month. The Indians finished a distant sixth and manager Kerby Farrell was fired. Bobby Bragan was brought in to manage in 1958 and he retained the coaches. The Indians were rebuilding and the lineup was in constant flux. Not surprisingly, the team struggled and Bragan was fired on June 26 with a 31-36 record. That fall Kress returned to Venezuela to manage Gavilanes, which finished 26-26. The 1959 Indians were a marked improvement over the '58 version, but fell five games short of Al Lopez's White Sox.

Kress was fired after the tumultuous 1960 season (slugger Rocky Colavito went to Detroit in a controversial trade for Harvey Kuenn). He did not stay unemployed very long. He was hired to help guide the expansion 1961 Los Angeles Angels. Angels manager Bill Rigney called him "one of baseball's top coaches," but Kress was fired at the end of the season. The brand-new New York Mets hired him to help in spring training and then manage in the Minors, probably at Syracuse. But Mets manager Casey Stengel kept Kress as a coach. No amount of coaching from Kress or anyone else helped the first-year Mets, who finished 40-120. In October, Kress returned to his home in the Canoga Park section of Los Angeles. He died of a massive heart attack on November 29. He was fifty-five years old. He is buried in Forest Lawn cemetery in Glendale, California.

Chapter 6. **Bill Lobe**

Joseph Wancho

Bill Lobe's contribution to a Major League team goes largely unnoticed to even the most knowledgeable baseball fan. His duties seem plain enough: warm up the starting pitcher and relievers if needed, in the bullpen. But the bullpen coach is an extension of the pitching coach, and can readily see if a hurler has his best stuff before he marches to the hill to meet the day's foes.

Cleveland starting pitcher Art Houtteman related an occurrence when he was warming up for a game in 1953 and was not pitching particularly well.

> I was warming up in the bullpen with Coach Bill Lobe, who is a great guy to work with. It was a Friday night and I was getting ready for a Sunday assignment. I felt exceptionally strong and quick. I was certain I had terrific stuff. But there was Lobe catching me like he was picking cherries. I couldn't understand it. It meant my ball was doing nothing. It bothered me.
>
> I changed the angle of my delivery just a little. I dropped it down just a bit. Then Lobe admitted he found it much harder to follow the ball. Either the delivery was harder to pick up, or the ball was moving more. Whatever it was, it made me effective once more. It was only a fine point, but it seemed to make all the difference, and it all happened just because Lobe was catching me so easy.[1]

William Charles Lobe was born on March 24, 1912, in Cleveland, the third of four children born to Louis Lobe, who owned a diner, and Florence Lobe. Bill's siblings were a sister, Florence; a brother, Joseph; and a younger brother, Edward.

Bill began his association with the Cleveland Indians at a young age. When he was fifteen years old,

Bill Lobe—Lobe was born and raised in Cleveland, serving as a Tribe batboy at League Park. A Cleveland sandlot star, he had a brief Minor League career before becoming bullpen coach of the Indians in 1948. (The Cleveland Press Collection, Cleveland State University Library)

Cleveland general manager Billy Evans hired him as one of the first batboys to work at League Park. (According to his obituary he was one of the first batboys in the Indians' history; batboys had been a regular feature on other clubs since the nineteenth century.) His responsibility was handling the bats of the visiting team, beginning with the 1927 season. He eventually became a member of the grounds crew.

Lobe was a standout on the Cleveland sandlots,

playing catcher for Poske Barbeque, one of the elite teams in the area. Because of his success, he was signed to a Minor League deal by the Indians and was sent to Springfield of the Class C Mid-Atlantic League for the 1939 season. He served as a backup to future Cleveland star Jim Hegan. But Lobe never advanced past the Class C level in three years. His best offensive year was at Thomasville of the Class D North Carolina State League, when he hit .213, collecting forty-five hits in 211 at-bats. "I couldn't hit enough to play pro ball," Lobe said in a 1952 interview. "I could hit well enough on the sandlots but not in the minors. Maybe it was just as well. Maybe I wouldn't have the job I've got today."[2]

With the United States fighting in World War II, Lobe entered the U.S. Army in March 1942. He rose to the rank of sergeant and served at a couple of camps, then settled in at Camp Barkeley, a training facility near Abilene, Texas. There he played for and managed the camp baseball team. In 1945 he was stationed in London, England.

After he was discharged, Lobe returned to Cleveland, where the Indians hired him as their batting-practice catcher in 1946. He became the full-time bullpen catcher in 1948, the season Cleveland won its second and, as of 2012, its last world championship.

Lobe developed strong bonds with several of the Indians. In particular, he was fond of Mel Harder, who was a star pitcher when Lobe was a member of the grounds crew and would drive Lobe home after ballgames. Together, they worked with the Tribe pitching staff in later years. "I never would have believed it if someone would have told me years ago that this would happen," said Lobe. "It's like a dream come true. Mel is the grandest guy in the world."[3]

Lobe caught some hard throwers in his day, particularly Bob Feller, Herb Score, and Bob Lemon. Jim Hegan typically went through about four catcher's mitts a year. Lobe broke them in during his bullpen work, warming up the heaters. One of the hardest throwers was Mike Garcia. "When I warm him up, he seems right on top of me," Lobe once said, showing off his red and swollen left hand. "I can imagine how he must look to the hitters. . . . His fastball stings, even through leather and sponge."[4]

The Indians set an American League record with 111 wins in 1954, but in an upset were swept by the New York Giants. As manager of the American League pennant winners, Al Lopez managed the American League All Star Team the following year. He named Lobe to his coaching staff for the midsummer classic, played in Milwaukee on July 13, 1955. Lobe's main duty was that of batting practice catcher.

Lobe retained his post as bullpen catcher through the 1956 season. He also did some scouting for the Tribe until 1960.

On September 25, 1953, Lobe married the former Olga Dolsak at St. Peter's Catholic Church in Cleveland. They did not have any children.

In the off-season, and in retirement, Lobe worked for the City of Cleveland Recreation Department. He also drove a truck for Dregalla Trucking Company in the off-season, and sold real estate for Pena Realty Company in suburban Euclid, Ohio.

Lobe died at his home in Euclid on January 7, 1969.

Chapter 7. A Seven-Year-Old's Perspective on the 1954 Indians

David Bohmer

It was quite a year to be a baseball rookie in Cleveland in 1954—not as a rookie player on the Indians team (though it must have been exciting to be Don Mossi, Ray Narleski, or Rudy Regalado and be heading to the World Series), but rather as a young boy paying attention to baseball for the very first time. I turned seven in June of 1954 on the same day as the trading deadline (not that it meant as much to me that summer as it would four years later when one of my childhood heroes, Roger Maris, was traded to the Kansas City Athletics). Discovering the Indians that summer of '54 began my lifelong love affair with the game of baseball and an unswerving loyalty to the Tribe that remains, decades after I moved from the Cleveland area.

My parents had moved to Parma Heights in 1940, when the little village was still as close to its farming roots as it was to its coming days as a fully developed suburb. By 1954 the community was booming, driven by the easy commuting distance to downtown Cleveland and the expanding Chevrolet and Ford plants that were close by. Just across from where we lived on York Road, Precision Realty was developing a large subdivision, one of many that were sprouting up in Parma and Parma Heights. Behind us on Pearl Road, construction was under way for a motel on the main road into Cleveland off the brand-new Ohio Turnpike.

Cleveland was thriving in 1954, benefiting from the post–World War II prosperity that dominated the decade. The 1950 Census counted close to a million people in the city itself, the largest population it would reach. While the car was becoming the main mode of transportation, it was still possible to drive toward the city on Pearl Road and catch the streetcar at the State Road car barn. I still remember going into downtown across the High Level Bridge and looking out the window at the Cuyahoga River valley below.

Downtown was thriving as well. My memories as a seven-year-old include seeing Santa Claus at Higbee's. It was still years before shopping malls were built and one could visit Santa at more convenient locations. While at Higbee's, my mother and I would also have lunch, which was served in a little metal stove. Even more than seeing Santa, that meal was the highlight of the visit. While downtown, we would also make a point of going over to Playhouse Square, perhaps to catch a movie, but especially to stop at the Sterling Linder Davis department store on Euclid Avenue to gawk at the fully decorated, six-story-tall Christmas tree.

The other non-baseball memory that paralleled the 1954 season was the Sam Sheppard murder case. From the Fourth of July on in 1954, the case seemed to dominate the news. Our family subscribed to both the *Plain Dealer* in the morning and the *Press* in the evening. My dad's sister, who lived in the other side of our double house, had the *News* delivered. It was still an era when the major source of local news was the newspaper, and it sometimes seemed to an impressionistic kid that the Indians and Dr. Sheppard were competing for top coverage.

While I remember scanning the papers every day to check out the box score, player statistics, and the standings, I remember only one picture: the image of bald-headed Vic Wertz bending forward for the camera with "we're in" written on his head. The image remains almost as fresh today as when I first saw it. It came, of course, in mid-September when the Tribe had clinched the pennant over the second-place Yankees.

At the time I was too young to understand that the 1954 Tribe had broken the three previous years of fan frustration, when the hometown team finished a close second to the consistently dominant Yankees. Into the twenty-first century, the 1954 Indians, who won 111 games, have held the best won-lost percentage (.721) in American League history. Perhaps even more special, for all the Yankee dominance of baseball during the 1950s, their best-performing campaign came in 1954, the only season during the decade in which they won more than 100 games. And with those 103 victories, the Yankees still ended up eight games out of first place!

Surprisingly, I don't recall going to any specific ballgame, but I do remember going to games in the cavernous Municipal Stadium with my dad and older brothers. It may also have been that summer when I first learned from my dad to keep score. Only recently did I discover that the style of scoring he taught me used some of the symbols originally developed by Henry Chadwick in the nineteenth century, even beyond the infamous "K" that survives today. Even now, I keep score using some of those symbols.

Going into the World Series in 1954, there seemed to be a confidence that the Tribe would dominate the Giants. Our starting pitching staff of Bob Lemon, Early Wynn, Mike Garcia, and Bob Feller was strong enough to dominate the Giants' bats. Even if one of the starters faltered, there was strong bullpen help from the likes of Art Houtteman, Hal Newhouser, Mossi, and Narleski. Interestingly, I still know all of the won-lost records of that pitching staff, the only team for which that is the case. I don't think there were any radios in my second-grade class, and in any case our teacher at the Pearl Road School probably would not have allowed us to listen. I do remember feeling jealous that my dad was going to Game Three, the first game of the Series in Cleveland, and that I couldn't go because of school.

While I didn't witness directly Willie Mays's catch in the first game, I have seen it so many times since that I sometimes feel as if I were there.

My most vivid memory of the 1954 Indians was following my two idols on the team, Al Rosen and Larry Doby. I admired them for two basic reasons: They were stars for the Cleveland team and they hit home runs a lot. Doby hit thirty-two during the season and Rosen twenty-four. It never occurred to me, a seven-year-old kid with parents who conveyed many of the stereotypical views of the fifties, that my two idols were Jewish and African American. I also recall seeing Doby making a leaping catch of a potential home run at the center-field fence and being impressed, as any seven-year-old would be, at his acrobatic talents. In fact, decades later, when National League President Bill White put me on the phone with Doby, I immediately became that kid again. All I could babble was how much I admired his great catches in center field.

I am sure that my recollections are probably very similar to those of other seven-year-olds growing up in Cleveland in 1954. Some memories are clear, others imprecise at best. I do remember sharing the disappointment with my family and friends when the Tribe ended their incredible season by dropping all four games to the Giants. With that disappointment, however, came the start of my passion for the game of baseball and, in particular, the Cleveland Indians. The 1954 season was the beginning of a love affair that, in spite of my living in or close to other Major League cities for most of my life, remains today.

Chapter 8. Timeline, April 13–April 30

Joseph Wancho

April 13—Chicago—INDIANS TRIUMPH IN OPENER, 8–2—Cleveland opens the season with an 8–2 win over the White Sox at Comiskey Park. Bobby Avila goes 4 for 6 and George Strickland goes 3 for 4 to pace the attack. Strickland and Wally Westlake each homer off Chicago starter Billy Pierce. Early Wynn gets the victory.

April 14—Chicago—LEMON DEFEATS WHITE SOX, 6–3—Cleveland sweeps Chicago in the short two-game series. Bill Glynn goes 4 for 5 and Al Rosen 3 for 5, each player driving in a run. Wally Westlake homers.

April 15—Cleveland—INDIANS DROP HOME OPENER, 3–2—The Tribe drops the home opener before 40,421. The Tigers score a run in the top of the eighth and ninth innings to claim victory. Ralph Branca gets the win in relief. Al Rosen homers and doubles, driving in both runs.

April 17—Cleveland—SOX WIN FIRST VICTORY; BEAT INDIANS, 8–1—The White Sox score five in the top half of the first inning and coast to their first victory of the season. They smack three home runs (Jim Rivera, Chico Carrasquel, and Ferris Fain). Bob Keegan gets the win. Outfielder Bob Kennedy is traded to Baltimore for outfielder Jim Dyck.

April 18—Cleveland—SHOWER OF 3 HOMERS LEADS TO WYNN ROUT—Chicago starter Billy Pierce K's six. Minnie Minoso hits a three-run homer in the five-run fifth inning. The game is called after six frames on account of rain. Sox win 6–2.

April 21—Baltimore—DOBY'S HOMER AFTER SINGLE BEATS TURLEY—The Tribe manages only two hits. Larry Doby drives in two with a homer in the top of the ninth inning of the 2–1 victory. Turley strikes out fourteen for the O's in a losing effort. Bob Lemon wins his second.

April 22—Baltimore—ORIOLES WHIP INDIANS, 4–1—The only Indians run is a bases-loaded walk to Larry Doby. Baltimore starter Duane Pillette strikes out six for the win. Mike Garcia loses for the second time.

April 23—Detroit—INDIANS LOSE SHIRTS, GAME TO TIGERS, 6–1—The start of the game is delayed one hour because the Indians' uniforms were misdirected from Baltimore. Once the game gets under way, Detroit starter Ned Garver scatters six hits for the win. Catcher Frank House doubles, driving in three runs.

April 24—Detroit—TIGERS WHIP INDIANS—Harvey Kuenn goes 3 for 4, scoring two runs, and Ray Boone hits a three-run homer. Bill Glynn, Bobby Avila, and Larry Doby each hit solo shots. Steve Gromek gets his third win on the season. The Tribe record is 3-6 on the season.

April 25—Detroit—INDIANS WHIP TIGERS, 10–9, ON PHILLEY HOMER—Wally Westlake homers twice, driving in four runs. Dave Philley hits a two-run homer in the tenth to snap a three-game skid. Don Mossi gets the win in relief, and Early Wynn earns a save.

April 29—Boston—REGALADO HURT AS INDIANS WIN, 6–3—Mike Garcia strikes out eight

Red Sox to claim his first victory. Al Rosen collects three RBIs and Dave Philley homers in the Tribe win at Fenway Park.

April 30—New York—INDIANS TRIP YANKS, 9–4—Cleveland scores five runs in the top of the tenth inning. George Strickland triples to plate two runs. Larry Doby homers. Bob Lemon raises his record to 3-0.

Chapter 9. **Bob Feller**

C. Paul Rogers III

AGE	W	L	PCT	ERA	G	GS	GF	CG	SHO	SV	IP	H	BB	SO	HBP	WP
35	13	3	.813	3.09	19	19	0	9	1	0	140	127	39	59	3	0

Bob Feller was a thirty-five-year-old veteran of fifteen Major League seasons in 1954 when the Cleveland Indians won 111 games and swept to the American League pennant by eight games over the New York Yankees. His fastball had lost a good deal of its luster, and manager Al Lopez had reportedly wanted to release him during spring training. Lopez, however, was overruled by general manager Hank Greenberg, who was worried about fan reaction, particularly since Feller had pitched pretty well in 1953, winning ten while losing seven.[1]

Still, Lopez was reluctant to rely on Feller and sat him on the bench until the third week of the season, when he started Feller in the first game of a doubleheader against the Washington Senators. Feller was gone by the fifth inning but escaped with a no-decision. His next opportunity was not until two weeks later, and this time he made it only until the third inning, again ending with a no-decision as the Indians won. Fortunately, Lopez gave him another chance a week later. This time Feller showed he had something left in the tank, pitching a complete-game 14-3 win over the Baltimore Orioles for the 250th win of his storied career.

After a complete-game loss to the White Sox, Feller got on to a roll, winning six consecutive starts to stand at 7-1 on July 21. Lopez was starting him every six days to great effect. In those six wins, he allowed a grand total of only seven runs. His fastball revived to the extent that, if not back to 1940s standards, it was above average. He had developed a sinker to go with his curveball and slider, and sometimes even broke out a knuckleball.[2] For the season, Feller finished with thirteen victories against

Bob Feller—Cleveland's all-time winner with 266 career wins, Feller has three no-hitters to his credit and an even more impressive twelve one-hitters in a career that spanned more than three decades. (National Baseball Hall of Fame Library, Cooperstown, New York)

just three losses. He threw nine complete games in nineteen starts and allowed only 127 hits in his 140 innings of work.

Feller was naturally quite anxious to win his first World Series game, accurately thinking the 1954 World Series would be his last chance.[3] Lopez originally penciled Feller to start Game Three against the New York Giants, the first game to be played in Cleveland. When the Indians lost the first two games in the Polo Grounds, however, Lopez opted in Game Three to start Mike Garcia, who had won nineteen games and had the lowest earned run average in the American League. Feller was hopeful of starting Game Four, but when Cleveland lost Game Three to go down three games to zero, Lopez selected twenty-three-game-winner Bob Lemon to go on short rest. Unhappily for the Tribe, that didn't work either, as the Giants won to sweep the Series.

Feller continued to be perplexed as to why Lopez did not use him at all in the Series, noting that Lopez used seven pitchers, including all the principal starters and relievers but him. In his second memoir, he pointed out that those seven gave up twenty-one runs in four games.[4] His real last chance for a World Series victory, he lamented, had been in 1948, the last time the Indians had been in the Series.[5] It was indeed, for the Indians would finish second in both 1955 and 1956, the last two years of Feller's career.

Robert William Andrew Feller was born on November 3, 1918, in Van Meter, Iowa, the first of two children to the former Lena Forrett, a schoolteacher and registered nurse, and William Feller, a farmer. The boy was perhaps the first to be raised by his father to be a Major League star.[6] Before little Bobby could walk, his father would roll a ball to him and use a pillow to catch the return tosses.[7] From the age of four on, playing catch with his father was a daily routine. By the time he was nine, Bobby could throw a baseball more than 270 feet.[8] Although he was an excellent hitter and fielder, his father saw his promise as a pitcher and set up arc lights in the barn so the two could play catch there during cold winter evenings.[9]

During the summer of 1930, when Bobby was eleven, the Van Meter High School team played several games against the elementary school team. Since Feller could throw harder than anyone else, he pitched and more than held his own against the older boys.[10] By the fall of 1931, Bill Feller and son took the extraordinary step of building a ballpark on the farm to give local players a place to play and to better showcase young Bobby's talent. Soon the field, which they called Oak View Park, was hosting games, charging twenty-five-cent admission, and sometimes drawing a thousand fans.[11]

Initially, Bobby played mostly shortstop for the Oak View team, batting .321 in the summer of 1933. In 1934, when he was fifteen, however, he began having exceptional success on the mound, striking out thirty-five batters in his first eighteen innings as a starter for Oak View. He was soon pitching for the American Legion team in nearby Adel as well, with similar results. His batterymate there was often Nile Kinnick, who later won the Heisman Trophy at the University of Iowa before being killed in World War II.[12]

The following summer, in 1935, after reportedly throwing five no-hitters for Van Meter High,[13] the sixteen-year-old Feller graduated to the semipro Farmers Union team in Des Moines, where the competition was tougher and scouts more plentiful. His meteoric rise continued. According to statistics kept by his father, Bob struck out 361 hitters in 157 innings that summer, allowing only 42 hits and compiling an ERA of under 1.00.[14]

In early September, Farmers Union traveled to Dayton, Ohio, for the national amateur baseball tournament. Before at least eight scouts, Feller pitched the opening game against Battle Creek, Michigan. He lost, 1–0, but allowed just two hits while striking out eighteen batters. Suddenly Feller was besieged with offers that included sizeable bonuses. He couldn't accept, however, for the fact was that he had secretly signed a contract with Cy Slapnicka of the Cleveland Indians earlier in July.[15] A Des Moines semipro umpire had tipped the Indians about Feller, and Slapnicka was dispatched to check out the young phenom.[16] He was impressed, and on July 21 Feller (and his dad, since Bobby was sixteen) signed for a bonus of one dollar and an autographed Indians baseball.[17]

Feller was to report the following spring to the Fargo-Moorhead Twins of the low-rung Class D

Northern League. While in Van Meter that winter for his junior year of high school, however, he somehow developed a sore arm. The Indians transferred Feller's contract to the New Orleans Pelicans of the Southern League, where he was placed on the "voluntarily retired" list while he finished his spring semester of school. After the school year, Slapnicka, whom the Indians had promoted to the equivalent of general manager, had Feller take the train to Cleveland, ostensibly to work in concessions but in reality so that the Indians could monitor the health of his arm.[18]

After a couple of weeks, Slapnicka arranged for Feller to start two games for the Rosenblums, a fast Cleveland semipro team sponsored by a clothing store. In the second game, he struck out sixteen while allowing only four hits. Then on July 6, Feller made his professional debut, entering an Indians–St. Louis Cardinals exhibition game in the fourth inning.[19] His first pitch was a fastball strike to Bruce Ogrodowski, a rookie catcher. Ogrodowski bunted the second pitch and was thrown out by third baseman Sammy Hale. The second hitter was Leo Durocher, the Cardinals' shortstop, who attempted to intimidate Feller, yelling, "Keep the ball in the park, busher." Feller did, striking Durocher out swinging on three fastballs. The third hitter, reserve infielder Arthur Garibaldi, did the same.[20]

In his three innings of work, Feller gave up an unearned run and struck out eight batters, including Rip Collins, Pepper Martin, and Durocher twice. On his second trip to the plate, Durocher told the umpire, "I feel like a clay pigeon in a shooting gallery."[21] Afterward, a photographer asked Cardinal ace Dizzy Dean if he would pose for a picture with the kid pitcher. Diz responded, "If it's all right with him, it's all right with me. After what he did today, he's the guy to say."[22]

Feller was still technically on the Rosenblums' roster and started one more game for them, losing 3–2 while striking out fifteen. Finally, on July 14, the Indians officially put him on the big league

roster, sending him to Philadelphia to join the club there. The seventeen-year-old's first official Major League appearance came a few days later, on July 19, in the eighth inning of a game against the Washington Senators in Griffith Stadium that the Indians were losing 9–2. Feller plunked the first batter, Red Kress, in the ribs with a wild curveball. Then, throwing only fastballs, Feller retired the side around two walks on a strikeout and two pop-ups to end his one inning of work.[23] His second appearance was six days later, on July 24 in Cleveland. With the Tribe ahead of the Philadelphia Athletics 15–2, manager Steve O'Neill brought the seventeen-year-old into the game in the eighth inning. In two innings, he gave up three hits and one run while striking out two. He got mop-up duty again two days later in the ninth inning of a 13–0 loss, allowing three hits, a walk, and two runs.[24]

O'Neill continued to use Feller sporadically in relief before giving him his first start, against the seventh-place St. Louis Browns on August 23 in Cleveland. The fireballer began by striking out Lyn Lary on three pitches, giving up a single to Harlond Clift, and then striking out the number three and four hitters, Moose Solters and Beau Bell. Pitching in ninety-degree heat, Feller continued to be overpowering and struck out a total of fifteen hitters in a complete-game 4–1 victory, one shy of Rube Waddell's American League record. He gave up six hits.[25]

O'Neill knew he had something special on his hands and resolved to start Feller about once a week for the balance of the season. Bob had control problems during his next two starts, losing both and failing to get out of the first inning against the Yankees on September 3. He then defeated the Browns again on September 7, striking out ten in a complete-game seven-hitter. On the 13th he defeated the Athletics 5–2 on two hits, but walked nine and allowed seven stolen bases. He was virtually unhittable that afternoon, striking out seventeen batters to set the American League record and tying Dizzy Dean's Major League record.[26]

Young Feller won two of his last three starts as the 1936 season wound down, with the Indians settling in fifth place with an 80-74 record. For his rookie year, the teenager threw sixty-two innings in fourteen appearances, including eight starts. He posted a 5-3 record, allowing 52 hits, with 76 strikeouts and 47 walks. His 3.34 ERA was the best on the club. After the season, Feller signed on for a brief barnstorming tour, pitching against Satchel Paige in Des Moines and traveling into the Dakotas and Canada.[27]

Although one would assume that Feller would not have a worry in the world after his impressive beginning, he in fact did. Pursuant to a complaint from E. Lee Keyser, the owner of the Des Moines Demons, the closest Minor League team to Van Meter, Commissioner Kenesaw Mountain Landis was investigating alleged irregularities in his signing by Cleveland, with the threat of declaring him a free agent.[28] After summoning Bob and his father to his Chicago office shortly after the end of the season, Landis waited until December to decide that Feller could remain Cleveland property.[29]

In the meantime, Feller spent the winter finishing high school, taking physics, English literature, American history, and government, before leaving for spring training in New Orleans.[30] The Indians and New York Giants annually barnstormed north out of spring training, playing games in places like Vicksburg and Jackson, Mississippi; Thomaston, Georgia; Decatur, Alabama; Little Rock and Fort Smith, Arkansas; Tyler, Texas; and Shawnee, Oklahoma.

Feller first pitched against the Giants in Vicksburg and in three hitless innings struck out six Giants, four in succession. Everyone was impressed except Giants shortstop Dick Bartell, who said, "He's not so fast. We've got several pitchers in the National League who can throw just as hard. I know he isn't as fast as [Van Lingo] Mungo." As the caravan moved on, Feller proceeded to strike out Bartell sixteen out of nineteen times. One sportswriter noted that Bartell went all the way to Fort Smith before he got a loud foul off Feller.[31]

Overall, Feller had a terrific spring and was dubbed the "schoolboy wonder" in several national publications. *Time* magazine put him on its April 19 cover, only the second time a baseball player had been so honored.

It all came to a screeching halt on April 24. Feller, in pitching to the first batter in his first start of the year, felt a sharp pain in his elbow when throwing a curveball. He managed to get by only with fastballs for six innings before finally telling manager Steve O'Neill that he had hurt his arm. The Indians sent him to several specialists, most of whom recommended rest. He made national news when he flew home in May to attend his high school graduation, but on his return to Cleveland he was still not ready to take the mound. Finally, in June, Cy Slapnicka sent Feller to A. L. Austin, a chiropractor just a few blocks from League Park, the Indians' home ballpark. He diagnosed a dislocated ulna bone as the problem, gave Feller's arm a sudden twist, and pronounced him ready to pitch after one more day's rest.[32]

Two days later Feller threw in the bullpen and was pain-free. He returned to action on June 22 with two innings of work and then on July 4 threw four innings against the St. Louis Browns. He was wild but as fast as ever, giving up three runs but only one hit. A week later he pitched an eight-inning complete game against the Tigers, losing 3–2. By late July he was back in the rotation, starting every fifth day. He was 0-4 in his first four starts, but still overpowering most of the time. In August he threw a twelve-strikeout, ten-walk game against the Yankees in Yankee Stadium. Later in the month he struck out sixteen Red Sox while walking only four and allowing just four hits.

For the 1937 season, Feller finished 9-7 despite his 0-4 start. In just under 149 innings, he allowed only 116 hits. His 3.39 ERA was second on the team to that of Johnny Allen, who won fifteen while losing only a single game that season. Feller's 150 strike-outs were fourth in the league even though he had missed three months of the season.

Incredible as it seems today, especially considering his sore arm, Feller again embarked on a barnstorming trip after the season, pitching against Paige and other top Negro League players. This tour was more extensive and wound through the hinterlands before arriving in Los Angeles.[33]

So high had been the expectations for Feller that the Associated Press had unfairly named him "flop of the year" for 1937.[34] The Indians still had faith in him and backed it with a salary of $17,500 for 1938, right in line with Joe DiMaggio and the highest-paid players on the Indians. New manager Oscar Vitt did not use Feller much in spring training, instead attempting to improve his delivery by shortening his leg kick in bullpen work.[35] He started the second game of the season, on April 20 in League Park against the Browns, and pitched the first of twelve one-hitters of his career.[36] The only hit was a sixth-inning bunt single that Billy Sullivan barely beat out.[37]

In late June, Feller defeated the legendary Lefty Grove of the Red Sox to run his won-loss record to 9-2 and, on the same day, was named to his first American League All-Star team. Still only nineteen years old, he was the youngest player named to the Midsummer Classic. Although he did not appear in the game, which the National League won 4–1, he was warming up in the bullpen to come in for the bottom of the ninth had the American League been able to tie the score.[38]

Feller was not as effective after the All-Star break as the Indians faded to third place. The Yankees ran away with the 1938 pennant, and as the season wound down, all attention was focused on Hank Greenberg's run at Babe Ruth's single-season home-run record of sixty. The season concluded on October 2 with Feller starting the first game of a Sunday doubleheader against the Tigers and Greenberg needing two home runs to tie Ruth. Rapid Robert lived up to his name that day, striking out eighteen

Tigers to set a new Major League strikeout record and steal the thunder from Greenberg, who went without a home run.[39] It was almost anticlimactic that Feller lost the game, 4–1.

For the year, his first full big league season, Feller won seventeen and lost eleven. His 240 strikeouts led the league as did his hard-to-believe 208 walks, which no doubt contributed to his 4.08 ERA.[40] All this and Feller was still a teenager. As if 278 innings weren't enough wear and tear on a nineteen-year-old arm, Feller took a brief barnstorming trip after the season.[41]

Feller was given his first Opening Day start in 1939 and defeated Detroit, 5–1, fanning ten.[42] Although the Indians were playing about .500 baseball, Feller had won five of his first six starts leading into his May 14 start against the White Sox in Cleveland. That day happened to be Mother's Day and Feller's mother was in attendance, along with his father and sister. In the third inning, Chicago third baseman Marv Owens sliced a foul ball into the stands, striking Mrs. Feller flush in the face above her left eye and shattering her glasses. Cleveland officials rushed her to the hospital while a visibly shaken Feller managed to complete a 9–4 victory.[43]

Undaunted, Feller continued to dominate the league, and by late June had put together an 11-3 record. On June 27 he started the first night game in Cleveland history, pitching against the Detroit Tigers. He proceeded to strike out thirteen batters and allowed only one hit, a fifth-inning humpback drive off the bat of the recently traded Earl Averill that fell in front of center fielder Ben Chapman.[44] By the All-Star break, Feller was 14-3 and a shoo-in for the Midsummer Classic. This time he pitched in the game, entering in the fifth inning at Yankee Stadium with a 3–1 lead and holding the National League scoreless in three and two-thirds innings of one-hit relief.[45]

While the Indians finished the season in third place, Feller established himself as the top pitcher in the American League. He led the league with

24 wins, almost 297 innings pitched, 246 strike-outs, 24 complete games, and fewest hits allowed per nine innings.[46] Still only twenty years old, he was the youngest starting pitcher in the league and the youngest ever to win twenty games.[47] Never one to turn down an extra payday, Feller headed back to California after the season to barnstorm up and down the California coast.[48]

In 1940 Feller was again the Opening Day hurler, this time with historic results. On April 16 in forty-degree weather in Comiskey Park in Chicago with his mother, father, and sister present, the twenty-one-year-old Feller tossed a no-hitter to win, 1–0. As of 2013, it remains the only Opening Day no-hitter in Major League history.[49] Feller continued to dominate as the Indians played themselves into the middle of the pennant race. On June 20 he defeated the Senators, 12–1, to push the club into first place. But while the team was playing well, at the same time Feller and others were revolting against their caustic manager, Oscar Vitt. The press got wind of the revolt and dubbed the team "the Crybabies."[50]

The team nonetheless held first place at the All-Star break. Feller, with a 13-5 record, was named to the All-Star team. He pitched two innings in the game, allowing one run in a 4–0 loss to the National League. In his next regular-season start, on July 12, he nearly had another no-hitter, allowing only an eighth-inning single to Dick Seibert of the Philadelphia A's.

The pennant race was a tight one and the Indians went into the final series of the season against the Tigers trailing them by two games.[51] Feller thus pitched the biggest game of his career to that point on September 27 in the first game of the series. The Tigers, essentially conceding the game and saving their best pitchers for the second and third games of the series, started unknown rookie Floyd Giebel. Although Feller gave up only three hits and two runs on a homer by Rudy York, Giebel pitched the game of his life and shut out the Indians to clinch the pennant for the Tigers.[52]

For the year, the twenty-one-year-old Feller won 27 games to lead the league, while losing 11. In one of the most dominating performances in history, he also led the league in six other categories, including strikeouts (261), ERA (2.61), innings pitched (320⅓), games (43), games started (37), complete games (31), and fewest hits per nine innings (6.9).[53] He finished second in the league MVP voting and was named the 1940 *Sporting News* Player of the Year. Even with his prodigious regular-season workload, Feller could not resist a brief barnstorming tour into Montana and North Dakota before returning home to Van Meter for the winter.[54]

The Indians' 1941 spring training was in Fort Myers, Florida, and there Feller began dating Virginia Winther, the daughter of a wealthy Chicago family who was attending college at nearby Rollins. The Indians had finally fired Oscar Vitt in the offseason, replacing him with Roger Peckinpaugh. The club played well out of the gate and held first place into early June when it began to slump. But Feller had a spectacular first half and by the All-Star break was 16-4. That earned him his first All-Star Game start, and he did not disappoint, striking out four and allowing only a single to Lonnie Frey in three innings.[55]

While the Indians stumbled to a tie for fourth place, Feller again led the American League with 25 wins, against 13 losses. He repeated as the league leader in most major categories including innings pitched (343), strikeouts (260), shutouts (6), games pitched (44), and games started (40).[56] Still only twenty-two years old, Feller now had 107 big league victories.

He would remain stuck on that number for three and a half years, thanks to World War II. On December 7, 1941, Feller was driving from Van Meter to Chicago to meet with Cleveland officials about his 1942 contract. When he heard on the radio about the attack on Pearl Harbor, he immediately decided to enlist in the navy and was sworn in at a navy recruiting office in Chicago on December 9.[57]

After a couple of weeks back home in Van Meter, Feller reported for basic training at the Norfolk Training Station in Virginia. When he completed basic training, he was given the rank of chief petty officer and became a physical-drill instructor. Beginning in March 1942, Feller played for the Training Station baseball team, playing Minor League clubs and other service teams.[58] Feller estimated that the team won 92 of about 100 games played that spring and summer.[59]

Feller, however, was not content with his light military duty and volunteered for gunnery school after he was turned down for pilot training because he failed a high-frequency-hearing test. He was assigned to the battleship Alabama, stationed in Norfolk,[60] where he learned in early January 1943 that his father had died. He was granted a ten-day emergency leave to attend the services. Also, as his father had wished, Feller went ahead with wedding plans and married Virginia Winther in Waukegan, Illinois, before returning to his ship in Norfolk.[61]

That spring and summer, the Alabama was dispatched to the British Home Fleet to escort convoys along the North Atlantic corridor.[62] In early August, the Alabama was called home to Norfolk and dispatched to the Pacific, traveling through the Panama Canal before arriving at Efate in the New Hebrides Islands on September 14. For the first time since the previous September, Feller was able to play some baseball, pitching for the Alabama's baseball team and playing first base for the softball team.[63]

Beginning in November, however, the Alabama went into combat and over the next six months saw action off the Gilbert Islands, the Marshall Islands, Truk, Tinian, Saipan, and Guam. While at sea, Feller occasionally played catch on deck, but in the main he was completely away from baseball. In late April and May, the Alabama went for refitting on the island of Majuro, where Feller was again able to pitch for the ship's baseball team. He threw forty-seven consecutive scoreless innings at

one juncture and continued to work on the slider he'd first developed in Norfolk.[64]

In early June the Alabama was out to sea again, participating in the invasion of Saipan. Feller participated in the Battle of the Philippine Sea, one of the most lopsided American victories in the war. In charge of a gunnery crew, he was in the heat of combat and later called the battle "the most exciting 13 hours of my life," adding, "After that, the dangers of Yankee Stadium seemed trivial."[65] The Alabama continued to see action in and around the Philippines until finally returning to Seattle for repairs and crew rotation in January 1945. Feller's combat duties were over.

After reuniting with his bride,[66] Feller received a leave in early February and visited his mother in Van Meter. He was then assigned to the Great Lakes Naval Training Station and in April succeeded Mickey Cochrane as manager of the base's crack baseball team.[67] During the summer of 1945, Feller pitched about 100 innings for Great Lakes, with the highlight coming on July 21, when he threw a ten-strikeout no-hitter before a crowd of ten thousand sailors.[68]

Finally, on August 21, one week after V-J Day, Feller received his honorable discharge from the navy. He had served for forty-four months and accumulated eight battle stars.[69] He was still only twenty-six years old.

Feller immediately signed a contract with the Indians for the balance of the 1945 season and was treated to a hero's welcome before his first start, on August 24, just three days after his discharge.[70] Before a crowd of more than 45,000 fans, Feller notched a complete-game 4–2 victory over the Detroit Tigers and their ace southpaw Hal Newhouser. Using his new slider with his fastball and curveball, Feller struck out twelve and allowed only four hits. It was his first big league game in almost four years, but he had announced in no uncertain terms that he was back.[71]

Feller made eight more starts for Cleveland in 1945, compiling a 5-3 record with a fine 2.50 ERA.

He struck out fifty-nine in seventy-two innings, allowing only fifty hits. His best game came on September 19 when, again facing the Tigers, he allowed only a bloop third-inning single by Jimmy Outlaw to finish with the sixth one-hitter of his career.[72]

Feller was eager to make up some of his lost income from the war and organized a monthlong barnstorming trip that featured a number of matchups against Satchel Paige and other Negro League stars.[73] Then on December 10, Virginia gave birth to the Fellers' first child, a baby boy they named Stephan and called Stevie.[74] In late January, Feller organized and held a "free school" in Tampa, Florida, for baseball players returning from the war. More than 180 former players attended the three-week course, and 66 eventually signed professional contracts.[75]

During spring training, Jorge Pasquel, a Mexican millionaire who was trying to create another major league south of the border, reportedly offered Feller a three-year contract at $100,000 a year to pitch in his new league. Feller was not anxious to leave the United States after two years in the Pacific and turned it down, telling the press, "No chili con carne baseball for me."[76] He opened the 1946 season with a 1–0 shutout of the White Sox. Then, in his fourth start of the year, he threw his second career no-hitter, this time against the New York Yankees in Yankee Stadium in another tense 1–0 win.[77] Those starts propelled Feller to one of the greatest seasons of pitching in Major League history. By the All-Star break Feller had fifteen wins, half the way to the coveted thirty.[78] He pitched one-hitters on July 31 and August 8 to bring his career total to eight, breaking Addie Joss's Major League record of seven.[79] On August 14 he surpassed his personal season strikeout record of 261 and set his sights on Rube Waddell's Major League record of 349.[80]

With eight games left in the season, Feller stood at 320 strikeouts. Of the next seven games, he started two on short rest and relieved in another to tie the record at 343 heading into the final game of the season against the Tigers. His opponent was Hal Newhouser, who sported a 26-8 record. A tired Feller didn't strike out anyone until the fifth inning, but then managed to fan five to break the record and finish at 348 strikeouts.[81] For the season, he finished with 26 wins against 15 losses. The sixth-place Indians won only 68 games, meaning that Feller was the winning pitcher in more than 38 percent of his team's wins.[82] He threw an incredible 371⅓ innings in 48 games and 42 starts, 36 of which were complete games. He also led the league with ten shutouts, and his 2.18 ERA was the third lowest in the league.[83]

While putting together this prodigious record, the tireless Feller was organizing an extensive postseason barnstorming trip in which "Bob Feller's All-Stars" would play thirty-four games in twenty-seven days. Feller rented two DC-3 airliners for the tour, which started in Pittsburgh and ended in Long Beach, California. Most of the opposition was provided by the "Satchel Paige All-Stars" with Paige and Feller toeing the mound for a few innings in virtually every game. In all, the tour covered around 13,000 travel miles and drew an estimated 250,000 fans.[84]

In January, Feller signed a contract with new Indians owner Bill Veeck for 1947, which at $70,000 plus attendance bonuses was reputed to surpass Babe Ruth's $80,000 salary as the largest in sports history.[85] Although Feller battled injuries in 1947 and elected not to pitch in the All-Star Game because of back pain, he put together another stellar campaign for the improving fourth-place Indians. He pitched two more one-hitters to bring his career total to ten, finishing the season with 20 wins against 11 losses. He led the league in games started (37), shutouts (5), strikeouts (196), and innings (299), and was second in ERA (2.68).[86] After the season, despite his heavy workload, Feller went barnstorming, again, competing mostly against Satchel Paige and other Negro League stars.[87]

With the Indians in a pennant race in 1948, Feller, at least for him, struggled during the first half of the season and was only 9-10 by the All-Star break.[88] He battled arm fatigue after the break and was inconsistent, sometimes showing his old form and sometimes getting rocked. On October 3, the last day of the season, manager Lou Boudreau sent Feller to the mound against Hal Newhouser and the Tigers with a one-game lead. If the Indians won, they would win the pennant. Feller did not survive the third inning, however, and the Indians lost, 7–1, forcing a one-game playoff with the Red Sox in Boston.[89]

The Indians won the playoff game, 8–3, behind the pitching of southpaw Gene Bearden, pitching on just one day's rest.[90] The following day, October 6, Boudreau tapped Feller to start the first game of the World Series against the National League champion Boston Braves. He was on his game and didn't allow a hit until the fifth inning before retiring nine more Braves in a row. He headed into the bottom of the eighth inning locked in a scoreless tie against Braves ace Johnny Sain, who had scattered four hits. In the eighth, Feller walked lead-off batter Bill Salkeld, who was replaced by pinch runner Phil Masi, who was sacrificed to second. With two out, Feller turned and picked Masi off second by at least a foot; the only problem was that umpire Bill Stewart called Masi safe. Unfortunately for Feller and the Indians, Tommy Holmes then singled to left, scoring Masi and sending Feller to a 1–0 defeat.[91]

Later, with the Indians leading the World Series three games to one, Feller toed the rubber for Game Five back in Cleveland with a chance to close out the Series. He was anything but sharp and struggled to a 5–5 tie into the seventh, when the roof really caved in on him and four relievers. The game ended in an 11–5 defeat. The Indians clinched the Series the next day in Boston, but Feller had the ignominy of being the losing pitcher in the only two games the Indians lost in the Series.[92]

Feller was no better than the third-best pitcher on the crack Indians staff in 1948, finishing with a 19-15 record and a 3.56 ERA.[93] He did start thirty-eight games, to lead the league, and although his strikeout total dropped to 164, that, too, was first in the league. After the season, Feller did not barnstorm, other than throwing seven shutout innings in an exhibition game to celebrate "Feller Day" in his hometown.[94]

Named Opening Day starter in 1949, Feller strained a shoulder muscle warming up and lasted only two innings. By the All-Star break, he was only 6-6 and was not named to the AL team for the first time since 1937 (excepting the war years). He finished the season 15-14 with a 3.75 ERA as the Indians, beset with injuries, fell to third place. In 211 innings, Feller's strikeouts fell to 108.[95] He improved to 16-11 in 1950, with his ERA dropping to 3.43. At thirty-one, Feller was no longer overpowering but was still a quality starting pitcher, and he was again named to the All-Star team.[96]

Feller started the 1951 season with a vengeance, and on June 30 he stood 10-2 with a league-leading ERA of under 3.00. Yankees manager Casey Stengel nonetheless left him off the All-Star team. The day after the team was announced, Feller answered the slight by pitching the third no-hitter of his career, defeating the Tigers 2–1.[97] Although Feller was not as sharp in the second half of the season, he still finished 22-8, leading the league in wins for the second-place Indians.[98]

Unhappily, Feller's 1952 season was a dud. He finished at 9-13 for the first losing record of his career. He also walked more than he struck out and gave up more hits than innings pitched, both also for the first time. His ERA was an unsightly 4.74, and his disappointing year had a lot to do with the Indians' second consecutive second-place finish behind the Yankees. Although he had long had his sights set on 300 career victories, Feller was now resigned to falling short of that mark.[99]

At thirty-four, Feller was able to bounce back in 1953, becoming a serviceable once-a-week starter. He won ten games, lost seven, and dropped his ERA more than a run to 3.59 as the Indians again finished in second place behind the Yankees. He continued his success as a weekly starter in the Indians' runaway 1954 pennant year,[100] but in 1955 was restricted to spot starting and long relief. Finishing 4-4, he had a very serviceable 3.47 ERA in eighty-three innings of work. He still showed flashes of his old self, throwing the twelfth one-hitter of his career, against the Red Sox on April 16.

Feller was back for more in 1956 and emerged from spring training as the Indians' fifth starter. But after one ineffective start in April and another in May, he was relegated to the bullpen, where he was used mostly in mop-up duty. The Indians threw a day for him on September 9, honoring him with a new car and various other gifts. President Dwight Eisenhower sent a telegram lauding Feller for his military service and work with charities, which "makes a fine example of American manhood."[101]

The final start of Feller's career was on September 30, the last day of the season. He pitched a complete game against the Detroit Tigers, losing 8–4 and failing to strike out a single batter. For the season, he appeared in only nineteen games and threw only fifty-eight innings, finishing 0-4 with a 4.97 ERA. Amid much speculation, Feller met on December 28 with Indians general manager Hank Greenberg. When he emerged he announced his retirement to the assembled press.[102] He was thirty-eight years old.

Although no one knew it at the time, Feller's wife, Virginia, had become addicted to barbiturates and amphetamines shortly after the war ended. For the last ten years of his playing career, Virginia was a constant worry and distraction for Feller. The couple had three sons and Feller had to hire a live-in maid to take care of them. Virginia had several stays in the Mayo Clinic but couldn't stem her addiction, which caused insomnia and other behavioral problems as well as stretching the family's finances. Finally, in 1971, the couple divorced.[103]

Feller did not slow down upon his retirement as an active player. He got into the insurance business in Cleveland and also joined Motorola as "consultant on youth activities," crisscrossing the country

supporting Little League programs by giving speeches and conducting baseball seminars and camps.[104] In August 1957 he appeared on the *Mike Wallace Interview* program on ABC Television and created controversy by roundly criticizing baseball's reserve clause.[105] He became the first president of the Major League Players Association and helped develop its first pension plan.

In 1958 Feller briefly joined the Mutual Radio Network to help broadcast the *Game of the Day*.[106] He was elected to Baseball's Hall of Fame in 1962, his first year of eligibility, receiving 150 of 160 votes cast.[107] After his divorce, Feller was married again in 1974 to Anne Thorpe, a woman he had met in church. He sometimes participated in old-timers' games and was a frequent guest at sports memorabilia shows around the country. In 1994 the Cleveland Indians erected a ten-foot bronze statue of him at their new Jacobs Field home, and in 1995 the Bob Feller Museum, designed by Feller's architect son, Steve, opened in Van Meter. Feller was still throwing a baseball every day well into his eighties and claimed to have thrown a baseball more often than any man in history.[108] The last time he pitched was at an exhibition game in Cooperstown in June 2009, at the age of ninety.

Feller was diagnosed with leukemia in August 2010 and died on December 15 of that year. He was ninety-two years old.

For his eighteen-year Major League career, Feller won 266 games against 162 losses.[109] At six feet tall and 185 pounds, he was on the short side for a right-handed pitcher by contemporary standards. Both Ted Williams and Joe DiMaggio labeled him the greatest pitcher either had ever seen.[110] Although he lost almost four full seasons to service in World War II during the prime of his career, he still led the American League in victories six times and in strikeouts seven times. With his three no-hitters, twelve one-hitters, 279 complete games, and forty-four shutouts, he was the dominant pitcher of his generation and one of the greatest of all time.

Chapter 10. **Dave Hoskins**

John Watkins

AGE	W	L	PCT	ERA	G	GS	GF	CG	SHO	SV	IP	H	BB	SO	HBP	WP
28	0	1	.000	3.04	14	1	3	0	0	0	26.2	29	10	9	0	1

When Dave Hoskins of the visiting Dallas Eagles warmed up before his start against the Shreveport Sports on the evening of June 9, 1952, he had reason to be apprehensive. Earlier that day, Hoskins, the Texas League's first black player, had received three letters threatening his life.

At the time, Louisiana was not particularly hospitable toward black ballplayers. Pending before the state senate was a bill that would have prohibited blacks and whites from participating together in any competitive sports event for which admission was charged. The bill's sponsor acknowledged that it was aimed at the Texas League in general and the Eagles in particular.[1]

According to each letter in turn, Hoskins would be shot if he sat in the dugout, set foot on the field, or took the mound. "I figured all three were from the same person," Hoskins said the following spring. "Probably someone just trying to scare me. I didn't tell Dutch Meyer, the manager of our club, because I was afraid he wouldn't let me start."[2]

Although Hoskins thought the letter writer was "only bluffing," he admitted being "a little scared" when he went to the mound. But he settled down and pitched a complete game for his ninth win of the season as the Eagles defeated the Sports, 3–2. The record crowd of 7,378 included 4,403 African Americans.

Dallas went on to a first-place finish, and Hoskins led the league in wins (22), complete games (26), and innings pitched (280). He finished second in earned run average (2.12), added two more wins in the playoffs, and was a unanimous choice for the Texas League all-star game. The next season, Hoskins made the jump from Double-A to the Cleve-

Dave Hoskins—Hoskins spent two years in the Majors, both with Cleveland (1953–54). He achieved a 22-10 record for the Dallas Eagles of the Texas League in 1952.

land Indians, making his Major League debut on April 18, 1953. He was thirty-five years old, soon to turn thirty-six.

Most baseball sources state that David Taylor Hoskins was born in Greenwood, Mississippi, on August 3, 1925. Two corrections need to be made: his middle name was Will, apparently after his father, and he was born in 1917. "His birthday was listed as 1925, but Dave knew that was a fib," a newspaper columnist once wrote, adding that he

51

was "age 36 or thereabouts" when he reached the Major Leagues.[3]

Dave was the third child of Will and Hattie Hoskins, joining two brothers in the family. The boys lost their mother in 1924, when Hattie passed away. By the time the federal census was taken in May 1930, Will had remarried and lived with his wife, Bertha, his three sons, and his aging parents in rural Leflore County, of which Greenwood is the county seat. The family later expanded with the birth of two daughters. Will Hoskins grew cotton, most likely as a sharecropper. Although Dave, then twelve, did not yet work, his two brothers, fifteen and eighteen, and the boys' grandfather joined Will in the fields.

Dave graduated from G. H. Jones Industrial School in Highlandale, about twenty miles north of Greenwood. His family soon moved to Flint, Michigan, birthplace of General Motors, and Dave found a job at the Chevrolet assembly plant. He also began making a name for himself as a baseball player.[4]

For four seasons in the Flint City League, Hoskins starred as a left-handed-hitting outfielder and right-handed pitcher. His performance attracted the attention of the Cincinnati Clowns, who in 1942 signed him to his first professional contract. Reportedly classified 4-F in World War II, he spent one season with the Clowns as an outfielder and part-time pitcher.

Hoskins saw duty with three more teams over the course of the decade: the Homestead Grays, the Chicago American Giants, and the Louisville Buckeyes. His best seasons were with the legendary Grays; in 1944, when the Grays won their eighth consecutive Negro National League pennant, he played right field, hit .324, and compiled a 5-2 record on the mound. Sportswriter Sam Lacy was impressed, listing Hoskins as one of nine Negro League players with potential to play in the Major Leagues.[5]

On August 1, 1948, Hoskins made his debut in Organized Baseball as an outfielder with the Grand Rapids Jets of the Class A Central League. He bat-ted .393 in forty-six games and, as the league's first black player, experienced harsher treatment than he would later encounter in the Texas League. In addition to enduring racial slurs, he had to avoid fastballs aimed at his head.

Hoskins returned to Grand Rapids in 1949 but was released after a few games. He then joined the Louisville Buckeyes of the Negro American League, hit .305, and made the all-star team before being traded to the division-winning Chicago American Giants for the playoffs. Hoskins's road to the Major Leagues also began that year, when Satchel Paige, then in his second season with Cleveland, arranged a tryout. "You better sign this boy," Paige told general manager Hank Greenberg. "He can hit. I know 'cause I never could get him out easy."[6]

Greenberg signed Hoskins to a Minor League contract, and in 1950 Cleveland sent him to Dayton in the Central League. Once again the target of opposing pitchers, he was hit in the head with a fastball and hospitalized. While recovering, he decided to focus on pitching. "I was tired of having pitchers throw at me," Hoskins said later. "I made up my mind I would start throwing at other guys."[7] Back on the team, he asked for and got a chance to pitch, but the results were unremarkable: a 0-2 record and a 6.43 ERA in fourteen innings.[8]

Hoskins was undeterred. Barnstorming with Paige that fall, he got a chance to pitch one day and notched several strikeouts with a sharp curveball. "Man, you're wasting your time in the outfield," Paige said. "With a curve like that you ought to be pitching."

At spring training in 1951, the Cleveland organization decided that Hoskins had progressed enough to stay on the mound. The decision paid off. Assigned to Wilkes-Barre in the Class A Eastern League, he posted a 5-1 record and a 3.60 ERA while also working as a part-time outfielder.

In early 1952 Dick Burnett, owner of the Dallas Eagles of the Double-A Texas League, made clear his intent to sign the league's first African American player. He believed that talented black athletes would not only improve the Eagles but also attract African American fans. After tryouts in Dallas and at spring training failed to produce satisfactory candidates, Burnett sought help from the Indians, with whom Dallas had a working agreement. Hank Greenberg recommended Hoskins.

Burnett got a bargain. Hoskins, the club's lowest-paid player, became the Texas League's top pitcher as the Eagles finished in first place and led the league in attendance, drawing African American fans to Burnett Field in large numbers. Attendance jumped by 16.8 percent in Dallas while falling 2.7 percent across the league.

The key to Hoskins's success, manager Dutch Meyer recalled years later, was the pitch that had impressed Satchel Paige. "Dave could throw a curveball through a knothole," Meyer said.[9] For good measure, Hoskins hit .328 in 128 at bats.

Apart from the death threats in Shreveport, Hoskins had fewer problems with opposing players and fans than he had experienced in the Central League. Bench jockeying was minimal and headhunting pitchers were rare. Crowds on the road were at times brutal, however, as some fans taunted and cursed him. In addition, the rules of the Jim Crow South were a constant presence on road trips, as well as in strictly segregated Dallas. Through it all, Meyer said, the pitcher was "a model of decorum" on and off the field.

Hoskins downplayed his pioneer role and the adversity he faced. "All in all," he said, "I had no complaints."[10] He cared much more about his relationship with his teammates, and there were no problems in that regard. "He was such a nice man, you couldn't not love the guy," first baseman Joe Macko said. They realized the pressure he faced as the league's first black player, and pitcher Joe Kotrany thought Burnett "got just the right player to take on the responsibility."

A fitting coda to the year came on its last day, when the influential *Chicago Defender* named nine individuals to its "honor roll of democracy" for 1952.

Among them was Hoskins, cited "for exemplifying the highest type of sportsmanship while pioneering as the first Negro to play in the Texas League and proving that qualifications can overcome racial discrimination."

Hoskins was among the pitchers reported to "figure prominently" in Cleveland manager Al Lopez's plans for the 1953 season. The team's strength was its "Big Three," starting pitchers Bob Lemon, Mike Garcia, and Early Wynn. But fourth starter Bob Feller had slumped to 9-13 in 1952, and bullpen depth was a concern.

Although the situation presented an opportunity for Hoskins, the odds were against him. Of the twenty-seven black Major Leaguers from 1947 through 1952, only five were pitchers—an apparent aversion toward African American hurlers that endured for years. Hoskins made the club as a reliever and spot starter and helped the Indians to a second-place finish behind the Yankees. His 9-3 record led American League rookies, and he finished with a 3.99 ERA in 112⅔ innings over 26 games.

Hoskins's best performance came on August 21, not long after his thirty-sixth birthday: a complete game at home against St. Louis that Cleveland won on Bill Glynn's two-out double off Harry Brecheen in the bottom of the twelfth inning. On September 7, Hoskins and Satchel Paige made history as the Tribe again hosted the Browns. It was the first Major League game in which both starting pitchers were African Americans. Neither lasted beyond the fourth inning, but Paige claimed bragging rights with two hits.

After Hoskins's strong rookie season, the Indians rewarded him with a "substantial" raise, and he was optimistic about 1954. He had pitched well for Roy Campanella's barnstormers, and manager Al Lopez was reportedly counting on him again in the dual role of reliever and spot starter. But as Cleveland won 111 games to take the pennant, Hoskins experienced only disappointment in what was to be his last Major League season.

The Indians were loaded with pitchers, and there was little room for Hoskins. Lost in the crowd, he made only one start and thirteen relief appearances, logged twenty-six and two-thirds innings, and finished with a 0-1 record and a 3.04 ERA. After clinching the pennant, the Indians announced that he would not be on the list of twenty-five players eligible for the World Series against the New York Giants. In his place was an extra catcher who had missed most of the season with an injury.

Hoskins's teammates made known their displeasure about the club's decision. In a meeting to allocate the players' portion of the World Series proceeds, they voted Hoskins a full share, worth $6,712.50. They also directed Feller, the Indians' player representative, to "express our concern" about a roster move that "deprived a worthy player of a distinction for which he, like all of us, worked so hard all season to attain."

At spring training in 1955, the competition among pitchers would be intense. The Tribe was expected to carry ten pitchers, and as a practical matter only one position on the staff was open. The heralded rookie Herb Score, a twenty-two-game winner at Indianapolis, was the top candidate to fill it. When the squad was trimmed on March 28 as the team broke camp at Tucson, Hoskins was among the players sent to Daytona Beach for reassignment. Some observers were surprised, and the pitcher was floored. As he told *The Sporting News*, he became "sick and nervous and couldn't sleep." Lopez explained that Hoskins would be better off at Indianapolis, the Tribe's affiliate in the American Association, where he could pitch regularly. That way, the manager said, "he can be sharp whenever we need him."[11]

The call-up never came. Hoskins pitched at Indianapolis in 1955 and played for seven other Minor League teams over the next five years, also squeezing in some winter ball. He began the 1960 season, his last, in Canada with the Montreal Royals of the International League and ended it in Mexico with the Double-A Poza Rica Petroleros. Fittingly, his best season was in 1958 when he returned to Dallas: 17-8 with a 3.18 ERA in 246 innings.

With his World Series check, Hoskins had purchased an eighteen-acre farm near Flint. After retiring from baseball at forty-three, Hoskins worked full-time for General Motors in Flint, drove a taxi to supplement his income, and enjoyed life on the farm with his wife, Cora, whom he had married in 1953, and their children. His first marriage had ended in divorce when his spouse asked him to give up baseball.

Rural life appealed to Hoskins, who enjoyed being outdoors. He grew a large vegetable garden, kept a few farm animals, and raised German shepherds for sale to law-enforcement agencies. He also hunted pheasant and played golf. A modest and unassuming man, he never bragged about his baseball accomplishments.

Hoskins made friends easily and loved music. His tastes were eclectic, ranging from jazz to country-western. He took an interest in cameras as well. With newsreel photographers at work one day at spring training, he took advantage of the break in routine to shoot his own movies. As might be expected of someone who worked for General Motors, he liked cars; during his time with the Indians, he drove a Cadillac. He also enjoyed nice clothes and was known as a sharp dresser.

On April 2, 1970, the fifty-two-year-old Hoskins was found slumped over the steering wheel of his taxi, parked outside a Flint coffee shop. He was pronounced dead at Hurley Hospital, having suffered a heart attack. A member of United Auto Workers Local 659, Hoskins was employed at the Chevrolet Parts Division at the time of his death. He was survived by his wife, Cora; daughters Ruchelle, Lynda, and Carolyn; son Maurice; and one brother and two sisters. He was buried at River Rest Cemetery in Flint.

In 2004 Hoskins was honored as one of the inaugural inductees to the Texas League Hall of Fame. Previously, he had been named to the Greater Flint Afro-American Hall of Fame, recognized "as the greatest Flint athlete to pitch professional baseball."

Chapter 11. **Don Mossi**

Mark Stewart

AGE	W	L	PCT	ERA	G	GS	GF	CG	SHO	SV	IP	H	BB	SO	HBP	WP
25	6	1	.857	1.94	40	5	18	2	0	7	93	56	39	55	1	0

One of the rarest things in baseball is a shut-down righty-lefty bullpen. Players, managers, and—let's face it—agents like relief roles defined. Today you have eighth-inning guys and ninth-inning guys. And if you're lucky, you have hurlers who can form a human bridge from the starters to those players. Having two closers—one to dispose of lefties, another to clamp down on righties—is either an unheard-of or an unaffordable luxury. The short list includes Eastwick and McEnaney, Gossage and Lyle, Hernandez and Lopez, and Dibble and Myers. From there you have to think really hard. Of course, fans of the Cleveland Indians can tell you who the originals were: Don Mossi and Ray Narleski, rookie roommates on the fabled 1954 American League champions.

Narleski, the flamethrower, didn't survive the 1950s. Mossi, the control artist, was a different story. He not only had a grand career as a reliever, he was a top starter for several seasons, too, and was still getting batters out in 1965. As memorable for his peculiar looks as for his pinpoint pitching, Don was the kind of guy every manager wanted on the team.

Donald Louis Mossi was born on January 11, 1929, in St. Helena, California, in Sonoma County, north of San Francisco. He grew up in Daly City, just south of San Francisco, and attended Jefferson High School. Like many other schools in the Bay Area, "Jeff" would produce several outstanding athletes and sports personalities—including Major Leaguers Ken Reitz and Tony Solaita, and NFL coaching legend John Madden.

During the summers, Don played on youth-league teams, typically made up of his schoolmates and

Don Mossi—A rookie in 1954, the left-handed Mossi teamed with right-hander Ray Narleski to give the Indians a superb one-two punch out of the bullpen.

neighborhood kids. He threw hard, hid the ball well, and had a lot of poise for a young left-hander.

The Cleveland Indians signed Mossi after his nineteenth birthday and assigned him to the Bakersfield Indians of the Class C California League for the 1949 season. Bakersfield may have seemed miles away from the Majors, but Mossi's spirits must have been buoyed by the knowledge that three seasons earlier, Mike Garcia had toiled for these same

Indians. Now he was elbowing his way into the Cleveland rotation.

Manager Harry Griswold guided Bakersfield to a first-place finish with an 85-54 record, largely on the strength of the league's top player, Earl Escalante. Escalante won twenty-eight games—ten more than anyone else in the loop—and provided a veteran presence for Mossi and the team's other young pitchers. Bakersfield's season ended when they lost in the first round of the playoffs. Mossi won 13 games and lost 9, fanning 149 California League hitters in 195 innings. He was projected as a strikeout pitcher, which made his 115 walks a matter of concern.

Mossi returned to Bakersfield in 1950. The Indians finished the year 61-79, in sixth place. Mossi went 11-10 in twenty-nine starts. His control issues were still present, but there was little else to complain about. As a twenty-one-year-old lefty, he was making progress and getting critically important innings under his belt.

In 1951 Mossi began with the Wichita Indians of the Class A Western League. Although he still struggled with bouts of wildness, he had refined his approach considerably, as witnessed by his 2.29 earned run average in 122 innings. He went 7-6 for Wichita and also pitched for Wilkes-Barre of the Eastern League, where he was equally effective in six appearances.

In 1952 Mossi was assigned to Dallas of the Double-A Texas League. One of five starting pitchers on the Eagles, he was a swingman in the four-man rotation, logging 42 appearances with 22 starts, and went 9-8 in 179 innings with a 3.42 ERA against the stiffer competition. He was still walking a batter every other inning.

The 1953 season was a pivotal one for Mossi. He found himself back in the Texas League, this time with the Tulsa Oilers, a Cincinnati Reds farm team. The Indians no longer had an affiliate agreement with Dallas, and Mossi was one of many Cleveland players at this level to be sprinkled around the Minors. Recognizing Mossi's resiliency, manager Joe

Schultz used him liberally in 1953. Mossi led the team in innings pitched with 201, going 12-12 with an ERA under 3.00. Lost in these statistics was the fact that he effected a significant change in his pitching style at Tulsa. He began experimenting with a three-finger grip instead of the traditional two, and found he could spot the ball without losing velocity or movement. This discovery could not have come at a better time, for the rules of Organized Baseball dictated that the Indians had either to promote Mossi to the Majors in 1954 or to waive him, for he had spent his fifth season in the Minors.

Thus, Mossi found himself in spring training with the Indians in 1954, pitching for a spot on the big league roster. Among the pitchers in camp were starters Mike Garcia, Early Wynn, and Bob Lemon. Among them they totaled fifty-six victories in 1953. Bob Feller, who at thirty-five no longer had his blinding speed, still had a killer curve and brought nearly two decades of professional mound experience to the fifth starter's job. The question for manager Al Lopez was who would get the fourth starter's role. The most likely candidates included Dave Hoskins, Bill Wight, Bob Hooper, rookie Dick Tomanek, and Art Houtteman. Mossi was never mentioned among the competitors for a rotation spot. He was pitching for his baseball life, and when he arrived at camp and saw the wealth of arms on the Cleveland roster, he literally started thinking about a second career. During the winters he had been working construction to support himself and his wife, Eunice, whom he had married in the summer of 1950. He showed a flair for carpentry and decided this would make a fine fallback profession. With the Indians he didn't have a particularly outstanding spring, but Indians manager Al Lopez was a shrewd judge of potential, and saw that Mossi had mostly licked his control problems, had a good fastball, and could clearly throw his curve for strikes. Both pitches were well above average for a rookie. To Lopez, keeping a competent two-pitch pitcher like Mossi in the bullpen was for more appealing than the prospect of letting him go.

Former catcher Lopez understood that left-handed hurlers were more effective against left-handed batters, and that right-handed pitchers did better against right-handed hitters. This was hardly revelatory information, but few managers until then were willing to build and then utilize a bullpen around this concept. The 1953 Indians had not had the arms to make this happen, particularly from the left side. The 1954 Indians did. Mossi joined veteran Hal Newhouser, signed by GM Hank Greenberg after being released by the Tigers, as the two southpaws in the Cleveland relief corps. Future Hall of Famer Newhouser performed in long relief for the Indians in 1954. Mossi, with his fastball and curve, newly minted pinpoint control, and ability to hide the ball from batters, functioned as the short man and sometimes-starter when Cleveland faced a tough left-handed lineup, or when Feller or Houtteman was unable to go.

The right-handed half of the bullpen was made up of Mossi's former Minor League teammates Dave Hoskins and Bob Hooper, along with Garcia, who warmed up quickly and could be used in emergencies. The man who stepped up and seized the mantle of short relief was fellow rookie Ray Narleski. The skinny New Jerseyan was a second-generation Major Leaguer. He had climbed the organizational ladder a step ahead of Don, but here they were, asked to close out the games that the previous year's bullpen had allowed to slip away. Narleski threw a white-hot fastball that enemy hitters found irresistible. He would take opponents up the ladder until they were swinging at pitches out of the zone, and either striking out or hitting harmless flies. Mossi and Narleski roomed together during the 1954 campaign.

Mossi may not have let it show, but going into his first big league campaign, surrounded by superstars and awash in impossibly high expectations, he was downright scared. He later said that the team's veterans helped him find his comfort zone, particularly Lemon and Feller. Of course, there wasn't much time for him to ponder his surroundings. The Ti-

gers and White Sox got off to blistering starts, while Cleveland found itself in the cellar after nine games.

Mossi finished the year with a 6-1 record in forty appearances, thirty-five of them in relief. He finished sixteen games as a reliever, seven of which qualified as saves (which were not a statistic in those days). In his five starts, Mossi went 2-1 and pitched two complete games. His only loss as a starter was inflicted by the Tigers in extra innings. In all, he hurled ninety-three innings, gave up fifty-six hits, and walked thirty-nine batters. He struck out fifty-five and turned in an excellent 1.94 ERA, contributing to the team's league-best 2.78 mark. Narleski was just as good, finishing nineteen games with thirteen saves and a 2.22 ERA.

The 1954 World Series was a watershed moment for baseball, though for reasons largely untold. For the first time, baseball fans were talking about the battle of the bullpens. Other pennant winners had relied on good relief pitching, but never before had two opponents in the Fall Classic boasted such impressive bullpens. Hoyt Wilhelm and Marv Grissom combined for twenty-two wins and twenty-six saves for the Giants, more than a match for the sixteen wins and twenty-seven saves shared by Mossi, Narleski, and Newhouser. As for Mossi, his role heading into the Series seemed clear. He would be used to quell the left-handed bats of Don Mueller, Whitey Lockman, and Hank Thompson.

In Game One, with the score tied 2–2, Mossi and his teammates watched Willie Mays reel in Vic Wertz's eighth-inning drive to deep center field, a play that turned out to be pivotal and famous. With a scoring opportunity lost, the Indians were focused on holding the Giants. In the tenth inning, starter Bob Lemon walked Mays, who stole second. Lemon issued an intentional pass to Thompson to create a force with one out.

Were the year 2004 instead of 1954, Mossi might have been inserted in the game to face left-handed pinch hitter Dusty Rhodes. Instead, Lopez left the right-handed Lemon on the mound, hoping he would induce a grounder for a double play. Rhodes homered to win the game.

Mossi saw action in the final three games of New York's jaw-dropping four-game sweep. In Game Two, one inning after Rhodes homered against Early Wynn in the seventh, Mossi took the mound and retired Lockman on a foul pop to first, Alvin Dark on a liner to second, and Thompson on a comebacker. The Indians put the first two runners on in the top of the ninth, but Johnny Antonelli retired the next three to preserve a 3–1 victory.

The Series switched to Cleveland for Game Three, but the Indians' luck failed to change. For the third contest in a row, Rhodes got the backbreaking hit, this one a two-run pinch single off of Art Houtteman in the third inning. Mossi took the mound in the ninth to mop up a 6–2 loss. He gave up two hits but retired the Giants with a double play and a strikeout of Rhodes, who had stayed in the game.

Game Four was a rout, with the Giants touching Lemon, Newhouser, and Narleski for four runs in the fifth inning to open a 7–0 lead. Mossi pitched the sixth and seventh, retiring six straight hitters as his teammates scored three times to make the game interesting. In the bottom of the seventh, Lopez lifted Mossi for Rudy Regalado, whose single to center cut the deficit to 7–4. Manager Leo Durocher brought Hoyt Wilhelm into the game, and he retired Dave Pope on a comebacker to end the inning. Antonelli, the Game Two starter, followed Wilhelm and finished off the Indians without allowing another run.

In four World Series innings, Mossi allowed a couple of screamers, but he held the Giants scoreless in his three appearances. Cleveland fans were left to wonder what might have been had Lopez matched Durocher lefty for lefty at the three key moments during the Series. Mossi's assessment of the Indians' loss was simple: "We were overconfident."

The law of gravity seized the Indians in 1955, as they finished with 93 wins—three behind the Yankees. With the exception of Al Smith, none of the hitters could reproduce his 1954 numbers. Nor could the Big Three, though Lemon tied for the AL lead with 18 wins. Lemon, Wynn, and Garcia accumulated 46 victories—19 fewer than the year before. Needless to say, Lopez counted more heavily on his bullpen, and once again Mossi and Narleski answered the call. They made 57 and 60 appearances, respectively, and combined for 13 wins and 28 saves. Mossi was sharp all year. In 81⅔ innings he gave up 81 hits, while he walked a meager 18 batters. He struck out 69 and had a 2.42 ERA to go with 4 wins and 9 saves. Herb Score, the rookie starter who won 16 games for the Indians that summer—and called games on TV and radio for decades—said often that he never saw a better lefty-righty duo than Mossi and Narleski in 1955. At season's end, Mossi even received a handful of MVP votes from the baseball writers.

An elbow injury nagged Narleski for much of the following season, as the Indians finished behind the Yankees in the pennant race yet again. Mossi finished 24 games, winning 6 and saving 11 in support of Wynn, Lemon, and Score, who won 20 games each. His ERA rose to 3.59, but his other numbers stayed more or less the same.

The 1957 season saw the departure of Al Lopez to the White Sox. Chicago ascended to second place while Cleveland, under Kerby Farrell, finished a game below .500, in sixth place. The starting staff disintegrated due to age and injury, the most notable event being the Gil McDougald line drive that destroyed Score's career. With Cleveland's acquisition of Hoyt Wilhelm, Farrell pressed Mossi into action as a starter twenty-two times in 1957. He responded with six complete games and a shutout. He went 11-10 with a pair of saves and an uncharacteristically high 4.13 ERA.

That July, Mossi was selected to play in his one and only All-Star Game. Called in to preserve a 6–4 lead in the ninth inning with two on and none out, he struck out Eddie Mathews looking, then allowed a ground single to left by Ernie Banks that plated a run. Gus Bell, running from first base, was thrown out trying to reach third base for the second out. Gil Hodges entered the game as a pinch hitter, and Bob Grim of the Yankees replaced Mossi. Hodges hit a liner to left, which Minnie Minoso snagged to end the game. After his All-Star appearance, Mossi had a rough July, dropping five straight at one point and getting roughed up by the Senators, Yankees, and Red Sox.

Mossi returned to the bullpen in 1958, as the Indians brought in a passel of new starters, including Mudcat Grant, Gary Bell, and Cal McLish. The new-look Tribe improved by exactly one win, finishing a game over .500, in fourth place. Mossi contributed seven wins and three saves, assuming more finishing duties after Wilhelm was waived and picked up by the Orioles.

Mossi had actually enjoyed his time as a starter in 1957, and although he helped make history with his relief work in 1954, he was never entirely comfortable going game to game without knowing if he'd be working or not. Thus, when the Indians dealt Mossi, Narleski, and infielder Ossie Alvarez to Detroit for Billy Martin and Al Cicotte prior to the 1959 season, Don looked forward to the change of scenery. There, he was reunited with a former Minor League manager, Bill Norman, and joined a starting staff that included Frank Lary, Jim Bunning, and Paul Foytack. The season got off to a disastrous start, as the Tigers limped to a 2-15 record. Norman was replaced with Jimmy Dykes and the ship was righted, as the Tigers went 74-63 the rest of the way. To the amazement of Tiger fans, Mossi turned out to be the star of the staff. He went 17-9, hurling 228 innings, giving up 210 hits, and walking 49. He tied for the team lead with three shutouts and tied with Milt Pappas for second in the American League with fifteen complete games.

The highlight of the year for Mossi was his five straight wins over New York. He and Lary, the famous "Yankee Killer," were a major reason why the Bronx Bombers slipped into third place. Mossi

actually preferred facing slugging lineups to teams that scratched out hits. He succeeded by changing speeds and locations and upsetting the timing of enemy hitters. Mickey Mantle, Elston Howard, and Bill Skowron were much easier for him to deal with than, say, Nellie Fox and Luis Aparicio. Besides, by that point, Mossi had lost a little off his fastball and was starting to feel the arm discomfort that would accompany him the rest of his career. Blowing the ball past power hitters wasn't really an option anymore. In fact, he had started working a changeup into the mix, if only to create the illusion of speed when he fired a fastball over the plate.

Mossi began the 1960 campaign by beating the Yankees twice more, running his personal string to seven. He completed 9 of 22 starts and had a 9-8 record when a sore arm ended his season in late August. The Tigers finished a disappointing 71-83, in sixth place. The team's pitching returned to form in 1961, as Lary won 23 games and Jim Bunning added 17. Mossi bounced back with a 15-7 mark during a relatively pain-free season, as he logged 240 innings and led the starters with a 2.96 ERA. The Tigers held first place for most of the first half, but relinquished their grip after the All-Star break to the Yankees. New York took the pennant with 109 wins to second-place Detroit's 101. If Mossi ever wondered how the Yankees felt the year Cleveland won 111, now he knew. Sometimes, it just wasn't your year.

By this time Mossi had appeared on enough bubble-gum cards to have caught the attention of millions of young fans, who marveled at his unusual visage. He did not have the classic country-boy good looks of a Mickey Mantle or the dark, handsome face of a Sandy Koufax. Don was, well, different. He had a long, slightly crooked nose, his eyes were close together, and his ears stuck out to the edges of the cardboard. Indeed, some of his teammates called him Ears. Others nicknamed him The Sphinx. Later, when these young fans grew up, they were less diplomatic. One said he looked like "Mount Rushmore on a rainy day." Bill James wrote that Don was the "complete ugly player. He could run ugly, hit ugly, throw ugly, field ugly, and ugly for power. He was ugly to all fields."

Well, Don could certainly *win* ugly. During that remarkable 1961 season, for instance, he proved it in a June game against the Indians. His former teammates launched no fewer than five home runs off him, yet he persevered and won the game. It took thirty-eight years for another Tiger, Jeff Weaver, to match Mossi's team record by allowing five dingers against the Boston Red Sox.

Alas, Detroit's aging rotation could not maintain its high standards in 1962, and the team sank to fourth place with an 85-76 record. Mossi, now thirty-three years old, made 27 starts and won 11 times against 13 defeats, with a 4.19 ERA. That wonderful 1961 season was starting to look like his last hurrah as a starter. This proved to be the case, as twenty-two-year-old Mickey Lolich usurped Mossi's spot in the rotation during the 1963 campaign. Don finished his tenth year in the Majors with a 7-7 record and a 3.74 ERA. No one was complaining about his control—he walked just 17 batters in 123 innings—but as far as the Tigers were concerned, he was nearing the end of the line.

Mossi reported to spring training in 1964 to find the Tigers were committed to dismantling their entire starting staff. He was sold to the White Sox in March—a vertical move, given Chicago's second-place finish the year before, and the fact that he would be reunited with Al Lopez. A fringe benefit of this arrangement was the chance to work with Ray Berres, the team's pitching coach. Berres was known for coaxing quality innings out of tired arms. Mossi and Frank Bauman served as the lefties in the Chicago bullpen during an enthralling summer. Hoyt Wilhelm was the team's primary closer, but Mossi got to finish seventeen games, picking up seven saves in the process. The White Sox, Orioles, and Yankees spent the summer in a death struggle for first place.

Mossi's season ended before the September stretch run began thanks to his recurring arm trouble. The White Sox finished one game behind New York. In a season of what-ifs for South Side fans, having a healthy Don Mossi available might have been one of the difference makers the team needed.

The White Sox released Mossi after the 1964 season. He caught on with the Kansas City A's the following spring. Although the team finished dead last with 103 losses, and Mossi's arm hurt almost all the time, he cherished his last summer as a big leaguer. In an effort to qualify Satchel Paige for a pension, owner Charles Finley signed him and planted him in the bullpen until he had enough days under his belt. Paige, who was pushing sixty at the time, regaled the relievers with fables from his Negro League days.

Mossi felt old and out of place in the youthful Kansas City clubhouse. His kids weren't much younger than his catcher, Rene Lachemann, or fellow pitcher Catfish Hunter. He threw his final pitch on October 1 against the White Sox, giving up the winning runs in a meaningless ballgame. His last big league season ended with five wins and seven saves, and a 3.74 ERA in fifty-one relief appearances.

That winter Finley sent Mossi a new contract, but he never signed it, choosing to retire instead. His final career numbers were 101 wins, 80 losses, and 50 saves. He completed one-third of his 165 starts and made 295 relief appearances. In 1,548 innings, he allowed 1,493 hits, walked 385, and fanned 932 batters. His career ERA was 3.43. Though never recognized for his defense, he handled 311 chances while committing just three errors. His .990 fielding percentage was the best in history at the time he retired.

Life after baseball mostly meant life without baseball. Mossi watched the occasional game on television and once appeared at a Giants Old Timers' Day at the behest of his old teammate, Al Rosen. Mossi coached some youth teams. Otherwise, his contact with baseball was minimal. He received a

MARK STEWART

fair number of letters and autographs from fans at his home in Ukiah, about three hours north of San Francisco. When fans sent him an extra card, he would set it aside for his grandchildren.

Over the years, when team physicians examined Mossi's slightly crooked arm, they surmised that he must have suffered an accident as a child. He could not remember one. If an accident did occur, it was a happy one. For Don Mossi could hurl a baseball with the best of them.

Chapter 12. Hank Majeski

Mark Hodermarsky

AGE	G	AB	R	H	2B	3B	HR	TB	RBI	BB	SO	BAV	OBP	SLG	SB	GDP	HBP
37	57	121	10	34	4	0	3	47	17	7	14	.281	.320	.388	0	5	0

Many baseball enthusiasts recall the bottom-of-the-tenth pinch-hit home run that gave the underdog New York Giants a dramatic win over the Cleveland Indians in Game One of the 1954 World Series. Many remember that Dusty Rhodes was the batter, that Bob Lemon was the pitcher, and that the ball barely cleared the 258-foot right-field wall. And most will not forget how Rhodes's homer and "The Catch" by Willie Mays two innings earlier established the direction and tone of the shocking sweep by the New Yorkers. What a good number of fans don't recollect, however, is the other pinch-hit home run in the Series or, more important, the hitter responsible for the round-tripper—Hank Majeski.

Hank Majeski played for the Indians during the twilight of an impressive thirteen-year Major League career. Before taking up duties as a dependable utility third baseman and second baseman for the Tribe from 1952 through 1955, Majeski, who debuted in the Major Leagues in 1939, had strung together five solid seasons at the plate and in the field, most notably for the Philadelphia Athletics.

Heeney—his nickname from childhood—enjoyed his best year in 1948 as the Athletics' third baseman (plus eight games at shortstop) when he batted .310, hit twelve home runs, drove in 120 runs, and set a Major League record with six two-base hits in a doubleheader. Considered one of the finest defensive third basemen of his era, in 1947 Majeski set an American League record with a .988 fielding average, making only five errors. (Don Money of the Milwaukee Brewers broke the record in 1974 with a .989 mark.)

In six Minor League seasons between 1936 and

Hank Majeski—Majeski played for six teams over three decades in the Major Leagues. An infielder, he hit .279 for his career.

1942, Majeski never hit less than .303. Playing for Eau Claire of the Class D Northern League on August 3, 1936, he went 7 for 7 (three singles, two doubles, a triple, and a home run). He reached the Major Leagues with the Boston Bees (the once and future Braves) in September 1939. Though his career numbers don't match those of the future All-Stars and Hall of Famers who also debuted in 1939—Hal Newhouser, Dizzy Trout, Mickey Vernon, Ted Williams, and Early Wynn—his numbers demand respect. In 3,421 at bats in 1,069 games, he batted .279, collected 956 hits, and knocked in 501 runs. In 1948 Majeski ranked in the top ten in most batting categories. In two consecutive years, 1947 and 1948, he led American league third basemen in fielding average. And in 1954 Majeski was a key role player in Cleveland's record-shattering pennant-winning season of 111 wins and 43 losses.

Majeski grew up during the Depression on Staten Island, New York, the son of Polish American parents, and never forgot his roots. Born on December 13, 1916, the son of a factory worker, he became a determined, talented, and humble athlete and later an esteemed coach and steady friend. Except for his baseball travels, throughout his life he never strayed far from the place he most loved—his home, Staten Island.

By the age of six, Henry was obsessed with baseball, as were most boys of his generation, and was called Shorty by neighborhood boys because of his short legs. Later he was nicknamed Heeney for reasons unknown. When Henry was eight, his father, who had worked at the U.S. Gypsum Co. plant on Staten Island making wallboard and paint, died, leaving five children. The oldest brother, Walter, assumed the role of father figure to Henry, brother Eddie, and their two sisters, Sadie and Sophie.

Young Henry dreamed of becoming a big leaguer as soon as he discovered baseball. A family friend gave him his first glove (it was being saved for a son who had died young) with these prophetic words: "Now you take it and become a big leaguer." When he was in the Major Leagues, he told a sportswriter he would "never forget" the day his first pair of baseball shoes arrived. He was eleven. "It was pouring rain, but I slipped into the kitchen, took some grease, rubbed it on the shoes, and ran around the block five times," he said.[1]

At Curtis High School, the alma mater of another baseball great, Bobby Thomson, Majeski had not yet achieved a growth spurt, standing only about five feet five. But his coach, Harry O'Brien, believed in him. Majeski said that "in high school I was too small to play anything but baseball. But Harry O'Brien felt I had the stuff to play on the team, and his confidence in me got me started."[2]

After high school, Majeski's chunky build, with his powerful neck and strong shoulders, made him appear bigger than his actual frame. He eventually grew to five feet nine and 180 pounds. (Al Simmons, a coach with the Athletics when Majeski was on the team, said, "Majeski's power is in his wrists. He snaps that bat pretty quick."[3]) Majeski aroused the interest of Major League scouts with his slashing line-drive hitting, excellent batting eye, and deft fielding at second base.

As with most players coming out of high school during Majeski's time, the road from amateur to professional baseball was winding and bumpy, even for the likes of the gifted Staten Islander. After he had spent two years playing sandlot baseball for the Staten Island team in the Police Athletic League, the Boston Red Sox signed Majeski to a contract in 1935 to play for Class D Eau Claire. The Chicago Cubs picked up the Eau Claire franchise, as well as Majeski, in 1936. In 1937, with Moline in the Class B Three-I League, Majeski hit .345. For Birmingham of the Southern Association in 1938, he batted .325. After the season the Bees bought his contract.

Boston manager Casey Stengel moved Majeski from second base position to third in 1939, and that's where he would primarily stay for the duration of his thirteen-year big league career. Majeski said Stengel did him a favor with the switch because "I probably could have played fast minor-league ball at second base for the rest of my life, but might never have made the grade in the majors at that spot."[4]

Majeski played in 106 games in his rookie season and batted .272. But a broken toe after the season and a stay in Stengel's doghouse resulted in a demotion to Newark of the International League in 1940. There, Majeski blistered opposing pitching, and in May 1941 the New York Yankees, for whom Newark was a farm team, purchased his contract from the Bees. He remained with Newark in 1942 and batted .345 with 121 RBIS. In 1943 he enlisted in the Coast Guard, and in June of that year he married Margaret McLaughlin, who was employed on Staten Island. Discharged from the Coast Guard, he began the 1946 season with the Yankees, but in June he was sold to the Athletics, and his career blossomed.

After three-plus seasons as the A's third baseman (in 1948 he batted .310, hit 41 doubles, and drove in 120 runs), Majeski was traded to the Chicago White Sox for pitcher Ed Kleiman. In 1950 he batted .309. In 1951 Chicago traded Majeski back to Philadelphia, and in 1952 the Athletics sent him to Cleveland, where he assumed a utility role before being traded to the Baltimore Orioles on June 27, 1955. After about a month the Orioles released him, and at the age of thirty-eight his playing career was over.

Majeski became a Minor League manager for the Indians, piloting the Daytona Beach Islanders of the Florida State League in 1956 and the Cocoa Indians (the franchise had moved) for part of 1957. He later managed the Oneonta Yankees (1966), coached at Wagner College on Staten Island and scouted for several Major League teams. He was a hitting instructor for the Houston Astros and Cincinnati Reds in 1966.

Majeski remained dedicated to baseball. Bill Klapach, a veteran Staten Island umpire and longtime friend of Majeski's, said he always participated in the annual Staten Island old-timers' baseball game and "loved to speak to kids about baseball." Majeski, a member of the Staten Island Sports Hall of Fame, never missed an induction ceremony. Klapach said, "Majeski was a fine gentleman who was proud to be from Staten Island."[5]

Bert Levinson, former baseball coach at Curtis High School on Staten Island, recalled how Majeski would "attend our practices and help the kids out with their batting and infield play. He would also show up when he could for some of our games and sit in the stands near the bench so as not to be a distraction to the team." Levinson added that Majeski would "always be there to distribute awards at the end-of-the-year Baseball Fair." Levinson said Majeski was a father figure to Bobby Thomson.[6]

Perhaps no one else can trace Majeski's rise to the Majors and his contribution to Staten Island baseball better than a former Minor League pitcher and close friend of his, Carmine "Lefty" DeRenzo. Living only five doors away from Majeski, DeRenzo eagerly followed his neighbor's progress toward stardom. Once after he injured his foot during spring training, Majeski asked for DeRenzo's help. "To help Heeney get his swing back in shape, we went to Curtis High School where I threw him batting practice four days in a row," DeRenzo recalled.[7]

Although Dusty Rhodes hit the more famous pinch-hit home run in the 1954 World Series, Majeski's blast had to feel extra special to him. His three-run shot in Game Four against Don Liddle with two outs gave the Tribe, down 7–0 at the time, some hope for a comeback.

Majeski died on August 9, 1991, at the age of seventy-four. He was survived by his wife, Margaret; a stepdaughter, Nannete; a sister, Sophie; four grandchildren; and seven great-grandchildren. He also left behind a host of memories for those lucky enough to have seen him play and to call him a friend.

MARK HODERMARSKY

Chapter 13. **Dale Mitchell**

Scott Longert

AGE	G	AB	R	H	2B	3B	HR	TB	RBI	BB	SO	BAV	OBP	SLG	SB	GDP	HBP
32	53	60	6	17	1	0	1	21	6	9	1	.283	.377	.350	0	1	0

The small town of Colony, Oklahoma, began as an agricultural settlement for Native Americans trying to adapt to a new way of life. In 1886 about 120 Cheyenne and Arapahos left their tribal lands in an attempt to assimilate themselves into the American culture. They became farmers, growing such staples as wheat and cotton. Six years after Colony was established, the land became open to settlers other than Indians. Several thousand people gathered in Washita County, settling in towns including Burns Flat, Corn, and Dill City. Early in the twentieth century, John H. Mitchell and his wife, Mary, rode their ancient covered wagon to become tenant farmers in Colony. The population at that time stood at around 200 to 250, most of them small farmers trying to scratch out a living through honest labor. Try as they might, many of the farmers were dirt-poor, the Mitchells among them. The town had a bank, a blacksmith shop, a newspaper, and a small hotel for the few travelers looking for a place to stay the night.

On August 23, 1921, the Mitchells celebrated the birth of a second son, Loren Dale. Their first child, Billy, had been born in 1906. The sparsely populated community had few children Dale's age to toss a football or baseball with. John Mitchell bought a first baseman's glove for his left-handed son to practice with. At times some of the nearby farmers would stop by the Mitchell farm and hit fly balls, which the eager young man chased across the wide-open land. Dale attended a two-room elementary school that had only about thirty students. There were no amateur teams to catch on with: there were not enough boys to cover the infield and outfield.

At the age of ten, Dale walked two miles to get to

Dale Mitchell—Mitchell was the starting left fielder on Cleveland's 1948 world championship team. He was second among starters with a .336 batting average that season.

school. Occasionally he hitched a ride when he could flag down a traveling cotton wagon. One day after school he was riding a wagon back to the Mitchell farm. The horse-drawn wagon stopped at the side of the road and Dale hopped off to walk the short distance home. He started to cross the road just as an automobile attempted to pass the stationary wagon. At that exact second a huge water truck came bearing down the highway directly at the auto. The driver of the car swerved sharply to his right to avoid the truck, but had no time to stop, and he hit the ten-year-old square on. Dale flew through the air and landed on the road unconscious. The three men at the scene rushed the young boy to a local hospital, where X-rays showed a broken left collarbone along with cuts and gashes on his face. Dale missed two months of school recovering from his injuries, but he healed well, returning to his daily regimen of basketball. He had much more speed and size than any of his classmates, and could get to the basket with relative ease.

As a teenager Dale enrolled in Cloud Chief High School, which had a district covering forty square miles. Despite the giant region to draw from, Cloud Chief had only about 160 students. But there were enough for a young athlete to compete at baseball, basketball, and track. Before he graduated, the "Cloud Chief Clouter" earned twelve athletic letters. He was all-state in basketball and set a state record in the 100-yard dash with a time of 9.8 seconds—not quite up to par with Jesse Owens, but a tremendous feat nonetheless. Knowledge of Mitchell's athletic accomplishments became widespread, which led to a visit from a professional baseball scout.

Hugh Alexander, a former outfielder for the Cleveland Indians, was the scout. Besides the standard contract, Alexander verbally offered the family monthly payments until their underage son graduated from high school and reported to his Minor League assignment. With a handshake agreement, the Mitchells put their signatures on the contract. All was well until about a month later, when the payments failed to arrive. Alexander claimed that somebody in the Cleveland front office decided to ignore the agreement as it was not specified in the contract. Angry with the turn of events, Dale refused to check in with Fargo-Morehead of the Northern League, where the Indians had placed him. Despite numerous phone calls, telegrams, and letters from the Indians organization, he declined to report unless the monthly payments arrived. He could not say anything publicly for fear of losing his amateur status for the remaining track season and the possibility of playing college sports. Years later Mitchell said the family had signed the contract because of

his father's poor health. They needed money immediately to help pay the medical expenses. All parties were willing to break the rules to help the elder Mitchell and let Dale continue with high school sports. However, the Indians' refusal to honor Alexander's offer created another problem. Like it or not, Dale was Cleveland's property, which meant he could not negotiate with any other professional team. So began a secret holdout that lasted an unheard-of seven years.

After graduation, Mitchell married his best girl, Margaret Emerson, a classmate at Cloud Chief. The newlyweds left Washita County to live in Norman, Oklahoma, a more convenient location for their future plans.

Since few people knew about the signed contract, Mitchell went ahead and enrolled at the University of Oklahoma. As a freshman in 1940 he was ineligible to play varsity sports, but the following summer he played semipro baseball with the Oklahoma Natural Gas club. Mitchell flourished there under the guidance of coach Roy Deal. Later he said, "I had a habit of stepping away at the plate and pulling the bat with my body. . . . Deal taught me how to spread my stance and hit with my wrists. This enabled me to hit outside balls and thus bat better against southpaw pitching."[1]

With an improved hitting stance, Mitchell had an excellent season as a sophomore for the Sooners, batting .420. He no longer played basketball, but still ran track. He seemed to be on the way to challenge the record books, but World War II was on, and the twenty-one-year-old was drafted and eventually sent to Europe for three years as a member of the Army Air Force. Serving as a quartermaster, Mitchell spent most of the war in England and France, remaining there until Germany surrendered in 1945. His son Dale Jr., who was two and a half years old at the time, remembered his dad arriving home, getting out of a car in full uniform with a duffle bag over his shoulder. It was the first time father and son had seen each other.[2]

SCOTT LONGERT

After his discharge from the army, Mitchell returned to college, where he played baseball once again. He had a spectacular season, batting a remarkable .507. At this point some much-needed good fortune came into play. The Cleveland organization entered into a working agreement with Oklahoma City of the Double-A Texas League. Needing some money to support a wife and young son, Mitchell took a deep breath, then approached the owners of the club about playing ball for them. He revealed the details about the 1939 contract fiasco along with his desire to end the marathon stalemate with the Indians. The owners were sympathetic to the plight of the ex-serviceman. They contacted the home office in Cleveland, asking the executives to assign Dale to Oklahoma City. Much to everyone's relief the request was granted, ending the seven-year holdout.

On June 3, 1946, Mitchell made his first appearance as a Minor League ballplayer. He likely had a case of nerves, going hitless in four at bats with two strikeouts. He recovered quickly, spraying base hits all around the Texas League and winning the batting championship with an average of .337. The Indians called him up in September. To help things go smoothly, the Oklahoma City owners accompanied their best player to Cleveland. They met with Indians owner Bill Veeck to explain the unusual circumstances that had kept Mitchell away from professional baseball for seven years. As Mitchell later said, "Veeck made amends." Veeck told Hal Lebovitz of the *Cleveland News*, "I couldn't let the world's record for determination go unrewarded!"[3]

Pleased with the Cleveland owner's generosity, Mitchell made his Major League debut on September 15, 1946, at Cleveland's Municipal Stadium. Batting second and playing center field, he lashed out three singles in five at bats, helping the Indians to an 8–1 victory over the Philadelphia Athletics. Mitchell played the final eleven games of the season, batting like a Hall of Famer. His average for the very short trial was an eye-opening .432. However, his fine hitting went virtually unnoticed. The

only excitement left for the sixth-place Cleveland team was Bob Feller's attempt to break the American League strikeout record, held at the time by Rube Waddell.

In 1947 Mitchell reported to spring training at Tucson, Arizona, a candidate for the center-field job. He had the necessary speed, but lacked the throwing arm and experience to claim the job. Tris Speaker, who was on the coaching staff, worked with the outfielders, and one could not hope for a better teacher than Speaker, who was one of the best center fielders in baseball history. Speaker paid great attention to his student, teaching Mitchell the correct way to break for line drives and flies. Mitchell spent much time learning how to get leverage in his throwing arm along with the proper way to field base hits. Reflecting on his time spent with the rookie outfielder, Speaker commented, "He was a grand pupil. I don't see how he can miss."[4]

The 1947 season opened with Mitchell in the starting lineup. A slow start by the team and its new outfielder resulted in a benching, then a demotion back to Oklahoma City. Mitchell did not handle the setback very well, sitting at home waiting for the Indians to call him back. He did not play a single game for the Minor League club. There he remained until June 2, when the Indians decided to bring him back for another look. An article in *Baseball Digest* later stated that Cleveland had violated a rule by sending a war veteran back to the Minors. The article mentioned that several teams put in a claim for Mitchell, forcing Veeck and manager Lou Boudreau to make a quick decision.[5]

With two outfielders injured, Mitchell returned to the lineup, this time in left field. He hit the ball everywhere: line drives to left-center, bouncing balls over the pitcher's mound, and singles between third base and shortstop. When he did not connect solidly, his great speed allowed him to beat out infield hits at a regular pace. He ran off a twenty-two-game hitting streak. Though not regarded as a power hitter, Mitchell surprised fans and teammates by one day launching a mammoth home run into the right-field grandstand at Municipal Stadium. He was reportedly only the fourth batter to accomplish the feat since the ballpark opened in the early 1930s.

Mitchell batted .316 in 123 games. In 493 at bats, he struck out only 14 times, an average of once every 35 trips to home plate. Speaker marveled at his student's ability to make contact, telling reporters, "The man has one of the best batting eyes in baseball."[6] With great bat control, Mitchell would frustrate American League pitchers for years to come.

In 1948 spring training Mitchell worked hard in left field, chasing fungoes off Speaker's bat. He would race to the outfield fence to grab high fly balls, then sprint toward the infield to snag line drives off his shoe tops. The extra fielding sessions helped him become a reliable fielder. Mitchell's hitting did not need much fine-tuning; he continued to drive the baseball to all parts of the ballpark. Teams would try to load up the third base side of the field against him, often moving the shortstop close to the hole, while the left fielder would stand a few steps away from the left-field foul line. This strategy had little success during the regular season. Mitchell concentrated on driving the ball to left-center or straight-away center, frustrating the defense. He told reporters, "I have learned to relax at the plate. When I feel I am getting tight I step out of the box and drop my bat. This has helped to get more power. I fool 'em now and get more punch in my swing."[7] Though he would never be known as a home run hitter, Mitchell began to hit for extra bases, collecting a fair number of doubles and triples. In the pennant-winning season of 1948, he finished with 30 doubles and 8 triples among his 204 base hits, second in the American League. His batting average of .336 left him in third place, behind only future Hall of Famers Ted Williams and teammate/manager Lou Boudreau. In 608 at bats, he struck out only 17 times. As a lead-off hitter, Mitchell fit perfectly in the batting order, getting on base for the likes of Joe Gordon, Larry Doby, and Boudreau.

But one of his best moments during the season occurred not at bat, but in left field. Playing at Detroit on June 30, Mitchell watched as fellow Indian Bob Lemon worked on a no-hit bid. In the seventh inning the Tigers' third baseman, George Kell, sent a drive to deep left field. Like the track star he was, Mitchell raced back to the fence, speared the ball, and crashed into the wall. He hit the ground hard but held the baseball, preserving Lemon's no-hitter.

A World Series win by the Indians over the Boston Braves in 1948 paid a winner's share of $7,000. Rather than throw the money around in celebration, Mitchell purchased farmland near his residence in Oklahoma. He bought 160 acres, which he leased to wheat farmers. He did this again with Series money in 1954 and 1956. He controlled the 480 acres the rest of his life, giving his family security after his playing days were over.

Though there would be no more postseason play for the Indians for six seasons after 1948, Mitchell continued to hit over .300 while playing a very good left field. In 1949 he swatted an amazing twenty-three triples, best by a wide margin in the Major Leagues, putting him three behind Joe Jackson and Sam Crawford for the highest total ever recorded in the American League. His 203 hits were tops in the junior circuit, nine ahead of runner-up Ted Williams. At this point Dale was collecting a salary of $18,500, a huge improvement over his rookie pay of $7, 000. Before he retired, his salary peaked at a very respectable $32,000.

Sportswriters sometimes asked Margaret Mitchell what was so unusual about her husband, if anything. Once she replied, "In the ten years we have been married, Dale has been what you might call a good, solid citizen. I have been waiting for something to happen [said with a smile]. That's what keeps me interested."[8] For his part Mitchell kept himself amused by playing golf and a mean gin rummy with *Akron Beacon Journal* reporter Jim Schlemmer. Asked by Schlemmer, the Indians beat reporter, to speak at a sports banquet, Mitchell agreed, saying he couldn't refuse because he already had too much of Schlemmer's money.

Early in the 1952 season, Mitchell found himself on the bench, replaced by a hot prospect named Jim Fridley. Manager Al Lopez thought he could generate more runs in the lineup with younger players like Fridley and Harry Simpson to go along with stalwarts Larry Doby and Luke Easter. Injuries to the latter two pushed the thirty-one-year-old Mitchell back in the lineup. He responded by going off on a rampage, hitting .395 during the month of August. For the season he finished with an average of .323, his best in four years.

Life was pretty good for the Mitchells. Unlike his father, who had struggled mightily to scrape out a living, Mitchell had done well in his baseball career. He had many good friends in the game, including Bob Kennedy, Bob Lemon, and Hal Naragon. He could now enjoy the fruits of his labor, renting roomy houses in Cleveland during the baseball season, then returning to Oklahoma for the winter. Son Dale Jr. recalled moving to northeast Ohio each April and finishing his school term there. Once summer vacation began, young Dale went to the ballpark every day with his father. He had his own Indians uniform and shagged fly balls with Mike Hegan and other players' sons. At times the coaches would throw batting practice to the boys before their dads took the field. Each summer Dale Jr. went on a road trip, usually to Detroit or Chicago. The only rule he had to obey was to keep away from Early Wynn and Bob Feller, who did not enjoy having children on the field while they practiced. Other than the one restriction, summers were a grand time for father and son.

The 1953 season was the last in which Mitchell, by then thirty-one years old, appeared in the everyday lineup. He responded with an average of .300 and a career best in home runs, thirteen. He spent his final three years with the Indians as a pinch hitter, getting no more than fifty or sixty at bats in each season. He made two plate appearances in the disappointing 1954 World Series, failing to get a base hit.

The 1956 season showed the thirty-four-year-old left fielder at the end of his career, hitting an all-time low .133. At the end of July 1956, the Brooklyn Dodgers claimed Mitchell for the waiver price of $10,000 plus a player to be named later. A week earlier the Dodgers and Indians had played an exhibition game in which Mitchell banged out a triple and a single. Brooklyn sorely needed a reliable pinch hitter. In his first at bat with his new club, Mitchell proved he still had some pop in his bat, delivering a single in the eighth inning to score Jackie Robinson with the winning run against Milwaukee. The Dodgers won the National League pennant and advanced to the World Series against the New York Yankees. In Game Five, Don Larsen was pitching a perfect game when Mitchell was sent up as a pinch hitter with two outs in the ninth inning. With the tension mounting, Mitchell took a ball, then a strike. He recalled years later, "I got a pitch to hit from Larsen. I think it was the second pitch, a hanging curve that I fouled off. If you miss your pitch you're out of business."[9] Larsen delivered one more time, a pitch off the outside corner. Umpire Babe Pinelli called it a strike, which gave the Yankee pitcher his perfect game. Mitchell turned to argue with the umpire, but Pinelli had already left. Doubters have insisted that the called third strike was nowhere near the plate. For the rest of his life, Mitchell insisted that the pitch was a ball. When you have nearly 4,000 at bats during your career and you strike out a minuscule 119 times, you may have something there. In 1986, on the thirtieth anniversary of the perfect game, *Good Morning America* invited Mitchell to come on the show and talk about the game with Larsen and Yogi Berra. Mitchell refused to go on, saying he was not going to travel across the country to talk on TV about striking out. After eleven years in Major League baseball with a career average of .312 and two All-Star game appearances, he had earned the right.

The strikeout was Mitchell's last at bat in Organized Baseball. He retired after the season and began a new profession in the oil business. Later he joined the Martin Marietta Corporation as president of its cement division in Denver. He retired in the early 1980s. He played a lot of golf and took part in many old-timers' games at Yankee Stadium. While visiting with old friends and former teammates, he became acutely aware of the number of former players who couldn't pay hotel and transportation costs. He gave money to several who were destitute. He did this for a number of years until the sadness of seeing his old buddies in such a depressing state proved too much for him, and he no longer went to the old-timers' games.

In October 1981 the University of Oklahoma unveiled its new baseball stadium, Dale Mitchell Field. An alumni game featured former Sooners and current Major Leaguers Mickey Hatcher, Bob Shirley, Jackson Todd, George Frazier, and Joe Simpson. Mitchell was honored in the dedication ceremony for his tireless efforts to raise money for the ballpark. Despite a stellar baseball career, Mitchell called this honor the biggest of his life. And why not? For a great collegiate athlete and student himself, what could be better than his alma mater paying him a tribute that would last for a lifetime?

Dale Mitchell suffered a severe heart attack and died on January 5, 1987, in Tulsa, Oklahoma. He was sixty-five years old. In 1973 he had had a bout with heart trouble but recovered to spend another fourteen years with his children and grandchildren. Mitchell had come a long way from a tenant farm in Colony, Oklahoma, to become an elite baseball player and a top executive in the business world. Though he accomplished much in life, baseball was never far from his thoughts. As he told a reporter in 1974, "You never leave baseball once you're in it. You always love the game."[10]

Chapter 14. Mike Garcia

Warren Corbett

AGE	W	L	PCT	ERA	G	GS	GF	CG	SHO	SV	IP	H	BB	SO	HBP	WP
30	19	8	.704	2.64	45	34	8	13	5	5	258.2	220	71	129	2	1

The Cleveland Indians boasted one of the strongest corps of starting pitchers in history in the early 1950s: Bob Feller, Bob Lemon, Early Wynn, and Mike Garcia. For a few years Garcia was at least the equal of his Hall of Fame stablemates, but the right-hander known as "The Big Bear" burned out early.

Edward Miguel Garcia was born in San Gabriel, California, on November 17, 1923. When he was two years old, his father, Merced, a Mexican immigrant, moved the family to the tiny farming community of Orosi, in the San Joaquin Valley. Merced owned a ranch and trained and bred horses. Mike said later, "I was one darned good vaquero."[1] He weighed less than 100 pounds when he was thirteen and wanted to be a jockey. He rode in one quarter-horse race for five dollars, but the horse threw him. He soon outgrew his riding dream.

He played for three years at Orosi High School and then transferred to the larger Visalia High for his senior year. A Cleveland scout, Willis Butler, saw him pitching semipro ball in Tulare and signed him for the Appleton Papermakers in the Class D Wisconsin State League.

Garcia posted a 10-10 record with Appleton in 1942, and then was called into service in World War II. He spent the next three years stringing telephone wires for the Army Signal Corps, including service in Europe.

After his discharge, the twenty-two-year-old was assigned to Bakersfield in the Class C California League in 1946. Called "Ed" Garcia by *The Sporting News*, he won twenty-two games and led the league in earned run average (2.56) and strikeouts (186). The next year he spent spring training

Mike Garcia—"The Bear" won twenty games or more twice in the twelve years he pitched in Cleveland. He led the American League with a 2.64 ERA in 1954.

with the Indians, who had figured out that his name was actually "Mike," but their veteran coach, Bill McKechnie, pronounced him not quite ready. He went to Class A ball in Wilkes-Barre, Pennsylvania, of the Eastern League. He made the postseason all-star team with seventeen wins and a 3.24 ERA.

In 1948 Garcia moved up to the Double-A Texas League with Oklahoma City. He pitched a one-hitter and a two-hitter among his nineteen victories for a losing team. Cleveland called him up in September and he made his big league debut on October 3, 1948, in the last game of the regular season. The Indians were playing for the pennant that day, but they fell behind Detroit's Hal Newhouser. Garcia and another rookie, Ernie Groth, mopped up. Cleveland finished tied with the Red Sox, beat Boston in a one-game playoff, and won the World Series, but Garcia, as a September call-up, was not eligible to play.

He made the Indians in 1949 and got his first start on May 22 against the Philadelphia Athletics. It was a disaster; he walked the first three men in the first inning and was relieved. Garcia notched his first big league win as a starter on May 30, when he shut out the St. Louis Browns, scattering six hits in the 5–0 Cleveland victory. His next start was not until June 12, when he made an emergency start against the Yankees after the scheduled pitcher, Early Wynn, came down with hives. Garcia held New York to one run before 77,543 fans at a Sunday doubleheader in Cleveland Stadium. That performance won him a slot in the starting rotation, and he blossomed into one of the American League's top pitchers. He led the league with a 2.36 ERA, pitched five shutouts, won fourteen games, and was named to *The Sporting News* rookie all-star team.

Because he spoke Spanish, Garcia was assigned to watch over another rookie, Mexican-born infielder Roberto Avila, who knew little English. They were roommates for several years. His veteran teammate Joe Gordon nicknamed him "Bear." Garcia explained that he wore his black hair cut short and "maybe I walk a little like a bear."[2] Maybe he was built a little like a bear, too. He stood six feet one and said his playing weight was between 215 and 220.

In 1950 Garcia fell off to an 11-11 record as his ERA swelled to 3.86. He struggled with knee and shoulder injuries and his mother died during the season. On January 13, 1951, he married Gerda Martin, whom he had met at the Cleveland ballpark. At first she didn't like his nickname, but eventually she bought him a tie adorned with bears.

The 1950 Indians featured a pitching Big Three of future Hall of Famers Feller, Lemon, and Wynn.

In 1951 Garcia made it a Big Four, beginning a four-year run as one of the game's best pitchers. Manager Al Lopez said. "Garcia was just overpowering."[3] When he broke into the Majors, he had a slider to go with his sinking fastball, but he said he didn't become successful until pitching coach Mel Harder taught him a curve. He liked to work to the inside and outside corners of the plate, "east-west" instead of "north-south" in pitcher-speak. Lopez recalled, "He threw such a 'heavy' ball, when you hit it, it felt like you were hitting a rock."[4] Ted Williams accused him of throwing a spitball, and years later Mel Harder told a reporter that Garcia had a good spitter.

In 1951 Cleveland began a six-year chase of Casey Stengel's Yankee dynasty. The Indians won only one pennant, but finished second every other season. The Yankees claimed five straight world championships from 1949 through 1953, and then won four more AL pennants and two World Series from 1955 through 1958.

In 1951 Cleveland finished five games behind the Yankees as Feller, Wynn, and Garcia each won at least twenty games and Lemon won seventeen. The next season the Tribe mounted their closest challenge. Most sportswriters picked Cleveland as the preseason 1952 favorite, because Yankee superstar Joe DiMaggio had retired and third baseman Bobby Brown, second baseman Jerry Coleman, and pitcher Whitey Ford were lost to military service.

The Indians won their first seven games and swept a three-game series from New York at Yankee Stadium in early May. Fighting off injuries to four of their eight regular position players and a slump by slugging first baseman Luke Easter, they managed to stay close to the Yankees.

Garcia beat New York four times during the season and pitched three straight shutouts in early September, finishing each game in under two hours. Feller had skidded to the worst season of his career, so Lopez used his new Big Three to start eighteen of nineteen games down the stretch, with Garcia's seven starts leading the way. Cleveland won sixteen of twenty games during a September home stand, but their ninety-three victories fell two short of the Yankees.

Lemon, Wynn, and Garcia each won twenty-two games. Garcia's 2.37 ERA was second in the league to New York's Allie Reynolds. His six shutouts tied Reynolds for the league lead. In addition to thirty starts, the Bear relieved in ten games and saved four of them, a statistic that was not computed until years later.

The Big Three won sixty-seven games and posted an ERA of 2.59, but their supporting cast lagged at 4.57. In fact, the Yankee pitching staff recorded the better ERA, 3.14 to 3.32 for the Indians. Casey Stengel said his club had another advantage that was usually overlooked: defense. The Yankees turned 199 double plays, the second-most in history, to 141 for Cleveland—58 extra outs for New York. Cleveland's155 errors tied the St. Louis Browns for most in the league. New York committed 28 fewer errors, another 28 extra outs. Those extra outs— batters the Yankee pitchers did not have to face— were more than enough to account for New York's two-win advantage.

Garcia signed his 1953 contract for a reported $30,000, compared to $45,000 for Lemon and $37,000 for Wynn. Feller, once baseball's highest-paid player, took a huge cut to $40,000, half his peak salary.

The Indians finished second for the third straight season in 1953, but there was no pennant race. The Yankees reeled off eighteen consecutive wins in May and June, including a four-game sweep in Cleveland, and wound up eight and a half games ahead. Lemon was the team's only 20-game winner (21), though Garcia had 18 and Wynn 17. *The Sporting News* editorialized, "Ever since they won the world championship in 1948 it has been one thing or another with the Indians. One year they had a superlative defense but not enough hitting. The next year they battered down the fences but

their infield fell apart. Only the pitching has been consistent."[5]

The planets finally aligned for Cleveland in 1954. They won 111 games, the most in American League history to that point, and finally gave the Yankees a taste of second place. Many observers, then and since, agreed with manager Lopez's assessment that his pitching staff was the greatest ever. Their 2.78 ERA was the lowest since the Lively Ball Era began in 1920. Lemon and Wynn each won 23 and Garcia added 19, plus 5 saves. He led the league in ERA for the second time at 2.64 and allowed the fewest base runners per nine innings of any AL pitcher. On May 16 he shut out the Athletics on one hit, one of his five shutouts. The victory was Cleveland's fifth straight and lifted them into first place, where, other than for a few days in June, they remained.

This time the Indians had depth behind the Big Three. A revived Feller went 13-3 and shared the fourth starting slot with newly acquired right-hander Art Houtteman, who finished 15-7. A pair of rookie relievers, left-hander Don Mossi and right-hander Ray Narleski, combined for 9 victories and 20 saves.

On July 4 Garcia left the game against the White Sox after two innings with a broken blood vessel in the middle finger of his pitching hand, although he had not given up a hit. Narleski relieved, and then gave way to Wynn in the eighth, with the Sox still hitless. With two out in the ninth, Minnie Minoso singled to break up the gem.

Garcia was chosen for the All-Star team for the third straight year, but he missed the game because of the injured finger. On July 26 Gerda gave birth to their first child, Michael Martin, called "Little Bear" by his father. On the same day Mike's father died at age sixty-nine.

With the pennant clinched, Garcia took a shot at his twentieth victory in the season's last game, but he said the rest of the lineup was "all the scrubbinies."[6] He pitched twelve innings against Detroit in a 6-6 tie before being relieved. General manager

Hank Greenberg said Garcia thought he was pitching for a bonus if he won, but he was being hit hard. Greenberg said he called the dugout for the only time in his front-office career and asked Lopez if he was trying to get the pitcher killed. The Indians eventually lost, but Greenberg said he paid Garcia the bonus anyway.

The 1954 team is renowned for its great pitching, but Cleveland also finished second in runs scored. Lopez pointed out that he had three power hitters in center fielder Larry Doby, third baseman Al Rosen, and first baseman Vic Wertz, a mid-season pickup: "So our game was to hold the other side with our good pitching and wait for somebody to sock one out."[7] The Indians' bench was strong enough to withstand injuries to Rosen, second baseman Avila, and shortstop George Strickland. Doby led the league with 32 home runs and 126 RBIs and Avila won the batting title at .341. (Ted Williams hit .345, but walked so many times that he did not get the 400 at bats required to qualify for the championship. As a result, the rule was changed to count plate appearances rather than at bats in future years.)

When the World Series opened, the Indians were heavy favorites over the National League champion New York Giants. Lopez set up a starting rotation of Lemon, Wynn, Feller, then Garcia. After New York took the first two games, the manager bypassed Feller and sent Garcia out for the third. He lasted only three innings, giving up four runs (one unearned) as the Giants won 6–2. He came back in relief the next day, pitching the final two scoreless innings as the Giants swept to an upset championship.

The Indians returned to their familiar home in second place behind the Yankees in 1955 and 1956, but Garcia stumbled. In 1955 he posted an ERA above 4.00 for the first time in his career and finished 11-13, completing only six of thirty-one starts. He took a reported $5,000 pay cut to $25,000. In '56 his ERA came down to 3.78, but his record was 11-12. Mike and Gerda celebrated the birth of their

second child, Lisa Inez, on September 24, 1956. Another daughter, Celeste, was born two days after Christmas 1957.

Manager Lopez left the Indians after the '56 season. Under new manager Kerby Farrell, the aging team finished sixth in 1957. The thirty-three-year-old Garcia rebounded with a 12-8 record and a 3.75 ERA. He tried out a knuckleball, but he relied mostly on curves and sliders. He said, "Every fast ball pitcher sooner or later has to come to the realization that his big one is gone. I have adjusted."[8]

By 1958 he was the last of Cleveland's Big Four. Feller and Lemon had retired, and Wynn was traded to the White Sox. During spring training Garcia slipped on a wet mound in Los Angeles and hurt his back. Because there was no room for him on the disabled list—each team could have only two players at a time on the list—Cleveland released him in May.

The club reportedly paid for surgery to correct a slipped disc, and he won a roster spot the next spring. In his first start, he shut out Washington for eight innings but lost on three unearned runs in the ninth. Cleveland writer Hal Lebovitz reported, "It was spine-tingling to witness the lineup of well-wishers who visited his locker to shake his hand."[9] But he pitched only seventy-two innings that season and was released in the fall.

Garcia said he was healthy and determined to continue pitching. Within weeks he signed with the White Sox, managed by Lopez and owned by former Indians' owner Bill Veeck. During the off-season he sliced off the tip of his right index finger while working on one of his midget racing cars, but it was healed by spring training. He quipped that the shortened finger gave him a natural slider.

His medical troubles were not over; he underwent an emergency appendectomy during spring training. The White Sox released him in May 1960, when rosters were reduced to twenty-five. He stayed with the team as a batting-practice pitcher and was reactivated when the rosters expanded September 1. He pitched just seventeen and two-thirds innings

WARREN CORBETT

in relief during the season and was released again in November.

Chicago invited Garcia to spring training in 1961, but Cincinnati's Vada Pinson hit him with a line drive that broke his leg. After recovering, Garcia worked out with the Washington Senators and was signed on July 19. He pitched sixteen times in relief, but was released before the season ended. At age thirty-seven, his baseball days were over.

Garcia had bought a dry-cleaning shop in the Cleveland suburb of Parma in 1955 and named it Big Bear Cleaners. After leaving baseball he ran the business, played some slow-pitch softball, served as commissioner of a local Little League, and continued to race his midget cars.

By 1983 he was suffering from diabetes and heart trouble and had shrunk to 180 pounds. "I'm 59. I feel like I'm 80," he told the Cleveland *Plain Dealer*.[10] The next year he was reported to be undergoing dialysis three times a week because of kidney failure. He had sold his business to pay his medical bills. The Sports Media Association of Cleveland and Ohio organized a benefit on December 2, 1985, to help him with those bills. Garcia and former teammates Feller, Lemon, and Wynn autographed limited-edition 16-by-20-inch prints that were sold for $100 each.

Mike Garcia died at 62 on January 13, 1986, his 35th wedding anniversary. Gerda and their three children survived him.

During his career Garcia won 142 games and lost 97. His 3.27 ERA was 17 percent better than the league average, after adjusting for the parks where he pitched, equal to that of Gaylord Perry and Bert Blyleven, who had much longer careers. Garcia was a workhorse, starting and relieving and finishing in the top four in innings pitched every year from 1951 to 1954. He is the only one of Cleveland's Big Four who is not in the Hall of Fame, because his prime lasted only six seasons, from 1949 through 1954. Analyst Bill James dismissed his low ERA as a product of "cold, cavernous Cleveland Memorial Stadium [*sic*], which at that time had a pitcher's mound higher than the white cliffs of Dover."[11] His more famous teammates enjoyed the same home-field advantage, but it was Garcia who recorded the staff's lowest ERA in four of those six seasons.

Joseph Wancho

May 1—New York—TRIBE NOTCHES FOURTH IN ROW—George Strickland goes 3 for 4, with three RBIS. The Tribe scores four unearned runs in the fifth inning, and Early Wynn backs his win with two RBIS.

May 2—Washington—INDIANS WIN 2 FOR 6 IN ROW—George Strickland drives in two runs and Al Rosen and Bobby Avila each collect two hits in the game one victory at Washington. Wally Westlake goes 4 for 6. He drives in three runs with a bases-loaded triple in the top of the tenth inning for a Cleveland victory and a sweep of the Senators. The Tribe moves into third place in the American League, one game back of Chicago.

May 4—Philadelphia—WILD THROW GIVES GARCIA THIRD DEFEAT—Gus Zernial singles in the bottom of the eighth inning to score the winning run in the A's 3–2 win. Cleveland third baseman Al Smith's throwing error in the sixth allows an unearned A's run. Mike Garcia strikes out seven in the loss. Al Rosen hits a solo shot. The six-game win streak is snapped.

May 5—Philadelphia—LEMON TRIPS A'S FOR 4TH IN ROW, 7–2—Dave Philley hits a three-run homer. Al Rosen goes 2 for 4, with two RBIS. Bob Lemon raises his record to 4-0. They pull within a game and a half of Chicago.

May 6—Philadelphia—WYNN TAKES 3D VICTORY, HALTS RALLY IN SIXTH—Larry Doby, Bobby Avila, and Al Smith have two hits apiece. Smith homers in the eighth inning. Early Wynn K's three

in the sixth inning, to preserve a one-run margin. Wynn strikes out nine for the game.

May 8—Baltimore—ORIOLES DROP 5 IN A ROW, LOSE TO INDIANS, 5–3—Starting catcher Hal Naragon knocks in three runs with a bases-loaded double in the fourth inning. Early Wynn saves the game for Mike Garcia. The Tribe wins their eighth in nine games on this eastern trip.

May 9—Baltimore—ORIOLES AND TURLEY BEAT INDIANS, 2–1—Gil Coan's single in the bottom of the tenth inning scores an unearned run. Art Houtteman does not record a strikeout in ten innings of work. The Tribe is held to four hits in the 2–1 loss.

May 10—Cleveland—PHILLEY'S 4-RUN DRIVE SINKS YANKEES—The Tribe scores all eight runs in the bottom of the first inning. Dave Philley's grand slam is the big blow. Don Mossi gets the win in relief. Mike Garcia gets the save.

May 11—Cleveland—YANKEES BEAT INDIANS, 5–3, ON BERRA'S DOUBLE—The Yankees score two runs in the top of the ninth inning to break the tie. Yogi Berra's double plates both runs. The Indians score two in the eighth, then load the bases with no outs. Allie Reynolds shuts the door and allows no runs to score. First baseman Rocky Nelson is sold to the Brooklyn Dodgers.

May 12—Cleveland—YANKEES SHADE INDIANS, 5 TO 4; SHARE THIRD PLACE—Andy Carey collects two RBIS on an eighth-inning homer. Yogi Berra and Irv Noren tally two hits apiece.

Eddie Lopat raises his record to 5-0 with the 5–4 win. The Tribe sells outfielder Jim Lemon to Washington.

May 13— Cleveland—TRIBE BAGS 6 IN 9TH INNING TO TIE SCORE—The Indians score six in the bottom of the ninth inning to tie the score. Al Rosen's double wins it in the eleventh. Dave Philley adds three RBIs and Rudy Regalado homers. "Prince Hal" Newhouser gets his first Cleveland win in relief, before a season-low crowd of 2,485 spectators.

May 14—Cleveland—STRICKLAND'S GRAND SLAM WINS, 5–2—George Strickland hits a grand slam in the first inning. Bob Lemon strikes out six to go to 5-0 on the year.

May 15—Cleveland—DOBY DRIVES IN DECIDING TALLY—Early Wynn strikes out seven as his record goes to 4-2. Al Rosen and Bobby Avila each hit home runs. Larry Doby singles in Dave Philley for the winning run in the eighth inning.

May 16—Cleveland—INDIANS SWEEP. TOP A'S, 12–7 AND 6–0 TO LEAD. GARCIA GIVES 1 HIT—The Tribe moves into a first-place tie in the American League with Chicago. Bob Chakales wins the opener in relief. Al Rosen homers. Jim Hegan goes 4 for 5, drives in four, homers, and scores twice. Mike Garcia one-hits the A's for his third win in the nightcap. Al Rosen homers, driving in three.

Chapter 16. Larry Doby

John McMurray

AGE	G	AB	R	H	2B	3B	HR	TB	RBI	BB	SO	BAV	OBP	SLG	SB	GDP	HPB
30	153	577	94	157	18	4	32	279	126	85	94	.272	.364	.484	3	7	3

Larry Doby is best remembered for becoming the first black player in the American League and the second in modern history in Major League baseball. When Doby made his Major League debut for the Cleveland Indians on July 5, 1947, he broke the league's color barrier less than three months after Jackie Robinson first played for the Brooklyn Dodgers.[1] In the face of racial prejudice, Doby remained a superior hitter and outfielder during his thirteen-season career, with selection to seven American League All-Star teams. "I had to take it," Doby said, "but I fought back by hitting the ball as far as I could. That was my answer."[2]

Lawrence Eugene Doby was born on December 13, 1923, in Camden, South Carolina. Larry's father, David, met his future wife, Etta, while playing baseball on the street in front of her home.[3] Biographer Joseph Thomas Moore wrote that the Dobys were "one of the most prosperous black families in Camden."[4]

David Doby was a stable hand, grooming the horses of many wealthy New Jersey families. The marriage, however, was strained because of David's frequent travel and Etta's strong attachment to her own mother, leaving young Larry often in the care of his grandmother, Augusta Moore. She recounted how Doby said that Augusta "made me go to church with her all the time. I liked what I heard in the Twenty-Third Psalm and the Ten Commandments. Somehow I got the feeling that the church helped black people to be themselves. I liked that feeling."[5]

When Larry was eight years old, his father died in a tragic accident. David had gone fishing on a day off, and he drowned after falling from a boat while fishing on Lake Mohansic, in upstate New York.

Larry Doby—Doby led the American League in home runs and RBIS in 1954. He was the first African American player in the American League in 1947. He was elected to the Baseball Hall of Fame in 1998.

His death began a tumultuous time for Larry, during which he moved frequently and was cared for by his aunt and uncle. Four years after his father's death, Larry and his mother left South Carolina and moved to Paterson, New Jersey.[6]

It wasn't easy for Doby in Paterson. "I was lonely living alone," he said. "But I just kept trying to be me."[7] In Paterson, Doby began following in the footsteps of his father, who had been a semipro ballplayer. He developed his skills playing sandlot baseball close to home, at the Newman Playground and on Twelfth Avenue. Doby lettered in baseball at Paterson Eastside High School, where he was one of about twenty-five black students in the school. He won letters in three other sports, a total of eleven in all. Initially, Doby had thoughts of finishing high school and then becoming a physical education teacher or perhaps a coach.[8]

Doby was more introspective than demonstrative, and his personality could confuse his teammates. As recounted by biographer Moore, high school teammate Al Kachuadurian never felt he could slap Doby on the back, and he thought Doby kept his teammates at a distance. "I remember distinctly that if things didn't go just right, he'd sulk. Deep down, he's a warm-hearted guy. But you didn't know if he was sulking at you personally, or whether he was sulking inwardly at himself." Doby, however, later countered that he wasn't sulking at all but had gotten accustomed to being alone based upon the circumstances in his life.[9] In some sense, Doby's self-reliance may have been mistaken for aloofness.

Even before graduating from high school, Doby began playing second base under the assumed name of Larry Walker in the Negro Leagues for the Newark Eagles. He was an immediate star, and team owners offered him $300 to play between high school and college. Although statistics from his first season are inexact, Doby believed he had batted around .400 during that summer.[10]

Doby enrolled at Long Island University. Part of his motivation was to play for renowned basketball coach Clair Bee. Another reason was to be able to visit Helyn Curvy, whom Doby had begun dating at Eastside High School when he was a sophomore.[11] Curvy's father had died, however, and responsibilities for taking care of her siblings prevented Curvy from attending any of Doby's high school baseball games. "But when I had a game," Doby recalled, "I'd take her brother George to the game with me, then I'd bring him back to her house."[12]

At the time, Doby had concern about being drafted into the military during World War II. He made the difficult decision to transfer from Long Island University to Virginia Union College, where he would play basketball for coach Henry Hucles. Doby believed he could transfer into an ROTC program there. Yet he was drafted into the navy at the conclusion of the basketball season. The mandated racial segregation of the military at the time left a deep impression on him. He was assigned to Camp Robert Smalls, the black division of the Great Lakes Naval Training Station, outside Chicago.[13]

Due in large part to his outstanding physical condition, Doby was able to become a physical education instructor there. He kept his baseball and basketball skills sharp by playing in the afternoons. Doby got to know future NFL Hall of Famer Marion Motley while on his tour of duty. Later, while stationed in the Pacific, Doby began what became a lifelong friendship with Washington Senators star Mickey Vernon. Vernon wrote to Senators owner Clark Griffith, touting Doby's playing abilities. After their military service was done, "[Vernon] sent me a gift of some bats when I started the 1946 season with the [Newark] Eagles," Doby recalled. "It was a gift I'll never forget."[14]

In 1945 general manager Branch Rickey of the Brooklyn Dodgers signed Jackie Robinson to a contract to play baseball in Montreal. The move made Doby reconsider his options, as playing baseball in the Major Leagues now seemed a possibility. "My main thing was to become a teacher and coach," Doby said. "But when I heard about Jackie, I decided to concentrate on baseball. I forgot about going back to college."[15]

Doby was honorably discharged from the military in January 1946. After playing two months of winter ball with the San Juan Senators for $500 a month at the invitation of Monte Irvin, a prewar teammate on the Newark Eagles, Doby subsequently rejoined the Eagles. Being close to home also allowed him to date Helyn again. "She told me if we didn't get married that year, 1946, to forget it," Doby said. "We got married on August 10, 1946, in Paterson."[16] The night of their wedding, the couple drove to Trenton, where Doby was scheduled to play. The game was rained out.[17] A few days later, Doby played in a Negro Leagues All-Star game against a team including Josh Gibson.

The Eagles went on to win the Negro Leagues World Series in 1946. Doby batted .272 with one home run in that series against the Kansas City Monarchs of the Negro American League. He tagged a runner out at second base for the second out of the ninth inning of the seventh game, and he caught a pop-up for the final out of the series. "To play the Monarchs in the World Series!" Doby later exclaimed. "They had Satchel Paige and all those guys. That was a great team. To beat those guys, you were in the upper echelon of baseball."[18]

With Doby's notoriety high after the 1946 championship season, Bill Veeck, the owner of the Cleveland Indians, took notice. Veeck, who had long been eager to racially integrate the American League, hatched a plan for Doby to join Cleveland right after the 1947 All-Star break. Doby had played the first half of the season with the Eagles, and he had hit a home run in his final Newark at bat. The Cleveland team quietly purchased Doby's contract and brought him to Cleveland. A scoop by local writer Bob Whiting forced the team to move up Doby's first game from July 10, which was the original intention, to July 5.[19]

Teammates, however, did not immediately welcome Doby, averting their eyes and not speaking to him as he made his entry to the clubhouse at Comiskey Park to meet with player-manager Lou Boudreau. "Shrug it off," Boudreau reportedly said.[20] Still, Doby in 2002 recalled, "I knew it was segregated times, but I had never seen anything like that in athletics. I was embarrassed. It was tough." As Bill White later noted, Doby had to go to the Chicago clubhouse to get a first baseman's glove, since none of his Cleveland teammates offered him one.[21]

Pinch-hitting for Bryan Stephens against Earl Harrist of the White Sox, Doby struck out in his first Major League at bat. On July 6, in the second game of that day's doubleheader, Doby made his only start of the season at first base. He got his first Major League hit, a single off Orval Grove in the third inning that also gave him his first RBI.[22] During that difficult first season, Doby batted only .156 in twenty-nine games with two RBIs. "It was 11 weeks between the time Jackie Robinson and I came into the majors. I can't see how things were any different for me than they were for him," Doby said.[23]

He had to wait until the start of the 1948 season to win a starting job in Cleveland's outfield. During his first full season, Doby hit fourteen home runs and had sixty-six RBIs. That fall, Doby became the first black player to hit a home run in the World Series when he connected off the Boston Braves' Johnny Sain in Game Four. His blast helped lead Cleveland to a 2–1 win and a lead of three games to one in the Series. A photo taken after the game showing Doby embracing Cleveland pitcher Steve Gromek has become one of the most famous in baseball history, symbolizing an erosion of racial divisions and Doby's acceptance as a member of his new team.

The 1948 season was the first of ten consecutive years in which Doby hit at least fourteen home runs and drove in at least fifty runs. He was selected to the All-Star team in every year between 1949 and 1955 and finished in the top ten in the American League MVP voting in 1950 and 1954. Doby's finest statistical season was 1952, when he led the American League in slugging percentage (.541), home runs (32), and runs scored (104). He hit for the cycle that year against Boston on June 4 at Fenway Park—the last time an American Leaguer accomplished that feat until Mickey Mantle did it in 1957.[24]

In 1954 Doby was Cleveland's most dominant offensive player, leading the American League in home runs (32) and runs batted in (126). He also played a stellar center field, committing only two errors in 153 games while finishing second in the league in put-outs. Doby's regular season success that year, like that of many of his teammates, did not extend into the World Series, as he was able to manage only two singles in the four games against the New York Giants. Still, for his regular-season efforts, Doby finished second in the 1954 American League Most Valuable Player award voting to Yogi Berra.

After the 1955 season, during which Doby battled a wrist injury, he was traded to the Chicago White Sox for Jim Busby and Chico Carrasquel. At the time, Chicago manager Marty Marion said that Doby's arrival was "the end of the search for a No. 4 hitter."[25] Marion later said, "This guy used to murder us when we played Cleveland. Last year, I definitely felt that, when we could get him out, we could handle the Indians. But we couldn't—and the record shows that they had a season break on us, 12-10."[26]

Doby immediately delivered with Chicago, hitting 24 home runs and knocking in 102 runs. During a nine-game winning streak in June 1956, Doby hit five home runs, leading White Sox owner Charles Comiskey to remark, "Larry Doby, he's our guy. You know, when we dealt for Doby, we weren't worried about Larry. We knew he'd come through."[27]

Doby was involved in one of the bigger melees of the 1957 season. In a game on June 12, Art Ditmar of the Yankees threw a pitch inside, causing Doby to fall to his knees. Both benches emptied, and Doby knocked Ditmar down with a punch to his jaw. Doby also got into an on-field fight with Billy Martin after the umpires had restored order. Doby, teammate Walt Dropo, and the Yankees' Enos Slaughter and Martin were all thrown out of the game. The Yankees, feeling that penalties against their players by the league were unjustified, paid all fines of their players assessed after the incident.[28]

After his power numbers faded a bit during the 1957 season, Doby was traded to Baltimore that December with Jack Harshman, Russ Heman, and Jim Marshall in return for Tito Francona, Ray Moore,

and Billy Goodman. Manager Al Lopez explained the deal, saying, "We wouldn't start another season with Doby because the fans are down on him."[29] A contemporary article noted that the fans often booed Doby at Comiskey Park, leading to resentment on Doby's part.[30] Doby never played with the Orioles, being traded again before the season began on April 1. This time he went back to the Cleveland Indians along with Don Ferrarese for Dick Williams, Gene Woodling, and Bud Daley.

By then, however, injuries had taken their toll, and Doby was a part-time player. In 1958 he hit thirteen home runs and batted in forty-five runs in only eighty-nine games. Just before the 1959 season, Doby was traded to the Detroit Tigers for Tito Francona. Finally, on May 13, 1959, he was purchased from Detroit by the Chicago White Sox for $30,000.

Chicago was Doby's last Major League stop as a player. By then thirty-five years old, he played in only twenty-one games, batting .241 with no home runs and only nine runs batted in. His final game in the Major Leagues was on July 26. Sent down to the White Sox's San Diego farm team in the Pacific Coast League, Doby fractured an ankle sliding into third base on a triple on August 23.[31] Doby finished his Major League career with a .283 batting average, 243 doubles, 253 home runs, and 970 RBIs.

In 1960 Doby signed with the Toronto Maple Leafs of the International League, but because of the lingering effects of his ankle injury, he was released in May without getting into a game. In 1962 he played for the Nagoya Dragons in Japan. He went on to coach with Montreal, Cleveland, and the White Sox.[32] He also owned a lounge and a liquor store in Newark, and he worked in the Essex County prosecutor's office in New Jersey for three years.[33]

During that time, Doby wrote letters to Major League teams seeking the opportunity to be a Major League manager. In 1971, when he was a batting coach for the Montreal Expos, Doby spoke of the possibility of managing in the Major Leagues in an interview: "The Expos know what I want to do," he said. "But they want me to work my way up. . . . They want me to wait. I don't mind waiting because right now I'm learning. But I can't wait for the rest of my life."[34] Doby remarked that he enjoyed working with kids in part because he had good training—he had five children of his own.

Doby received the chance to manage in 1978, becoming the second black manager in Major League history when he took over the White Sox. He succeeded Bob Lemon, who was fired, but took over the Yankees and led them to the pennant. Doby's time managing was filled with frustration, however, as he had a record of only 37-50 during the portion of the one season in which he managed during his career. Doby cited injuries for the team's failures, saying, "When you have to use people you hope can play, rather than those you know can play, you are in a bad situation."[35]

He also maintained strong feelings about why he had to wait until the age of fifty-three to receive the Chicago managerial job: "Why did it take this long? You tell me. I don't mean to sound prejudiced, but you can look at the system and see that, until I was named (to replace Lemon on June 30), there was no black manager in the major leagues."[36]

After the 1978 season, Doby was fired as the team's manager. "I can't truly say what kind of manager I was or could've been because I didn't have enough time," he said. "I thought I could have been successful. I thought I had those intangibles."[37]

After his managerial career was over, Doby remained active with Major League baseball. He was an administrator for the Former Players Licensing Branch of Major League Baseball, helping to license people or companies that wanted to use players or their trademarks for card shows or speaking engagements.[38] In 1995 Doby was named special assistant to American League president Gene Budig, who said at the time, "Few have done more for Major League Baseball than Larry Doby, and we are excited about having him associated with us."[39] Doby later was also named to the Baseball World board.[40]

In 1997 the Indians retired Doby's No. 14 on the fiftieth anniversary of his Major League debut. He became the fifth Cleveland player to be so honored, joining Bob Feller, Earl Averill, Mel Harder, and Lou Boudreau.[41] A banner was displayed in left field on July 5, 1997, at Jacobs Field, showing Doby and Jackie Robinson, saying "50 years: 1947–1997." At the ceremony, Hank Aaron said to Doby, "I want to thank you for all that you went through, because if it had not been for you, I wouldn't have been able to have the career that I had."[42] In 1998 Doby was elected to the Baseball Hall of Fame by the Veterans Committee.[43]

Doby's health plagued him in retirement. He battled a cancerous tumor in 1997 and had to have a kidney removed.[44] Helyn, his wife of fifty-five years, died in 2001 after a six-month battle with cancer.[45] Larry Doby died of cancer in Montclair, New Jersey, on June 18, 2003. More than three hundred mourners attended his funeral at Trinity Presbyterian Church.[46] He is buried in Montclair. He was honored posthumously by appearing on a U.S. postage stamp released in July 2012.[47]

Chapter 17. George Strickland

Mel Marmer

AGE	G	AB	R	H	2B	3B	HR	TB	RBI	BB	SO	BAV	OBP	SLG	SB	GDP	HBP
28	112	361	42	77	12	3	6	113	37	55	62	.213	.314	.313	2	10	1

George "Bo" Strickland was the starting shortstop on the 1954 Cleveland Indians team that won the American League pennant and compiled one of baseball's finest records ever, 111-43. He went hitless (0 for 9) in that season's World Series, the only one he ever played in, as the Indians were swept by the New York Giants. Strickland was a good glove man, a utility infielder highly regarded for his defense, who despite being a weak hitter (.224 career batting average) played ten Major League seasons.

The New Orleans native had his finest season in 1953, when he turned 103 double plays and hit .284. In 1955 he eked out only a .209 batting average but had the highest fielding percentage for shortstops in the Major Leagues, .976. Strickland was credited with helping to turn around the Indians' defense and being a significant factor in the team's 1952 and 1959 pennant runs. After his playing career ended, Strickland scouted for one year and coached for ten with the Indians, the Minnesota Twins, and the Kansas City Royals. In 1964 he became the first New Orleans native to manage in the Majors when he filled in for an ailing Birdie Tebbetts.

Strickland kept a low profile as far as the general public was concerned, but to those who knew him, he was a loyal friend with a great sense of humor. Later in life, when he attended sports luncheons in New Orleans with retired athletes, said a New Orleans sportswriter, "He was often the life of the party, and had the group in stitches. Everybody wanted to sit next to George."[1]

George Bevan Strickland was born on January 10, 1926, in New Orleans. His father, Harry L. Strickland, was a police officer assigned to Pelican Stadium where the New Orleans Pelicans of the

George Strickland—Strickland was a steady presence at shortstop for the Indians in the 1950s, and also filled in at second base. He managed parts of two years for Cleveland (1964 and 1966) and coached for over ten years in the Major Leagues.

Southern Association played. His mother, Imelda (Bevan) Strickland, was a homemaker. George had a sister, Rita, six years older, and a brother, Harry L. Jr., four years older.

The Strickland family lived in the Third Ward, the crowded central business district in the Crescent City. "Like many families then, ours was poor due to the Great Depression. We didn't have a radio, so we played a lot out of doors," Strickland told an interviewer. His favorite activities were baseball, basketball, and fishing. His earliest memory of playing ball was of his father taking him to a wide median on a major street and spinning bottle caps at him to hit with a sawed-off broom handle.[2]

George got his nickname, Bo, for having numerous "bobos" (scratches, scrapes, and bruises) when he was a child. "When I was little," he related, "I liked to visit my grandma at the casket factory where she worked, and her boss said he'd never seen a little fella with so many bobos. The nickname stuck and everyone started calling me Bobo, later shortened to Bo."[3] But by the time he was a ninth-grader and tried out for his S. J. Peters High School baseball team, he preferred to be called by his middle name, Bevan. Strickland didn't make the team in the ninth grade, but he made the varsity as a sophomore in 1941. His coach, Dave Dahlgren, liked his fielding ability. "He might be small," said Dahlgren, "but just try to get a ball past him!"[4]

The 1941 Peters nine made its way to the New Orleans City high school finals. Teammate Mel Parnell, a future Boston Red Sox star pitcher, said the team "was so good, we took things easy; we fooled around too much and were beaten."[5] The next year, though, with Strickland as the team captain, Peters won the city title. Strickland was still growing; he didn't reach his adult height of six feet one and weight of 175 pounds until a few years later.[6]

In 1943 Strickland played American Legion ball with Aloysius Jax Post. The team won the Legion tournament regional finals at Cape Girardeau, Missouri, then finished fourth in the national finals at Miles City, Montana. Strickland made the All-Legion second team as a utility infielder,[7] and shortly afterward he signed a contract with the New Orleans Pelicans, a Brooklyn Dodgers farm team. He played in only three games for the Pelicans, and then, before the 1944 season began, he was drafted into the U.S. Navy. He spent sixteen months on the Pacific island of Saipan as a mailman specialist. While he was there, his older brother, Harry, an

army paratrooper, was killed in action in the Pacific.[8] Discharged from the navy in May 1946, Strickland returned to the Pelicans, who had become a Boston Red Sox affiliate. He resumed playing third base and batted .242 in seventy-eight games.

Strickland went to spring training with the Red Sox in 1947, where he competed for a backup infield position, but eventually was sent to Scranton of the Class A Eastern League, where he displayed a strong arm but batted .235 in his first full Minor League season. He had difficulty at third base coming in on infield taps and eventually switched positions with Scranton shortstop Fred Hatfield, a move that benefited both players.[9] Strickland started the 1948 season with Scranton, but he was promoted after several weeks to the Triple-A Louisville Colonels and given the regular shortstop job. He fielded well but batted just .237. The next season Strickland was sent back to Double-A ball, the Birmingham Barons in the Southern Association. For Strickland it was a wake-up call that led to his best season in the Minor Leagues. He hit .261 in 128 games for the Barons and was named the Southern Association's second-team all-star shortstop. After the 1949 season, the Pittsburgh Pirates selected Strickland in the Rule 5 draft. The Pirates were regarded as one of baseball's worst teams then, but Strickland didn't care, because "they wore major-league uniforms!"[10]

Strickland made the Pirates squad in 1950, but his Major League debut was delayed until May 7 after a recurrence of a fungal infection he had suffered in the army. In his debut, against the Dodgers in Brooklyn, he entered the game as a defensive replacement in the eighth inning. He did the same the next day and got to bat but drew a walk. On May 14, he hit a two-run pinch-hit single in the ninth inning off the Chicago Cubs' Paul Minner that won the game, 6–5. But he played sparingly, appearing in just twenty-three games, and started only six games at shortstop. He was 3 for 27, for a .111 batting average.

In 1951 the Korean War and the resultant draft of young players worked in Strickland's favor. Since he had served in World War II, he would have been among the last to be called for duty. Eight games into the 1951 season, the Pirates traded shortstop Stan Rojek, and with Danny O'Connell serving a two-year army hitch, Strickland became the starting shortstop. He played in 138 games, hit just .216, led the team with 83 strikeouts, and made 37 errors, second only to New York Giants rookie Alvin Dark's 45. Most of Strickland's errors occurred because he rushed his throws, and not because of poor fielding. Playing in Pittsburgh's Forbes Field, he got into the bad habit of trying to pull everything, which resulted in lots of strikeouts and easy fly balls to left field. Hitting coach Paul Waner tried to teach him to "hit the ball where it was pitched," to little avail.

The woeful Pirates desperately needed hitting. Then they drafted Dick Groat, a local boy who was an All-American basketball player and all-conference baseball player at Duke University, and Strickland became expendable. On August 18, 1952, hitting .177, he was traded to the Indians with pitcher Ted Wilks for second baseman Johnny Berardino and $50,000. Later the Pirates also received Minor League pitcher Charles Sipple. Tony Cuccinello, the Indians' infield coach, liked Strickland and had recommended that the team acquire Strickland. A former National League coach, Cuccinello had watched Strickland and felt that he had the "soft" hands necessary to be a good fielder, and that his throwing faults could be corrected.

The Indians were built on offense—they could easily accommodate Strickland's lack of offensive production to shore up the infield. They were last in the league in turning double plays, and each infielder led the league in errors at his position. On August 24, 1952, the Indians committed seven errors, handed the Senators seven runs, and lost, 9–8. Manager Al Lopez inserted Strickland at shortstop the next day. He didn't get a hit, but he turned three nifty double plays, and the team won behind Bob Lemon, 7–2. The next day he broke a scoreless tie with the Philadelphia Athletics and smacked his first home run as an Indian, a two-out, two-run shot off Bobby Shantz. On September 27, against the Detroit Tigers, he burnished his fielding credentials by taking part in five double plays, tying a record at the time that has since been broken. With Strickland as the regular shortstop, the Indians became part of the race for the American League pennant, which eventually was won by the New York Yankees.

Strickland had his most productive year in 1953, batting .284, and leading American League shortstops in turning double plays with 103. Then, in the marvelous season of 1954, he slipped back to his usual level (.213), but contributed more than his share of timely hits. Early in the season the *Cleveland Plain Dealer* noted that though he had only sixteen hits at the point, he had fifteen RBIs.

On July 23 Strickland's jaw was broken in a game in Yankee Stadium when he was hit by a throw from Yankees pitcher Marlin Stuart while sliding into third base. He was out for more than a month and lost fifteen pounds. He missed five weeks and didn't return until September 5. He never got his timing back at the plate, and in the World Series, in which the Indians were swept by the Giants, he was hitless in nine at bats.

In Game Three he made a throwing error in the first inning that let in the first run in the 6–2 loss to the Giants. Some sportswriters suggested that he was out of position in the third inning when the Giants' Don Mueller executed a perfect hit-and-run play. Others came to his defense, saying that it was normal for a shortstop to cheat toward second base when he is looking for a double-play ball, and that Mueller, one of the finest place hitters in the game at the time, had pushed the ball perfectly through the vacated spot. Strickland was replaced at shortstop in Game Four by Sam Dente, who had started forty-eight games at shortstop during the season.

In 1955 Strickland struggled at the plate again (.209) but led American League shortstops in fielding percentage. In 1956 he turned thirty years old and lost his starting shortstop job when the Indians obtained shortstop Chico Carrasquel in a trade over the winter. Strickland was relegated to a utility role. He filled in at shortstop when Carrasquel's bat went cold, or for Bobby Avila at second base when Avila's back was sore. He played in eighty-five games and batted .211.

Strickland hit well in spring training of 1957 and was named the outstanding player of camp. He was moved to second base but was injured early in the season. In September he replaced Carrasquel when Chico was benched for "not charging ground balls," but overall Strickland's playing time was greatly diminished (eighty-nine games).

In 1958, at the age of thirty-two, Strickland asked to be placed on the voluntarily retired list. He and Lorraine had adopted a child, John Thomas, their first. His diminished playing time, and a new manager, Bobby Bragan, also influenced the decision. In Strickland's absence, the Indians converted center fielder Woodie Held into a shortstop. Strickland, meanwhile, took a job selling sporting goods at the Maison-Blanche department store in downtown New Orleans. That fall he applied for a job working in the pari-mutuel windows at the Fair Grounds race track in New Orleans that fall and winter. (He sought and received permission from the baseball commissioner's office, which in general frowned on players working in the gambling world.) Strickland worked at the race track until he retired in 1988 as assistant manager of the pari-mutuel department. Meanwhile, though, in 1959, after spring training had begun, he asked the Indians to reinstate him as a player. The Indians allowed him to compete for a job as a nonroster player. Strickland played well in spring training and was added to the roster. He continued to hit well, though everyone expected his average to plummet as it almost always did. Cleveland stormed out of the gate that year to the lead in the American League. Strickland played a major part in it. The infield consisted of Vic Power at first base, Billy Martin at second, Strickland at short, subbing for Woodie Held (recovering from surgery), and Randy Jackson at third. Near the end of May, Strickland was batting .355. Billy Martin said the best season he ever had as a fielder was 1959 when he had Strickland at short and Vic Power at first.[11]

Then Strickland pulled a leg muscle and was replaced by Granny Hamner at shortstop. Soon Woodie Held was back at shortstop, and Strickland moved to third base. The Indians stayed in the thick of the pennant race until a series at the end of August when they lost four straight to the Chicago White Sox, dashing their hopes for winning the pennant.

In April 1960 Strickland returned for another season with the Indians as insurance to play shortstop if the Indians had to move Woodie Held to center field in case Jimmy Piersall hadn't signed. Piersall signed late and played center field, but an injury to Held gave Strickland yet another opportunity to play shortstop for fourteen games. He also filled in at third base for fourteen games and at second base for two games. His batting average plummeted to its usual anemic state. When Held returned to play shortstop, the writing was on the wall; there was no need to keep Strickland. He played his final game on July 23, 1960. He had a career batting average of only .224, but his skill in the infield allowed him to play 971 games over ten seasons.

Strickland was the last remaining member of the Indians who'd played for the team before Frank "Trader" Lane began as general manager in November 1957. "They said I was brittle, but I lasted ten years in the majors and that's something I'm proud of," he said years later.[12]

After he was released, Strickland scouted National League clubs for the Indians in 1960. Sam Mele, a friend from his days in the Red Sox's Minor League system who was then the Minnesota Twins manager, added him as the third base and infield coach for the 1962 season.

On October 13, 1962, Birdie Tebbetts returned as the Indians' manager. His first move was to hire Strickland from the Twins. On July 10 Tebbetts was out sick, and Strickland filled in as manager, becoming the first native of New Orleans to manage in the Major Leagues. After Tebbetts recovered, he went back to his third base coaching duties. In 1964, when Birdie Tebbetts again took ill, Strickland again filled in.

In December of 1965 Strickland was reported to be the top candidate to manage the Chicago White Sox, but Eddie Stanky got the job. On August 19, 1966, Tebbetts was fired as manager of the Indians and Strickland succeeded him. The Indians went 15-24 under Strickland. His overall record as an Indians manager was 48-63. Joe Adcock was named manager the following season, 1967, and Strickland went back to coaching third base. His last season coaching for the Indians was 1969. In 1970 he joined his Indians friend Bob Lemon as a coach with the Kansas City Royals. When Lemon was fired after the 1972 season, Strickland was also released, and he retired from baseball for good. He told Lemon not to call him even if he got another job (Lemon did get another job, managing the Yankees), because he was going home to New Orleans to be with his family. He'd earned the maximum pension after twenty years in the Major Leagues. He had also continued to work at the Fair Grounds race track.

For a decade or so Strickland was a popular speaker for a group that met for lunch every week in New Orleans. The group included former pitcher Mel Parnell, Louisiana baseball historian Arthur Schott, sportswriter Peter Barrouquere, retired football players, a boxing referee, and a racehorse trainer.

"Everything in baseball turned out the best for me," said the modest, soft-spoken baseball lifer with an infectious enthusiasm for the game. He died on February 21, 2010. He was survived by his son, John Thomas Strickland, and his family, and was buried in Greenwood Cemetery, New Orleans. His beloved wife, Lorraine, had predeceased him by five years.

Chapter 18. **Cleveland Stadium (1932–96)**

Tom Wancho

Cleveland Stadium— The venerable Stadium was home to both the Cleveland Indians and the Cleveland Browns from the 1940s through the 1990s. Contrary to popular belief, it was not built in hopes that the city would have a venue to host the Olympics. (The Cleveland Press Collection, Cleveland State University Library)

I am gone and forgotten. People who sat in my seats rarely recall me fondly, if they remember me at all. When the wrecking ball began to demolish my sixty-four-year-old sides in December 1996, there was no public outcry to save me. It was a slow, painful death, memories cascading underneath the rubble that occasionally brought Cleveland sports fans a reason to celebrate, and hope.

Although I was officially kicked to the curb after Art Modell moved the Browns to Baltimore following the 1995 NFL season, my demise began decades earlier. Anyone who went to see the Indians or Browns play from the 1970s on could see the wear and tear that living by icy Lake Erie had taken on me. Peeling paint, crumbling concrete, inoperable escalators and elevators, uncomfortable seats, flood-ed restrooms, misnamed luxury boxes, obstructed views were always a part of me but had become more noticeable, and a general coldness that lasted well beyond winter peppered my résumé.

I wasn't always that way.

During my first baseball game, a July 31, 1932, Sunday showdown against the Philadelphia Athletics attended by baseball royalty and 76,979 fans, I was praised for what I was, not what I would become. Baseball's first commissioner, Judge Kenesaw Mountain Landis, commented, "This stadium is perfect. It is the only baseball park I know where the spectator can see clearly from any seat. Look at those people out there (he said pointing to the crowded center-field bleachers); they can watch every play."[1]

Landis turned around in his box seat near the Indians' dugout and swept the grandstands with his hand. "Not a barrier to block anyone's view. Comfortable chairs. This is perfection." Obviously, the Commish never saw a game from beyond the box seats.

John Heydler, the National League's president, said, "Marvelous. It is the last word in baseball parks. A great thing for baseball. And one should not forget to give (Indians president) Mr. (Alva) Bradley credit, either."[2]

And this from Thomas S. Shibe, Athletics president: "This was built for baseball. I wish we had this in Philadelphia for the last three World Series."[3]

Before the Beginning

According to the October 1985 Inventory Nomination form for a listing on the National Register of Historic Places, "Cleveland Municipal Stadium was designed by the progressive city administration as a multipurpose structure to accommodate the great surge in attendance at baseball and football games and other public spectacles that occurred with the rise of the automobile."[4]

The nomination form goes on to read, "Since then, in addition to baseball and football, the range of activities at the stadium has included religious convocations, the Metropolitan Opera, the Beatles, circuses, rodeos, big bands, tractor pulls, and polka festivals."[5]

It is interesting that the "great surge in attendance at baseball and football games" was mentioned in the application. From 1922 through 1931, the Indians averaged 491,227 fans per year to League Park, good enough for a fifth-place average in the eight-team American League during that span. In fact, 1931 was the only year during that decade that the Indians finished as high as third in attendance, behind the New York Yankees and Philadelphia Athletics. Attendance figures for the Cleveland franchise (1920–23) in the fledgling National Football League are sketchy.

If You Build It . . . Who Will Come?

Constructed on a landfill that stretched the Stadium two hundred feet farther into Lake Erie, the facility was completed in 370 days at a cost to taxpayers of $3,035,245. Although 21 percent over budget, the cost overruns were attributed to the addition of a scoreboard, sound system, and infrastructure around the facility, including bridges, railroads, and road work.

The Stadium's first sporting event took place two days after work had been completed. The heavyweight bout between champion Max Schmeling of Germany and Young Stribling was witnessed by 37,000 fans on the night of July 3, 1931. Schmeling scored a fifteen-round TKO. The remainder of the summer of '31 brought a Shriners convention and the "Grand Summer Opera Week" to the new edifice by the lake.

The Indians played the rest of their home games at the Stadium following their July 31, 1932, "opener" and their entire 1933 home schedule as well. But after attendance dipped in 1933 to 387,936—nearly 100,000 less than the 483,027 they attracted in 1931, their last full season at League Park—owner Bradley moved the club back to League Park for all but one game during the 1934–36 seasons.

Under pressure from city leaders, unhappy while their 80,000-seat stadium sat vacant, Bradley agreed to play most doubleheaders and other games expected to draw larger crowds at the Stadium. The Tribe didn't move downtown full time until 1947, after Bill Veeck purchased the club.

Ten years before that, the Cleveland Rams played exactly one game—the first in franchise history—at the Stadium, drawing 20,000 fans for a 28–0 loss to the Detroit Lions on September 10, 1937. Because the Stadium "was too big and the rent too high,"[6] when the Rams won their only NFL championship in 1945, all of their home games were at League Park, though they did play the title game at the Stadium.

According to Rams public relations director Nate Wallack,

Our season-ticket sale was nothing (in) those days. Maybe 200 at the most. We put the championship seats on sale and immediately we sold 30,000 and we had another week to go before the game. The weather was beautiful. It looked as though we'd sell out the Stadium. Then a blizzard. I mean an awful one. It ended our sale. Now Bill Johns, our business manager, was worried about the field. He wanted to keep it from freezing. He got in his car and set out toward Sandusky, stopping at every farm to buy hay. He wanted to cover the field with it. He bought over 1,000 bales.

The day of the game the temperature dropped to zero. I sat in the press box and the windows got so steamed we couldn't see. All the writers had to get out into the stands and freeze. Me too. A water pipe broke in the upper deck and cascading water turned to ice immediately—a frozen waterfall. The fans burned the hay and even the wooden bleacher seats to keep warm. One fan froze his feet and didn't realize it until he started to walk home after the game. An ambulance had to be called. The game was so exciting, though, the fans stayed to the end. We sold about 35,000 tickets and 29,000 showed.[7]

The Rams' 15–14 victory over the Washington Redskins was the team's last game in Cleveland. Mickey McBride, a Cleveland taxicab magnate, purchased a franchise for the new All-America Football Conference, to be named after its head coach, former Massillon and Ohio State head man Paul Brown. McBride signed a long-term lease to play home games at the Stadium. Typical of the doom that would frequent Cleveland professional sports teams, the Rams moved to Los Angeles *after* winning a championship.

Home Sweet Home

The Stadium entered an unprecedented period of success after the Browns and Indians became its

Cleveland Stadium II—Chief Wahoo proudly displays the upcoming schedule outside the stadium. (The Cleveland Press Collection, Cleveland State University Library)

chief tenants beginning in 1946 and 1947, respectively. The Browns won every championship during the four-year history of the All-America Football Conference, with three of those wins taking place on the Stadium's turf. The Indians set a baseball attendance record in 1948, drawing 2,620,627 fans as they won Cleveland's second—and to date, last—World Series. The Tribe captured Games Three and Four at the Stadium before wrapping up the title at Braves Field in Boston. Noteworthy in the Game Five home loss was a then World Series–record crowd of 86,288 who had hoped to see the Clevelanders wrap the series up at home.

While the 1950s remained kind to the Browns, the Indians began a slow descent that concluded with a remarkable tumble down the American League standings during the latter decades of the twentieth century. Despite posting a then all-time American League best 111-43 record in 1954, the Tribe was swept in that year's World Series by the New York Giants. The last World Series game played in Cleveland Stadium was seen by 78,102 disappointed fans.

The Browns entered the NFL in 1950 and promptly captured that season's title with a 30–28 Christmas Eve victory over the . . . Rams, who returned to the Stadium for the first time since leaving for Los Angeles five years before. Cleveland appeared in six of the next seven NFL title tilts (going 2-4), including a 1955 championship at the Stadium. The Browns' 27–0 shutout over the Baltimore Colts at the Stadium on December 27, 1964, remains the last championship captured by a Cleveland professional sports franchise.

Cleveland Stadium Spectacles

Whether it was sports or other events, the Stadium provided a backdrop for a multitude of memorable moments. Ted Williams hit his 500th home run there on June 17, 1960. The Indians' Len Barker pitched the tenth perfect game in Major League Baseball history against the Toronto Blue Jays on May 15, 1981. Joe DiMaggio's fifty-six-game hitting streak ended there on July 17, 1941. Bob Feller whiffed a then record eighteen Detroit Tigers on October 3, 1938, from the Stadium's mound. The first Monday Night Football game ever played pitted the Browns against Joe Namath's Jets on September 21, 1970, from the Stadium. Four MLB All-Star Games were held at the Stadium.

Cleveland Stadium was also home to 10¢ Beer Night and "The Drive" engineered by John Elway. The Browns ended up on the wrong end of another playoff game against the Oakland Raiders on January 4, 1981, after quarterback Brian Sipe had a pass intercepted at the east (open) end of the Stadium when a field goal would have won the game. That led to a joke: What do a Billy Graham Crusade and a Cleveland Browns game have in common? Answer: Eighty thousand fans leaving the Stadium murmuring, "Jesus Christ."

The End

Stadiums are public gathering places, often for sporting events. They are steel, concrete, grass, dirt, seats, and scoreboards. What transpires within their walls brings fans together, be it in victory or defeat. Some fans have fond memories of the Cleveland Municipal Stadium. It represents their youth, possibly the site of their first Major League or NFL game. Its decrepitude, warm beer, and cold hot dogs are also part of the collective memory bank.

Over time, the Stadium became known as the "Mistake by the Lake." After its demolition, the old Stadium's reinforced concrete was dumped in Lake Erie and used as a barrier reef for fishermen. Like Luca Brasi from *The Godfather*, it sleeps with the fishes.

Chapter 19. **Jim Hegan**

Rick Balazs

AGE	G	AB	R	H	2B	3B	HR	TB	RBI	BB	SO	BAV	OBP	SLG	SB	GDP	HBP
33	139	423	56	99	12	7	11	158	40	34	48	.234	.289	.374	0	15	0

The Cleveland Indians of the early 1950s, including the 1954 team, were well known for their Big Four starting rotation, consisting of Bob Feller, Bob Lemon, Early Wynn, and Mike Garcia. But when asked which superstar pitcher was the best, Yankees manager Casey Stengel said, "Give me that fella behind the plate. He's what makes 'em."[1]

Stengel was referring to Jim Hegan, the Indians' longtime catcher, who had a reputation for excellent defense. Hegan's catching prowess and game-calling ability helped the Tribe have one of the game's most dominant pitching staffs from 1947 to 1956. Beyond his success on the field, Hegan was one of the Indians' most popular players, among both his teammates and the Cleveland fans. He spent fourteen of his seventeen Major League seasons with the Indians and never lacked for job security, despite a career batting average of just .228.

James Edward Hegan was born on August 3, 1920, in Lynn, Massachusetts, a few miles north of Boston, to John and Laura Hegan, a working-class Irish couple. His father was a policeman. Family was the focal point of the Hegans' lives. John sang in a barbershop quartet, and any time they were all together after dinner, they would gather to sing in the living room. Emphasis on family and an affinity for barbershop quartets remained with Jim for the rest of his life.

The Hegan family—Jim had two sisters and four brothers—also possessed a substantial amount of athletic ability. Jim's youngest brother, Larry, played basketball and pitched for his high school baseball team despite having a deformed hand. His oldest brother, Ray, was a very good football player and received a scholarship to Dartmouth.[2] Jim starred

Jim Hegan—One of the great defensive catchers of his era or any other, Hegan was given much credit for the success of Cleveland's great pitching staffs in the 1940s and 1950s. He served as a coach for more than twenty years for both the New York Yankees and Detroit.

in baseball, basketball, and football in high school. He was the only one in his family to play a sport professionally.

"He was a tremendous, all-around athlete," said Hegan's son Mike, who followed his father into baseball, had a twelve-year Major League career, and has been a play-by-play broadcaster for more than three decades. "He quit playing football in his sophomore year because I think he knew he wanted to play baseball professionally. My mother and others have told me that he was an outstanding receiver in football." Mike said his father was a center in basketball and played semipro in the off-seasons in Boston for a forerunner of the Boston Celtics, before the NBA was created.[3]

Hegan met his future wife, Clare, at Lynn English High School. He was a senior and she was a sophomore. It took little time for them to realize that they wanted to get married, and they were wed in 1941.

Jim and Clare had three children, Mike, Patrick, and Catharine. Mike was the oldest, born in 1942, seven years before his brother, Patrick, and twelve years before his sister, Cathy. Mike played for three teams during a fifteen-year playing career before becoming known to another generation of Indians fans as a TV and radio broadcaster for Indians games.

Like most young families, the Hegans had to work hard to make ends meet. Before moving from Boston to Cleveland, the family shared a house with Clare's sister, across the street from Clare's parents.

"My dad was very much a family man," Mike said. "He puttered around the house. Even when he was semi-retired, he and my mom spent a lot of time together, shopped together, and vacationed together. He had good friends, but they were basically his family. Family was most important to him."[4]

Hegan broke into professional baseball in 1938, when the Indians offered him a contract at the age of seventeen.[5] He played in the Minor Leagues with Springfield of the Class C Middle Atlantic League in 1938 and 1939, and split the 1940 season between Oklahoma City of the Texas League and Wilkes-Barre of the Eastern League. He played for the same two teams in 1941 and was promoted to the Indians in September. His debut with Cleveland, on September 9 against the Philadelphia Athletics, must have been a daunting event for Hegan; he was assigned to catch Bob Feller. But the rookie went 2 for 5 with a home run and drove in three runs, and the Indians won, 13–7, as future Hall of Famer Feller earned his twenty-third victory of the season.

After the game, manager Roger Peckinpaugh told Hegan, "Nice game," which Hegan later said was "like handing me $1 million."[6] Sportswriters were equally complimentary; the Cleveland Plain Dealer said that "although Feller is one of the most difficult pitchers in the major leagues to catch, Hegan handled him perfectly and performed like a veteran."[7]

Hegan's debut was a sign of a promising career to come, although the realization of that career took some time. In 1942 he played in sixty-eight games and batted only .194 in 170 at bats as Otto Denning and Gene Desautels handled the bulk of the catching. With the United States fighting in World War II, Hegan was away serving in the Coast Guard from 1943 through 1945. He returned to the Indians in 1946 and batted.236 in 271 at bats while splitting the catching duties with Sherm Lollar and Frankie Hayes.

Hegan became the starting catcher in 1947, though he was hobbled by manager Lou Boudreau's decision to call the pitches from his position at shortstop. That angered the pitchers and stung Hegan, though he advised the pitchers not to rebel. The Indians went 80-74 but didn't fulfill expectations. Owner Bill Veeck nearly fired Boudreau as manager.[8]

Before the 1948 season, Boudreau told Hegan to forget about the previous season and gave him the duty of calling pitches. The Indians posted a team ERA of 3.22, leading the American League, and proceeded to win the pennant and World Series. Perhaps Boudreau's demonstration of confidence boosted Hegan's offensive production; he had his best season with the bat, hitting .248 with career highs in home runs (14), RBIs (61), and doubles (21). He finished nineteenth in the American League Most Valuable Player voting, ahead of notable players like teammates Feller and Larry Doby and fellow catcher Yogi Berra of the Yankees. (Boudreau won the MVP award.)

After the Indians defeated the Braves in the World Series, team owner Veeck praised Hegan, saying, "There isn't a better catcher in the league."[9] Judging from the performance of Indians pitchers during Hegan's years as the everyday catcher, few could argue with Veeck. From 1947 to 1956, the Indians led the American League in ERA six times. In those ten years, a Cleveland pitcher won twenty games seventeen times. Hegan caught three no-hitters, one of only fourteen catchers to do so, as he was the receiver for Don Black's no-hitter in 1947, Bob Lemon's in 1948, and Bob Feller's third in 1951. (One of the fourteen, Jason Varitek, caught four.[10])

The most spectacular pitching staff during Hegan's tenure, of course, was the one from the 1954 team. That year, the Indians led the American League with a sparkling 2.78 ERA. With such a dominant staff leading the way to a 111-win season, losing the World Series in a four-game sweep to the Giants was hard to take, particularly for Jim.

"The 1954 year might have been the most satisfying and the most frustrating for him, simply because they won 111 games but didn't win it all," Mike Hegan said. (The Indians were swept by the New York Giants in the World Series.) "They were not the best baseball team, yet they were. All those guys from that team just kind of shake their heads. It just might have been a quirk of fate, the way it worked out."

The Hegans relocated permanently to Cleveland in 1954 after spending off-seasons in the Boston area. The family moved to their new home in Lakewood, just west of the city, and Hegan joined in a business venture with Cleveland Browns quarterback Otto Graham. Eventually they opened a store, Hegan-Graham Appliance, on Euclid Avenue in downtown Cleveland that sold sporting goods, luggage, and jewelry in addition to appliances, and urged customers to "Get the right pitch before you buy."[11]

Hegan made several noteworthy headlines during the 1954 season. One memorable day was September 12, when the Indians swept a doubleheader against the Yankees before a crowd of 86,563 at Cleveland Stadium. Hegan caught both games, a complete-game 4–1 victory for Bob Lemon and a complete-game 3–2 victory for Early Wynn. Six days later, he hit a solo home run for what turned out to be the deciding run in the pennant-clinching victory in Detroit.

The headlines weren't as favorable in Game One of the World Series against the Giants at the Polo Grounds in New York. In the eighth inning, with the score tied at 2–2 and two Indians on base, Willie Mays made his famous catch of Vic Wertz's long drive to center. Most people say the catch took the wind out of the Indians' sails. In reality, the Indians had a better chance to score three batters later, but the wind literally ruined their chance to score. Hegan came to bat with the bases loaded and two outs and hit a long fly to left, but the wind knocked down what might have been a grand slam.

"It looked like a homer, but the wind, blowing toward the right, pulled the ball in so that Monte Irvin was able to make the catch," Indians manager Al Lopez said after the game.[12] Irvin said, "[The ball] was out of my sight. Gone. It missed the scoreboard by a fraction of an inch and fell into my glove."[13]

The same wind didn't do the Indians any favors in the bottom of the tenth, when Dusty Rhodes's short fly ball stayed fair down the right-field line for a three-run homer, giving the Giants a 5–2 victory and setting the stage for their sweep.

That 1954 season was one of Hegan's best. He batted only .234 but hit eleven home runs and a career-high seven triples, and led American League catchers in fielding percentage (.994). He repeated the feat in 1955 (.997) while committing only two errors.

At thirty-three, Jim was entering the latter stages of his career. He had two more seasons as the Indians' regular catcher. In each of those seasons, the Indians finished second to the Yankees, just as they had done each season from 1951 to 1953. Hegan had established himself as one of the most popular players on the team. In 1953 he was honored with a Jim Hegan Night at Municipal Stadium. Little League catchers wore his uniform number, 10, and when he switched to 4, they switched too.[14]

Hegan was popular with his teammates too. Often they would join him in barbershop quartets on train rides during road trips. Hall of Fame pitcher Bob Lemon was his roommate and best friend. They roomed together for seventeen years, starting in the Minor Leagues when they were both eighteen. The two were complete opposites. Lemon was an avid socializer who loved to crack jokes and often came in late after having a few too many. Hegan was more reserved and was one of the few players who didn't drink.

"Lem was always so full of fun," Clare Hegan once said. "He'd wear a fake arm and shake somebody's hand and the arm would come off. Jim was quiet. He was dignified, even when he was young. He was almost embarrassed when people recognized him as being a major leaguer."[15]

"You couldn't have two any more different personalities," said Mike Hegan. "People used to say that they would invite Jim out with the guys after the ballgame because he would make sure they would get home. He was this day and age's designated driver."

With young catcher Russ Nixon waiting in the wings, the Indians traded Hegan to Detroit before the 1958 season. After brief stints with the Tigers, the Philadelphia Phillies, and the San Francisco Giants in 1958 and '59, Hegan's playing career seemed to be over. He and Otto Graham had closed the appliance business after Graham went to the Coast Guard Academy to coach football. Hegan then went to work as a salesman for a trucking company. But in the spring of 1960 he got a call from his old manager, Lou Boudreau, who was now managing the Chicago Cubs. One of the Cubs' catchers, Dick Bertell, was injured, and Boudreau wanted Hegan to join the Cubs as a backup catcher. After discussing the opportunity with Clare, he accepted Boudreau's offer. "I was a senior at St. Ignatius [in Cleveland] at the time, and the two of us would go up to Lakewood Park with a bag of balls," Mike said. "I threw him batting practice every day for about a

week. After the Cubs returned from a road trip, he joined the team."

Hegan played his first game for the Cubs on May 28 and hit a home run in his second at bat. But he played sparingly, and the Cubs released him on July 27. Hegan quickly signed with the Yankees as a bullpen coach to replace Bill Dickey, who was ill. Dickey had been a Hall of Fame catcher with the Yankees and had once famously said of Hegan, "When you catch like Hegan, you don't have to hit."[16]

The Yankees placed Hegan on their active roster in September. Though he didn't appear in a game, manager Casey Stengel still thought highly of Hegan's ability, telling the *New York Times*, "Hegan still is a very fine catcher, especially in moving around and getting under foul balls."[17]

After Ralph Houk replaced Stengel in 1961, Hegan remained with the Yankees. He coached with the team for sixteen seasons, from 1960 to 1973 and in 1979–80. As of 2012 he had the third-longest tenure among Yankees coaches, trailing only Frank Crosetti (1946–68) and Jim Turner (1949–59, 1966–73).[18]

Mike Hegan played for the Yankees in 1964, 1966, and 1967. During their time together Jim almost joined Mike on the active roster. "There was one year when somebody got hurt and there were some rumors of activating my dad," Mike said. "But he didn't want to do it, and it wasn't because I was on the team. Had that happened, we would have been the first father-and-son combination to play on the same team." Ken Griffey Jr. and his father, Ken Sr., became the first, playing together on the Seattle Mariners in 1990. Still, the Hegans achieved a couple of feats rare for father-son duos. They each played on a World Series–winning team, with Jim playing for the 1948 Indians and Mike for the 1972 Oakland Athletics. They were the first father-and-son tandem to be chosen for the All-Star Game; Jim was picked five times and Mike once.[19]

"I was able to watch him in action and operate," Mike said. "He was really Ralph Houk's right-hand man. Everywhere Ralph went, he went. I would call him an assistant pitching coach more than anything else. That's basically what he was."

Mike said he didn't receive favorable treatment from his father while with the Yankees. "He was the same in his relationships with players, whether they were teammates or from a coaching perspective, or even a parenting perspective. He was always consistent."

Mike said his father's personality and tall stature helped make him an effective coach. "For that age, he was kind of a big guy, six three or six four [he was six feet two, according to Baseball-reference.com], so he had a commanding presence," Mike said. "He didn't say much, but when he did say something, you took the hint. That's the way he was. If you were to talk to guys like Feller and Lemon over the years, that's the way he was behind the plate as well. Everybody said that he was a very strong leader."

Jim died at the age of sixty-three on June 17, 1984, after a heart attack. His legacy for defensive excellence at the catcher position remains well intact. His teammates marveled at his ability. "He was so good that if you crossed him up nobody knew it," Herb Score recalled after Hegan died. "He had the best hands I ever saw. If I crossed him up he might not tell me until three days later."[20] Mike Garcia once said of him, "If a foul ball went in the air and stayed in the ballpark it was an automatic out. He didn't stagger around under it. He went right to the spot of the ball."[21]

Mike Hegan said his father took pride in his game-calling and defensive ability. "He took pride in that aspect of the game, knowing it was a strength," Mike said. "He was a great athlete, and that transferred behind the plate in his ability to catch the baseball, block balls, and have an outstanding throwing arm. People still say he never dropped a pop fly behind home plate. Bob Lemon shook him off once. The batter then hit a home run, and Lemon never shook him off again."

Hegan's love of the game and his drive to succeed undoubtedly helped him achieve his success. "He loved baseball," Clare once said. "He couldn't believe people were paying him to play."[22]

"He was a perfectionist," Mike said, and recalled when his father took up golf and joined Avon Oaks Country Club, west of Cleveland. "My dad started playing and gave it up because he grew frustrated that he couldn't excel at it. If he couldn't do something, he would walk away from it instead of being frustrated by it."

Fortunately for Cleveland fans and Tribe pitchers, Jim Hegan loved baseball and perfected the art of catching. He continues to be and always will be remembered as one of the greatest and classiest players ever to wear a Cleveland Indians uniform.

Chapter 20. Timeline, May 17–May 31

Joseph Wancho

May 18—Cleveland—INDIANS BEAT BOSTON, 6–3, AS ROSEN HITS 2—Bob Chakales is credited with his second win in a relief appearance in three days. Al Rosen homers twice and tallies three RBIs. Ted Williams leaves the bases loaded twice for Boston.

May 19—Cleveland—LEMON TRIPS BOSOX FOR 6 IN ROW, 5–3—Al Rosen homers for the fifth consecutive game. Bob Lemon wins, going to 6-0. The Tribe opens a one-game lead on New York after their seventh consecutive win.

May 21—Cleveland—INDIANS' 3 HITS SHADE ORIOLES, 2–1; 8TH IN ROW—The Tribe attack musters three hits. Al Smith and Al Rosen each drive in a run. Early Wynn whiffs six for his fifth win of the season.

May 22—Cleveland—INDIANS TAKE NINTH IN ROW ON HIT IN 10TH—Al Rosen's solo shot wins it in the tenth inning. Rudy Regalado goes 3 for 5 and knocks in two runs. Mike Garcia evens his record at 4-4.

May 23—Cleveland—INDIANS WIN TWO FOR 11 STRAIGHT, 14–3, 2–1—Rudy Regalado and Dave Philley each collect four RBIs. Philley homers. Al Rosen tallies three RBIs. Bob Feller wins the opener for his first win of the year and notches his 250th career win. Al Rosen's eleventh homer ties the game in the bottom of the ninth inning. Art Houtteman backs his victory in the nightcap with a double in the bottom of the twelfth inning to score the winning run. The Cleveland win streak reaches eleven games. They sweep four games from Baltimore.

May 25—Chicago—CHISOX END TRIBE'S 11-GAME STRING, 4–2—The Indians' eleven-game win streak is snapped as Bob Lemon loses his first game of the season. Billy Pierce fans seven. Sherman Lollar goes 2 for 4 with an RBI. Minnie Minoso, Ferris Fain, and Cass Michaels each drive in a run. 43,039 cram into Comiskey Park.

May 26—Chicago—SOX WIN 5–4, BEAT INDIANS ON MICHAELS SINGLE IN 9TH—Cleveland drops their second game in a row at Chicago. Ferris Fain knocks in two runs, and Cass Michaels's single wins it in the bottom of the ninth inning. The White Sox swipe five bases and close to a half-game behind Indians.

May 28—Cleveland—INDIANS, WYNN WIN, 3 TO 0, ON ROSEN HOMER—Larry Doby goes 3 for 4, with a run scored. Al Rosen homers and drives in two. Early Wynn wins his sixth game. The game is played in an hour and forty-seven minutes.

May 29—Cleveland—LEMON WINS 7TH, BLANKS TIGERS, 12–0—Rudy Regalado and Larry Doby both homer, driving in two runs. Bobby Avila goes 3 for 4, drives in two, and scores two runs.

May 30—Cleveland—INDIANS WHIP TIGERS, 3 TO 1—Dave Philley drives in two runs, and Mike Garcia wins his fifth game. The lone Tiger run is unearned. The Indians sweep the three-game series from Detroit.

May 31—Cleveland—HEGAN'S HOMER GIVES INDIANS SPLIT—Minnie Minoso and Ferris Fain each homer and drive in two runs to key the White

Sox's 6–4 win in the DH opener. Bob Keegan wins his seventh game. In the second game, Jim Hegan and Dave Philley each homer, and Bobby Avila goes 3 for 5, scoring twice. The Tribe splits the Memorial Day doubleheader before 39,997. Cleveland remains ahead of Chicago by one game.

Chapter 21. **Dave Philley**

Cort Vitty

AGE	G	AB	R	H	2B	3B	HR	TB	RBI	BB	SO	BAV	OBP	SLG	SB	GDP	HBP
34	133	452	48	102	13	3	12	157	60	57	48	.226	.308	.347	2	16	0

Equally at home rounding the bases or rounding up cattle, Dave Philley played Major League baseball with the same no-nonsense efficiency he successfully utilized in operating his 557-acre ranch and managing his other business enterprises.

David Earl Philley was born on May 16, 1920, in Garret's Bluff, a suburb of Paris, Texas, in the northeastern part of the state. He was the second son of Maxie and Leila Philley. Maxie played semipro ball in East Texas, while older brother Noel and younger brother Frank each had brief professional careers. On many a summer day in the Red River valley, young Dave could be found playing sandlot baseball. He generally played on Boys Club Field, where hitting one out of the park counted for only a double. "You could hit the ball two blocks and it was still two bases," he once told his hometown newspaper.[1]

Dave threw right-handed and batted left until a fall from a tree cracked a bone in his left arm. The injury made it impossible for the eight-year-old to swing from his natural left side. To keep playing, he learned to hit right-handed and became adept enough to switch-hit after the arm healed. He was mostly a catcher, but was versatile enough to play several other positions, even taking the mound to pitch on occasion. Philley was a standout in football and track at Chicota High School, where he also excelled at boxing and became a local Golden Gloves champ.

Chicago White Sox scout Hub Northern signed Philley in 1940 as a catcher. Farmed out to play for the Marshall Tigers in the Class C East Texas League, Philley was converted to an outfielder to take advantage of his fine speed and long, graceful strides. After hitting .264 for Marshall, Philley played in 1941 for the Monroe White Sox of the Class C Cotton States League, where he posted a .346 batting average, made a brief stop with Shreveport in the Texas League, then was brought up for a seven-game look-see with the Chicago White Sox in September. Manager Jimmy Dykes cautiously inserted him into the lineup against the Washington Senators. The Washington correspondent for *The Sporting News* reported, "A rookie named Dave Philley played left field for five innings and escaped without serious injury."[2] As an outfield newcomer, Philley completely missed one ball hit in his direction. Later, a scorching line drive barely missed his head, prompting Dykes to "remove the youngster before being charged with manslaughter." (But not before Philley hit a double, walked twice, and scored four runs as the White Sox romped, 12–4.) Philley carried the tattered news clipping in his wallet for many years.

Philley entered the army after the 1941 season, and except for a few early 1942 games with St. Paul in the American Association, he served until the end of World War II. "I was proud to join the army when the war broke out and I never regretted my decision," he told a baseball researcher many years later.[3]

Discharged from the service in 1946, Philley hit .329 with Triple-A Milwaukee and .363 in seventeen games with the White Sox late in the season. The jury was still out on Philley. He became the White Sox's regular center fielder in 1947, hitting .258 in 143 games. His twenty-one stolen bases were the second best in the league. On occasion, he'd showcase his strong throwing arm and overall versatility by competently filling in at third base. An impressed

Dave Philley—Philley, shown here after hitting a home run against the Yankees, was much-traveled, playing for eight teams in his eighteen-year career. (The Cleveland Press Collection, Cleveland State University Library)

White Sox general manager Frank Lane commented," I don't know how he'll do, but I'll say this: He'll give it a battle. He's not afraid of anything."[4]

Philley had married Nell Marie Bratcher, a native of Leonard, Texas, on June 11, 1942, and the couple settled into Paris, Texas. Sons Bill and Paul later completed the Philley family. Over the years, Dave partnered with his brother Noel in several local business ventures, including the cattle farm, a Tucker auto dealership, an insurance agency, and a Humble Service Center.

The six-foot, 188-pound Philley posted a .287 mark in 1948, followed by a consistent .286 average in 1949. He realized he hit about 100 points higher from the left side and decided to start the 1950 season solely as a left-handed batter. The experiment ended when Yankees left-hander Tommy Byrne plunked Philley during a contest at Yankee Stadium. Dave resumed switch-hitting and finished the season with a .242 average and a career-best fourteen home runs.

Former White Sox skipper Jimmy Dykes was running the Philadelphia Athletics in 1951 when the A's

acquired Philley, along with outfielder Gus Zernial, in a seven-player deal also involving the Cleveland Indians. (Minnie Minoso moved from the Indians to the White Sox in the trade.) By now Philley had become an accomplished flyhawk, and his old field boss had no qualms about his improved defensive skills—or his defending ability. On numerous occasions, Philley saved his diminutive manager from surly pitchers and argumentative catchers. A bench-clearing brawl generally resulted in Dave's interceding by gruffly stating, "All right, you want to fight somebody—fight me. Let him alone. He's an old man." "Well, that took me down a peg or two," Dykes once commented. The hard-playing Philley confidently stated, "I never look for trouble."[5] But teammates and opposition alike agreed that he never ran from it either.

Philley posted identical .263 averages in 1951 and 1952 and enjoyed his most productive offensive season with the A's in 1953, when he hit .303 in 157 games. The strong-armed Philley led league outfielders in assists three times during his American League tenure. Dykes noted, "He has always been a sort of a ballplayer's ballplayer, faster than most and with a stronger arm than the majority." Philley also practiced hard to become an exceptional bunter and usually led the A's in sacrifices.

After his fine 1953 season, Philley held out for more salary than the Athletics offered in 1954. The A's said they couldn't meet Philley's salary demands, and traded him to Cleveland before the start of the season. Dave learned of the deal while negotiating a cattle sale in Oklahoma and couldn't have been happier with the news. "With Cleveland, I'll have a chance at the pennant. They're nice people and fine players. It's a real break for me," he told his hometown newspaper. Cleveland general manager Hank Greenberg said, "He's fast of foot, a good defensive man and an outstanding hustler. We've got another solid outfielder who can be very helpful to us. He's the kind of ballplayer we've been looking for."[6]

Philley liked to win and called himself "the most hated player in the American League." He added, "I play so hard to win that if a man gets in my way, I go into him, knock him down. If I was a manager and one of my men didn't go into the second baseman to break up the double play, I'd fire him. That's part of team play."[7]

The 1954 Indians may have been pennant bound, but Philley proceeded to have the worst season of his career, hitting only .226. "But Cleveland teammates and fans agree that the Paris outfielder was the man who built the pennant fire under the Redskins," a Paris sportswriter commented in an admiring if ethnically offensive tribute.[8] It was the only World Series appearance of Philley's career that October, as the New York Giants swept the Tribe in the Series. Philley started the first and third games, against Giant right-handers. In the first inning of the first game, at the Polo Grounds, he narrowly missed a two-run homer when his drive to deep right was hauled in at the fence by the Giants' Don Mueller. Later in the game his sharp drive struck a pitcher and resulted in an out.

Further down in the 1954 standings, the former St. Louis Browns, in their inaugural season as the Baltimore Orioles, finished a dismal seventh. The O's went from bad to worse as 1955 opened, going 20-53 under new manager Paul Richards. Desperate to add offensive punch, Richards was surprised to find the thirty-five-year-old Philley available and promptly plucked the big Texan off the waiver list. This acquisition immediately sparked the team. "He's too good a hitter to be fooled consistently," explained Richards. "That's the penalty a line drive hitter must pay. Too many of those drives go straight into the gloves of the opposition. I'm not worrying about him."[9] Philley went on to hit .299 for the Orioles, primarily playing left field and third base. The Orioles improved to a 37-44 record after his arrival, earning him Most Valuable Oriole honors, as voted by the media. Back home in Paris, appreciative townsfolk celebrated Dave Philley Day in October, when family, friends, and associates honored him during the halftime ceremonies of the Paris-Gainsville high school football game.

In May of 1956 the Orioles traded the well-traveled Philley to the White Sox in a six-player deal. With Chicago he added first base to his growing résumé of defensive positions. On June 23 the White Sox won their sixth game in a row, 2-0 over New York, and moved within three games of the league-leading Yankees. Both runs came in a sixth-inning spurt that began after the fiery Philley was struck on the shoulder by a pitch from right-hander Bob Grim and charged the mound. Philley was thrown out of the game, but the White Sox proceeded to get the only two runs of the game. The White Sox trounced the Yankees the next day and moved within two games of the top, but at the end of the season they were twelve games behind the pennant-winning New Yorkers.

Philley was next shuttled to the Detroit Tigers in 1957. His .400 average as a pinch hitter was the highest in the Major Leagues. Dave enjoyed playing at Briggs Stadium, where, he said, he was able to see the ball very well. Overall, he hit .295.

Philley made his initial National League appearance when he was sold to the Philadelphia Phillies before the 1958 season. Acquired specifically as a pinch-hitting specialist, the thirty-eight-year-old veteran was still agile enough for outfield or first base duties. He feasted on National League pitching to the tune of a .309 batting average in ninety-one games. The hard-charging veteran broke his nose on May 17 when he dove into the first base stands chasing a foul ball; the collision kept Philley out of the lineup for just six days. He had eighteen hits as a Phillies pinch hitter, with eight coming consecutively at the end of the season. "Hitting, I guess you'd call it a battle of wits up there," he told his hometown paper. "You learn more about pitchers. You have to keep learning."[10]

Philley extended his streak to nine in a row, then a National League record, when he connected in his first appearance of 1959. He elaborated on his approach to pinch hitting in a 1959 interview with Ed Wilks of the Associated Press. "I walk to the plate with all the confidence in the world. I figure I've got only one shot at it. I relax as much as possible, yet manage to bear down. Of course it helps to know the opposing pitchers. I study them as much as I can."

After a productive .291 mark in 1959, Philley was sold to the San Francisco Giants in May of 1960. After hitting only .164 in thirty-nine games, he was reunited with the Orioles and old manager Paul Richards on September 1. Although obtained specifically for pinch hitting, the veteran was immediately pressed into the starting lineup after left fielder Gene Woodling suffered an injury. Philley hit .265 in fourteen games for Baltimore.

In 1961 the Baby Birds of Baltimore sprouted wings and started to fly, winning ninety-five games and finishing a very respectable third. A solid group of youngsters was supported by forty-one-year-old Dave Philley. Coming off the bench, he laced twenty-four safeties to establish an American League record. Overall, he posted a .250 average in ninety-nine games. Despite his pinch-hitting prowess, he was released by the Orioles at the end of the season. By then old boss Paul Richards had been hired away from the Orioles to develop the expansion Houston Colt .45s. Richards signed Philley as a free agent in March 1962 and on the same day traded the veteran to the Boston Red Sox, where Philley wrapped up his big league career. He went on to manage in the Houston organization and also served as an instructor and scout in the Red Sox system.

Overall, Philley's 1,700 hits in 6,296 at bats produced a lifetime batting average of .270, with eighty-four home runs, in a career spanning World War II to the Kennedy administration. Philley was a competitor on the field and strived to improve every aspect of his game. A believer in top physical conditioning, he was a proponent of fingertip push-ups, as taught to him by Ted Williams. He always got plenty of sleep and strictly adhered to training rules. The strongest drink he'd consume was soda pop and his only admitted vice was smoking an occasional cigar. In retirement, Philley continued to run his expansive cattle ranch east of Paris, Texas. He also became an active community leader and held local elected posts. He enjoyed fishing and quail hunting with fellow Major Leaguer and Paris native Eddie Robinson. Often in demand as an after-dinner speaker, he would happily appear before youth and church groups.

Philley was a devout Baptist. An article in his hometown paper commented, "Dave is a walking testimonial to the fact that you don't have to be a sissy to be a Christian. He speaks frankly about his religious views, and has no patience with major league idols who set bad examples for their fans with partying and carousing."[11]

"I figured I'd play five or six years," said Philley. "I had one thing on my mind and that was to play big-league ball. Nothing was going to interfere with that."[12]

Philley was at his ranch on March 15, 2012, when he died from an apparent heart attack; he was ninety-one years old.

Chapter 22. **Bob Lemon**

Jon Barnes

AGE	W	L	PCT	ERA	G	GS	GF	CG	SHO	SV	IP	H	BB	SO	HBP	WP
33	23	7	.767	2.72	36	33	1	21	2	0	258.1	228	92	110	4	6

As Bob Lemon watched Willie Mays make his historic catch in Game One of the 1954 World Series against the Cleveland Indians, he may have recalled another spectacular catch by a young center fielder eight and a half years earlier. That was the day, April 16, 1946, when rookie outfielder Bob Lemon saved Bob Feller's Opening Day victory over the Chicago White Sox.

With one out and the tying run on second in the bottom of the ninth, Feller was hanging onto a 1–0 lead when Chicago pinch hitter Jake Jones sent a drive to right-center field. Lemon, playing the right-handed batter to hit to straightaway center, sprinted to his left as the ball tailed away from him. At the last second he dove and fully stretched out his left arm to make the catch. He sprang to his feet, threw to second, and doubled off base runner Bob Kennedy, who had already rounded third, for the final out of the game. It was Lemon's first Major League game as an outfielder, and he sported bruises on his elbow, chin, and chest to show for his effort. Feller called it "the greatest outfield play I have ever seen."[1]

Though he became one of the top pitchers of his era, Lemon said he would have preferred a career as an everyday player rather than as a starting pitcher with nothing to do for three out of four days. Much was made of his refusal to wear a toeplate, a standard part of a moundsman's equipment, until well after he had become a star pitcher. But Lemon said the fact that he could make more money as a pitcher finally convinced him he should give up any thought of returning to the outfield. Still, throughout his career, he continued to work out during infield practice at third base, his position when he first came to the Major Leagues.

Bob Lemon—A converted pitcher, Lemon won twenty or more games seven times in his career. He won two games for the Indians in the 1948 World Series.

Lemon was hardheaded, but also a hard worker. Soft-spoken, but with a cutting wit. A devoted family man who spent long hours in bars. A power hitter in the Minor Leagues who couldn't hit the change-up in the Majors. A loyal friend of George Steinbrenner, but twice a victim of the dictatorial Yankee owner's managerial ax.

Robert Granville Lemon was born in San Bernardino, California, on September 22, 1920. His father, Earl, worked for an ice company in Long Beach and operated a chicken farm. A former Minor League shortstop, Earl made sure that his son had the best baseball equipment available. His mother, Ruth, also was an avid baseball fan. In his Hall of Fame induction speech, Lemon mentioned that he had beaned his mother one day in the driveway while showing off his curveball.

Baseball was central to Bob's life growing up in Southern California. He pitched and played the infield for Woodrow Wilson High School in Long Beach, and attracted the attention of scouts for the Cleveland Indians. After graduating, the seventeen-year-old Lemon signed with the Indians for $100 a month.

Although Lemon later said he was signed as a pitcher, he took the mound for only one inning in 1938 for his first team, Oswego in the Class C Canadian-American League, because the team was overloaded with pitchers. He hit .312 with seven home runs and a .450 slugging percentage in seventy-five games for the club, primarily as an outfielder. He also appeared in several games for Springfield (Ohio) of the Class C Middle Atlantic League.

Setting pitching aside, Lemon played shortstop and the outfield for Springfield and for New Orleans of the Southern Association the following year, combining for a .300 average in 132 games. Switching to third base in 1940, he injured his knee and struggled at the plate with Wilkes-Barre in the Class A Eastern League, but he bounced back to hit .301 for the same club the following year.

Lemon got a September call-up from the Indians in 1941 and made his first Major League appearance as a late-inning replacement for Ken Keltner at third base in a 13–7 victory over the Philadelphia Athletics on the 9th. He got his first hit three days later against Washington when he singled as a pinch hitter against a future teammate and member of the Indians' Big Three, the Washington Senators' Early Wynn.

After failing to make the big league club in spring training of 1942, Lemon was sent to the Indians' top farm team, Baltimore of the International League, where he found his power stroke. Despite having hit only sixteen home runs in his first four Minor League seasons, he was billed as a left-handed power hitter, and with the Orioles he didn't disappoint. Lemon stroked twenty-one homers and drove in eighty runs during his year with the Orioles, though his batting average dropped to .268. He also impressed with his fielding at third base and started a triple play on a grounder to third on Opening Day.

While his future looked bright, the United States was now at war, and other duties called. Lemon enlisted in the navy after the season and served for three years. While in the service, he married Jane H. McGee on January 14, 1944, and they remained together for fifty-six years. They had three sons.

Lemon's reputation as a prospect continued to spread during the war years. He starred for teams at naval bases in California and Hawaii. Other big league players and coaches in the service got to watch Lemon hit, field, and pitch. Though he received glowing reviews for his pitching skills, his coach in Hawaii, Billy Herman, kept him in the infield because of an abundance of pitchers. As a result, in 1945 with the Fourteenth Naval District Circuit in Hawaii, Lemon played third most of the time, tied for second in the league with fourteen home runs, and was fifth in MVP balloting.

With the war over, spring training of 1946 gave the six-foot, 170-pound twenty-five-year-old his first real opportunity to stick with the Major League club. Adding to his chances was the fact that incumbent third baseman Keltner, also returning from military service, was holding out and management was entertaining trade offers for him. Manager Lou Boudreau cited the young Lemon as a prime candidate if a replacement was needed at third because of his batting punch, speed, and arm.

Keltner eventually agreed to a contract and remained with the team, leaving no room at third for Lemon. In addition, it was discovered that Lemon's fielding at the hot corner was of less than Major

League quality. So Boudreau shifted him to center field to get him into the lineup. Lemon's showing as one of the Tribe's top hitters in the exhibition season earned him a spot in the starting lineup as the Opening Day center fielder, setting the stage for his game-saving catch to preserve Feller's shutout.

But Lemon struggled against Major League pitching and soon lost his job in the outfield. "I could hit anything else they threw at me, but not the change-up, and the word got around pretty quick," he said in later years. "Pretty soon that's all I saw. Fastball out of the strike zone. Curveball out of the strike zone. Then the damned changeup."[2]

Based on reports about Lemon's performance while pitching for navy teams, Boudreau decided to give him serious consideration as a pitcher. In his first start, on June 3, 1946, he lasted only three and two-thirds innings in a 3–2 loss to the Philadelphia A's. Lemon showed promise the rest of the season, posting a 4-5 record and a 2.49 earned run average in thirty-two appearances, including five starts, but he suffered from control problems, walking sixty-eight and striking out only thirty-nine in ninety-four innings. His .180 batting average virtually ensured that if Lemon had a future in the Majors, it would be as a pitcher. After the season, he joined Feller's barnstorming team as a utilityman on a thirty-game exhibition tour against Satchel Paige's Negro All-Stars.

Still battling control problems, Lemon had a poor spring training in 1947. He was placed on waivers early in the season, but when he was claimed by Washington, the Indians decided to hold on to him and have coach Bill McKechnie help him work on his control. Although Lemon later gave credit to Mel Harder and Al Lopez, two veteran teammates in 1947, for helping him through this difficult period, McKechnie got all the plaudits when Lemon emerged as one of Cleveland's best pitchers in the second half of the season. His mound work helped the team finish strong and move into fourth place. In thirty-seven games, including fifteen starts, he

was 11-5 with a 3.44 ERA. He also batted .321 with a .607 slugging percentage.

The pennant-winning season of 1948 saw Lemon develop into a star. In spring training he introduced a "sidearm crossfire fastball" to go with his devastating curve and slider, and the hitters were mystified. Lemon and Feller led the Indians to a fast start, and both were named to the All-Star team. On June 30 Lemon tossed a 2–0 no-hitter against the Detroit Tigers, the only no-hitter of his career. Future teammate Art Houtteman was the losing pitcher.

Lemon suffered a mild concussion on July 15 when a throw by Athletics second baseman Pete Suder hit him on the head as he scored on Dale Mitchell's double in the fifth inning. He shook it off and went back out to pitch in the sixth, but he yielded two hits and a walk, and Boudreau removed him. He then came back to pitch in relief three days later.

By September, Lemon's energy was spent and he contributed only two wins during the last month of the season. He regained his steam for the World Series, leading his team with two victories and a 1.65 ERA in sixteen and one-third innings as Cleveland bested the Boston Braves in six games.

Lemon was named the American League's Outstanding Pitcher for 1948 by *The Sporting News* on the merits of his 20-14 record and 2.82 ERA. In his thirty-seven starts, he tossed a league-leading ten shutouts.

The following year, with Boudreau's endorsement, Lemon decided to take it easy in spring training to avoid a repeat of his September slumber of the previous year. He responded with another excellent season, finishing at 22-10 with a 2.99 ERA. He also hit a career-high seven home runs. But the Indians fell to third place. Lemon now was undeniably the ace of the staff, as Feller had an off year. Lemon was only two years younger than Feller, but Rapid Robert seemed to be aging rapidly, while the younger Bob still had his best days ahead of him.

Early in 1950 Lemon reportedly told general manager Hank Greenberg that he wouldn't take less than $50,000 for the coming season, but he came to terms in March for a salary estimated at about $35,000. The season turned out to be his busiest yet as he led the league with thirty-seven starts, tied for the league lead with twenty-two complete games, relieved in seven games, and went 6 for 26 as a pinch hitter. He played in seventy-two games, and fatigue again plagued him in September. He upped his victory total to a league-leading twenty-three with eleven losses and led the league in strikeouts with 170, but his ERA climbed to 3.84. He was again named the league's Most Outstanding Pitcher by *The Sporting News.* Meanwhile, the Indians dropped another notch in the standings, to fourth place.

(Late that season the Indians had two Bob Lemons. They called up James Robert Lemon, a power-hitting outfielder in the Minors who had been known as Bob. When he joined the Indians, he asked to be called Jim. He played only briefly for Cleveland but had a twelve-year career, mostly with the Washington Senators and Minnesota Twins, and hit 164 home runs.)

Al Lopez took the reins as manager of the Indians in 1951, and the team rose to second place, largely on the pitching of three twenty-game winners. Lemon wasn't one of them. Feller returned to his old form with a 22-8 record, while Mike Garcia and Wynn each won twenty. Lemon struggled to 17-14 and 3.52 as a back injury in May bothered him for the rest of the season. Earlier in the year he received what he had asked for in 1950, signing for more than $50,000, which made him the highest-paid pitcher in baseball. At year's end, it was rumored that he was being offered as trade bait for Ted Williams.

Another second-place finish followed in 1952, and Lemon rebounded with a record of 22-11 and a 2.50 ERA. He led the league with twenty-eight complete games and 310 innings pitched, and tied Garcia for the league lead with thirty-six starts. Wynn added twenty-three victories while Garcia won twenty-two, but Feller dropped to 9-13.

Lemon was Cleveland's only twenty-game winner in 1953, but Garcia and Wynn also posted solid years and the club's hitting improved as the Indians finished second once again. Now thirty-two, workhorse Bob showed no signs of slowing down, again leading the league in innings pitched on his way to a 21-15, 3.36 season. On Opening Day he pitched a one-hitter and hit a home run to beat the White Sox, 6–0. By this point, he had developed a knuckleball that moved so unpredictably that the catchers couldn't handle it, so he was afraid to use it in a game. Lopez also advised him not to use the knuckleball, saying he didn't need it.

Before the 1954 season, a national survey of writers voted Lemon both the most conceited and the wittiest player on the Indians. During the off-season, he helped out at his father's gas station and, later, at the ranch they bought together. He also had found time to appear in 1952 in the movie *The Winning Team,* which starred Ronald Reagan as Grover Cleveland Alexander. Lemon played the role of pitcher Jesse Haines and also served as Reagan's stand-in.

Now possessing an outstanding change-up to go with his sinking fastball, amazing curve, and baffling slider, Lemon was generally considered the number one man in Cleveland's Big Three of Lemon, Wynn, and Garcia. "I suppose that the slider is the pitch I've relied on most during these last few years. I didn't have to work to develop it, as I did to develop a good curve," Lemon said.[3] "I don't try to throw a sinker. My fastball sinks naturally. I've always assumed my short fingers do it."[4]

In his prime, Lemon was remarkable in the consistency of the numbers he put up season after season—twenty-one to twenty-three wins, an ERA around 3.00 or below, and among the league leaders in starts, complete games, and innings pitched. Such was the case in 1954, as he went 23-7 with a 2.72 ERA and led the league in complete games with twenty-one. It was his sixth twenty-win season, and for the third time he was named the American League's Most Outstanding Pitcher by *The Sporting News.*

"No statistic, though, could capture the man's competitive fire, his bulldog nature that made him the Indians' most-feared pitcher—and hard-luck first-game loser—in the World's Series," sportswriter Bob Broeg wrote.[5]

In June, Lemon tore a rib muscle and was out for several weeks. When he came back, he won seven straight to raise his record to 16-5. He beat the Yankees four times during the season.

Lemon was the logical choice to start Game One of the World Series against the New York Giants, and he pitched a strong game through nine innings. He said the home run pitch he threw to the Giants' Dusty Rhodes in the tenth inning was a good one—a curveball low and slightly outside—but the lefty pinch hitter was able to pull it just over the short right-field wall at the Polo Grounds. In an unusual public display of emotion, Lemon sailed his glove high in the air after the ball cleared the wall. A Cleveland writer quipped that the glove traveled farther than Rhodes's homer. Coming back on two days' rest for Game Four, Lemon struggled and was charged with five earned runs in four innings, giving him a 6.75 ERA for the Series, which the Giants swept.

Cleveland fell three games short of the Yankees in 1955 as none of the Big Three won twenty, though each had a solid season. Hampered by two serious leg injuries, Lemon still recorded eighteen victories, which tied him with Whitey Ford and Frank Sullivan for the most in the league. (It was the first time the American League had no twenty-game winners.) Still making around $50,000, Lemon remained the highest-paid pitcher in the Majors, but he was only the second-highest-paid Indian behind Ralph Kiner. At the end of the season, GM Greenberg proclaimed a new Big Three: Herb Score, Ray Narleski, and Don Mossi.

Lemon posted his seventh and final twenty-win season in 1956, going 20-14 with a 3.03 ERA and tying Billy Pierce for the league lead in complete games with twenty-one. Although Wynn and Score also won twenty and the Tribe pitching led the league in

ERA, the team was fifth in the league in runs scored and dropped further behind the Yankees, finishing in second place, nine games back. With two months left in the season, Lemon pulled a muscle in his right thigh while reaching for a bad throw as he covered first, and the injury nagged him the rest of the way. Now almost thirty-six years old, he commented that while he'd pulled muscles before, "This is a new spot. It must be old age."[6] He recorded his 200th victory on September 11, a 3–1 win over the Orioles, and his own two-run homer, the thirty-sixth of his career, accounted for the margin of victory.

As the Indians tumbled to sixth place in 1957, Lemon had his first losing season since 1946. He finished at 6-11 with a 4.60 ERA. He had one of his best games on May 7, when he was brought in to relieve after Herb Score was felled by Gil McDougald's line drive. Lemon pitched eight and one-third innings and gave up just six hits to claim the 2–1 victory. Lemon developed bone chips in his right elbow late in the season, but he continued to pitch. "We were chin-high in injuries. I didn't want to be a liability," he said.[7] The elbow was operated on in November, and twenty pieces of bone and tissue were removed.

Lemon struggled to recondition his arm in 1958, to no avail. He made what turned out to be his last Major League start on April 22, when he gave up five singles before leaving the game in the second inning, and he was placed on the disabled list the next day. The plan was for him to work back into shape with the San Diego farm club, but Commissioner Ford Frick, in a new strict policy to crack down on abusive practices by teams, ruled that he couldn't work out with either the Major or the Minor League club while on the disabled list. "I'll have to pitch to my son, Jeff, in our backyard, I guess," Lemon said.[8] He returned for a few more games in relief, including a game in June when he pitched five innings and said he felt pain only when he swung and missed. He finished the season in San Diego, where he was 2-5 with a 4.34 ERA in twelve games.

In 1959 the thirty-eight-year-old Lemon gave up all hopes of a comeback early in spring training and became a Minor League pitching coach for the Indians. In 1965 and 1966, he managed Seattle of the Pacific Coast League and was named Minor League Manager of the Year when he led the California Angels' farm team to the pennant in 1966. He also coached for the Phillies (1961) and Angels (1967–68), and managed Vancouver of the PCL in 1969.

Lemon later managed in the Majors for nine seasons. His managerial career followed a similar pattern everywhere he went—take on an underachieving team, lead it to success, and then get fired the next year. In 1970 he was named manager of the floundering Kansas City Royals in June 9 after serving as the team's pitching coach. The Royals rebounded and climbed to second place in the AL West in 1971, earning Lemon the Manager of the Year award. But after a disappointing fourth-place finish in 1972, he was ousted by owner Ewing Kauffman after being quoted as saying he was looking forward to retirement so he could leave baseball for some remote island. The comment most likely was tongue-in-cheek, and Lemon claimed he was misquoted. Nevertheless, Kauffman said he wanted a younger manager, and he hired Jack McKeon.

Lemon managed Sacramento of the PCL in 1974 and Richmond of the International League in 1975 before being named pitching coach for the New York Yankees in 1976. He was voted into the Baseball Hall of Fame that year. In his induction speech he summed up his outlook on baseball and life: "If you lose, you can't help it. You've done a good job. You've tried the best you could. And I didn't take it home. I would leave it at a bar on the way home someplace."[9]

Lemon got a second chance at managing in the Majors when Bill Veeck hired him in 1977 to guide the Chicago White Sox, a last-place club the prior year. Again, Lemon was named Manager of the Year when he lifted the team to a surprising ninety wins and a third-place finish. But the club strug-gled the following year, and Veeck fired him midway through the season. That's when Lemon ran off to join the circus. In New York, the Martin-Jackson-Steinbrenner Circus was generating daily headlines. After Billy Martin made his famous remark about Reggie Jackson and George Steinbrenner, saying, "One's a born liar, the other's convicted," Steinbrenner forced Martin into a tearful resignation. On July 25, less than a month after he was fired by Veeck, Lemon was hired by Steinbrenner as the Yankees' manager. In fourth place at the time Lemon took over, the Yankees surged to 48-20 the rest of the way, won a memorable one-game playoff over Boston, and defeated the Los Angeles Dodgers in six games in the World Series.

Lemon's low-key style seemed to be just what the team needed. Outfielder Jay Johnstone said, "Lem's sort of like an Andy Griffith character. You know, 'Take it easy, don't panic, we'll think of something.'"[10] Another Yankee player, unnamed, said, "Lem just puts you out there and lets you play. He never overmanages. If you can't play for him, you can't play for anybody."[11] But the circus continued. Only five days after Lemon was hired in 1978, an announcement was made that he would become general manager after the 1979 season and Martin would return as manager in 1980. Martin didn't have to wait that long.

Tragedy struck the Lemon family shortly after the 1978 World Series when Bob and Jane's young-est son, Jerry, was killed in an automobile accident. According to Steinbrenner, Lemon lost his motivation after that.

With the team suffering from injuries and off to a sluggish 34-31 start in 1979, Steinbrenner decided to pull the plug early on Lemon and replaced him with Martin. The Yankees fared slightly better under Martin, but could manage only a fourth-place finish. Lemon continued to work as a scout for the Yankees until Steinbrenner called for him once more late in the 1981 season. This time, manager Gene Michael drew Steinbrenner's ire when he would not apologize for saying Steinbrenner was always threatening to fire him. Commenting on his decision to hire Lemon, Steinbrenner said, "He has the one quality that means so much to me, loyalty. If you needed one word to describe Bob Lemon, it would be 'decent.'"[12]

When he was rehired as manager, Lemon said, "When (Steinbrenner) replaced me before, it may have been more for my own good. With the problems I had, some of the incentive was lost. After he did it, he explained to me how he thought I felt. It took me a while to realize that he was right. . . . When I went home, I really missed (managing). It was just a case of getting myself back together."[13]

Although the team finished only 11-14 under Lemon, the Yankees earned a playoff berth in the unique strike-shortened 1981 season because of their first-place showing in the first half. They made it all the way to the World Series, but they lost in six games to the Dodgers.

Lemon came under fire for some questionable moves in the Series, including lifting Tommy John for a pinch hitter with the score tied 1–1 in the fourth inning of the final game, but the club announced that he would remain manager in 1982, with Michael returning the following year. Like Martin, Michael didn't have to wait that long. After only fourteen games and a 6-8 record in 1982, Lemon was sent back to California to return to scouting duties, and Michael was named manager once again.

Lemon returned to his home in the Bixby Knolls section of Long Beach, where he had lived with his wife since 1949. He reportedly remained on the Yankees' payroll under a lifetime contract awarded by Steinbrenner after the 1978 World Series.

The Indians retired Lemon's No. 21 in 1998. He had compiled a 207-128 record with a 3.23 ERA in thirteen seasons. He was named to the American League All-Star Team each year from 1948 through 1954 and was the first manager to win a world championship after beginning the season as the manager of a different team. A left-handed batter, he was one of the best-hitting pitchers ever in the Majors, and his thirty-seven home runs were one short of the record, held by Wes Ferrell.

Bob Lemon died at a nursing home on January 11, 2000, at the age of seventy-nine, after several years of failing health. He was survived by his wife, Jane, and two sons, Jeff and James.

Though he was always regarded as unflappable, Lemon told a reporter late in life that he had suffered inside. "I had ulcers like everybody else," he said.

"I've had a hell of a life," Lemon said. "I've never looked back and regretted anything. I've had everything in baseball a man could ask for. I've been so fortunate. Outside of my boy getting killed. That really puts it into perspective. So you don't win the pennant. You don't win the World Series. Who gives a damn? Twenty years from now, who'll give a damn? You do the best you can. That's it."[14]

Chapter 23. **Rudy Regalado**

Steve Johnson

AGE	G	AB	R	H	2B	3B	HR	TB	RBI	BB	SO	BAV	OBP	SLG	SB	GDP	HPB
24	65	180	21	45	5	0	2	56	24	19	16	.250	.333	.311	0	5	4

Rudy Regalado is one of the few players—perhaps the only player—to have participated in the College World Series, the Caribbean World Series, the Junior World Series, and the Major League World Series. He was successful on the diamond on every level from high school to the Major Leagues. In his career, he was in the company of some of the greatest players in baseball history. His is a unique story of one man whose dreams came true.

Rudy's story starts in Mexico. His grandfather, Stephen, and grandmother, Maria, emigrated from there to the United States. They settled in El Paso, Texas, where Rudy's father, Manuel, was born in 1897. The family eventually moved to Los Angeles, where Stephen found work with the Los Angeles trolley system.

Manuel married Maria Gutierrez from Guadalajara, Mexico, and they had five children, a daughter and four sons. Maria was an admirer of a romantic silent movie star of the 1920s, so when son number four was born on May 21, 1930, she named him Rudolph Valentino Regalado.

Perhaps it was the prejudice of the time or just a misinterpretation of his name, but sportswriters would refer to him as Mexican-Italian or just Italian. "No," he said, "we're all Mexican!"[1]

Manuel and Maria worked in a terra-cotta factory, Manuel as a kilnsman and Maria as a laborer. Later Maria worked as a housekeeper. The 1930s and '40s were tough on the family economically, and Manuel lost his job several times. The family had to move three times before Rudy was in the sixth grade. Eventually, times got better and Manuel found a job that he kept for twenty-five years.

Manuel had a love of baseball and played on and

Rudy Regalado—A rookie in 1954, Regalado played well for the injured Al Rosen. He knocked in twenty-four runs in limited playing time.

managed teams in the Los Angeles area. His enthusiasm for the sport spread to all his children. He would make baseballs out of socks wound with tape and string and pitch to Rudy. "They would twist and turn, and I guess I learned how to hit the curveball," he said. Rudy's sister, Nellie, played softball at Glendale High School. His oldest brother, Gregory, played in 1946 for Visalia in the California League.

Rudy was a standout shortstop at Glendale High School. Coached by Bud Teachout, a former pitcher for the Chicago Cubs, he hit .390 in his sophomore year, .425 in his junior year, and a whopping .561 his senior year.

Players from several area high schools would meet on Saturdays in Griffith Park for pickup games. The boys would coach and umpire their own games. The level of play was high enough to attract the attention of Babe Herman and Casey Stengel, among others.

In 1947, his senior year, Regalado was one of two high school players selected from the Los Angeles area to be a part of the USA All-Stars, teams made up of players from across the country that played a game in New York's Polo Grounds. Honus Wagner and Oscar Vitt were the coaches for Rudy's team. Also on the All-Stars were future Major Leaguers Billy Harrell, Gino Cimoli, Harry Agganis, Bill "Moose" Skowron, and Don Ferrarese. Babe Ruth was there, too. "He sat in the first row. He was kind of feeble, but he threw out the first ball from the stands," Regalado said in a telephone conversation in 2011.

By vote of the high school coaches, Regalado was named to the California Interscholastic Federation's All-CIF Baseball Team three years in a row. Among the other players selected were future Major League stars Del Crandall and Dick Williams.

Rod Dedeaux, the longtime baseball coach at the University of Southern California, encouraged Regalado to stay in school and get his education before going into a professional baseball career. Rudy graduated from high school in 1947. He enrolled at Glendale Junior College, where he played on the baseball team and batted .375. The next year Dedeaux got him a baseball scholarship at USC. "We didn't have much money," Regalado said. "My dad couldn't afford to send me to a university. Rod was like my second dad. He really helped me out. He got me a job on campus. . . . I was grateful for that." Regalado was paid about $150 a month. Out of that he paid $75 for tuition and $72 to the Kappa Sigma fraternity house for room and board. "So I had three bucks to live it up with!" he recalled.

Dedeaux installed Regalado at first base. He immediately made an impact, batting .411 his first (sophomore) year and winning the California Intercollegiate Baseball Association batting championship. He followed that with another outstanding year as a junior, batting .375.

In 1949 USC won its conference championship, beat Colorado State to win the West Coast championship, and went to the College World Series in Wichita, Kansas. The Trojans lost to Wake Forest, beat St. John's of New York, then lost again to Wake Forest and were eliminated from the tournament.

Among Regalado's teammates at USC were four players who spent some time in the Major Leagues. Wally Hood Jr. pitched two games for the New York Yankees, Hank Workman played two games at first base for the Yankees, Gail Henley was in the outfield for fourteen games with Pittsburgh, and Jim Brideweser spent seven seasons as an infielder, mostly with the Yankees. Another teammate, Bill Sharman, played in the Minor Leagues but became famous with the Boston Celtics.

The Korean War began in June 1950. In September, Regalado's National Guard unit, the Fortieth Infantry Division, was activated and he was sent to Japan. While in Japan, he was the player-manager on the Fortieth Division GI championship baseball team, which played Japanese teams from Hokkaido, Sendai, Osaka, and Yokohama. From Japan the division was sent to Korea, where it was close to the front lines for several months. Regalado's unit, the 223rd Regiment, was involved in the Inchon landing in January 1952. One of his jobs was keeping the records of soldiers who had been killed.[2] "That was a tough job because one of the names that came across my desk was a guy I had played against in high school," he recalled. He was promoted to corporal before returning to the United States in May 1952.

After his discharge, Regalado still had a year of college eligibility left and wanted to go back to USC. Along with several other USC players, he spent the summer with the Fergus Falls Red Sox of the semi-pro West Central League. One night Cy Slapnicka, the legendary scout for the Indians, who had signed Bob Feller, visited Rudy and offered him a $10,000 bonus to sign with the Indians. Regalado called Rod Dedeaux and his father for advice. Told that the Indians were offering a $10,000 bonus, Dedeaux said, "Forget your last year at USC; you can always make it up. Take the money," Regalado recalled.

Regalado began his professional career in 1953 with the Reading Indians of the Class A Eastern League. The powerhouse team, which had nine future Major Leaguers, including Rocky Colavito and Herb Score, won the league championship. Regalado was not around for the finish. After batting .318 in eighty-nine games, he was promoted to the Triple-A Indianapolis Indians, where he played in thirty-six games and batted .325.

The next year, Regalado wrote his way onto the Cleveland roster. The Indians held spring training in Tucson, Arizona. Rudy had been assigned to Indianapolis, which was to train in Daytona Beach, Florida. He sent a letter to Indians general manager Hank Greenberg asking if he could work out in Tucson on his way to Florida. Greenberg agreed and Regalado joined the Indians, where he soon established himself as a reliable infielder and hitter. "He's going to stay with us a while. I like him a lot," said manager Al Lopez.[3] In the Indians' first intrasquad game, Regalado hit a home run and a single. Increasingly impressed, Lopez tried Regalado at third base, although he was given little chance there, as All-Star Al Rosen seemed firmly entrenched. Regalado also worked at second base, as Bobby Avila was a brief holdout and, after he reported, came down with stomach troubles. There was also talk of moving Regalado to first base, although it was pointed out that there were already three players vying for that position—Luke Easter, Bill Glynn, and Rocky Nelson. The discussion continued throughout spring training. Though several prospects were sent to the Minor League camp at Daytona Beach, Regalado remained in Tucson.

Because he was supposed to have been in Daytona Beach, Regalado's bats had been sent there. He had to borrow bats from other players. Asked whom he borrowed from, he said, "I don't remember. They were good bats because they worked." On March 8, against the Chicago Cubs, he hit two home runs, a double, and a single. The next day he hit two more home runs, another double, and another single against the Cubs, and his batting average for the exhibition season stood at .591 (13 for 22) with eleven runs batted in. (But at second base he was having trouble with the pivot on double plays.)

Press speculation heightened. There was talk of moving Rosen to first base and installing Regalado at third. On March 24 Regalado hit another home run against the Cubs, and on the 25th he hit two more. *Plain Dealer* sportswriter Gordon Cobbledick wondered if Regalado could be a spark for the Indians.[4]

On March 28 Regalado hit another pair of home runs and two singles against the New York Giants. He was hitting .481 with nine home runs and nineteen RBIs. In the *Cleveland Press*, Frank Gibbons referred to him as "Rudy the Red Hot Rapper."[5] The speculation that Rosen would be moved to first base and Regalado would take over at third grew serious.

Then, inexplicably, Regalado was virtually benched. He got little playing time for the rest of spring training. Cobbledick criticized the team for not playing him.[6] He urged the Rosen switch, but noted that Rod Dedeaux said Regalado's natural position was at first base.

On April 6 the Tribe purchased Regalado's contract from Indianapolis. As spring training ended, the *Plain Dealer* called Regalado the best hitter and the most surprising player of spring training.[7] The *Press* featured a cartoon that depicted Al Lopez being asked by everyone from the bellboy to the cab driver where he intended to play Rudy.[8]

The season began on April 13 with the Indians

STEVE JOHNSON

in Chicago to face the White Sox. Regalado made his first Major League appearance when he was inserted as a pinch runner for Hank Majeski in the eighth inning. His first appearance at home and his first appearance at the plate came on April 17, when he replaced Avila at second base late in the game. He went hitless in one at bat and had two assists at second base.

On April 25 it was announced that the much-discussed Rosen-Regalado switch would take place. That afternoon Al Rosen moved to first base and Regalado was at third base in his first Major League start. In a 10–9 extra-inning victory over Detroit, Regalado hit a double and two singles and scored twice. He walked in the tenth inning and came home on Dave Philley's home run. In the field he had two put-outs and one assist.

On the 29th, in the sixth inning of a game with the Boston Red Sox at Fenway Park, Regalado pulled a muscle in his right leg as he ran to first base on a sacrifice bunt. It was May 6 before he could work out again at third base. He got back into the lineup for a game against the Yankees on May 12 when he pinch-hit and struck out.

On the 13th Regalado hit his first Major League home run, off the Washington Senators' Mickey McDermott. He was part of a rally in the ninth that sent the game into extra innings. The Indians prevailed in the eleventh, 8–7.

On May 20 there was a report that Regalado's leg "remains tender."[9] Nine days later he hit his second home run, against Detroit's Ralph Branca. "He threw me a curve that didn't curve very much, and I hit it over the left field fence. So, Bobby Thomson and I have something in common," Regalado said. It turned out to be his last home run in the Major Leagues.

Regalado continued to hit for a while but then slumped and was benched. Thereafter he appeared mostly as a pinch hitter. "They started throwing the curveball to me," he said in 2011. "I'd never seen such great curveballs as they had in the big leagues."

The Indians were on a tear, winning games at a torrid pace. The Yankees kept pace for a while, but in a critical doubleheader in Cleveland late in the season, the Indians won both games and the Yankees were through. The pennant-winning Indians finished with 111 wins. Regalado got into all four games of the World Series as the Indians were swept by the Giants. To an interviewer in 2011, he admitted to "a little bit of terror and nervousness" at coming into a Series game.

In Game One, Regalado ran for Vic Wertz in the tenth inning. He got the first of his three World Series at bats in Game Two, hitting into a force play in the ninth inning. Regalado pinch-hit for Art Houtteman in Game Three and grounded out to third. In the seventh inning of Game Four, with Cleveland trailing 7–3, Regalado pinch-hit for Don Mossi and singled in a run off Don Liddle. "It was a slider and I hit it hard, right through the box." Regalado's RBI was the Indians' last Tribe postseason RBI for forty-one years.

After the series, Regalado took his $6,712.50 World Series share back to California, where he reentered USC. (He gradually acquired his credits, finishing his degree in physical education in 1956.) That winter he played for the Rosabell Plumbers, a semipro team in Los Angeles. They won the Triple-A Baseball League championship in December.[10]

In 1955 Regalado failed to make the Indians in spring training. He was sent back to Indianapolis, where he continued to hit, ending the year with a batting average of .316 with nine home runs. He was called up to the Indians for only ten games. After the season, he joined the Tomateros de Culiacán team in the Mexican Pacific League. Other American Major League players were there, too. The Indians' Russ Nixon and Hank Aguirre were teammates. The team won the league's seasonal championship with a record of 33-25.[11]

In 1956 Regalado was again in Indianapolis, hitting .322 with fourteen home runs in ninety-five games. He played only sixteen games for Cleveland.

They were his last Major League games. At Indianapolis he roomed with Roger Maris, and the two players remained close friends until Maris's death in 1985. The Indianapolis club was a powerhouse; twenty-four of the team's players had had or would have Major League experience. The Indians defeated Minneapolis and Denver to win the league championship, then swept the Rochester Red Wings of the International League in the Junior World Series. Regalado was 8 for 16, with a home run, triple, and double.[12]

In November, Regalado started the winter season in the Dominican Republic on the Estrellas Orientales team. "One of our outfielders got hurt. I called Roger [Maris] and he said he just got married. 'Congratulations,' I said. 'Why don't you come down here and spend your honeymoon.'"[13] And he did.

Regalado did not spend much time with the Marises. After a month in the Dominican Republic, he left to join the Leones de Caracas team in the Venezuelan Professional Baseball League. The team won the championship of Venezuela and qualified for the Caribbean World Series, which was held in Havana. The Leones beat Puerto Rico, then lost to Panama. It was a double round-robin tournament, and when they lost to Cuba, they were out of contention. Regalado hit .292 in the tournament (7 for 24).[14]

Regalado was optioned to the San Diego Padres of the Pacific Coast League for the 1957 season. Playing with such future Indians as Gary Bell and Mudcat Grant, Rudy had another good year at the plate, hitting .306 with fifty RBIs and eight home runs. He was named the best third baseman in the Minor Leagues, and he appeared on TV's *Ed Sullivan Show*. (This was his second appearance on the show, the first being after the 1954 World Series.) After the season, Regalado returned to Venezuela, this time with the Pampero club, where he won the league batting title with a .368 average.[15]

Midway through the 1959 season, Regalado was traded to the Seattle Rainiers of the Pacific Coast League. The sixteen home runs he hit for both teams were the most he ever hit in a season. After the 1960 season, the Rainiers sold Regalado's contract to Jersey City. Rather than travel across the country, Rudy hung up his spikes.

Back in California, Regalado met an executive of XETV, a television station based in Tijuana, Mexico, that served the San Diego market. The executive, Julian Kaufman, offered him a ninety-day trial as a salesman at $400 a month if he would also play shortstop for the station's softball team. "It wasn't until years later I figured that those ninety days would be just about the end of the softball season!" Regalado said. The ninety-day trial turned into a twenty-five-year career.

During the 1954 season, through Hal Naragon, an Indians backup catcher, Regalado had met Marilyn Hall, a third-grade teacher in the South Euclid–Lyndhurst school system, outside Cleveland. In 1958 Marilyn moved to La Jolla, California, to teach. The couple were married on February 11, 1961. "Thank God she liked baseball!" Regalado said. They had three sons. Two, Perry and Gary, went into teaching. The third son, Rudy, was a two-time All-American golfer at Redlands University and became a salesman for the Cleveland Golf Company. A nephew, Samuel Regalado, is a college professor and has written a book on Latin American baseball.

The Regalados invested in apartment houses in the San Diego area. It proved to be a lucrative opportunity and gave them financial security. After retiring from XETV and the apartment business, they moved to the small desert community of Borrego Springs, where they bought a condominium that overlooks a golf course.

They keep busy, Rudy said in 2011, playing golf on the course, driving for Meals on Wheels, and reading Scripture to nursing-home patients. Deeply spiritual, they are active in their church and several charitable organizations.

On September 18, 2010, the Seattle Mariners invited Regalado to throw out the ceremonial first pitch before their game with the Texas Rangers.

STEVE JOHNSON

The game was to "pay tribute to the contributions Latin American players have made to the game of baseball."[16] "I warmed up . . . for about nine days," throwing tennis balls against a wall by their condo. "So I was ready!" The Mariners flew Rudy and Marilyn to Seattle. He was given a jersey with "Marineros" on the front and his name and No. 8, his old Indians number, on the back. When the moment came, he stood on the mound and threw a perfect strike.

Chapter 24. **Ray Narleski**

Joseph Wancho

AGE	W	L	PCT	ERA	G	GS	GF	CG	SHO	SV	IP	H	BB	SO	HBP	WP
25	3	3	.500	2.22	42	2	19	1	0	13	89	59	44	52	2	2

The hot days of summer strolled lazily by Cleveland in 1954. The Indians were looking to sweep the visiting Chicago White Sox on the July Fourth holiday and make it four straight victories over the Pale Hose and seven straight overall. Cleveland was flexing its muscles, in first place with a four-and-a-half-game lead over the New York Yankees in the American League standings, and showing no signs of letting up.

Besides its stellar pitching rotation, Cleveland's success could be credited to two unheralded rookies in the bullpen. The pair of relief specialists offered manager Al Lopez the luxury of bringing in either Don Mossi, a left-hander with a sweeping delivery and a big curve, or Ray Narleski, a right-hander who presented a contrast to Mossi's style by throwing inside with heat.

Narleski got to the ballpark early this Sunday, arriving in the morning at the urging of bullpen coach Bill Lobe. "Funny thing about it, he was so wild I was afraid to stand up to the plate," said Lobe. "The day before I told him he might be getting rusty and we decided to come out early."[1] Narleski took to the outfield to shag fly balls. He was not anticipating any early work, as Mike Garcia was the scheduled starter for Cleveland. The Bear could eat up innings, with 258⅔ pitched by the end of this season.

But after Garcia retired the first four batters he faced, a blood vessel ruptured on the middle finger of his pitching hand and forced him out of the game in the second inning. Enter Narleski, who responded to the early SOS from Lopez by tossing five and two-thirds innings of no-hit ball and earning his second victory of the season. He struck out five and gave up just one run, on a walk, a wild pitch,

Ray Narleski—The hard-throwing right-hander complemented the left-handed-throwing Don Mossi coming out of the Indians' bullpen. Narleski's nineteen saves in 1955 led the league.

a ground out, and a throwing error in the eighth inning when, by his own admission, he was tiring. "After I walked Sherman Lollar to start the inning, I just didn't know where the ball was going," Narleski said after the game.[2] Early Wynn, in one of only four relief appearances that season, worked the final two innings, giving up the only White Sox hit, a single by Minnie Minoso with two outs in the ninth inning, and preserving the 2–1 victory for Narleski.

Ray Narleski performed at a high level for five seasons in Cleveland. Eventually, arm trouble curtailed his career, but his ability to pitch fast and with precision to the batter made him a feared competitor.

Raymond Edmond Narleski was born on November 25, 1928, in Camden, New Jersey. He was one of five children born to William E. and Marie Narleski. Bill Narleski, known as Cap, was a utility infielder for the Boston Red Sox in 1929 and 1930, had a long Minor League career, and played on many semipro teams when Ray was growing up. The family moved many times in southern New Jersey and spent some time in Chester, Pennsylvania, not far from New Jersey. Ray's younger brother Ted was a star offensive back for UCLA in the early 1950s. Later he played in the Indians' farm system for three seasons.

Ray starred in baseball and football at Collingswood (New Jersey) High School. However, because of the family's many moves, he turned nineteen years old before the start of his senior season and was ineligible to play. Many of the scouts who were following Narleski believed he was not playing because of injury, and their interest waned. However, Indians scout Billy Whitman knew the real reason why Ray was idle and signed him after graduation. Part of the deal was that Bill Narleski would be taken on as a scout. There was also a verbal agreement that Narleski would be given a pact with Triple-A money after one year of playing Class A ball. Narleski also found the time to get married before he embarked on his pro career, exchanging "I do's" with his high school sweetheart, Ruth May Gilbert.

Narleski started his pro career at Wilkes-Barre of the Eastern League, where his 2-10 record prompted manager Bill Norman to feel that he may have been over his head in Class A. But Norman saw potential in the young pitcher. "He showed a lot of promise because he could really hum that seed," Norman later recalled.[3] But the Indians didn't keep their end of the verbal agreement, and Narleski decided to sit out the 1949 season. He soon found out that Cleveland general manager Hank Greenberg, who had been unaware of the promise made to Narleski, could be just as stubborn. To keep in shape, Narleski played semipro ball while working at the RTC Shipbuilding Company.

Bill Norman, still managing at Wilkes-Barre, counseled Narleski and eventually persuaded him to return to baseball. Narleski got a slight pay raise and restarted his career in 1950 at Cedar Rapids of the Class B Three-I (Illinois-Indiana-Iowa) League. His record improved there, and in 1951 at Dallas in the Texas League. In 1952 the Indians moved him up to Triple-A Indianapolis, and after going 11-15 that season, he flourished in 1953 under manager Birdie Tebbetts. The veteran catcher noted that Narleski would sail through the opposition's lineup for two or three innings and then get shelled. Figuring that Narleski could flourish as a reliever, Tebbetts asked Greenberg to approve the switch. Greenberg, recalling the contract squabble with Narleski, told Tebbets, "I don't care what you do with him."[4] Narleski also balked at the idea, fearing his salary would be cut because he wouldn't pitch as many innings. Assured that Greenberg had no intention of reducing his pay, Narleski agreed to Tebbetts's plan. "I accepted it because I had to, but I didn't get paid for it, and that's the part I didn't appreciate," Narleski said years later. "I always felt I was underpaid."[5]

Narleski, now twenty-five, made the Indians' roster out of spring training in 1954, and he and Mossi anchored a superior bullpen. Though the common intelligence is that a team can never have enough pitching, Cleveland had almost too much. The Big Four of the starting rotation were Bob Lemon, Early Wynn, Mike Garcia, and Bob Feller. Lemon and Wynn led the American League with twenty-three wins apiece, while Garcia was the ERA king at 2.64. Add to the mix thirteen wins for an aging Feller and fifteen for Art Houtteman, and the rotation was indeed formidable. Besides Narleski (3-3, 2.22 ERA,

13 saves) and Mossi, the Indians also signed veteran Hal Newhouser to shore up the bullpen.

A game against the Yankees at Yankee Stadium on June 2 typified the strength of the bullpen. Wynn started but was taken out in the first inning by manager Al Lopez after giving up four runs without getting an out. His replacement, Mossi, surrendered three more runs in the first inning, putting the Indians in a 7–0 hole after one inning. But a parade out of the bullpen, including Narleski, Bob Hooper, Garcia, and finally Newhouser, no-hit New York the rest of the way. Cleveland climbed back in the game and tied the score on a home run by Bobby Avila in the ninth inning, then winning, 8–7, when Al Smith homered in the tenth.

"Narleski's fastball takes off," said catcher Jim Hegan. "He throws it around the letters and it usually moves in on a right-handed batter and away from a left-hander. When he gets it high enough, it's almost impossible to hit."[6]

On offense the Indians were led by Avila, Larry Doby, and Al Rosen. They won 111 games, an American League record that stood until 1998, and finished ahead of New York by eight games.

Cleveland was heavily favored to beat the New York Giants in the World Series, which began at the Polo Grounds in New York. A superstitious fan might have been alarmed when the team, amid a throng of well-wishers, departed from the train terminal on Track 13. Superstition may have been as good a reason as any to explain how the Indians were swept in four games. The Series began on a Wednesday and was over by Saturday. It was a complete collapse. The Indians hit .190 and their pitchers posted a 4.84 earned run average. Giants bench player Dusty Rhodes contributed three timely hits, including two home runs, and Willie Mays's catch off Cleveland's Vic Wertz in Game One has gone down in baseball legend. Narleski pitched in Games Three and Four, giving up one run in four innings.

The save became an official statistic in 1969, when Narleski had been out of Organized Baseball for a decade. The criteria for which a pitcher is credited with a save has been amended a handful of times over the years. At first a pitcher got a save simply for finishing a winning game, without getting credit for the victory. There was no requirement for the number of innings pitched or what the on-base situation was when the pitcher entered. Retroactively, Narleski has been given credit for fifty-eight saves in his six Major League seasons; and if it were an official statistic in 1955, he would have led the American League with nineteen.

Narleski and Mossi became close friends and roomed together on the road. Their careers were bounded by honing their trade in the bullpen, side by side. Although both pitchers preferred to be in the starting rotation, relief work would be their calling for now. (From 1957 through 1959, the last season on the Detroit pitching staff, Narleski made forty-nine starts.) But in their early days, Cleveland manager Lopez made full use of the pair, never hesitating to pull a starter at the slightest hint of an oncoming predicament. "I know they'd do well if I started them every four days," Lopez said in 1955, "but I hate to take them out of the bullpen. They're more valuable there, at least right now since we have plenty of starters."[7]

It was almost impossible to see a story written about one player that did not include the other. Their success earned them many nicknames during their years in Cleveland. Among them were the Toss Out Twins, the Gold Dust Twins, and the Tremendous Two. "Finding them was like finding gold dust," said first baseman Vic Wertz. "Because of them we cashed in on pennant gold last year and if we do it again they'll deserve the credit."[8]

Wertz's words were almost prophetic. In 1955 Herb Score injected some youth and a blazing fastball into the rotation. Besides his nineteen (unofficial) saves, Narleski had a 9-1 record. After sweeping a doubleheader from Washington on September 13, Cleveland held a two-game lead over New York in the standings. But the Tribe could not close the deal, losing six of nine down the stretch while the Yankees won nine of eleven.

Hal Lebovitz, who covered the Indians for the *Cleveland News,* wrote, "They just ran out of gas, carrying an immense load of problems. The bullpen did a terrific job, but Narleski tired under the strain. (Outfielder Al) Smith had no chance to rest. A few key men had to carry the load—and they ran out of gas in the home stretch, that's all. The other Indians let Smith and Narleski down by not taking up the slack. These two men carried the ball all season and their tremendous effort was wasted because their teammates couldn't carry the burden the one time they had to."[9]

Lebovitz had a point on Narleski's tiring. Ray led the league in appearances with sixty, while Mossi pitched in fifty-seven games. Combined, they took the ball for just under two hundred innings. Narleski finished sixth in the Most Valuable Player voting.

Narleski improved on those numbers early in the 1956 season. From May 25 to June 20, he did not surrender an earned run in twenty-four and two-thirds innings pitched. But on July 2, he pulled a muscle in his right elbow and missed two months. He had been selected to participate in the All-Star Game, but he was forced to sit it out. He returned in early September and wound up the season with a sparkling ERA of 1.52 in thirty-two games.

Lopez left the Indians after the season to take the reins of the Chicago White Sox. In his six seasons at the helm in Cleveland, the Tribe had never finished lower than second place. Greenberg promoted Kerby Farrell from Triple-A Indianapolis to steer the ship. The change in managers was among the factors that led to the Indians' dropping to sixth place in 1957. The pitching staff suffered an unfortunate loss when Score was hit in the eye with a batted ball on May 7. Then Lemon had bone chips removed from his elbow, further thinning out the rotation.

Narleski pestered Farrell for a chance to start, and Farrell acquiesced. From July 21 through August 8, Narleski won four of six games started, with

no losses. Mossi also got some starts, and he and Narleski combined for thirty-seven starts. "He deserves to remain a starter," Farrell said of Narleski. "He's done a great job for us, really saved our lives. But taking him out of the bullpen hurts, too."[10] Narleski ended the year with an 11-5 record and an ERA of 3.09. He also had sixteen "saves." In a relief appearance on June 23 in Washington, Narleski socked the first and only home run of his Major League career. (He also hit one in the Minors.) The Washington blast, a three-run shot off the Senators' Russ Kemmerer in the eighth inning, provided the winning margin in a 7–5 victory.

Kerby Farrell was replaced after one year by Bobby Bragan. Bragan had previously managed in Pittsburgh, to no great avail. He was the choice of the new general manager, Frank Lane. Lane had replaced Greenberg, who rejoined Lopez two years later in Chicago.

Lane, known for the multiplicity of his trades, got to work right away. He sent Wynn and Smith to Chicago, and Hegan to Detroit. Lane was just warming up. If anything, he was impetuous, showing Bragan the door after sixty-seven games. Former Yankees and Indians great Joe Gordon assumed control—or as much control as a manager had under Lane.

The Indians were said to be pursuing a second baseman, and it was reported that they had their eye on New York's Bobby Richardson. The *New York World-Telegram and Sun* reported that a trade involving Narleski and Richardson was a done deal. An agreement was never reached, which illustrated that even swaps that Lane didn't make made headlines.

In 1958 Narleski was thrown into the revamped pitching rotation with Cal McLish, Gary Bell, and Mudcat Grant. He recorded a 13-10 mark, pitching in 183⅓ innings. He was named to the AL All-Star team, and pitched one-hit ball in three and one-third innings. A muscle popped in his forearm as he threw a curveball. He had a hard time strengthening the arm unless he soaked it in the whirlpool.

After the All-Star break, Narleski was returned to

his familiar role as a reliever. "Frank [Lane] moved me back to the bullpen to knock me out of being a 20-game winner," he said. "I didn't want to go back to the bullpen. I was a starter and then refused to sign a 1959 contract with the Cleveland club."[11]

In the off-season the Indians were still trying to find a way to fill their need at second base. On November 20 Narleski, Mossi, and infielder Ossie Alvarez were traded to Detroit for second baseman Billy Martin and pitcher Al Cicotte. Narleski was thrilled with the move, as he always felt he was not being used correctly in Cleveland. Lane commented that Narleski and Mossi won just five games between them after Joe Gordon's arrival, and that they just did not figure in the team's plans. Detroit general manager John McHale said he hated to give up Martin, "but we feel Narleski and Mossi will win more games for us than Billy did."[12]

Joining the Tigers, Narleski was reunited with Bill Norman, his Minor League skipper who was now the head man in the Motor City. "We know that one of our big problems last year was in bullpen help," Norman said. "When one of our starters weakened, we were in trouble. With Narleski and Mossi to come in and bail us out, I think we will be a lot better off."[13]

But for Norman, Narleski, and the Tigers, the 1959 season did not unfold as they might have hoped. The Tigers wobbled out of the gate with a 2-15 record and Norman was fired. Narleski had been nursing a bad back since spring training, and his performance on the mound reflected the pain he felt. He posted a 4-12 record with a 5.78 ERA. His back never did heal properly. After surgery in 1960 to repair a disk, he was hospitalized for six weeks. He was on the disabled list for the entire 1960 season. In 1961 Detroit planned to send him to Triple-A Denver. Narleski refused the reassignment, and he was released on March 31, 1961. After six seasons and more than 700 innings pitched, he finished his career with a record of 43-33 and an ERA of 3.60. He also totaled fifty-eight unofficial saves.

In retirement Narleski played semipro ball in New Jersey and Delaware. He went to work as a mechanic/truck builder for H. A. DeHart Trucks in Thorofare, New Jersey. He and Ruth had three sons, Ray Jr., Steven, and Jeffrey. Steve Narleski signed with the Indians and spent a few years in their Minor League chain.

Narleski lived out his retirement years in Camden, New Jersey. "What the hell, I had a great career," he told a writer in 2006. "OK, I am bitter about a couple of things . . . and it's not just that they kept me in relief. If they had just paid me what I was worth, I would not have been pissed off about not starting, although I know I could have been successful and made a lot more money. If that's having an attitude, so be it, I had one."[14]

Ray Narleski passed away from natural causes on March 29, 2012.

Chapter 25. Timeline, June 1–June 15

Joseph Wancho

June 1—INDIANS TRADE CHAKALES FOR WERTZ—Cleveland trades relief pitcher Bob Chakales to Baltimore for outfielder Vic Wertz. Manager Al Lopez says that Wertz will be "good insurance."

June 2—New York—SMITH'S HOMER UPSETS YANKEES, 8–7—The Yankees score all of their seven runs in the first inning. Hank Bauer drives in two runs. Larry Doby clouts a three-run shot in the third inning and Bobby Avila homers in the ninth frame. Al Smith's HR in the tenth wins it. Newhouser is credited with the win in relief.

June 3—New York—YANKEES BEAT INDIANS, 2–1, ON COLLINS' HOMER—Eddie Lopat raises his record to 6-1, scattering eleven hits for the win. Joe Collins hits a solo shot in the eighth to win it.

June 4—New York—YANKS BEAT TRIBE, BOMBERS CUT INDIANS LEAD TO 7 POINTS—Yogi Berra hits a three-run homer in the first inning. Mickey Mantle goes 1 for 2 with two RBIs, walks three times, and scores twice. Cleveland and Chicago are in a virtual tie atop American League.

June 5—Philadelphia—GARCIA WINS TWO-HITTER IN 11TH—Mike Garcia notches his sixth win, whiffing seven A's hitters. Dave Philley hits a solo homer in the seventh inning. The Indians score three runs in the top of the eleventh inning to win 4–1.

June 6—Philadelphia—INDIANS BEAT A'S TWICE, HOLD LEAGUE LEAD—The Tribe scores both runs in the second inning, courtesy of two triples (Dave Philley, George Strickland), each fol-

lowed by a sacrifice fly (Bill Glynn, Jim Hegan). The offense manages only three hits in a 2–1 win in the first game, as Bob Feller gets the win. Art Houtteman backs his fourth victory with a home run in the second game. Larry Doby also homers. Hal Naragon drives in three runs in a 7–5 win.

June 8—Washington—SENATORS JAR INDIANS, 5–2; 2 HIT GAME—Eddie Yost tallies three RBIs for the Nats, and Early Wynn strikes out nine in a 5–2 defeat. Mickey McDermott throws a two-hitter and wins his fifth game for Washington.

June 9—Washington—GARCIA'S FIVE-HITTER BLANKS NATS, 1–0—The only run of the game is an unearned fielder's choice in the seventh inning. Garcia wins his seventh victory. The shutout is the fourth by the Indians' pitching staff.

June 10—Washington—DEAN STONE OF SENATORS JARS INDIANS, 8–4—Rookie Dean Stone wins his fourth game in a row. Roy Sievers and Mickey Vernon each collect two hits and an RBI. Tom Umphlett knocks in three runs to lead the Nats. Doby hits a two-run HR in the loss.

June 11—Boston—HOMERS, HOUTTEMAN JAR RED SOX, 6 TO 2—Larry Doby hits a three-run home run in the first inning. Wally Westlake and George Strickland also homer. Art Houtteman strikes out five for his fifth win on the year.

June 12—Boston—INDIANS BEAT RED SOX, 4 TO 3; TAKE OVER LEAD—Bob Feller strikes out eight for his third win. He registers his 2,500th career strikeout. A bases-loaded single in the seventh inning by Larry Doby plates two. The Indians score three in the frame. Cleveland regains the lead atop the American League.

June 13—Boston—INDIANS SEIZE TWO, 4–1, 8–1—The Tribe takes two from Boston for their fifth straight Sunday sweep of a DH. Wally Westlake goes 2 for 3, with a homer, two RBIS, a run scored, and a walk. Early Wynn strikes out seven in the opener of the DH. Rudy Regalado goes 2 for 5 with three RBIS, and Vic Wertz goes 2 for 4 with an RBI in the nightcap. Mike Garcia earns his eighth win.

June 14—Boston—INDIANS SWEEP RED SOX SERIES—Larry Doby goes 3 for 5 and drives in two. George Strickland hits a three-run homer. Al Smith hits a solo home run. The Cleveland offense bangs out twenty-two hits. Bob Lemon wins his eighth as the Tribe sweeps the five-game series at Fenway Park.

June 15—Cleveland—INDIANS RIP NATS, 9–3—Cleveland scores six runs in the bottom of the eighth inning. Al Rosen's pinch-hit double is the key hit. Hank Majeski goes 3 for 5 with a double. Rudy Regalado drives in two runs.

Chapter 26. **Sam Dente**

Jack Morris

AGE	G	AB	R	H	2B	3B	HR	TB	RBI	BB	SO	BAV	OBP	SLG	SB	GDP	HBP
32	68	169	18	45	7	1	1	57	19	14	4	.266	.319	.337	0	5	0

It's ironic that a player who's best remembered for the slogan "We'll win plenty with Sam Dente" would have played almost half his career for two organizations synonymous with losing, the St. Louis Browns and the Washington Senators.

It was during his three-year Senators tenure from 1949 through 1951 that the slogan was first seen on a sign, but the prediction didn't really come true until Dente was signed by the 1954 Cleveland Indians. His play as a utility infielder, ultimately taking over the starting shortstop job when regular George Strickland went down with a broken jaw, was a big part of the Indians' 111-win season.

Dente, a five-foot-eleven, 175-pound right-hander, was often called in the press a "good-field, no-hit" infielder. For only two seasons did he hold down a steady position with a Major League club. What kept him in the Majors was a rifle arm combined with the athletic ability to play all of the infield positions well. In his prime, he was the ultimate utility infielder.

He was a fiery competitor, quick to anger—mostly at himself. He was a serial water-bucket kicker, often being fined for ruining a dugout water bucket after striking out.[1] The practice eventually came to an end in one game when someone filled the water bucket with sand.[2] But Dente was also the clubhouse comedian, keeping the locker-room mood light with his hijinks.[3]

Samuel Joseph Dente was born on April 26, 1922, in Harrison, New Jersey, to Italian immigrant parents Joseph, a railroad laborer, and Lena Dente. Both of his parents immigrated to the United States in the 1890s. Sam was the youngest of six children, with four sisters and a brother.[4]

Sam Dente—"Win plenty with Sam Dente" was the cry for Tribe fans in 1954. He played well in place of the injured George Strickland. He is the grandfather of pitcher Rick Porcello.

Dente excelled at two sports as he grew up. He was a fine center half for the Kearny High School soccer team.[5] He was so good that after high school, Dente played professionally in the American Soccer League for the Kearny Americans.[6]

But Dente also shined at baseball. He played shortstop for Kearny High and, in 1941, was a finalist in the *New York World-Telegram*'s Most Valuable Baseball Player contest for high school players from New York and the vicinity.[7] More than fifty years later, the *Newark Star-Ledger* named Dente to its high school baseball All-Century team for the 1940s.[8] Dente also honed his skill in the American Legion junior ball program.[9]

Naturally, a player of Dente's ability started to draw attention. The first person to talk to him was Jack Tighe, player-manager of the Muskegon Reds in the Detroit Tigers organization and a neighbor of Dente's in Kearny. In 1941 Tigers general manager Jack Zeller offered Dente a bonus for signing and sent him to Newark and Jersey City, where he worked out with the Tigers' International League team, the Buffalo Bisons.[10]

What happened next is up to dispute. In 1950 *The Sporting News* reported that the Tigers cut Dente after watching him bat against hard-throwing Virgil Trucks, who amassed four Minor League no-hitters before starting a seventeen-year Major League career. But Dente told *Baseball Digest* in 1954 that Bisons manager Al Vincent never allowed him to bat when he was with the team, yet Vincent reported to the Tigers that he wasn't much of a hitter.[11]

Whatever happened, the Tigers weren't interested in keeping Dente. The Red Sox jumped in. Their scout Jack Egan signed Dente to a contract and sent him off to the Owensboro Oilers of the Kentucky-Illinois-Tennessee League.[12]

Dente had little trouble adjusting to the Kitty League offensively, batting .273. But he struggled defensively playing shortstop for the Oilers. In seventy-seven games, he committed forty-four errors for a .901 fielding percentage.

But the Red Sox saw enough potential that they moved Dente to Greensboro in 1942. At Greensboro he improved his defense but struggled with the bat. Yet despite his hitting only .209, he found

himself moved up another classification, this time to Scranton for the 1943 season.

In Scranton, Dente again struggled with the bat, but World War II soon intervened. In February he was classified as 3-A ("men with dependents, not engaged in work essential to national defense").[13] On June 11 he enlisted in the army at Wilkes-Barre, Pennsylvania.[14]

Unlike many other Major and Minor Leaguers, Dente didn't play baseball during the war. He was sent to Europe, where he manned an antiaircraft gun for much of the war.[15] Because he bent over the firing piece, it cost him his hearing in his left ear.[16] He was kept in the army until March 1946.[17]

Dente managed to make it to training camp after his discharge and was placed back with Scranton for the 1946 season, as were many of his former 1943 teammates who had gone away to the war. As a result, Scranton was loaded with talent.

Instead of playing shortstop, Dente was moved to third base. He, and the Scranton Red Sox as a whole, had a tremendous season. Dente hit .289 in 134 games and proved an asset in the field.

Scranton easily won the Eastern League regular-season championship by eighteen and a half games and then steamrolled through the playoffs to the EL championship. Dente's teammate Sam Mele was named the EL Most Valuable Player. Dente finished eighth in the voting.[18]

After the season ended, the Red Sox swapped seven players to Louisville for seven players slated to be with Louisville in 1947. Dente was one of the latter group.[19] *The Sporting News* proclaimed that he had "a fine minor league reputation" and was a "sure fielder and thrower and a fair hitter."[20] Boston Red Sox manager Joe Cronin called Dente "promising."[21] His career was definitely on the upswing. On January 22, 1947, Dente signed a contract to play for the Red Sox, but not before the Red Sox told him in no uncertain terms to quit professional soccer.[22]

At camp, he found himself in a battle for the third-base job with Frank Shofner and Merrill Combs.[23] *The Sporting News* wrote that Dente had the "strongest gun" of any infielder in the Red Sox camp.[24] But his hitting held him back, and Shofner soon had the inside track on the job as camp came to a close.[25]

According to *The Sporting News*, when the Red Sox broke camp and started barnstorming home, Dente was left behind at their camp in Sarasota, Florida, "until the situation became clearer."[26] Eventually, the Red Sox sent Dente and catcher Ed McGah to Louisville for the start of their season.[27]

Dente caught fire almost immediately at Louisville. By July 9 he was hitting .311. The Red Sox, on the other hand, were struggling to find an adequate third baseman.[28] Shofner hadn't panned out and, in their desperation, the Red Sox had tried five other players at third base. On July 10, 1947, Dente became the seventh to play the position.[29]

In his first game, Dente faced Detroit Tigers pitcher Hal Newhouser, a future Hall of Famer. He singled twice against Prince Hal, and the press wrote that he had "played sensationally" at third base.[30] Dente went on to start forty-two straight games for the Red Sox at third base. He was seen as a stabilizing presence at third base after two years of a revolving door at the position.[31]

Cronin continued to praise his new third baseman for his defensive abilities, calling him the team's best defensive third baseman since Cronin became the manager of the Red Sox in 1935.[32]

But Dente still was a liability with the bat. *Sporting News* correspondent Jack Malaney wrote, "It appears that Dente is not ready for Major League pitching."[33] By season's end, Dente was hitting only .232. The Red Sox, who finished third in the American League, were looking to upgrade at several positions, so on November 18 they traded Dente, pitcher Clem Dreisewerd, Minor League infielder Bill Sommers, and $65,000 to the St. Louis Browns for pitcher Ellis Kinder and infielder Billy Hitchcock.

Meanwhile, the Browns were interested in Dente primarily as a shortstop. Dente, eager to win the starting job, went to camp early in San Bernardino, California.[34]

Despite the successful integration of baseball in 1947, Organized Baseball was still holding its collective breath, worried that an incident might occur on the field between a white and a black player that would have racial implications. It was an incident involving Dente that proved that, as far as play on the field goes, it would be business as usual.

It occurred during a spring-training game between the Browns and the Cleveland Indians at Wrigley Field in Los Angeles. While Dente was playing shortstop, Larry Doby accidentally spiked him while stealing second. There was no altercation between the two players, though Dente had to leave the game to be tended to.

While the spiking may not seem a big deal given today's sensibilities, it warranted a full story in *The Sporting News* with the headline "Negro Spikes White Rival—and That's the Whole Story." The publication wrote of the incident, "Civilization's stumbling progress toward true maturity passed at least a minor milestone at Wrigley Field."[35]

While Dente didn't crack the regular lineup at the start of the season, he still helped the Browns to a surprising winning record as June began. He batted over .300 in mostly pinch-hitting and utility roles.[36] The Browns, however, soon fell into their normal pattern and finished the season thirty-seven games back of the Cleveland Indians. Dente had a good season as a spot starter for regular shortstop Eddie Pellagrini. Dente started fifty-seven games at shortstop and four at third base. He hit .270 in ninety-eight games for the Browns.

But the Browns, always in the mood to trade a player especially when they received cash in return, traded Dente to the Washington Senators on October 4 in exchange for pitcher Tom Ferrick, infielder John Sullivan, and $25,000. Dente wasn't sad to move from St. Louis to Washington. Years later he told author Eric Stone, "I wasn't (in St. Louis) very long, thank God. We had some nice guys but absolutely no chemistry. Everybody went his way. No team unity. I was very happy to leave."[37]

When the 1949 season started, Dente was the Senators' starting shortstop. Despite the changes, the Senators got off to a bad start. After dropping a doubleheader to the Philadelphia Athletics, the Senators stood at 3-11 and in the midst of a fourteen-game road trip. Things looked bleak. But the Senators won nine straight games before dropping their last game of the road trip.

When the Senators arrived back in Washington, there was an auto parade waiting to take them to Griffith Stadium. Thousands of people lined the route.[38] Along the parade route, people held various signs. One sign in particular was reported in the newspapers: "We'll Win Plenty with Sam Dente."

While the slogan didn't exactly come true in 1949 for the Senators, it was Dente's best season as a Major Leaguer. Playing in 153 games, he batted .273 and drove opposing teams crazy with his ability to get the bat on the ball. In addition, he cracked the first of his four Major League home runs, off the St. Louis Browns' Red Embree on June 1.[39]

In July, *Sporting News* correspondent Shirley Povich wrote that Dente "is now recognized as the most valuable player on the club."[40] Povich later declared that getting Dente from the Browns was the "smartest trade" made by the Senators that year.[41]

Everything seemed to be going Dente's way. His hometown of Harrison, New Jersey, presented him with a new car at Yankee Stadium between games of a doubleheader in August.[42] And in a critical, must-win game for the Boston Red Sox at the end of the season, Dente played a superb game against his former team, handling thirteen chances perfectly.[43] At the end of the game, the Senators carried Dente off on their shoulders.[44]

While Dente had a good season with the bat, it wasn't as good defensively. He led the league in errors. Yet despite Dente's fielding, Senators owner Clark Griffith declared him "an untouchable" in the off-season.[45] Right before spring training, Griffith

raised Dente's salary.[46] Clearly, Dente was a popular player both with the fans and with the Senators' front office.

When the season began, Dente was the Senators' starting second baseman. But at the end of May, the Senators obtained second baseman Cass Michaels in a trade with the White Sox. Michaels, who had hit .308 in 1949, would add another good hitter to the Senators' lineup. So with Michaels penciled in at second, Dente moved back to shortstop. He struggled with the bat throughout 1950. He finished the season with a .239 average. These weren't the numbers the Senators were looking for from Dente, who had started every game of the season. Shirley Povich wrote that he "was the biggest disappointment on the Senators."[47] And there were plenty of disappointments to go around as the Senators finished in fifth, thirty-one games behind the Yankees.

So going into the 1951 season, Dente would have to earn his position. The Senators brought in a couple of shortstops from the Southern Association, Atlanta's Gene Verble and Chattanooga's Willy Miranda, to challenge Dente in spring training.[48] He didn't handle the pressure well, going hitless in eighteen straight games in spring training.[49] Toward the end of spring training, he started hitting again and entered the season with optimism. But his hitting woes continued through the beginning of the season. Manager Bucky Harris replaced him with both Verble and Miranda, but they hit even worse than Dente.[50] By June 6 Dente was hitting a paltry .218. Harris was trying everything to shake up his Senators, who were second- to-last in team batting in the American League.

Finally, in late June, the Senators called up shortstop Pete Runnels from Chattanooga. Runnels was tearing up the Southern Association, batting .356.[51] Dente went to the bench for much of the rest of the season as the Senators staggered toward a seventh-place finish. Only the lowly Browns kept them out of the cellar. Dente finished the season with a .238 batting average.

On November 27, 1951, Griffith and Harris gave up on Dente, trading him to the White Sox for short-stop Tom Upton. The White Sox had received Upton earlier in the day in a trade with the Browns.[52] The White Sox brought Dente to spring training in Pasadena, California, to compete for their third base job. They had played seven different third basemen in 1951 and were hoping to solidify the position in 1952. Vying for the job in training camp were Dente, Hector Rodriguez, Mel Hoderlein, Minnie Minoso, Rocky Krsnich, and Bob Dillinger, who had played seventy games at third for the White Sox in 1951.[53]

With all the third basemen in camp, rumors of trades swirled. Dente was reported to be headed to the Detroit Tigers.[54] But in the end, Dente stuck with the White Sox, winning a utility infielder position, helped by his .354 batting average in spring training.[55] He filled in at every infield position as the White Sox battled in a pennant race. He even played six games in the outfield—by far the most versatile player in the American League that season.[56] But he played in only sixty-two games and finished the season with a .221 batting average, easily his worst hitting season in the Major Leagues, as the White Sox finished in third, fourteen games behind the Yankees.

After the season, Dente worked at the Brooklyn Division of the American Baseball Academy, which was a baseball program aimed at juvenile delinquents.[57] Teaching baseball would become a passion of his through the years. He often worked camps throughout the rest of his career and years beyond.

In 1953 Dente again made the Opening Day roster as a utility fielder and played in two games before the White Sox sold him to the Indianapolis Indians, a Cleveland Indians affiliate, on May 5.[58] Dente thrived under Indianapolis manager George "Birdie" Tebbetts. By mid-June, he had already put together a nineteen-game hitting streak and a thirty-seven-game errorless streak at shortstop, nine games short of the American Association re-

cord. In all, he had 219 chances without an error during the streak.[59]

When the Indians' second baseman, Bobby Avila, was injured, rumors abounded that Cleveland general manager Hank Greenberg would call up Dente. But the Indians' front office didn't want to further weaken Indianapolis, which was in the midst of its own pennant race. Indianapolis, with Dente, eventually fell out of the pennant race but finished fourth and made the playoffs, only to lose in the first round to eventual champion Kansas City. It wasn't for lack of trying on Dente's part. He hit .524 in the six-game series.[60] After the season, he was voted most popular player by the fans.[61]

The Cleveland Indians wasted little time in getting Dente onto their roster. They sent outfielder Mike Lutz and cash to Indianapolis for Dente and pitchers Marion Murszewski and Don Mossi.[62] When Dente reported to spring training in 1954, he found he was in competition with Hank Majeski and Owen Friend for two utility infielder spots.[63] Friend eventually lost the battle and Dente found himself back in the big leagues.

On April 2 the *Cleveland Plain Dealer* ran a story in its "Batting Around" column about Dente and the signs from his Senators day that read "Win plenty with Dente."[64] It would mark the resurrection of the slogan as the Indians' magical 1954 season progressed.

Dente was forced into a starting role in June, when second baseman Bobby Avila went down with an injury.[65] While starting, Dente struggled with the bat, then was hurt when he collided with teammate Dave Philley while chasing a pop fly. The injury put him on the shelf for ten days.[66] After he rejoined the team, other than a few spot starts to relieve the slumping George Strickland, Dente was on the bench again.[67] But the Indians were in the midst of the pennant race, and Dente would play a big part in their success.

Dente's personal life was on a high as well. He went home over the All-Star break to visit his new-born daughter, Patricia, for the first time.[68] With the new addition to the family, he bought a home in Clifton, New Jersey.[69]

Then Dente's big break came on July 23 when Strickland's jaw was broken by a ball thrown by New York Yankees pitcher Marlin Stuart as Strickland slid into third base.[70]

With Dente playing shortstop and outfielder Vic Wertz stepping in at first base, Yankees manager Casey Stengel called the patchwork Indians' infield the "lousiest" he had ever seen in the Majors. "None of 'em can move five feet," said Stengel.[71] But even with a patchwork infield, the Indians played well. After Strickland went down, the Indians won ten of their next fourteen. Dente helped, batting .250 during that stretch.[72] Despite being riddled with injuries, the Indians, behind their fine pitching staff, won twenty-six games in August.[73]

Even more remarkable was the fact that midway through August, Dente fractured his finger yet kept playing. The only people to know of the break were Cleveland manager Al Lopez and the team doctor and training staff.[74] Even GM Hank Greenberg was in the dark on the injury.[75] The team doctor told him playing couldn't make it worse. "The finger hurt for about a week," Dente told sportswriter Hal Lebovitz. After he broke his finger, the Indians went 20-6 and Dente batted .266.[76]

Dente played some of the best baseball of his career while replacing Strickland. On September 1 he was batting .276 and was second in the American League in fielding percentage at shortstop. To top it off, he hit his fourth (and last) Major League home run off the Yankees' Whitey Ford.

After the Indians won the American League pennant, Greenberg, in *Life* magazine, wrote, "Sam Dente . . . did all the things our star, George Strickland, did before suffering the broken jaw."[77] Al Lopez was even more impressed. He said that Dente was "the fellow who gave us the greatest lift when we needed it the most."[78] In sixty-eight games, Sam batted .266 and drove in nineteen runs.

With Strickland back at full strength, Dente sat the bench for most of the World Series against the New York Giants. He got into Game One as a defensive replacement for Strickland in the eighth inning and had a sacrifice bunt in the tenth inning in the Indians' 5–2 loss. In Game Two he again was a defensive replacement in the eighth. He saw no action in Game Three.

In Game Four, with the Giants on the verge of a four-game sweep, Lopez started Dente for Strickland. Strickland had been hitless for the Series and Lopez needed a spark. Dente didn't fare much better than Strickland, going 0 for 3 with a walk and a run scored as the Giants won, 7–4, and swept the Series.

In spring training in 1955, the Indians, looking to upgrade their utility-infielder positions, brought in veteran Eddie Joost to compete with Dente.[79] Joost, who never signed a contract with the Indians, left halfway through camp to sign with the Red Sox.[80] So Dente entered the 1955 regular season again as one of the Indians' backup infielders.

By mid-May, Dente was back in the starting lineup when Strickland was injured and out for three weeks.[81] Meanwhile, the Indians, tired of Strickland and his injuries, attempted to deal Strickland, pitcher Art Houtteman, and Dente to the White Sox for Chico Carrasquel. The White Sox nixed the deal, asking for Larry Doby instead.[82] Dente was also rumored to be coveted by the Baltimore Orioles, but nothing came of it.[83]

Unlike 1954, Dente didn't play well in replacing Strickland in 1955. By June 22 his batting average stood at .210 in forty games. After that, Dente played little, getting into thirty-three games the rest of the season. He did manage to pull his batting average up to .257 by season's end, but it was clear that the Indians, who had finished second, three games back of the Yankees and sixth in AL team batting, were looking to make changes in the infield.

On October 17 Dente was sold to the Indianapolis Indians.[84] In November he told Hank Greenberg that he wouldn't be going to Indianapolis. "I feel that I can help several major-league clubs," he said.[85] Dente also needed only thirty-five days of Major League service to become a ten-year man and improve his pension status.[86]

Dente's hearing problems from his time in the army became so bad that he underwent an ear operation.[87] The operation left him with vertigo. "My sense of balance was affected," he later remembered.[88] On top of that, his wife, Marie, needed an expensive operation as well. They were forced to sell the family home to finance the operations.[89] Dente did find work after the 1955 season as a salesman, working with the Yankees' Joe Collins at a Newark clothing store.[90]

On February 16, 1956, the San Diego Padres of the Pacific Coast League purchased the rights to Dente.[91] Padres GM Ralph Kiner, who was an old teammate of Dente's, wanted Sam to replace Buddy Peterson, who had left to go to the White Sox.[92]

But in March, still plagued by issues following his ear operation, Dente announced his retirement.[93] "I had to stay idle in 1956 while recovering from the operation," he said a few years later.[94] He subsequently had one more operation to correct his progressive deafness.[95]

By August he was feeling good enough to ask for his release from the Indians.[96] It's unclear whether the Indians granted him his release, but *The Sporting News* said in September that Dente had informed Greenberg he would be making a comeback in 1957.[97]

The comeback never occurred. The Indians insisted on sending him first to the Minors, while Dente wanted to be placed on the Major League roster.[98] Out of baseball, Dente become a salesman for various companies through the 1950s and 1960s. He worked for a construction firm in Clifton[99] and a medical drug firm in Newark.[100] In his spare time, he participated in baseball clinics.[101]

In the late 1960s Dente began working at Merit Mailers, a direct-mailing house in Newark, where he became a vice president.[102] He worked there until

his retirement. Dente had moved to West Caldwell, New Jersey, after the 1955 season and remained there until his death on April 21, 2002, five days shy of his eightieth birthday. He died at Mountainside Hospital in Montclair, New Jersey.

Dente was remembered a few years after his death when his grandson, Rick Porcello, was taken in the first round of the 2007 free-agent draft by the Detroit Tigers.[103] Another grandson, Jake Porcello, was drafted in the forty-eighth round by the Tigers in 2009. Jake decided to attend Seton Hall University instead.

To the end of his life, though he played on some terrible teams, Sam was best remembered for the catchphrase "Win plenty with Dente." While reminiscing on his career in 1973, Dente told the *Cleveland Plain Dealer*, "I still hear the 'Win plenty with Dente' slogan quite often."[104] And in 1954, the Cleveland Indians certainly did.

Chapter 27. 1954 Cleveland Indians by the Numbers

Dan Fields

2nd, 3rd, 5th, and 6th

Rank in voting for the AL Most Valuable Player Award by Larry Doby, Bobby Avila, Bob Lemon, and Early Wynn, respectively. Lemon and Wynn were the only pitchers in the league to finish in the top ten.

2.64

League-leading ERA by Mike Garcia. Bob Lemon (2.72) finished third and Early Wynn (2.73) fourth.

2.78

Team ERA by the Indians, the lowest in the AL since 1918. Indians pitchers held opponents to a .232 batting average and .297 on-base percentage, both league lows.

3

Home runs (including a grand slam) in consecutive at bats by Bill Glynn in a 13–6 win over the Detroit Tigers on July 5, in the first game of a doubleheader. He also drove in a runner on a sacrifice fly, for a total of eight RBIs during the game. The utility infielder had only five home runs and eighteen RBIs all season.

5

League-leading number of shutouts pitched by Mike Garcia. Early Wynn tossed three shutouts.

8

Runs scored by the Indians before a batter was retired in the bottom of the first inning, against the Baltimore Orioles on July 6. The Indians scored three more runs in the inning and won 11–3.

8

RBIs by Indians players in the 1954 All-Star Game, before a crowd of some 69,000 in Cleveland on July 13. Al Rosen hit a three-run homer and a two-run homer, Bobby Avila drove in two runs with a single and a sacrifice fly, and Larry Doby hit a solo homer. The AL topped the NL, 11–9, with the two teams combining for thirty-one hits—an All-Star record that was not matched until 1992.

21

League-leading number of complete games by Bob Lemon. Early Wynn had twenty complete games.

23

League-leading number of wins each by Bob Lemon and Early Wynn.

32

League-leading number of home runs by Larry Doby. The Indians led the AL with 156 homers.

89-21

Record by the Indians against teams other than the New York Yankees and the Chicago White Sox. The Indians swept the Boston Red Sox in eleven games at Fenway Park and won the season series 20–2.

111

Wins by the Indians, topping the previous AL record of 110 wins by the 1927 New York Yankees.

126

League-leading number of RBIs by Larry Doby. AL Most Valuable Player Yogi Berra of the Yankees finished second with 125.

.190

Batting average by the Indians as they were swept in the World Series by the New York Giants. Vic Wertz had eight hits in sixteen at bats, but no other Indians player had more than three hits.

250

Career wins by Bob Feller on May 23. He threw a complete game as the Indians beat the Orioles, 14–3, in the first game of a doubleheader. Feller had a 13-3 record in 1954.

270⅔

League-leading number of innings pitched by Early Wynn.

.341

League-leading batting average of Bobby Avila. The Mexican native became the first foreign-born batting champion. Ted Williams of the Red Sox hit .345 but finished fourteen at bats short of qualifying for the title.

.721

Winning percentage by the Indians, with 111 wins against only 43 losses. The .721 mark is still an AL record; the 1998 New York Yankees and 2001 Seattle Mariners later won more games, but with the benefit of a 162-game schedule.

.995

League-leading fielding percentage as center fielder by Larry Doby. Jim Hegan led AL catchers with a .994 fielding percentage.

2,500

Career strikeouts by Bob Feller on June 12, in a 4–3 win over the Red Sox. When he threw his 2,581st and last strikeout in 1956, he trailed only Walter Johnson and Cy Young for career K's.

86,563

Attendance at a September 12 doubleheader in Cleveland against the Yankees—a new Major League record. The Tribe swept the Yanks, 4–1 and 3–2.

Around the Majors in 1954

0

Hits against Jim Wilson of the Milwaukee Braves on June 12 in a 2–0 complete-game victory over the Philadelphia Phillies.

1st

Career home run by Hank Aaron on April 23, as the Braves beat the St. Louis Cardinals 7–5 in fourteen innings.

4

Home runs by Joe Adcock of the Braves on July 31 in a 15–7 win over the Dodgers. Adcock also hit a double, finishing with eighteen total bases—a Major League record that stood for forty-eight years.

4

Passed balls by Giants catcher Ray Katt in the eighth inning of a game against the Reds on September 10. Knuckleballer Hoyt Wilhelm was on the mound. Two runs scored on passed balls as Cincinnati won 8–1.

5

Home runs by Stan Musial of the Cardinals in a doubleheader against the Giants on May 2. Musial hit three homers as the Cards won the first game 10–6 and then two more as they lost the second game 9–7. Among those in attendance was eight-year-old Nate Colbert, who in 1972 would match Musial's feat by smacking five homers in a doubleheader while playing for the San Diego Padres.

5

Black players starting for the Dodgers in a game against the Braves on July 17—the first time in Major League history that the majority of a team's starting lineup was black. The Dodgers won 2–1 in eleven innings.

8th

Year in which Stan Musial of the Cardinals led the NL with doubles, with forty-one in 1954. Musial scored 120 runs that year to tie for the NL lead for the fifth time.

13

Runs scored by the Dodgers in the eighth inning versus the Reds on August 8. Twelve of the runs came when the Dodgers had two outs and no one on base, and Gil Hodges had three plate appearances that inning. The Dodgers won 20–7.

17

Consecutive games in which Ted Kluszewski of the Reds scored a run, from August 27 through September 13. The streak tied the modern-day NL record set by Rogers Hornsby in 1921.

19

Sacrifice flies by Gil Hodges of the Dodgers, a Major League record that still stands.

20

Wins by AL Rookie of the Year Bob Grim of the Yankees, against only six losses.

29

NL-leading number of complete games by Robin Roberts of the Phillies. Roberts also led the NL in wins with twenty-three.

32

Double plays grounded into by Jackie Jensen of the Red Sox—a Major League record that was not topped until 1984, when Jim Rice of the Red Sox grounded into thirty-six double plays.

49

NL-leading number of home runs by Ted Kluszewski of the Reds, including thirty-four at home. Kluszewski also topped the NL in RBIS with 141. The sharp-eyed slugger struck out only thirty-five times all year.

58

Consecutive games on base by Duke Snider of the Dodgers. This modern-day NL record was matched by Barry Bonds in 2003. Snider tied for the NL lead in runs (120) and total bases (378) in 1954.

102

RBIS by Roy Sievers of the Washington Senators despite a batting average of only .232.

136

AL-leading number of walks received by Ted Williams of the Red Sox in only 117 games. Williams also led the league in on-base percentage (.513) and slugging average (.635).

716

Plate appearances by Wally Moon of the Cardinals—a record by an NL rookie that stood until 1984. Moon, the NL Rookie of the Year in 1954, scored 106 runs, collected 193 hits, and had a batting average of .304. He also hit a home run in his first Major League at bat on April 13.

1,715

Attendance on September 19 at the last home game of the Philadelphia Athletics, who lost 4–2 to the Yankees. After the 1954 season, the Athletics moved to Kansas City.

46,354

Attendance on April 15 at the first home game of the Baltimore Orioles, who beat the White Sox 3–1. After the 1953 season, the St. Louis Browns moved to Baltimore and became the Orioles.

Chapter 28. Jim Dyck

Greg Erion

AGE	G	AB	R	H	2B	3B	HR	TB	RBI	BB	SO	BAV	OBP	SLG	SB	GDP	HBP
32	2	1	0	1	0	0	0	1	1	1	0	1.000	1.000	1.000	0	0	0

Jim Dyck's Major League career was relatively short and undistinguished. It spanned six years, four of which involved stints in the Minors, only one season with more than 400 at bats and a mediocre .246 average. In his brief stint with the 1954 Indians, Dyck had only two plate appearances. Yet during his career Dyck helped set a Major League record, saved a no-hitter, played for a pennant winner—and became the answer to a baseball trivia question. Dyck also represents something that is largely lost to baseball: the career professional player. Dyck began playing ball in 1941 with the Norfolk Yankees of the Western League. His last game came with the Vancouver Mounties of the Pacific Coast League in 1961. Like so many young men of his generation, Dyck's career was interrupted by military service during World War II.[1]

Dyck, of German extraction, was born in Omaha, Nebraska, on February 3, 1922, the son of Cornelius (Connie) Dyck, a bank teller, and his wife, Mary Jane.[2] Jim was the second of three brothers. Jack, the oldest brother, died in a car accident at the age of eighteen. Art, the youngest, followed Jim into professional baseball.[3] When Jim was young, the family moved to Jefferson City, Missouri, where his father opened Dyck's Bowling Alley. The business complemented Connie's talent for bowling, a skill passed on to Jim and Art, who each came to be excellent bowlers.[4]

Both Jim and Art fared well in baseball and basketball during high school and junior college. While Jim was attending Jefferson City Junior College, his performance with the state amateur champion Jefferson City Red Birds attracted the attention of Major League scouts.[5]

Jim Dyck—Dyck, a reserve outfielder, spent most of 1954 playing in the Minors for Richmond. His one at bat in Cleveland was a hit and drove in a run.

In September 1940, after a New York Yankees tryout camp in Kansas City with over 300 hopefuls, Dyck was one of twelve offered a contract by Yankees scout Bill Essick, who negotiated with Dyck to pitch for Norfolk (Nebraska) in the Class D Western League the following April.[6] From there, it took Dyck ten years to make the Majors, his progress impeded by military service in World War II.

In 1941 Dyck put together a respectable 9-6 record at Norfolk and played a few games in the outfield. The next spring he reported to the Fond du Lac Panthers in the Class D Wisconsin State League. While the right-hander's pitching fell off, he showed talent with the bat; of the eighty games he played in, only twenty were as a pitcher and forty-two were at third base as he sported a non-pitcher-like .273 batting average.[7] That year Dyck also met his future wife. One evening a Panthers fan took her friend to a ballgame. After the game, the friend introduced Charlotte Jane Holmes to Dyck, and they hit it off immediately.[8]

Dyck might have continued to climb through the Yankees organization, but twenty-year-olds stood little chance of continuing to play baseball in the early 1940s. World War II was in full stride and Dyck, like hundreds of other ballplayers, was called into the service, joining the Navy Air Corps as did his brother Art.

Jim Dyck Jr. recalled that his father's baseball skills served him well in basic training: "One of his proudest moments was setting the record for the obstacle course. The first obstacle was a log that everyone crawled under. He told me he did a standup slide under the log and came up running. He never looked back and set the record." Dyck moved on to officer's candidate school, was commissioned an ensign, and was assigned to flight school. After winning his wings, he was assigned to the USS *Windham Bay*, a support carrier in the Pacific. Before shipping out, Dyck married Charlotte on October 25, 1944. Their marriage spanned fifty-four years and produced two children, a son, James Jr., and a daughter, Jamey.[9]

On the *Windham Bay*, Dyck flew new Corsair fighters to the larger battle carriers and returned with planes in need of repair. Dyck and his fellow *Windham Bay* pilots had the right to turn down any plane determined not to be flyable, a decision often based on less than precise information. These return flights were not always routine. Dyck recalled several instances when a fellow pilot took off never to be seen again.

Dyck's combat experience was limited to several isolated strafing runs on enemy-held islands. Like so many other servicemen, he shared little of his experiences. Observing how this ultimately affected his father's playing career, Jim Jr. said, "I always felt being in the service cost him those years in the Majors, and a pension as well. He ended up just a few months short of the necessary time to qualify but he was never bitter about that. He always took things in stride. He was just that kind of guy."[10]

Discharged after the 1945 season, Dyck was assigned in 1946 to Joplin in the Class C Western Association, where he hit .364 and earned a late-season promotion to Quincy of the Class B Three-I League. He was now a third baseman; pitching was no longer in his future. (The career of Jim's brother Art took the opposite path; in 1943 he played first base in Class D as a Yankees' farmhand, but when he returned to baseball after the war, it was as a pitcher. Art advanced as high as Triple-A Syracuse before his career ended after eight seasons in 1953.)

For Jim, progress was slow through the loaded Yankees organization. By 1947 he had played for Kansas City and Newark teams, New York's top farm teams, where his performance, while solid, was not outstanding enough to warrant promotion to the Majors. Dyck was with one of the most talent-competitive organizations in baseball.

On December 5, 1949, Dyck caught a break. He was acquired by the St. Louis Browns in the Minor League draft. Dyck had gone from one of the top organizations in the Majors to one of the poorest, but after two solid seasons with the Browns' San Antonio farm club in the Texas League, batting .321 in 1950 and hitting twenty-seven home runs in 1951, he made the Major Leagues.

Dyck often played ball during the winter. After the season, he and Charlotte traveled to Venezuela, where he began play in the Venezuela League and became caught up in a politically turbulent situation. The Venezuelan president was assassinated in Caracas, and within hours rumors swirled around the capital that foreigners staying at the Hotel Savoy were celebrating his death. A contingent of police swept down on the Savoy, gathered up fifteen players, herded them into trucks, and took them to the local police station. Along the way, as *The Sporting News* reported, they were, "punched, shoved, herded along with the flat side of a machete." The situation seemed ominous, as the police were armed with pistols, rifles, and machine guns. At the station, their identity as baseball players was verified, and they were returned to the hotel. Within days of the incident, most of the players left the country despite apologies from local government officials and "$500 to forget the incident."[11] Unlike most, Dyck let the incident pass. He explained, "They apologized for their mistake and I played in Caracas again. Can't beat the climate, the pay and there is no travel."[12]

Dyck started spring training with the Browns in 1951 but was sent back to the Missions. The team made it into the postseason playoffs. Dyck was a major offensive force, leading the league with 127 RBIS, and was named the league's Most Valuable Player.

Dyck got a call-up to the Browns after the season along with teammate Bob Turley, who had been named the league's Pitcher of the Year. They made their Major League debuts in the last week of the season as the Browns were wrapping up a last-place finish. Dyck played his first game on September 27, starting at third base against the Detroit Tigers in front of just 560 fans. He went 0 for 4. Altogether he played in four games, getting one hit in fifteen at bats. At the age of twenty-nine, Dyck had reached the big leagues.

Once again Dyck was invited to the Browns' spring training camp with an outside chance to make the team. While he had exhibited speed and hitting skill, there seemed to be a question about his fielding. His ability to make the team was enhanced when several outfielders, including Roy Sievers, were injured during exhibition games. Manager Rogers Hornsby shifted Dyck from third base to the outfield; he responded with timely hitting and ability in the field and made the Opening Day roster.

The Browns, long the doormat of the American League, were in dire financial straits at the time. Fewer than 300,000 fans had come to see them play in 1951. Thanks to owner Bill Veeck's numerous promotional efforts, attendance improved in 1952 but not to a financially sustainable level. This and a seventh-place finish led to another poor season for the Browns.

But Dyck had a decent rookie season. On May 2 he hit his first Major League home run, off Bill Henry of the Boston Red Sox. As the year progressed, Dyck was shifted to third, as others were found wanting at the position. His play improved to the point that new manager Marty Marion called him "a standout" who "gets better with every game."[13] In July and August he hit eight home runs, capped off by a two-homer game against Chicago on August 12. The first home run tied the game in the eighth; the second won it in the eleventh.

Continuing to do well, Dyck was honored with a "Jim Dyck Day" on September 14 at Sportsman's Park between games of a doubleheader with the Athletics. A contingent from Jefferson City, the state capital, including Missouri's lieutenant governor, was on hand and Dyck was presented a red Buick and fishing gear. The Browns were swept by Chicago.[14]

For the season Dyck hit .269. He was second on the team to Bob Nieman in home runs with fifteen, and his .450 slugging average placed him among the top fifteen in the American League. Dyck was named to *The Sporting News*'s 1952 Rookie All-Star Team alongside such other notables as Eddie Mathews, Hoyt Wilhelm, and Dick Groat.

The Browns were satisfied with Dyck's performance. Marion observed, "Dyck is one of those 'naturals' a baseball manager dreams about. He plays any position—and plays it well—and while he is not a bulldog type . . . Jim's aggressive in his own way."[15] Bill Veeck repeatedly described Dyck as one of his set players for the coming season. He backed up his praise with practical application. Dyck and seven other players were invited to Veeck's office during the off-season for "lunch," which turned into an impromptu contract-signing session, with Veeck, always the promoter, singing the praises of all concerned and arguing the Browns' chances for the coming year.[16]

Dyck went into the 1953 season with an upbeat attitude: "I've come to the conclusion that next year I should do all right. After listening to the wise boys explain that it's to a pitcher's advantage to learn the league and know the men he's facing, so that he can improve himself after, say, a year, I've decided that the same theory works in the case of the batters. What's wrong with a batter studying the opposing pitchers and getting to know them better, so that he learns their style and knows how to hit against them after that first year."[17] While he planned to fish during the off-season, he also looked beyond his playing days, opening a billiard parlor with his father in Jefferson City.[18]

All the encouraging off-season talk could not mask the inevitable truth: that Veeck was no longer able to sustain the Browns if they remained in St. Louis. Word spread that he was actively trying to shift the franchise to Milwaukee or Baltimore. Stymied by the intransigence of American League owners, Veeck was forced to sell out—but not without enduring a lame-duck season as a target of ire for outraged Browns fans.

The 1953 season also was a disaster for Dyck. He got off to a slow start, and by early May was hitting in the .140s with just one extra-base hit. On May 6 he was still mired in a slump when Marion gave lightly regarded reliever Bobo Holloman a start against the Philadelphia A's. Holloman had an 0-1 record with an 8.44 ERA, but he threw a no-hitter in his first Major League start, before 2,473 fans. While most of the defensive focus was on a nice fielding play by shortstop Billy Hunter in the eighth to snuff out a hit, Holloman didn't forget an earlier play made while the game was still scoreless. When he said, "I owe it all to God, Hunter, and Dyck," Holloman was referring to Dyck's "leaping, twisting catch" at the left-field wall in the second inning of a ball off the bat of Gus Zernial.[19] (About two months later, Holloman was out of the Majors, his no-hitter the only complete game he ever threw in the big leagues.)

Dyck's performance failed to improve appreciably. Marion thought his poor hitting might have been related to not having played winter ball. "Last year he came to us after playing winter ball and he was real sharp. Maybe that has been the difference in his play," the manager said.[20] By the end of May, Dyck had been replaced in the starting lineup and played sporadically thereafter. There was one highlight: On July 16, with only two home runs to his credit, Dyck came to bat against the Yankees at Sportsman's Park. Clint Courtney and Dick Kryhoski had just hit back-to-back home runs. Dyck hit a third. The three homers in succession tied a Major League record that was not broken until the Milwaukee Braves hit four in a row in 1961.[21]

One of Dyck's teammates that season was the storied Satchel Paige. Paige, as Dyck recalled after his career, marched to his own beat, having just a passing knowledge of his teammates. Dyck was out of the lineup the day after he had had a particularly good day at the plate and happened to sit next to Paige in the bullpen. Paige said to nobody in particular, "Why aren't they playing that boy who was in left yesterday?" Dyck responded. "Well, that was me." "Then you ought to be out there today," the blasé Paige advised.[22]

The Browns stumbled through the '53 season, at one point losing fourteen games in a row. With their crowds frequently under five thousand, it became apparent that they were not long for St. Louis. On September 27, the last day of the season, with the team down 2–1 to Chicago and with two outs in the bottom of the eleventh inning, Dyck came to bat and flied out to center field, thus becoming the last player ever to bat for the hapless team. As if to epitomize the futility of the franchise, the Browns had run out of baseballs during the game and had to use what was left of scuffed-up balls. The ball Dyck hit had a large cut in it from previous use. Fans who had booed the team all season long had to wait only two days to learn that the St. Louis Browns were no more. Under pressure from the rest of the league's owners, Veeck sold out to a group that got permission from the owners to move east and become the Baltimore Orioles.

If the Browns finished on a dismal note, so did Dyck. After he had exhibited such promise the year before, his average had fallen off to .213, with just nine home runs. Under new manager Jimmie Dykes in Baltimore, his position was tenuous. The manager seemed to give Dyck short shrift, saying that "out of Don Lenhardt, Jim Dyck, and Dick Kokos and about 20 youngsters we're bringing to camp [we] ought to come up with a good left fielder."[23] The year before, Dyck had been counted a mainstay. One of twelve outfielders on the Orioles' spring training roster, Dyck found himself in a highly competitive environment. And he was the oldest.

The 1954 season was just four days old when Dyck was traded to Cleveland for outfielder Bob Kennedy. While Indians manager Al Lopez indicated that he would use Dyck as insurance in the outfield and as a pinch hitter, the likes of Larry Doby, Al Smith, and others made him expendable, and he was sent to Richmond before getting into a game. Called up late in the season, Dyck pinch-hit twice, drawing a walk once and singling against the Detroit Tigers.

Oddly enough, Dyck's two appearances for Cleveland paid him more per at bat than any other appearance in his professional career. By the time of his recall, Cleveland had clinched the pennant. For having been on the Indians, even though briefly, Dyck was awarded $1,500 from the players' portion of the World Series revenue. For Dyck that translated to $750 per plate appearance with Cleveland.

As the 1955 season dawned, Dyck faced the same level of competition in the Cleveland outfield. He was again expendable, and was sold outright to the Indianapolis Indians of the American Association. Dyck proceeded to tear the league up in an effort to get back to the Majors. He was leading the league in hitting in early July, and Cleveland moved to recall him. The Indians were in the thick of another pennant race and needed pinch-hitting help. But Dyck found his path to Cleveland blocked by baseball bureaucracy. Commissioner Ford Frick voided the recall because a team could not sell a player's contract to a Minor League affiliate and buy him back until other teams had a chance to obtain him in the draft. He had originally been sold to Indianapolis because he had already been optioned the maximum three times. Dyck pleaded his case with Frick, arguing that he was being deprived of a pay raise and a possible share of World Series money. Frick told Dyck that rules were rules and had to be enforced.[24] Indians general manager Hank Greenberg, embarrassed by his miscue, promised Dyck that he would try to sell him to another Major League team. Greenberg made good on his promise and arranged Dyck's sale to his former team, now the Orioles. Dyck left the American Association with a .378 average—more than forty points higher than the eventual batting champ. (Dyck had only seventy-eight games and 317 plate appearances, not enough to qualify for the title.) The Orioles, in last place and in need of offensive help, immediately put him into the lineup.

Dyck picked up with the Orioles right where he left off with Indianapolis. He crafted a thirteen-game hitting streak, and by the end of July was hitting .359. Among the reasons for the resurgence, he credited playing just one position, outfield, and hitting to all fields, instead of trying to pull the ball in every at bat, his new approach becoming the proper one for the cavernous Memorial Stadium.[25] Eventually he cooled off and ended the season with a .279 batting average. On September 19 he hit a grand slam against the White Sox; it was the last home run of his Major League career.

Dyck led the Orioles in hitting during 1956 spring training, but he was one of many vying for a position on the team. At thirty-four, his age and lack of power worked against him. Manager Paul Richards, also the general manager, was on the lookout for young prospects and power hitters, and he saw Dyck as expendable. Dyck later said, "I could see the handwriting on the wall in Baltimore."[26]

Off to a slow start and playing sparingly during the first month of the season, Dyck was sold to the Cincinnati Redlegs. He welcomed the trade to a team that was contending for the pennant. "This club certainly has the potential to go all the way," Dyck wrote to the *Jefferson City Post-Tribune*. He said Redlegs manager Birdie Tebbetts had advised that Dyck would be his number one pinch hitter against left-handers. Optimistically, he said, "If I can adjust myself to coming off the bench cold and get a few base hits in the clutch . . . I may be here until I am 40."[27]

Not about to dent the starting outfield of Gus Bell, Wally Post, and Frank Robinson, Dyck had to adapt to being a bench player, a tough adjustment for one who had for the most part been a regular. It was an adjustment he could not make. After eleven at bats and just one hit, as well as being thrown out at home three times, Dyck was sent to the Nashville Vols (Southern Association) as partial payment for infielder Tommy Brown. His last game in the Majors came on July 22 as a pinch hitter against the Pittsburgh Pirates. He struck out.

Dyck played only one game for the Vols. As his reentry to the Majors in 1955 had been marred by a bureaucratic mishap, so was his exit. When Brown reported to the Redlegs with a sore arm, the deal was nullified. It took the Redlegs two weeks to sort out the resultant muddle, and they eventually sent Dyck to the Seattle Rainiers in the Pacific Coast League.[28]

Dyck spent the rest of his playing career in the PCL, either for the Rainiers or the Vancouver Mount-

ies. Jim Jr. recalled what his father said of those years: "My dad played because he loved the game. I don't think he ever really grew up. He always said he never worked, he was paid to play a kids' game. Back when he was playing, lots of players ended their careers playing in the PCL. They made good money in the PCL and the quality of the baseball was major league."[29]

Dyck's last season was with Vancouver in 1961. He was a player-coach under future Orioles manager Billy Hitchcock. At the age of thirty-nine, playing part-time, Dyck retired after the season. He had coaching offers, and the Dodgers organization considered him for the manager's position with Spokane, but he turned them all down and happily retired to the bowling business. As much as he enjoyed playing baseball, he shunned coaching, which he believed would require him to get into the political aspect of the game. Perhaps most important, he had two young children, James Jr. (born in 1953) and daughter Jamey (1954), and he felt that being absent on long road trips would not be conducive to their upbringing. For the Dycks it was the correct decision. His son recalled the many times he spent with his father bowling, fishing, or hunting, creating lifetime memories.[30]

While playing in the Pacific Coast League, Dyck had gained an appreciation for the Northwest. He and his brother Art decided to move to Cheney, Washington, where they opened a bowling alley. Eventually Jim Jr. joined the business. Dyck's running of Cheney Bowl was in keeping with his lifelong interest in bowling. As a young man he had won the Missouri all-state events when he was seventeen, and his skills never left him. In 1996 he was elected to the Spokane Bowling Hall of Fame.

On January 11, 1999, at the age of seventy-six, Dyck died of cancer. He was survived by his wife, Charlotte, and their two children.

Dyck was not a Major League star, but he loved and respected the game, and in twenty-one years he was never kicked out of a game for improper conduct. He served his country to the detriment of his playing career. And in a profession where ego often trumps personal obligations, Dyck placed family as the highest priority, leaving a legacy more powerful than any batting exploit.

Chapter 29. **Bob Chakales**

Bill Nowlin

AGE	W	L	PCT	ERA	G	GS	GF	CG	SHO	SV	IP	H	BB	SO	HBP	WP
26	2	0	1.000	0.87	3	0	0	0	0	0	10.1	4	12	3	0	0

Major League right-hander Bob Chakales was one of five sons born to Edward Peter and Blanche Wiggs Chakales (in order: Robert, Charles, Dwight, and twins John and James). Bob was born on August 10, 1927, in Asheville, North Carolina. His mother worked in retail, selling women's clothing, and his father—known as Eddie Pete—worked in a number of fields: in the restaurant business, selling shoes, and as a brakeman with the railroad. Times were tough in the Depression, and though both of Bob's parents had jobs in Asheville, when Bob was in the fifth grade the family moved to Dunn, North Carolina. That's where Eddie Pete had one of the first Krispy Kreme doughnut shops, the company having opened in North Carolina in 1937.

Two of Eddie Pete's older brothers were born in Greece, Bob said. Eddie Pete himself was born in Pittsburgh, where the family seems to have first settled after coming to the United States in 1902. Eddie Pete's father, Peter, worked in confectionery manufacturing.

Bob hadn't played any organized baseball in Asheville, but he played a lot of true sandlot ball. "We used to stitch corncob parts together to make balls," he said in a communication before his death in February 2010, adding that he also spent some time reading about Babe Ruth. (Not long before Ruth died, Bob was able to meet the Babe at a special event and shake his hand.)

Baseball became more interesting to Bob after the move. "When I moved to Dunn, I found that baseball was a big deal. I was talked into joining the Kneepants League [a competitor to Little League for children aged ten to twelve]." Bob told his son

Bob Chakales—Chakales won two games for the Indians in 1954, then was traded to Baltimore for Vic Wertz.

James that his interest grew when he saw his name posted on the stats sheet at the local barbershop. "Every week the baseball stats were prominently displayed for everyone to see. I was hitting so well I could get a free lollipop anytime I wanted." Clearly, this was a rewarding sport.[1]

Bob (or Chick as he was known in childhood) played as a third baseman in Dunn, and also played American Legion ball, again at third—the position where the team had the greatest need. Then, in the final game of the season, when the games had piled up and the team needed an extra pitcher, Bob's coach asked him to pitch. He did well, winning his first outing, and was told, "Next year, you're our pitcher." Before the next year rolled around, the Chakales family moved again—to Richmond, Virginia, where Eddie Pete opened a Greek restaurant. Before they left Dunn, Eddie Pete's leg was crushed when a co-worker on the railroad forgot to switch tracks properly. While laid up, he thought more about the war. Eddie Pete tried to enlist but the damaged leg kept him with 4-F status.

The family pronounces their last name "Shackles"—though the Greek pronunciation would be slightly different, more like SHACK-a-lees. Bob would occasionally boast lightheartedly, "First there was Hercules, then there was Socrates, but along came Chakales, the Greatest Greek of all!"[2]

The American Legion team at Dunn wanted Bob back so badly that the mayor himself, Herbert Taylor, called and offered him room and board to return for another season. Once Bob agreed to return to Dunn, the mayor drove to Richmond and chauffeured him in a new Chrysler Imperial, which at the time, the 1940s, was riding in style. Bob opened the American Legion season with victory in an eighteen-strikeout performance. He wound up pitching Dunn into the state finals. He was named outstanding pitcher of the tournament.[3]

It wasn't without the fright of his life, though, Bob told his son James. The mayor owned a funeral home and that's where Bob lodged. That was all well and good until a heavy downpour came. The funeral home had a tin roof and this was one of those storms "with raindrops so heavy you could weigh them." It was during World War II, and these heavy raindrops were pounding down on the roof so hard it sounded like bullets striking. He was upstairs and there were dead people laid out in the funeral home downstairs. Bob was so petrified he leapt out of bed, ran downstairs, and saw one of the newly dead pop up from a table (this can happen with a combination of rigor mortis and post-mortem contraction of tissue and tendons). Before

Bob knew it, he just ran out of the funeral home, without a clear destination—just running across town during the rainstorm. Bob added succinctly, "A funeral home is no place for a young person to spend their summer."

Baseball wasn't the only sport at which Bob excelled at the state level. James recalled, "Marble shooting was a big deal, especially in the South. I remember as a kid collecting marbles, and he would tell me, 'Let me show you how you shoot marbles.' Even then, he was thirty years older than me, he could lay a marble on the floor and he could fire a marble off his thumb and hit another marble every time." When Bob was a youth, he went all the way to the top, winning the North Carolina state marble-shooting contest. He might have gone further, but was too fearful of traveling out of state, so the runner-up was selected instead to represent North Carolina in later competitions.

While in Richmond, Bob met Granny Hamner, a fellow ballplayer his age and a future Philadelphia Phils Whiz Kid, who pushed for Bob to enroll at Benedictine High School, a small private Catholic boys' school with strong sports programs. The headmaster, Father Dan, drove south to Dunn to scout Bob and decided he would be a great addition to Benedictine. Bob became the quarterback on the football team and was named All-State in basketball and baseball. "We only had sixteen in my graduating class and we competed against all the major high schools," Bob said, "but we won a lot of state championships using kids from all four grade levels. Granny was a great friend and one heck of a ballplayer."

It was a real boon to the family that Hamner had "recruited" Bob. His tuition was gratis—and even though it was a military school, Bob was not required to wear the military uniform. The sports uniforms were sufficient. The school apparently drew quite well, having good athletes on its teams. "Father Dan used to always say, 'I am going to get my money out of you,'" which he did by assigning Bob menial tasks, and "when I was a senior he told me that he got all his money back."

A news report in the *Christian Science Monitor* in 1944 said that Robert Chakales had struck out ninety-nine batters in sixty-nine innings for Benedictine High "despite a sore arm."[4] The following spring the *Richmond News-Leader* reported that a vote of coaches had named Chakales, a guard, as captain of the all-military-academy basketball team in Virginia.[5] Bob was selected All-State in baseball, basketball, and football. On the ball field that spring, he won eight games in a row, including a no-hitter, and led all Richmond batters in hitting with a .523 average.[6]

Young Chakales was offered scholarships to a wide variety of colleges across the South, but before accepting any he responded to a telegram from the Philadelphia Phillies offering a tryout before general manager Herb Pennock at Shibe Park. He told Cleveland sportswriter Hal Lebovitz that Pennock had told him the Phillies would match any offer.

On June 4, 1945, an Associated Press dispatch reported that the Phillies had signed the seventeen-year-old to a contract with a reported $7,500 bonus and an additional $4,000 earmarked for his college education. There's a good family story behind the signing. Bob's son James told it the way he heard it:

Connie Mack had come to Richmond from Philadelphia, and was in my grandfather's home—my dad's home—getting ready to sign Dad to a contract. He offered him $4,000, which at that time was still a lot of money. The phone rings, and Branch Rickey was on the other end. My grandfather answers the phone and says, "Mr. Rickey, hi." [Rickey] said, "We want to offer Bob a contract to play professional baseball for the Dodgers." [Branch Rickey wanted Bob for his hitting ability.] And he goes, "Well, that's interesting. Connie Mack is here right now." Rickey replies, "He is? What's he offering?" The great Greek negotiator says, "He's offered five thousand." "Just

tell Bob to sign with us right now. $5,500." So my grandfather goes back and joins Connie Mack and my dad and says, "I've got Branch Rickey on the phone. He just offered $6,500 for Bob to sign with the Dodgers." And Connie Mack said, "Whoa. That's a lot of money. I don't think we can do that. I'll tell you what, just sign right here and we'll offer $7,000." My grandfather says, "Okay, let me tell Mr. Rickey." He goes, "Mr. Rickey. Connie Mack just said $8,000." They went back and forth raising the signing bonus to $11,000 from the Athletics until Connie Mack sees what happening and says, "We are out of this business— you can sign with the Dodgers," and walked out the door. Then Branch Rickey felt his limit was reached so he backed out.

Bob ended up signing with the Phillies through representative Jocko Collins. Bob did get the money he wanted: $11,500, which at that time made Bob a huge bonus baby.[7]

It was most fortuitous that Rickey chose to call while Mack was in the home, as Bob's value was established. Although the Phillies provided him with money for college education, he never did go to college. The college fund was, however, put to good use. The great Greek negotiator, Eddie Pete, used the $4,000 to pay off his mortgage. Bob told his dad he would earn that money back by playing ball. Instead of college, Bob went to the Phillies' Class A affiliate, the Utica Blue Sox. He lost his first three games, though one was a 2–0 home loss to the visiting Hartford Senators. The powers that be decided to have the seventeen-year-old get his feet wet one level lower on the ladder, and he went to Class B Wilmington, Delaware, where he pitched in the Interstate League for the Wilmington Blue Rocks. Bob posted a 13-5 record, despite a 5.06 earned run average, and was one of the best batters on the team, hitting .327. He was listed as six feet one and 185 pounds. Between his high school season and his first professional summer, Bob had thirty pitching decisions—a lot of pitching for someone who was still just seventeen years old.

Despite all the innings he accumulated, Chakales was booked for postseason baseball in October 1945, for the Richmond All-Stars against the touring Tommy Holmes Major League All-Stars team. His postseason didn't last long. World War II was just over, but there was still a need to cycle in new soldiers, while letting those who had served come home, and on November 9, 1945, Chakales passed his physical and was inducted into the army. Fort Lee in Virginia was glad to have a pitcher going for its team, even though in his first outing, on April 10, 1946, Bob showed the rust from inactivity as he was pounded in a 10–1 loss to the Wilkes-Barre Barons, described in the press as "an ex-servicemen's aggregation." By early August, though, the Fort Lee Travelers had established themselves as state semipro champions and flew to the national semipro tournaments in Wichita, Kansas. Chakales had been 7-3 with 119 strikeouts and was hitting well in the army, too—.340. He was elected to the All-America semipro team. Branch Rickey hadn't forgotten the young pitcher, but Philadelphia Phillies president Bob Carpenter declined a couple of offers Rickey made that December that were specifically aimed at acquiring Bob.

His service commitment complete, Chakales began pitching for Utica again in April 1947, first beating the Hartford Chiefs in May in the Connecticut state capital, 5–2. He shut out the Pioneers in Elmira, 1–0, with a three-hitter on June 3. Bob had mixed results throughout the season, but a highlight was a one-hitter he crafted against the Williamsport Tigers on September 5. Chakales later characterized the 1947 campaign to Hal Lebovitz: "Ah was as wild as a March Hare. Just wild. Ah don' know what made me wild. I won seven and lost five."[8] His ERA was again over five runs a game, 5.36, and he walked seventy-six batters in ninety-four innings.

Chakales tried out with the Phillies in Clearwater, Florida, during spring training in 1948, and was again assigned to begin the season pitching for

Utica, but he hurt his arm trying to work a curveball. "I was trying to snap a curve and I snapped my arm. My arm was really sore. I told them about it and they said, 'Keep throwing—it'll work out.' Instead it got sorer and sorer. I could hardly lift the ball."[9] The advice was not atypical for the day, and many pitchers found their careers cut short as a result. Chakales was 1-2 with Utica, but with a much-improved ERA of 3.71.

Once more, he was moved to a lower level and was sent to Maine, joining the New England League's Portland Pilots in early June. A three-hit 12–0 shutout of the Lynn Red Sox on June 15 was noted by the AP. *The Sporting News* reported on his winning both halves of a doubleheader against Manchester on August 27, the first a one-hitter and the second after coming on in relief.[10] For Portland he was 12-7 with a 3.16 ERA.

A scout working for the Cleveland Indians, Latimer "Laddie" Placek, saw Bob pitch a game for Utica that stuck in his memory. "I liked what I saw," Placek told the Tribe's front office (Laddie was their head scout in the state of Ohio). "He's fast, he's worth a gamble."[11] So the Indians pounced and took Chakales in the Minor League draft on December 10, 1948. Chakales was taken by Oklahoma City, part of the Cleveland system. (Phils owner Carpenter did get back $3,000 of his bonus money as a result.)

In 1949 Chakales played with the Single-A Wilkes-Barre Barons into May and was advanced via option to Oklahoma City of the Double-A Texas League on the 14th. Despite the move, Bob spent most of the season pitching for the Barons, right into the championship game against the Binghamton Triplets in the Governors Cup finals on September 25. He pitched one-hit relief in that game, but the damage had already been done, and Whitey Ford won it for the Triplets. It really hadn't been that successful a season for Chakales. For Wilkes-Barre he was 6-10 with a 5.25 ERA. He blamed it on the sore arm he'd developed in '48 and it left him with a poor disposition. He acted out. "Ah became a playboy," he said in the Southern drawl Hal Lebowitz attributed to him. "I learned how in the Army. I got out of shape." Placek wasn't pleased; he contacted Bob over the wintertime. "Laddie wrote about how he believed in me an' how I was lettin' him down. He wrote that he had more confidence in me than I had in myself."[12]

The arm got better, and perhaps Placek's letter supplied a little more motivation. Chakales became the main moundsman for the Barons in 1950 and threw the Eastern League title-clinching game on September 1 with a 4–2 win over Hartford. He was an all-star that year with a 16-5 record and a superb league-leading 2.04 ERA. Nine days later the Indians announced that they'd obtained him from their Wilkes-Barre affiliate. The Barons easily beat Binghamton, four games to one, for the Governors Cup. After the season, Chakales was named the top pitcher in the Eastern League.

Chakales reported to Tucson for spring training in 1951 with the Indians. Hal Lebovitz of the *Cleveland News* was much taken with the young ballplayer, calling him "a likable rookie with a friendly smile . . . as colorful as Dizzy Dean . . . something like a character in a Ring Lardner yarn." He brought 10 suits and 17 pairs of pants to camp, 25 shirts, and "at least 50 pair of socks." Asked why he was lugging around so much clothing with him, he drawled, "Man, I didn't come here just for a visit. I came here to stay."[13] He was touched up for a wind-blown double by Yankees rookie Mickey Mantle, in relief of Early Wynn during the exhibition season's first game, but he got his feet wet. At the end of March, manager Al Lopez said he felt the Tribe bullpen could make a difference in 1951 and cited Al Olsen, George Zuverink, and Bob Chakales as joining the veterans Steve Gromek, Sam Zoldak, and Jess Flores.

Chakales debuted in Cleveland on April 21, 1951, giving up one hit in one inning of work, the third pitcher in a lost cause as Ned Garver of the Browns beat the Indians, 9–1. His first start came on May 6, a 4–2 win over the visiting Washington Senators. He started off a little wild, granting six bases on balls in the first four frames, but settled down to win the game. On May 13 Bob was added to the starting rotation as a fifth or sixth starter. He contributed with the bat with what proved to be his only big league home run in a game against the White Sox that ended in a 4–4 tie when time ran out in the tenth inning, conforming to an agreement reached in advance that allowed the Indians to make their train. On Memorial Day Chakales had his first complete-game win, despite giving up nine hits and six walks; he'd parceled them out judiciously. He drove in two runs as the Tribe took the Tigers, 3–1. Chakales was a good batter; over his four seasons with the Indians, he hit .353 in thirty-four at bats. After his seven seasons of Major League ball, he held a .271 average.

Bob's best Major League pitching effort, a 2–0 four-hit shutout of Detroit, came on the same day that Bob Feller no-hit the Tigers in the first game of a doubleheader. Bob laughed as he told his son James that when he did something that was headline worthy, Feller threw a no-hitter on the same day. The Tigers got some revenge five days later against the Tribe, rolling up thirteen runs (more than they'd scored in their first eleven games of the season when facing the Indians), including six hits and four runs off Chakales in relief of losing pitcher Bob Lemon.

Chakales's last start of 1951 came on August 22, when he "blew up completely" in the seventh, allowing three more runs to the Senators, and left the game down 5–2; the Indians won it in fourteen, 6–5. Had they made the World Series, he would have been on the eligible list, but the Indians finished second; after the season, Chakales earned a full share of the second-place money. His name came up in trade talks over the winter—catcher Birdie Tebbetts raved about him—but on February 2 GM Hank Greenberg announced that Chakales and Lou Brissie had re-signed, both with increased pay. Greenberg had earlier assured Chakales that he would not be traded and would work every fifth day in the Tribe's rotation. That still didn't prevent the Indians from trying (in vain) to spring Sam Mele free from the Senators by dangling Chakales and Bob Kennedy in front of Washington in early March. A month later the Senators came back offering lefty Mickey Harris for Chakales. No go. Meanwhile Bob was working as the player-coach of the Dixie Containers basketball team in Richmond.

In spring training of '52, Chakales told the *Sporting News* correspondent in Tucson that by his own assessment he had improved 15 percent over the year before! He explained, "I did it with my mind." Chakales went on to say that manager Al Lopez had told him he needed to work on his curveball if he wanted to guarantee his future with the Indians. He asked Tebbetts how to better his curveball, and Birdie answered with one word: "Think." So, Bob said, "I'd lie in bed at night and just think about my curve. The trouble was I'd let it go too close to my chest. I kept thinking about releasing the ball at arm's length and when I came out here for training I threw the curve just the way I thought about it." Birdie had inspired success via visualization.[14]

Chakales had just one start for the Indians in 1952, winning the next-to-last game of the season. He spent most of the year in Indianapolis, playing for the Indians' Triple-A club. The only drawback, he said, was that he'd planned to get married in Richmond on one of the Indians' trips to Washington to take on the Senators. Now it was going to cost him extra to travel from Indianapolis to Richmond to keep the appointment. The marriage to Anne Mackenzie came off, on June 7, though manager Gene Desautels hit Chakales with a fine for reporting back late.[15] Chakales labored with a 5.12 ERA in Indianapolis. He was recalled nonetheless on September 2. His first game back was the following day, and he loaded the bases in the sixth. Lou Brissie relieved him, and Brissie's first pitch was hit for a grand slam by Detroit's Don Kolloway. In a season wrap-up, sportswriter Ed McAuley comment-

ed from Cleveland that Chakales was the youngster most likely to succeed in 1953. The Indians did broach a trade with Boston, a massive one involving Dale Mitchell, Ray Boone, Bobby Avila, and Chakales to the Red Sox for Dick Gernert, Dom DiMaggio, and Billy Goodman, but Red Sox general manager Joe Cronin replied, "I wouldn't give Billy Goodman for the entire Cleveland team."[16]

In 1953 Bob opened the season with the big league ball club and played most of the year with the Indians, though appearing in only seven games before he was optioned to Indianapolis on July 23, his record with Cleveland being 0-2 with a 2.67 ERA in twenty-seven innings of work. He got into only eleven games with Indianapolis and was 4-2 with a 3.91 ERA. He was recalled on September 9 but saw no further action. That winter he pitched for Gavilanes in the Venezuelan League.

The 1954 spring training season started off a little rocky, and in the second game of the exhibition season, Chakales saw his infielders commit errors on four consecutive balls. He summoned them to the mound, and then tried to lighten the mood by asking if the fix was in. The Indians won the game, 23–10, over the Giants.[17] However, Bob was ready for the season. He opened the 1954 campaign in Cleveland, where he helped the Indians off to the best season in baseball history (111 victories in a 154-game season). He picked up his first decision of '54 for the Indians on May 16, winning the first game of a doubleheader over the Athletics. He won again on May 18, beating the Red Sox.

Bob's 2-0 record and ERA of 0.87 made him more marketable. The Indians went to the World Series in 1954, but without Chakales. On June 1 Cleveland traded their twenty-seven-year-old pitcher to the Baltimore Orioles for Vic Wertz, in a deal that has been considered the blockbuster trade of 1954.[18] He left a first-place team for a team in last place at the time of the trade. Wertz reportedly had a strong dislike for batting in Baltimore, which pushed the Orioles into seeking a trade. Looking back on things, it seems like an uneven swap, but Chakales was considered an ambitious young pitcher with great potential. Orioles general manager Art Ehlers believed that he could become a regular in the starting rotation. He had not been able to get enough work with the Indians. They had too good a team. With such a superior staff (Wynn, Lemon, Garcia, Houtteman, and Feller), Chakales just wasn't going to have enough opportunity to break into Cleveland's rotation. He felt a little regret fifty years after the fact: "I was never as sharp and I could be, since pitchers went the distance back then. When I pitched a lot, I was good; when I didn't, I was not. I think I got out of shape for a while, too, just waiting for 'the call.'"[19] Indians manager Al Lopez knew how hard it had been for Chakales to crack the rotation; the 1951 and 1952 teams had three 20-game winners on the staff. "With any other major-league team, he would be a starting pitcher," Lopez allowed.[20]

Given a start for the Orioles on June 4, Chakales lasted but two and two-thirds innings, giving up four earned runs and losing to Philadelphia. He started six games for the Orioles and relieved in thirty-two others—winning in back-to-back extra-inning relief jobs on June 26 and 27. There was an odd occurrence in Detroit on July 11. Al Aber of the Tigers had a perfect game going and had set down seventeen Orioles until Chakales singled in the sixth. When Cal Abrams followed with a double, Bob had scored—until he was ruled out for failing to touch second base in his haste. Inning over. The final was 2–1, Tigers.

On August 6, Chakales first really met Ted Williams. It was in Baltimore's Memorial Stadium and the score was tied in the top of the tenth. With two outs, Ted came to the plate. Bob's son James recounted the story his father told him:

Ted was on a hot streak but Bob had gotten him out earlier. The manager called time and asked Bob if he wanted to walk Ted; of course he said no. Bob had Ted 0-2 in the count with two fast-balls. He threw a low inside slider as a waste pitch and Ted got under it and popped it up. Bob was walking off the mound and glanced back to see the right fielder drifting to the foul pole. The lazy pop-up went over the fence just out of the reach of the right fielder's glove. Bob was so mad he chased Ted Williams around the bases calling him every name and expletive that came to mind—the one that could be printed was: "You lousy, cheap-shot artist, you lucky bum, you will never get another hit off me." Later [when he was traded to the Red Sox] he asked Ted if he was mad at him for chasing him around the bases and for what he said. Ted just gave that smirky smile of his and said he had forgotten all about it.[21]

With Baltimore, Bob was 3-7 in 1954, though his 3.73 ERA was slightly better than the team average.

On December 6, Chakales was packaged in a seven-player trade. He went from the Orioles to the Chicago White Sox with infielder Jim Brideweser and catcher Clint Courtney for pitchers Don Ferrarese and Don Johnson, catcher Matt Batts, and infielder Fred Marsh.

Chakales got very little work in the first part of 1955, and then he and Courtney packed their bags once more—on June 7 they were again traded as part of a threesome, this time joining outfielder Johnny Groth, all three packed off to Washington for one man, outfielder Jim Busby. In his short time with the White Sox, Bob had thrown twelve and one-third innings and given up eleven hits and six walks, but only two runs (1.46 ERA). After announcing the swap, Chicago general manager Frank "Trader" Lane enigmatically characterized Chakales as a "pitcher of parts."[22] It was a big gamble for Lane. Busby was hitting but .230 at the time, though his outfield defense was cited. He hit .243 the rest of the year. For Chakales it was another trip down the standings. The White Sox spent some time in first place that summer, and the Senators spent time in the cellar. Chakales was hit hard on the left knee by an Enos Slaughter liner in mid-July but picked up his first win of the season, and was back in action a week later.

Washington manager Chuck Dressen made Bob his main man for relief, but he struggled. Over the wintertime, Bob explained to *Washington Post* writer Bob Addie that he'd felt tired throughout the summer of 1955. "My arm was dead," he said, "and I felt as if I was a sleepwalker most of the time." A thorough physical included a fluoroscope examination that revealed the cause. "I was oozing poison from my appendix. They cut it out and I began to feel like living again. I did a lot of throwing this winter to test the arm and it feels great."[23]

Addie's interview with Chakales wasn't the only news the pitcher generated during 1956 Grapefruit League play in Orlando. A later column explained how Bob was driving an electric golf cart on the Dubsdread Country Club course when, negotiating a narrow wooden bridge near the eighth hole, the cart tipped over and dumped fellow right-hander Hal Griggs in the drink.[24] Bob had fully recovered from the appendectomy but pulled a muscle in the springtime; nonetheless, he started the season well. Throwing an unanticipated seven and two-thirds innings of scoreless three-hit relief against his old Washington teammates on May 3 earned Bob his second win of the season, just four days after five and one-third innings of one-hit relief against his former Orioles mates gave him his first victory, on April 29. He was, at age twenty-eight, the old man on the Senators' staff.

On May 8, Chakales stumbled, giving up five earned runs while recording only one out, but on the 11th there was another lengthy relief stint—six innings of two-hit ball against the Red Sox. His longest effort was ten innings of five-hit relief in a seventeen-inning loss to Kansas City on May 23, but Bob was long gone from the game before the denouement. By early June he was considered the "surprise performer" with a 1.97 ERA through his first sixteen outings. He pulled a tendon in his

elbow, however, and suffered a sore arm for much of the year. He soldiered through the season, however, appearing in a club-high forty-three games.

Asked about what seemed to be an unusually high number of sore arms reported in the press, Chakales forthrightly admitted in 2009 that some of them may have been a little manufactured for popular consumption via the newspapers:

> My junior year in high school, I probably overpitched. Pitched a lot. I had one sore arm in the minor leagues, and had a couple after leaving the Indians. I didn't have many sore arms in the big leagues. Let me tell you, I told a lot of people I had a sore arm when I was with Cleveland because I was young and embarrassed I wasn't playing. I thought I should have been playing; I had to have a reason. I wasn't going to tell them I wasn't good enough, or whatever. I wasn't going to say anything bad about the management. I just said my arm was sore.

These were still the days when there was always someone ready to take your place.

During the off-season Bob opened his own restaurant in Richmond, called Blair's. It was his second venture in the field, having owned and operated one on Maryland's Eastern Shore in the winter of 1955. Another job he had done fairly early was—as he put it—to take an ax and "cut trees down in front of billboards. I thought it was the best way to work on my swing and keep my strength." The work was for Ted Turner's young company, Turner Outdoor Advertising. He also sold automobiles, as did a lot of ballplayers.

President Dwight D. Eisenhower threw out the ceremonial first pitch of the 1957 season, and Chakales took over from there, pitching on Opening Day against Baltimore. He threw seven innings and gave up four runs, but left with the lead. He himself had driven in the fourth and fifth Senators runs with a two-out triple in the bottom of the fourth. The O's beat the Senators' Camilo Pascual in the eleventh inning, and to his credit, Ike stayed for the whole game. Chakales didn't quite last the month, though. On April 29 the Senators sent him and pitcher Dean Stone to the Red Sox for infielder Milt Bolling, pitcher Russ Kemmerer, and outfielder Faye Throneberry.

Red Sox pitching coach Boo Ferriss was high on Chakales. "We were fortunate to add a pitcher of Chakales' experience," he told Ed Rumill of the *Christian Science Monitor.*

> He has the stuff and he has a book on the hitters. He has that valuable know-how. He knows what he's doing out there. The only real bad pitch on his record is that three-run homer by Frank House in the second game at Detroit last week. But I'll tell you something about that pitch. It was a waste ball. The count was nothing and two and Bob threw one too high for a strike. House's strength is a pitch at waist height or lower. But this time, for some reason, he went after the high pitch and hit it into the seats. It will probably never happen again.[25]

Bob got to see part of Ted Williams's amazing .388 season, in the year Ted turned thirty-nine, but not the whole of it. On August 1 the Red Sox purchased 16-7 Murray Wall from Dallas and optioned Chakales to their San Francisco Seals farm club. There was one odd incident in Sacramento, when the umpire ordered Bob to change his pants during a game. It was in the midst of a three-hit shutout he was administering to the Solons, and the Sacramento manager complained that Bob kept "going to his pants" as though there were a foreign substance there that he was using to benefit his pitching; Bob was deemed clean and finished the shutout. After the Coast League season ended, he was brought back to Boston, where he appeared in one final game, on September 17. Ted Williams pinch-hit a game-tying homer in the bottom of the eighth, Billy Klaus drove in the go-ahead run, and Chakales earned the save with a 1-2-3 top of the ninth. In what

proved to be his final Major League appearance, Bob actually took Ted Williams's place. Pinch-hitter Ted had homered (the 452nd of his career) deep into Fenway's right-field seats, tying the game, and Chakales took his place in the batting order, throwing the ninth inning and setting down the three men he faced. During Bob's year at Boston, he and Williams became close. Bob often stayed in the hotel room registered for Williams to shield Ted from the media. They continued to see each other after they retired from baseball. During five straight years in the 1970s, Bob and Ted met during the Preakness horse race in Baltimore. At his death Bob still had a book Ted gave him, *The Art of Pitching,* with an inscription from Ted: "Bob, I always loved it when you were pitching . . . because I knew I'd get a hit, your friend Ted." Bob often teased Ted about leaving the bases loaded twice against him. Before memorabilia was big, Ted signed his official Genuine Louisville Slugger with his name engraved and gave it to Bob. Not knowing the value of the bat, his son James broke the gift from Ted in a sandlot game. "All Dad said was, 'I wish you did not do that, Ted gave me that bat.' Nothing else was said again."

On January 14, 1958, the Red Sox announced the outright sale of Chakales to Minneapolis, which had replaced San Francisco as Boston's top farm club. After he gave up thirteen earned runs in seventeen innings, laboring under illness, Minneapolis had seen enough and sent Chakales away—but for Bob it was a bit of a treat to find himself sent to his hometown team, the Richmond Virginians, part of the Yankees' system, managed by Eddie Lopat. On June 8 just one Sandy Amoros single in the second inning deprived him of a no-hitter against Montreal, one of four shutouts by Bob during the season. He still hoped to return to the Majors, and Lopat said there were several teams that could well use him. Chakales was only thirty, and he declared, "Lopat has taught me more about pitching than I ever knew." He was telling Chakales to be more aggressive in the strike zone and not give the hitters a chance to relax. Though he said he felt the best he'd felt in three seasons, he served out the full year in the Minor Leagues.

That December, Richmond sold Chakales to the Toronto Maple Leafs. He became involved in strike talk, as one of two player representatives for the International League. With seven seasons of Major League experience, he was selected to represent the IL players, who were angling for the implementation of a pension plan, and the 160 members of the International League Baseball Players' Association were being urged to neither sign their 1959 contracts nor report to spring training unless the owners agreed to submit the proposal to arbitration or at least discuss it. Chakales was outspoken on the subject: "They say minor-league ball is deteriorating and no wonder. There is a great deal of discontentment in the league. All the players live for is the first and 15th of the month to collect their pay checks. Most of them don't earn enough to support their families and are looking for outside jobs to supplement their income. Added to that, they have no security."

They were looking to create a pension that would entitle the players to collect fifty-nine dollars per month in their old age. "I thought I could benefit as well," he said in 2009. "I went to New York with a lot of confidence and left knowing that Major League Baseball was a huge powerful organization and the Minor Leaguers had no chance. Too much money, power, and influence." Asked if it might have hurt him to have been a leader, he felt it might have. "There was not a strike, but I left work to negotiate. In effect, I was the only one who went on strike. I still had a lot of good pitching ahead of me, but could not make it up again. I can't say it hurt me; although I felt I was still better than some of the guys who were still pitching." With sixteen seasons of professional baseball under his belt, and the one year—1946—he spent in the army, Chakales admitted to being a little steamed. "I was mad then, but got over it after a while. I loved the sport and

felt I never got to show I would have been a twenty-year player."

Chakales's opportunities may have been limited, but he wasn't blackballed from baseball entirely, and he got in a fairly full season for the unaffiliated Toronto Maple Leafs in 1959 (13-10, 4.04). The Indians took on Toronto as their Triple-A affiliate in 1960, and Bob was back in the Cleveland system, going 9-3 (3.74). In 1961 he split the season, 3-1 for Toronto and then 4-3 for the Hawaii Islanders (in the Pacific Coast League, affiliated with the Kansas City Athletics). The 1961 season was his last in professional baseball. His last time pitching against Major Leaguers was in an exhibition game in Toronto on July 14, 1961, when he pitched a 3-0 three-hit shutout against the California Angels.

In the Minor Leagues, Chakales was 113-73 with a 4.11 ERA. As in the Major Leagues, he'd been used more as a reliever than a starter, with 162 of his 295 appearances coming in relief roles, but most often in long relief (over his Minor League career, combining starts and relief roles, he averaged an impressive five-plus innings a game). In the Majors, Bob was 15-25 (4.54 ERA), starting 23 of his 171 games and averaging just a little over two and one-third innings per appearance.

After baseball, Chakales sold insurance for Markel Insurance, a local agency in Richmond. The Markels, he said, were great sportsmen and very good businessmen. At the time he retired from playing ball, they owned part of the Richmond Virginians. Bob loved golf and thought about going pro, "but my 1 handicap was nothing compared to those greats. I was in the beer league and they were playing for champagne."

One of his uncles, Broaddus Wiggs, told him about a new golf course concept called Lighted Night Golf—par 3. They contacted the United States Golf Association, found out how to register as a contractor, and built a par-3 course in Richmond. A general contractor from Charlotte, Ray Costin, heard about the course and reached out to Chakales. The two formed a partnership and began to build par-3 courses. Then requests came for Bob to build championship courses; he started with a nine-hole championship course and then went on to build course after course, in the end building nearly two hundred golf courses and becoming president of the Golf Course Builders Association of America. Chakales built the original TPC Sawgrass Course in Ponte Vedra Beach, Florida. Presumably, he designed wider bridges over water hazards than the one he'd failed to successfully negotiate in Orlando in the spring of 1956!

Golf-course construction was a busy life, with a lot of travel. "I was gone more than I wanted to be. I was good at what I did, but fearful I would not get that next job—so fortunately I had many offers so I kept my plate full." Like many busy men, Chakales had some regrets at missing a few too many family events, but he considered himself blessed to have "five wonderful children (Sandra, Robert, James, Dabney, and Susan) and a patient and loving wife who is still as beautiful as the day I met her."

Three of Bob and Anne's five children continued with athletics after high school. Bob Jr. swam at the University of Alabama with Olympic Silver Medalist Jack Babashoff; Dabney played tennis and basketball at Meredith College; and James played baseball for Bobby Richardson at the University of South Carolina. James came close to playing professional ball as well. Bob recalled that Boston Red Sox scout Mace Brown was one of the scouts who wanted to sign James out of high school (he witnessed James throw a twelve-inning, one-hit, twenty-strikeout performance in the American Legion state championships), but Bob said, "No. James is going to college—something I did not do." James went on to throw a couple of no-hitters in American Legion ball and then played with Mookie Wilson and other All-Americans on teams that made it to the College World Series final game twice (1975 and 1977).

Bob Chakales died on February 18, 2010, in Richmond. He was eighty-two years old. He is buried in Westhampton Memorial Park in Richmond.

Chapter 30. Timeline, June 16–June 30

Joseph Wancho

June 16—Cleveland—INDIANS GET 3 IN 7TH; JOLT SENATORS, 5–1—Rudy Regalado goes 3 for 4 and drives in two runs. Bobby Avila collects two RBIS. Don Mossi strikes out eight in a rare start and earns the decision.

June 17—Cleveland—NEED ONLY 5 HITS TO SINK NATS—Dave Philley knocks in two runs on two sacrifice flies. Wally Westlake knocks in two runs. Early Wynn fans seven for his eighth victory.

June 18—Cleveland—GARCIA RUNS TRIBE STREAK TO NINE, 2–0—Mike Garcia strikes out seven to blank the Bosox. Larry Doby goes 2 for 4 with an RBI and a run scored. Cleveland sits four games up on New York and Chicago.

June 19—Cleveland—RED SOX HALT TRIBE AT 9 IN ROW, 6–3—Cleveland's winning streak is snapped at nine games. Sammy White goes 2 for 3 with two RBIS. Jackie Jensen goes 3-4, scores twice, and slugs a solo shot. Ellis Kinder gets the win.

June 20—Cleveland—INDIANS SWEEP, 3–1, 9–2; LEAD BY FOUR—Al Smith homers in the game. Rudy Regalado and Dave Philley each bat in a run. Bob Feller goes the distance in the opener. Larry Doby and AL Smith each club three-run home runs in the nightcap to pace the Tribe to a DH sweep of the Red Sox. Houtteman posts zero K's in his seventh win.

June 22—Cleveland—A's DEFEAT INDIANS, 4–1; NO. 1 FOR SIMA—Al Sima backs his first win with two RBIS and gives up one unearned run. Joe Astroth goes 2 for 3, with an RBI.

June 23—Cleveland—INDIANS BLAST 3 HOME RUNS; BEAT A's, 5 TO 2—Al Rosen and Larry Doby each smack two-run homers. Bob Lemon backs his ninth win with a solo shot.

June 24—Cleveland—A's AND PORTOCARRARO BEAT CLEVELAND, 5–1—Lou Limmer and Joe DeMaestri each homer to pace the Athletics' attack. Arnie Portocarraro whiffs six.

June 25—Cleveland—49,808 GROAN IN NEW YORK'S 7-RUN THIRD—Joe Collins goes 3 for 5, with four RBIS and a homer. Gene Woodling goes 3 for 4 and drives in three runs. Allie Reynolds whiffs eight to raise his record to 9-1. He blanks the Tribe, 11–0.

June 26—Cleveland—YANKS WHIP INDIANS IN SLUGFEST, 11–9—Gil McDougald homers and Mickey Mantle homers and doubles to pace the Yankee attack. Bobby Avila hits two home runs for the Indians. Al Smith and Jim Hegan also homer. The Yankees pull within two games of Cleveland, with Chisox one game back.

June 27—Cleveland—NEWHOUSER HALTS YANKS AS INDIANS HIKE LEAD, 4–3—Wally Westlake goes 2 for 3 with two RBIS and a homer. Dave Philley also homers. The Indians salvage one win from the series. The three-game series against New York draws 143,782 fans to Cleveland Stadium.

June 29—Baltimore—HOUTTEMAN VICTORY, 5–1—Every player in the starting lineup for Cleveland gets a hit. Avila knocks in two runs. George Strickland homers. Cleveland snaps Baltimore's

five-game winning streak. Art Houtteman notches his eighth win.

June 30—Baltimore—GARCIA BEATS ORIOLES
FOR 10TH VICTORY—Mike Garcia shuts out the
Orioles 2–0, scattering four hits. Larry Doby hits
a solo home run in the third inning.

Chapter 31. **Al Rosen**

Ralph Berger

AGE	G	AB	R	H	2B	3B	HR	TB	RBI	BB	SO	BAV	OBP	SLG	SB	GDP	HBP
30	137	466	76	140	20	2	24	236	102	85	43	.300	.404	.506	6	14	3

As Rose Rosen watched her son Al play with other kids, she frequently held her breath as Al coughed and painfully inhaled as if each gulp of air was his last. This asthmatic youngster did not seem destined to become a Major League baseball player. Rather, it looked as if he would end up in some office as a clerk or administrator. But he was resolutely determined to be a great athlete. Rosen did not only succeed as a ballplayer, but he was also a fine boxer and became an excellent Major League executive.

Rosen once talked of his encounter with Elmer Yoter, a Minor League manager. Yoter told Rosen to go get a lunch pail or he would never make it. Yet toughness and determination were hallmarks of Al Rosen's character and allowed him to succeed beyond anyone's expectations.

Born Albert Leonard Rosen, in Spartanburg, South Carolina, on February 29, 1924, he was the son of Louis and Rose Rosen. As described by his mother, Al's father was a "handsome ne'er do well" who ended up deserting the family after only a few years of marriage. Due to Al's asthma, the family moved to Miami when Al was only eighteen months old, providing a climate that Rose Rosen said was healthier for him. Rose worked as a salesperson in a dress shop while Al's Polish-born grandmother, Gertrude Levine, looked after his brother Jerry and him. Encouraged to try sports, Al soon showed he had good athletic ability. As he grew up, his asthma disappeared.

The neighborhood where Rosen lived in Miami was a hardscrabble one. It was in the southwest part of the city known as Little Havana. The Rosen clan was the only Jewish family in his neighborhood, and

Al spent his childhood engaged in many fights due to his ethnic origins. Toughness became his mantra as he grew up.

Rosen's Jewish background also led to some skepticism about his athletic abilities. Rosen once said his high school football coach asked him why he was going out for football when he was Jewish. He later said he was determined that every Jew in America would be proud of him because of his achievements.

On one occasion, columnist and TV host Ed Sullivan wrote that Rosen was a Catholic because he always marked a cross on home plate each time he came to bat. Rosen responded that "it was not a cross but an x" and that he wished his name was "more Jewish" so no one would mistake him for being Catholic.

Rosen, an accomplished boxer, took no guff from anyone on the playing field, and players avoided most confrontations with him. One time, someone on the Chicago White Sox called Rosen a Jew bastard. Rosen walked over to the Chisox dugout and calmly asked whoever called him that name to step forward. No one accepted his invitation.

Rosen normally went by the nickname Flip, which some said was gained as a loose-wristed softball pitcher while a teenager. Others say it was the way that athletic Rosen passed a basketball.

In high school, Rosen became an outstanding baseball player. He looked up to Lou Gehrig and Hank Greenberg, who also was Jewish, as his favorite players. Rosen briefly attended the University of Florida in 1941 and 1942 before opting to leave school to try professional baseball. He was signed to the Thomasville, North Carolina, team in the North Carolina State League, the lowest level in

Al Rosen—The League and *Sporting News* MVP in 1953, Rosen was a fan favorite and one of Cleveland's all-time best run producers. Here, he connects on one of his two home runs in the 1954 All-Star Game as Brooklyn's Roy Campanella looks on. Note Rosen's broken right index finger, indicated by the arrow. (The Cleveland Press Collection, Cleveland State University Library)

the Minors, and earned ninety dollars a month before World War II intervened. Al joined the navy in 1942 and saw action in the South Pacific. He navigated an assault boat in the initial landing on Okinawa in the bitter battle for the island. In 1946 he left the navy as a lieutenant and returned to his emerging baseball career.

Al began in earnest to continue his quest to make it to the Majors. Because the Thomasville club was under contract to the Indians, Rosen remained property of the team. He was assigned by the Indians in 1946 to play for the Pittsfield Electrics in Pittsfield, Massachusetts, a team in the Canadian-American League. He batted .323 with fifteen homers and eighty-six runs batted in and was voted the league's outstanding rookie. He gained a new nickname, the "Hebrew Hammer," for his fine Minor League hitting.

In 1947 Rosen moved to the Oklahoma City Indians of the competitive Texas League. There he set the league on fire by batting .349, with 186 hits, 141

runs batted in, and a slugging percentage of .619. Rosen was voted the league's Most Valuable Player and had what was considered one of the finest seasons in Texas League history.

Rosen, a third baseman, was competing for a position against the aging but still-formidable Ken Keltner, who had won the hearts of the Indian fans with his sterling play and for his defensive gems that helped stop the fifty-six-game hitting streak of Joe DiMaggio in 1941. Keltner held on to third base and Rosen was sent down to the Kansas City Blues, a Triple-A team in the American Association.

On July 26 and 27, 1948, Rosen clouted five consecutive homers for Kansas City. Batting .327 that year, Rosen was voted the league's Rookie of the Year. At the end of the 1948 season, Rosen was recalled to the Indians and served as a pinch hitter for the American League champions in the World Series, going 0 for 1 against the Boston Braves.

In 1949 Rosen played twenty-three games for the Indians but spent most of the year with the San

Diego Padres of the Pacific Coast League. Rosen played there with several future Major Leaguers, including Minnie Minoso and Luke Easter.

In 1950 Ken Keltner was finally slowed by age and relinquished the third base position to Rosen. Cleveland fans, who still adored Keltner, at first were skeptical of the change. But Rosen rose to the challenge and set a rookie record at the time by blasting 37 homers to take the AL home run title. Rosen also led the league in assists with 322. Batting .287, Rosen walked 100 times, drove in 116 runs, and scored 100 runs with an on-base percentage of .405.

Rosen's assault on American League pitching tailed off in 1951. Playing in all 154 games, he tied a Major League record by slugging four grand slams. But his average slipped to .265, and he belted only 24 home runs, although still managing to drive in 102 runs.

Unhappy with his 1951 performance, Rosen took a long vacation to South America and then returned to prepare his mind and body for the 1952 season. He worked on getting his legs in shape. He had played golf in previous years, but this year he instead worked out at the Miami Minor League ballpark to stay in condition. He was told by another well-known athlete, golfer Sammy Snead, that it was best to give up golf to be a better baseball player.

In 1952 Rosen improved his performance. He scored 101 runs, had 171 hits, and drove in 105 runs with a .302 batting average. This was a glimmer of what he would accomplish in 1953.

Nineteen fifty-three was Rosen's banner year. Sparked by a lusty .336 average, Rosen barely missed out on the Triple Crown. On his last at bat, he apparently had beaten out a ball hit to third base that would have given him the Triple Crown. Umpire Hank Soar felt otherwise and called Rosen out. After the game, Soar was questioned about the call. "He missed the bag," Soar said. Rosen agreed he would have been safe had he not missed the bag. Thus Mickey Vernon, who batted .337 with Washington, won the AL batting championship. Rosen

slugged 43 homers and drove in 145 runs and had to settle for those titles.

Rosen's was unanimously voted the American League's Most Valuable Player in 1953, the first player since Hank Greenberg in 1935 to receive all first-place MVP votes. As Milton Gross of the *New York Post* put it, "Against the backdrop of provincialism usually shown in this voting, the landslide not only is unprecedented, but the most sincere sort of testimonial to the prematurely graying twenty-eight year old after only four [full] seasons of big league baseball."

Injuries began to hamper Rosen during the 1954 season, limiting him to only 137 games. Rosen still managed to hit .300, slam 24 homers and drive in 102 runs, the fifth consecutive year Rosen had driven in at least 100 runs. More troubling, Cleveland fans started to get on him. However, Rosen did win the MVP award in the All-Star game that year after hitting consecutive home runs in the exhibition. More meaningfully, his Indians team won the 1954 AL pennant with a then record 111 victories before falling to the New York Giants in the World Series.

In 1955, playing in only 139 games, Rosen batted a lowly .244, driving in only 81 runs and hitting 21 homers. The 1956 season was no better. Rosen batted .267 with 15 homers and 61 runs batted in.

Suffering from chronic injuries, Rosen decided to call it quits as a player after the 1956 season. Among those ailments were a broken finger and a back injury caused by a rear-end collision while driving. Ironically, a falling-out with his former idol Greenberg, then the Indians' general manager, contributed to his decision to retire. When the 1956 season ended, Greenberg wanted to slash Rosen's contract by another $5,000 after cutting it previously from $42,500 to $37,500. Rosen also had suffered a broken finger after the Indians forced him to make a position switch to first base in 1955. Rosen was upset with Greenberg, and their relationship went downhill.

Playing a total of 1,044 games, all with Cleveland, Rosen batted 3,725 times, scored 603 runs, pounded out 1,063 hits, belted 192 homers, and drove in 717 runs with a lifetime batting average of .285. Al's World Series statistics are unimpressive, as he went 3 for 13 during his 1948 and 1954 appearances. Rosen was only thirty-two years old when he retired. His pride would not let him go on playing and turn in what he considered sub-par performances.

Baseball life seemed over for Rosen as he traded in his uniform for a stockbroker's pinstriped suits. For seventeen years in Cleveland, the investment business was Al's life. Most of his time was spent with Bache and Company, where he eventually rose to manager of the Cleveland office. But baseball was still in his blood, and he helped the Indians as a batting instructor each spring and by sitting on the club's board of directors.

By 1973 Rosen had left the investment business for a job with Caesar's Palace in Las Vegas. After five years at the casino, New York Yankees owner George Steinbrenner asked Rosen to become president and chief operating office of the Yankees. Rosen accepted the offer in 1978 and spent a triumphant yet tumultuous year working with Yankees manager Billy Martin and Steinbrenner.

According to an article by Howard Cosell, Rosen and Martin had made a gentleman's agreement just before the All-Star game in 1978 to stick together against some of the decrees issued by Steinbrenner. Martin then made his infamous remarks about slugger Reggie Jackson and Steinbrenner, that "one's a born liar; the other's convicted." Either Rosen was forced to fire Martin or Martin resigned. Either way, Rosen replaced Martin with an old friend, former teammate Bob Lemon. The Yanks went on to win the 1978 AL pennant and World Series. Media sources believed Rosen spent more time in 1978 settling feuds between Martin and Steinbrenner than on baseball matters.

In 1979 Martin had returned as Yankee manager. Martin told Steinbrenner that he would no longer communicate to him through Rosen, complaining that messages passed through Rosen were distorted. Now that Rosen had effectively been removed as a barrier to Steinbrenner, Martin outranked everyone in the front office.

The first real test of who had Steinbrenner's ear occurred when Rosen authorized that a game between the Yankees and California Angels be played earlier in the day to accommodate a national telecast. Martin wanted the game to start at its regular time, and Steinbrenner sided with Martin. The so-called gentleman's agreement between Rosen and Martin was officially dead. Rosen's duties were almost entirely now business-related and the baseball part was taken from him. Rosen chafed under this situation, one of a long line of executives in the Yankees office who felt limited by Steinbrenner's micromanaging. Al resigned on July 19, 1979, only a year and a half into his Yankee position.

After Rosen left the Yankees, he was hired as supervisor of credit operations at another casino, Bally's in Atlantic City. But Rosen's tenure there was troubled when he authorized a $2.5 million loan to four casinos that had been defrauded in a scam. Five people were arrested in a probe. Rosen was not arrested but admitted that he had used bad judgment in authorizing the loans.

Rosen was not out of baseball for long. Two weeks after the Houston Astros lost a playoff series to the Philadelphia Phillies in October 1980, Al Rosen replaced Tal Smith as Astros president and general manager. However, this experience did not start happily for Rosen, due to the controversial nature of Smith's firing. The Astros had just completed the team's first playoff appearance since the franchise had launched in 1962. The playoff series was exciting and well played, and Smith had been named Major League Executive of the Year.

Rosen encountered a hostile press and a hostile fandom. Astros owner John McMullen, already not well liked in Houston, suffered an insurrection from the team's twenty limited owners for forcing out Smith, and McMullen eventually ceded sole authority to make decisions regarding the club. Rosen was on the hot seat again. Tony Siegle, an assistant to Smith whom Rosen kept as part of his administrative staff, had this to say: "General Santa Ana received a friendlier welcome from the state of Texas than Al did."

McMullen and the minority stockholders were at constant odds, with many shareholders wanting to oust Rosen and reinstate Smith. Adding to the tumult, Rosen learned he would need open-heart surgery. Rosen underwent the operation and came through successfully.

Unfortunately, Rosen never had much control over Astros affairs. Rosen, considered a conservative general manager, was constrained by ownership in his attempts to deal players. Through all the infighting, the team was relatively successful in Rosen's time there. The Astros finished third in the National League West in 1981, fifth in 1982, third in 1983, second (tied with Atlanta) in 1984, and third in 1985, winning a total of 386 games and losing 372 games. Rosen eventually left the team in September 1985.

That same month in 1985, Rosen was hired as president and general manager of the San Francisco Giants, a last-place team that year. He helped resuscitate a moribund franchise through his dealings, culminating in an NL West title in 1987. Rosen's stint with the Giants lasted through the 1992 season. During his tenure, the Giants won 589 games while losing 475. In 1987 Rosen was chosen Major League Executive of the Year. The Giants again finished first in the National League West in 1989 and won the NL Championship Series against the Chicago Cubs but were swept in the World Series by the Oakland A's, 4 games to 0.

Rosen then retired to his home in Rancho Mirage, California.

Rosen's personal life had been stricken with tragedy on May 4, 1971, when his wife, the former Teresa (Terry) Ann Blumberg, fell to her death from the Warwick Hotel in Philadelphia under mysterious circumstances; married in 1952, they had three children. Understandably, Rosen prefers not to talk about this painful event.

Al and his second wife, Rita (née Kallman), who calls him Flip, have been married thirty-four years. Rosen occasionally consults for baseball teams, including a stint with the Yankees as special assistant to the general manager in 2001 and 2002. When he is feeling good, he plays golf. Rosen, born on February 29, jokes that he doesn't get to celebrate his birthday that often.

In 1994 the Indians held a special celebration honoring Rosen's 1953 unanimous MVP Award, and all five of Rosen's children were in attendance at Jacobs Field. In 2006 Rosen also was inducted into the Indians' Hall of Fame. Rosen also is a member of the Cleveland Hall of Fame, the Jewish Sports Hall of Fame, and the Texas League Hall of Fame.

Al's strength and determination to overcome any and all obstacles was the key factor in his rise to becoming a star ballplayer and his success as a baseball administrator. Physical and mental toughness served Rosen well through all his many life challenges: desertion by his father as a toddler, asthma as a youngster, racial taunts for his Jewish background, skepticism about his baseball abilities, and his later travails as a Yankee and Astros executive. He indeed was "one tough Jew," as Rosen once said of himself, and was a ballplayer and person that all could admire.

Chapter 32. **Wally Westlake**

Bob Hurte

AGE	G	AB	R	H	2B	3B	HR	TB	RBI	BB	SO	BAV	OBP	SLG	SB	GDP	HBP
33	85	240	36	63	9	2	11	109	42	26	37	.263	.337	.454	0	8	2

The small town of Gridley, California, was established five years after the Civil War ended. It would become known for its agriculture, eventually becoming the "Kiwi Capital of the United States." The Northern California community would also be successful in growing such other crops as peaches, plums that would become prunes, rice, and walnuts. Gridley became the birthplace of another homegrown product: Wally Westlake. In 1947 the Pittsburgh Pirates baseball club would plant this California product in the outfield of Forbes Field with the hopes of bountiful harvests for years to come. He became a staple in Pittsburgh from 1947 to 1951.

Named after his father, Wally Westlake was born November 8, 1920, of good old English-Irish stock to Waldon Thomas Westlake and the former Helen Holland. Honest, hard-working people whose families had settled in Northern California in the 1880s, Waldon and Helen had three boys and a girl whom they taught to respect others and their property as well as the animals they hunted. Wally became an avid fisherman and hunter. Jim, the Westlakes' youngest son, played in the Minors and had one at bat with the Phillies on April 16, 1955.

Wally carried his parents' lessons with him as he progressed in professional baseball. Stunned by the viciousness and ignorance of some people, he witnessed several instances of anti-Semitism and racism. Westlake recalled how Hank Greenberg, his teammate in 1947, struck up a relationship with a young Jackie Robinson. Hank, who had experienced anti-Semitism first-hand, became one of Robinson's biggest supporters.[1]

Westlake played at the Christian Brothers High

Wally Westlake—Westlake was a reserve outfielder for Cleveland in 1954, but he was an all-star with Pittsburgh in 1951.

School and the local American Legion League in Sacramento, where the family had moved when he was six years old. His play caught the attention of a scout named Ted McGrew, and he was invited to a Brooklyn Dodger tryout camp in Fresno. He would sign as an amateur free agent in 1940 and start his professional career with Class A Elmira of the Eastern League. He appeared in only one game for the Pioneers, without a plate appearance. In a recent phone interview, Wally confessed that he was overmatched. The young man wanted to quit and go home. Fortunately, he did not and finished up the year playing at Class C Dayton of the Mid-Atlantic League. Westlake played in thirty games, hit a couple of home runs, and batted .176. Although these were terrible numbers, the future Major Leaguer felt comfortable with the level of competition. He spent the entire 1941 season with the Merced Bears of the California League and did reasonably well, hitting .265 with eighteen home runs and eighty-five RBIS over 136 games.

The young slugger from Sacramento earned a promotion to Class Double-A in 1942 to play for the Oakland Oaks, managed by John Vergez, of the Pacific Coast League (PCL). Westlake hit for an average of .268, clubbed seven round-trippers, and produced fifty-seven runs while playing in 169 games. His stats for the 1942 season showed the possibility of a bright future. The *Los Angeles Times* on April 5, 1942, reported the following: "For Oakland, Hugh Luby singled through the box and scored on a triple by Wally Westlake, the rookie outfielder who was one of the home run leaders of the California League last semester."[2]

World War II interrupted his career, taking the young man from 1943 to 1945. While his father saw action against the Germans in France during World War I, Wally would never leave California. He would humorously refer to himself as a "Broadway" soldier.

Westlake returned to the PCL in 1946. The league had been upgraded to Triple-A classification. That year he played for the legendary Casey Stengel. After fulfilling his military requirement, Wally enjoyed a fine season. He credited the "Old Professor" with teaching him more about being a baseball player, both as a batter and as an outfielder, than he ever

had known before. "There wasn't a move that any player made that Old Case didn't see and talk about afterward. A smart kid never made the same mistake twice. You just can't help but listen to him. But don't laugh at some of his strange mutterings. He won't go for that. He was smart!"[3]

The Oakland squad finished in second place that season, four games behind their California rivals, the San Francisco Seals, managed by Lefty O'Doul. Westlake enjoyed a campaign in which he achieved a .315 average, seven homers, and fifty-seven runs driven in. The Oaks advanced to the PCL championship against the San Francisco club by defeating Los Angeles, only to lose to the Seals four games to two.

Westlake's play at Oakland must have made an impression on Ray L. Kennedy, then the general manager of the Pittsburgh Pirates. The Pittsburgh papers reported on September 25, 1946, the Pirates purchased the young outfielder for cash and a player to be named later. The Pirates sent pitcher Johnny Hutchings to Oakland to complete the deal. Wally was twenty-six and married to the former Rosie Bier.

The Pirates began the 1947 season under new ownership. Barney Dreyfuss's widow decided to sell the club for $2.5 million. Frank McKinney, John W. Galbreath, and Tom Johnson became the club's new owners. They made an intriguing transaction by coaxing former Detroit Tiger great Hank Greenberg out of his short retirement. Part of the bait, aside from making him the first $100,000 player in the National League, was to move in the left field fences at Forbes Field by thirty feet, creating Greenberg Gardens. In his only season in Pittsburgh, Greenberg would manage just twenty-five dingers due to a nagging back ailment. While the shorter dimensions did not seem to help the old slugger's performance, it was advantageous for a young slugger named Ralph Kiner. Ralph would become a disciple of Greenberg and under his tutelage would launch fifty-one homers to tie the Giants' Johnny Mize for the National League lead that year. Another batter in the same outfield would also find the altered dimensions to his liking. "Hank Greenberg, who led the American League in home runs last season with 44 and then moved to the National, where the home run leader (Kiner) hit only 23, is finding the going tough. He isn't even leading his own Pittsburgh club in homers, much less the National League. Wally Westlake of the Pirates has clouted three homers compared to Greenberg's two, and Ralph Kiner, who was the league's home run champion in 1946, hasn't hit one yet."[4]

Of course, Kiner went on to lead the league in home runs, as the dismal Pirates finished the season at 62-92 to tie the Phillies for seventh place. Westlake would complete his rookie season with seventeen round-trippers, sixty-nine runs batted in, and a .273 batting average. This fine debut attracted the attention of none of other than Branch Rickey, the general manager of the Brooklyn Dodgers. Rickey's desire was mentioned in the "Daniel's Dope" column in the *New York World Telegram*: "Reports involving the Dodgers and the Pirates in a trade which would bring Waldon Westlake to Ebbetts Field for Eddie Miksis are founded almost on wishful thinking. Pittsburgh would be glad to take Miksis but it had no intention of trading Westlake." Ralph Kiner became one of Westlake's biggest backers, calling him "the most underrated player on the team."[5]

The Pirates went to great lengths to improve their club for the 1948 season. During the off-season, they acquired first baseman Johnny Hopp and second baseman Danny Murtaugh from the Boston Braves. Then from Brooklyn they picked up Stan Rojek, who had spent his time with the Dodgers as Pee Wee Reese's backup, in addition to Dixie Walker, the "People's Cherce." After a contract dispute, Westlake became the final player to sign for the upcoming season. Finally, the Pirates hired Billy Meyer to take over the club from Billy Herman.

The 1948 season proved successful for several reasons. Meyer won Manager of the Year honors for guiding the Pirates to a fourth-place finish with an 83-71 record, leaving them eight and a half games

behind the Boston Braves. Kiner tied Johnny Mize for the National League home run title with forty, as Greenberg Gardens were renamed "Kiner's Corner." Wally Westlake improved upon his rookie season by batting .285 with seventeen home runs and sixty-five RBIs. He hit for the cycle on July 30 during a 10-5 victory over the Dodgers.

Unfortunately, 1949 confirmed what many Pirate fans feared, that the team's success was due to career seasons by several players. Many would fall back to earth, returning the team to the second division of the National League. The Pirates fell to 71-83 to finish in sixth place, twenty-six games off the pace. Even with the disappointing season, Kiner again led the National League in homers, many landing in Kiner's Corner. Westlake improved upon 1948. He would play in 147 games, tag 23 homers, drive in 104 runs, and finish with a batting average of .282. He hit for the cycle on June 14, 1949, for the second time in his career. The *New York Times* wrote that "Wally Westlake scored practically a one man victory tonight as he rapped a homer, a triple and a ninth inning double to lead the Pirates to a 4–3 victory over the Braves."[6] His single was not included in the *Times* account since it did not result in a run.

Branch Rickey became the general manager of the Pirates to start off the new decade. Ever since his Brooklyn Dodger years he had been aware of Westlake's value. During an interview while riding in a car to attend a luncheon honoring Happy Chandler, Rickey told his companions, "We're going to use as many of the kids this year as we possibly can." "The Mahatma" pointed to Wally Westlake as an example. He felt that Westlake was the only player on the roster that would bring fair value on the trade market. Although Kiner was a major star and desired by several teams around the league, Rickey neither liked him as a player nor believed trading him could justify the loss at the gates that a Kinerless team would spell. The Pirate GM's assessment of Westlake's value might have been valid, but his lack of appreciation for Kiner was unwarranted if not irrational.

In 1950 the Pirates' fortunes sank quicker than an anchor being dropped in the middle of the ocean. Wally put together another fine season for the club. He hit one more home run than the previous season with 24, knocking in 95 runs to go with a .285 batting average. His roommate, Ralph Kiner, also had a good season: 47 home runs to lead the league, 118 RBIS, an average of .272—and the Player of the Year Award from *The Sporting News*. Unfortunately, no starting pitcher posted a winning record, and the team finished in the cellar, at 57-96 and thirty-three and a half games behind the Philadelphia Whiz Kids.

The next year's home opener was held on April 17, 1951. That day 25,894 fans poured through the turnstiles of Forbes Field to brave snow flurries and forty-degree temperatures to watch the Pirates play the St. Louis Cardinals. While the fans sat in flurries, they did not realize that they were witnessing the start of a different flurry on the playing field. That day Westlake sent one high over the Longines clock in left field for a 5–4 Pittsburgh victory. Wally was beginning what was arguably his best season at the plate while employed by the Pirates.

Then on June 15, 1951, papers reported that the Pirates had announced a trade with the St. Louis Cardinals. Pittsburgh sent Westlake and Cliff Chambers to the Cards for Howie Pollet, Joe Garagiola, Bill Howerton, Ted Wilks, and Dick Cole. Although Chambers had pitched a no-hitter that season, he became expendable with a series of ineffective starts. Wally Westlake, on the other hand, was having a torrid season at the plate. At the time of the trade, Wally had hit sixteen homers and driven in forty-five runs while posting a .282 batting average and a .569 slugging percentage. Columnist Joe Williams expressed surprise at Rickey's deal involving Westlake at the trading deadline: "Rickey surrendered Wally Westlake in a five-man deal with the Cardinals, a move which invited press box crit-

icism. Next to Ralph Kiner, Westlake was the Pirates' strongest bat. There is no record that Rickey ever lost his shirt in the baseball market."[7] Williams felt that any change by the Pirates was likely to be a good one. Westlake tailed off to finish the year with twenty-two home runs, eighty-four RBIS, and a .266 batting average. Wally revealed in conversation that the trade had affected him psychologically.

At the age of thirty-one, Wally Westlake attended spring training with a team other than the Pirates. Indeed, suddenly reduced to the status of a journeyman player, he spent the 1952 campaign on three different teams. He appeared in twenty-one games for the Cards, hitting no home runs, driving in ten runs, and batting a very disappointing .216. Next he was swapped to the Cincinnati Reds along with Eddie Kazak for Dick Sisler and Virgil Stallcup. The *New York World Telegram* quipped that the transportation costs for the traded players were about the cheapest in the history of the game. That afternoon the Cards were playing at Ebbets Field, while the Reds were at the Polo Grounds. Westlake played in eighty-nine games with Cincinnati. He launched three home runs, drove in fourteen runs, and hit a terrible .202. The vagabond finished his season in the American League with the Cleveland Indians. In twenty-nine games, he accounted for a homer, nine RBIS, and a .232 batting average.

Before the trade to Cleveland, Westlake was asked where he would like to play if traded to the American League. Some thought that his choice would have been the Yankees, especially with the chance of being reunited with Casey Stengel, his former manager in the PCL and one that he credited for saving his career. Hank Edwards, a teammate of his at Cincinnati, recommended the Indians for several reasons: the number of veterans on the club, the ballpark, and the management. Wally would be reunited with Hank Greenberg, his old teammate who was now the general manager at Cleveland. In a telephone interview, Westlake expressed a deep respect for Greenberg, as both a hitter and a person. Edwards also informed him that the Cleveland ball-park was as nice a place to play as any available in the National League. At the same time, Wally professed his love for Wrigley Field: "You almost wanted to give some of your money back to play there!"[8]

Coincidentally, Westlake was sold on August 7, two days after the Reds played an exhibition against the Indians to benefit local sandlot teams. Like another trade involving Westlake, this one saved on travel expenses. It was said that the Tribe was seeking a dependable, experienced outfielder for their stretch drive, and Greenberg noticed that Westlake was available on the waiver line. To make room for him, the club sent rookie outfielder Jim Fridley to Indianapolis of the American Association. At the time, Fridley was having a more successful season than Wally but did not provide the same level of defense. The trade was consummated for $25,000 with two players to be named later. The newspapers pointed out how Westlake was languishing in a horrible season before the trade. To such criticism Wally replied, "I've got no alibis, and I'm just not hitting. I don't know why. I'm in good shape, my weight is down and I feel fine but I'm just not hitting the ball. I can't even hit in batting practice." He went on to express his pleasure at the opportunity to play with the club. "I know we've got a good chance to win the pennant and I'd like to do my share."[9]

With the 1952 season behind him, Westlake went to spring training with the Indians in 1953. He wanted to prove why the Indians were smart in obtaining him. Wally would flourish in his role as an additional outfielder. The vet rekindled the ability that seemed lost from his days in Pittsburgh. He hit a homer on May 5, 1953, to break up a shutout by Whitey Ford. Later in the month one of his home runs helped defeat the White Sox. Then in August he went on a hitting tear. It started with a game played on July 31 against the Philadelphia Athletics. Wally posted a batting line of five hits, which included a homer and four runs batted in. Such clutch hit-

ting was reminiscent of his earlier playing days in Pittsburgh. The *Chicago Daily Tribune* reported on August 28, "Wally Westlake hit a homer in the 11th inning with a man on base to give the Indians a 4–2 victory over the rival Yankees." The report continued, "Westlake, inserted in the 10th inning as a rightfield replacement got his sixth homer of the season off left hander Bob Kuzava, who took over in the eight."[10] The *New York Times* reported the continuance on September 3: "Wally Westlake walloped a pair of home runs tonight to pace the Indians to a 6–3 victory over the Athletics. Westlake, a spare outfielder until he started to hit recently, belted both homers off of Harry Byrd and drove in 3 runs. He has hit 8 four baggers this year." Unfortunately, even with Westlake's exploits, the Indians finished with a 92-62 record, good enough for second place and eight and a half games behind the Yankees. Westlake finished with a batting average of .330, nine homers, and forty-six RBIs in only eighty-two games.

The 1954 season was magical for the Cleveland Indians, who won 111 games, the American League record at the time. Ironically, the end of the preseason would be prophetic as to the outcome of the 1954 season. Before the 1947 season, Bill Veeck had decided to move the Indians' spring training site to Arizona from Florida. In his biography Veeck explained, "I had already made up my mind to get out of Florida. By arranging for the Giants to come to Arizona with us, I was able to move the next team I had down South, the 1947 Indians, to Tucson."[11] The two teams began a tradition of playing exhibitions throughout Texas and other southern states as they traveled north. This type of travel seemed to appeal to Westlake, who performed some hitting heroics along the way. On April 4, 1954, he hit a home run off Sal Maglie to tie the score in the seventh inning, and his double drove in two more runs, leading the Indians to an 8–4 victory over the Giants. He hit another home run the following day in a 10–8 victory.

Wally started the season as the regular left fielder for the Tribe, but Lopez would eventually bench him in favor of Al Smith, who was faster and could bat leadoff. Then Cleveland experienced a rash of injuries that brought Westlake back into the regular lineup. He returned on June 11, 1954 as the Indians won 6–2 at Boston. Westlake had a homer and a single. He played in left field and batted out of the six-hole. Wally went on a streak that produced sixteen hits in fifty-one at bats through June 27. During that span he collected two doubles, three homers, and twelve RBIs. Before this stretch, he had played in only thirty-nine of the Indians' first eighty-eight games. Even with his lack of playing time, the jovial outfielder served as a positive influence in the clubhouse. Wally was well liked in the clubhouse, as he seemed to have only kind words for everyone. While he was reduced to a limited role up to and after the stretch, Westlake still had twenty-six RBIs.

Wally recapped his career in an interview for the July 7, 1954, issue of *The Sporting News*. Much of the interview centered on how he bounced around the National League before finding a home in the "junior" circuit. Cleveland correspondent Hal Lebovitz pointed out that the Indians took a chance on him because they needed a quality outfielder. It probably did not hurt that former teammate Hank Greenberg was the general manager. When he was asked about his reaction toward the National League's letting him pass waivers, he replied, "I was surprised that somebody DID want me. I was darn grateful."[12] Of course, the Indians were the grateful ones. At the age of thirty-three, the National League cast-off played a valuable role in the Indians' efforts to end the Yankees' dominance.

The July 7 article contained a little-known story. While in a slump during the 1953 season, Wally unknowingly partook in being filmed. At the time this was considered revolutionary. Al Lopez and Hank Greenberg hired the Cleveland Browns' photographer to film Westlake in early July of 1953. Wally walked into the clubhouse prior to a night game, when a clubhouse boy informed him that Hank Greenberg wanted to see him. He expected the worst and walked into the room, only to see Greenberg, Lopez, and a movie screen. "Sit down Wally. We would like to show you some films."[13] The movies were of him in early July, when he was in a batting slump. Greenberg, Lopez, and Westlake critiqued the action on the screen, and after thorough analysis, they determined that his swing was both too quick and too long. Their solution was for him to open up his stance.

Like magic, Wally broke out of his slump. While the films might have helped, he was not ready to give them all of the credit. He did see a benefit to them. "I hope they do more movie taking. I think it would be a good idea to take movies of a batter when he is going well too. Then comparisons could be made."[14] He felt, too, that movies should be taken of great hitters like Williams, Musial, and Kiner.

Also in the interview Westlake called it a privilege and a pleasure to play in the Major Leagues, especially to have roommates like Ralph Kiner and Al Rosen. He noted that they were both highly intelligent men. Wally said that both were all business on the playing field. The difference was that Kiner never showed emotion between the white lines, while Rosen did not take it lightly if he missed a pitch.[15]

Of course, Rosen had already established himself as one of the top hitters in the American League. In 1953, after becoming Westlake's roommate, however, he had one of the greatest years any third baseman ever had and was named Most Valuable Player. Westlake refused to take credit. In fact, he was grateful to Rosen: "He helps me more than I help him . . . he's always encouraging me."[16]

Westlake finished the 1954 season with eleven homers and forty-two runs batted in to compile an average of .263 for eighty-five games. The Indians won the American League pennant, finishing eight games ahead of the rival Yankees. This would be the only year that Casey Stengel would ever win over a hundred games, but ironically he wound up in second place. The New York Giants swept the Indians in that year's Fall Classic.

On June 15, 1955, the Orioles traded Gene Woodling and Billy Cox to Cleveland for Westlake, Dave Pope, and cash. By July 9, 1955, he was released after posting a dismal .125 average, no homers, and one RBI in twenty-four at bats.

The next stop for the journeyman was the Philadelphia Phillies. He appeared in only five games in 1956, all as a pinch hitter, and struck out three times. He played the balance of 1956 with Sacramento of the PCL, appearing in ninety games, batting .273, hitting twelve home runs, and driving in fifty. On February 15, 1957, at the age of thirty-six, Westlake hung up his cleats for good.

With his baseball career over, the former Major League outfielder joined the sales force for Tidewater Oil. The work did not suit him. He eventually became employed by A. Teichert & Sons Construction Company, working there as a lead laborer. Being outside was to his liking. Each year the company would conveniently shut down during duck season. Wally would spend this time outdoors, fishing and hunting. One of his favorite fishing spots was located on the Smith River along the Oregon/California border. "We would fish from the bank, use spinning tackle and fresh roe for bait." His favorite fish to catch was steelhead. He landed an eighteen-pound monster with spinning tackle and a twelve-pounder with a fly rod![17]

Westlake still lives in Sacramento. He has five children: Patricia, Constance, Steve, Cathleen, and Joseph. Each of them lives nearby. His beloved wife, Rosie, now lives in an assisted living facility. During his career, Wally was well liked by his teammates. Wally admitted, "I wasn't a great player but a good one."[18] He recounted how it was an honor to put on the uniform. Baseball also allowed him to meet many people in and out of the sport. For example, when he played for Pittsburgh and Bing Crosby was a part owner, he would hunt on Crosby's ranch outside of Las Vegas and also at his place

in Redding, California. He felt privileged to play for several different managers: Casey Stengel, Billy Herman, Marty Marion, and Al Lopez. Willie Mays was the best player he ever saw. Ewell Blackwell was one of the toughest pitchers he ever faced: "Guys would come down with stomach aches when he was schedule to pitch."[19] He had kind words for Bob Lemon and Robin Roberts, whom he considered the most intelligent hurlers of his era. As a Major Leaguer, he also considered himself lucky to play with and against several great hitters like Greenberg, Kiner, Williams, and Musial.

Waldon Thomas Westlake considered the 1954 season and playing on a team that went to the World Series the highlight of his career. "It was a great bunch of guys and of course you enjoyed winning every day."[20] The *Baseball Encyclopedia* shows lifetime totals of 958 games played, 3,117 at bats, 848 base hits, 127 homers, and 539 RBIs with an average of .272. As Wally would say, it was fun.

Chapter 33. **Dick Tomanek**

Thomas Ayers

AGE	W	L	PCT	ERA	G	GS	GF	CG	SHO	SV	IP	H	BB	SO	HBP	WP
23	0	0	.000	5.40	1	0	0	0	0	0	1.2	1	1	0	0	0

Signed as a teenager, Dick Tomanek reached the big leagues after serving in the U.S. Marines and pitching in the Minor Leagues for less than three years. He went on to amass more than 100 Major League appearances with the Cleveland Indians and Kansas City Athletics. More than half of those appearances came in 1958, when Tomanek split the season between the two teams and served a valuable role as a reliever and spot starter for both clubs.

Richard Carl Tomanek was born on January 6, 1931, in Avon Lake, Ohio, about fifteen miles west of Cleveland. He was the fourth child born to William and Elizabeth Tomanek. He was commonly called Dick and was also known by the nickname Bones. He was signed by the Indians before the 1950 season and began his professional career at the age of nineteen. A left-handed pitcher, Tomanek stood six feet one and his playing weight was listed as 175 pounds.

Tomanek began his Minor League career in 1950 with the Pittsfield Indians, Cleveland's affiliate in the Class C Canadian-American League. Tomanek finished with the third-lowest earned run average on the team at 3.80. The only regular starter with a lower ERA was Brooks "Bull" Lawrence, who also went on to pitch in the Major Leagues. Tomanek finished with a 6-8 record in sixteen starts and five relief appearances for the seventh-place team. One of only two nineteen-year-olds on the staff, Tomanek walked 142 batters in 123 innings.

Tomanek missed the following year and part of 1952 while serving in the marines. Discharged in the middle of the 1952 season, he reported to the Reading Indians of the Class A Eastern League.[1]

Dick Tomanek—A local product from Avon, Ohio, Tomanek pitched relief in his five-year career with Cleveland and Kansas City.

The youngest pitcher on the team, Tomanek posted a 2-5 record with a 3.35 ERA and made progress on the control issues that had been his Achilles's heel in 1950. Although he still walked more than a batter every other inning, he halved his walk rate from 1950, giving up forty-four bases on balls in seventy-eight innings. Tomanek and former Pittsfield teammate Brooks Lawrence had a hard time breaking into Reading's veteran rotation; Tomanek got only nine starts.

Tomanek made big strides the following season with the Indianapolis Indians of the Triple-A American Association. He made twenty-three starts and went 13-8 with a 3.11 ERA and three shutouts. He showed that the progress he made with his control during the previous season was sustainable, walking 98 batters in 165 innings. He struck out 158 batters and continued to be difficult to hit, as he surrendered only 127 hits. Playing under the tutelage of manager Birdie Tebbetts, a former Major League catcher and future Indians manager, the twenty-two-year-old Tomanek struck out the most batters per inning and surrendered the least hits per inning of any pitcher on the club and had the lowest ERA of any Indianapolis starter.

His fine season caught the eye of the Cleveland front office and Tomanek was called up to Indians in September. His Major League debut came in a start on September 25 against the Detroit Tigers at Cleveland Stadium, with the Indians sitting in second in the American League but unable to catch the first-place Yankees. Tomanek held the Tigers scoreless as the Indians built a 7–0 lead. He surrendered a three-run home run to Ray Boone in the seventh inning, but retired six of seven batters in the last two innings and recorded a 12-3, complete-game victory, allowing six hits, walking six, and striking out six.

The Indians had high hopes for Tomanek at the beginning of the 1954 season. In an off-season column for the *Milwaukee Journal,* manager Al Lopez said,

> In addition to [Rocky] Nelson and [Gale] Wade, our outstanding rookie may turn out to be a young left-handed pitcher named Dick Tomanek. You may recall that Tomanek pitched one of our late season games against Detroit and showed a great deal of poise as he defeated the Tigers. . . . What was particularly impressive to us was the poise the youngster showed when he was in serious trouble in the early innings. . . . He has a fine

fastball and if he can supplement this with an effective curve ball he may be an outstanding pitcher within the next two or three years.[2]

But Tomanek pitched only once for the Indians in 1954, on April 17, entering a game against Chicago in relief in the first inning with the White Sox already leading, 5–0. He retired the first five batters he faced before allowing a home run to Ferris Fain and walking Bob Boyd. Jose Santiago was summoned in relief. Tomanek didn't pitch again for Cleveland for more than three years.

Tomanek had a sore elbow after that performance, and the team physician, Don Kelly, diagnosed it as "curve ball pitching disease" that had resulted in pulled elbow muscles.[3] After missing several months, Tomanek was sent to Indianapolis, where he posted a 6-9 record with a 4.29 ERA. For the first time in his career, Tomanek allowed over a hit an inning, and he walked 53 in 107 innings. The Indians won the American Association title by 10½ games.

Indianapolis was Tomanek's home for the next two seasons. He found it difficult to break into Cleveland's rotation, headed by Early Wynn, Mike Garcia, Bob Lemon, and Bob Feller. In 1955 Tomanek's ERA rose to 5.25 and his record fell to 7-13. He walked 104 in 168 innings, allowed 19 home runs, and threw 14 wild pitches, both totals exceeding those of his previous two seasons combined.

With Indianapolis in 1956, Tomanek made only thirteen appearances, winning two games and losing three, and walking only thirteen batters in forty-six innings. His performance put him back on the Indians' radar, and he made Cleveland's bullpen out of spring training in 1957. The season did not begin well; Tomanek surrendered six runs in three and two-thirds innings in his first two appearances. He entered May with a 14.73 ERA and was a peripheral member of the bullpen, pitching only four times in Cleveland's first twenty-two games. He bounced back in his next seven appearances, giving up only three runs in fourteen and two-thirds innings, striking out sixteen, and walking four. To-manek picked up his first win of the year, and his first Major League victory in nearly three and a half years, against the White Sox on May 24. That was followed by his first Major League loss in June. To-manek was inconsistent in July, pitching six and two-thirds scoreless innings in two appearances but giving up thirteen runs in four and two-thirds innings in two more games. He picked up his second win of the year on August 23, with a scoreless tenth inning against the Yankees. He was used infrequently toward the end of the season, pitching only three innings after September 1. Tomanek finished the year with a 2-1 record and a 5.68 ERA in sixty-nine and two-thirds innings. He struck out fifty-five batters while walking thirty-seven.

Tomanek began 1958 back in Cleveland's bullpen, surrendering a pair of runs in his first appearance but holding the opposition scoreless in his next two. On April 24 he started against the White Sox, allowed four runs in four and one-third innings, and didn't get the decision as the Indians won the game.

Subsequently, Tomanek returned to the bullpen and had one of the busiest stretches of his career, with six appearances between May 9 and 18. On May 13, after Tomanek allowed three runs in two innings, manager Bobby Bragan called him the team's "biggest disappointment."[4] Tomanek seemed to respond to his manager's criticism, as he threw six scoreless innings of two-hit relief on May 16. Perhaps owing in part to that strong effort, he was handed another start on May 21, against the Boston Red Sox. He went twelve innings and surrendered just a Jackie Jensen home run and a second run that was unearned. In his complete-game victory, secured by a walk-off home run by Minnie Minoso, Tomanek allowed only four Red Sox to reach second base. It was perhaps his finest performance in the Majors.

After the game, Bragan said, "That was a masterful pitching job against the team that I figure as the best we've met."[5] Tomanek was asked if he had heard Bragan's earlier criticism and he responded,

"I heard about it. Maybe it did shake me up a little, made me more determined." However, he added, "I'm not doing anything different. My control has been better and that always helps."[6]

Bragan complimented Tomanek's stuff, saying it was probably second only to Herb Score's on the staff, but he was not as fond of Tomanek's approach on the mound. "When he gets out there in a tough situation, he throws the ball in the dirt or fools around with his slider when his fastball is his best pitch. . . . Sometimes he seems plain scared out there."[7]

Tomanek immediately got two more starts, but he didn't match his results against the Red Sox, and the Indians lost both games. In early June he returned to a swingman role, alternating between starting and relieving. Tomanek lost two starts, although he did throw an eight-inning complete game. On June 8 he notched a victory in relief over the Yankees with one and two-thirds scoreless innings.

On June 15, the day of the trading deadline, Tomanek was dealt from his home-state Indians along with outfielder Roger Maris and first baseman Preston Ward to the Kansas City Athletics for utility-man Woodie Held and outfielder/first baseman Vic Power. The Athletics would come to rely heavily on Tomanek's presence in the bullpen during the second half of the season.

Tomanek quickly made a positive impression on his new team; he didn't allow a run in his first five appearances and recorded a save with two and two-thirds innings of strong relief against the Red Sox. He picked up two quick victories for his new club; the second was particularly deserved as he spun five innings of one-run relief against the Yankees in a 12–6 victory.

Another career highlight came on July 4, as Tomanek recorded two saves in a doubleheader (retroactively, because saves were not a Major League statistic then). He threw two scoreless innings against the White Sox to pick up his second save of the year during the first game of a doubleheader. Because he looked so good in the first game, he was summoned again from the bullpen during the second game and threw a scoreless ninth for his second save of the day.

On July 18 Tomanek made his first start for the A's, and he responded with a complete game in a 2–1 victory over the Yankees. Tomanek gave up eleven hits, but he didn't walk a batter and struck out four. Tomanek, who surrendered the run in the ninth inning, almost became the first left-hander to shut out the Yankees in nearly two years. (Herb Score had recorded the last shutout on August 21, 1956.) Tomanek didn't fare as well in a start against New York ten days later, and took the loss to even his record at 5-5.

August was the busiest month of Tomanek's Major League career; he made fourteen appearances, all out of the bullpen. Tomanek finished 5-5 for the Athletics and 7-8 for the season with a 4.50 ERA. He had five saves and threw three complete games in his eight starts. He struck out 92 and walked 56 in 130 innings. With fifty-four appearances, Tomanek was the second-busiest pitcher in the American League, finishing one appearance behind Washington's Tex Clevenger. He led the league with nine wild pitches.

Tomanek began 1959 in Kansas City's bullpen, but he spent much of May at the back of the bullpen, entering during the latter stages of losses and finishing the game. In four games he pitched seven innings and allowed six earned runs and three homers.

Tomanek went on the disabled list with a sore arm and didn't pitch again until August 7.[8] He pitched in five games that month, often in the same mop-up role he had in May. His most notable appearance came on August 23, in the first game of a double-header against Washington. In a game Kansas City lost, 7–3, Tomanek entered in the fifth and finished the game with five innings of one-hit relief, giving the bullpen some necessary rest.

On September 7 Tomanek entered a 4–4 tie against the White Sox in the third inning and allowed back-to-back homers, retiring only one of the four batters he faced, and left with the Athlet-ics behind 7–4. He took the loss, and those were the last runs he surrendered in the Major Leagues. After three scoreless innings in two appearances, Tomanek entered a game against the Indians in the bottom of the ninth inning on September 26 with the Athletics leading 8–4, two outs, and two runners. He gave up a single to Jim Baxes, loading the bases, but retired Carroll Hardy on a grounder to shortstop and picked up his second save of the year. Tomanek never pitched in the Majors again.

He finished the year with a 6.53 ERA and an 0-1 record in sixteen appearances, finishing the game twelve times and picking up a pair of saves. In twenty and two-thirds innings, Tomanek allowed 27 hits, walked 12, threw 5 wild pitches, and struck out 13. He allowed 6 home runs.

In the off-season Tomanek was sold to Dallas–Fort Worth, Kansas City's American Association affiliate. He pitched the entire season for the Rangers and led the team with twenty-seven starts. The last-place Rangers had the league's highest ERA, and Tomanek's 4.08 ERA was the second lowest among the eight pitchers who started at least ten games for the team. Tomanek led the team in innings pitched (181) and had a 7-11 record. Tomanek never pitched again in Organized Baseball after that season.

Tomanek worked for B. F. Goodrich Chemical Company after his baseball career ended. He retired in 1990. He continues to live in Avon Lake, Ohio, his birthplace, as of this biography's completion.[9]

Chapter 34. Dave Pope

Tom Heinlein

AGE	G	AB	R	H	2B	3B	HR	TB	RBI	BB	SO	BAV	OBP	SLG	SB	GDP	HBP
33	60	102	21	30	2	1	4	46	13	10	22	.294	.354	.451	2	2	0

Although he spent just two full seasons in the Major Leagues, Dave Pope played in one of the most memorable games in baseball history. It was the game that featured "the catch," Willie Mays's spectacular play on a ball hit by the Cleveland Indians' Vic Wertz in the eighth inning of Game One of the 1954 World Series, with the score tied 2–2 and runners on first and second, that saved the game for the New York Giants. Two innings after "the catch," in the bottom of the tenth inning, Pope, playing right field for the Indians, could only wonder what might have been after having leaped for a fly ball hit by Dusty Rhodes that landed just beyond his reach down the right-field line and into the seats for a game-winning home run. The Giants went on to sweep the series from the Indians in four straight. "There was just a slight breeze out there that day towards the stands," Pope recalled. "If the wind had not been blowing, I believe I would have caught the ball. After all, the ball just hit on top of the cement. . . . When you look at a hit like Dusty Rhodes's, which was what—200-and-something down the right field line? And when you think of a 250-foot home run and you think of a 410-foot out, it's just something that doesn't seem to match. But that's the way the game goes."[1]

David Pope was born on June 17, 1921, into a family of fifteen children, in Talladega, Alabama. His father, Willie, was a farmer and married to Sussie, according to the 1930 U.S. Census. Pope's family moved north to Liberty, Pennsylvania, just outside Pittsburgh, when he was young and he grew up there. As a youth he practiced baseball in a way he had for years thought was unique until he discovered later in life that he was not alone, that he

Dave Pope—Pope was a reserve outfielder in his four-year career with Cleveland and Baltimore.

was in fact in good company. "I . . . didn't think that anyone else had even experienced what I did in my young days—in my childhood days—and that is hitting bottle caps and broomsticks. I listened to [Hank Aaron] and he said that he did, that's the way he learned to hit, also."[2]

Pope starred in baseball and basketball at Liberty High School. After graduating in 1939, he entered the University of Pittsburgh, where he played baseball for three years. He had intended to become a doctor but instead joined the army during World War II. Following his discharge from the army, after having served for a year, he began his baseball career. In his first season, in 1946, he played in the Negro Leagues, first with the Homestead Grays and later with the Pittsburgh Crawfords.

Pope married Nellie Archie on October 9, 1947. They had four children together—three daughters (Linda, Elaine, Sharyon) and a son (Vincent)—and later had ten grandchildren and three great-grandchildren.

In 1948 Pope signed on with Farnham of the Quebec Provincial League, an independent semipro league at the time, where he played, along with one of his brothers, Willie, for two seasons. By 1949, regarded by some as the golden year of Quebec baseball, the Provincial League had become famous as a refuge for baseball's dispossessed. "Former Negro League players [Terris McDuffie, Quincy Trouppe], young Latinos [Victor Pellot Power, Roberto Vargas], displaced major leaguers from the war years [Walter Brown. Tex Shirley], local, home-grown talent [Roland Gladu, Paul Calvert]–all were welcome."[3]

Farnham, meanwhile, had become a solid part of the Provincial League, having emerged as a good baseball town during the war. Known for its link with the black baseball community, Farnham fielded interesting if not always successful teams, later gaining national recognition when in 1951 it became the first team in Organized Baseball to have an African American manager, Sam Bankhead.[4]

Pope performed well in his two seasons with Farnham. Although his team finished last in 1948, he batted .361, belting 23 home runs and knocking in 72 runs in 98 games. He kept up the pace in 1949, again batting over .300, with 19 home runs and 77 RBIs, as he helped lead Farnham, despite finishing fifth (out of six teams) in the regular season with a 42-55 mark, to the championship series, where it pushed the heavily favored Drummondville Cubs to the series limit of nine games.[5]

The Drummondville team featured several players who would become Major Leaguers, including Vic Power and Sal Maglie, who was playing there because he had been banned from Organized Baseball for playing in Jorge Pasqual's Mexican League. Maglie, who five years later took the mound for the Giants in that famous Game One of the '54 World Series, pitched for the Cubs in the deciding game of the Provincial League's championship series. It looked as though Pope's Farnham team was going to upset Maglie and the Cubs and win the series, as it held a 1–0 lead into the seventh inning. However, Drummondville exploded for five runs and went on to win the championship.[6]

After his two years in Quebec, Pope was signed in 1950 as a free agent by the Cleveland Indians. Hank Greenberg, the Hall of Fame slugger and at the time general manager and part owner of the Indians, was credited in those years with having sponsored more African American players than any other baseball executive, and as a player had welcomed Jackie Robinson publicly in 1947. For Pope, having grown up in an integrated Pennsylvania town and having just played two seasons in an integrated Canadian league, Organized Baseball took some adjusting to. "When I first joined the Indians, the integration had not really caught on at that time in sports and a very disappointing situation was in spring training," Pope said of his first spring training in the Indians' farm system.

> There were two separate buildings for players to live in, one was for the white ballplayers to live in, one was for the black ballplayers. That would not have been so bad, but the place that the black ballplayers lived in was an emptied tool shed . . . maybe about 30 by 30 or something of that nature. There were eight of us and we were in double bunk beds in that building while the other ballplayers had—they weren't luxurious but they were facilities in what they called the "Wigwam." We were in the teepee, they were in the wigwam.[7]

While segregation was an unfortunate part of life off the field, Pope remembered few if any racist incidents on the field, recalling that his teammates, both black and white, were friendly with one another. Reflecting on his experience playing in 1952 for the Indians' Indianapolis farm team, he said the desire to win and the need to perform together as a team did more to bring a team together than racial differences did to drive them apart.[8]

Pope's first stop after being signed by Greenberg was at Wilkes-Barre in the Class A Eastern League, where he played for two seasons, 1950 and 1951. He batted .268 in 1950 and led the Eastern League in triples with 18. In 1951 he batted .309 with 15 home runs and 95 RBIS, and again led the league in triples (13), as well as in runs scored with 113.

Pope was moved up to the Triple-A Indianapolis Indians in 1952 and had arguably his best minor-league season: Batting a league-leading .352, he collected 167 hits, 49 for extra bases (29 doubles, 7 triples, 13 home runs), and 79 RBIS in 126 games. He reeled off 18- and 15-game hitting streaks, played well in the outfield, and was named to the postseason all-star team. He got a brief midseason call-up to the Indians, making his debut on July 1 shortly after turning thirty-one (though some accounts at the time listed him as twenty-seven). He left an impression—and the game—in his first appearance: "His zeal for the game was apparent the first time he took the field when he crashed into the (concrete facing of the) right field wall and suffered a chest bruise while chasing a foul ball."[9] Pope was forced to leave the game because of the injury. He stayed with the parent club for two weeks before returning to Indianapolis to finish the Minor League season.

Pope was back in Indianapolis for the 1953 season and batted .287 in 154 games, with 172 hits, 101 runs, 33 doubles, 14 triples, 24 home runs, and 88 RBIS. After two solid seasons at Indianapolis, he had shown he was ready to move up to the Major Leagues. In 1954 he made the Cleveland roster, a team that would win 111 regular-season games and play in the World Series.

Though not a regular, Pope played an important role in 1954. He batted .294 as a reserve and hit .381 in twenty-four pinch-hitting appearances, reaching base eleven times.

The capture of the pennant by the 1954 Indians interrupted the Yankees' spectacular run of championships under manager Casey Stengel. Pope saw similarities between those Yankee teams and the '54 Cleveland club.

Stengel had two ballclubs where he could just close his eyes and pull off the bench and say, "Go ahead in there." Well, in '54, Cleveland was much similar to that. We didn't have two ballclubs, but we had a lot of extra ballplayers who were performers. Al Lopez had not too much of a problem that year with doing things because whoever he called, the team didn't lose that much. Guys like myself, like Sam Dente, Wally Westlake, Hank Majeski—some of them had been regulars and stars before but they were on their waning years and some of us had never reached that level of stardom, but that year every one had a good year. It didn't matter what happened, if Lopez needed a pinch hitter or if he needed a shortstop to play or whatever he needed, it was there. The players produced for him.[10]

Pope felt the Indians' coaching staff also had a significant impact on the team's success. "I think that the guys who made that club were the coaches: Tony Cuccinello, Red Kress, Mel Harder, and Bill Lobe, and guys like that who kept the team on the prod and kept 'em loose, so to speak. I think that the coaches contributed much more than people give them credit for doing, as far as the morale of the ballclub and so forth."[11]

While Pope played a limited role in the World Series, going 0 for 3 with a walk and a strikeout, his play during the season led manager Lopez and the press to believe 1955 held a lot of promise for him. "The quiet, industrious Dave Pope needs only to display an improvement on defense to capture the right field post," a correspondent for The Sporting News wrote. "He has a strong arm and good speed, but he has had moments of uncertainty as a flychaser. 'It's all a matter of experience,' points out Lopez. 'He isn't accustomed to the ball parks and that makes a big difference in outfield play. You've got to know the lights and shadows.' He mentions the sudden development of Al Smith in the outfield. 'It could happen to Dave, too,' the manager hopes. 'He has all the tools.'"[12]

During the off-season Pope continued to work on his game, returning to the Venezuelan League to play with Santa Maria. It was his fourth season in a winter league; he had played in Puerto Rico for San Juan in 1951–52 and 1952–53, and with Gavilanes in the Venezuelan league in 1953–54. In Pope's two years in the Venezuelan League, he got in nearly 450 at bats, hitting a league-leading .345 in 1953–54 and .322 in 1954–55.[13] With the Indians in 1955, Pope was batting .298 in thirty-five games with six home runs, including a grand slam, when on June 15 he was traded to the Baltimore Orioles along with outfielder Wally Westlake for outfielder Gene Woodling and third baseman Billy Cox. (Cox refused to report to his new team, so the Orioles sent cash to Cleveland to complete the trade.) Though he played more frequently for the Orioles than he had for the Indians, his hitting and home-run production fell off, and his average for both teams was .264 with seven home runs. In May of the following season, the Orioles traded Pope back to Cleveland for outfielder Hoot Evers. Pope played in just 37 games for Baltimore and Cleveland combined in 1956, spending most of the season back at Indianapolis, where he hit .302 with 25 home runs and 76 RBIs in 100 games. It earned him a return call-up to Cleveland late in the season, but it would be his last, as he played in his final Major League game on September 30.

"I left Cleveland in '57 (for the San Diego Padres in the Pacific Coast League) and I certainly thought that I was going to get another chance in the big leagues because the way I left was rather disappointing," Pope told interviewer Brent Kelley.

That year I think I had an excellent spring training. In the first place, I didn't feel that I should have been the person to go the minor leagues, because I felt that I performed as well as any of the outfielders on the ballclub. I didn't understand all of that other stuff about opportunities to play in the big leagues, how many years you had in the big leagues, the seniority system, and all that kind of stuff. I just felt that the best ballplayer ought to be out on the ballfield, and that wasn't the case; but I did have a good spring training, and I felt that I should not have gone to San Diego that year.[14]

Playing with the PCL Padres in 1957 and 1958, Pope was a model of consistency, with statistics nearly identical both years. In 1957 he batted .313 with 18 home runs and 83 RBIs in 129 games, and in 1958 he hit .316 with 19 home runs and 96 RBIs in 142 games.

Pope was rankled that he did not get a chance to return to the Majors.

After I didn't get the opportunity to come back after the first years—that was '57—and winning the Most Valuable Player Award for the San Diego club, also, I began to get a little frustrated at that time because I felt that if the Cleveland Indians were not going to bring me back to the big leagues, that I should have been released or sold to some other ballclub. Later, I found out that there were opportunities for that to happen, but they didn't sell me. In fact, Hank Greenberg (Cleveland general manager) came out there and we had a talk about that and he told me that he had an opportunity to sell me to a couple ballclubs but he felt that he didn't want to get rid of the best ballplayer in the Pacific Coast League. I couldn't understand his reasoning there, so we got into a little heated conversation about that.[15]

Then after the 1958 season, the Indians did deal Pope, to Toronto of the International League. He played for Toronto in 1959 and for the Houston

Buffs of the American Association in 1960, batting in the .270s both seasons. Back at Toronto in 1961, he was a part-time player before retiring at the age of forty.

After retiring, Pope worked in a job-counseling program with the Cleveland Recreation Department. He coached amateur baseball and was an active member of First Zion Baptist Church in Cleveland. He later became a supervisor for the Equal Employment Opportunity Commission, then retired in 1994. Five years later, on August 28, 1999, Pope died of leukemia at the age of seventy-eight in Cleveland. He is buried at Lake View Cemetery.

Reflecting on his career, Pope told Brent Kelley, "I hear people talk about great feats that they've done; I never remembered those. I never bothered about statistics. I never bothered about batting averages or anything. When I read the paper the next day, I read the important parts about winning and losing and that was about it."[16]

Chapter 35. Timeline, July 1–July 13

Joseph Wancho

July 2—Cleveland—INDIANS HIKE LEAD TO 4 ½ GAMES; TAKE TWO FROM CHISOX, 3–2, 5–4—Doby goes 2 for 4 with two RBIS. He hits a solo home run in the sixth inning. Feller scatters four hits for his fifth win in the opener at home. Doby hits a three-run homer in the fifth inning of second game, and paces the sweep of Chisox. Wynn registers his ninth victory. Cleveland extends their lead to four and a half games over New York, five games over Chicago.

July 3—Cleveland—PINCH SINGLE BY MAJESKI ENDS BATTLE—Majeski's pinch-hit single to left field in the bottom of the fifteenth inning plates two runs for the victory over the White Sox. Doby and Westlake homer. Newhouser wins in relief.

July 4—Cleveland—TRIBE RUNS STREAK TO SEVEN, 2–1—Doby homers to lead the offense over the Chisox. Narleski gets the win in relief, combining on the one-hitter with Garcia and Wynn.

July 5—Detroit—INDIANS WHIP TIGERS, 13–6; THEN LOSE, 1–0—Bill Glynn hits three homers and collects eight RBIS to lead the offense, which collected fourteen hits in the opener at Detroit. Larry Doby adds three hits and two runs. Harvey Kuenn's homer in the bottom of the eleventh inning lifts the Tigers in the second game.

July 6—Cleveland—11-RUN SALVO, 15 RED-SKINS BAT IN FIRST INNING—Bill Glynn and Wally Westlake each drive in three runs and Glynn adds a home run. Early Wynn captures his tenth win. Cleveland scores all eleven runs in the first inning.

July 7—Cleveland—INDIANS WHIP ORIOLES, 6–1—The Tribe scores all their runs in the second frame, aided by four free passes from Bob Turley. Bobby Avila goes 2 for 4, with two RBIS. Mike Garcia improves his record to 11-5.

July 8—Cleveland—FELLER'S 5TH STRAIGHT HIKES LEAD TO 4—Jim Hegan and Wally Westlake each hit a home run. Bob Feller K's six to claim his sixth win, and adds an RBI single. Cleveland sweeps the Birds in the three-game series.

July 9—Chicago—CHISOX CUT TRIBE'S LEAD TO THREE, 8–3—Jim Rivera hits two solo home runs. Nellie Fox and Chico Carrasquel add two RBIS apiece for the White Sox. Chicago scores four runs in the bottom of the seventh inning. Bob Keegan raises his record to 12-3.

July 10—Chicago—INDIANS HELD TO SIX HITS BY TWO HURLERS—Jack Harshman backs his shutout effort with two hits and an RBI in Chisox's three-run second inning. He strikes out five batters. Sandy Consuegra earns the save. The Tribe strands eleven base runners.

July 11—Chicago—TRIBE LEAD CUT TO HALF GAME, 3–0, 8–2—Billy Pierce whiffs seven, while Minnie Minosa and Matt Batts homer to lead the White Sox to victory in the first game of the twin bill. Virgil Trucks completes the sweep of the Indians at Comiskey Park with his twelfth win. Ron Jackson hits a three-run homer. Johnny Groth drives in two runs. The Indians lead the Yankees by a half game at the All-Star break.

July 13—Cleveland—AL WINS ALL-STAR GAME, 11–9—Al Rosen homers twice and drives in five runs. Larry Doby homers once. Bobby Avila goes 3 for 3 with two RBIS. Attendance for the game was 69,751.

Chapter 36. **Luke Easter**

Justin Murphy

AGE	G	AB	R	H	2B	3B	HR	TB	RBI	BB	SO	BAV	OBP	SLG	SB	GDP	HBP
38	6	6	0	1	0	0	0	1	0	0	2	.167	.167	.167	0	0	0

I've seen a lot of powerful hitters in my time but for sheer ability to knock a ball great distances, I've never seen anybody better than Easter—and I'm not excepting Babe Ruth.

—Del Baker

Luscious "Luke" Easter was born August 4, 1915, at 8:15 p.m. in Jonestown, Mississippi.[1] During his playing career and later in life, Easter would equivocate on his birth date. Indians general manager Hank Greenberg once said, "No one knows how old Luke really is. No one, that is, but Luke himself, and sometimes I'm not sure that he knows."[2] He first claimed to have been born August 4, 1921, in St. Louis, Missouri, then changed to the same date in 1913 and 1914. On August 17, 1963, during one of a series of Luke Easter Days at Rochester's Silver Stadium, Red Wings club president Morrie Silver offered Easter $10 for every year of his age, prompting Luke to announce that "my baseball age is 42, but my real age is 52," placing his birth in 1911 (and netting him $520). The 1915 date is substantiated by a birth certificate, census research, and Easter's Social Security application, as well as an inscription in the Easter family Bible.[3]

Luke was the fifth of ten children born to James and Maude Easter. At the time of Luke's death in 1979, he still had six surviving siblings: brothers Robert, Julius (J. C.), and Wilbert, and sisters Minnie (married name Blanks), Ruby (Hayes), and Izell (Tillis).[4] Two other siblings died young. His father, who had attended the Tuskegee Institute and who, like his son, cut an imposing figure at six feet one, 210 pounds, was a farmer in Jonestown, a town of

Luke Easter—Easter was the *Sporting News* MVP in 1952, as he hit 31 home runs and drove in 97 runs. He is credited with hitting the longest home run in Cleveland Stadium history, a 477-foot clout on June 23, 1950.

four hundred, but in 1919 the family relocated to St. Louis, where James's brother found him work shoveling sand in a glass factory. Maude died of tuberculosis in 1922, when Luke was seven. Luke attended St. Louis public schools and went to the same high school as fellow Negro Leaguer Quincy Trouppe, three years his elder. Luke dropped out, however, after the ninth grade, and spent his time playing ball. J. C. Easter relates that he and Luke used to play with a broomstick and bottletops.[5]

Easter first took part in Organized Baseball in 1937, when he played outfield and first base and batted cleanup for the St. Louis Titanium Giants. The Giants were sponsored by the American Titanium Company. Easter and the other players worked for the company year-round, but they were given time off to play ball. The St. Louis Stars had previously been the top black team in the city, having succeeded the St. Louis Giants in 1922, and they won three Negro National League championships between 1928 and 1931. After 1931, however, the league was dissolved, and the Stars with it. In their absence, the Titanium Giants had become an elite club, defeating six Negro American League teams in exhibitions 1940 and regularly winning 90 percent of their games. Indeed, when an attempt was made in 1937 to reestablish the St. Louis Stars under different management in the new Negro American League, the experiment lasted only two years, largely due to competition with the Giants. Luke's teammates in St. Louis included Sam Jethroe, Jesse Askew, and Herb Bracken. Askew once said that "Easter was unlucky in not getting an earlier shot at the Negro Leagues, primarily because he played poorly in exhibitions against teams like the Kansas City Monarchs."[6]

In 1941 Easter and several teammates were traveling in Jethroe's car to a road game. The car crashed, and Easter suffered a broken ankle.[7] This ended his 1941 season, and the Giants were disbanded the following year. Later in his career, Luke would deny having played baseball before 1946, claiming instead that he'd only played softball, a claim that some have labeled mythmaking.

By the beginning of 1942, World War II had broken out, and Easter, like many players, was drafted into the war effort. The National Archives and Records Administration lists him as being inducted on June 22, 1942, and stationing at Fort Leonard Wood, Missouri . He spent thirteen months in the army before being discharged on July 3, 1943, because of his ankle injury.[8] He later found work in a "war chemical plant" in Chicago in the summer of 1945.[9] At the end of 1945, with the war over, he spoke with "Candy" Jim Taylor, manager of the Chicago American Giants. Taylor directed him to Abe Saperstein, who was a major baseball promoter before founding the Harlem Globetrotters. Saperstein was starting a new team, the Cincinnati Crescents, and he invited Easter to join it.[10] The Crescents did not succeed in gaining admission into the Negro American League, and instead spent the 1946 season barnstorming across the country, competing against many Negro League teams. Statistics are not widely available for the 1946 Crescents, but the March 30, 1949, *Sporting News* reported that Easter had batted .415 with 152 RBIs; it has also been said that Easter hit 74 home runs, although that number is not verified. He also hit one of his more famous home runs, a ball that reached the center-field bleachers of the Polo Grounds in New York against the Cubans. As teammate Bob Thurman said, "He hit it halfway up the stands, about 500 feet. The thing about it—it was a line drive."[11]

As he was throughout his career, Easter was a fan favorite in Cincinnati, and in 1947 he was signed to the Homestead Grays for a reported $1,100 a month,[12] making him one of the highest paid players on the team. The Grays sought a replacement in the lineup and at the box office for Josh Gibson, who'd died of a stroke the previous winter. In fact, Buck O'Neil writes that "we [i.e., the Negro Leagues] wanted to get Luke away from the St. Louis Stars [*sic*] long before he went to the Grays, but he didn't want to leave home. He had a pretty good job there as a security guard."[13] The team already featured Hall of Fame slugger Buck Leonard; outfielder Bob Thurman, who would later play five seasons with the Cincinnati Reds; pitcher John "Needle Nose" Wright, who later received a tryout with the Los Angeles Dodgers; and Wilmer Fields, who pitched and played third base, and who won eight MVP awards in different leagues in his career. In 219 at bats in 1947, Luke hit ten home runs and held a .311 batting average, while playing the outfield (since Leonard was at first base). The following year he recorded a batting average of .363, and his thirteen homers tied him with teammate Leonard for the league lead (Leonard also took home the batting title that season, with a .395 average). He also led the NNL with sixty-two RBIs. Most impressively, in only fifty-eight games, the six-foot-four, 240-pound Easter legged out a career-high eight triples, helping the Grays to a Negro League World Series championship. After the season, he was chosen to play in the 1948 East-West All-Star Game. The year 1948 also saw Luke's marriage to twenty-four-year-old Virgil Lowe, a Cleveland native. Some sources claim that Virgil was his third wife, yet there is no reference to any other wives in any of the available documents.[14] He and Virgil would remain married until Luke's death, thirty-one years later.

Meanwhile, Easter had also been playing winter ball in Puerto Rico, Venezuela, and Hawaii for the prior three years.[15] Statistics for these seasons are difficult to come by, but over three years playing for Mayagüez in Puerto Rico, he amassed 48 home runs, 145 RBIS, and a .330 batting average, leading the league in home runs each season.[16] His best season was 1948–49, when he was named MVP, batting .402 as the team won the championship. Easter also later played for Hermosillo of the Mexican Pacific Coast League in 1954–55, leading the league with twenty homers, and for Caguas in Puerto Rico in the winters of 1955–56, leading the league in home runs at the age of forty-one, and in 1956–57.[17]

By 1949 Major League Baseball was slowly becoming integrated, and Bill Veeck signed Easter to a contract with the defending champion Cleveland Indians on February 19.[18] The Indians already featured Larry Doby, the first black player in the American League, as well as Satchel Paige. Easter, who had told Veeck that he was twenty-seven, was first assigned to Cleveland's Pacific Coast League affiliate in San Diego. He was only the second black player to appear in the PCL, but he assured San Diego president Bill Starr that "everybody likes me when I hit the ball."[19] That spring, however, he injured his right knee in an on-field collision, then had the same kneecap broken by a pitch. Despite the injury, he played on to packed crowds, with fans flocking to the park to see him hit. Researcher Rick Swaine claims that the average attendance in his first ten games was over 34,000; Goodrich reports, perhaps more realistically, that the total attendance of his first seventeen games, home and away, was a record 101,492. Some clubs were even obliged to sell standing-room-only tickets in the outfield when San Diego came to town. In one three-game stand in Los Angeles, Easter hit six home runs, and fights broke out at the gates as fans clamored to watch him hit. Frank Finch, writing in *The Sporting News,* reported that the crowds to see him take batting practice were equaled only by those that turned out to see Stan Musial, Ted Williams, and Ernie Lombardi.[20] On the field, however, Easter did have to deal with racial discrimination. Some suggested that the pitch that had broken his knee in the spring had been intentional, and in a game against Portland, pitcher Ed Liska threw at him eight times in a single at bat, including two that sailed behind the batter. Easter responded in his next at bat with a 450-foot shot to dead center that narrowly missed Liska's head on its way out of the park.[21]

The Padres, also featuring future Major Leaguers Max West, Al Rosen, and Minnie Minoso, ended up in the championship series for the year. By the end of June, however, the pain in Luke's broken right knee had become insurmountable, and the Indians had him undergo surgery. Only six weeks later, still hobbled, he would join the Indians, making his Major League debut on August 11. According to *The Sporting News,* PCL owners estimated a loss of more than $200,000 in revenue for the league after his departure,[22] and the Indians were forced to part with the popular Allie Clark in order to make room for him on the roster. Easter became the eleventh black player in MLB history. Bob Feller was the winning pitcher in relief that day as the Indians defeated the White Sox 6–5 in a twelve-inning game that lasted nearly four hours. Luke played in twenty-one games in 1949 and hit just .222 with no home runs. Bill Veeck, as he was wont to do, had created a great deal of publicity for Easter, and Cleveland fans did not take well to his early struggles. *The Sporting News* named him "the most booed player in the history of Cleveland Stadium." Tris Speaker pointed to the racial tension of the era, saying, "The poor guy came up under the worst possible conditions. . . . [He] had nothing to do with the condition that made him the target of the boo birds."[23] Easter replied that "I hear them and I don't hear them . . . if I hit, they'll like me. If I don't hit, I don't deserve to be in the lineup."

Spring 1950 found Easter embroiled in a competition for the starting first base job with popular veteran Mickey Vernon. He performed well in spring training, leading the team with a .333 average and batting in fourteen runs. Perhaps his most memorable shot, however, was an out: in a game between the Indians and the Browns, St. Louis pitcher Ned Garver thrust his glove in the way of an Easter line drive and was knocked off his feet by its momentum.[24] Despite the strong spring, however, Vernon started the year at first, with Easter in the outfield. Still slowed from his knee surgery, Easter's struggles at the plate continued early on, as did the booing, until May 6, when he blasted his first home run, off of Allie Reynolds of the Yankees. He went on to post a .280 batting average that year, with 28 home runs and 107 RBIs. Particularly noteworthy was a 477-foot home run he hit into the second deck in right field at Cleveland Stadium on June 23, 1950, off Joe Haynes of the Senators, said to be the longest ball ever hit there.[25] He also was able to finish the season playing first base, as Mickey Vernon was traded to Washington to accommodate him.

And, as was inevitable, by the end of the year Easter had won over the hostile Cleveland crowds with his powerful swing and his endearing demeanor. He was a regular unannounced spectator at local sandlot games, and signed endless autographs for the children who came to watch him play. On the field, though, Luke's struggle for acceptance continued, as he led the league in HBP.

Again in 1951, Luke was injured early, this time tearing a tendon in his left knee; but despite missing thirty games, he managed to hit 27 home runs and 103 RBIs, both team highs. The year was also significant for Easter due to the replacement of manager Lou Boudreau with Al Lopez, who had little use for immobile infielders—or, according to researcher Rick Swaine, for black players in general. Luke, riddled with injuries and illness as well as deteriorating vision, started extremely poorly for the 1952 Indians, and he was demoted to Triple-A Indianapolis after hitting just .208 through sixty-three appearances. In Indianapolis, however, Luke caught fire, hitting .340 with six home runs and twelve RBIs in only fifty at bats. He was quickly brought back to Cleveland, and he stayed hot for the rest of the season, hitting twenty homers in the second half of the season. At the end of the year, he was named the American League's Most Outstanding Player by *The Sporting News*. Hank Greenberg marveled, "His comeback is the most amazing thing I've ever seen. Six weeks ago . . . the snap in his swing was gone completely. They thought he'd never come back."[26]

Easter signed a contract for $20,000 at the beginning of the 1953 season and had high hopes of replicating his 1952 success. Unfortunately, he was struck by a pitch in the fourth game of the season, breaking a bone in his left foot. The injury hobbled him for the remainder of the season, and he was only able to appear in sixty-eight games. He was released on October 1 but was invited back to spring training the following year, when he was again slowed, this time by an infection in his toe. He had six pinch-hit at bats for Cleveland before being optioned to the

Minor Leagues when the club had to make its final roster cuts in early May. His final big league appearance came on May 4. Though Easter was initially bitter at being demoted, he ended up playing very well. He played fifty-six games with the Padres and sixty-six with Ottawa, batting .348 in his time in Canada. Between Ottawa and San Diego he managed to hit twenty-eight home runs, but he was released by the Indians after the season. "Had Luke come up to the big leagues as a young man, there's no telling what numbers he would have had," said Al Rosen.[27]

Despite his success in the Majors, Luke Easter inarguably received his greatest acclaim and adulation as a Minor Leaguer. Just as he had in St. Louis, Cincinnati, San Diego, and Cleveland, Easter became a local legend with his home run hitting and his likeable personality. In 1955 he started with the Charleston (wv) Athletics of the American Association, where he tied for third in the league in home runs with thirty. The following year, Easter signed a $7,500 contract with the newly independent Buffalo Bisons of the International League. Buffalo had just declined to renew their contract with the Detroit Tigers and were struggling with community ownership. The signing of Easter, the first black player on the team since Frank Grant in 1888, was their first important acquisition, and he did not disappoint.[28] Although the 1956 Bisons finished twenty-one and a half games out of first, Easter hit .306 and led the league with 35 homers and 106 RBIS. More important, he helped capture the city's interest for the game with countless public appearances, a crucial task for a community-owned team.[29] He played even better in 1957, hitting forty home runs for the Bisons, who by this time had signed a player development contract with the Kansas City Athletics. Among those forty home runs was one that has become perhaps the most famous of all of Big Luke's famous blasts. Buffalo baseball historian Joe Overfeld tells the story in *100 Seasons of Buffalo Baseball*:

The explosion occurred on the evening of June 14, 1957. It was mild and windless, and there was a trace of haze in the air. In the fourth inning of the second game of the evening's double-header, Columbus left-hander Bob Kuzava delivered what he later called "a perfect pitch"—a knee-high fastball on the outside of the plate. Easter swung, timed the pitch perfectly and sent it soaring high and deep to center field. As the ball disappeared into the haze, there was a mighty roar from the crowd as many fans realized at once what had happened: Luke Easter had just become the first batter ever to hit a ball over the centerfield scoreboard. As Easter completed his lumbering home run trot, dead-pan all the way, the cheering and applause reached decibel levels never previously attained in the old park.[30]

The center-field fence at Offerman Stadium was 400 feet from home plate, and the scoreboard towered 60 feet in the air. The ball had traveled in an arc of approximately 550 feet. It concluded by crashing triumphantly through the window of Irene Luedke, who lived across the street from the stadium, and who "thought for sure someone had dropped an atom bomb on the roof."[31] After the game, Easter boldly predicted, "If my legs hold out, I'll do it again," and incredibly enough, he did, just two months later. Offerman Stadium saw its last game in 1960, and Easter went down in history as the only man ever to clear that scoreboard—having accomplished it twice. His tremendous power caused teammate Joe Astroth to remark to the customs inspector at the airport in Havana, "You, Mr. Inspector, are face-to-face with the greatest home run hitter since Babe Ruth . . . there is no one alive who can hit a ball the distance with Luke Easter."[32]

Luke played his third year with Buffalo in 1958, hitting 38 homers and driving in 109. After the season, however, the Bisons signed an agreement with the Philadelphia Phillies, who had important plans for prospect Francisco Herrera. Herrera, a big, right-handed first baseman, made Easter expendable. Several weeks into the 1959 season, on May 14, Easter was sold to the Rochester Red Wings for $100.[33] He responded by paying tribute to the fans of Buffalo, and made the ninety-mile trip down the interstate to Rochester, where the last chapter of his baseball career was to play out.

In the remainder of the 1959 season, Luke managed to hit 22 home runs and drive in 76 runs. He followed with 14 home runs in 1960, 10 in 1961, 15 in 1962, and 6 in 1963, his last full season. By this point, Easter was practically immobile, although he would not suffer any further injuries after leaving the Indians in 1953. Even as his hitting faltered, however, he managed to become perhaps the most popular player in Red Wings history. Long-time Rochester writer George Beahon wrote, "Foul weather or fair, he never denied an autograph. During those years, after I filed stories from the press box to the morning paper, I would see Luke still around the clubhouse or the parking lot, signing his name and making friends for the franchise."[34] Luke Easter Night in 1960 drew more than eight thousand fans, who saw Luke receive "a color television set, fishing equipment, a $300 wrist watch with diamond numerals, a movie camera, luggage, and even a frozen turkey and five pounds of sausage."[35] In fact, Easter had started his own Luke Easter Sausage Company several years prior, and would regularly make gifts to his teammates in appreciation of strong performances.

Easter appeared in ten games as a pinch hitter in 1964 before finally deciding to hang up his cleats, twenty-six years after his debut with the St. Louis Titanium Giants and fifteen years after breaking into the Majors as a thirty-four-year-old rookie. He remained with Rochester for the remainder of the season as a coach; Major Leaguers Boog Powell, Curt Blefary, and Pete Ward all credited Easter with helping in their development.[36] After the 1964 season, Luke moved back to Cleveland with his wife, Virgil.[37] Aside from a short coaching stint with the

Indians in 1969, necessary to qualify for pension benefits, he would never work in baseball again.

After returning to Cleveland, Luke immediately set to work again, though no longer in baseball. Former Negro Leaguer Frazier Robinson, in his autobiography, writes about having often gone to a café that Luke had opened in Cleveland called the Majestic Blue Room. He recalls that "he had a lot of jazz acts at his club, and it was a pretty popular place in Cleveland."[38] He also took a full-time job polishing airplane parts for TRW. Though he worked the night shift, Luke soon gained the confidence of his coworkers and was named chief steward of the Aircraft Workers Alliance.

It was in his capacity as union steward that Easter, in typical selfless fashion, came to his tragic end. He often cashed paychecks for fellow employees who could not make it to the bank. On March 29, 1979, he was carrying a small handgun for self-protection, though at other times he procured a police escort.[39] Easter stepped out of a Cleveland Trust Company branch in Euclid, Ohio, at 9:00 a.m., carrying a bag full of cash. His *New York Times* obituary from March 30, 1979, reports that he had $5,000 in the bag, while Daniel Cattau says $45,000. In either case, he was accosted by two gunmen in the parking lot at East 260th Street and Euclid Avenue. One of them was a former TRW employee who knew about the arrangement Luke had with his coworkers. They demanded the money from him. When he refused, they shot him several times in the chest; the *New York Times* obituary says that it was "a sawed-off shotgun and a .38-caliber revolver", while Cattau attributes it to a .357 Magnum. The gunmen were captured after a high-speed car chase, their pockets filled with the stolen cash.[40] Luke was dead on arrival at the hospital.

On April 3, 1979, the baseball fans in Cleveland poured en masse into Mt. Sinai Baptist Church to pay their last respects to the legendary man. More than 4,000 people filed by the casket, and over 1,000 attended the funeral ceremony itself. Former teammates Bob Cain and Mike Garcia were pallbearers; ex-Indians Al Rosen and Bob Lemon, longtime Cleveland sportswriter Hal Lebovitz and Indians team president Gabe Paul were among those serving as honorary pallbearers. Following the service, Easter was interred at Highland Park Cemetery. Besides his wife Virgil, Luke's survivors included six siblings, and six children (sons Terry Lee, Luke Jr., Travis, and George, and daughters Nana and Marla), two of whom (George and Marla) he and Virgil had adopted. He also had three grandchildren at the time of his death.[41]

Easter has been posthumously honored by many of the organizations to which he contributed as a player. He was a charter member of the Rochester Red Wings Hall of Fame in 1989 and also became a member of the Greater Buffalo Sports Hall of Fame in 1997. His plaque reads, "Buffalo fans have always worshiped their sports heroes, but few have ever attained the near mythical stats accorded to Bisons great Luke Easter." In Cleveland, a local ballpark was renamed in his honor, and a statue of him stands in front of it today. His wife became the first vice president of the Cleveland Baseball Federation, of which Luke had earlier been chairman.[42] The most lasting impression of Luke Easter, however, lives in the minds of the countless fans who saw him club pitches far into the night, for whom he signed autographs, with whom he laughed, and whom he inspired with his infectious enthusiasm and unwavering kindness.

Nearly everyone who ever saw Luke Easter play has a story about a seemingly impossible home run that he hit. Many, such as his colossal shots in the Polo Grounds in New York, Municipal Stadium in Cleveland, and Offerman Stadium in Buffalo, have become part and parcel of baseball mythology. Any attempt to recount Easter's life, however, should place the most emphasis on the impressions he made upon the people who had the pleasure of meeting him, no matter how briefly. He was adored by teammates and fans in every city he played in,

even as one of the first black players in the PCL, the Major Leagues, and the International League. His demeanor was always positive, and he refused to be discouraged by the racism he often encountered. Joseph Thomas Moore, in his biography of Larry Doby, reports that the two players often had different ideas on how to breach the color issue: "They were as different from each other as Doby and [Satchel] Paige had been. While Doby was totally serious on the field, Easter relaxed and enjoyed his new status . . . as a big leaguer." Luke once told Doby, "Look, Larry, you fight just half the world and leave the other half to me."[43]

Away from the stadium, Luke was a partier and a gambler, a clotheshorse and a lover of fine food and cigars. Kevin Nelson has an apt description of Easter in *The Story of California Baseball*: "Everything about Easter was big—his home runs, his personality, his luxury Buick automobile. He liked for his teammate Artie Wilson to act as chauffeur and let him sit in the back seat so that when he was driving around town people would think a big shot was passing by. A woman who knew him (and there were more than a few of those) described his free-spending, party-loving personality as 'flamboyant.'"[44]

Luke was a serious card-shark, quickly winning back large sums for teammates on the road when the need arose.[45] He was also an impeccable dresser who took special care to keep his shoes shined and his pants pressed. James Goodrich reported in a 1950 interview that, "though Luke is an exceptionally large man, he eats only normal meals. His special appetite is for cereals and vegetable dishes."[46] He also enjoyed going to watch gangster movies and listening to jazz; Jim Fridley recalls Luke introducing him to Louis Armstrong.[47]

His social life aside, however, it is difficult to sum up the admiration and affection that Luke inspired in those who saw him play or shook his hand during his long baseball career. Minnie Minoso once recalled, "He was such a nice man. I didn't speak good English, so he'd take me to restaurants and other places and translate for me."[48] Buffalo historian Joe Overfeld recalls that when Easter died, "for many it was as though the life of a member of the family had been suddenly and tragically snuffed out."[49] Luke always had time for an autograph, a handshake, a photograph, or a smile. He was once fined at a Minor League game in Minneapolis for opening the gates to the stadium to let in children who couldn't afford tickets.[50] One often hears Easter compared to Babe Ruth. The comparison goes further than their similar power at the plate, for like Ruth, Luke had the ability to relate to all who watched him play, at home or on the road. It is with this intense enthusiasm and caring in mind that one can best understand the great baseball life of Luke Easter.

Chapter 37. **Early Wynn**

David L. Fleitz

AGE	W	L	PCT	ERA	G	GS	GF	CG	SHO	SV	IP	H	BB	SO	HBP	WP
34	23	11	.676	2.73	40	36	4	20	3	2	270.2	225	83	155	0	2

Chicago fans were outraged when the White Sox traded their most popular player, Minnie Minoso, to Cleveland in December 1957 with Fred Hatfield for Early Wynn and Al Smith. Wynn was a thirty-seven-year-old right-handed pitcher who had posted a losing record for the Indians that season, and his best days appeared to be behind him. However, Wynn joined Billy Pierce to give the White Sox a formidable one-two punch at the top of their rotation, and his Cy Young Award–winning performance in 1959 led the club to its first American League pennant since 1919. Four years later, at age forty-three, he became the fourteenth member of baseball's 300-win club.

Early Wynn Jr., whose family claimed Scotch-Irish and Native American heritage, was born in Hartford, Alabama, on January 6, 1920, to Early Wynn Sr. and his wife, Blanche. Hartford is a small town surrounded by peanut and cotton fields in Geneva County, which borders the Florida Panhandle in the southeastern part of the state. Early Jr., whose father was an auto mechanic and a semipro ballplayer, earned ten cents an hour hauling 500-pound bales of cotton after school. He concentrated on baseball after breaking his leg at a high school football practice, and at age seventeen he traveled to Sanford, Florida, to attend a baseball camp operated by the Washington Senators. Legend has it that Early, a husky six-footer who weighed about 200 pounds, arrived at camp in his bare feet. He did not, said Early years later to writer Roger Kahn, "but I was wearing coveralls."[1] A Washington scout, Clyde Milan, was impressed with his fastball and signed Early to a contract. The young pitcher dropped out of high school and began his professional career in 1937

Early Wynn—Wynn was named the Cy Young winner and *Sporting News* Pitcher of the Year when he won twenty-two games for the White Sox in 1959. He was elected to the Hall of Fame in 1972.

with the Senators' Class D Florida State League farm team in Sanford.

After a 16-11 season in Sanford, Early advanced to the Charlotte Hornets of the Class B Piedmont League, where he remained for the next three years. The Senators gave him a trial in Washington at the end of the 1939 season, though Early was not yet ready for Major League action, going 0-2 in three games. He spent all of 1940 in Charlotte, and a good season at Springfield in the Class A Eastern League in 1941 (16-12, 2.56) brought him to Washington to stay. In 1942 he made twenty-eight starts for the Senators, posting a 10-16 mark with a 5.12 ERA as a twenty-two-year-old with little more than a fastball in his arsenal.

In 1939 Early married Mabel Allman, from Morganton, North Carolina, and the couple had a son named Joe Early Wynn. Tragically, the marriage ended prematurely. In December of 1942, Mabel was killed in an automobile accident in Charlotte, where the Wynns lived during the winter months. Early was left with a baby to raise, with the assistance of his relatives. He won eighteen games for Washington in 1943, but fell to 8-17 in 1944, leading the American League in losses. He married Lorraine Follin that September, shortly after entering the United States Army. Wynn served in the Tank Corps in the Philippines during World War II. He spent all of the 1945 season and part of the next in the military before rejoining the Senators.

At this time, Wynn owned an impressive fastball, but had only a mediocre changeup to complement it. He was inconsistent, posting a 17-15 log in 1947 and an 8-19 mark in 1948. Still, he was undeniably talented, and the Cleveland Indians coveted his services. Bill Veeck, the Cleveland team owner, tried to acquire Wynn in a trade before the 1948 season, but he was rebuffed by Washington owner Clark Griffith. In December 1948 Veeck acquired pitcher Joe Haynes, Griffith's son-in-law, from the Chicago White Sox. Veeck then offered Haynes to the Senators for Wynn, and Griffith agreed, sending first baseman Mickey Vernon along with Wynn for Haynes, pitcher Ed Klieman, and first baseman Eddie Robinson.

The Indians figured that Wynn would become a big winner if he could develop more pitches, and the club assigned pitching coach Mel Harder to teach Wynn how to throw a curve and a slider. "I could throw the ball when I came here [to Cleveland]," recalled Wynn years later in *The Sporting News*,

"but Mel made a pitcher out of me."[2] By mid-1949 he had mastered the curve and slider, and he began to use a knuckleball as an off-speed delivery. With a new array of pitches at his command, Wynn joined the ranks of the top hurlers in 1950. He won eighteen games and led the American League in earned run average that season with a 3.20 mark.

Early, nicknamed "Gus," got along well with his teammates, but he was a grim, scowling presence on the mound. "That space between the white lines—that's my office, that's where I conduct my business," he told sportswriter Red Smith. "You take a look at the batter's box, and part of it belongs to the hitter. But when he crowds in just that hair, he's stepping into my office, and nobody comes into my office without an invitation when I'm going to work."[3] With his large frame, grizzled appearance, and willingness to knock down opposing hitters, Wynn stood out as one of the most intimidating pitchers in the game. Roger Kahn, in his book *A Season in the Sun*, described how the pitcher once brushed back his teenaged son, Joe Early, during a batting practice session at Yankee Stadium. "You shouldn't crowd me," snarled the elder Wynn. As he explained to Kahn, "I've got a right to knock down anybody holding a bat."[4]

He hated losing, and he was never afraid to throw at batters who got too close to the plate, or hit line drives at him. Some called him a headhunter, but Early regarded close pitches as part of the game. "If they are going to outlaw the inside pitch," said Wynn in an article he wrote for *Sport* magazine in 1956, "they ought to eliminate line drives and sharp grounders hit through the pitcher's box."[5] To those who suggested that he would throw at his own mother, Early famously replied, "I would if she were crowding the plate."[6] One day, Mickey Mantle drilled a liner through the box for a single. Early then threw several pickoff attempts at Mantle's legs. "You'll never be a big winner until you start hating the hitter," he told rookie pitcher Gary Bell, according to a 1959 article in *The Sporting News*. "That guy with the bat is trying to take away your bread and butter. You've got to fight him every second."[7]

His toughness and durability made Wynn part of one of the greatest pitching rotations of all time in Cleveland, with Wynn, Bob Lemon, Bob Feller, and Mike Garcia all posting twenty-win seasons during the early 1950s. Under the tutelage of Mel Harder and manager Al Lopez, Wynn won twenty games or more in a season four times for Cleveland, and he anchored the rotation that led the Indians to the American League pennant in 1954. In the World Series that year, the New York Giants defeated Wynn in the second game, as he gave up three runs in seven innings and lost by a 3-1 score. Wynn did not have the chance to pitch again in the Series, as the Giants swept to the title in four games.

Wynn made his permanent home in Nokomis, Florida, where he and his wife raised his son, Joe Early, and their daughter, Shirley. He spent his leisure hours hunting, driving powerboats, and flying his own Cessna 170 single-engine plane. Beginning in 1955, Wynn produced a regular column for the *Cleveland News*, titled "The Wynn Mill," and donated the money he earned from the effort to the Elks Club in Nokomis. Though he had dropped out of high school, Early wrote without the assistance of a ghostwriter, and his frank assessments of umpires, league policies, and his own management rankled Cleveland team officials and strained his relationship with general manager Hank Greenberg.

Early notched another twenty-win campaign in 1956, but in 1957 he posted his first losing season in Cleveland (14-17, with his ERA leaping from 2.72 in 1956 to 4.31) despite leading the league in strikeouts (184). The careers of both Bob Feller and Bob Lemon drew to a close during this time, and perhaps the Indians believed that the thirty-seven-year-old Wynn was fading as well. On December 4, 1957, the team traded Early and outfielder Al Smith to the Chicago White Sox for outfielder Minnie Minoso and infielder Fred Hatfield. The White Sox inserted a clause in his contract that prohibited the pitch-

er from writing for newspapers, but the team compensated him for the lost income. Reunited with his old Cleveland manager Al Lopez, who had been released by the Indians and hired by the White Sox, Early compiled a 14-16 record in 1958, leading the league again in strikeouts (179).

He was still a tough competitor, sometimes throwing chairs in the locker room after losses. Early hated to be taken out of games, though his advancing age often made it necessary to use relievers to finish his wins. In 1992 Al Lopez described Wynn's competitiveness to biographer Wes Singletary. "So this one day Early was arguing with the umpire," said Lopez, "when I came out there and he threw the ball at me, hitting me in the stomach. It was more of a flip/toss but the press played it up. I said give me the goddamned ball and don't be throwing it at me. After the game he came and apologized to me. I said, 'Early, I know how you feel but the people upstairs, the fans and media, they see that and think you're mad at me.' I told him don't get mad at me, get mad at the guys who are hitting."[8]

Early had suffered from gout since the 1950 season, and he pitched in pain for the last half of his career. Still, he kept in good shape, and his fastball remained sharp as he approached his fortieth birthday. Lopez kept Early at the top of the Chicago rotation, and in 1959 everything clicked for both Wynn and the White Sox. On May 1, the thirty-nine-year-old pitched a one-hit shutout against the Boston Red Sox, and hit a home run that provided the only scoring in the 1-0 victory. He led the league in innings pitched, started the first All-Star Game (from 1959 to 1962, Major League Baseball held two All-Star Games each year) for the American League, and won a league-leading twenty-two games, pitching the White Sox to their first American League flag in forty years. His twenty-first win of the season, a 4–2 victory over Cleveland on September 22, clinched the pennant and set off a night of celebration on Chicago's South Side. At season's end, Wynn won the Major League Cy Young Award and finished third in the American League Most Valuable Player balloting behind teammates Nellie Fox and Luis Aparicio.

The White Sox faced the Los Angeles Dodgers in the 1959 World Series, and Wynn pitched seven shutout innings in the opening game, teaming with reliever Jerry Staley to defeat the Dodgers by an 11–0 score. However, he struggled in the fourth contest, played at the Los Angeles Coliseum before 92,650 fans. Wynn failed to complete the third inning of a game that the White Sox eventually lost, 5–4, though Staley was the losing pitcher. In the sixth game, played in Chicago, a six-run Dodger rally in the fourth inning knocked Wynn out of the game and saddled him with the Series-ending defeat.

Wynn's 13 wins in 1960 left him with 284 career victories, and the pitcher announced his intention of joining the 300-win club before his retirement. He pitched well in 1961, with eight wins in his ten decisions, but arm soreness, caused by gout, ended his season in July. He gave up eating meat in an attempt to control his gout problem, but the pain persisted, causing problems with his legs and right hand. He fell short of his 300th win in 1962, posting a 7-15 record while relying mostly on a slider and a knuckleball. His seventh win, a complete-game effort against the Senators on September 8, was the 299th of his career, but Early failed in three subsequent attempts to gain his 300th victory. The White Sox were convinced that the forty-two-year-old pitcher had reached the end of the line, and in November the team released him.

The White Sox invited Early to their 1963 spring training camp, but he failed to make the team. He returned home to Florida, where he stayed in shape and waited for a call from another club. A few teams offered Wynn one-game contracts, seeking to capitalize on his quest for 300 wins, but he held out for a season-long deal. In June his old club, the Cleveland Indians, signed Early for the rest of the season and put him in the starting rotation. On July 13, in his fourth start of 1963, he pitched five innings

against the Kansas City Athletics and left the game with a 5–4 lead. Reliever Jerry Walker held the Athletics scoreless the rest of the way, giving Wynn his 300th, and final, win. He was the first man to win 300 games in the American League since Boston's Lefty Grove reached the mark in 1941.

Wynn started only one more game for Cleveland and retired at the end of the season, ending his career with a record of 300-244 and an ERA of 3.54. Wynn remained with the Indians, succeeding Mel Harder as Cleveland's pitching coach in 1964. He moved to the Minnesota Twins in 1967, and then managed in the Minor Leagues for several years. In 1972, in his fourth year of eligibility, Early was elected to the Baseball Hall of Fame. He had been disappointed in not gaining the honor earlier, once calling the institution the "Hall of Shame" in an interview. After his election, Wynn told *The Sporting News*, "I would have been happier if I'd made it the first year. I don't think I'm as thrilled as I would have been if that had happened. But naturally I'm happy. So is my wife. We've had a long wait."[9]

Early Wynn worked as a broadcaster for the Toronto Blue Jays and the Chicago White Sox after his election to the Hall of Fame, and he also owned a restaurant and bowling alley for a time. He fully expected to be the last of the 300-game winners, and often referred to himself in such terms in interviews. Nineteen years passed between Wynn's final victory in 1963 and Gaylord Perry's ascension to the 300-win club in 1982. As it was, Early saw six pitchers, including Perry, surpass his total during the 1980s. By the end of the 2008 season, Early was one of twenty-three pitchers with 300 wins or more.

Wynn retired during the mid-1980s and resided in Nokomis, Florida, until his health began to fail following the death of his wife, Lorraine, in 1994. Early suffered a heart attack and a series of strokes during the final years of his life, and spent his remaining days in an assisted living center in Venice, Florida, where he died on April 4, 1999, at age seventy-nine.

Chapter 38. **Hal Naragon**

Tracy J. R. Collins

AGE	G	AB	R	H	2B	3B	HR	TB	RBI	BB	SO	BAV	OBP	SLG	SB	GDP	HBP
25	46	101	10	24	2	2	0	30	12	9	12	.238	.300	.297	0	0	0

Hal Naragon gave up two years of his professional baseball career when he was drafted into the marines in 1951. Like many players of his era, he was proud to serve his country. His story is not unique in that respect. Yet, unlike many players, Hal thought that he was lucky. With his atypical unselfish and positive personality, Hal said that his time in the marines was "a good thing."[1] Still, luck is nothing without talent and hard work. In fact, Naragon's story is one Horatio Alger could have written. Like Alger's characters, Naragon experienced success through hard work, courage, determination, and concern for others. Yet, don't tell him this. He would say it was all luck. But it's a story any American boy might dream: A young boy grows up in small-town Ohio, plays professional baseball for his hometown team, goes to the World Series, and marries his high school sweetheart. It is exactly this quietly effective personality that served him well not only as a player for the Cleveland Indians but also later as a respected bullpen coach.

Harold Richard Naragon was born October 1, 1928, the third of four children, to Dwight and Dorothy Naragon in Zanesville, Ohio. When he was in the seventh grade, his parents moved to Barberton, Ohio, outside of Akron, "because there were more jobs there during the war," he said.[2] Hal essentially never left Barberton again. He is exceptionally proud of his hometown. In fact, he is quick to recite the city's proud sporting history, which includes figures such as Glenn "Bo" Schembechler, the famous University of Michigan football coach, who began his own sporting career on the Barberton High School baseball team as a teammate of Naragon's, and Bob

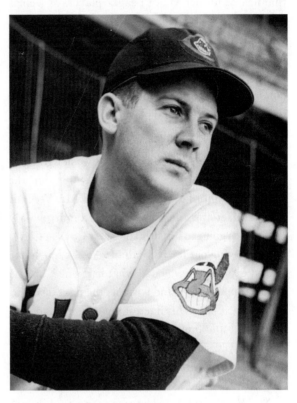

Hal Naragon—A local product from Barberton, Ohio, Naragon was a backup catcher in his career. He was a coach with Minnesota and Detroit in the 1960s.

Addis, the first Barberton High School graduate to sign a contract with a Major League Baseball team (with the New York Yankees as an amateur free agent in 1943).

Despite this pedigree, while Hal was in high school, the Barberton Magics were not always successful. According to the 1944 Barberton High School yearbook, "The 1944 season was unsuccessful in wins and losses, but a green team gained valuable experience for another season."[3] Naragon, a right-handed-throwing, left-handed-hitting freshman catcher, nonetheless earned his varsity letter. The 1946–47 school year proved to be a good one for "Haddie" Naragon, as he was referred to in the yearbook. To begin with, Hal spent the summer of 1946 playing on a Class A baseball team in Akron that fielded former Major League players as well as college players. One day, a friend on the team told Hal that a group of guys were driving up to Cleveland to try out for "Mr. Veeck," the new owner of the Cleveland Indians. Bill Veeck had decided to conduct open tryouts throughout Ohio to increase interest in the team. Hal played well at the tryouts, earning a contract. But, as he tells the story,

> I was not supposed to be there. I wasn't going to graduate until next year and couldn't sign the contract until I graduated. I asked Mr. Veeck if I could let him know my decision tomorrow. My dad was going to kill me if he knew I was in Cleveland trying out for the Indians. So, I came home and explained to my dad what happened, and he drove up to Cleveland with me the next day. Mr. Veeck explained his interest in me to my dad, and my dad told him I had not graduated from high school yet, so Mr. Veeck asked if I would give the Indians the opportunity to sign him the following spring. My dad asked, "Will a handshake do?" Mr. Veeck said yes. The two men shook hands and that was that.[4]

Back in Barberton, 1947 was declared "the year of sports champions."[5] In the winter, Hal was on the basketball team and helped the Magics get their first Ohio State Athletic Association trophy for winning the district championships. The Magics lost to Ashtabula in the regional tournament. Then there was the baseball season. The 1947 team, described in *A Bicentennial Remembrance: Barberton Ohio the Magic City*, as "the greatest group of athletes ever to play together on a single team in the City," won all of their games during their regular season with three shutouts and one no-hitter. They were

district and regional champions and lost the state championship game in extra innings. "The team's slugger was Hal Naragon, who could be counted on to hit one 'out of the park' every third game. People still speak of those 'Naragon shots.'"[6] Even at the beginning of that "magical" season, the *Barberton Herald* published an article, "B.H.S. Baseball Team Captures Three Contests," referring to Naragon as a "fixture behind the plate" and "a good sticker as well as a receiver."[7] Naragon posted a .444 batting average in his senior year and batted over .400 for his school career.

Naragon graduated from high school on June 5, 1947, and was ready to begin his career with the Indians. He signed in the spring of 1947 and in July headed off to Pittsfield, Massachusetts, to play for the Pittsfield Electrics of the Class C Canadian-American League. It was his first time away from home, but Hal was ready to be a professional baseball player, the only career he said he ever wanted.[8] By April 1948 he was the first-string catcher for Harrisburg of the Class B Interstate League where, according to his hometown *Herald*, "Down in Harrisburg Naragon has been credited with having one of the best throwing arms ever seen in those parts working from behind the plate."[9] In midseason he was sent down to Watertown, New York, of the Class C Border League to work on his hitting but went back up to Harrisburg when he began to improve. That year was important for Naragon in at least two ways. First, Fred Gerken, manager of the Watertown team, helped him improve his hitting, and second, in what Hal says was the most important and best decision he ever made, on October 10, 1948, he married his high school sweetheart, Joanne Schake, in Barberton, Ohio.

Naragon ended the 1948 season with a .195 average at Harrisburg, but was back with the Senators for 1949. Muddy Ruel, the Indians' assistant farm director, sang Naragon's praises, saying, "If anyone in this camp has a chance to become a solid major leaguer it's Hal Naragon. He has a very fine chance to become a good catcher. He has the physique and the natural aptitude of a catcher, and he has a sure pair of hands when he comes to catching foul flies," and he was "willing to learn."[10] That willingness to learn helped him immensely as he worked his way up to playing for Oklahoma City in the Texas League in 1950, and by 1951 he was in spring training with the Indians. After spring training, he was sent to San Diego of the Pacific Coast League and earned a call-up to the Indians at the end of the season. Continuing his Horatio Alger dream of a life story, he singled in his at bat as a pinch hitter in his first game as a Major League player on September 23 at Briggs Stadium. He then played in two more games before the season ended—enough to keep his name in the minds of his coaches as the Korean War intervened.

After the season, Naragon was drafted into the marines and was stationed at Quantico, Virginia. He was discharged in December 1953. Asked if he felt his career suffered during those years, Hal responded, "I didn't miss a thing. In fact, I got stronger physically during those years. I always thought everything I have done has been a positive experience."[11] After his discharge, the Indians' general manager, Hank Greenberg, sent him to Panama to play winter ball.

Naragon started the 1954 season with the Indians and was part of the winningest team in American league history to that point (111 victories). He became friends with all-star outfielder Dale Mitchell, who Naragon says was the person who helped him the most in his baseball career. Naragon recalls, "Mitchell came up in 1946 and was a really great player. When I arrived in '54, he asked me if I wanted to room with him. It was a pleasant surprise to be asked by him." Mitchell became an important part of his baseball life. "He helped me a lot with my hitting," Naragon said.[12] Looking back on his career, the 1954 season was important to Naragon not only because it was his first full season in the Major Leagues and the team went to the World Se-

ries, but also because it was in that season that he had his best moment as a player. The left-handed-hitting Naragon remembers, "We were playing the Philadelphia A's at Connie Mack Stadium. It was the top of the tenth inning and the bases were loaded. I hit a triple off of a left-handed pitcher! This was a big deal because we were struggling during that part of the season to win."[13] The front page of the *Cleveland Plain Dealer* declared "Naragon's Triple Wins for Indians," and the author continued to explain Naragon's feat. "With the Indians' clutch slipping and their pennant machine stalling badly, Hal Naragon performed a hasty repair job tonight."[14] The rookie catcher finally had made his mark.

The Indians won that game 4–3 on August 25. They went on not only to set the record for the most wins for a season but also to play in the World Series against the New York Giants. Naragon maintains that the Indians would have won had the series started in Cleveland, but instead they were swept by the Giants. When asked which he thought was more important, setting the record for most wins or going to the World Series, Naragon chose the World Series. "Winning the pennant and playing in the World Series was a great thrill and the record was secondary to going to the World Series. They [the Indians] had a lot of veterans and they came close to going to the World Series before, so it was good to see them succeed. There were five rookies that came up that year and the older fellas were really good to us and gave us a lot of encouragement. They were real good to us."[15]

Most remarkably for him during that season, he caught four future Hall of Fame pitchers—Bob Feller, Early Wynn, Hal Newhouser, and Bob Lemon. When asked who was the most fun to catch, who was the easiest to catch, and who was the hardest to catch, Naragon mentioned Lemon and Wynn as being easy to catch but added that no one threw a knuckleball, so no one was difficult. Then he laughed and said, "As long as I got to play in the Major Leagues it was all easy."[16] Playing backup to Jim

Hegan, Naragon finished the season with a .238 batting average and a perfect 1.000 fielding percentage in forty-five games. After the season, he returned to Panama to play winter ball, and in 1955 he played fifty-seven games with a batting average of .323. In 1956 and 1957, still in a backup role, he hit .287 and .256, respectively, playing in about fifty games each season. He was sent back to San Diego for the 1958 season, coming back to play with the Indians for only nine plate appearances.

On May 25, 1959, Naragon was traded by Cleveland with pitcher Hal Woodeshick to the Washington Senators for catcher Ed Fitz Gerald. Of the team's lackluster record in Washington, Hal said, with his characteristic tact, "We had some good players there, but maybe we didn't all belong together on the same team."[17] Hal moved in 1961 to Minnesota when Calvin Griffith relocated his franchise from Washington to become the Minnesota Twins. In his first year with the Twins when they returned to Washington to play the expansion Senators, he hit the last sacrifice bunt in Griffith Stadium on September 21, 1961, in the seventh inning. That first year in Minnesota was one of Naragon's better years hitting (.302 in fifty-seven games as a backup to Early Battey), but it was no roster guarantee. In 1962 he had only thirty-five at bats, and played his last game on August 5 of that season. He was released by the Twins on October 19, 1962, having played his entire ten-year career in the American League. (Asked what he thought of not having ever played in the National League, he chuckled and with his usual humbleness replied, "I was glad to be playing in any league."[18])

During an era in baseball history when players spent their off-seasons working, Naragon was no exception, spending his winters working at the rubber factory in Barberton. However, when his playing career was over, Hal was not quite ready to return to the factory. The Twins named Naragon their bullpen coach. As a coach, Naragon found another calling. In 1965 the Twins won the American League

pennant only to lose the World Series in Game Seven against the Los Angeles Dodgers' unhittable Sandy Koufax. From 1965 to 1969, when he left baseball, Hal worked in tandem with pitching coach Johnny Sain, moving with Sain to Detroit when both were released by the Twins after the 1966 season.

According to Naragon, "There were some disagreements—we had a great time in Minnesota—but some people thought that John only got along with the pitchers, which was not true. John, in his career, he always seemed to have a run-in with the managers or different ideas than the managers."[19] What it came down to was that Sain and manager Sam Mele could not work together any longer and, "because Naragon supported Sain strongly," Mele also asked for Naragon's release. *Sports Illustrated* quoted Twins pitcher Jim Kaat, who won twenty-five games for the Twins in 1965, as calling the firing of Sain and Naragon "the Great Mistake." Kaat added, "This is the worst thing that could happen to our club at this time. Every move John Sain and Hal Naragon made was in the best interest of the Minnesota Twins. . . . Hal Naragon was the last instrument of communication between Mr. Mele and the players. Now there is complete division."[20]

The combination of Sain and Naragon proved just as effective in Detroit as Minnesota. When they arrived for the 1967 season, the Tigers had just finished in third place in 1966, but the 1967 season found them climbing. They finished second, only one game behind the Boston Red Sox. With a great pitching staff and a future Hall of Famer, Al Kaline, in the outfield, the Tigers could not be denied in 1968. Toward the end of that memorable 1968 season, longtime Detroit sportswriter Watson Spoelstra wrote, "There's no question that Sain and his close friend and associate, coach Hal Naragon, know about as much as anyone on pitching. They are dedicated baseball men with a low-key selling job."[21] Spoelstra reported that during the 1968 off-season Naragon was given a vote of confidence by the Tigers when they signed him for the 1969 sea-

TRACY J. R. COLLINS

son. Spoelstra quoted pitcher Mickey Lolich as saying, "Sain and Naragon are my boys. They know how to get a guy straightened out."[22] The Tigers were not as successful in 1969; Naragon finished the season with them and retired from professional baseball. Writers had always said that "Naragon goes where Sain goes," but when Sain landed with the Chicago White Sox in 1971, Naragon had already decided to try something different.[23] "Could I make a living outside of baseball, was always at the back of my mind, and when John went to Chicago, I decided it was time to answer that question for myself," he says.[24]

Naragon returned to Barberton, to live with his wife and their only child, Pam. He did indeed make a living outside of baseball. "I am proud to say that I owned the largest and best sporting goods store in Barberton, Ohio. Of course, it was also the only sporting goods store in Barberton."[25] According to Barberton historian PhyllisTaylor, Naragon bought the local sporting goods store in 1974. He sold the business and retired in 1990. He remains active in charitable fundraising events through an association of Major League alumni and watching the Barberton Magics play baseball on Naragon Field, built in 2000 and named in his honor in April 2006. He also enjoys playing golf with his two grandsons and his wife, a team they affectionately call "the family foursome." Lately, he keeps himself busy enjoying his first great-grandchild, who was born in 2010.

When asked what he thought his best attributes were as a coach, he laughed and said, "I had trouble with that question. I asked my wife and she said I was a good listener. I guess I was a positive thinker. I learned in pro ball that folks started off negatively because they were so used to hearing criticism, but I thought the power of positive suggestion was much stronger. At a 1965 Twins reunion in 2005 Jerry Kindall said I was very even-tempered and it was always a new day with me. John [Sain] was a very positive person too and we were a good team."[26]

Watson Spoelstra, in a June 22, 1968, article for *The Sporting News*, called Naragon "the quiet man who ran the bullpen."[27] This quiet effectiveness, love of baseball, and good-natured positive attitude is not only evident in reports of interviews with players during his career, but it is also clear in the tone of his voice. "I have met some wonderful people playing baseball," Naragon said. "I don't think anything else I could have done would have put me in contact with as many good people."[28] Such people include Naragon himself, by all accountants a truly good man among baseball's alumni.

Chapter 39. 1954 All-Star Game

Rick Huhn

Can an All-Star game energize a baseball team and significantly influence a pennant race? A slumping 1954 Cleveland Indians team was about to find out. The All-Star battle between the two Major Leagues, the twenty-first in an annual rivalry that began in Chicago in 1933, was about to be waged on the shores of Lake Erie in Cleveland on the afternoon of July 13 at Municipal Stadium, the home of the American League's Indians. A vast majority in the throng of 68,751 in attendance that day, the second-largest crowd to that point in All-Star Game history, were fans of the hometown club. Almost all of those Tribe fans entered the stadium with a nervous hitch to their step. Over the past weekend they had watched in horror as the Indians' league lead shrunk to less than a game over the dreaded New York Yankees as the Tribe was swept in four games in Chicago by the White Sox, themselves in third but three back. Particularly troublesome to Tribe faithful were the rash of injuries troubling many of their stars such as 1953 AL Most Valuable Player Al Rosen, second baseman Bobby Avila, and pitchers Bob Lemon and Mike Garcia.

Despite the Indians' recent swoon, the City of Cleveland and all of northern Ohio tingled with anticipation during the weeks preceding the big event. The almost daily reports of fan voting for the starting lineups shared newspaper space from Independence Day weekend on with headline-grabbing reports of the sensational murder of thirty-one-year-old Marilyn Sheppard, wife of prominent local physician Sam Sheppard. When the final tally—4,272,470 votes strong—was released on July 4, the right side of the AL's infield would be manned by Al Rosen at first and Bobby Avila at second. In the two previous All-Star Games, Rosen had played third base. His selection to man first this time around, where by the rules he must play at least three innings, rather than his normal spot at third was due to the early-season switch in which he ceded his former position to rookie sensation Rudy Regalado. That experiment failed when the rookie fizzled and Rosen had returned to third. Nonetheless, the fans voted him in at first with a total of 1,452,736 votes, second only to highly popular St. Louis Cardinals outfielder Stan Musial, who led the National League and all of baseball with 1,468,377 votes in locking up a position in right field.[1] Future Hall of Famers selected for the AL's starting lineup were Mickey Mantle and Yogi Berra of the Yankees, in center field and behind the plate, respectively. In addition to Musial, future Cooperstown enshrinees earning starting nods for the NL were all members of the Brooklyn Dodgers: Jackie Robinson in left field, Duke Snider in center field, and Roy Campanella catching.

The managers for the two squads were a study in contrasts, yet both would also eventually take their place in the game's Hall of Fame. The NL squad was under the direction of rookie manager Walter Alston of the Brooklyn Dodgers. Alston had earned his spurs in the Dodgers' farm system, stepping into the parent club's slot following the 1953 season when manager Chuck Dressen and his boss, Walter O'Malley, fell out over the length of Dressen's contract. Since the Dodgers had won the 1953 NL pennant, the job of managing the senior circuit's top players in the All-Star Game belonged to his successor. Alston was clean-cut and soft-spoken. The Ohio native was forty-two. His opposite in more ways than one

was Casey Stengel of the Yankees, just over twenty years Alston's senior. The New Yorkers' skipper was a curmudgeon—a living, breathing circus sideshow. Yet he performed his act with a wise man's twinkle and a truckload of baseball acumen. All he had done since 1949 when he arrived back in New York, where he had once both played and managed, was lead his charges to five consecutive World Series titles. The fact his club had in 1949 dethroned the Indians, winners in 1948 of only the franchise's second world championship, and had kept them back in the pack ever since was a particularly sore point with Tribe fans. They saw the irascible Stengel as a major source of their problem. He was the one man whom most Clevelanders loved to hate. Yet here he was, surprisingly the losing manager in his four previous All-Star managerial efforts, directing the AL All-Stars just as his own club pressed ever closer to the top of the league standings. Many in the stands would not know whether to cheer or boo the man and probably planned to do a bit of both.

According to the rules, the opposing managers completed each twenty-five-man squad by naming the pitching staff, including the starter, and a complement of substitutes who often rivaled the starters in star power. They would also appoint a coaching staff. Once again, future members of the Hall of Fame dotted the landscape. In that vein Stengel selected one of his own, Whitey Ford, and the Indians' Bob Lemon for the pitching staff. He added second sacker Nellie Fox (White Sox) and Detroit third baseman George Kell, as well as outfielders Larry Doby (Indians) and Ted Williams (Red Sox) to the position players. For his NL pitching staff, Walt Alston chose future Hall of Famers Robin Roberts of the Phillies and Warren Spahn of the Braves. His bench included several more who were on their way to baseball immortality, including shortstop Pee Wee Reese (Dodgers) and second baseman Red Schoendienst (Cardinals) in the infield and twenty-three-year-old Willie Mays (Giants) in the outfield. One of Alston's coaches, fiery Giants manager Leo Durocher, would one day earn a plaque in Cooperstown as well.

As game day approached, there was one bit of controversy. A story out of New York during the voting period quoted Al Rosen as saying that if elected, he would not play, due to a broken right index finger that remained stiff and continued to swell, throwing him into a lengthy slump. Rosen, concerned the statement would cost him votes, hotly denied making any such statement. To the contrary, he told reporters, "I would be greatly honored to be elected to the All-Star Game [*sic*] and I would be proud to play in it."[2] Rosen, it appeared, would play. On the other hand, several members of Stengel's crew had to bow out due to injury. Injured first baseman Ferris Fain of the White Sox was replaced by future Hall of Famer Mickey Vernon of the Senators. As it turned out, George Kell was injured as well. His spot was taken by Dean Stone, the Senators' rookie left-hander. On July 4, Indians hurler Mike Garcia broke a blood vessel in the middle finger of his pitching hand, forcing him from the roster. An ailing hip benched Stengel's own hurler, Allie Reynolds. Pitcher Sandy Consuegra of the White Sox took their place on the pitching roster. Rather than add another pitcher, Stengel added Yankee outfielder Irv Noren to fill out the squad.

As game day approached, the only item of pregame maneuvering that remained was selection of the starting pitchers. Once again Casey Stengel went to a familiar well, naming his crafty lefty Whitey Ford. The twenty-five-year-old was playing in the first of his ten All-Star Games. Many thought Bob Keegan of the White Sox would be Casey's choice, since the Yankee skipper had inserted Ford into a three-inning relief role just two days before on Sunday. Nonetheless it was Ford to start things off. Alston countered with Philadelphia's Robin Roberts. The brilliant right-hander, a still youthful twenty-seven, was starting his fourth All-Star Game in the past five years. The match-up between Ford and Roberts promised to be a great one. It lived up to its billing. In the middle of the third, the game was scoreless. Ford had tossed three masterful innings;

the only NL hit was a second-inning safety by Stan Musial. Robin Roberts had pitched two scoreless innings himself and the fans were settled back in their seats for more of the same in the bottom of the third when the junior circuit began turning up the heat. Left fielder Minnie Minoso, the exciting Cuban outfielder who had started out his career as a Cleveland Indians player and now played for the White Sox, worked Roberts for a lead-off walk. Then Bobby Avila, like teammate Rosen playing with an injured hand, singled. At this point Roberts settled down, retiring Mantle and Berra. The next man up was Rosen, who had added to his frustration entering the game by striking out in the first inning with two men aboard. Down a strike, Rosen swatted Roberts's next pitch over the wall in left-center field. That home run and the one that followed immediately thereafter by Tigers third baseman Ray Boone, another former Tribe performer, were the twentieth and twenty-first gopher balls served up by Roberts that season. It represented the first time in All-Star history that a pitcher had surrendered back-to-back home runs. Rosen's blast was by far the unlikeliest of the pair, as he discussed after the game.

Despite his previous comments regarding his desire to play, as game time approached and his batting problems persisted, it seems Rosen had decided to approach Stengel and offer to leave the game after his first at bat. Stengel listened to the offer and went so far as to check it out with baseball's commissioner, Ford Frick. Said Casey, "I asked the commissioner and he says it's okay if he [Rosen] don't go three innings like they're supposed to but we'll have to tell you guys [the press] all about it." Then Rosen struck out. It made sense that this was his exit tune. If he wanted to be removed, perhaps now was the best time. For the competitive Rosen, however, it was just the opposite, as "that strikeout made me mad and, maybe, I forgot about the finger." He had hardly slept the night before the game and awoke on game day with his finger even more painful than before, "scared to death about being the All-Star game goat." He wanted to honor the fans by starting, "but I figured I'd be out of there after one time at bat. Probably would have been, too, if it hadn't been for that strikeout. I couldn't leave after that. I wanted at least one more crack at it."[3] And crack it he did. Fueled by that four-bagger and Boone's solo blast, the third inning came to an end with the AL holding a 4–0 lead.

Whitey Ford had set a fine example for his pitching mates through three innings. Now Casey Stengel turned the mound duties over to Sandy Consuegra, the late entry from the White Sox who was in the midst of a career-best season in which he would go 16-3. Things started well when he retired the first batter, and then soured quickly. After retiring shortstop Alvin Dark of the Giants, he surrendered five consecutive hits, the most damaging a double by Jackie Robinson. The barrage produced four runs and left Robinson at second. Consuegra was replaced mid-inning by Bob Lemon, another of the Tribe's walking wounded, as he battled a right side injury. It was the seventh time Lemon had been chosen to represent the AL. He responded by retiring the first batter he faced, Roy Campanella. Then Alston pinch-hit outfielder Don Mueller of the Giants for Robin Roberts. He singled home Robinson. By the time the NL took the field in the bottom half of the fourth, they led 5–4.

The floodgates were now open, and hitters wielding heavy bats continued to wade in. The second-largest crowd to date in All-Star history was about to see a batting display like no other. In the bottom of the fourth, the AL tied the score against Giants lefty Johnny Antonelli, the run scoring on a sacrifice fly by Bobby Avila. In the fifth, Cincinnati Reds muscleman Ted Kluszewski hit a two-run homer off of the Senators' Bob Porterfield. In the bottom half of the inning, the AL countered when Yogi Berra singled off Antonelli and the now totally rejuvenated Al Rosen followed with a two-run blast to deep left field, his second four-bagger of the game. The twin blasts equaled an All-Star record shared at the

time by Pittsburgh's Arky Vaughn (1941) and Ted Williams (1946).[4] The inning ended with the two leagues still knotted, but now at seven apiece. Porterfield held the NL at bay in the top of the sixth, allowing the AL to stake a one-run lead as Indians players continued to shine when Bobby Avila's single drove home Ted Williams. The score remained the same as the game entered the eighth inning.

In the top of the eighth, the plot thickened in what some baseball scholars have labeled "one of the more interesting innings in All-Star history."[5] Bob Keegan, another White Sox hurler having his best season (16-9), replaced Bob Porterfield. Like his teammate Consuegra, he retired the first batter he faced, and then ran into serious trouble. After Willie Mays singled, Keegan struck out Campanella, but then pinch-hitting outfielder Gus Bell of the Reds continued to add a decidedly Ohio flavor to the contest by launching a mighty two-run blast to deep right-center field. The NL was up 9–8 and looking for more when the very next batter, Cardinals infielder Red Schoendienst, raced all the way to second as Minnie Minoso dropped his fly ball after a long chase down the right-field line. Alvin Dark's infield single moved Schoendienst to third and sent the ever-dangerous left-handed batter Duke Snider to the plate. Stengel had seen enough. He replaced the right-handed Keegan with rookie replacement Dean Stone, a lefty.

The switches in playing personnel set the scene for one of the most controversial plays in All-Star history. The count on Snider stood at 1-1 when suddenly Schoendienst headed for home. The six-foot-four Stone delivered the ball to Berra. Schoendienst was called out by the home plate umpire, the NL's Bill Stewart. Leo Durocher, exhibition game be damned, went berserk. He was joined by his first-base counterpart Charlie Grimm of the Milwaukee Braves. The pair, as well as Walter Alston upon his arrival, argued that young Stone had balked. Alas, their heated pleas were to no avail. The top half of the eighth inning was history, but at least the NL had forged a lead, 9–8. Later, the still fuming Durocher stated his position. "That call was a disgrace," he said. "Every person in the ball park saw the play except the one that should have. He [Stewart] just missed it, and it cost us one run and no telling how many more. . . . Stone saw him [Schoendienst] on his way and he never completed his motion at all. He just threw it home—and even then it was close."[6] Bill Stewart, the only one whose opinion counted, saw it differently. "I saw the entire play perfectly and there was no doubt in my mind about it at all." According to Stewart, as soon as Stone saw the man on third break for the plate, he lowered his hands to belt level and speeded up his motion by not bringing the ball over his head, a permissible move. "He quickened up his motion and just came to a brief stop—but that's all right."[7] Unfortunately for Durocher and the NL, Stewart held serve.

Now it was gangly Gene Conley's turn to quiet the AL's big guns. The Braves hurler, who stood six feet eight and at twenty-two had already played one season of basketball in 1952–53 for the Boston Celtics of the National Basketball Association, was not up to the task. After retiring one batter, he faced pinch hitter Larry Doby, the regular center fielder for the Indians. It had been a Cleveland sort of day. There was no reason that should change now. Doby hit the game's second pinch-hit round tripper and the first ever for an AL performer. The solo shot to left field tied the game, 9–9. It also seemed to shake Conley up. He proceeded to load the bases; the third base runner was none other than Al Rosen, continuing his magical day by drawing a walk. A grim-faced Walt Alston went to his bullpen yet again, bringing in Carl Erskine of the Dodgers. Since Erskine threw from the right side, Stengel went with the percentages. He brought in the Senators' slick-fielding first baseman Mickey Vernon to bat for the right-handed Ray Boone. The strategy failed, Vernon taking a called third strike. Now there were two outs and Nellie Fox, second sacker for the White Sox, was at the plate. Fox, no power

hitter—entering the season he had hit but seven home runs in a seven-year career—was enjoying his best year at the plate. Just when it appeared Erskine might get out of it, Fox lifted a blooper into center. It dropped in, scoring two of Casey's "boys," Mantle and Berra. When the next batter popped up, the inning was over, but the damage was done. The AL lead was 11–9 heading into what well might be the NL's last time at bat.

In the top of the ninth, Stengel made a number of defensive moves, including switching Rosen to his natural position at third. This allowed the AL to keep Vernon in the game at first. Virgil Trucks, yet another White Sox pitcher, entered the game, hopefully to close it out. This is exactly what he did, as after issuing an opening walk to Duke Snider, he retired the side in order. The final score was 11–9 and the overwhelmingly pro-AL crowd could issue a mighty cheer and finally catch their breath at the same time.

In the locker room the participants discussed the "heroics" of Nellie Fox. Alvin Dark had the best shot at catching the wounded duck. "I went for it," he told reporters, "but it seemed to keep on going as if the wind were carrying it. I just couldn't catch up." His infield companion, Red Schoendienst, also might have had a play, but he thought Dark would make the catch.[8] Perhaps Leo Durocher, never at a loss for words, summed it up best. "Home runs all over the place. So what beats us? A lousy 98-foot chip shot."[9]

Durocher was right about one thing. It had been a hitter's game and a fan's delight. Arch Ward, the Chicago journalist who had originally planted the seed for this annual event, was in attendance and in accord. He called it "the best ever."[10] Indeed, the batting statistics were impressive. The teams totaled twenty runs on thirty-one hits, both All-Star records. The four AL homers and total of six tied All-Star Game records. In addition the AL's seventeen hits set a record, as did the nine runs by the NL (most by a losing team). The hitting led to a pair of new pitching marks for most pitchers used by two teams (thirteen) and the most pitchers used by one team (the AL's seven).[11]

In yet another odd feature of the contest, the winning pitcher was Dean Stone. The NL led 9–8 with two men out in the top of the eighth inning when the young Senators hurler relieved Bob Keegan. That was the lead when the inning ended after Stone threw a ball and a strike, and Schoendienst made his unsuccessful mad dash for the plate. When the AL went ahead in the bottom of the eighth, Stone was the pitcher of record. He did not pitch in the ninth, but when the AL's lead held, Dean Stone had garnered a piece of All-Star history without officially facing a batter. The scorer's decision to credit Stone with the victory occasioned some criticism. The official scorer, Ed McAuley of the *Cleveland News*, told readers he spent forty minutes going over the rule book. He concluded that under the rules the only way Virgil Trucks, who pitched the AL ninth, could have been credited with the win was if Stone's performance had been brief and ineffective. According to McAuley, "Stone's term certainly was brief. But it wasn't ineffective."[12]

The individual and collective performances of the Cleveland Indians on the AL squad were certainly not ineffective either. Bob Lemon had pitched admirably during his brief stint (no runs, one hit in two-thirds of an inning, although the hit allowed an inherited runner to score), but it was the hitters who really shone. Indians players banged out seven hits in eight official at bats, hit three home runs, scored four times, and drove in eight of the eleven runs tallied by the AL. Avila was 3 for 3, scored a run, and batted in a pair for his part. Doby hit a solo home run when he had his turn as a pinch hitter.

And then there was Al Rosen. His five appearances at the plate brought three base hits and a walk, including two home runs. He drove in five runs while scoring two of his own, the former tying an RBI single-game record set by Ted Williams in 1946. The record still stands. Interestingly, af-

ter the game, Rosen credited Williams's advice as the key to his slump-breaking performance. After Rosen struck out his first time up, he asked Williams for his help. "The Splendid Splinter" recommended Rosen choke up on his bat to help him get it around quicker.[13] He followed the advice, and Al Rosen had a "splendid" day of his own. It would be 1962 before baseball selected an MVP for its all-star clashes, but few would argue that hometown hero Al Rosen was the clear-cut winner in 1954.

The Indians were a slumping ball club entering the All-Star break. Only a fraction of the team had performed on June 13 in Municipal Stadium, but those that did were energized. They were a big reason that Casey Stengel finally broke his All-Star managerial jinx. Yet the win perhaps carried a heavy price tag. Those Indians bats had come alive on his watch. The Yankee major domo knew more than ever he was in a fight for the duration. "Now I got to work on that half-game lead Cleveland's got us by," he said after the game.[14] His dugout opposite, the Tribe's Al Lopez, on the other hand, was elated. The exploits of his men represented "(a) great thing for our club. It'll shoot the whole team up. . . . We're over our rut and ready to start a winning streak."[15]

Happily for the Indians, Lopez was correct. Over the next fifty games, his club won thirty-nine, tied two, and lost but nine. The post–All-Star break surge increased the Cleveland lead over the Yankees to five and one-half games on the way to a best-ever AL season record of 111-43 and an eight-game margin over the second-place New Yorkers. In the lead for his front-page post–All-Star Game write-up, sportswriter Harry Jones of the *Plain Dealer* told readers, "The Indians may not win the world series [sic] and they may not even win the pennant, but at least they won an All-Star game yesterday."[16] As it turned out, Tribe fans would have to settle for two out of three. But, indeed, it was some run. And it all may just have been ignited by a perfectly timed and most conveniently located Major League All-Star Game.

Chapter 40. Timeline, July 15–July 31

Joseph Wancho

July 15—Philadelphia—WYNN'S 3-HITTER TRIPS ATHLETICS, 4–0—Early Wynn blanks the Athletics on three hits. Bobby Avila, Jim Hegan, Al Smith, and Al Rosen each stroke a double.

July 16—Philadelphia—INDIANS ROUT A'S, 9–3, RETAIN LEAD—The Tribe offense bangs out eighteen hits. Sam Dente goes 3 for 4, with two doubles and three RBIS. Bobby Avila hits two doubles and gets an RBI. Dave Philley homers. Al Smith goes 4 for 6 with a triple and an RBI. Bill Glynn goes 2-5 with a triple and two runs scored. Mike Garcia records his twelfth win.

July 17—Philadelphia—FELLER'S 2-HITTER SWEEPS SERIES, 6–0—Bob Feller throws a two-hitter against the Athletics, fanning six batters. Feller gets two hits, including a double. Al Rosen drives in two. In spite of the sweep, the Tribe leads Yankees by a half game.

July 18—Washington—AVILA SETS PACE IN 7–4 VICTORY; NATS BAG OPENER, 8–3—Eddie Yost goes 3 for 5 with a double, a triple, a HR, and an RBI. Ed Fitz Gerald knocks in two runs. Johnny Pesky goes 2 for 5 with a run scored and an RBI in the first game. Rosen hits a two run inside-the-park homer in the nightcap. Avila doubles and collects two RBIS. Don Mossi gets the win in relief.

July 19—Washington—MITCHELL'S PINCH HIT BEATS NATS, 4–3—Larry Doby goes 3 for 5, with two runs. Al Rosen goes 2 for 5, with three RBIS and a double. Dale Mitchell's pinch hit in the top of the seventh inning gives the Tribe a 4–3 lead. Wynn raises his record to 12-7. Narleski gets his sixth save.

July 20—Boston—16-INNING TIE, 5–5—The game is suspended at 12:57 a.m. after the completion of the sixteenth inning due to the league curfew rule. Bobby Avila smacks two home runs, and Al Rosen and Larry Doby each stroke their sixteenth home run of the season.

July 21—Boston—INDIANS TIE, 7 TO 7: GAIN ON YANKEES—Game called after the eighth inning on account of rain. Jim Hegan hits a three-run home run. George Stickland goes 2 for 3, with a run scored. Larry Doby cranks his seventeenth homer on the year.

July 22—Boston—INDIANS SWEEP RED SOX, HOLD LEAD, 6–3, 5–2—Vic Wertz hits two home runs and drives in four runs. Bob Feller raises his record to 8-1, striking out six hitters. Wally Westlake and Al Smith both go deep with solo home runs as Cleveland sweeps the twin bill at Fenway Park. Bob Lemon wins his tenth.

July 23—New York—INDIANS ROUT YANKS 8–2, TO HIKE LEAD—Larry Doby goes long twice on solo shots. Al Smith hits a three-run homer and racks up five RBIS. The Tribe plates four runs in the top of the seventh inning to take command of the game. Early Wynn collects his thirteenth win.

July 24—New York—DOBY'S HOMER IN 10TH TOPS YANKS—Larry Doby smacks a two-run homer in the tenth inning, winning the game. Jim Hegan strokes a solo homer. Bob Lemon garners his eleventh win in relief. Ray Narleski saves his seventh game of the year.

July 25—New York—YANKS NIP TRIBE. CAR-EY HITS WITH THREE ON IN 11TH—Andy Carey's single wins it for the Bombers in the eleventh inning. Attendance is 57,259 at Yankee Stadium. Bob Grim wins his eleventh in relief of Whitey Ford. The Tribe's lead over New York is cut to one and a half games. Chicago slips to six games back.

July 27—Cleveland—INDIANS HIKE LEAD; ROSEN AND WERTZ RAP HOME RUNS—Al Rosen and Vic Wertz both club homers. Wertz collects three RBIS. Bob Lemon pushes his record to 12-5 with the 6–3 win over Boston.

July 28—Cleveland—WYNN NAILS 14TH AS INDIANS WIN, 2–1—Early Wynn goes to 14-7, whiffing seven. Wertz goes 2 for 3 with an RBI. Rosen drives in a run and scores a run. Cleveland leads the Yankees by two and a half games.

July 29—Cleveland—RED SOX WIN, 10–2, JEN-SEN BATS IN 6 RUNS—Jackie Jensen smacks two home runs. Ted Williams also goes deep, as they combine for eight RBIS. Billy Goodman goes 3 for 4, scoring twice. Bobby Avila homers for the Tribe.

July 30—Cleveland—INDIANS HIKE LEAD; HOUTTEMAN TOPS NATS TO WIN 10TH—Jim Hegan goes 2 for 4, with four RBIS, two runs, and a home run. Larry Doby hits his twenty-first homer. Art Houtteman goes the distance for his tenth win.

July 31—Cleveland—LEMON'S THREE-HITTER BEATS NATS, 6–0—Dave Pope, Bobby Avila, Larry Doby, and Al Rosen combine to go 7 for 14, with six RBIS and three runs. Larry Doby and Al Rosen each homer. Bob Lemon scatters three hits, strikes out four, and wins his thirteenth game.

Chapter 41. **Al Smith**

Gary Livacari

AGE	G	AB	R	H	2B	3B	HR	TB	RBI	BB	SO	BAV	OBP	SLG	SB	GDP	HBP
26	131	481	101	135	29	6	11	209	50	88	65	.281	.398	.435	2	2	7

Al Smith was an accomplished ballplayer whose Major League career spanned twelve seasons with four American League teams. Primarily an outfielder, he played six positions as a Major Leaguer and was a fine defender with a strong arm and good speed. Smith finished with a .272 lifetime batting average, hit 164 home runs, and reached base nearly 36 percent of the time. He also made two All-Star teams and played for two pennant winners (both managed by Al Lopez). He hit a career-best .315 in 1960 and posted his biggest power numbers—twenty-eight homers and ninety-three RBIS—in 1961. But despite his considerable on-field accomplishments, he will always be best remembered as the unwitting subject in one of baseball's most lasting images: the "beer-bath" photo from Game Two of the 1959 World Series. When Smith died in 2002, his obituary in the *New York Times* was headlined, "Al Smith, 73, Dies; Was Doused in Series."

Alphonse Eugene Smith was born on February 7, 1928, in Kirkwood, Missouri, a St. Louis suburb. He grew up a fan of both local big league teams, the Cardinals and the Browns, and his hero was Cardinals outfielder Joe Medwick. Nicknamed "Fuzzy," Smith was a versatile, multitalented athlete at Douglas High in Webster Groves, Missouri. The MVP of the baseball team, he also starred in football, basketball, and track, and was a Golden Gloves boxing champion in the 160-pound division. Smith scored thirty-three touchdowns in one football season and was reputed to have scored ten touchdowns in one game.

Upon his graduation in 1946, Smith signed with the Negro American League's Cleveland Buckeyes.

Because he was only seventeen, his mother had to sign his contract. In his first full season with the Buckeyes, in 1947, Smith was moved from his natural position of third base to shortstop and batted .285. He led the league with twenty-seven doubles and eleven triples, and finished second with twelve home runs. The Buckeyes, managed by Quincy Trouppe, posted a pennant-winning 54-23 record and played in the Negro League World Series (losing to the New York Cubans). Smith changed positions again in 1948, this time to the outfield. That summer, he caught the eye of Cleveland Indians scout Laddie Placek, who had been dispatched to League Park to evaluate pitcher Sam "Toothpick" Jones. On July 11, Placek signed both Jones and Smith to Major League contracts.

Smith was sent to Class A Wilkes-Barre in the Eastern League, becoming the league's first African American player. He hit .316 the rest of the way, and then .311 with the same club in 1949. Smith later said of Wilkes-Barre manager Bill Norman, "He was a thoroughbred. He said he was down there to train and get ballplayers ready to go to the big leagues and if anyone didn't like the idea that I was playing they could get up and leave."[1]

In 1950 Smith earned a promotion to San Diego in the Pacific Coast League, where he spent the next two seasons. In 1952 Smith moved once more, this time to Indianapolis in the American Association, where he played under Birdie Tebbetts, another manager who helped Smith integrate the team. "He was *the* man," Smith recalled, "When he'd tell you something you believed it. He's the kind of guy that if he knew you played good, it didn't make no difference what color you were. He threw all that

out the window."[2] Smith finally received the call to the Indians after posting a .332 average in the first half of the season, and he debuted in the Majors on July 10, 1953.

Although Jackie Robinson famously broke the Major League color barrier in 1947, many teams still had no black players. The Indians were a stark exception. In '47, then owner Bill Veeck had signed Larry Doby as the American League's first black player, and when Al Smith reported to the team in '53—by which point Veeck was gone—it had four black players: Doby, pitcher Dave Hoskins, outfielder Harry Simpson, and first baseman Luke Easter. Al Smith always held Veeck in high regard, calling him "the greatest man I ever met in baseball," and added, "No one ever treated me better than Bill. I observed him closely and he's one of the smartest men you'll meet anywhere in any kind of business. A great human being, too."[3]

In 1954, his first full season with the Indians, Smith beat out veteran Dale Mitchell for the everyday job in left field. Batting lead-off, he hit .281 and scored 101 runs on a team that set an Amer-

ican League record with 111 wins. Game One of the World Series started with Smith being drilled in the ribs by New York Giants ace Sal Maglie. In Game Two, Smith entered the record books by hitting a home run on the very first pitch of the game, thrown by Johnny Antonelli, becoming one of only three players in Major League history to accomplish this feat. Nevertheless, the heavily favored Indians were swept by Leo Durocher's club in four games.

In 1955 Al Smith ranked as one of the American League's best players. His numbers included 22 home runs, 77 RBIs, and 123 runs scored, the latter figure leading the league. He earned his first trip to the All-Star Game. After the season, he finished third in the MVP balloting, behind Hall of Famers Yogi Berra and Al Kaline but ahead of Ted Williams and Mickey Mantle.

Smith's numbers fell off substantially in 1956 as the Indians won eighty-eight games and finished well behind the Yankees. His offensive decline continued in 1957 (.247 batting average) as the Indians fell into the second division. What's more, Smith was rankled when new manager Kerby Farrell informed him he'd be playing third base in 1958—rankled enough to ask for a trade.

The Indians honored that request. On December 4, 1957, Smith and star pitcher Early Wynn were sent to the White Sox for Minnie Minoso and Fred Hatfield. White Sox fans were unhappy about the trade that cost them longtime favorite Minoso, and they took out their frustrations on Smith, who was booed continuously throughout that season and the next. Trying to help, White Sox owner Bill Veeck staged an "Al Smith Night" on August 26, 1959, against the Red Sox. Anyone with the name Smith, Smythe, Schmidt, or Smithe was admitted free and given a button that read, "I'm a Smith and I'm for Al." Smith responded with a forgettable game: 1 for 4 with a strikeout, and he dropped a seventh-inning fly ball that led to a couple of unearned runs on the way to a 7–6 loss. Veeck's plan had backfired . . .

Or had it? The disastrous game seemed to spark Smith. As Veeck recounted in his book *Veeck as in Wreck*, "Over the last six weeks of the season, he led our team in home runs and runs batted in, and won game after game with the clutch hit in the ninth inning or in extra innings."[4] Like many other stories in Veeck's book, this one is perhaps a bit exaggerated; there were only four weeks in the season after Al Smith Night, and over that span Smith batted .255 and drew exactly two walks. But he did hit six homers and drove in eighteen runs, and one of those home runs did come in the pennant-clincher, on September 22 (though it was a solo shot in a 4–2 victory).

In the first game of the World Series, the White Sox beat the Dodgers 11–0 behind Early Wynn. They lost Game Two, though, which has forever been remembered for Al Smith's embarrassing "beer bath," a single instant that seemed to epitomize the White Sox's frustrations throughout the Fall Classic. In the fifth inning, Smith drifted back to Comiskey Park's left-field fence in pursuit of Charlie Neal's deep drive. As Smith watched the ball disappear into the stands, a fan named Melvin Piehl, sitting in the first row, knocked over his beer and thoroughly drenched the startled left fielder. "It hit the bill of my cap and came down the side of my face," Smith recalled. "It was in my nose and everywhere. At first, I thought the guy dumped it on purpose, but the umpire told me he just tipped it over to get the ball. I wouldn't have caught the ball anyhow. It made the third row."[5]

In a 2000 interview, Piehl, a motor oil company executive, said he was sitting next to his wife and his boss's wife along with a group of his company's top salesmen. In the excitement of the moment, Piehl tried to catch the ball, he claimed, so "it wouldn't hit my boss's wife."[6] The incident was captured by *Chicago Tribune* photographer Ray Gora, stationed near the third-base dugout with a new camera developed to shoot rocket launches from Cape Canaveral. The camera was equipped with a 70-millimeter lens, and every picture it took looked like a close-up. Gora's camera captured the mishap in an eight-part sequence that was featured in newspapers nationwide the next day. Al Smith had involuntarily played a memorable role in World Series history.

Smith kept a blow-up of the famous photo in his Chicago home, and once facetiously remarked that he had signed copies of the picture 200,000 times. At the fortieth anniversary celebration of the 1959 team, Smith said of the incident that had long overshadowed his fine career, "All these years, I've never made a dime off of it. Everywhere I go, that's all the people bring up. Maybe I should make T-shirts and sell them."[7] (A remorseful Melvin Piehl shunned publicity, and once declined a guest appearance on TV's *I've Got a Secret*.)

In any event, that was not Smith's only memorable moment in Game Two. With the Sox trailing 4–2 in the eighth inning, Smith came up with Earl Torgeson on second base, Sherm Lollar on first, and nobody out. As Smith later told author Bob Vanderberg, "I was up there to bunt. We were trying to get runners over to second and third. I bunted and fouled it off. Bunted again, and fouled it off."[8]

GARY LIVACARI

With the bunt off, Smith doubled to left-center field. Torgeson scored, but the slow-footed Lollar, waved around by third-base coach Tony Cuccinello, was out at home by a lot. Smith wound up on third base but was stranded there, and the game ended in a 4–3 Sox loss, thanks to perhaps the most infamous coaching decision in franchise history.

Smith rebounded offensively in 1960, hitting .315 (second in the AL) and making his second trip to the All-Star Game. With the return of Minoso to the White Sox that year, Smith willingly moved to right field so that fan favorite Minoso could play left. In 1961 Smith continued his resurgence and hit twenty-eight homers, his career high. But Bill Veeck had sold the team to John Allyn, and Smith ran into trouble with new general manager Ed Short. According to White Sox historian Richard Lindberg, Smith balked at yet another (proposed) move to third base, and was also upset when "they asked him to work as an offseason ticket salesman for the ballclub."[9]

These ill feelings eventually resulted in a trade to Baltimore, on January 14, 1963: Smith and Luis Aparicio to the Orioles; Hoyt Wilhelm, Dave Nicholson, Peter Ward, and Ron Hansen to the White Sox. After one season in Baltimore, Smith was traded back to the Indians, his original team, but was released on August 5, 1964, with a .162 batting average in sixty-one games. Picked up as a free agent shortly afterward by the Red Sox, he still didn't hit, and played his last game in the Majors on October 4.

Smith had married Mildred Winston on February 12, 1956, and they remained together until Smith's death, forty-six years later. After the end of his baseball career, Smith worked for the city of Chicago, managing the park district's baseball program, with ex-Cub pitcher Dick Drott, from 1966 through 1981. In addition to his baseball duties, he also served as supervisor of recreation at Ogden Park, on the city's South Side, and worked as a part-time community relations representative for the White Sox. Upon retiring, he became an excellent golfer and consistently shot in the low eighties.

Al Smith died on January 5, 2002, at St. Margaret Mary Hospital in Hammond, Indiana. He was seventy-three and succumbed to cardiac arrest after arterial surgery. In addition to his wife, Mildred, he was survived by two sons, Al Jr. and Dan; two daughters, Deborah Bender and Maria Chalkey; a brother and three sisters; and eleven grandchildren.

At the time of Smith's death, his White Sox teammate Billy Pierce said, "Al was a very good teammate. Al was always quiet. He never said a lot, but with his actions, he did a lot. He helped us tremendously in 1959 to win the pennant. Unfortunately, people remember him for having the beer spilled on him during the World Series, but they forgot that he drove in a lot of runs for us. He was just a very good player and a real gentleman."[10]

White Sox fans will always be grateful to Al Smith for his contributions to the pennant-winning team in 1959. But he is also fondly remembered in Cleveland. In 1993 he was enshrined in the Ohio Baseball Hall of Fame, and in 2001 he was honored as one of the "100 Greatest Indians of All Time." A fine ballplayer and a dedicated husband and father, Al Smith deserves a better fate than to be remembered simply for being doused in beer.

Chapter 42. **Vic Wertz**

Mark Armour

AGE	G	AB	R	H	2B	3B	HR	TB	RBI	BB	SO	BAV	OBP	SLG	SB	GDP	HBP
29	94	295	33	81	14	2	14	141	48	34	40	.275	.344	.478	0	4	0

In the biggest baseball game of his life, the opening contest of the 1954 World Series, Vic Wertz hit a 420-foot triple to right, a 400-foot double to left-center, and two line singles, while driving in all of his team's runs. In his other at bat, with two runners on in a tie game in the eighth inning, he crushed a 450-foot line drive to the outer reaches of the Polo Grounds, well over the head of the opposing center fielder. Unfortunately for Wertz and his Cleveland Indians, the opposing center fielder was Willie Mays, perhaps the only man in baseball history who could have run the ball down. And run the ball down Mays did, sprinting with his back to the plate toward the faraway bleachers and catching the ball like a football wide receiver hauling in a long pass.

For Willie Mays, "The Catch" became one of the central stories in a career filled with amazing deeds. But it also became the central story in the career of Wertz, a very good ballplayer who spent much of the remainder of his life talking about his long out. Were it not for Mays's sensational play, Wertz would have registered the first five-hit game in World Series history, a feat later accomplished only by Paul Molitor in 1982. But when people recall the 1954 World Series, and Vic Wertz's notable though ultimately losing role in it, only one play comes to mind.

Victor Woodrow Wertz was born on February 9, 1925, in York, Pennsylvania, about a hundred miles west of Philadelphia, the youngest of five children (Dorothy, Paul, Doris, and Helen preceded Vic) born to Paul (who was Pennsylvania Dutch) and Manerva Wertz. The family lived on Cedar Street when Vic was born, and later moved to West Market Street across from the West Side Hospital. When Vic was

Vic Wertz—Acquired in midseason for Bob Chakales, Wertz added much-needed offensive punch to a corner position for the Indians.

eleven years old, the family relocated to Reading, about sixty miles to the northeast. Paul Wertz had a variety of careers over his lifetime, including hardware store owner, insurance salesman, farmer, and house painter. Manerva was an accomplished seamstress, working in her home. Paul and Manerva were members of the Church of the Brethren.

Vic did not play baseball until after he moved to Reading, but he took to it quickly, starring for Gregg Post in American Legion ball and at Reading High School,[1] both of which won state championships with Wertz. In 1941 he was first scouted by Ed Katalinas of the Detroit Tigers, who watched him hit two home runs and a double during his first visit. "That was enough for me," recalled Katalinas. Wertz got a few bonus offers from other clubs, but he chose Detroit, which offered no bonus money, because he had been a fan of the Tigers ever since their World Series victory over the Cubs in 1935. He signed on July 1, 1942.[2]

Wertz was not a power hitter in high school or in his early days as a professional—he was a pitcher and fleet-footed outfielder. He debuted with Winston-Salem (Piedmont League), and hit just .239 in sixty-three games with no home runs. A left-handed hitter, he often hit to the opposite field and used his speed to help get on base. The next season, at Buffalo (International League), he was hitting .222 in eighteen games before he was drafted into the army. He was still just eighteen years old.

Wertz spent three years with the Eighty-First Infantry Division, including twenty-two months in the Pacific. He did not see combat. "I played quite a bit of baseball over there," he recalled. In fact, he later said that he changed his swing after observing Enos Slaughter while overseas. Wertz began to pivot his body and pull the ball toward right field.[3] He returned to Buffalo in 1946, bigger, stronger, and three years older. In 139 games, he hit .301 with 19 home runs and 91 RBIs. In 1947 he made the Tigers' roster for the first time.

A good spring and an injury to Dick Wakefield got Wertz a spot in the Opening Day lineup on April 15, hitting fourth no less, and he responded with two hits, including a double off the St. Louis Browns' Denny Galehouse in his first at bat. He played 102 games his first year, mainly in left and right fields, and batted .288 with six home runs. He hit his first round-tripper off Bob Muncrief in St. Louis on Au-

gust 13. On September 14 at Washington, he hit for the cycle in a 16–6 Tigers victory.

The next season in a similar role, Wertz fell to .248 with seven home runs. By this time he had become frustrated with manager Steve O'Neill for platooning him, and he went to general manager Billy Evans asking to be traded. Instead, Evans, at the direction of owner Walter Briggs, gave Wertz a $3,500 bonus as a gesture of faith in his abilities. O'Neill was fired in the off-season and replaced with Red Rolfe, and a great spring earned Wertz the right-field job. This time he kept it, starting all 155 games for the Tigers in 1949, and breaking out with 20 home runs, 133 runs batted in (third in the league), and a .304 batting average. His breakout performance earned him his first All-Star Game, in which he played three innings.

Wertz was no longer the slim speedy player who signed with the Tigers in 1942. He now carried 200 pounds on his six-foot frame, mainly around the chest and shoulders, which slowed him down in the outfield. The cause, he confessed, was that he loved to eat—he could and often would eat a huge sandwich any time of day or night. But Wertz's most striking physical feature was his total baldness. "It's that darn South Pacific salt water that did it," he complained. "I used to have nice curly hair." He was sensitive enough about it to keep his hat on as much as he could, and dreaded having to take his hat off for the National Anthem.[4]

Having broken through, Wertz remained a productive slugger for several years, though there were more setbacks along the trail. He had another big season in 1950, clubbing twenty-seven home runs and thirty-seven doubles while driving home 133 runs and batting .308. Over a five-game stretch beginning July 27, Wertz hit seven home runs, going 13 for 17 with four doubles and six walks in addition to the homers. In Wertz's first pennant race, the Tigers led the league for most of the summer and as late as September 15, but ended up three games behind the Yankees. In 1951 Wertz again hit twenty-seven home runs, and batted .285. He started the All-Star Game for the American League, finishing 1 for 3 with a fourth-inning home run off Sal Maglie in Wertz's home ballpark of Briggs Stadium.

Wertz married Bernice Wineka early in his career, and the couple had two children, Terence and Patricia. Their marriage ended in the early 1950s, and in June 1952 Vic married Lucille Caroll Caleel, a Lebanese American woman who would be his life partner. Caleel was a Tigers fan who went to Briggs Stadium to root for George Kell, but ended up meeting and falling for Wertz.[5] Lucille had a dramatic effect on Wertz's life and career, talking him through his occasional slump or career crisis. One early influence for Lucille: she persuaded him to own up to his lack of hair. "You're one of the few guys in baseball who has a bald head," she told him. "Make it your trademark." After that, Wertz began to leave his cap off more often.[6] "I consider my head a real asset," he later said.[7]

The Tigers fell to fifth place in 1951, and then to eighth (last) in 1952 with a 50-104 record. The highlight of Wertz's 1952 season was undoubtedly the game-ending home run he hit in Detroit on May 15—the game ended 1–0, and it gave teammate Virgil Trucks a no-hitter. Wertz was hitting .246 with seventeen home runs on August 14 when he was abruptly sent to the St. Louis Browns as part of an eight-player deal, with the Tigers getting ace pitcher Ned Garver. Detroit general manager Charlie Gehringer was blunt in his analysis of the deal: "Vic is one of those outfielders who must hit .300 or be a liability. When he didn't hit, he hurt us."[8] As for the Browns, they were having their typically poor season, but would still finish one spot ahead of the Tigers. "We simply had to have more punch," said St. Louis manager Marty Marion.[9] Wertz hit .346 in the last six weeks for the Browns, and finished at .277 with twenty-three home runs for the season. In 1953 he was the Browns' best hitter, with nineteen home runs, seventy RBIs, and a .268 average for a last-place squad.

The Browns became the Baltimore Orioles in 1954, and Wertz was their Opening Day right fielder. He hit poorly for the club, .202 in twenty-nine games, before being traded on June 1 to the Indians for pitcher Bob Chakales. This was a dramatic change of fortune for Wertz, as Cleveland was in the midst of a great season, one in which they would set the American League record with 111 wins. Wertz was thrilled. "Imagine what a surprise that was to me," he said. "I really had been down in the dumps for two seasons."[10]

The Indians were not in need of outfielders, but a short time after Wertz arrived, manager Al Lopez asked him to try first base, a position he had never played. Truth be told, Wertz had never been a good outfielder, and by 1954, at the age of twenty-nine, he was big and immobile and fit to play first base. He would remain at the position for the rest of his career. Whether it was the change of team or position or something else entirely, Wertz regained his batting form over the last half of the season. He eventually settled in to the number five spot in the order, behind Larry Doby and Al Rosen, and hit fourteen home runs and batted .275 in 295 at bats. "He's a fine boy to have on your club," said a grateful Lopez, "very conscientious, a hustler with a good influence on the team as a whole."[11]

When the Indians faced off against the New York Giants in the World Series, the oddsmakers favored the Indians because of their gaudy won-lost record. But it was the Giants who won the World Series in four straight games, starting with their ten-inning victory in Game One, when Wertz made four hits and nearly five. In fact, Wertz kept hitting, finishing 8 for 16 for the Series, including a home run off Ruben Gomez in Game Three. No other Indians player had more than three hits for the entire Series, and Wertz had four of the club's total of nine extra-base hits. He put together a great four games, but unfortunately had little help.

Nonetheless, Wertz entered 1955 rejuvenated, a key member of a great team. In the event, it would be a very difficult year. He hit fourteen home runs in seventy-four games, missing several days in May with a sprained neck, and a month in early summer with a jammed thumb, before being hit with a more serious ailment in August. He played a game on the 24th before being struck with what was thought to be a forty-eight-hour virus, but when his temperature soared and severe pain set in the next night, he was hospitalized and diagnosed with poliomyelitis, more commonly known as infantile paralysis or polio. Polio was a dreaded disease in the 1950s, responsible for paralysis and death in thousands of people just in the United States. "Ten days later the physical pain started to leave but it was replaced by a mental anguish," Wertz recalled. "I honestly didn't think of baseball. My fear was that I'd be a cripple and all that meant to my future."[12] Fortunately for him, Wertz's strain was nonparalytic, though still serious.

Wertz was in bed for weeks before he began to walk again, exhausted after just a few steps. He had lost twenty pounds, but slowly began to gain both strength and weight. Wertz credited his wife, Lucille, with staying upbeat and taking a lighthearted approach. "She accused me of 'jaking,'" he laughed. "Her bright talk and high spirits made me feel as though I'd never been sick."[13] He received 14,000 letters, many of them from children. By late winter Wertz was exercising, and, miraculously, he showed up at spring training determined to get his job back.

On April 17, 1956, Wertz took his place in the Indians' Opening Day lineup, fully recovered from his serious illness. Though often rested as a precaution, he played 136 games and belted a career-high 32 home runs while driving in 106 runs. He had a very similar season in 1957, playing in 144 games while hitting 28 home runs with 105 RBIs, and batting .282. On September 14 at Fenway Park he drove in a career-high seven runs, in a 13–10 loss to the Red Sox. Boston's Dick Gernert also drove in seven runs, the only time in baseball history two opponents had each driven in seven runs in a game.

Remarkably, Gernert and Wertz were both products of Reading High School and the Gregg Post American Legion team, though Gernert was four years younger.

Wertz was thirty-two in 1957, but showed no signs of slowing down as a middle-of-the-order slugger. He had another medical setback the next spring, though not nearly as serious as polio. While sliding into second base in a spring game, he fractured his ankle. He came back four months later but mainly pinch-hit, getting just forty-eight plate appearances for the season. Though the ankle healed, the Indians now had Vic Power at first base, leading them to trade Wertz (and outfielder Gary Geiger) to the Red Sox for star outfielder Jimmy Piersall. In 1959 Wertz played part-time, hitting .275 with 7 home runs, but was a more regular player again in 1960, responding with 19 home runs and 103 RBIs in 443 at bats. It was his fifth 100-RBI season. He started just 110 times at first base, but also finished 10 for 18 as a pinch hitter, including a grand slam off Don Newcombe, one of three grand slams he hit that season, of the ten he hit in his career.

The thirty-six-year-old Wertz slowed down a bit in 1961, hitting eleven home runs in ninety-nine games and losing most of the first-base job to Pete Runnels. In September the Red Sox sold him in a waiver deal to the Tigers, where it had all begun. In the waning days of the season, Wertz pinch-hit six times. In 1962 he became a great pinch-hitting specialist, getting fifty-three at bats in that role, and batting .321 with three home runs. For the season he hit a robust .324 in 105 at bats.

Wertz finally reached the end of the line in 1963, starting 0 for 5 with the Tigers, drawing his release, and then finishing 6 for 44 (with three homers) for the Twins. "If he didn't have a single hit," said Minnesota manager Sam Mele, "Wertz would be an asset to our club. He gives us character." At the end of the season, Wertz retired from baseball.

Vic and Lucille settled in the Detroit area, where many years earlier he had established a beverage distributorship. Although the couple did not have any children together, Vic remained close with his own two children, and also with his siblings, nieces, and nephews. He was very outgoing and fun-loving, and made a lasting impression on everyone who spent time with him.

Although he missed baseball, Wertz took to his next career as well as he did to his first. Vic Wertz Distributing Company became a Miller Beer distributor in Mount Clemens, Michigan. He won numerous company awards and his company ended up with the biggest share of the Detroit market. "I love the work," Wertz said in 1979. "I could take some time off, but I don't want to. We work our tails off. This is a very competitive business and I consider my employees to be like a team."[14]

Wertz also made a lasting contribution to the Michigan branch of the Special Olympics when he organized an endurance snowmobile ride in northern Michigan. The riders collected pledges for their annual ride to benefit the charity. The organization, now called Wertz Warriors, held their first ride in 1982 and as of 2012 were still going strong, raising over $7.5 million through the years for Special Olympics Michigan Inc. (SOMI).

Wertz died on July 7, 1983, just fifty-eight years old, while undergoing heart surgery at a Detroit hospital. He had suffered a heart attack the day before, his second in less than a month. Among those who remembered him fondly was the man with whom he was inextricably linked. "Vic was a very good player," said Willie Mays, "but he often said nobody knew about him until he hit the ball, and I caught it. I'm very sorry that a very good friend of mine died. I played golf with Vic a while ago, and he looked very good."[15]

Chapter 43. **Hal Newhouser**

Mark Stewart

AGE	W	L	PCT	ERA	G	GS	GF	CG	SHO	SV	IP	H	BB	SO	HBP	WP
33	7	2	.778	2.51	26	1	15	0	0	7	46.2	34	18	25	0	0

"Prince Hal" Newhouser had the unique distinction of being baseball's best pitcher during the 1940s—as well as its most unpopular player. An uncompromising perfectionist who was as hard on himself as his teammates, he was famous for his hot left arm and mercurial temperament. Whether Newhouser was mowing down enemy hitters or smashing a case of Coke bottles against the clubhouse wall, he was given a wide berth by opponents and teammates alike. Hal began his baseball career as a gangly, wide-eyed teenager and finished as one of the smartest scouts in the game. In between he made a few friends and plenty of enemies, left a lifetime of memories for baseball fans in Detroit, and was part of the Indians' lights-out bullpen during their historic 1954 campaign.

Harold Newhouser was born on May 20, 1921, in Detroit, Michigan. His parents were first-generation immigrants. His father, Theodore, was a draftsman in the automotive industry. He had been a gymnast in his native Czechoslovakia. His mother was Austrian. Newhouser got his athleticism from his father and his serious (some would say sour) disposition from his mother.

The Newhousers had moved to Detroit from Pittsburgh before Hal was born. Although there was good, steady work during the Great Depression, the family still struggled to make ends meet. Despite the fact that Hal and his four-years-older brother, Dick, were exceptional athletes, the Newhousers showed little interest in sports other than gymnastics. Even after Dick was signed to a contract by the Tigers and played a couple of seasons of Minor League ball, his parents didn't know much about baseball and didn't care. Dick left the game

Hal Newhouser—The Detroit Tigers great was a welcomed boost to the Indians' bullpen. Newhouser was elected to the Hall of Fame in 1992.

in his second year after he was beaned and suffered a fractured skull.

The scout who signed Dick was Wish Egan, a man who sought to corner the local market on baseball talent. Through Dick, Egan got the inside track on Hal, a skinny left-hander who could whip a baseball with tremendous force, and who already seemed to have the grim, competitive makeup of a pro pitcher as he entered his teen years. Hal was deadly serious at all times. Teammates and sportswriters later noted that he had no sense of humor.

Hal Newhouser was a true survivor. He took every manner of odd job, including selling papers, setting pins in a bowling alley, and collecting empty bottles for the penny deposits. During the winter he would wander over to the coal yard and collect discarded flakes in a gunnysack to take home. When the mercury plummeted, every little bit helped—especially if it was free.

As a boy Newhouser also survived several serious injuries. He punctured his stomach when he fell off a woodpile onto a metal spike. He received a nasty head injury when another boy hit him with a brick. During a basketball game he got a bad floor burn and then obsessively picked at the scab until he got blood poisoning. He got several deep gashes playing football, too. A deep scar under his right eye became more noticeable as he grew older. By the time he was in the Majors, he could look downright scary.

When Newhouser was fourteen, he listened to the radio as Goose Goslin drove Mickey Cochrane home with the winning run in the 1935 World Series. He decided that day that he wanted to pitch for the hometown Tigers. Newhouser was already playing softball in a fast-pitch league, pitching and playing first base. Bob Ladie, who coached a top sandlot team in Detroit, suggested that he try throwing a baseball. Young Hal took the mound for the first time at fifteen. Over the next three seasons, he won forty-two games and lost only three times.

Newhouser developed an explosive but hard-to-control fastball and good overhand curve. He also gained a reputation as a perfectionist with an explosive temper. He expected the best from himself as well as his teammates. When his fielders booted a ball, when his hitters failed to give him the runs he needed, he took it very personally. He was a difficult teammate to say the least; later, during his heyday with Detroit, he was characterized as the most unpopular man in the locker room.

But ballplayers will put up with a lot if you win,

and win he did. At Egan's suggestion, he quit the baseball team at Wilbur Wright Trade School and pitched American Legion ball instead. His fellow students at Wright signed a petition asking him to reconsider, but he had his sights set on a bigger prize. Against this higher grade of competition, Newhouser was simply fantastic. During one stretch he won nineteen games in a row and pitched sixty-five scoreless innings, striking out twenty or more hitters five times. Also at Egan's insistence, he quit the school basketball team—after being captain for two seasons—so he could focus on baseball.

The Tigers decided to sign seventeen-year-old Hal in the summer of 1938, right after he returned from the American Legion tournament. But by then the secret was out and other teams—most notably the Indians—were hovering. Wish Egan had the inside track and he used it to close the deal on the evening of August 6. Egan got the boy's signature on a contract and paid him a $500 bonus in $100 bills. Hal gave $400 to mom and dad, and socked away $100 for himself in case he didn't make it as a pro. Plan B was to go to an industrial school to study tool and die work.

A little while after Newhouser signed the contract, he was walking down the street when the Indians' head scout, Cy Slapnicka, pulled up in a shiny new car. He offered Newhouser a $15,000 bonus and the car. Hal was crushed. Slapnicka had been late because he was picking up the car!

At virtually the same time, the Tigers were engineering the departure of manager Mickey Cochrane, replacing him with Del Baker. When Egan—who had known Iron Mike since he arrived at Detroit—heard the news, he was unmoved. "A couple of years from now the Tigers will win pennants no matter who manages them," he told his secretary. "Today I've just signed the greatest left-handed pitcher I ever saw."[1]

Newhouser reported for duty the following spring to the Tigers' Minor League club in Alexandria, Louisiana. He dominated batters at two Minor League stops that summer, first in the Evangeline League with Alexandria and then with Beaumont of the Texas League. He logged a total of 230 innings on his teenage arm. Later Newhouser felt that had he been brought along more slowly, he would not have experienced the arm and shoulder problems that began plaguing him in his late twenties.

Newhouser won his first game as a pro, striking out eighteen batters, and then seven more before earning a promotion to Beaumont. He won his first four games with his new team before Texas League batters figured they could wait him out and force him to groove his pitches when he was behind in the count. Newhouser lost thirteen in a row at one point and the Tigers were getting alarming reports about the eighteen-year-old's temper. Egan stepped in at this point and suggested that he join Detroit, mostly so they could keep an eye on him.

Newhouser joined a team led by pitchers Schoolboy Rowe, Tommy Bridges, and Bobo Newsom. He was part of a youth movement that included Dizzy Trout and fellow teenager Fred Hutchinson. It was manager Del Baker's plan to work the youngsters into the rotation and phase out Roxie Lawson, Vern Kennedy, and George Gill—all whom had been traded away by the time Newhouser reached the Majors.

Newhouser appeared in one game in 1939. On September 29 he started, giving up three hits and four walks in five innings in the second game of a doubleheader against the Indians. The game was called on account of darkness, and Newhouser took the loss. It was one of seventy-three suffered by the Tigers that year against eighty-one victories. Detroit obviously had superb pitching, but the Bengals' offense was in flux. Hank Greenberg and Rudy York supplied ample power, while veteran Charlie Gehringer was a perennial .300 hitter. The rest of the lineup was good but not great, peppered with the likes of Birdie Tebbetts, Barney McCosky, Pinky Higgins, and Pete Fox.

Which made what happened in 1940 all the more remarkable. Baker needed York's bat in the lineup every day. A catcher by trade, York did not offer the receiving skills of Tebbetts and thus had functioned primarily as a backup player and pinch hitter. Baker moved Greenberg to left field and stationed York at first base. York exploded with a 33-homer, 134-RBI season, while Greenberg held his own in left and came within a dozen points of winning the Triple Crown.

The veterans on the Tigers' pitching staff took full advantage of this firepower, with Newsom, Bridges, and Rowe combining for a 49-17 record. Newhouser was in the rotation most of the year, making twenty starts and going 9-9 with a 4.86 earned run average. Every outing was an adventure. When he threw the fastball for strikes and located his curve, he was tough to beat. When his control was off, it was painful to watch him. These swings were not always game to game. Sometimes they were inning to inning.

As a nineteen-year-old in the thick of a pennant race, "Prince Hal" was not always in control of his emotions. In his wilder moments, he would pace around the mound, trying to regain his composure, worried what the veterans were thinking. Often he would peer into the stands, searching for the large hat worn by his mother, who sat along the right-field line when she attended games at Briggs Stadium. His father never saw him pitch at Tiger Stadium—he was working during the afternoons and the Tigers were a noted holdout where night baseball was concerned. (Later, Newhouser bought his folks a house in Asbury Park, New Jersey, where they opened a small pattern-making business.)

After being pulled from a game by Baker, Newhouser was like a hurricane (his alternate nickname was Hurricane Hal). He would throw tantrums in the clubhouse that reminded baseball people of another volatile southpaw, Lefty Grove. Once, he destroyed an entire case of Coke, smashing each bottle against the locker-room wall. Over the years Newhouser would become so irate that he demanded that the Tigers trade him. After cooling off, he would always come to his senses.

Even in calmer times, Newhouser could be tough to take. As tradition dictated, the Tigers had Newhouser room with Rowe, the veteran who had grown up in the Detroit system. All Newhouser wanted to talk about was the minutiae of pitching. He drove Rowe crazy.

Every one of those nine wins in 1940 turned out to be precious. The Tigers and Indians battled all summer, while the juggernaut Yankees—a last-place team in May—came around and made a spirited dash for first place in September. The smart money was on the Indians until a player revolt against manager Ozzie Vitt destabilized the clubhouse. In the end Detroit survived to win the pennant by a game over Cleveland and two over New York.

The World Series against the Reds was a tight affair that went the full seven games. Newhouser did not see the light of day, and watched from the dugout as Cincinnati took the final two games by scores of 4–0 and 2–1.

The law of gravity caught up with the Tigers and Indians in 1941, as both teams tumbled into a fourth-place tie with sub-.500 records. Missing from the lineup was Greenberg, one of the first ballplayers drafted in advance of the Second World War. That left York as the club's sole power source, and not surprisingly, his numbers declined.

Once again Newhouser was part of the Detroit rotation, this time going 9-11 with a 4.79 ERA. It was essentially a repeat of the previous season. He ran hot and cold, fanning hitters when he got ahead in the count, and getting knocked all over the park when he fell behind. On the upside, Hal, now twenty, married his girl, Beryl, in 1941. They had met at a party a couple of years earlier.

On December 5 Detroit fans got good news when the military announced that it was discharging all men over the age of twenty-eight. They had exactly two days to rejoice about the return of Hammering Hank before the Japanese attack on Pearl Harbor plunged America into war.

Newhouser's wartime plans involved being sworn into the Army Air Force on the mound at Briggs Stadium. However, he failed his physical after doctors heard the swoosh of a mitral valve prolapse. He was classified 4-F, unfit for duty. Newhouser tried on other occasions to slip through the medical screening as Greenberg had (originally, he too was 4-F due to bad feet), but the stethoscope told doctors all they needed to know, and Hal was excused from service.

Newhouser made the best of his situation, pitching well enough against the league's dwindling offensive talent in 1942 to make his first All-Star Game. No one suspected it at the time, but this would be the first of six straight All-Star selections. Newhouser was not easy to score on, as witnessed by his 2.45 ERA. But the Tigers lineup had been decimated by the draft and struggled mightily to generate runs. The result was an 8-14 record for Newhouser. He completed eleven games and also functioned as the team's closer at times, racking up five saves. The Tigers finished below .500 again, in fifth place.

Newhouser's control was the big issue. More often than not it was horrible. In 1943 former catcher Steve O'Neill replaced Baker as manager and brought in Paul Richards to handle the young staff. Richards, who was already establishing himself as a baseball guru, would be charged with squeezing the long-awaited potential out of Newhouser and his teammates.

The new manager and catcher were exasperated by the number of walks Newhouser issued in 1943—a league-high 111 in just over 195 innings. He worked his way in and out of trouble constantly, running up big pitch counts and getting pulled for pinch hitters in the middle innings, which drove him crazy. His moodiness and frustration grew even worse. At season's end, Newhouser's record was a dismal 8-17. Had the war not been taking a heavy toll on Major League rosters, Newhouser probably would have been farmed out, released, or traded.

As Newhouser headed into the 1944 season, he had to make an important career decision. He was

34-52 at this point, and a source of great frustration to his teammates and Tigers management. His father had secured an off-season job for him as an apprentice draftsman at Chrysler headquarters and he showed enough promise to be offered a full-time job with a very attractive salary. He agreed that it was a good opportunity, but he informed his parents that he would give baseball one more shot.

Newhouser sensed that O'Neill and Richards had much to teach him. Trout and Virgil Trucks, another product of the Tigers' farm system, had made the transition to effective Major League starters. Detroit, whose pitching was getting thinner and thinner, really needed Hal to "grow up" and join them atop the rotation.

When Newhouser arrived at the wartime spring-training camp in Indiana, Richards told him that he was a thrower. "I'm going to make you a pitcher," he said.[2] By this time Newhouser was a three-pitch pitcher, with a fastball, curveball, and changeup. Richards taught him how to throw a slider. Back then the pitch was known somewhat derogatorily as a nickel curve, but in Newhouser's hand it was a sharp-breaking pitch that looked enough like his fastball that batters couldn't handle it.

Another part of the transformation involved teaching Newhouser to harness his emotions. Whatever Richards said and did worked miracles. Newhouser became a completely different pitcher, on the mound and in the clubhouse. Meanwhile, Richards managed to turn Trout into a top pitcher, too.

Newhouser led the Tigers into battle during one of the weirdest seasons in AL history. Two second-division clubs, the Boston Red Sox and St. Louis Browns, joined the Tigers and Yankees in a wild four-team race that lasted well into September. Boston faded after losing key players to the army, but the Browns and Yankees kept pace. The only reason New York didn't run away with the race was Newhouser. He beat them six times that season.

The Browns shocked the Yankees in a late-season series to put them out of the running, and with two days left Detroit and St. Louis sported identical 87-65 records. Newhouser won his start—victory number 29, which led the Majors—but the Browns won, too. Trout, whose season was every bit as good as Newhouser's, took the mound on the final day and lost to the Senators. In St. Louis the Browns scored a comeback win over the Yankees to nail down the pennant.

After the season, the MVP vote was a toss-up between Newhouser and Trout. Dizzy had 27 victories to Newhouser's 29, but had made 40 starts, logged 352⅓ innings, and had an ERA of 2.12. Trout actually received more first-place votes than Newhouser, but Hal won the overall voting by four points to cop the trophy by a narrow margin. Newhouser had led the Majors with 187 strikeouts and had an ERA of 2.22. He twirled 6 shutouts to Trout's 7, and also saved 2 wins for Detroit; thus, he had a hand in a total of 31 victories.

While Trout was never as good again, Newhouser continued his assault on American League batters. In 1945 he led the AL with 313 innings pitched, 29 complete games, 212 strikeouts, 8 shutouts, and a 1.81 ERA. He won 25 times and lost 9, with a couple of saves on top. Rarely has a pitcher gone through a season with the total command Newhouser enjoyed. His strikeout total seems tame by modern standards, but at the time, the second-place finisher, Nels Potter of the Browns, had 83 fewer.

The Tigers welcomed Hank Greenberg back at midseason and also reacquired outfielder Roy Cullenbine in a trade with the Indians early in the year. Cullenbine established himself as the team's table-setter, while Greenberg got into seventy-eight games and regained his swing in time for another thrilling four-way pennant race.

Hal may have alienated his teammates at times, but they knew he was a gamer. Toward the end of 1945, his back began to spasm and the team decided that he should stay in Detroit while the Tigers made their final eastern trip. When they arrived in New York, general manager Jack Zeller revisited this decision and phoned Newhouser to ask him to fly to New York. The Tigers pitchers were exhausted, and the thinking was that Newhouser might be able to fool the Yankees for a couple of innings before they realized he wasn't himself. Newhouser threw a curve to Charlie Keller and practically passed out from the pain, so he stuck with a fastball and changeup. Newhouser ended up blanking the Yankees on four hits that afternoon.

The Tigers rolled into Washington in late September with a half-game lead on the surprising Senators and with plenty of bumps and bruises. Eddie Mayo had a sore shoulder. Greenberg was limping on a sprained ankle. And Newhouser's back was killing him. He lasted only one inning before leaving the first game of a crucial twin bill. The Tigers rallied to win 7–4 and took the nightcap 7–3 behind Trout, who won his fifth game in two weeks. They split the next day's doubleheader.

The Senators finished their schedule the following week with eighty-seven wins, a game behind the Tigers. Detroit, however, was unable to clinch because of four consecutive rainouts. The weather finally cleared with the Tigers needing one win to clinch and avoid a playoff with the Senators. Virgil Trucks, who missed the entire year in the navy, was released in time to start the final game for Detroit. He allowed one run over five-plus innings, but got into trouble in the sixth. Newhouser came in from the bullpen and wriggled out of a one-out, bases-loaded jam to preserve a 2–1 lead. The pesky Browns scored single runs off Newhouser in the seventh and eighth to take a 3–2 lead. In the ninth inning the Tigers loaded the bases and Greenberg hit his most famous home run, a shot into the left-field stands that won the game for Newhouser and the pennant for Detroit. Newhouser ended up leading the Majors in wins, strikeouts, and ERA, pitching's version of the Triple Crown. This time Newhouser was a central character in the World Series. The Tigers opened the Series against the Chicago Cubs in Detroit with Hal on the mound. He got

absolutely clobbered in a 9–0 rout, giving up seven runs before being yanked in the third inning. The Tigers had played terrible defense behind Newhouser, but he blamed himself for this one. He had not made good pitches when he needed to.

The series seesawed back and forth and was tied at two games apiece when Newhouser redeemed himself in Game Five with an 8–4 complete-game victory. Hal was called upon three days later to start Game Seven. The Tigers staked him to five runs in the top of the first inning—highlighted by a bases-clearing double by his catcher, Paul Richards—and Newhouser kept Chicago under control for nine innings, scattering ten hits and striking out ten for an easy 9–3 victory. With the exception of the Game One debacle, Newhouser just blew the Cubs away in the series. In twenty and two-thirds innings, he fanned twenty-two batters and walked only four.

After the Series, Newhouser was named the league MVP again. In doing so he became the first—and still the only—hurler to win back-to-back Most Valuable Player awards. Newhouser later admitted that he tried hard to win the second award. He knew how tough it was for a pitcher to win it, and he was determined to win it twice.

The winter of 1945–46 brought some interesting developments in the baseball world. Jorge Pasquel decided to take advantage of all the returning baseball talent and transform his Mexican League into a Major League. The key was luring a few big names south of the border. There was no bigger name in baseball than Prince Hal Newhouser. Pasquel offered him $200,000 to pitch for three seasons, with a $300,000 signing bonus.

For a player who had missed a big payday once, this seemed too good to pass up. Newhouser felt a lot of loyalty to the Tigers, and informed Briggs that he was being wooed by Pasquel. The Tigers gave him a $10,000 bonus to stay with the club, with a promise of much more after the season, when his new contract came due. Worried that he might be banned from baseball if the Mexican League imploded, Newhouser took the Detroit offer and never looked back. The Tigers did give him a big raise, to more than $60,000 a year.

The 1946 season belonged to the Red Sox, who celebrated the return from military duty of Ted Williams by winning 104 games and running away from the league. The Tigers finished second, twelve games out. Newhouser was again the top pitcher in the AL, winning a league-best twenty-six games and taking the ERA crown again with a 1.94 mark. Any doubts that the returning stars would expose him as an inferior pitcher were erased by his stellar season. Although Williams won the MVP award, Newhouser finished close on his heels in second place.

The Tigers had a wonderful starting staff in 1946. Trout, Trucks, and Fred Hutchinson combined to go 45-33 and rarely gave up more than three runs a game. Meanwhile, Greenberg was the top power hitter in the league, and the team had just acquired George Kell, a future batting champion, at the suggestion of Hal's old mentor, Wish Egan. They also had Dick Wakefield, one of the brightest young stars in baseball. Detroit fans had plenty to look forward to.

After the 1946 season, the Tigers chatted to the Yankees about pitching. New York had failed to win a pennant for a fourth straight year and the Tigers were loaded. Hal's name came up in conversation and so did Joe DiMaggio's. Was a trade of these two stars specifically discussed? Rumors that it did have circulated ever since.

The 1947 Tigers finished in second place, twelve games out, for the second year in a row. This time they were looking up at the Yankees. The missing piece to their puzzle was Greenberg, who had gotten into a fight with management over his salary and abruptly retired. The Tigers sold his contract to the Pirates, where he played one final season. Meanwhile, the Detroit offense became a black hole. No Tiger hit twenty-five homers or knocked in or scored a hundred runs. Kell was the only regular over .300.

With little offensive support, Newhouser's record dropped to 17-17. He still had a tremendous season, completing 24 of his 36 starts, fanning 176 batters, and turning in an ERA of 2.87. Though he had been a big leaguer for nearly a decade, he still had moments of teen-like frustration. During a game at Briggs Stadium in August, O'Neill attempted to remove Newhouser in the third inning after he gave up five runs to the Red Sox. Hal insisted he had his good stuff and simply refused to leave the mound. O'Neill later fined him $250 for his obstinacy—the first fine he had doled out as Tigers manager. It was also the first time Newhouser had actually ever been fined, despite having done untold damage to clubhouses around the league.

If anyone was qualified to judge his own stuff, it was Newhouser. Long before teams used videotape and analyzed pitching motions, Hal had film shot of his games through an expensive lens. He would run the movies at home between starts looking for flaws in his motion and also in his grip. Toward the end of his frustrating 1947 campaign, he purchased a second projector and ran films side by side on two screens. One film showed him during his big years of the mid-1940s. The other had his most recent starts. After hours of study, he noticed a slight difference in his follow-through. He corrected the flaw and won three of his final four decisions. He later discovered that he had been playing with a broken right foot.

The Tigers faded from the first division in 1948, finishing a respectable 78-76 but in fifth place. The offense was the problem again. This time they were without Kell for a long stretch of the summer, and rising stars Hoot Evers and Vic Wertz weren't ready to carry the club. For his part, Newhouser had another stellar season. He led the AL with 21 wins and, with 143 strikeouts, was top man on a Detroit staff that finished first in strikeouts. A decade's worth of innings had taken the edge off Newhouser's fastball, but he still got it to the plate in the nineties and had become quite adept at locating his big curve.

On June 15 the Tigers became the last American League team to install lights. Owner Walter Briggs was a staunch proponent of day baseball, and even after the first night game, he told reporters he did not envision the club playing too many of them. Newhouser was on the mound to deliver the first pitch against the Philadelphia A's at 9:30 p.m. He allowed two hits in a 4–1 victory, later ranking this night among his top baseball thrills. More than 50,000 people were in the stands, and the team received a long, loud ovation after the final out. It was one of the few bright spots in a season that saw Detroit finish eighteen and a half games out of first place.

Newhouser did figure in the 1948 pennant race. On the season's final day, he faced Bob Feller. These were always exciting matchups, and although Feller typically got the best of the Tigers when they faced each other, Newhouser did have one of his most memorable moments on this particular occasion. Newhouser's shoulder was aching and he was throwing on one day's rest, but he pitched one of the best games of his life, winning 7–1 in front of a deflated crowd at Municipal Stadium. The victory prevented the Tribe from clinching the pennant, and forced them into a one-game playoff with the Red Sox, which they won. Newhouser's twenty-first victory put him one ahead of both Bob Lemon and Gene Bearden, Rapid Robert's teammates.

The 1948 season was Newhouser's last as a twenty-game winner. The shoulder pain he felt that day never really went away. Over the years doctors and trainers tried everything they could to diagnose and relieve the pain. By Newhouser's own estimate he was X-rayed more than 100 times during his career. He had shots in his neck, a tooth pulled, and every type of chiropractic maneuver in the book.

Newhouser labored through the 1949 campaign, winning eighteen times, often on sheer guile. Red Rolfe, the old Yankee star, was now the manager. He squeezed decent years out of fellow veterans Trucks and Hutchinson, and got twenty-five wins from young starters Art Houtteman and Ted Gray.

The Tigers got big years out of Wertz and Kell to finish twenty games over .500, in fourth place.

Detroit continued its winning ways in 1950. The Tigers battled the Yankees, Red Sox, and Indians all year, but finished in second place three games behind the pennant-winning New Yorkers. Newhouser went 15-13 but could no longer count on his fastball to get him out of trouble. His ERA soared to 4.34.

From their fine showing in 1950, the Tigers tumbled into the second division the following year. Newhouser spent half the season unable to pitch because of shoulder woes, going 6-6 in fourteen starts. The smooth, rhythmic movement that had characterized his delivery was gone. For a player so concerned with form, it was sheer torture. Newhouser didn't win a game after the All-Star break and was unable to make any starts after mid-July. During the year he was offered a job with a Detroit company for $30,000 a year but turned it down without revealing the firm's name. He wanted to keep pitching.

Newhouser also wanted to keep working with kids. He was a fountain of information on his craft and actually wrote a book entitled *Pitching to Win*. He also had established a kids club in Detroit and a few other cities called Hal's Pals. He met with members on his off days and before games when he wasn't pitching. He also collected used equipment and sent it to the different clubs after the season. Through these interactions he developed a taste for scouting, no doubt spurred by the memory of Wish Egan. Hal had been a pallbearer at Egan's funeral in April of 1951.

The Tigers cut Newhouser's salary by the maximum 25 percent for 1952, but he refused to sign the contract GM Charlie Gehringer sent him until he was sure he could pitch without pain. He went to Lakeland, Florida, at his own expense a month early and began working out. While some ballplayers would have cringed at the thought of extra work in the spring, Newhouser was a great believer in intense training. Forty laps around the park were just a warm-up for him.

When Newhouser was confident he could make it through the season, he made a fascinating proposal to the team. He was due $31,000 for 1952. Instead, he asked for a five-year deal for $100,000. If for some reason he could not pitch, the salary would cover him as a Minor League pitching instructor or Major League coach. The Tigers had a long-standing rule against multiyear contracts. After careful consideration they turned him down.

Newhouser managed to make nineteen starts in 1952 but was only marginally effective. He went 9-9 with a 3.74 ERA, and toward the end of the year lost his starting spot to young Billy Hoeft. Newhouser's final victory of the season was also his 200th. It turned out to be his last as a Tiger. The following season he made it into only seven games. He was 0-1 with a 7.06 ERA for Detroit.

Newhouser was released by the Tigers before the 1954 season and decided it might be time to retire. His old teammate Hank Greenberg was GM and part owner of the Indians. Greenberg offered him a chance to unretire and make the club as a reliever. Newhouser took it. The move to the bullpen could not have been an easy one for Hal. He was nothing if not pragmatic, but he also was famous for not wanting to leave the mound. At times the ball had to be pried from his hand while he pleaded his case.

The signing turned out to be brilliant. Everything went right for Cleveland during the regular season. Newhouser pitched primarily in long relief, winning seven games and saving seven others against just two losses. His ERA was a neat 2.51. Newhouser was part of a lights-out bullpen that featured a pair of twenty-five-year-old call-ups, Don Mossi and Ray Narleski. Between this threesome they accounted for 16 wins and saved 27 of the Tribe's record 111 victories that season. (Saves were not an official statistic at that time, and the 27 were compiled in later years.) The Giants shocked the Indians in the World Series, scoring a four-game sweep. Newhouser saw action in Game Four. He relieved Lemon in the fifth inning but failed to retire the two batters he faced.

With his final seven victories, Newhouser moved ahead of two Rubes—Marquard and Waddell—into eighth place all-time on the list of victories by left-handers. Hal made just two appearances in 1955 before he was released. His final numbers were 207 wins and 150 losses with a career ERA of 3.06. Newhouser led the American League in wins four times in five seasons and in strikeouts, complete games, and ERA twice. He also was the top man in shutouts one season.

Hal Newhouser stayed in baseball, scouting for many years in Michigan—not a job for the fainthearted, given the state's April temperatures. He worked for the Orioles, Indians, Tigers, and Astros in the four decades after his retirement as a player. His first discovery was Milt Pappas in 1957. He spotted the right-hander at Cooley High in Detroit and connected him with the Orioles. Pappas would make the big club after just a handful of Minor League starts and star as one of the Baby Birds for Newhouser's old catcher, Paul Richards. A couple of years later, Newhouser signed Dean Chance for the O's. Chance later won a Cy Young Award with the Angels.

Newhouser's last employer was the Houston Astros. He quit after the Astros overrode his suggestion to make Derek Jeter the first pick in the 1992 draft. Houston took Phil Nevin instead. Newhouser had watched Jeter play many times and got to know his family—the kid was a lock, he told his wife, Beryl, even at the $1 million bonus many thought it would take to lure the shortstop away from the University of Michigan. "No one is worth a million dollars," Hal told his boss, Dan O'Brien, "but if one kid is worth that, it's this kid."[3]

Over the years Newhouser suffered the indignity of being passed over by Hall of Fame voters not for his lack of talent, but for the talent drain in baseball during the years in which he excelled. He was what baseball people disdainfully referred to as a

Wartime Pitcher. They conveniently ignored the fact that in the postwar years 1946–50, he averaged just under twenty wins a season. In his last year of eligibility he received 155 votes, his best showing by far but still far short of what he needed.

As the years passed, Newhouser became more philosophical about this slight. He half-understood what the voters were going through—even those on the Veterans Committee who had tried to hit against him. For several years he listened to the radio on the day the Hall of Fame enshrinees were announced, but after too many years of not hearing his name, Hal stopped listening.

After more than three decades of eligibility, Newhouser finally got the call from Cooperstown in 1992. He cried when he heard the news—not because he had made it, but because his mother, ninety-two, was still alive to see her son receive his just rewards.

Newhouser was the first Detroit-born Tiger to reach Cooperstown. He went into the Hall of Fame with pitchers Tom Seaver and Rollie Fingers and Bill McGowan, the late umpire. Among those passed over by the Veterans Committee that year were Phil Rizzuto, Nellie Fox, Earl Weaver, Joe Gordon, Leo Durocher, and Vic Willis—all of whom would later make it—and Gil Hodges, who as of 2013 was still waiting.

A few years later Newhouser began suffering from emphysema and heart problems, but lived to see his No. 16 retired by the Tigers. He died on November 10, 1998, at Providence Hospital in Southfield, near his home in Bloomfield Hills. He was survived by Beryl and his daughters, Charlene and Cherrill, as well as his brother, Richard.

The story around baseball during Newhouser's MVP years was that he learned to control his temper the day he learned to control his fastball. Sometimes it was the other way around. Soon it became baseball lore. Hal was nothing if not honest, and always made a point of refuting this theory.

"That's nonsense," he liked to say. "I'll be hot-headed all my life. That's just the kind of guy I am." He was quick to add, "I didn't win because I controlled my temper. I controlled my temper because I began to win. . . . There's no use getting mad when you're winning!"[4]

Chapter 44. **Bill Glynn**

Richard Marsh

AGE	G	AB	R	H	2B	3B	HR	TB	RBI	BB	SO	BAV	OBP	SLG	SB	GDP	HBP
28	111	171	19	43	3	2	5	65	18	12	21	.251	.297	.380	3	4	0

Even the Detroit Tigers faithful were cheering Cleveland first baseman Bill Glynn on as he stepped into the batter's box in the eighth inning on July 5, 1954. Glynn was having the greatest game of his Major League career in the first game of a doubleheader at Detroit's Briggs Stadium. In his first three at bats, Glynn hit three home runs and drove in seven runs. Facing Ralph Branca in the third inning, Glynn hit a grand slam down the right-field line. Batting with one on in the fifth inning, he hit a homer to right field. In the seventh inning, Glynn hit a solo homer to right-center off Dick Weik.

When Glynn came up again in the eighth inning, the bases were loaded, and he was staring baseball immortality in the face. If he hit another homer he would become the seventh player in the Major Leagues to hit four home runs in a game. Another round-tripper would also give him eleven runs batted in in the game, tying a record set by the New York Yankees' Tony Lazzeri in 1936. Glynn bashed the ball 440 feet to deep center field, only to see Detroit outfielder Bill Tuttle snatch the ball at the fence; the runner on third scored after the catch, Glynn's eighth RBI in the game. The final score was Cleveland 13, Detroit 6.

The Indians did not fare as well in the second game, losing 1–0 in eleven innings. Glynn was unable to sustain the magic, going 0 for 5. Afterward, he said, "I wish I could've saved a homer for the second game."[1]

William Vincent Glynn, who played for three seasons with the Indians in a four-year Major League career, was born on June 30, 1925, in Sussex, New Jersey. He was the oldest child born to Vincent and

Bill Glynn—Mostly a defensive player, Bill Glynn carved out a good career in the Pacific Coast League after his days in the Major Leagues.

Helen Glynn. Vincent supported his family working as a laborer. A premier athlete at Franklin High School, Glynn lettered as a first baseman in baseball, a running back in football, and a forward in basketball. He played against a future Indians teammate, Larry Doby, in basketball and baseball at the state tournament level. (Doby's team, Eastside High School of Paterson, won in both sports.)

Glynn graduated from high school in 1942 and, with the United States in World War II, he entered the army, where he was trained as an infantryman. Stationed at Leghorn, Italy, for twenty-one months, he spent some of his free time playing baseball and softball, drawing the attention of several Major League scouts.

In 1946, after his discharge, Glynn was signed by the Philadelphia Phillies scout Chuck Ward and was assigned to Americus of the Class D Georgia-Florida League. Glynn was considered by Phillies scout Gil Smith to be the finest prospect in the league, as he hit .328 with 104 RBIs and was named to the all-league team, inspiring an Americus sportswriter to pen this ode: "It's Glynn again, the ball's on the wing again. Let us sing again the praises of Glynn."[2]

In 1947 and 1948, Glynn played for the Utica Blue Sox of the Class A Eastern League. The 1947 team was considered by many to be the best team Utica ever had, posting a 90-48 record and finishing ten games ahead of second-place Albany. His batting average fell to the .260s in both seasons, but his slugging continued; in 1947 he hit two home runs in the Blue Sox's pennant clincher.

The Phillies promoted him to Triple-A Toronto in 1949. They considered him Major League ready defensively. He had nineteen home runs for the Maple Leafs but was hitting only in the .260s, principally because he had trouble against left-handers. Farm director Joe Reardon believed that Glynn would overcome this problem, and Glynn was a September call-up to the Phillies, playing in eight games and getting his first Major League hit off the St. Louis Cardinals' Gerry Staley on September 20.

Back at Toronto in 1950, Glynn hit twenty-five home runs but batted only .234. The Phillies switched their Triple-A affiliation to Baltimore in 1951 and Glynn played that season for the Orioles, who were two years away from their return to the Major Leagues. He continued his impressive fielding, but his offensive numbers were unimpressive: .249, 14 homers, and 51 RBIs in 143 games.

After the season, the Phillies sent Glynn to Sacramento of the Pacific Coast League for outfielder Gerry Scala. Sacramento was looking for a power-hitting first baseman. Player-manager Joe Gordon had Glynn bat just ahead of him so that he could offer advice from the on-deck circle. Glynn responded, hitting .306. Gordon and several scouts recommended Glynn to Cleveland. In midseason the Indians needed a first baseman, and on July 15 they purchased Glynn for Minor Leaguers Dino Restelli and Ben Taylor. Glynn backed up Luke Easter (named the American League Player of the Year by *The Sporting News* in 1952) at first base and also pinch-hit.

As the 1953 season began, the Indians were once again considered to be a major contender for the pennant, having finished just two games behind the Yankees in 1952. The Indians' expectations for Glynn were high. General manager Hank Greenberg said that if Glynn had been with the Indians at the beginning of the 1952 season, the Tribe would have been stronger at both first base and right field and would have easily made up the two games.

Less than a week after the season began, on April 18, Luke Easter broke his foot, and Glynn became the starting first baseman. "He'll give us some speed in the infield and he's dangerous at the bat," Greenberg said. "He won't hit the long ball as often as Luke, but he gives it a battle."[3] Greenberg's assessment of Glynn's power (or lack of it) was accurate. It wasn't until May 31 that he hit his first home run, in an 8–1 victory in Detroit.

When Easter returned in mid-June, Indians manager Al Lopez said that he had to put Luke back on first, because one homer was worth more than three singles on the power-starved Indians, "especially with a club with as little speed as ours." Lopez added, "When the ball is hit out of the park, the runners can creep around the bases and still score."[4] Meanwhile, Glynn worked on his hitting weaknesses. Teammate Hank Majeski helped teach him the finer points of bunting and showed him how to employ a more open batting stance. Glynn was a good pupil, realizing that he might not be successful in every at bat.

The Indians played the Yankees on July 30, Yankee manager Casey Stengel's sixty-third birthday. Glynn spoiled Stengel's day by driving a triple to center field to plate Wally Westlake with the winning run in the eighth inning of the Tribe's 4–3 victory.

By August 6 Glynn was hitting so well that Lopez was considering moving him to right field to keep both him and Easter in the lineup. On August 22 Glynn smashed a three-run homer as Mike Garcia defeated St. Louis, 4–1.

Before the 1954 season, some of Cleveland's sportswriters did not expect Glynn to make the team. Although the competition at first was fierce with Easter, Glynn, and newly acquired Rocky Nelson, first base was still regarded as the weak spot for the Indians. Lopez kept repeating that the starter at first would be the person who hit the best in spring training. Because of his previous injuries, Easter quickly became a nonfactor and was optioned to the Minor Leagues after six unsuccessful pinch-hitting appearances. (He never played in a Major League game again.) The competition came down to Nelson and Glynn. Glynn had a tremendous spring, hitting .333 with two home runs, eight RBIs, and eleven runs scored; the *Cleveland Plain Dealer* dubbed him the most improved hitter on the team. By contrast, Rocky Nelson was playing himself off the Tribe, and was sold to Brooklyn on May 11. So, in the big surprise of the spring, Glynn emerged as Cleveland's Opening Day first baseman.

Opening Day in Chicago on April 13 saw Glynn go 1 for 3 in Cleveland's 8–2 win. Perhaps the game foreshadowed his future, as Hank Majeski batted for him in the eighth. The next day Glynn went 4 for 5, all singles. He turned in the defensive play of the game, nabbing Ferris Fain's smash to end the game in the Tribe's 6–3 victory. All of his hits came off left-handers, whom he usually could not hit. The following day, the 15th, the Indians hosted Detroit in their home opener, and Glynn was 2 for 4, although Cleveland lost, 3–2.

After nine games, Glynn, at .419, was leading the American League in batting but had only one extra-base hit, a home run. To generate more offense, Al Lopez benched him, moving Al Rosen from third to first and installing rookie Rudy Regalado at third. Glynn became Rosen's defensive replacement.

The Indians made a deal on June 1 that altered the season for Glynn, when they acquired first baseman Vic Wertz for pitcher Bob Chakales. "I think Vic can do us a lot of good," said Lopez. "He's going to be good insurance."[5] Eventually, the offense Wertz injected into the lineup made it impossible to sit him down. Glynn was relegated to backup duty.

Glynn regained the starting job against the White Sox on July 2, the start of a four-game series.[6] "We'll need all the defense we can get against the White Sox. They like to run and bunt," Lopez said in explaining the move. However well it aided Cleveland's defense, the switch to Glynn also gave the Indians an edge at the plate, as Glynn continued his domination of Chicago's pitching (he hit .381 against them for the season). In the four-game series, a sweep by the Indians, Glynn went 7 for 19. Cleveland then traveled to Detroit, and Glynn's three-homer performance came in the first game of that series on July 5.

Glynn continued to play regularly through July 19, supplying steady defense but generating little offensive punch. From July 22 to the end of the season, Glynn was used primarily as a defensive replacement and as a pinch runner for Wertz. (His only starts were in the last two games of the season.) The system worked for the Indians, as the Tribe benefited from Wertz's lethal stick and Glynn's exceptional glove in the late innings.

In the World Series, Glynn pinch-hit in two games. In Game One, he struck out in the tenth inning. In Game Three, Glynn doubled and scored in what turned out to be his last Major League at bat. The Indians sold Glynn to Indianapolis in 1955. He was there about a month, and then was sent to the Seattle Rainiers of the Pacific Coast League. Glynn hit and fielded well for Seattle and then the San Diego Padres. When San Diego traded Glynn to

Birmingham of the Southern Association after the 1958 season, he retired. He and his family relocated to California, where he worked a retail milk route for Dairy Mart for fourteen years. In 1974 he became a retail supervisor for the Alta Dena Dairy in City of Industry, California. In 1976 he was inducted into the Sussex County, New Jersey, Sports Hall of Fame.

In retirement, Bill Glynn resided in San Diego with his wife, Dolores, whom he married on December 9, 1950. They have two sons, Bill Jr. and Patrick.

He passed away on January 15, 2013.

Chapter 45. Timeline, August 1–August 15

Joseph Wancho

August 1—Cleveland—INDIANS SWEEP NATS' SERIES, 3–1, 5–4—The Tribe scores three runs in the sixth inning of game one. Larry Doby, Al Rosen, and Vic Wertz each knock in a run. Early Wynn strikes out nine to up his record to 15-7. Dave Pope goes 4 for 5, with two runs. Bobby Avila goes 3 for 5, with one run. Vic Wertz homers. The Indians sweep visiting Washington. "Prince Hal" picks up the win in game two in relief, and knocks in the go-ahead run in the bottom of the seventh inning.

August 3—Cleveland—YANKS TRIP INDIANS 2–1, BEFORE 60,643—Whitey Ford strikes out six batters and scatters four hits for his eleventh win. Yogi Berra knocks in both of the Yankee runs.

August 4—Cleveland—AVILA'S HOMER JARS YANKS, 5–2—Bobby Avila belts a three-run homer in the bottom of the third inning. Vic Wertz also homers. Bob Lemon raises his record to 14-5. Attendance is 58,091.

August 5—Cleveland—YANKS HIT 3 HOMERS TO CUT TRIBE'S LEAD—Mickey Mantle hits two solo shots. Joe Collins also homers. Bob Grim raises his record to 14-4. Johnny Sain records his twenty-second save. Larry Doby hits his twenty-fourth homer and drives in both runs. New York closes the gap to a game and a half.

August 6—Cleveland—GARCIA GAINS 13TH—Mike Garcia beats the A's for the fourth time of the year. He raises his record to 13-5, striking out five Athletics. The Bear goes 2 for 4 at the plate, driving in and scoring a run. Larry Doby and Sam Dente each collect two RBIS.

August 7—Cleveland—FELLER'S 9TH VICTORY IS A 4-HITTER, 5–1—Larry Doby hits a three-run homer in the fifth inning. Dave Pope goes 3 for 4 and drives in two runs. Bob Feller goes to 9-2. The victory is Feller's third consecutive win over Philadelphia.

August 8—Cleveland—INDIANS WIN 2 FROM A'S, LEAD BY 4 GAMES—Bob Lemon goes to 15-5 and hits a two-run home run. Bobby Avila knocks in two runs. The Tribe wins the first game, 7–2. Art Houtteman backs the win in the nightcap with two RBIS. Larry Doby goes 2 for 2, with three RBIS, and smacks his twenty-sixth homer. Wally Westlake goes 3 for 3, doubles, and scores two runs. The Tribe sweeps the A's in the double dip and the series. The Yankees lose in Detroit.

August 10—Detroit—TIGERS CUT TRIBE LEAD TO 3 GAMES—Ned Garver blanks the Indians on five hits and fans six for his tenth win. Wayne Belardi goes deep with a solo homer. Al Kaline goes 3 for 4, triples, drives in a run, and scores one. The crowd of 53,778 is the largest in two years at Briggs Stadium.

August 11—Detroit—INDIANS BAG 2 UN-EARNED RUNS TO WIN—Mike Garcia strikes out five Tigers and scatters four hits for his fourteenth win, shutting out Detroit, 2–0. Sam Dente registers the only RBI for the Indians. Shortest game of the year, 1:45.

August 12—Detroit—LEMON WINS 16TH: TRIBE LEAD IS CUT—Al Rosen hits a three-run homer and Sam Dente goes 3 for 5 with two RBIS. Vic Wertz homers in the second frame. Bob Lemon raises his record to 16-5 in the 10–1 victory over Detroit. The Yankees sweep the doubleheader from the A's to pull within two and a half games of the lead.

August 13—Cleveland—TRIBE'S 14 HITS GIVE FELLER 10TH, 9–4—The Tribe swats six doubles (Vic Wertz two, Dave Pope, Jim Hegan, Al Rosen, Al Smith). Dave Pope goes yard for his first home run on the year and drives in three runs. Bob Feller raises his record to 10-2.

August 14—Cleveland—INDIANS WHIP ORIOLES, 4 TO 3; YANKS WIN, 3–1—Hal Naragon's single to right field scores Dave Pope for the win in the eleventh inning. Bobby Avila swats a three-run home run. Don Mossi picks up his fifth win in relief.

August 15—Cleveland—INDIANS WIN TWO FROM BALTIMORE; BOOST LEAD TO 3—Larry Doby smacks his twenty-seventh homer, a three-run shot in the sixth inning. Art Houtteman wins his twelfth as Cleveland takes the opener of the double dip, 5–2. Mike Garcia strikes out five to raise his record to 15-5 on the year. Avila goes 3 for 4, doubles, with two RBIS and a run scored. Mike Garcia backs his win with an RBI as Cleveland sweeps Baltimore in the four-game series.

Chapter 46. José G. Santiago Guzmán

Edwin Fernández

AGE	W	L	PCT	ERA	G	GS	GF	CG	SHO	SV	IP	H	BB	SO	HBP	WP
25	0	0	.000	0.00	1	0	0	0	0	0	1.2	0	2	1	0	0

During the 1954 season, the Cleveland Indians enjoyed a very healthy pitching rotation, including great hurlers like Bob Feller, Mike García, Early Wynn, and Bob Lemon, but they had other great throwers in their Minor League farm clubs, among them José Santiago. From 1949 through 1953, Santiago was one of the best pitchers in Cleveland's Minor League system. He compiled a record of 77-47, with an earned run average of 2.93.

José G. Santiago Guzmán was born on September 4, 1928, in Coamo, Puerto Rico. His father was José Regino Santiago, from Coamo, and his mother was Eleuteria Guzmán from the southern town of Juana Díaz. He attended Ponce High School, and then he moved with his parents to New York, where he graduated from high school in Brooklyn. In 1949 José and Matilde Luciano-Rangel of Ponce were married in New York. They had two daughters, Matilde and Judith.

In New York, Santiago, a skinny right-hander with a strong arm and a lightning fastball, played amateur baseball with the Puerto Rican Stars and a team in Brooklyn. In 1946 he went to Puerto Rico with a New York team to play games against two teams, Juncos and Mayagüez. In the series, Santiago pitched a one-hit shutout. That year he was signed to a contract by Martiniano García, owner of the Ponce Lions of the Puerto Rico Winter League. The contract, for the 1946-47 season, included a $1,000 bonus.

Santiago was voted Rookie of the Year after posting a record of 8-2 and an ERA of 3.09. He excelled in crucial games and was a fan favorite. Later he played for the San Juan Senators, where he made a great duo with former New York Yankees reliev-

José Santiago—Santiago won twenty-seven games for Dallas in the Texas League, earning a call-up to the Indians in 1954.

er Luis Arroyo. For San Juan, Arroyo and Santiago often worked Sunday doubleheaders with one pitching in the morning and the other in the afternoon, a nightmare for the opposition batters. Santiago played a total of sixteen seasons in Puerto Rico, also suiting up with the Mayagüez Indians and the Santurce Crabbers.

In 1947 the New York Cubans of the Negro National League signed the eighteen-year-old Santiago. Playing on the same team as the Cuban hurler Luis Tiant Sr., one of the pitching greats of the Negro Leagues at the time, Santiago started six games in 1947 and 1948, winning three and losing two.

During the Indians' 1949 spring training camp, the legendary pitcher Satchel Paige told him, "You have a nickel curve but your fastball's worth a million." In an interview, Minnie Minoso acknowledged that Santiago had recommended him to the Cleveland Indians.

Before the 1949 season, Santiago signed with the Indians, and that season, with Dayton of the Class A Central League, he won 16 games and lost 12 with a team-leading 2.60 ERA in 211 innings pitched. He pitched for Wilkes-Barre in the Class A Eastern League in 1950 and 1951, in the latter year earning the Pitcher of the Year award as he led the league leader in wins (21-5) and ERA (1.59). Near the end of the 1951 season, he was promoted to Triple-A San Diego, where he was 1-5 with a 6.75 ERA.

In 1952 and 1953, Santiago pitched for Dallas, the Indians' Texas League affiliate. In 1952 he won fourteen games and lost seven with a 2.83 ERA, and in 1953 he was 13-11 (3.47.) In 1954 he made the Indians' roster out of spring training. His stay with Cleveland was brief—one game. Santiago pitched in relief on April 17 against the Chicago White Sox, allowing an unearned run in one and two-thirds innings. Optioned to Triple-A Indianapolis, he pitched in one game, then jumped his contract to play in the Dominican Republic.

Although Santiago had built a solid record in the Minors, it was difficult to break into the Indians' pitching rotation, and in the days before free agency, players had few options. Santiago was unhappy and believed he was not being treated fairly. He did not have a healthy relationship with Hank Greenberg, the Cleveland general manager, who Santiago said never gave him a real opportunity.

According to Santiago's account, at a boxing match in Chicago he was introduced to Francisco

Martínez-Álvarez, owner of the Escogido Baseball Club in Dominican Republic and a cousin of Dominican dictator Rafael Leonidas Trujillo. Martínez offered Santiago a $12,000 contract to play with his team. Santiago, who was making about $5,000 with the Indians, accepted the proposal and went to Santo Domingo to play ball. Greenberg complained to Commissioner Ford Frick, who decreed that if Santiago or anyone else played in Santo Domingo, he would be declared ineligible to play in Organized Baseball. But Santiago's punishment did not last long. Rodrigo Otero-Suro, the baseball commissioner in Puerto Rico, intervened, and Santiago was reinstated.

Santiago returned to Indianapolis in 1955, and in July the Indians recalled him. He pitched thirty-two and two-thirds innings in seventeen games, all in relief, and recorded a 2-0 mark with a 2.48 ERA. In May 1956 the Indians sold Santiago's contract to the Kansas City Athletics, for whom he made five starts, his first in the Majors, winning one game and losing two before being sent down to Triple-A Columbus. He never returned to the Major Leagues again. His record in twenty-seven games was 3-2, with a 4.66 ERA in fifty-six innings pitched.

From 1957 to 1959, when he left Organized Baseball, Santiago pitched for three Minor League teams, Buffalo and Havana in the International League, and San Antonio in the Texas League. In his eleven seasons in the Minor Leagues, he won 112 games and lost 83, with a career earned run average of 3.22, with 12 shutouts. In seven of his eleven seasons, his winning record reached double figures.

Santiago played in the Puerto Rico Winter League for sixteen seasons, three of them after he left Organized Baseball. In all, he won 107 games and lost 97. On December 6, 1956, he pitched a seven-inning no-hitter. He played in six Caribbean Series (1951, '52, '53, '57, '58, and '59). In 1951 Santiago won two games to help the Santurce Crabbers win the championship. In 1957, when Cuba won the Series with a record of 5-1, Santiago shut them

EDWIN FERNÁNDEZ

out 6–0, allowing only three hits. His best games were against Cuba.

After his baseball life, Santiago became an entrepreneur. He was a successful boxing promoter. He was also active in the horse-racing industry as the owner of the Panta Stable, whose horses won a number of major races. Though he retired as a player, Santiago never said goodbye to baseball. He owned the Caguas Criollos of the Puerto Rico Winter League for several years. In 2012 he lived in San Juan.

The nickname "Pantalones," which in Spanish means pants or trousers, was given to Santiago after José struck out the side with the bases loaded in the ninth inning during a Winter League game between the Ponce Lions and the Caguas Criollos. Santiago was relieving in the ninth, and the next morning Emilio E. Huyke, a newspaper sports editor, wrote: "Santiago had a lot of pantalones"— meaning he had lots of guts to do such a performance. Since then, he has been called Pantalones.

In the 1957 Caribbean Series in Havana, Santiago shut down the Cuban powerhouse 6–0. The announcer Eladio Secades said, "To blank the Cubans in their hometown you need to have pantalones."

In 1987 Santiago was inducted into the Puerto Rico Sports Hall of Fame for his achievements in baseball. He has also been inducted into the Caribbean Series Hall of Fame.

Chapter 47. **Bob Kennedy**

Philip A. Cola

AGE	G	AB	R	H	2B	3B	HR	TB	RBI	BB	SO	BAV	OBP	SLG	SB	GDP	HBP
33	1	0	0	0	0	0	0	0	0	0	0	—	—	—	0	0	0

Bob Kennedy, whose sixteen Major League seasons included one inning for the 1954 Cleveland Indians, was a journeyman pro who managed only a .254 batting average in his career with the Indians, Chicago White Sox, and three other teams. Kennedy isn't likely to find a niche in the Baseball Hall of Fame. In a way this is too bad, because if Kennedy gained admittance into the Cooperstown shrine, he would bring with him a number of distinctions. In no particular order:

Kennedy was born in Chicago just as the Black Sox scandal was unfolding.

He did *not* play against Buck Weaver, one of the Black Sox. (That will be explained.)

In 1940 he was the first teenager to play in 150 games in a season.

He was one of just three players to serve in the military in World War II and then be recalled to serve in the Korean War. (The other two were Ted Williams and Jerry Coleman; all three were fliers.)

He had the last at bat by a Brooklyn Dodger before the team moved to Los Angeles.

He was a coach, manager, scout, and front-office executive for thirty-five years.

Robert Daniel Kennedy was born on the South Side of Chicago on August 18, 1920. As he grew up into a strong, hard-throwing teenager playing amateur ball in and around Chicago, there were times he was held out of games because one of the banned Black Sox, Buck Weaver, was playing that day. According to Bob's son Terry, himself a Major League player and Minor League manager, Bob was held out of those games by his coaches because anyone

Bob Kennedy—Obtained in mid-1948 from the Cubs, Kennedy hit .301 to help the Tribe to the pennant and the World Series in 1948. He managed the Chicago Cubs in the 1960s.

who played in a game with Weaver could be banned from the Major Leagues, and Bob was thought to have a future in the big leagues.

As a youth Kennedy was a top pitcher, throwing numerous no-hitters in American Legion ball, and it was clear that his strong arm was noticed. Only sixteen years old, he was signed as a third baseman in 1937 by the hometown White Sox, who were seeking to curry favor with a dwindling fan base following nearly two decades of second-division teams. The White Sox sent him to play for the Vicksburg (Mississippi) Hill Billies in the Class C Cotton States League. He struggled against professional pitching, batting just .192 in forty-one games with no home runs. A clear sign that the White Sox had their eye on him was the fact that despite his difficult start, Kennedy was promoted before the end of the season to the Dallas Steers of the Class 1A Texas League, at that time the second highest classification in the Minor Leagues. In Texas he hit better, raising his average to .300, but still with no power (just one extra-base hit in sixty at bats).

In 1938 Kennedy played for the Longview Cannibals in the Class C East Texas League. The line-drive hitter batted .261 in 136 games and tied for the league lead with 14 triples. He led the league in put-outs and assists at third base and it was becoming clear that fielding and throwing were his strengths, although he made forty-one errors that season. In 1939 Kennedy played again in the Texas League, for the Shreveport Sports. He was making more contact (.284 average with eight home runs). The White Sox called Kennedy up in September and he made his Major League debut on September 14, 1939, at the age of nineteen, making an out as a pinch hitter. He stood six feet two (six feet three, according to some sources) and weighed about 190 pounds.

In 1940 White Sox manager Jimmy Dykes moved third baseman Eric McNair to second base and installed the teenage Kennedy at third base. Kennedy played in 154 of the team's 155 games (one no-decision) at third base and led the team in at bats. Kennedy was a consistent if unspectacular performer, hitting .252 with three home runs and fifty-two RBIs. He led the league with 178 put-outs and 33 errors at third base. Perhaps surprisingly, he received three points in the American League Most Valuable Player voting, tied with Charlie Gehringer and Joe Gordon for twenty-third place. He would never again receive any consideration for MVP.

In 1941 Kennedy's batting average plunged to .206 with one home run and twenty-nine RBIs, and he played in only 76 games. In 1942 he played in 113 games, 16 of them in the outfield, and batted .231. From 1943 through 1945, during World War II, he served in the Marines as a pilot and flight instructor. (He trained Ted Williams at Pensacola, Florida, and they both played on the base team.) In June of 1945 he married Claire Ellensohn. Back with the White Sox in 1946, Kennedy, with his strong throwing arm, found a home in the outfield, and raised his batting average to .258 and to .262 in 1947.

On June 2, 1948, Kennedy was traded to the Indians for outfielder Pat Seerey and pitcher Al Gettel. With Cleveland he was a reasonable contributor in the team's successful run for the pennant and the world championship, batting .301 while playing part-time in the outfield and in a handful of games at first base and second base. In the World Series, Kennedy was used as a defensive replacement in three games, and he had an RBI single in Game Two.

Kennedy looked fondly upon his time in Cleveland, specifically referring to the 1949 through 1951 seasons as the best of his career. His batting average improved. He was the regular right fielder those years, but also returned to third base for twenty-one games in 1949. He started a triple play from right field in 1950. In 1952, after playing in twenty-two games, Kennedy was recalled to military service during the Korean War, as were Williams and Jerry Coleman. Kennedy returned to the Indians in 1953 and played in 100 games, batting .236.

As the Indians embarked on their 111-victory 1954 season, Kennedy appeared in only one early-season game in left field, and on April 17 he was traded to the Baltimore Orioles for Jim Dyck who, like Kennedy, played both outfield and third base. Kennedy did well for the first-year Orioles, belting the franchise's first grand slam off Allie Reynolds of the Yankees on July 30. He had a solid year as a backup third baseman and outfielder, batting .251 in 106 games. But at the age of thirty-three, he was on the downside of his career and did not play as a regular again as he switched teams each year from 1954 through 1957.

Kennedy played in twenty-six games for the Orioles in 1955 before being sold back to the White Sox on May 30. With the White Sox he appeared in 83 games, hitting .304. Overall in 1955, playing in 109 games at first, third, and the outfield, he tied his career high with nine home runs. Early in the 1956 season Kennedy was traded along with infielder Jim Brideweser and pitcher Harry Byrd to the Detroit Tigers for infielder Fred Hatfield and outfielder Jim Delsing. Just before Opening Day in 1957, he was released by the Tigers and immediately signed with the White Sox for his third stint back home. He played little, and on May 20 he was sold on waivers to the Brooklyn Dodgers. He played in only nineteen games for the Dodgers, but was in the starting lineup on the last day of the season—the Brooklyn Dodgers' last game before they became the Los Angeles Dodgers. It was at Philadelphia's Shibe Park on September 29, and Kennedy batted fifth and played left field. He went 0 for 4, and in his last at bat, also the last ever by a Brooklyn Dodger, Kennedy flied out to center field to end the game, a 2–1 loss for the Dodgers. It was also the last at bat of Kennedy's sixteen-year playing career. He was released by the Dodgers on October 15. He had played in 1,484 games and batted .254 with 63 home runs and 514 RBIS.

The Indians hired Kennedy as a scout, and a year later they promoted him to assistant farm director. Kennedy did a good job in these roles for the Indians. In 1962 he was named the manager of Salt Lake City in the Pacific Coast League, an affiliate of both the Indians and the Chicago Cubs. The next season he was hired as a coach on a unique Cubs team.

Innovative ideas do not always lead to the best results, as was shown with the Cubs in 1961 and 1962. Tired of losing, team owner Philip Wrigley decided to hire four "head coaches" in 1961 who would alternate as managers or "head coaches." They were Vedie Himsl, Harry Craft, El Tappe, and Lou Klein. In 1961 the so-called College of Coaches led the Cubs to a seventh-place finish with a record of 64-90. In 1962, with three "head coaches" (Tappe, Klein, and Charlie Metro), the Cubs finished seventh again with a 59-103 record, forty-two and a half games behind the first-place San Francisco Giants and "good" enough to finish eighteen games ahead of the record-setting expansion Mets. In 1963 Wrigley's innovation was scrapped and Kennedy was named the lone manager of the Cubs.

The forty-two-year-old Kennedy proved to be a good field general, turning the Cubs around to an 82-80 finish, seventeen games behind the pennant-winning Dodgers, and in seventh place in a ten-team league. Though a strong nucleus of a club was developing with Ernie Banks, Ken Hubbs, Ron Santo, Lou Brock, and Billy Williams, things went bad in 1964. National League Rookie of the Year Hubbs was killed in a plane crash in the off-season, and the Cubs were frustrated with young Brock, trading him in June for eighteen-game-winner Ernie Broglio. This looked like a great trade for the Cubs, but history revealed it to be a stellar trade for the Cardinals, as Broglio soon faded and Brock went on to a Hall of Fame career with the Cardinals. The Cubs slipped to eighth place under Kennedy with a record of 76-86. Kennedy managed the 1965 Cubs for fifty-eight games, leading them to a record of 24-32 (there were two ties) before moving to the front office as an assistant to the general manager.

After the season, Kennedy moved on to the Dodgers' system. In 1966, after an off-season managing an Arizona Instructional League team for the Dodgers, he managed the Dodgers' farm team at Albuquerque to a third-place finish and a spot in the Texas League playoffs. This earned Kennedy a Major League coaching job with the Atlanta Braves in 1967 under manager Billy Hitchcock. The Braves had a talented team but finished seventh, and Hitchcock and his staff were fired. Kennedy was quickly hired to manage the brand-new Oakland Athletics, relocated from Kansas City. The A's had experienced a miserable end to the 1967 season in Kansas City as players rebelled against a suddenly ineffective manager, Alvin Dark, and finished in last place at 62-99. Kennedy was hired as a steadying force, and he led a promising young A's team to a huge improvement, finishing 82-80 in sixth place. Then, without explanation, Kennedy was fired by mercurial team owner Charlie Finley.

In 1969 Kennedy went back to scouting with the Cardinals. In 1970 general manager Bing Devine promoted him to director of Minor League operations. In 1972 he was promoted to director of player personnel. During this time Kennedy's oldest son, Bob Jr., was drafted as a right-handed pitcher by the Cardinals. Young Bob played in the Minor Leagues for five seasons and later worked for his father as a scout for the Cubs and Astros. Bob Sr. stayed in his front-office job until he returned to scouting in 1976 for the Cardinals.

Once again it was back to Chicago (for the fifth time) in 1977 as Phil Wrigley hired Kennedy as the general manager. The Cubs were again mediocre in the mid-1970s after making a run at the pennant in 1969. The Cubs showed early promise in '77, leading the National League East from May through July, but they eventually faltered and finished 81-81 and in fourth place. During the 1977 season, Bob's youngest son, Terry, was drafted in the first round by the Cardinals after an All-American season at Florida State in 1976. (He was named *The Sporting News* college player of the year.) Terry was a catcher and had a fourteen-year career with the Cardinals, Padres, Orioles, and Giants. Bob remained the Cubs GM through 1981. They finished no higher than third place and in last place twice during that time, including the strike-shortened 1981 season, after which Kennedy was fired.

From 1982 through 1985, Kennedy worked as vice president of baseball operations for the Houston Astros under general manager Al Rosen (whom he had backed up at third base for the Indians many years earlier). The Astros were on the verge of winning a division and contending for a pennant, but it would happen after Rosen and Kennedy departed for San Francisco in 1986.

From 1986 through 1992, Kennedy served under GM Rosen as the vice president of baseball operations for the Giants. Success and a big turnaround for the Giants happened quickly with a division title in 1987 (they lost to the Cardinals in the playoffs), and then a pennant in 1989 followed by a sweep at the hands of the A's in the World Series noted for being delayed for ten days by a major earthquake in San Francisco as Game Three was about to begin. The 1989 pennant was only the second in Kennedy's career as a player or executive. Kennedy retired in 1992 at the age of seventy-two, along with his sixty-eight-year-old friend and colleague Rosen, after fifty-six years in professional baseball.

Kennedy spent his retirement in Mesa, Arizona, where he had moved his family years earlier. He died in 2005 at the age of eighty-four.

Chapter 48. **Mickey Grasso**

Cort Vitty

AGE	G	AB	R	H	2B	3B	HR	TB	RBI	BB	SO	BAV	OBP	SLG	SB	GDP	HBP
34	4	6	1	2	0	0	1	5	1	1	1	.333	.500	.833	0	0	1

Of the eight Major Leaguers who were prisoners of war in World War II, only one also played in a World Series.[1] He was Mickey Grasso, who played in four September games for the 1954 Indians and was behind the plate in the tenth inning of World Series Game One when Dusty Rhodes hit a walk-off home run.

Newton Michael Grasso was born on May 10, 1920, in Newark, New Jersey. His parents, Carmen and Lena Grasso, had emigrated from Italy to settle in Newark. The 1930 U.S. Census lists an older brother, Michael, and a younger brother, Bernard. Newton was an outstanding ballplayer in grade school and on the sandlots of Newark; as a fifth-grader, he was good enough to sub on the eighth-grade team. He was later voted All-City catcher in the grade school category.

Newton was a pitcher in high school, where his talent was recognized by Newark Bears general manager George Weiss, who recommended a move off the mound. A tryout with the Trenton (New Jersey) Senators of the Class B Interstate League was arranged by Newton's uncle Bob Ciasco; the club was managed by former Washington Senators great Goose Goslin. On April 7, 1941, among a crowd of two hundred eager prospects, Grasso showed enough potential to warrant his first professional contract. Goslin signed the newcomer and planned to use him at second base; however, an injury to the regular catcher necessitated a move behind the plate. The right-handed-hitting Grasso stood six feet tall and weighed in at 190 pounds. Teammates nicknamed him Mickey, after noticing a resemblance to Hall of Fame catcher Mickey Cochrane.

When Pearl Harbor was attacked on December

Mickey Grasso—Grasso primarily served as a backup catcher over his seven-year career, mostly with Washington. (The Cleveland Press Collection, Cleveland State University Library)

7, 1941, Mickey heard the call to duty. He enlisted in the army on January 20, 1942, and reported to Fort Dix, New Jersey, for basic training. Grasso was assigned to North Africa with the Thirty-

Fourth Infantry Division, and was taken prisoner by Rommel's retreating army on February 17, 1943. Sergeant Grasso's unit was surrounded by ten thousand German soldiers, heavily equipped with tanks and howitzers. According to Burton Hawkins of *The Sporting News*, the lieutenant in charge quizzed his sergeant, "Mickey, shall we fight or go along with 'em?" Grasso answered, "Man, don't be crazy." After the war, Senators manager Bucky Harris heard this story and commented, "Right there I could've told you Grasso had the makings of a smart catcher."[2]

The prisoners were flown to Italy and transported by rail to Furstenberg, Germany, where they settled into Stalag IIIB. Mickey was held captive along with six thousand others for two years, three months, and ten days. In the early part of the war, German prison camps were run in the same efficient manner as the German army. Captured soldiers were systematically sent to camps based on branch of service. Once interned, the prisoners were separated according to rank. The prison camps varied in size; all were equipped with a parade ground, where prisoners gathered twice a day to be counted.

The United States and Germany had signed on to the Geneva Convention, which stipulated proper conduct toward prisoners of war. The Germans adhered to the code and generally treated those captured in accordance with the rules and regulations. Exercise and recreation was encouraged and the parade area was generally ample size for games of baseball or softball. POWs had access to sports equipment provided through the Red Cross. Massive numbers of gloves, bats, and balls were collected in the United States and shipped overseas, ultimately arriving at prison camps. Mickey and his prison mates at Stalag IIIB made frequent use of the equipment.

Prisoners felt it was their duty to escape. Grasso was involved in three failed attempts, each warranting a brutal beating at the hands of the guards. He finally managed to escape on April 20, 1945, about two weeks before the Germans surrendered. The Russian army was closing in on German forces near the camp. Grasso's captors ordered prisoners moved farther from the ground fighting. By this time, the German army was short of personnel, and most guards were poorly trained older men. On the evening on the evacuation, Mickey was one of ten prisoners who simply ran off while the guards snoozed. The escapees marched through towns, led by a prisoner fluent in German. When stopped by German officers, the leader said it was a work detail; the explanation seemed plausible and the trip resumed. Happening upon a dilapidated boat, the group climbed aboard and paddled across the Elbe River to the safety of the American side, where they were met by American forces. It took some convincing, but finally the American soldiers, with rifles drawn, believed the interlopers were prison camp refugees.

After being liberated, Grasso weighed sixty pounds below his normal playing weight, and the repeated beatings at the hands of camp guards left him frail. Acclimating to peacetime, he returned to Trenton and started the long climb through the Minor Leagues, hoping to once again become a prospect. His compensation as a POW amounted to $1,195, or almost a dollar a day.

In 1946, after a brief trial with the New York Giants, Grasso was assigned to their Jersey City farm team, hitting .228 with 13 home runs in 106 games. He became Jersey City's regular catcher in 1947, posting a .268 average with 16 home runs. After the season he was sold to the Pacific Coast League Seattle Rainiers for the then staggering sum of $20,000.

At Seattle in 1948, Grasso could proudly boast of having a 5,000-member fan club. He commented that he "made 1,000 friends by giving away 1,000 baseballs that belonged to the club." Behind the plate, he led league catchers with eighty-one assists, while batting .261 with five home runs.

Grasso enjoyed another fine season at Seattle in 1949, hitting .251 and again leading league receivers with seventy-four assists. During the season, he was ejected twenty-three times, drawing $1,100 worth of fines. This aggressiveness caught the attention of Washington Senators manager Bucky Harris, who recommended that his club purchase the fiery competitor. Harris had managed the PCL San Diego Padres in 1949 and remembered his first encounter with Grasso, when the strong-armed catcher picked off Luke Easter after the Padres' first baseman poked a single. Mickey described the action this way: "It was a hot afternoon and Easter looked sleepy to me, so I caught him napping."[3]

Grasso thought that Coast League umpires were "thick-headed and thin-skinned." He once got the hook for merely telling an ump to throw a new ball back to the pitcher himself. One day, Mickey didn't do or say anything prior to being thrown. When Grasso protested, the umpire said "he was thumbed for what he was thinking."[4]

Settling in with Washington in 1950, Grasso shared the catching duties with Al Evans. He played in seventy-five games and hit a career-high .287. One day the hot-tempered catcher was ejected for contesting a call by umpire Ira Gordon. Mickey flung his mask into the air, strategically flipping it far enough to miss the man in blue. After Gordon ordered the catcher to the sidelines, Grasso began unhitching his shin guards, slowly flinging each into the air. The second landed on the umpire's head, resulting in a $200 fine. In 1951 Grasso split time behind the plate with Clyde Kluttz. He played in fifty-two games, and his hitting slumped to .206.

In 1952, even though his production at the plate was weak (.216, just nine extra-base hits), Grasso played in 115 games, more than any other Senators catcher. He and umpire Larry Napp had a confrontation during spring training. As was the spring training practice in those days, Napp was assigned to travel with the Senators. One day his car broke down, and Grasso, who was traveling on the team bus, offered Napp the use of his new car to drive to a game in Fort Myers. During the game Grasso argued a called strike and Napp tossed him. After the contest was over, Mickey boarded the team bus

and saw Larry getting into the car. Grasso shouted, "I hope you get a flat tire," when he suddenly came to his senses and blurted, "What am I saying? It's my car."[5] Grasso's vendetta against the men in blue was reportedly attributed to beatings he received as a prisoner of war.[6]

In Boston on May 14, 1952, before a Senators game with the Red Sox, Grasso was honored by the American Prisoners of War Association. The slightly embarrassed Grasso slowly sauntered to home plate and received a lifetime membership in the organization.

Fiery as he was, Grasso didn't actually get tossed from a Major League game until a July 3, 1952, doubleheader in Washington against the Yankees. Trouble brewed in the first game when New York right-hander Tom Morgan clipped Mickey on the hand with an inside pitch. Later a fan interfered with a foul pop-up that would have been an easy play for Mickey. In the nightcap he poked a base hit, then was called out trying to reach third base on another hit. After a long and loud protest, Grasso was thrown out by umpire Larry Napp.

Grasso's batting style drew criticism from Nats owner Clark Griffith during spring training in 1953. Although he hadn't managed in more than thirty years, Griffith took the liberty of trying to tutor his catcher through manager Bucky Harris. "Stanley, tell that big galoot to stop swinging for home runs," and added, "I mean Grasso." Harris agreed and diagnosed the problem as Grasso lunging to take a big swing, when he could just as easily use his arms to poke singles and doubles in spacious Griffith Stadium.[7] Grasso also got a batting lesson from the Senators' secretary and treasurer, Judge E. B. Eynon. Grasso and the judge were discussing golf when Mickey lamented how manager Harris wouldn't permit golf during the season for fear it could adversely affect a player's batting stroke. He didn't find an ally in Eynon, who agreed golf could disrupt Mickey's swing. Responded Mickey, "I can't see how it could hurt, I'm hitting only .220 as it is."[8]

Grasso lost his starting job in 1953. On May 10, while conversing in the dining car of the train taking the team home from Philadelphia, the players started discussing league opponents. Mickey remarked how Pirates third-string catcher Ed Fitz Gerald had impressed him since their days in the Pacific Coast League. Apparently Bucky Harris agreed, and three days later Washington plucked Fitzgerald off the waiver list. On May 19 Grasso suffered a split finger and the newcomer was pressed into action. Fitzgerald hit a robust .350 and stayed in the lineup, even after Mickey healed.

The 1953 season ended with Grasso batting only .209 in sixty-one games; on the last day of the season, he was instrumental in helping teammate Mickey Vernon clinch the American League batting title. The Senators' first baseman was leading rival Al Rosen of the Indians, .337 to .336. In the eighth inning, the first three Nats hitters collaborated to go down in order and not give Vernon another trip to the plate. Grasso led off with a clean double, but "wandered" off second for the first out. Keith Thomas was out stretching a single into a double. Eddie Yost reached for a pitch out of the strike zone and popped up.

Mickey became a holdout in January 1954 when the Senators tried to cut his salary by $3,000. On January 20 he was traded to the Cleveland Indians for catcher Joe Tipton. "I am very happy about the trade," Grasso said.[9] The Nats acknowledged that the deal cost them a fiery competitor, who was extremely popular with the fans. *Washington Post* sportswriter Shirley Povich lamented, "With Grasso in there, the Nats were never a dull team. He was a good catcher too, a bundle of fire behind the plate and an arm that held terror for all base runners in the league."[10] The trade spread was extremely unpopular with Washington fans. Criticism even disrupted front-office family life, as club vice president Calvin Griffith's nine-year-old daughter, Corinne, entered a state of depression over the deal. Griffith commented, "Mickey wasn't much at the plate, but

he sure hit it off in the personality league with the kids and the women."[11]

Grasso came to terms with Indians GM Hank Greenberg during a long phone conversation. Cleveland restored his salary to $14,000, and Mickey was delighted at how Greenberg even paid for the long-distance call.

The 1954 Indians, managed by Al Lopez, sought a capable receiver to back up star catcher Jim Hegan. On March 24, during an exhibition game against the Chicago Cubs at their Mesa training center, Grasso broke his left ankle sliding into second base. The ball had been hit to shortstop Ernie Banks; Grasso thought Banks would step on second for the force, but Banks fielded the ball and threw to first, making the slide unnecessary. The Indians won the spring contest, 12–2, but lost their backup catcher.

Sportswriter Bob Addie of the *Washington Post* opened his column on April 11, 1954, by noting that Grasso, as a Senator, spent much of his time in Washington visiting hospital patients. Now it was time for fans to reciprocate by sending a card to "a nice guy who always took time out to help others."[12]

Hampered by the ankle injury, Grasso ended up catching only the four September games, hitting a single and a home run in six at bats. In Game One of the World Series against the Giants, Jim Hegan was taken out for a pinch hitter in the top of the tenth inning. In the bottom of the inning, Grasso replaced Hegan and was behind the plate when Willie Mays stole second base, setting the stage for the game-ending pinch home run by Dusty Rhodes. The Giants went on to sweep the Indians. Bob Lemon gave up Rhodes's home run, and Giants' coach Chuck Dressen later said Mays's stolen base was due to Lemon not holding him on first.

Demoted to the Minors by the Indians after the season, Grasso was drafted by the Giants, the organization where he started. Manager Leo Durocher remembered Mickey from the previous spring, when the Giants and Indians toured together, and coveted his aggressive play. But Mickey was released after appearing in only eight games, with no hits in three at bats.

Grasso made Minor League stops at Indianapolis, Miami, and Chattanooga before calling it a career after the 1958 season. His big league tenure spanned parts of seven seasons; he posted a lifetime batting average of .226.

In retirement, Grasso ran several successful restaurants and also worked in the horse-racing industry. He married in July of 1959 and a daughter arrived in October 1961. He died of a heart attack on October 15, 1975, in Miami.

Chapter 49. **Bobby Avila**

John Stahl

AGE	G	AB	R	H	2B	3B	HR	TB	RBI	BB	SO	BAV	OBP	SLG	SB	GDP	HBP
30	143	555	112	189	27	2	15	265	67	59	31	.341	.402	.477	9	9	1

Cleveland Indians general manager and Hall of Fame first baseman Hank Greenberg once said of Bobby Avila, "He has that something extra that makes a great hitter. Call it competitive instinct. . . . He's always fighting the pitcher, never choking up and never giving an inch. . . . In a tough spot, I'm always glad to see Bobby coming to the plate."[1]

"Everybody knows who Avila was in Mexico," said former Los Angeles Dodgers great Fernando Valenzuela. "He was an inspiration, of course, for Mexican ballplayers to follow to the States and play in the major leagues. He did a good job. Everybody knows and recognizes what he did."[2]

With the 1954 Indians, Avila played the best baseball of his eleven-year Major League career.[3] He led the American League in hitting (.341) and received *The Sporting News* American League player of the year award. His extraordinary 1954 performance made him the first Mexican-born player in history to lead the American League in batting.[4]

Roberto Francisco (Gonzales) Avila was born on April 2, 1924, in Veracruz, Mexico.[5] He had four sisters and three older brothers. His father, a lawyer, wanted Bobby to also become a barrister. While at a preparatory school in Veracruz, Bobby excelled in many sports, including baseball, soccer, and basketball. When he was fourteen a professional soccer team, Espana Club of Veracruz, offered him an opportunity to play left wing. For about seventy dollars a month and with his father's approval, Bobby joined the club and traveled throughout Mexico as a professional soccer player.[6]

Avila decided the following year to concentrate his athletic efforts on baseball and signed with the semi-

Bobby Avila—The *Sporting News* MVP in 1954, Avila led the league in hitting with a .341 average in 1954. Later, he served as mayor in his native Veracruz, Mexico.

pro Cordoba club. At the time, baseball in Mexico suffered from a lack of good instructors and coaches. Fortunately for Bobby, an older brother, Pedro, played baseball, and taught him the game. Although he started as one of Cordoba's pitchers, he switched to second base in order to get more playing time.

In 1943 the Mexican League offered Avila a contract to play for the Puebla club. He and his father remained at loggerheads over his future. He partly addressed his father's concerns by agreeing to also enroll at the University of Mexico to study engineering. Avila signed with Puebla for seven hundred pesos a month.

In 1946 Avila emerged as one of the league's top hitters, finishing with a .340 average. He also played Cuban baseball and performed well. Major League scouts noticed and several made offers to him. Reportedly, the Brooklyn Dodgers even brought him to their spring training camp to evaluate him.

Avila later said that most of the offers were in the area of $6,000 to $10,000. Rather than jump at the offers, he decided to stay put. The following year Avila led the league in hitting, with a .347 average. The Indians' Cy Slapnicka, who scouted and signed many great baseball stars over his career, extensively evaluated the five-foot-eleven, 170-pound Avila. He recommended that the Indians offer Avila a $17,500 bonus to sign. With the full support of his once skeptical father, Bobby signed.[7]

Cleveland assigned Avila to its Baltimore affiliate in the Triple-A International League. In 1948 he played in fifty-six games for the Orioles and hit .220.[8] At first his unfamiliarity with English significantly hampered his transition to American baseball. His first Minor League manager, Tommy Thomas, described Bobby as a "stranger in a strange land."[9]

Avila went from Mexican stardom to American anonymity. He struggled both socially and professionally. His self-confidence plummeted. "[It] was very hard for me at first," he said later. "Any Latin ballplayer who comes here must fight the language."[10] To make matters worse, Avila also suffered a hernia, which had to be corrected with off-season surgery.[11]

Avila began with Cleveland in 1949 and roomed with pitcher Mike Garcia, U.S.-born but of Mexican heritage. Garcia remembered, "At first, Bobby didn't speak a lick of English. All he would do was point and say, 'Como se llama eso?' meaning 'What's that?'" On the Major League roster only because of Major League requirements related to his signing bonus, Avila used his time on the bench in 1949 to learn the English language and American customs.[12] He appeared in thirty-one games, only one as a starter, had only fifteen plate appearances, and finished with a .214 average.[13]

In 1950 Joe Gordon, the Indians' hard-hitting and slick-fielding second baseman, suffered an injury and Avila made the most of his unexpected opportunity.[14] Appearing in eighty games and getting 201 at bats, he ended the year with a .299 average.[15] Gordon was released after the season and Avila became Cleveland's regular second baseman in 1951, playing in 141 games and hitting .304.[16] He had the best batting day of his career on June 20, 1951, hitting a single, a double, and three home runs (one inside the park) against five different Boston Red Sox pitchers.[17]

In a seemingly minor move, the Indians in 1952 obtained veteran utility infielder Hank Majeski from the Chicago White Sox. Cleveland assigned Majeski to room with Avila. The two quickly became good friends. "He (is) like a big brother to me," Avila said. "He helps me more than anybody. He makes you think you can do it. Sure you have to have the ability, but he help(s) me all (of) the time."[18] Avila responded positively to this new environment by hitting .300, scoring 102 runs, leading the league in triples (11), and making his first appearance in an All-Star Game.[19] With his All-Star appearance, he became the first Mexican-born player to be picked for the honor.[20]

Although Avila increasingly felt comfortable playing in Cleveland, he maintained his strong ties with his friends and family in Mexico. On his Major League salary, he supported his mother, his wife and two children, and his widowed sister and her son. In addition to his direct dependents, Bobby often received requests for financial help from other friends. According to Majeski, "In every town we go to people gather around him and he's always picking up the tab. After every payday, you ought to see the number of money drafts he sends to Mexico."[21]

Avila was now an international (United States, Cuba, Mexico) baseball star. In Mexico and Cuba, he went by the popular nickname "Beto," short for Roberto. Beto adorned all of his autographed baseball pictures and even his bats. The name Beto never caught on in the United States, so he went with the nickname Bobby. He ended up with two sets of bats in Cleveland: his Bobby bats and his Beto bats.[22]

Avila suffered a slight drop in his hitting production in 1953. In 141 games, he finished with his lowest batting average (.286) in four years.[23] On the field, though, Avila led all American League second basemen with a fielding average of .986.[24] Building on the footwork skills he used in soccer, he became very adept at turning the double play. He also used his soccer training to perfect the art of sliding into a base while simultaneously attempting to kick the baseball out of the fielder's glove. This angered some opposing players, who threatened retaliation.[25]

Within the framework of the Indians' spectacular 1954 season, Avila surged to the best year in his eleven-year Major League career. He led the league in hitting with a batting average of .341 and was the only Indian regular to hit over .300. (Al Rosen hit exactly .300.)

Avila's 1954 batting title has been the subject of some controversy, particularly among Boston Red Sox fans. During 1954 spring training, the legendary Ted Williams broke his collarbone diving for a ball and missed thirty-seven games. In addition, opposing pitchers walked him 136 times. The missed games and walks combined to give Williams 386 official at bats. Although he finished with a .345 average, to be eligible for a batting championship at the time, a player had to have 400 at bats.[26]

However, Avila also had both a significant injury and a possible suspension to address. After his unusually good start with the bat, he suffered a broken thumb on June 3. He remembered, "Hank Bauer slid into second and broke my thumb." At the time of his injury, Avila's average was .396.[27]

Avila played five games after his injury before deciding to get his increasingly sore right thumb

X-rayed. The film revealed a chip fracture near the joint. The doctor put a splint on the injury and told him not to play for at least a week. He also told Avila "not to shake hands" for a while.[28]

When Avila resumed playing, he found he couldn't swing the bat as well as he had earlier. Over the next month, his average dropped to .307. As the thumb got better, his average climbed and he finished at .341. Noting that confidence at the plate is a key factor in good hitting, Avila said that if he had not had the injury he could have hit for an even higher average.[29]

In addition to his injury, on June 4 Avila made contact with home-plate umpire Bill Grieve while arguing a third-strike call. Umpire/player contact incidents required a ten-day suspension. Upon his review, however, Baseball Commissioner Ford Frick decided that the incident was minor and could have actually been accidental. Instead of a suspension, the commissioner gave Avila a warning and fined him $100.[30]

Avila also hit a career-high fifteen home runs in 1954. Although that may seem modest, *The Sporting News* noted that thirteen of the fifteen either tied or won games in the late innings.[31] Avila played in his second All-Star game, which that year was played in Cleveland. He went 3 for 3 and drove in two runs in the American League's 11–9 victory.[32] Avila also led the league in sacrifice hits (19) and scored a career-high 112 runs.[33]

Yogi Berra was voted the Most Valuable Player in the American League that year, but Avila received several postseason awards. *The Sporting News* selected him as its AL Player of the Year and Major League All-Star second baseman. The Cleveland Baseball Writers named him their Man of the Year.[34]

When the Indians won the pennant, Avila faced the daunting task of satisfying a huge number of World Series ticket requests from Mexico. *The Sporting News* reported that he even got a call from the president of Mexico, who wanted tickets for himself and all of his cabinet members.[35]

Avila hit only .133 (2 for 15) as the Indians were swept by the New York Giants in the World Series. *The Sporting News* said the poor hitting of Avila and teammate Larry Doby made them the "top patsies" of the Series.[36] Reflecting on the Giants' sweep of the heavily favored Indians, Avila said, "You know how it is in baseball. Most of the breaks went for them and they beat us."[37]

In 1954 Avila, with the permission of General Manager Greenberg, became a part-owner of the Mexico City Reds of the Veracruz Winter League. After the World Series, he received a hero's welcome when he returned to Mexico to begin his player/owner duties.

Mexican officials met Avila in Nuevo Laredo at the U.S.-Mexican border and gave him a motorcycle escort all the way to Mexico City (900 miles).[38] As the Reds were not doing well, Avila also took over as their manager.[39]

In 1955 Avila's batting average dropped to .272, nearly seventy points below 1954. Several factors combined to produce these disappointing results. Before the season, Avila held out for a salary increase from $20,000 (including bonus) to $32,000. On March 25 he became the last Indian holdout to sign. He ended up with $27,500 and additional bonus opportunities of $2,000. The heavily publicized holdout embarrassed the Indians, particularly Greenberg.[40]

The Indians' trade of his roommate, mentor, and close friend Hank Majeski to Baltimore in early July had a negative effect on Avila's hitting. Although the trade made sense for the Indians, Avila had always praised Majeski for helping him keep his hitting focus.[41]

Injuries also played a role in Avila's slump. He suffered a sprained right toe early and missed several games.[42] In mid-July he had a corneal cyst surgically removed from his right eye. The surgery was publicly characterized as minor. However, it wasn't until mid-September that Avila acknowledged he felt comfortable at the plate again.[43] Although his batting average tumbled, he was again selected to play on the AL All-Star squad. For the second year in a row, he led the league in sacrifice hits (18).[44]

When the season ended, Avila returned to Mexico to play. This time his team won the Veracruz League pennant. Early in the winter season he signed teammates Early Wynn and Bob Lemon and White Sox outfielder Jim Rivera. Wynn and Lemon made only a few appearances, but Rivera played a full season.[45]

Avila again held out in the spring of 1956. He agreed via phone to a base salary of around $25,500 and reported three days after the Indians started their spring training. Greenberg took his frustrations with Bobby's negotiating tactics public.[46] Avila's batting average again dropped sharply, from .272 to .224. The Indians requested that he try eyeglasses when hitting. He wore glasses the last week of the 1956 season, but the results were inconclusive. He and the Indians agreed that he would have an eye exam during the winter.

The Indians began the 1957 season with a new manager, Kerby Farrell. Because of his poor 1956 hitting, Avila played no winter ball in Mexico. To the Indians' surprise, he showed up at spring training without glasses. He said his doctor's eye examination revealed he did not have any problems.

By the end of May, Avila's batting average stood at .211. Greenberg told him to see the Indians' eye doctor, who told him he was nearsighted and needed glasses. The first time he wore his new glasses, Avila got three hits. Although he steadfastly refused to wear glasses on the field, he wore them while batting. He finished the year with a .268 batting average.[47]

In 1958 Frank "Trader" Lane succeeded Hank Greenberg as the Indians' general manager, with Bobby Bragan as the manager. Lane said second base was one of the infield positions where the Indians needed to start a rebuilding effort.[48] Throughout the season, Lane frequently used Avila's name when he spoke publicly about possible trades. Within this fluid framework, Avila ended up playing eighty-two games at second base and thirty-three games at third base. He ended the season with a .253 batting average and a .349 on-base percentage.[49]

After the season, Lane traded Avila to the Baltimore Orioles for pitcher Russ Heman and $30,000. After playing in twenty games for the Orioles in 1959, he was sent to the Red Sox for the waiver price in mid-May. Avila played in twenty-two games for Boston and was put on waivers again. The Milwaukee Braves selected him to replace their ailing second baseman, Red Schoendienst. Bobby played in fifty-one games for the Braves, who were in a tight pennant race, which they lost to the Los Angeles Dodgers in a one-game playoff after the close of the regular season. For his three teams, Avila played in ninety-three games and ended with a .227 season average and an OBP of .314.[50]

After the 1959 season, Avila was the player-manager of the Jalapa team in Mexico. Recovering from a slow start, it lost the pennant on the last day of the season in a controversial game.[51]

The 1959 season was Avila's last in the Major Leagues. At the start of 1960, the Braves optioned the thirty-five-year-old Avila to their farm team in Louisville, which in turn optioned him to the Mexico City Tigers of the Mexican League.[52] The Tigers won the pennant as Avila hit .333 and scored a record 125 runs.[53] It was his last season as a player. During his eleven seasons in the major leagues, he played in 1,300 games, had 4,620 at bats, produced 1,296 hits, and registered a batting average of .281 and an on-base percentage of .359.[54]

In October 1960 Avila was named the president of the former Veracruz League, which in his honor was named the Roberto Avila League.[55] In 1971 he was elected to the Mexican baseball hall of fame as a player.[56] Two Mexican League stadiums were named after him: Estadio Beto Avila (capacity 7,782) in Cancun and Parque Beto Avila (capacity 9,000) in Veracruz.[57]

In 1980 Avila began a new career, as a Mexican lawmaker. He was elected the mayor of Veracruz and then to the Mexican Congress, where he served two three-year terms. He also remained active as a businessman and busy grandparent. He had four children and ten grandchildren.[58] On October 26, 2004, Avila died in his hometown, Veracruz, of complications from diabetes and lung disease. He was eighty years old.[59]

Avila may have summed up his baseball career best: "I loved the game. And I was real honest about my job. Nobody could ever say they saw Bobby Avila drunk or playing around. I was honest about my career and I gave it everything I had."[60]

Chapter 50. **Joe Ginsberg**

Mel Marmer

AGE	G	AB	R	H	2B	3B	HR	TB	RBI	BB	SO	BAV	OBP	SLG	SB	GDP	HBP
27	3	2	0	1	0	1	0	3	1	0	0	.500	.667	1.500	0	0	1

In Detroit's Briggs Stadium on April 17, 1951, Opening Day, 43,470 fans braved thirty-nine-degree weather to watch the Detroit Tigers host the Cleveland Indians. For the Tigers, veteran third baseman George Kell was out with an injury. Indians first baseman Luke Easter also was injured but started and played five innings (with two singles) before being removed for a pinch runner. The Tigers' catcher, Joe Ginsberg, a twenty-four-year-old product of Detroit's Cooley High School and the city's sandlots, had been up with the Tigers before, but this was his first Opening Day since the Tigers signed him in 1944. For Ginsberg, it was the realization of a dream to finally be in the Opening Day starting lineup and play in front of family and friends after five years in the Minors and two years in the army.

Though the hometown team lost a heartbreaker, 2–1, on an unearned run in the top of the ninth, Ginsberg, according to manager Red Rolfe, played well despite going hitless in three at bats.

It was eleven years before Ginsberg started another big league opener: April 13, 1962, in New York, his birthplace, when he was with the brand-new New York Mets and started their home opener, played before 12,447 fans. He went hitless (0 for 4) that day also.

In the eleven years between those opening games, Ginsberg was an everyday player for just two seasons, 1951 and 1952. After that, he was a backup catcher for five Major League teams and two in the Minors. The fact that Ginsberg stayed in the big leagues for thirteen seasons, even though mostly as a backup, attested to his love of the game as well as his value to his teams.

Joe Ginsberg—Ginsberg served as a backup catcher during a career that spanned three decades and seven teams.

Born in New York City on October 11, 1926, he was adopted as an infant by Joe and Rose (Cohen) Ginsberg. His given name was Myron Nathan Ginsberg, but he was called Little Joe after his father, and the name Joe stuck.[1] The family of three moved to Detroit, where his father ran a saloon at Michigan and Third, five blocks from Briggs Stadium. Though the Ginsbergs were Jewish, Joe had no formal religious training and was not bar-mitzvahed.[2]

Besides playing baseball and basketball at Cooley High School, Joe played Legion baseball, where he was spotted and signed by Tigers scout "Wish" Egan in 1944. No bonus was reported.

The five-foot-eleven, 180-pound Ginsberg broke in with the Jamestown (Pennsylvania) Falcons of the Class D Pennsylvania-Ontario-New York League. One of his teammates was sixteen-year-old center fielder and future Hall of Fame infielder Nellie Fox. Ginsberg did most of the catching, but found himself playing left field by the end of the season. On June 5, 1944, Ginsberg's hit drove in the winning run in the fifteenth inning of a game against Wellsville. He batted .271 with four home runs. At seventeen, Ginsberg was just nine and a half months older than Fox. The Falcons finished in second place in the regular season, and won the league championship by winning all seven of their playoff games. Ginsberg started six of the games, all in left field.[3] By season's end Ginsberg was listed as an outfielder and assigned to Buffalo for the 1945 season.[4] Instead, he was drafted and wound up serving in the army in the Philippines.

Ginsberg, described as "a hard-hitting catcher hitting .417 in an Army League in Manila,"[5] was not recruited to play baseball in the army; he learned of the Manila Dodgers team from a buddy.[6] He asked for a tryout and made the team but did not play until regular catcher Joe Garagiola suffered a broken finger. Ginsberg quickly made the most of his opportunity. On January 2, 1946, before a crowd estimated at 25,000 GIs, the most exciting game was a 2–1 Manila Dodgers victory over the touring National League All-Stars. Ginsberg drove in the winning run with a single in the fourteenth inning.[7] (One of his strengths was his ability to perform well in clutch situations.)

Discharged from the army, Ginsberg began the 1947 season at Triple-A Buffalo under the tutelage of Bisons manager Paul Richards but was sent to Class A Williamsport and finished the season there. In ninety-two games, he hit only .220. He played fourteen games in the outfield. In 1948 he returned to Williamsport and began the season on a high note, hitting safely in thirteen of his first fifteen games, including two pinch hits.[8] His .326 batting average was just one point behind the league leader, teammate Bruce Blanchard, and Ginsberg was voted to the league All-Star team.[9] At the end of the season, Ginsberg was called up to the Tigers and made his Major League debut on September 15, 1948, starting at home against Washington Senators right-hander Milo Candini. Wearing uniform No. 1, Ginsberg caught his Williamsport teammate Lou Kretlow in a 4–2 victory, went 1 for 4, and made a throwing error on a stolen base by Gil Coan. Ginsberg caught ten September games and the Tigers won eight of them, including two dramatic come-from-behind victories.[10]

Ginsberg quickly became a fan favorite. But the organization did not know what to make of the left-handed-hitting catcher with an excellent batting eye and good speed but not much power. His clutch performance and handling of pitchers intrigued the officials but did not convince them that he was the Tigers' catcher of the future. They said Ginsberg would be their starter if he played well, but they still signed a nineteen-year-old power-hitting catcher, Frank House, in the off-season for a bonus reported to be high as $75,000. They also had veteran catchers Aaron Robinson and Bob Swift. Under the bonus rule at the time, House had to stay on the Tigers' roster. It was obvious that one catcher would have to go. Ginsberg was sent to Toledo, where he batted .283 and pleased manager Eddie Mayo with his catching. Still, he was caught in the Tigers' catching logjam and was sent to Toledo again. He hit .336 in sixty-three games for the Mud Hens and .232 in thirty-six games for Detroit.

Ginsberg looked good during spring training in 1951, and manager Red Rolfe rewarded him by giving him the Opening Day assignment. (A few days earlier he had served as a pallbearer at the funeral of Wish Egan, the scout who had signed him for the Tigers.) Platooning with Robinson and Swift, he caught ninety-five games (starting eighty-one of them) and batted .260 with eight home runs, the most he ever hit in a season. That season, and throughout his career, his clutch hitting was exemplary, and he was a good base runner, "not your typical catcher who hit into a lot of double plays," Rolfe once said.[11] On July 7, 1951, he had four hits, including a home run, and five RBIs in a 13–7 victory over Cleveland. On August 5, in a Tigers' doubleheader sweep at Boston, Ginsberg tripled in the tiebreaking run in the first game and doubled in the winning runs in the second game.

After a second-place finish in 1950, the Tigers fell to fifth place in 1951. Aaron Robinson was cut loose in August, leaving Ginsberg, Swift, and young Frank House still on the roster. With the possibility that House could be called up by the army for the Korean War, the Tigers obtained catcher Matt Batts in a six-player trade with the St. Louis Browns in February and said he would probably be the first-string catcher. Batts was a 200-pounder with a rifle arm. Though it was a blow to Ginsberg, he good-naturedly joked that "there would not be any fighting over the job because (Batts) is too big for me."[12] The Tigers finished in last place with an abysmal 50-104 record (manager Rolfe was fired in July). Ginsberg had a couple of the team's few highlights. On May 14 he caught the first of Virgil Trucks's two no-hitters that year (Batts caught the second, on August 25). And on July 14, Ginsberg, hitting just .185 at the time, broke up Vic Raschi's no-hitter with a home run in the eighth inning in an 11–1 loss at Yankee Stadium.

Batts had an excellent spring in 1953, which made Ginsberg expendable. On June 15 he was traded to the Cleveland Indians in an eight-player deal in which the Tigers obtained two-time All-Star Ray Boone. The Indians already had two fine defensive catchers, Jim Hegan, thirty-two years old, and Joe Tipton, thirty-one. Still, Ginsberg, twenty-six, hoped that he would get a chance to show what he could do. He made his Indians debut on June 16 pinch-hitting for Tipton, and flied out. He started the next day against Philadelphia's Harry Byrd and got two hits. On the 18th he started again and got two more hits. In his first two weeks with the Indians, he was 6 for 17 (.353). He finished the season with a .290 batting average. Yet the following season, he had played in only three games by late May, so he went to traveling secretary Spud Goldstein and told him he'd like more playing time. "It was the only time in my career that I ever popped off," Ginsberg said in an interview in 2010. "I was young, and I wanted to play. Spud told me, 'We have just the thing for you, Ginsy.' The next thing I knew, I was on a train headed to Indianapolis."[13]

The 1954 Indianapolis Indians had one of the finest Minor League teams of the decade, with players like Herb Score and Rocky Colavito. Hank Foiles was the everyday catcher, but he shared playing time with Ginsberg after Joe arrived. Ginsberg hit .291 in fifty-nine games. The team finished first in the American Association by ten and a half games, but lost in the playoffs to Louisville.

In 1955 there was a logjam at the catching position in Indianapolis. Foiles was gone, but veterans Matt Batts and Mickey Grasso, plus a couple of young receivers, were there. Ginsberg wound up in Seattle of the Pacific Coast League as the starting catcher for his old batterymate, Fred Hutchinson, now the manager of the Seattle Rainiers. Ginsberg had an outstanding season, and it began on Opening Day, April 5, in Oakland, when his grand slam broke a 2–2 tie as the Rainiers won, 8–2.[14] Seattle went on to win the league championship, and Ginsberg was named the PCL's Player of the Year. On September 10 he and pitcher Lou Kretlow were sold to the Kansas City Athletics. In 1956 he hit .246 as Tim Thompson's backup, and in August he was traded to the Baltimore Orioles for catcher Hal Smith. Ginsberg got off to an awful start for his new team by going 0 for 26 before hitting two singles on the last day of the season to wind up 2 for 28, for an .071 batting average. At the suggestion of manager Paul Richards, he began wearing eyeglasses in 1957. He and Gus Triandos were the only catchers, so Ginsberg got more playing time (eighty-five games) and hit a respectable .274. But in 1958 and 1959, Ginsberg's ninth and tenth seasons in the Majors, were down years; he hit just .211 in 1958, followed by a career-low .181 in '59. Most of the press he received was for attempting to catch the knuckleball of Orioles hurler Hoyt Wilhelm.

On May 1, 1960, Ginsberg got a key hit to help beat the Yankees. But earlier, Richards had acquired veteran left-handed-hitting catcher Clint "Scrap Iron" Courtney to platoon with Triandos, and Ginsberg was released on June 15. Three days later he signed with the Chicago White Sox, managed by Al Lopez, his former skipper with Cleveland. On June 25 Ginsberg helped his new team defeat the Red Sox, 7–6, by going 3 for 4 with a double, a walk, a sacrifice hit, two RBIS, and three runs scored. He hit .253 in limited duty with the White Sox, played little at the start of 1961, and was released on May 15. Two days later he was signed by the Red Sox to back up Jim Pagliaroni and Russ Nixon. He got into only nineteen games and hit .250 in twenty-four at bats, with five runs batted in. After the season he was released by the Red Sox, and on January 30, 1962, he signed with the Mets. Though Ginsberg caught the home opener, he got into only one other game before he was released on May 1.

In June he caught on with the Denver Bears, a Tigers affiliate that needed a catcher because the regular catcher, Bill Freehan, had been shifted to first base when the first baseman was hurt. Ginsberg played in forty-six games, hit .214, and retired as a player after the season.

After baseball, Ginsberg became a salesman for the Jack Daniel's distillery, covering Michigan. He became an avid golfer and enjoyed participating in charity tournaments. He divided his time between Michigan and Florida before he and his wife, Donna, retired to Southwest Florida, where a number of former Tigers had located. Ginsberg appeared at a few Tigers fantasy camps and remained friendly with many ex-teammates, especially Virgil Trucks, whose no-hitter he caught in 1952. With Trucks, he appeared at the Tigers' Comerica Park on July 8, 2007, for a ceremony honoring Tigers pitcher Justin Verlander for his no-hit game of June 12, 2007.[15]

Joseph Wancho

August 17—Cleveland—AVILA'S HIT CAPS STO-RYBOOK FINISH—Bob Lemon pitches his way to a win, his seventeenth victory. Bobby Avila collects two hits and an RBI. The Indians score two runs in the bottom of the ninth inning for the win. Lemon's single scores Wally Westlake to tie the game, and Bobby Avila's hit to score Dave Philley wins it, 4–3.

August 18—Cleveland—WYNN NAILS TRIBE'S 8TH IN ROW, 4–0—Al Smith smacks a three-run homer. Bobby Avila also homers. Early Wynn scatters six hits and blanks the Tigers as he hurls his way to his sixteenth win. The Yankees keep pace with their ninth win in a row.

August 19—Cleveland—ABER CLICKS: FELLER WINS OPENER, 4–3—Dave Pope and Vic Wertz both go deep with homers. Bob Feller wins his eleventh game in the first game of the doubleheader, 4–3. Ray Narleski posts his tenth save. Bob Nieman clubs a homer in the seventh inning of the second game. The Tigers smack six doubles (Al Kaline 2, Harvey Kuenn, Wayne Belardi, Hoot Evers, and Nieman) to gain the split of the doubleheader, 8–2. Aber whiffs five on the way to a win. The Yankees top the Athletics to cut the lead to two and a half games.

August 20—Baltimore—INDIANS TRIUMPH, 7–2—Doby goes 2 for 5 with three RBIs. Al Rosen smacks his twenty-first home run. Sam Dente drives in a run. Art Houtteman wins his thirteenth game.

August 21—Baltimore—LEMON WINS 18TH, 4–1—Jim Fridley lines into a triple play in the bot-tom of the fourth inning, Lemon to Avila to Wertz. Larry Doby hits a base-loaded triple in the sixth inning. Bob Lemon goes to 18–5.

August 22—Baltimore—INDIANS LEAD BY 5 ½ AFTER 12–1 VICTORY; YANKS FALL AGAIN—The Indians' offense bangs out twenty hits. Jim Hegan, Vic Wertz, Al Rosen, Larry Doby, and Bobby Avila each tally two RBIs. Early Wynn scatters three hits and raises his record to 17-9. The visiting Tribe sweeps Baltimore, and Boston sweeps New York at Fenway Park.

August 24—Philadelphia—A'S DEFEAT CLEVE-LAND, YANKS WIN—Jim Finigan goes 3 for 4, with an RBI and a double. Johnny Gray registers his second Major League win. The Tribe has lost two of the last fourteen; both times, Mike Garcia was the Cleveland starting pitcher.

August 25—Philadelphia—NARAGON'S TRIPLE IN 10TH WINS—Hal Naragon's triple scores Bill Glynn for the winning run in the top of the tenth inning. Al Smith smashes his tenth homer. Bob Lemon wins to raise his record to 19-5.

August 26—Washington—SMITH HITS HOMER FOR 2–1 VICTORY—Early Wynn pitches his way to an 18-9 record. He gives up an unearned run to the Senators. Al Smith goes yard for a solo HR.

August 27—Washington—INDIANS LOSE IN 10TH, 3 TO 2, YANKEES WIN—Bob Feller sur-renders one earned run in loss. Mickey Vernon's single scores Pete Runnels from first base in the tenth inning, as Dave Philley boots the ball in right field. Bobby Avila goes 4 for 5. Al Smith and Larry

Doby each knock in a run. The Yankees close the lead to three and a half games.

August 28—Washington—CLEVELAND'S RALLY BEATS SENATORS, 5–2—Bobby Avila goes 3 for 4, with two RBIS. Larry Doby goes 3 for 4, with one RBI. The Nats turn five double plays in the contest. Mike Garcia goes to 16-7 on the year.

August 29—Boston—LEMON WINS 20TH; JOLT BOSTON, 6–2, 8–1. LEAD BY 4 GAMES—Bob Lemon goes the distance for his twentieth win, striking out seven. Larry Doby and Vic Wertz each belt a homer. Bobby Avila knocks in two runs. The Tribe takes the opener of the double dip, 6–2. Art Houtteman strikes out five in the nightcap for his fourteenth win, scattering six hits over nine innings. Vic Wertz and Al Rosen each smack solo shots and drive in two runs. Houtteman goes 2 for 4 and knocks in two runs. The Tribe sweeps the twin bill with an 8–1 victory in the nightcap. The Indians lead the Yankees by four games.

August 30—Boston—INDIANS BEAT RED SOX, 5–4—Cleveland scores all five of its runs in the top of the seventh inning. Hank Majeski's three-run round-tripper is the big blow. Hal Newhouser wins in relief. Mike Garcia records his fifth save.

August 31—New York—INDIANS BEAT YANKS, 6–1: LEAD BY 5 ½—Dave Philley goes deep for a three-run shot in the eighth inning. Al Rosen goes 2 for 4, with an RBI and two runs scored. Early Wynn's record climbs to 19-9. Attendance at Yankee Stadium is 58,859.

Chapter 52. Cleveland Indians World Championships, 1920 and 1948

Joseph Wancho

The trivia question came up while the Cleveland Indians announcers were filling time during a rain delay in the early 1980s: What did the 1920 and 1948 Cleveland Indians world championship teams have in common? Answer: Both teams were led by a player-manager (Tris Speaker in 1920 and Lou Boudreau in 1948).

But the player-manager aspect was not the only connection between these two teams. Both fielded future members of the Baseball Hall of Fame at shortstop and center field. And both teams received outstanding pitching performances from unheralded players. And of course, like all great teams, both of these had their own unique personality. For a city and a franchise that has enjoyed just two World Series titles in its history, let's start with a look back at that 1920 squad.

Spoke's Team

As the Cleveland Indians departed from their spring training home in New Orleans, they looked to be the team to beat in the American League. At least that is what the beat writers and reporters who covered the teams in the junior circuit seemed to believe. Although such polls are informal and really don't mean all that much, it was a mild surprise that the Tribe was the odds-on favorite to finish on top of the standings. But Tris Speaker's nine was given the nod by the baseball scribes in 1920 despite the strong teams that Chicago and Detroit fielded. Philadelphia manager Connie Mack was in agreement with the writers. "There's a mighty fine fellow (Speaker) and I would like to see him make good. And I think he will. I'm picking the Indians and I generally pick the winners," said Mack.[1]

Cleveland featured strong starters in Jim Bagby, Stan Coveleski, and Ray Caldwell. The three were so strong that combined they won 75 of the team's 98 victories. Each recorded 20 or more wins, Bagby leading the way with 31 victories and 30 complete games. The rest of the staff was made up of journeymen, and except for Dick Niehaus and Joe Boehling, there was not an experienced southpaw on the team. The lack of a lefty seemed to be the only potential mound glitch on the Indians.

The rest of the team was an offensive juggernaut, led by the triumvirate of Charlie Jamieson, Elmer Smith, and Speaker in the outfield. Steve O'Neill was a fine catcher and a formidable batsman. The infield was solid up the middle with Ray Chapman at shortstop and Bill Wambsganss at second base. The corner positions were anchored by Doc Johnston at first base and Larry Gardner manning the hot corner. Of the starting lineup, only Wambsganss (usually called Wamby) and Johnston did not exceed a .300 batting average. And Johnston did not miss by much, stroking the horsehide at a .292 clip. The team average was .303.

Speaker employed the platoon system at certain positions, and he had the bench to do it. George Burns spelled Johnston at first base. Joe Evans and Smoky Joe Wood were able replacements when needed in the outfield. And then there was always Jack Graney, who at the age of thirty-four was still a dangerous offensive threat.

There was a new rule that banned pitchers from using a foreign substance on the baseball. This included spit, mud, and emery. A list was submitted with the names of seventeen pitchers who depended on the spitball, and thus were allowed to throw it until their careers ended. Coveleski and Caldwell were two of the seventeen.

Cleveland opened the season at home, splitting a two-game series with St. Louis. An estimated crowd of just under twenty thousand attended the opener at League Park, located on the east side of Cleveland. Coveleski blanked the Browns, 5–0, as the Tribe backed him with a thirteen-hit attack. The Indians then won nine of their next eleven, finding themselves percentage points behind Chicago and a half-game up on Boston as the day's schedule concluded on May 2.

A week later the Indians won four of five from the White Sox at Chicago. Coveleski won his sixth and seventh games of the season. He bested Eddie Cicotte in a 4–3 victory for number seven. Smith went 3 for 4, driving in two runs, and Speaker added an RBI and a triple. The Tribe had taken six of eight from the White Sox in the early going. The Indians found themselves atop the league with a 14-6 record and a half-game lead over Boston. As good as Coveleski was, Bagby was even better. He started the season at 8-0 before finally dropping his first, a relief outing against the White Sox on May 29. He did not lose a game he started until June 4, a 7–6 loss to the Browns at League Park.

The team closed the month of May winning nine of twelve, and found itself out in front of the pack with a three-and-a-half-game lead over both Boston and New York. Predictably, Jamieson and Speaker led the offense in May, hitting .385 and .392, respectively. Speaker also contributed ten doubles and twenty-seven RBIs, both marks club highs for the month. O'Neil chipped in with thirty hits and a .345 average for the month.

The 1920 season ended the Deadball Era, and there was evidence that perhaps a different type of baseball was now being used in Major League games. For instance, from May 29 to June 4, which included two doubleheaders, the Tribe scored sixty-six runs on 116 hits. Another factor was Babe Ruth smacking home runs left and right for his new team, the Yankees. By August 11 he had eclipsed the twenty-nine homers he hit the year before for Boston, on his way to swatting fifty-four for the year.

After Bagby lost to St. Louis on June 4, Niehaus and Coveleski also fell to the Browns. They found themselves tied with New York, each sporting 28-16 records at the end of the day on June 6. But the Indians won twelve of their next fifteen games, including three of four from the Yanks at League Park. An overflow crowd of 29,266 squeezed their way into the stands for the second game, only to see Bob Shawkey shut out the Indians 14–0. Ruth smacked his seventeenth home run, over the right-field wall, stroked a double, and drove in two runs. Ping Bodie drove in three runs, and Cleveland starter George Uhle lasted only one-third of an inning.

The White Sox were not through either, and after getting swept by Chicago in early July, the Tribe found themselves one game behind the Yankees, while the White Sox were lurking in third place, three and a half games behind, on July 6.

On a trip east, Cleveland won four of five at Fenway Park, but lost three of four to the Yankees. The Indians' only victory was a 4–2 win. The game went eleven innings, and Bagby went the distance to earn his twentieth win. Gardner's triple scored Chapman and Wood to provide the needed margin of victory. The team returned home to topple the White Sox, as Coveleski outdueled Lefty Williams for his sixteenth win. The Indians closed the month by sweeping Boston at home in a four-game series. In the finale Guy Morton surrendered only one hit as Boston scored its only run via a wild pitch in the first frame. The Tribe won 2–1. Heading into August, the Indians led the Yankees by three games and the White Sox by five and a half.

New York headed to Cleveland for a crucial four-game set on August 9–13. The Yanks trailed the Indians by four and a half games, and as the season was growing long, they could not afford to lose ground. And they didn't, sweeping the Tribe, as Shawkey started and won both the first and last games of the series. A crowd estimated at close to twenty-seven thousand crowded their way into League Park for the second game, only to see the Yankees score three runs in the top of the tenth inning to win 7–4. Bob Meusel and Duffy Lewis delivered key run-scoring singles. When the Indians dropped a 5–3 game to Urban Shocker and the Browns, they found themselves in a virtual tie with New York.

The team departed Cleveland for its final eastern road trip of the season on August 15. The Indians' first stop was the Polo Grounds and a three-game set with the Yankees. Unbeknownst to anyone at the time, the series would mark one of the greatest tragedies, not only in baseball, but in all of professional sports. In the fifth inning of the first game, on August 16, Ray Chapman was struck in the head by a pitch from Yankees pitcher Carl Mays. He was rushed to St. Lawrence Hospital, where he was operated on after midnight. X-rays revealed a depressed fracture on the left side of Chapman's skull and a fracture on the right side. Once in surgery it was discovered that Chapman had a triple fracture to the left temple, and that pieces of bone had been driven into his brain. He was pronounced dead at 4:30 a.m. on August 17.

Boston and Detroit led a petition drive to ban Mays from the league. The submarine-style pitcher had hit fifty-five batters (including Chapman) to that point in the sixth year of his Major League career, and he was considered a bit reckless. Speaker did not blame Mays, though, stating that he did not believe Mays intentionally threw at Chapman. Instead, he said he thought Chapman had time to duck out of the way of the pitch, but he never moved. To Speaker it seemed that Chapman stood at the plate in a sort of trance. Thousands of mourners jammed St. John's Cathedral in downtown Cleveland to attend the funeral.

As the Indians continued their trip, they lost a doubleheader at Boston, getting shut out by the Red Sox in both games, 12–0 and 4–0. After losing four out of five games in the series, they moved on to Phil-

adelphia and lost two more to the A's before righting the ship against Washington, winning three of four contests. As August came to a close, the Indians found themselves in second place, a half-game behind Chicago and a half-game ahead of New York.

The team needed help, and a shot in the arm following the death of "Chappie." Two Minor League deals supplied the boost and helped carry the squad through the final month of the season.

The first deal sent pitchers Niehaus and Tony Paeth to the Sacramento Senators of the Pacific Coast League for left-handed pitcher John Walter "Duster" Mails. Mails had posted an 18-17 record for the Senators at the time of the deal. He made his first start for the Indians on September 1 and beat Washington on the strength of a two-hitter. In all, he made eight starts in September, and his record was a 7-0 with an ERA of 1.85. He also beat Chicago with a three-hitter on September 24, providing a key win down the stretch.

To replace Chapman, the Indians turned to the New Orleans Pelicans of the Southern Association, with whom they had an unofficial working agreement. They signed left-handed-hitting Joe Sewell for $6,000. Sewell hit .329 for the season and proved adequate in the field. He was a mainstay in Cleveland for years, eventually being enshrined at Cooperstown in 1977.

Cleveland had a one-and-a-half-game lead over Chicago on September 21 as the White Sox came to League Park to open a three-game series. Back in Chicago, a grand jury had been convened to investigate whether seven current members of the White Sox conspired to throw the 1919 World Series. (Arnold "Chick" Gandil had retired after the 1919 season.) The White Sox did not seem to be bothered by the allegations, and they won two of three from the Indians to close to within a half-game. As Cleveland was sweeping a four-game series in St. Louis, indictments were being handed up on several White Sox players. On September 28 Chicago owner Charles Comiskey announced that the players who were being investigated would be suspended from the team indefinitely. The Indians finished the year in Detroit, winning two of four from the Tigers, while the depleted Chicago squad lost two of three to the Browns to end their season.

Cleveland claimed its first pennant and headed to the World Series to face the Brooklyn Robins. Brooklyn, which finished seven games ahead of the second-place New York Giants, was returning to the Series for the first time since claiming the pennant in 1916. The Robins were a formidable foe, with Zack Wheat, Burleigh Grimes, Rube Marquard, and Doc Johnston's brother Jimmy, who manned the hot corner for the Robins.

The 1920 Fall Classic was a best-of-nine format and began with three games in Brooklyn. The Tribe lost two of three to the Robins, with Coveleski getting the only win, in the Series opener. Grimes came back to post a shutout in Game Two, scattering seven hits. Brooklyn right fielder Tommy Griffith went 2 for 4 and drove in two runs. Wheat knocked in the other run. Sherry Smith pitched a three-hitter in Game Three for a 2–1 victory. He got all the support he needed when the Robins scored two runs in the bottom of the first inning, with Wheat and Hi Myers driving in a run apiece. Wheat collected three hits in the game.

The Tribe took control of the Series when the teams moved to Cleveland, winning Game Four with Burns getting a key pinch hit in the third inning that plated two runs. The Indians then dismantled the Robins in Game Five. A key play occurred in the fifth inning when, with runners on first and second base and no outs, Brooklyn pitcher Clarence Mitchell lined out to Wambsganss. Wamby converted the out into an unassisted triple play. Bagby got the win and backed his outing with a three-run homer in the fourth inning, the first pitcher to do so in the World Series. Elmer Smith also homered, stroking the first grand slam in Series history. The Indians cruised to an 8–1 victory. Mails and Coveleski pitched shutouts in Games Six and Seven to give Cleveland its first world championship since it entered the American League in 1901.

A Veteran Team

Unlike the 1920 edition of the Cleveland Indians, the 1948 squad wasn't expected to finish higher than third in the American League. When *The Sporting News* made its annual predictions in the April 21 issue, the Indians were placed behind Boston and New York. Ed McCauley of the *Cleveland News* wrote, "Enough improvement over last year to suggest third-place finish."[2] The Indians had finished fourth in 1947, seventeen games back of New York.

But a series of player moves after the 1946 season had laid the foundation for success in 1948. The Indians sent pitcher Allie Reynolds to the Yankees for second baseman Joe Gordon. Several weeks later, the Indians and Yankees were trade partners again, with second baseman Ray Mack and catcher Sherm Lollar moving to New York and outfielder Hal Peck and pitchers Al Gettel and Gene Bearden heading to Cleveland. Gordon provided leadership and credibility because of the success he'd had in New York, where he had helped lead the Yankees to five pennants. He led the Tribe in home runs in both 1947 and 1948. But the real surprise was Bearden, who pitched with Oakland of the Pacific Coast League in 1947, posting a 16-7 record. The tall, strapping left-hander tied for Cleveland's team lead in victories with twenty in 1948.

On July 5, 1947, Larry Doby made his Major League debut with Cleveland, becoming the first black player in the American League. Although he was a second baseman for Newark in the Negro National League, he was relegated to pinch-hitting duties in twenty-four of the twenty-nine games he appeared in that season, hitting .156.

In 1948 the Tribe's everyday lineup was stocked with veterans at every position, with the exception of Doby, who found a new home in center field. Gordon and Lou Boudreau at shortstop were a formidable keystone combo. Eddie Robinson roamed first base while Ken Keltner was stationed across the diamond at third. Third-year man Dale Mitchell played left field and Bob Kennedy held down the right-field position. Jim Hegan was considered one of the best receivers in the league behind the plate. Allie Clark and Thurman Tucker were both capable reserves.

Bob Lemon, Bob Feller, and Bearden started the bulk of the team's 156 games, toeing the rubber in a combined 104 starts. Satchel Paige, Steve Gromek, Sam Zoldak, and Don Black all contributed as starters and relievers. Russ Christopher led the team with seventeen saves. (Saves were not an official statistic until 1969.)

The Indians opened the season at Cleveland Stadium as Feller blanked the St. Louis Browns on two hits for a 4–0 win. Hegan went 3 for 3, driving in three runs. He hit the first homer of the season, a two-run shot in the fourth inning. The turnstiles were busy as a crowd of 73,163 witnessed the shutout.

But the Indians did not stop there, as they won their first six games, making it a perfect month in April. During a three-game sweep of the Tigers in Detroit, Keltner put on his hitting shoes, smacking four home runs and driving in eight runs. After dropping four in a row to begin May, the Tribe went 17-7 for the rest of the month. On May 10 Doby collected four hits in a 12–7 win over Boston at Fenway Park. He drove in two runs, scored three, and hit his fifth home run of the year. Bearden got his first start on May 8, topping the Senators 6-1 on a three-hitter. For the month, he posted a 4-1 record and a sparking ERA of 1.24. After splitting a doubleheader with the Browns on May 31, the Indians found themselves one game behind Philadelphia and in second place of the American League standings.

After taking three of four games on the road at New York (June 11–13), Cleveland took over first place, leading Philadelphia by three games. But the Red Sox came to town and swept the Indians three straight. The second game was blown wide open by a pair of two-run homers off Feller, one by Ted Williams and the other Bobby Doerr, in a 7–4 loss. Cleveland then lost three of four to New York at home (June 21–24). In the third game, Tommy Henrich smashed a grand slam in the top of the eleventh inning as the Yankees went on to win 5–1 before 65,797 customers. The Indians' lead over the Yankees was down to one and a half games. The month did end on a good note when Bob Lemon hurled the ninth no-hitter in the team's history, beating the Tigers 2–0 at Briggs Stadium. Lemon struck out four and walked three batters.

From July 3 to 24, Dale Mitchell put together a twenty-one-game hitting streak. During the streak he batted .443, with eight doubles and three triples. He drove in eleven runs. On July 9, Leroy "Satchel" Paige made his Major League debut, tossing two innings in relief of Lemon in a 5–3 loss to St. Louis. Heading into the All-Star break, the Indians sat atop the standings, a half-game ahead of the Athletics, and two and a half games over New York.

The Fifteenth All-Star Game was played at Sportsman's Park in St. Louis on July 13. The Indians were well represented in the midsummer classic, with Lemon, Feller, Keltner, Boudreau, and Gordon all being selected to the team.

After winning three of four in Washington (July 18–20), the Wahoos lost five of six in a trip through New York and Boston (July 21–25). By month's end Cleveland was tied with New York for third place, two games off the pace. The streaking Red Sox went 18-3 from the break until the end of July to catapult into first place.

It was anybody's pennant to win over the last two months of the season, with two games separating the Red Sox, Athletics, Yankees, and Indians.

Bearden picked up his ninth victory of the year on August 5, shutting out the Senators 3–0. He hit his first Major League home run in the third inning, and Hegan added two solo shots in the win. From August 12 through 20, Cleveland finally got a streak going, stringing together eight wins in a row. During the streak, Satchel Paige authored two shutouts, both over the White Sox. The first was on August 13 at Comiskey Park, a 5–0 win. The second was a tight 1–0 contest on August 20 at Cleveland Stadium. A couple of reserve players played big roles on August 18, when Sam Zoldak shut out St. Louis, 3–0. Allie Clark went 3 for 4 and scored all three runs.

Larry Doby put together his own twenty-one-game hitting streak from August 22 through September 16, during which he batted .345, hit three homers, and drove in thirteen runs. He also stroked four doubles and three triples in this period.

But Boston was building steam as the last month played out. The Red Sox went 20-3 from August 20 through September 11. Cleveland went on an 11-3 run from August 30 to September 11. Not to be outdone, New York was also playing solidly, going 22-6 from August 17 to September 11. When the day's action was completed on September 11, the Red Sox led second-place New York by three games, and Cleveland was in third, three and a half games back.

On September 11 Lemon won his twentieth game, beating the Browns 9–1. Kennedy, Gordon, Tucker, and Hegan all doubled and Keltner drove in three runs. From September 16 to 22, the Indians won seven games in a row, the last a 5–2 win over Boston. The win gave Feller, who struck out six, his seventeenth win of the campaign. Keltner blasted his twenty-eighth homer of the year, a two-run job in the first inning. The win pulled Boston and Cleveland into a tie for first place with 91-55 records. The Yankees were a half-game off the pace at 90-55.

Cleveland and Boston were both 5-3 to finish September. For the Tribe, Bearden and Feller each won two games down the stretch on their way to each winning nineteen for the season. New York wrapped up the month with a 4-4 record, losing the final two games of the season to Boston. Cleveland and Boston finished the schedule with identical 96-58 records.

A one-game playoff was set at Fenway Park on October 4. Boudreau sent Bearden to the hill, and Boston skipper Joe McCarthy tabbed Denny Galehouse to start for the Bosox. Cleveland jumped out to a 5–1 lead in the fourth, courtesy of a three-run homer by Keltner. Boudreau added two solo shots of his own. Bearden went the distance, striking out six batters on the way to his twentieth win of the year. Cleveland punched its ticket to the Fall Classic with an 8–3 win.

Cleveland did not need to travel far to meet its opponent in the World Series, the Boston Braves. Game One was scheduled for October 6 at Braves Field. The Braves had finished six and a half games ahead of the favored St. Louis Cardinals and were looking for their first world title since 1914. They fielded a solid team with Eddie Stanky at second base and Al Dark at shortstop. Outfielders Tommy Holmes and Jeff Heath, along with infielders Earl Torgeson and Bob Elliot, were formidable hitters. (Heath, a former Indian, had broken his ankle in a game four days before the end of the season, and was out of the World Series.) Johnny Sain, Warren Spahn, and Bill Voiselle formed a dreaded pitching staff for opposing teams. Game One was a pitching duel, with Sain besting Feller 1–0. Sain struck out six and walked none, as Holmes singled home pinch runner Phil Masi from second base with the winning run in the bottom of the eighth inning. It was only the second hit given up by Feller in the game. (In a controversial decision by an umpire just before the hit, Masi had been called safe on a pickoff play even though he appeared to be out.)

Lemon won Game Two, 4–1, and the series shifted to Cleveland for the next three games. The Cleveland crowd was ready, as the attendance for the trio of contests attracted 238,491. Bearden shut out the Braves 2–0 in Game Three, scattering five hits. Steve Gromek beat the Braves in Game Four, 2–1, as Boudreau and Doby drove in a run apiece. The stage was set for Cleveland to wrap up the Series at home, and a then record crowd of 86,288 turned out to get in on the party. But Spahn was better than Feller, and the Braves walloped the Tribe, 11–5, forcing a return to Boston.

Lemon and Bearden combined to wrap up the world championship for Cleveland, beating the Braves 4–3 at Braves Field. Lemon was credited with the win. Gordon hit a solo shot in the sixth inning, and Boudreau, Hegan, and Robinson were each credited with an RBI.

World Series championships in Cleveland can be summed up in one phrase: few and far between.

Chapter 53. **Rocky Nelson**

David L. Fleitz

AGE	G	AB	R	H	2B	3B	HR	TB	RBI	BB	SO	BAV	OBP	SLG	SB	GDP	HBP
29	4	4	0	0	0	0	0	0	0	0	1	.000	.000	.000	0	1	0

Rocky Nelson—Rocky Nelson was a member of the 1960 Pittsburgh Pirates, hitting a home run in Game Seven of the World Series. (The Cleveland Press Collection, Cleveland State University Library)

Rocky Nelson came to Cleveland in the spring of 1954 with an impressive pedigree. He had won the Most Valuable Player award in the International League in 1953 and followed it up with a fine performance in the Cuban Winter League, where he won the batting championship. The Indians expected Nelson to win the starting position at first base, but the Minor League sensation struggled mightily in spring training and, though he made the Opening Day roster, he appeared in only four games for the Indians. He failed to hit safely in four times at bat, and in mid-May Cleveland sent Nelson back to the Minor Leagues, from which he eventually emerged to play backup roles with the Brooklyn Dodgers, St. Louis Cardinals, and Pittsburgh Pirates.

Born in Portsmouth, Ohio, on November 18, 1924, Glenn Richard Nelson, called Spike as a child, was the second and last child of Marshall and Esta (Sunday) Nelson. Marshall worked as a catcher in a steel mill when Glenn and his brother, Alfred, two years older, were young. But by 1940 he held a job as a processing clerk in a WPA program. (The Works Progress Administration was a New Deal creation that put unemployed Americans to work on public projects.) As a youth, Glenn was a batboy for the Portsmouth Red Birds, a St. Louis Cardinals farm club in the Mid-Atlantic League. A left-handed pitcher who stood five feet ten, he starred on the baseball team at Portsmouth High School and was signed by the Cardinals in 1942. Nelson earned his nickname in a Cardinals training camp when teammate Whitey Kurowski bounced a ball off his head during a pepper game. Nelson was unhurt, and Kurowski tagged him with the name Rocky, which he carried for the rest of his life.

Cardinals general manager Branch Rickey, enamored of Nelson's hitting skill, shifted the youngster to first base and sent him to Johnson City in the Appalachian League. The seventeen-year-old batted .253 that season, then enlisted in the U.S. Army on February 20, 1943, and served three years, including time in the Pacific theater during World War II. Returning to the Cardinals organization in 1946, Nelson won the Piedmont League batting title for Lynchburg in 1947. On August 20 of that year, he married Alberta Burns of Portsmouth in a pregame ceremony at home plate.

Nelson wore out Minor League pitching and, after hitting .303 for Rochester in 1948, earned a shot in the big leagues with the Cardinals in 1949. He shared the first-base job with Nippy Jones, but batted only .221 with four homers in eighty-two games, driving in thirty-two runs. The Cardinals, hampered by weak offensive production at the first-base position, lost the pennant to the Brooklyn Dodgers that year by one game. Sent down to Columbus in 1950, Nelson battered American Association pitching for a .418 average in forty-eight games, but he hit poorly after his recall to St. Louis. He was quickly earning a reputation as a Minor League superstar who could not, for whatever reason, break through at the Major League level.

The Cardinals gave up on Rocky after another slow start at the plate in 1951 and traded him to the Pittsburgh Pirates in May. He hit better for the Pirates, posting a .267 average, but his lack of power (one homer in seventy-one games) led the club to put him on waivers in September. The White Sox picked Nelson up, then sent the twenty-seven-year-old player to the Brooklyn Dodgers, where he spent the 1952 season recovering from a broken leg and backing up Gil Hodges at first base. He played little, batting only forty-six times and going hitless in four World Series plate appearances, and found himself back in the Minor Leagues with Brooklyn's top farm team, the Montreal Royals, in 1953.

Despite his troubles, Rocky was popular with fans and teammates. He was a colorful individual and clubhouse prankster with one of the most unusual batting stances in the game; as Jim Murray of the *Los Angeles Times* described it, his stance was "right out of a lithograph from the archives of baseball—right foot at right angles to the left foot, knees bent. It was so archaic that a magazine once devoted a whole, fascinated story to it on the notion it was obscene to have this kind of a stance without a handlebar mustache to go with it." Murray also wrote that Rocky "was a marathon talker who chain-smoked evil-smelling Cuban rope cigars. He even smoked them in bed, and roomie Gino Cimoli once told me he got tired of answering excited calls from hotel switchboards who thought the room was on fire."[1]

In Montreal, Nelson suddenly found his power stroke. On a team managed by Walter Alston and filled with future Major Leaguers including Tommy Lasorda, Don Hoak, and Dick Williams, Nelson led the International League with 34 home runs and 136 runs batted in, earning Most Valuable Player honors. This performance established Nelson as a hot prospect once again, but because Gil Hodges owned the first-base job in Brooklyn, Rocky would have to play elsewhere to establish himself in the Majors. In October 1953 the Dodgers sent Rocky to the Cleveland Indians for pitcher Bill Abernathie and a reported $15,000.

The Indians had finished second to the pennant-winning Yankees in 1953 despite a glaring weakness at first base. Luke Easter, the veteran first sacker, was thirty-seven years old and could no longer play the field, while Bill Glynn, a slick glove man

DAVID L. FLEITZ

who had led the league in fielding percentage, was a mediocre hitter best suited to a role as a late-inning defensive replacement. Manager Al Lopez hoped that Nelson, the Minor League slugging sensation, could fill the first-base hole and provide more power for the Cleveland offense. Walter Alston gave Nelson a strong recommendation. "I don't see how he can miss if he plays the kind of first base for Cleveland that he did for me all year," Alston told *The Sporting News*.[2]

Rocky welcomed the opportunity. "In my opinion," he said in February of 1954, "I've never had a chance in the big leagues to stay in the lineup long enough at one time to show what I could do."[3] But he got off to a bad start in spring training, hitting poorly and fielding worse. In a game against the New York Giants in Tulsa, Oklahoma, Rocky failed to catch two pop-ups and misplayed a line drive into a three-base error. Lopez nonetheless remained hopeful. "I'm going to keep him on first, especially after an exhibition like that," said the Cleveland manager. "If I jerked him out of there now, I would really ruin his morale."[4] In mid-March, Lopez offered encouragement. "I'm sure he can do better than he has shown so far," he told the press. "I know he's a good glove man, but he hasn't even been impressive in the field. That's what makes me think he's pressing, trying too hard."[5]

As Rocky's spring average fell to the .150 level, another newcomer, infielder Rudy Regalado, impressed the Cleveland management with his strong hitting and fielding. Regalado quickly became the darling of the local sportswriters, while Lopez and general manager Hank Greenberg considered a plan to move star third baseman Al Rosen to first base, with Regalado on third. Nelson earned a spot on the Cleveland roster, but watched from the bench on Opening Day as Bill Glynn, who hit well in spring training, played first. Nelson entered the game in the eighth inning as a defensive replacement but did not bat, as the Indians pounded the Chicago White Sox, 8–2.

The presence of Regalado, and an unexpected season-opening hot streak by Glynn, spelled the end for Nelson in Cleveland. He played in four games as a pinch hitter and late-inning replacement, with no hits in four times at bat, then spent the next few weeks on the bench. In late April, after Glynn's bat cooled down, the Indians moved Rosen to first base and inserted Regalado into the lineup at third. Nelson was the odd man out. He had failed his fifth Major League trial, and on May 11 the Indians returned Rocky to his previous club, the Montreal Royals. "Well, if I must play in the minors," said a disappointed Nelson, "I'd rather play with Montreal than with any other team."[6]

A few years later Nelson expressed his dissatisfaction with Cleveland management. "They gave me the position in the spring, sure, but they didn't spend all that money just to find out if I could hit in the spring," he told *Sports Illustrated* in 1958. "They bought me because of the great season I had in Montreal in '53. I've never been a good hitter in the spring. I need to get to know the pitchers. Even in the minors, what little hitting I do in the spring, I do against pitchers I've seen before. I never hit the new ones right at first. And that's the way it was up there. Just about the time I was learning what they could throw, I was on the bench. And then I was back at Montreal."[7]

Cleveland coach Red Kress had a different perspective. "You should have seen him that spring," said Kress. "He was tighter than a drum. Just plain nervous. He looked terrible; he couldn't even catch the ball. And at the plate, it wasn't some particular pitch that he couldn't hit. He couldn't hit strikes." Al Lopez agreed. "Rocky talked a lot," said Lopez, "and he gave the appearance of being nonchalant. But I think part of this was just a coverup. Inside he must have been burning."[8]

Predictably, Rocky turned into a slugger again upon his return to the Minor Leagues. Though he missed the first few weeks of the 1954 International League season, he led the circuit in home runs that year, and in 1955 he won the Triple Crown and another Most Valuable Player award. A .394 average in 1956 earned him another call-up to Brooklyn (where he was reunited with his old Montreal skipper, Walter Alston), but Nelson failed once again to stick with the club. "It was a complex of some kind," said Fresco Thompson of the Dodgers. "Rocky looked just as bad for us as he looked good down in the minors."[9] Nelson developed an unfortunate knack for hitting long, arching fly balls over the right-field fence just barely foul. "If they had just moved the foul pole over about ten feet," one writer quipped, "Rocky would have broken Ruth's record in a breeze."[10] The Dodgers sent Nelson on waivers to the Cardinals, and at season's end St. Louis sold his contract to Toronto of the International League.

In Toronto, Nelson won his second Triple Crown and third MVP Award in 1958. This performance earned him another shot with Pittsburgh, a club that already owned two established first basemen in right-handed batter Dick Stuart and lefty slugger Ted Kluszewski. Rocky performed so well in spring training, however, that manager Danny Murtaugh kept all three first sackers on the roster as the 1959 season began.

Nelson started slowly, as usual, and served exclusively as a pinch hitter in April and early May while Kluszewski went on a tear. Eventually, however, Rocky's bat came around, while Kluszewski went cold, batting .188 in June and .095 in July. Nelson claimed the backup first base job, cementing his hold on the position with two homers against the league-leading San Francisco Giants on August 24, leading the Pirates to a 6–0 win. The next day Pittsburgh management traded Kluszewski to the Chicago White Sox. Rocky batted .291 for the Pirates in 1959 with six homers, a performance that assured him a spot on the roster to start the 1960 season.

Solidly entrenched as Dick Stuart's backup, the thirty-five-year-old Nelson enjoyed his finest Major League campaign in 1960. One memorable performance came on July 5, when he led off the ninth inning against the Braves in Milwaukee with the Pirates down 2–0. Nelson belted a homer off Carlton Willey, igniting a rally that put Pittsburgh ahead, 3–2. The Braves tied the score in the ninth, but in the tenth Rocky belted his second round-tripper of the day, a two-run shot off Joey Jay that proved the winning margin in a 5–4 Pirates win. In all, he played in ninety-three games for the Pirates in 1960 with fifty starts at first base, all against right-handed pitchers. He batted .300 with seven home runs, providing important support as the Pirates won their first pennant in thirty-four years and earned a World Series berth against the New York Yankees.

Though the Yankees named right-hander Art Ditmar as their starting pitcher for Game One of the Series, manager Murtaugh gave Dick Stuart the starting assignment at first base. Nelson started the second game, collecting two singles in five at bats against right-hander Bob Turley as the Pirates fell by a 16–3 score. He appeared as a defensive replacement in Game Five and struck out as a pinch hitter in Game Six, but with Turley on the mound in the deciding seventh game, Murtaugh put Nelson in the lineup in the cleanup spot. In the first inning Rocky smacked the biggest hit of his career, a two-run homer that gave the Pirates an early lead.

Nelson almost emerged as the goat of the Series. With one out in the top of the ninth inning and the Pirates leading 9–8, the Yankees had Gil McDougald at third and Mickey Mantle at first when Yogi Berra hit a sharp grounder to Rocky at first base. A 3–6–3 double play would have ended the game and given the Pirates the world championship, but instead of throwing to second, Nelson stepped on first to retire Berra, then turned his attention to Mantle, who was caught only a few feet away from him. Mantle somehow eluded Rocky's tag, twisting his way around the Pirates' first sacker and diving safely back to first as McDougald scored to tie the game. Fortunately for Nelson, all was forgotten when Bill Mazeroski led off the bottom of the inning with his Series-winning walk-off homer.

Nelson's hitting fell off sharply in 1961, and the Pirates released the thirty-seven-year-old at season's end. He played one more year in the Minors, then retired from the game and opened a painting business in his hometown of Portsmouth, Ohio. He and his wife, Alberta, who had adopted a son in 1958, lived in Portsmouth until his death at the age of eighty-one on October 31, 2006.

Chapter 54. **Art Houtteman**

Warren Corbett

AGE	W	L	PCT	ERA	G	GS	GF	CG	SHO	SV	IP	H	BB	SO	HBP	WP
26	15	7	.682	3.35	32	25	3	11	1	0	188	198	59	68	3	1

Pitcher Art Houtteman was known as "Hard Luck" Houtteman—and that was before he nearly died in a car wreck and before his baby daughter was killed in another wreck.

Arthur James Houtteman was born in Detroit, Michigan, on August 7, 1927. His grandfather, Joseph, had emigrated from Belgium. They had called themselves "HOOT-uh-man" until a relative told his father that only the black-sheep side of the family used that pronunciation. Thereafter they were the "HOWT-uh-mans."

His father, also named Arthur, was a longtime player in the city's fast sandlot leagues. Arthur Sr. was pitching a game on the afternoon that his wife gave birth to their only son. When the news arrived at the ball field, the new dad tossed his glove in the air and vowed that the boy would be a big leaguer by the time he was seventeen.

Young Arthur signed with the Tigers sixteen days after his seventeenth birthday. Scout Wish Egan had been following him for two years at Catholic Central High School, in American Legion ball with Thomas A. Edison Post 187, and on the sandlots, where his father played right field in one of his starts. Egan brought the teenager to Briggs Stadium several times to work out with the big leaguers. In a scouting report, he praised the right-hander's "perfect pitching motion."[1] The Tigers signed Houtteman for $20,000, beating out a half-dozen other clubs.

He went to spring training with the Tigers in 1945 along with another Detroit sandlot product, left-hander Billy Pierce. Most Major Leaguers were serving in World War II, but the seventeen-year-olds were too young for the military draft.

Houtteman spent the early weeks of the season

Art Houtteman—Houtteman, acquired from Detroit, was a solid contributor to a deep pitching staff.

with the Tigers' top farm club at Buffalo in the International League. He was called up when the big league club's pitching staff was thinned by injuries. He worked just twenty-five and one-third innings of relief and lost his only two decisions. Detroit won the American League pennant behind pitchers Hal Newhouser and Dizzy Trout, who were exempt from military service because of health problems, and the late-season slugging of Hank Greenberg, who had been discharged after more than four years in the army. The teenager did not pitch as the Tigers beat the Chicago Cubs in the World Series.

He went back to Buffalo in 1946, when most war veterans returned to the Majors. Still only nineteen years old, he posted a 16-13 record and led the league in strikeouts.

He began 1947 in Buffalo, but was recalled in July. In his second start, shortly after his twentieth birthday, he shut out Washington on five hits. General manager Billy Evans crowed, "In 40 years I've never seen a better pitching job by a first year pitcher. We now know that Houtteman is really a big leaguer."[2] Next time out, he beat Boston on five hits and then shut out the St. Louis Browns on September 6. Manager Steve O'Neill said Houtteman had learned to throw a sinking fastball along with his curve and sidearm crossfire. He finished with a 7-2 record and an excellent 3.42 ERA. He also batted .300.

O'Neill put him in the starting rotation in 1948, but the season turned into a nightmare. Houtteman lost his first eight decisions; the club never gave him more than five runs. That's when the nickname "Hard Luck Houtteman" first hit the headlines. He got his first victory in relief, but he had to drive home the winning run himself to beat Washington in ten innings. In his next start he defeated Philadelphia in an eleven-inning five-hitter. Then he held Cleveland to just two runs on June 30. Emblematic of the way Houtteman's season was going, the Indians' Bob Lemon pitched a no-hit shutout that day.

Houtteman didn't win another game. He finished 2-16 for a team that went 78-76. Detroit writer H. G. Salsinger insisted he was the victim of "bad luck not bad pitching."[3] He started twenty games, relieved in twenty-three more, and was effective enough to earn ten saves, a statistic that was not computed until years later. O'Neill remained confident in the twenty-one-year-old, predicting, "He'll be a big winner someday."[4]

The year 1948 had been bad; 1949 started even worse. During spring training in Lakeland, Florida,

he was returning from a dance at Florida Southern College when his convertible collided with a fruit truck. The crash fractured Houtteman's skull. At first his survival was in doubt, but he was able to talk to reporters within a few days. One of his passengers, Arthur Falls (a cousin of future Detroit sportswriter Joe Falls), was also seriously hurt; two women in the car came away with minor injuries. Houtteman was sent home to recuperate. An ambulance was waiting for him at the Detroit train station, but he sneaked away and caught a cab to Henry Ford Hospital.

Houtteman returned to the mound on May 21, barely more than two months after the accident. He won fifteen games and lost ten, and his 3.71 ERA was a half run better than the league average. The Tigers' new manager, Red Rolfe, said, "Arthur has developed a beauty of a slow curve to go with his fast ball and his crossfire pitch."[5] At twenty-two, he was living up to his promise.

After the season the Philadelphia Sports Writers Association honored him as the year's "Most Courageous Athlete." Bob Hope got most of the laughs at the January banquet, but Houtteman quipped, "All a fellow has to do to get on this dais is to get hit by a five- ton truck."[6]

He took another step forward in 1950: a 19-12 record and 3.54 ERA in 274 ⅔ innings. In his only All-Star Game appearance, in July at Chicago's Comiskey Park, Houtteman pitched three innings but gave up a game-tying home run to Ralph Kiner in the ninth. The National League won on Red Schoendienst's fourteenth-inning homer off Houtteman's friend and roommate, left-hander Ted Gray.

Houtteman pitched a one-hitter against the Browns on August 19, facing the minimum twenty-seven batters. Jim Delsing singled in the second inning and was caught stealing. The two men Houtteman walked were erased in double plays. He twice failed to gain his twentieth win in September, but he was the Tigers' ace as they finished second, three games behind the Yankees.

The day after the season ended, October 2, Houtteman married Shelagh Marie Kelly of Rahway, New Jersey. They had met the previous year when he and some teammates spent an off-day at the famous Grossinger's resort in New York's Catskill Mountains, where Shelagh was a swimmer in the aquatic show. Two days after the couple returned from their honeymoon, the groom was drafted into the army.

Houtteman had once been classified 4-F (medically ineligible for the draft) because of a high school knee injury. He later groused that he was drafted only because he was a prominent athlete; the Yankees' top rookie, Whitey Ford, was also called into the army that fall as the Korean War intensified, and Willie Mays got his draft notice the next spring. But when Houtteman reported to Camp Pickett, Virginia, he was declared unfit for combat because the noise of gunfire gave him severe headaches. Doctors said that was likely a lingering effect of his skull fracture. He was put on limited duty pitching for the camp baseball team. After eleven months—when the baseball season was about over—he received a medical discharge.

Houtteman came home to his wife and first child, Sheryl, who had been born in August. He signed a 1952 contract for a reported $22,000. Manager Rolfe predicted, "Artie should be our best pitcher."[7]

On April 2, 1952, Shelagh was driving the baby and Art's mother home from spring training when her new Cadillac ran off a mountain road near Benton, Tennessee, and rolled over twice. Seven-month-old Sheryl was thrown from the car and killed.

Returning to the Tigers after burying his daughter, Houtteman was one out away from a no-hitter against the Indians on April 26. Catcher Joe Ginsberg called for a curve, but Houtteman shook him off and threw a fastball to outfielder Harry Simpson—and Simpson singled to left. Houtteman said, "This was the only pitch I shook Ginsberg off the whole game." For years afterward, fellow Detroiter Ginsberg said, he would rag Houtteman: "If you'd listened to me, I'd have you in the Hall of Fame."[8]

For the rest of the season, Hard Luck Houtteman was back in town. He lost twenty games against eight wins, even though he gave up less than one hit per inning and didn't walk many batters (65). His 4.36 ERA was worse than average, but he was the victim of weak run support. Detroit was shut out in four of his losses and scored only one or two runs in four others. His misery had plenty of company: the Tigers lost 104 games and finished last for the first time in their history.

After the season, general manager Charlie Gehringer acknowledged that Houtteman might be traded if the right offer came along, but Gehringer was not giving up on him. "Art has always had good stuff," he said, "much too good to be a 20-game loser."[9]

Houtteman spent the winter selling cars and making public appearances for the Tigers. He got off to a feeble start in 1953; he gave up twenty runs, including five homers, in his first twelve and two-thirds innings and lost six straight decisions. At the June 15 trading deadline, he was swapped to Cleveland in an eight-player deal that boiled down to Houtteman for infielder Ray Boone and veteran pitcher Steve Gromek. Indians manager Al Lopez praised his "very live arm," adding, "Houtteman had all the equipment to win, but he wasn't winning. He had an excellent fast ball, a good curve and slider. All he needed was to regain his confidence; to get back in the groove." Of his last two tough seasons in Detroit, Houtteman later said, "I began to experiment, try new things and that's the scourge of all pitchers. Soon you get completely lost. That's what I became— lost and bewildered." He said Lopez and Cleveland's pitching coach, Mel Harder, "did a complete overhaul on me."[10] Lopez soon moved him into the starting rotation, demoting the Indians' fading superstar, Bob Feller, to spot duty. Houtteman finished 7-7 for Cleveland with a 3.80 ERA.

On February 22, 1954, he and Shelagh celebrated the birth of daughter Hollis Ann, who was called Holly.

The 1954 Indians won an American League record 111 games behind a pitching "dream team" and knocked off the Yankees, who had claimed five consecutive World Series championships. Future Hall of Famers Bob Lemon and Early Wynn each won twenty-three games with ERAS under 3.00; Mike Garcia led the league with a 2.64 ERA and won nineteen. The thirty-five-year-old Feller rebounded with a 13-3 mark. Houtteman shared the fourth spot in the rotation with the no-longer-Rapid Robert. He posted a 15-7 record and 3.35 ERA in twenty-five starts, but was the most obscure member of the staff, so obscure that a 2004 biography of Feller refers to him as a left-hander.

The Indians' 2.78 ERA was the lowest in the American League since the long-ball era began in 1920. They allowed only 504 runs, by far the fewest in the league. Although the club is celebrated for its pitching, Cleveland finished second to the Yankees in runs scored.

In the World Series against the Giants, the Indians ran into two superstar performers: Willie Mays, whose back-to-the-plate grab of Vic Wertz's long fly ball in Game One is known simply as The Catch; and Dusty Rhodes, a superstar for a week, who hit two home runs and drove in seven. The Giants swept the Series in four games. Houtteman relieved Garcia with Cleveland trailing in the fourth inning of game three and gave up one run in two innings.

Houtteman had been a major contributor to a record-setting team, but he lost his starting job in 1955 to the fireballing left-handed rookie Herb Score. Score made Cleveland's Big Three starters a Big Four, with a 16-10 record and a league-leading 245 strikeouts. Houtteman served as a reliever and spot starter and won ten games.

The Houttemans' son, Jeff, was born December 29, not without drama. A friend, Detroit Lions football star Leon Hart, was visiting their home when Shelagh suddenly went into labor. The two men delivered the baby in the kitchen. Another daughter, Sharon, was born in 1959.

In 1956 Houtteman was Cleveland's forgotten man. He pitched only twenty-two times, mostly in relief. Kerby Farrell replaced Lopez as manager in 1957, and Houtteman immediately landed in his doghouse. Farrell reamed him out in front of his teammates after a poor performance in spring training. The Indians put him on the trading block but drew no serious offers, since other teams knew the club was desperate to get rid of him. In May he was sold to the Baltimore Orioles for a reported $20,000. *Cleveland News* sportswriter Hal Lebovitz called him "a pitcher of considerable promise but who somehow has yet to cash in on it."[11] He was still a few months short of his thirtieth birthday.

Houtteman was battered in four relief appearances with Baltimore and was sent down to Vancouver of the Pacific Coast League. The Orioles recalled him late in the season. He pitched the last of his 325 Major League games on September 22. His career record was 87-91 with a 4.14 ERA.

Baltimore released him just before Opening Day in 1958. He worked out with the Tigers and signed with their AAA farm club in Charleston, West Virginia. He pitched two straight shutouts in midseason and finished with a 3.25 ERA, but a 7-9 record, for the American Association pennant winner. The Kansas City Athletics gave him a spring tryout in 1959, but decided to go with young pitchers and released him, despite what one reporter called an impressive spring showing. He caught on with Portland in the Pacific Coast League, winning six games and losing nine with a 3.69 ERA. After the season, he quit baseball at age thirty-two.

Houtteman tried his hand at television that winter, reporting sports for a Detroit station. Then he started a new career as a sales executive with Paragon Steel in Detroit. He stayed with the company until he reached retirement age. In 1973 the *Detroit News* reported that he owned three Arabian show horses. He seldom attended ball games, but joined other former Tigers in 1999 at the final game in Tiger Stadium (known as Briggs Stadium in his day).

Art Houtteman died at his home in the Detroit suburb of Rochester Hills on May 6, 2003, of an apparent heart attack. He was seventy-five. Shelagh, their three children, and six grandchildren survived.

Chapter 55. **Bob Hooper**

Joseph Wancho

AGE	W	L	PCT	ERA	G	GS	GF	CG	SHO	SV	IP	H	BB	SO	HBP	WP
32	0	0	.000	4.93	17	0	8	0	0	2	34.2	39	16	12	1	0

It was the kind of trade that barely got noticed. A few lines buried within the stories of the daily newspaper and perhaps mentioned in the "transactions" column in the back of the sports section. During the season it might have been mentioned on the local sportscast, with some statistics mixed in. But the news that Cleveland had traded pitcher Dick Rozek and a Minor League player to the Philadelphia Athletics for pitcher Bob Hooper barely caused a ripple. It was, after all, December 19, 1952, and even baseball fans were more caught up in the hustle and bustle of the holiday season than the swap of a little-used pitcher (Rozek) and a Minor League infielder (Bobby Wilson) for a pitcher with a history of arm trouble (Hooper).

The Indians were in position to challenge the New York Yankees for the American League flag in 1953. Their staff had boasted three twenty-game winners in 1952 (Bob Lemon, Mike Garcia, and Early Wynn). Tribe skipper Al Lopez was forced at times to use the Big Three, as they had come to be known, in various relief roles. He was hoping that the addition of Hooper and perhaps Dave Hoskins would improve the team's second-line pitching.

The Indians found out soon enough how their new pitcher would fare. Cleveland opened the 1953 season in Detroit, winning the opener 6–0. In the second game, both teams were swinging the lumber, and the score was 9–8 in favor of the Indians at the end of five innings. Starting pitcher Mike Garcia gave up seven runs in four innings, and relief man Ted Wilks pitched a scoreless fifth inning.

Into the game came Hooper. He shut the door on the Tigers, surrendering just two hits over the final four frames. Hooper showed some moxie in

Bob Hooper—Hooper, who pitched mostly in relief for the Indians for two years, led the Athletics in wins in 1950 (15).

the eighth inning. The Tigers' Owen Friend hit a shallow fly ball to center field. Center fielder Larry Doby, second baseman Bobby Avila, and shortstop Ray Boone all converged on it. None of the three could make the play, and Friend, seeing that second base was unguarded, raced to the bag. Hooper hustled to the base and took the throw from Doby. He applied a backhand tag on Friend, erasing the runner for the third out. He was awarded the victory in relief. "See, I told you," said Hooper. "I told you that when the season started my arm would be good and strong. My arm feels fine. No pain at all."[1] Lopez, who had intended to use Hooper for only an inning or two, was elated with his new pitcher's early success. "It was one of those games that could have gotten away and have been a pain to remember later on," said Lopez. "We've had too many like that the last two years. Hooper landed this one."[2]

Robert Nelson Hooper was born on May 30, 1922, in Leamington, Ontario. It is unclear what circumstances brought Hooper to live in New Jersey with his uncle and aunt, Mr. and Mrs. William Herdman. The Herdmans lived in South Orange, where William made a living as a butcher.[3] Hooper attended grade school and then Columbia High School, both in South Orange.

Hooper was signed by the New York Giants out of high school. Over the next two years, he played for five teams in leagues ranging from Class D to A-1 (he played for four of the teams in 1942), with a 10-9 won-lost record. He served in the U.S. Army Air Corps from 1942 to 1945, training as a pilot.

After he was discharged from the service, Hooper returned to the Giants' farm system. He was unable to post a winning record until 1948, when he went 20-9 with a 2.45 earned run average at Jacksonville of the Class A South Atlantic League. After that breakout season, he was drafted by Detroit and was assigned to the Buffalo Bisons of the International League, where he went 19-3 in 1949, including an eleven-game winning streak as the Bisons, managed by Paul Richards, finished in first place but lost to Montreal in the playoff finals.

Hooper got a break when the Philadelphia Athletics purchased his contract after the season. Three of the starters on manager Connie Mack's mound corps were southpaws (Bobby Shantz, Lou Brissie, and Alex Kellner) and Mack was looking to even the rotation out with a right-hander. Not only did Hooper start twenty games in 1950, but he relieved in twenty-five others, earning him the nickname the Leamington Workhorse.

The Athletics were 52-102, finishing in last place in the American League. Of those 52 victories, 15 belonged to Hooper, who was the only Athletics pitcher to record double-digit wins. (Eleven of his victories came against second-division teams.) He also showed control problems, walking 91 in 170 innings while striking out 58 batters. It was a trend that would hamper him for most of his Major League career.

Hooper developed a sore arm in spring training in 1951 that was brought on by a pinched nerve. It became a yearly occurrence that he would develop arm trouble of some sort in camp after the off-season. The Athletics improved to 70-84 in 1951 under new manager Jimmy Dykes (Mack had retired), and Hooper was 12-10, lowering his walk total to 61 in 189 innings. He was a thorn in the side of Chicago and his old friend, White Sox manager Paul Richards, that season. He stopped Chicago's fourteen-game winning streak on June 2, scattering five hits and striking out three in the 5–1 win. On June 15 he stopped the Chisox again, halting their road winning streak at fifteen. This time Hooper went into extra innings in the 4–3 Athletics win. On July 15, with Chicago trailing league-leading Boston by one game, Hooper shut down the White Sox yet again. He surrendered one unearned run in a 3–1 victory. His three-run homer with two out in the top of the ninth backed his fine pitching performance.

"He helped me, I'll tell you," said mound mate Joe Coleman. "He taught me how to throw a slider, and he had a great one. It's thrown like you throw a football. You grip down on the outside of the ball and the ball slides across the plate. To the batter, it looks like a fastball, and then all of a sudden, it's gone."[4]

Hooper's twelve-victory season was the last in which he reached double digits in the win column. He suffered constant shoulder and arm injuries that earned him more innings coming out of the bullpen than as a starter. "Towards the end of his career he had shoulder problems," said Joe Coleman. "That bothered him a lot. It's what they call rotator cuff today. They didn't have a cure at that time. Today they can take care of it in no time."[5]

After he was traded to Cleveland, Hooper was given cortisone shots that relieved his pain for a brief time. But the Indians were hoping Hooper would give them some productive innings in relief, as their starting rotation was not only set, it was supreme. "Those guys won 20 games a year. The only time you could pitch for them was in doubleheader," said outfielder Barney McCosky, a teammate of Hooper's in both Cleveland and Philadelphia.[6]

In 1953 Cleveland finished second to New York for the third consecutive year, Hooper contributing five victories, all in relief. The next season the Indians finally knocked down the Yankees' door, breaking through with a then record 111 victories (43 losses) and winning the American League pennant. Hooper appeared in seventeen games but did not record a decision. He was seeing less time with the emergence of Don Mossi and Ray Narleski getting regular calls from the bullpen by manager Lopez. Nor did he make an appearance in the World Series against the Giants, who swept Cleveland in four games.

Cincinnati purchased Hooper's contract just before the 1955 season. "Both Birdie (Tebbetts) and I think Hooper's worth the gamble," said Reds general manager Gabe Paul. "Birdie, you know, played on the same club with him and knows what to do."[7] But Hooper was ineffective for the Reds. He made his last Major League appearance on May 14 in relief against the Brooklyn Dodgers. He surrendered six hits, three walks, and seven runs in just two-thirds of an inning. His career record was 40-41 with an ERA of 4.80.

Meanwhile, Hooper's old friend Paul Richards had been named general manager in Baltimore in an effort to right the Orioles' losing ways. Richards was given complete control of the baseball operations, and he hired Hooper to manage in the Minor Leagues. From 1957 to 1960, Hooper managed Baltimore farm teams in the lower Minors.

After his days were done on the diamond, Hooper returned to New Jersey. During his playing days he had taken courses at the Panzer College of Physical Education. He received a bachelor's degree in education from Panzer, which has since merged with Montclair State University. Hooper taught physical education at the Washington School in New Brunswick and at New Brunswick High School until he retired in 1979.

Hooper died on March 17, 1980, after a heart attack. He was survived by his wife, Helen Coyle Hooper, and their daughter, Barbara.

Joseph Wancho

September 1—New York—YANKEES WHIP INDI-ANS, TRAIL BY 4½—Eddie Lopat raises his record to 12-4. Yogi Berra goes 3 for 4, with two RBIS and two runs scored. Eddie Robinson's pinch-hit double plates two in the fourth inning.

September 2—New York—INDIANS LOSE, 3–2—The Yankees score all three runs in the sixth inning. Mickey Mantle slams a solo shot. Two errors by Vic Wertz at first base open the door for the other two runs. Bob Lemon surrenders one earned run and is tagged with the loss. Whitey Ford K's five as his record improves to 16-7. More than 141,000 see the three-game set at Yankee Stadium. The Indians' lead shrinks to three and a half games.

September 3—Chicago—DOBY HITS HOMER AS INDIANS EDGE CHICAGO, 3 TO 2—Larry Doby goes 3 for 5, with two RBIS, and slugs his thirtieth homer. Bob Feller surrenders one earned run and wins his twelfth game.

September 4—Chicago—WHITE SOX TALLY 5 UNEARNED RUNS—George Kell hits a homer and drives in two runs. Minnie Minoso and Ed McGhee each collect two RBIS to lead the Chi-sox to an 8–5 win. The White Sox score five runs in the sixth inning, courtesy of two Tribe errors (Bill Glynn, Bobby Avila). Early Wynn, who gives up two earned runs, is the tough-luck loser. Jack Harshman wins his fourteenth.

September 5—Chicago—TRIBE WINS, 8–2, RAISES LEAD TO 4½—Bobby Avila goes 4 for 5 with two RBIS. Vic Wertz smacks a two-run shot and scores twice. Dave Philley knocks in two RBIS.

Narleski pitches two and two-thirds innings of relief for the win, whiffing five.

September 6—Baltimore—INDIANS SPLIT WITH ORIOLES, RETAIN LEAD OF 4½ GAMES—Bob Lemon goes the distance in Cleveland's 6–1 win, capturing his twenty-first victory. Lemon also triples and scores a run. Al Smith goes 4 for 5 with an RBI and scores three runs. Dave Philley goes 2 for 4 with an RBI. The Orioles win the nightcap, 3–2 in ten innings. Dick Kryhoski's single to left field scores Bob Chakales with the winning run. Cleveland wins nineteen of its twenty-two games against Baltimore this season.

September 8—Cleveland—WYNN HURLS 20TH TRIUMPH, 5–2, OVER A'S—Early Wynn goes the distance for his twentieth win. Vic Wertz homers. Bobby Avila, Larry Doby, and Al Rosen all collect an RBI.

September 9—Cleveland—INDIANS TAKE 5½-GAME LEAD IN 100TH VICTORY—A bases-loaded walk to Hal Naragon scores pinch runner Dave Hoskins for the 4–3 win in the bottom of the eleventh inning. Al Rosen goes 3 for 5 and scores a run. Dave Pope homers. Hal Newhouser gets the win. Cleveland wins eighteen of twenty-two from Philadelphia this season.

September 10—Cleveland—INDIANS BEAT RED SOX, 4–2, GARCIA NAILS 17TH VICTORY—Mike Garcia goes the distance to run record to 17-8, fanning six Red Sox. Jim Hegan goes 2 for 3 with an RBI, scores two runs, and hits a solo shot. Vic Wertz, Larry Doby, and Bobby Avila tally an RBI apiece.

September 11—Cleveland—INDIANS WIN NO. 102, HIKE LEAD TO 6½—Art Houtteman blanks the Red Sox for his fifteenth win, 3–0. Vic Wertz homers. Al Rosen and Bobby Avila each knock in a run. The Yankees drop an extra-inning affair to Chicago, to drop six and a half back. Cleveland wins twenty of twenty-two games against Boston this season.

September 12—Cleveland—86,563 SEE INDIANS SWEEP TWO—Cleveland takes double dip from the Yankees before record crowd. The Indians score two in the bottom of the seventh inning and one in the bottom of eighth inning to pull ahead in the first game. Al Rosen goes 2 for 3, 2 RBIS. Lemon pitches nine innings, striking out five for his twenty-second win, a 4–1 victory. Cleveland scores all three runs in the fifth inning of the second game. Wally Westlake knocks in two runs with a double. Early Wynn whiffs twelve Yanks for his twenty-first win and a sweep of New York, 3–2. The Tribe extends lead to eight and a half games over the Yankees.

September 14—Cleveland—INDIANS WIN 105TH, SCORE 4 IN FIRST TO JAR NATS, 4–2—Mike Garcia notches his eighteenth win, while Ray Narleski earns his eleventh save. The Indians score all four runs in the first frame. Wally Westlake, George Strickland, Hank Majeski and Dave Pope all drive in a run.

Chapter 57. **Ken Coleman**

Curt Smith

The 1966 Boston Red Sox finished ninth. The next year's 100-to-1 team wrote "one of baseball's great rags-to-riches stories," said the *New York Times*'s Joseph Durso, by waving a last-day pennant. Pinching himself, Ken Coleman did not believe it. In the Boston clubhouse, garbed in champagne, he told a listener, "This is, if I may add a personal note, the greatest thrill of my life." In New England, no pennant race will ever rival The Impossible Dream. But half a country away, many recall Coleman in a different light: as the mid-century voice of Bob Feller and Rocky Colavito and Otto Graham and Jim Brown in Cleveland's huge lakefront bowl.

For most of the two decades after World War II, Ken Coleman embodied Ohio's two major sports. He telecast the 1954–63 baseball Indians, including a then American League record 111-43 titlist. From 1952 to 1965, he broadcast radio's, and then TV's, National Football League Browns, then left for Boston. All heard a voice silken and restrained, which never split an infinitive or dangled a participle—"a beautiful horn," said Boston Bruins announcer Bob Wilson, "and, oh, Ken played it well."

Ken's score began on April 22, 1925, in Quincy, a Boston suburb fifteen minutes from Fenway Park and his first icon, Jimmie Foxx. At age twelve, a BB-gun accident cost him an eye, and Coleman traded heroes: Double X for the Braves' and Red Sox's first regular broadcaster, Fred Hoey. From 1926 to 1938, Hoey carried each team through New England: "the first to work on a network [Yankee, also Colonial] covering the game, giving the play-by-play of the home games of both Boston clubs," said *The Sporting News.* "He has one of the biggest daily fol-

Ken Coleman—A fan favorite in Cleveland for his play-by-play calling of the Indians and Cleveland Browns. (National Baseball Hall of Fame Library, Cooperstown, New York)

lowings of any announcer in the country because of the large number of stations served."

To millions, Hoey *meant* Boston's two-headed baseball Janus. He forged a style later followed by the Red Sox' Curt Gowdy via Coleman and Ned Martin to the twenty-first century's Joe Castiglione: respect and understatement over schlock, kitsch, and shtick. "Because of a general attitude toward sports and listening habits developed from certain announcers, different regions are receptive to varying styles," said *TSN*'s Jack Craig. Coleman brought the same style to Ohio: "Just the facts, ma'am" trumped a wild and crazy guy.

Coleman's father, William, alternately a military man and a night watchman, died of a heart attack in Ken's high-school senior year. (His mother, Frances, was a housewife.) After graduation, the son, eighteen, joined the army in 1943, served in Burma, and aired Indian rugby, cricket, and soccer on Armed Forces Radio, saying, "*You* try performing with twelve thousand troops listening." Released, he studied oratory at Curry College outside Boston, worked at a 250-watt Worcester radio station, and later aired golf, bowling, basketball; Boston University, Ohio State, and Harvard football; and Vermont's Northern Baseball League, fighting the "urge to be Hoey, to . . . especially [use] his phrase, 'He throws to first and gets his man!'"

In the film *On the Waterfront*, Marlon Brando mourned, "I coulda been a contender." In 1952 Coleman and Lindsey Nelson contended for Cleveland Browns radio play-by-play. "We were the finalists," Ken said. "They didn't want a native, but a fresh face from outside Ohio." Out of the blue, Nelson, a Tennessean, took a job with NBC. Coleman took the Browns' 125-station network—his port the 78,000-seat Municipal Stadium on Cleveland's North Rim.

"The field was far away, but you were on the roof, looking down, so the view was beautiful," Coleman said, likening it to watching a chess match. Paul Brown was the Browns' namesake, founder, and "the greatest coach of all time," Ken felt. He invented the draw play, was first to hire a full-time coaching staff, and sired the two-minute drill. Quarterback Otto Graham took Cleveland to ten straight title games, throwing "long and feathery or short and hard—whatever was necessary." The Browns regularly led the NFL in attendance, evoking much to cheer: In fourteen years, Coleman aired seven champions, did eight network title and two College All-Star games, and called each pro touchdown (126)

by the man who ran the football better than anyone has, or is ever likely to, Jimmy Brown.

One Sunday: "He is gone for the score! Eighty yards and the place is going crazy!" Coleman bayed. Another: "Jim Brown trying the left side! And Jim Brown is running! Getting his blockers and coming down the *right* side!" Of a screen pass, "At the 20, 30, 40, 45, still going, Jim Brown, one of the greatest runs we've ever seen him make! It's a touchdown: an 83-yard play!" A rival said, "Brown says he isn't Superman. What he means is that Superman isn't Jim Brown." Jack Buck liked No. 32's Boswell: "People [came to] identify Coleman with [Red Sox] baseball, but he's the best football announcer I ever heard."

Brown played professionally from 1957 to 1965, Coleman the only person, he said, to see the fullback's every game. "Naturally, you remember the long runs," he said. "But what stands out is what Jim'd do with five minutes left, the Browns up by seven, have the ball, and Brown runs out the clock. He'd go four, then six, 14. Eighty thousand in Cleveland [a.k.a. Municipal] Stadium knew he'd get it." The visiting team did, too, some thinking that the end justified the means. One Sunday Cleveland beat the New York Giants. After the game Coleman observed that Brown's face around his eyes was bloated. "Jim, I couldn't get over how you looked—what's going on?" Ken later asked.

"When we got down into the dirt part of the infield, some of the Giant linemen threw dirt into my eyes," Brown said. "They wanted to get me mad enough to get in a fight and thrown out of a game, but I wouldn't go for it."

Coleman stared.

Brown, staring back: "I'll tell ya one thing. If it ever happens again, I'm going to kill 'em—a one-time shot. Never again will anybody go after my eyes." No one did, said Coleman, who helped the Browns turn *en famille*.

Son Casey became a summer training camp water boy, later a Cleveland sportscaster: WTAM morning host; WJM four-time Emmy sports anchor; Browns play-by-play; and Indians host, ending each show, "I'm rounding third and heading home." In Orville, Ohio, Bobby Knight and his father *locked* their house each Sunday when the Browns were televised—"priorities," Ken laughed. Such fidelity challenged the Indians when Coleman joined them in 1954, telecasting each away game on WXEL, Channel 8, by sponsor Carling Brewing Company, in a time when "one company could afford to sponsor most, if not all, your coverage."

Coleman broadcast when Chicago's Jack Brickhouse sold Hamm's Beer; Philadelphia's Byrum Saam, Phillies cigars; and the Yankees' Mel Allen, Ballantine Beer and White Owl cigars. In Cleveland, Carling's "Mabel, Black Label" beer outpitched them all. Later, Ken recalled how in Ohio people would still "come up and say to me, 'Hey, Mabel!'" He also grasped how baseball and football were separate but equal. "Both popular, but you can't do them the same. With football you spend the whole week preparing. In baseball, you're immersed in it day in and out." Rhythm differed, too. Coleman's football delivery reflected "22 people in motion at the same time." Baseball's was more conversational. Ken neither screamed nor condescended, defined TV as picture plus action, and believed in "not telling the audience what it already saw."

Unlike most of his Indians suzerainty, there was a lot to see in 1954. Improbably, Coleman aired it with Hoey's successor, the 1940–42 and 1946–50 Red Sox announcer. "I listened growing up after Fred left," Ken said. "Jim [Britt] seemed so erudite—of all the broadcasters I've heard, with the greatest command of language"—lyric, musical, unpredictable, but not hyperbolic: as Huston Horn wrote of Mel Allen, an "indefatigable hinged-in-the-middle tongue." Many thought Britt savvy. Some felt him snooty, panning the average Joe.

Britt telecast the 1954–57 Indians with Coleman by necessity, not necessarily choice. By 1950 Narragansett Beer had sponsored each Hub team since

1945 on WHDH. Late that year it inked a Braves-only pact on WNAC's Yankee Network, making Britt pick one club or the other. Incredibly, Jim chose the Braves over Ted Williams's Red Sox—said Coleman, "a terrible misjudgment as to the relative popularity of the teams." Sox owner Tom Yawkey countered—"He wanted to do this anyway," said Ken—by making *all*, not just home, coverage *live*, naming Curt Gowdy Britt's successor.

Britt "never recovered from what he'd done to himself," said Coleman. In 1953 the Braves absconded for Milwaukee, deserting Jim. "When they left, there was *nothing* left for Britt. He stumbled around a year, then came to Cleveland"—Jim refusing to go along to get along.

Local dialect pronounced the name of 1950s Indians All-Star second baseman Bobby *Ah-VEE-la*. Britt preferred *AH-vee-la*. "We got every kind of calls and letters," said Coleman. "People didn't like it."

Carling Brewing's chairman said, "You know, Jim, in view of the local colloquialism, we should probably call him *Ah-VEE-la*, like most fans want."

The chairman's name was Ian Bowie, as in *row*. Britt said, "All right with me, Mr. Bowie," as in *boo*.

In 1958 Britt returned to WHDH "haunted by the Red Sox' 'what if,'" said Hub broadcaster Leo Egan. Axed again, Britt moved to Detroit, St. Petersburg, and Sarasota, braving a divorce, unemployment, and arrests for drunkenness. He died in 1980, less tragic than forgotten, at home in Monterey, California. "In truth," Ray Fitzgerald wrote, "life had turned its back on him a long time ago." Coleman called himself "different in many ways" from Britt. "Jim was disputatious, mercurial. I guess I was more serene. But we had this in common. Our first year we win a league record 111 games, then afterward not much to tell."

In 1954 Douglass Wallop wrote *The Year the Yankees Lost the Pennant.* Cleveland led the American League in earned run average (2.78) and home runs (156). Bob Lemon, Feller, Mike Garcia, and Early Wynn went 78-29. Larry Doby's greatest year

(32 homers and 126 RBIs) helped. Municipal Stadium even housed the All-Star Game. Al Rosen added two homers and five RBIs. Doby, pinch-hitting, homered. "The day [11-9 final], crowd [68,751], and hitting [31 hits off 13 pitchers] had everything," said Coleman. "Like the year."

In August, Cleveland won an AL-record-tying twenty-six games. On September 12, a big-league-record 86,587 jammed the bowl, Lemon and Wynn beating New York, 3–2 and 4–1. Each year but 1954, the 1951–56 Indians placed second to the Yanks. "All the frustration climaxed on the Yankees' train back to New York City," said Allen. "Stengel was heckled by drunks on platforms in Pennsylvania and Buffalo. Casey never forgot it to the last day of his life." The Indians clinched on September 18. On the 25th they flayed Detroit, 11–1, for symmetrical victory 111, topping Murderers' Row's 110. The record lasted till New York's 114-48 in 1998. The Pinstripes would not go away.

Audio preserves Ken's pace, formality, and detail. "Larry Doby, born in South Carolina, but known across the country." "Bobby Avila, who may win the batting title [he did, at .341], has already won the league's respect [189 hits didn't hurt]." "Early Wynn, a Renaissance man off the mound [pilot and investor], bare-knuckled on it." "Another great play by the magic wand [George Strickland at shortstop]!" "The Big Bear [Mike Garcia] fans a second straight hitter." "Al Lopez, the thinking man's manager." Listening, you wonder how the Tribe lost the World Series, let alone each game.

Walter Alston was asked what he learned in twenty-two years as a Dodgers manager. "You make out your lineup card, and strange things happen." What was stranger than the 1954 World Series? "We had this 'unstoppable this, Hall of Fame pitching that,'" said Ken. The Giants seemed mismatched until the eighth inning of the Series opener: one out, two on, two-all. The Polo Grounds twinned a vast center field (483 feet) and pygmy right (257). New York's Don Liddle relieved Sal Maglie, where-upon Vic Wertz hit deep to center, prompting Willie Mays to race with his back toward the plate. "I don't want to compare 'em," Mays mused of his play, over the shoulder, to preserve the tie. "I just want to catch 'em."

Earlier, Giants manager Leo Durocher had called utilityman Dusty Rhodes "useless." Mays and Hank Thompson now walked to start the tenth. Rhodes pinch-drove a fly 200 feet shorter than Wertz's down the right-field line. In almost any other park, Wertz's out goes deep. Rhodes's pop fly dies. Instead, Dusty struck the seats: 5–2. Next day Rhodes again homered: New York, 3–1. In Cleveland, New York completed the sweep, 6–2 and 7–4; thousands stood behind the wire inner fence. Rhodes had four hits and seven RBIs. Leo now thought him useful. "In many ways," said Coleman, softly, "the franchise was never quite the same."

Baseball forbids local-team Series TV coverage to protect network exclusivity. Thus, Coleman watched 1954's by TV or from the stands. He felt the opener a metaphor for baseball's DNA—anticipation. "Anything can happen, and here did—a ridiculously short homer, outrageously long out." For much of the decade the Tribe anticipated another Series, but kept finishing behind New York. One fan put skipper Lopez's picture in her kitchen. "Lopez, you do as I tell you, or I'll use this on your head," she said, bashing Al's photo with a rolling pin. In his quiet way, Coleman grew as stymied.

"For a long time I think we had as much talent," he remembered. "The difference is that in September the Yankees'd buy or trade for a veteran who put them over. We were so close year after year. Then, invariably, an unhappy end." In 1956 Herb Score won twenty games. On May 7, 1957, Gil McDougald's liner careened off Score's right eye. The paladin was never again a star. Rocky Colavito was a slow but fetching slugger. In 1959 the Rock hit forty-two homers, Ken not yet having coined "They usually show movies on a flight like that." Tito Francona thumped .363. Cal McLish won nineteen games.

The Tribe vied till losing a four-game August series to Chicago, Cleveland's last contention until 1995. In 1960 general manager Frank Lane traded Colavito for Detroit batting titlist Harvey Kuenn. "I'm getting steak for hamburger," he bragged. Few said well-done of dealing Cleveland's greatest pinup since Lou Boudreau.

The 1960–67 Tribe teams never drew a million people, missed the pennant by fewer than fifteen games, or hinted that faith might last past June. Hating the bogus, Coleman found humor in reverse. One night, the now Tiger Colavito retreated to the wall. "Back goes Wally against the rock," Coleman said, then: "For those of you interested in statistics, that was my 11th fluff of the year. It puts me in third place in the American League." The '48ers had drawn a record 2,620,627. "Then the Browns started winning, the Indians weren't, and the crowds weren't there," Ken said. As bad, "twenty thousand in Municipal seemed like ten people." Once 15,000 people attended a Yankees game. Cleveland hosted the 1963 All-Star Game, just 44,160 visiting. Tribe attendance fell to 562,507. Ghosts draped the spectral air, short foul lines, and bleachers in another state.

Ironically, only radio seemed immune. After 1954, TV's Coleman did as few as twenty-five games and as many as fifty-seven a year, mostly on weekends or at night. After Britt, he partnered with Bill McColgan (1958–60), Harry Jones (1961), and Bob Neal (1961–62), sponsored by Carling, Standard Oil, Society National Bank, and Richman Bros., among others. Radio's Jimmy Dudley, by contrast, did every game: 154 a year before 1961, then 162. By 1957 he had forged a huge fifty-two-outlet network, including six in the Yankees' Western New York and fifteen in the Pirates' Western Pennsylvania. Increasingly, Dudley became interest's life-preserver—"So long and good, ya heah"—his voice stirring anyone who loved a story told with beauty and panache.

"Dudley had an advantage Ken didn't," said Joe Castiglione, who aired the 1979 and 1982 Indians.

"Radio is an anecdotal-telling medium. TV is not." Jimmy also had an oil and water challenge: 1957–61 partner Neal. Dudley was soft, quick, and fairly sang even ads: "Garfield-1, 2-3, 2-3," of an aluminum siding firm. Neal was loud, brash, and hated being number two. They never talked on the air, or off. Point: Neal blocked Dudley's view of a game by raising a briefcase lid on the countertop. Counterpoint: Jimmy cracked peanuts into a mike as Bob did play-by-play. Neal switched to TV by necessity—said Dudley, "We'd have killed each other otherwise"—proving that Coleman could get along with anyone. "Ken and Jimmy were consolation," said Castiglione, "something to hang on to"—Arcturus or Cassiopeia in Cleveland's stormy sky.

In 1964 Ken left the Indians to focus full time on football, his timing still sure: that December the Browns won the NFL championship, blanking Baltimore, 27–0. His last Browns broadcast was Jim Brown's farewell—also Ken's eighth pro football title game: Green Bay 23, Cleveland 12—in January 1966. Brown retired to Hollywood. At his peak as an institution, Coleman revisited the points of his past. Replacing Gowdy, the Red Sox chose the Quincy scion, who told himself, "You lucky stiff, going back to my roots, taking Britt's and Hoey's job."

In March 1966 Coleman was introduced at a press conference as the Red Sox's new prosopopeia. Boston finished ninth. Incredibly, 1967 made baseball cool again, revived the Boston American League Baseball Company, and filled Fenway Park with nightly peals. In July the Sox forged a ten-game road winning streak, 10,000 people waiting at Logan Airport to greet the team upon return. As special were pilots from the Hub to Nova Scotia tracing a late-season West Coast game by light in homes below. "It is late on a late-summer night in 1967," wrote the *Herald*'s Kevin Convey. "The house is dark except for the flashlight beside my bed. It is quiet except for my transistor, in a whisper. Ken Coleman didn't just call baseball games. He called my summers."

On August 13, two and a half games bunched five teams. By September 30, Minnesota led the Red Sox by one game with two left at Fenway. Stores closed. Churches opened. All knew the truth and consequences. Boston hit in the two-all sixth. "And [George] Scott hits one deep into center field! This one is back! This one is gone!" Ken cried. Sox: 6–4. Next day they encored, 5–3. At a minimum, Boston had forced a playoff for its first pennant since 1946.

"[Afterward] the players came into the clubhouse. Some were crying, some yelling, and I was trying to interview," Coleman said. A radio aired in the background. Detroit could force the playoff by taking a doubleheader against California. Instead, it lost Game Two, 8–5. The *Boston Record American* cover blared "CHAMPS!" and a drawing of two red socks. Jim Lonborg went 22-9. Carl Yastrzemski transcended myth: Triple Crown/MVP 44 homers, 121 RBIs, and .326. To Coleman's death, 1967 cried *gotcha* to Ken's heart. "People talk about upsets," he said. "They're child's play compared to this."

Later, Convey recalled that year—and the flashlight beside his bed. "There will be other summers. And I will listen to other announcers. But I will never stop hearing Ken Coleman." He and Gowdy used another medium to televise each NBC World Series game in Boston. "Talk about coming full circle," Coleman said of sharing the Fall Classic with his predecessor. Another graced the 1970s. In 1972 Ken moved solely to Sox TV. Dismissed in late 1974, he returned to Ohio to televise the Reds. Then, in 1979, released from a final year at Cincinnati, Coleman again took the Logan Airport shuttle to Fenway, many expecting him to man Red Sox video. Instead, he did radio through 1989.

"Kinder, gentler" before George H. W. Bush coined the term, Coleman encouraged 1980–82 partner Jon Miller to use his skill at mimicry: "I think you have something not many people have, and you should do it on the air." Ken called the end of professional baseball's longest game (1981, Rochester-Pawtucket); Yaz's final game (1983); and

Roger Clemens's then single-game strikeout record (20, 1986). He lunched with Ronald Reagan in the White House; used colleague Ned Martin's Walkman to mime Frank Sinatra on a flight; and called Bill Buckner's muff of Mookie Wilson's grounder, refusing to hear his broadcast for two years. As executive director of the Sox official charity, the Jimmy Fund, Coleman helped the Children's Cancer Research Foundation—now the Dana-Farber Cancer Institute.

By 1989, he hosted radio's *Ken's Corner* of poetry and inspiration, had founded the BoSox Club, and was an eight-time Ohio Sportscaster of the Year and a twelve-time American Federation of Television and Radio Artists honoree. He also had a heart attack, soon announcing his retirement, Fenway's TV booth later put in his name. That year future Hall of Fame president Jeff Idelson was a Red Sox booth statistician intern. He left the Fens grasping why Voices become a beach bud, mountain messenger, and pillow pal: "A radio broadcaster has to remind you of sitting around a fire, hearing tales." Ken did.

On October 1, 1989, Coleman ended his final game by thanking "the fans of New England for their support, their friendship, their patience and loyalty over the years," and for the Jimmy Fund, "which has been a most meaningful part of my professional life." He concluded: "This is Ken Coleman, rounding third and heading home." Retired, he wrote variants of "Take Me Out to the Ballgame," sung by Broadway's and future Yankees' Voice Suzyn Waldman: "And if I can't actually be there, then give me the action by Curt, Ned, and Ken." Ken finished a fifth book—his favorite, *The Impossible Dream*—and again did Harvard football, which recalled 1968's last-quarter Crimson miracle versus Yale—"This, of course," Coleman had said, "is *The* Play of *The* Game"—tying the score with seven seconds left. Half an hour later the student *Crimson* headlined: "Harvard Wins, 29 to 29."

In 2000, the man who never confused his tenses, ended a sentence with a preposition, or patronized his audience made the Red Sox Hall of Fame. Coleman died on August 21, 2003, at seventy-eight, leaving sons Casey, deceased in 2006 of pancreatic cancer, and William; daughters Kerry, Susan, and Kathleen; and former wife Ellen. Upon Ken's death, a tear fell in Ohio.

Chapter 58. Jim Britt

Mort Bloomberg

Jim Britt was the radio and television voice of both the Boston Braves and the Boston Red Sox in 1948, an enviable position he held from 1939 until the Red Sox began to broadcast road games as well as home games and therefore required a full-time broadcaster of their own.

In an era when several of the major radio stations in Boston competed nightly for the attention of sports fans, the most listened-to program on the air was "Jim Britt's Sports Roundup" from 6:15 to 6:30 on WNAC. It consisted of a mix of straight reporting, commentary, and in-studio interviews with newsmakers, and finished up with Jim's signature expression at the end of his program, "Remember, if you can't take part in a sport, be one anyway, will ya."[1] From today's vantage point, that tagline sounds cornball, but in the pre-television era it helped accelerate him into Boston's number one sports personality on the air in the 1940s.

Jim Britt was born in San Francisco in 1911. The well-to-do family (his father was chairman of the board of the Burroughs Corporation) moved to Detroit when Jim was eleven. Jim received a bachelor of arts degree from the University of Detroit (where his brother, a priest, would later become president), majoring in English and philosophy with a co-minor in speech and history. After graduation, he earned a law degree at the University of Southern California but chose not to take the bar exam. Always interested in speech, singing, and sports, he returned to Detroit to teach public speaking and debating in local high schools.

His entry into radio was accidental, not in one of the many ways open to those interested in media jobs today. He accepted a dare from the univer-sity's football coach to become better behind the mike than the current announcer, who Britt thought was horrendous and had declared emphatically as much to the coach.

Full-time radio work began in 1935 with Notre Dame football and basketball games. Then came two years of Buffalo Bisons baseball doing home games live and road games via telegraphic recreation with Leo Egan. A native Buffalonian, Egan came to Boston after the 1938 hurricane. He wrote for the *Boston Herald* and broadcast baseball and football for thirty years (many pigskin clashes being from atop Harvard Stadium). Ironically, Leo was the person who persuaded Jim to audition for an opening as sports director with WNAC and its Yankee Network. This network was a federation of radio stations from Maine to Connecticut and had nothing to do with the Bronx Bombers.

Britt got the job on November 10, 1939, and became Frankie Frisch's replacement as the voice of New England baseball. During his one year at the mike, Frisch had proven unable to fill the shoes of immensely popular local broadcast legend Fred Hoey and eagerly accepted the chance to return to the diamond as manager of the Pittsburgh Pirates.

Britt began to broadcast home games of the Braves and Red Sox in 1940 with Tom Hussey as his sidekick. Few other baseball announcers have covered two teams at the same time. Their partnership continued until the 1942 All-Star break when Britt received his induction notice from the navy. He served as an intelligence officer in the Pacific for the next three and a half years, an assignment not without risk. At one point, the bomber in which he was flying suffered a midair collision with another American aircraft. Britt was one of eight survivors.

Britt's return to civilian life allowed him to go back to cover Boston baseball games, now available on WHDH. Listeners welcomed the intelligent, smooth, and fluent sound of his voice again because play-by-play announcers assigned by the station in his absence were just not in his league. Reflecting back to when he was thirteen years old, *Sporting News* columnist Wells Twombly reminisced, "Jim Britt . . . makes baseball sound better than red-haired girls with freckles."[2] Ken Coleman, who broadcast for Boston in later years, recalled it as a treat when Britt returned to the booth. "There's no doubt in my mind that of all the broadcasters I've ever heard, and this includes network newspeople, no one had more of a command of the English language than Jim."[3]

Both Twombly and Coleman succeed in putting into words exactly what my own sentiments were. Jim Britt represented Braves baseball for me in the late '40s and early '50s. Thanks to him, I became such a devoted fan of the team that their move to Milwaukee in 1953 was like a death in the family. I still have vivid memories of hiding my portable radio underneath the covers at night listening to him describe yet another heroic comeback staged by the Braves during their victorious pennant chase of 1948. The losses piled up progressively from 1949 to 1952, but the drama in his voice always gave me fresh hope that the outcome of tomorrow's contest would be better.

Just a few months before what would become the final season of National League baseball in Boston, I wrote to Britt asking how best to pursue my lifelong dream. He took time from what must have been a busy schedule to offer me this advice during my sophomore year in high school: "Most important for either a sports broadcasting or sports writing career—get a good, well-rounded education. Go to college, if you can. There's no possible substitute. Then make the rounds of the various small radio stations and/or newspapers to get a job. It may be

hard to break in. But the job is interesting and well worth all the time and trouble to get started. Good luck in whatever you do, wherever you go."[4]

Boston's first baseball telecast occurred on June 15, 1948, with Britt and Hussey calling a contest between the Braves and the Cubs on Massachusetts' pioneer television station, WBZ-TV. Channel 4, as it was known then, had transmitted its inaugural program—a fifteen-minute newscast—a scant week before this historic event from Braves Field.

As the new medium grew, more games on the Braves (and soon the Red Sox) schedule were carried via television. The original broadcasting tandem remained intact through 1950, although Leo Egan and Bump Hadley also appeared from time to time. Hadley came from Lynn, Massachusetts, and capped a sixteen-year pitching career with three World Series appearances for the New York Yankees in the late 1930s. His legacy forever will be tied to fracturing Mickey Cochrane's skull with an errant pitch that ended the future Hall of Famer's career. Years after this incident, Bump's trademark closing to his popular sports show on WBZ was "Heads up and keep pitching."[5]

When Tom Yawkey announced that his ball club planned to air road games in 1951, Britt could no longer broadcast for both the Braves and the Red Sox. He was given his option as to which team to broadcast. His decision to go with the Braves was criticized by many. Even Britt second-guessed himself. However, in hindsight it arguably was not a bad choice given the remarkable success the Braves would enjoy later in the '50s and the hard times the Red Sox had during the same period.

Did Jim evaluate the young talent in the Braves' farm system in 1950 (Mathews, Logan, Buhl, Bruton, Conley) and foresee that they would benefit the team in Boston over the next decade while the Red Sox had stars who were aging (Williams, DiMaggio, Doerr, Pesky, Stephens), making the American League outfit more likely to suffer decline? I think he did and, more important, there were upcoming

MORT BLOOMBERG

threats to Britt's physical and psychological well-being that renders the Braves versus Red Sox dilemma inconsequential.

The counterview is that the poor judgment he exercised might have been somewhat attributable to the erosion in his health, making the issue vital and far from inconsequential. Without knowing either Britt's rationale to stick with Boston's National League entry or what the aftermath would have been had he chosen the Red Sox, there is no way to tell for sure.

The Red Sox hired Curt Gowdy, who at the time was Mel Allen's junior partner with the Yankees, and retained Tom Hussey. With Narragansett Brewery as their chief sponsor ("Hi neighbor, have a 'Gansett"[6]), they continued to carry their games on WHDH, where they stayed until 1975.

As for the Braves, their 154-game schedule moved to WNAC and was sponsored by Ballantine (remember the three rings?). Britt's backup during the Tribe's final two seasons in the Hub was Les Smith, a journeyman news and special features host at the station. Their sister station, Channel 7, showed home games periodically. The Braves broadcast duo was joined there by an always unintentionally amusing and sometimes seemingly inebriated Bump Hadley. Bump was that generation's answer to Ralph Kiner with gaffes like "that ball is going, going . . . and caught by Sam Jethroe in short center field."[7] This is not to say that Britt was without his own shortcomings. Leo Egan saw Britt as "sort of a Felix Unger type—quirksome, picky."[8] He remembers once when three times in the same game Britt miscalled fly balls as home runs. Egan characterized Britt as "very professional, very difficult. But, God, he was articulate."[9]

Britt was the first broadcaster associated with a local children's cancer charity adopted by the Braves known as the Jimmy Fund, benefiting the Children's Cancer Research Foundation (now Dana-Farber Cancer Institute). His tireless work to help eliminate childhood cancer established a tradition among Boston broadcasters that is followed to this day. Britt's future broadcasting colleague in Cleveland, Ken Coleman, became an especially avid advocate for the Jimmy Fund upon his return to Boston. Ken later served as executive director of the Jimmy Fund from 1978 to 1984. Current Sox play-by-play man Joe Castiglione has carried on in the tradition as a spokesman for the Jimmy Fund since first partnering with Coleman in the mid-1980s, as has Joe's former protégé Uri Berenguer-Ramos, the Spanish radio voice of the club. A cancer survivor and former Dana-Farber patient, Uri knows the importance of the Sox–Jimmy Fund partnership better than anyone.

The size of Britt's audience increased in scope as he did the 1946, 1948, and 1950 World Series on radio; the 1949, 1950, and 1951 Series on television; the first nationally televised football game in 1949; seven All-Star baseball games; and several major college football bowl games during this time span. But his stardom fell as quickly as it rose, mirroring the fortunes of the team with which he was affiliated most closely during the postwar era before its abrupt shift to Milwaukee. Since the newly transplanted Braves wanted homegrown talent behind the mike, the Triple-A Milwaukee Brewers' Earl Gillespie got the nod over Britt. After a year's involuntary sabbatical, Jim joined forces with Ken Coleman to do Indians telecasts for the next four years, beginning with Cleveland's triumphant march to the pennant in 1954.

Then began a peripatetic spiral downward for the voice of three teams that earned the right to play in the World Series: 1946 Red Sox, 1948 Boston Braves, and 1954 Indians. It was back to Boston as a news anchor and bowling program host prior to being fired by WHDH-TV. Drinking problems, which led to arrest more than once, and a divorce took their toll, especially when these incidents were splashed across the front page of the *Boston Daily Record* tabloid. Most telling was an eye injury that ended his sportscasting career.

Progressively longer periods of unemployment ensued. He drifted from Boston to Detroit to St. Petersburg to Sarasota and finally to Monterey, California, where he was found dead in his apartment by the police on December 28, 1980, at the age of seventy, with no known next of kin. His brother had predeceased him about two months earlier.

In Curt Smith's latest opus, *Voices of Summer*, the author ranks Britt 78th among the 101 all-time best baseball announcers. That placement is just ahead of Joe Angel (San Francisco Giants and Orioles) and right behind Bob Starr (Angels and Red Sox). Joe Morgan and Russ Hodges represent more famous benchmarks, listed 60th and 51st, respectively, by Smith.

Shortly after Britt's death, Ray Fitzgerald of the *Boston Globe* wrote that "life had turned its back on him a long time ago."[10] And maybe some of his detractors who called him arrogant, uncompromising, perfectionistic, thin-skinned, or unwilling to admit mistakes were secretly tickled that it had.

In his prime, Jim Britt was the king of New England sports radio and early television. He was bright, knowledgeable, and very articulate, took pride in his professionalism, and had a dry sense of humor. He once told radio/TV sports director and announcer Ted Patterson that his credo was "report the game, don't play it."[11] And that he did so objectively, although there was a hard- to-pinpoint pro-Braves and pro-Red Sox quality to his voice that hometowners could sense.

Even during his off-peak years in Cleveland, he never let serious alcohol and marital problems color his description of the game.

A mostly forgotten figure today, the final truth of the matter is that there was an admirable strength of character that defined Jim Britt's work, although not his life.

Chapter 59. **Jimmy Dudley**

Joseph Wancho

In a 1984 interview, former Cleveland Indians broadcaster Jimmy Dudley was reflecting on the 1954 team. They had set an American League record with 111 wins, but were swept in the World Series by the New York Giants, leaving many fans scratching their heads and asking, "What happened?" Thirty years later, Dudley was still searching for the answer to that question. "I've been trying to figure that out ever since it happened," said Dudley. "I guess it was just one of those things, a 10,000-to-1 shot. Destiny must have wanted the Giants to win."[1] It seemed as good an explanation as any; a more substantial explanation did not seem forthcoming, not even after thirty years.

"That 1954 team was not only the best I ever covered, it was also the best group of guys," Dudley continued. "They did everything together, on and off the field. They won together and lost together, although they didn't lose very often. There were no cliques. The 1954 Indians were a fun-loving team, a loose team, which was either another reason why they were so good, or the result of their being so good."[2]

"Don't forget, Al Rosen broke a finger and George Strickland was out for six weeks with a fractured jaw. But Vic Wertz (at first base) and Rudy Regalado (at third base) stepped in for Rosen and did well and Sam Dente played the best ball of his career when Strickland was out. It was a great team."[3]

Even after the Tribe was swept in four games, Dudley said, there were no excuses: "There were no alibis, which should tell you something else about that team."[4]

Dudley was the eyes and ears of Indians fans for twenty years. His ability to intertwine the call of the

Jimmy Dudley—Dudley's southern twang made him instantly recognizable to the radio audience as he brought a nice and easy pace to every game. (National Baseball Hall of Fame Library, Cooperstown, New York)

game with storytelling was a unique gift that only the greatest of broadcasters can provide to their listeners. Even though four decades have passed since Dudley called the action on the field, he is still revered as the greatest announcer the team ever had. And he is closely associated with the great Indians teams of the 1940s and 1950s.

James R. Dudley was born on September 27, 1909, in Alexandria, Virginia. He was the fifth child born to Mr. and Mrs. William Dudley. William Dudley owned his own farm in Gills Creek, located in the Blue Ridge foothills of Virginia. Jimmy was a good, all-around athlete as a child. Later he competed in baseball, football, and basketball at the University of Virginia. He graduated from college with a degree in chemistry, which landed him a job at DuPont.

But boredom set in while Dudley was at DuPont, and a friend suggested that with his voice he might want to give radio a try. Dudley took his friend's advice and started his broadcasting career in Charlottesville, Virginia, in 1937. From there he bounced around the East, making stops in Washington, Syracuse, and Pittsburgh. Eventually he made his way to Chicago and went to work at powerhouse station WIND in 1942. "When he was a Cubs announcer in those days, I was Hal Totten's briefcase carrier," he told the author of a book on broadcasters. "I was sort of his 'gopher'—I'd do the odd jobs–and once in a while he'd let me do play-by-play, but for no more than an inning, tops."[5] It was valuable experience for Dudley, but with World War II on, he went into the U.S. Air Force, putting his career on hold while he flew in India.

Dudley moved to Cleveland after the war to announce hockey games for WJW, which also happened to be the Indians' flagship station. Fate smiled on him in June 1947 when he was assigned to broadcast a sandlot game at Cleveland Stadium being broadcast by the station. George Creedon, the head of Standard Brewing Company, which had just acquired the rights to air the Indians' games, was listening to the broadcast and was impressed by Dudley. He told Indians owner Bill Veeck that he wanted Dudley to do the Indians' games. Veeck agreed, and Dudley became the play-by-play announcer for the Indians in 1948.

Dudley's first on-air partner was Jack Graney, who had been an outfielder for the Indians in the Deadball Era. Graney was a fine player and an excellent announcer. He was a master at the "re-creation" of Major League games and was the first former ball-player to make the transition from the field to the announcer's booth. "Jack was my first air partner and the one that did the most to help me," said Dudley. "He told me that 85 percent of people who listen to baseball broadcasts either know more about the game or think they know more about it than you do. And I never forgot what he said."[6]

For Dudley, taking over the announcing in 1948 was as if he were in baseball heaven. The Indians won the world championship that year after a thrilling American League pennant race and a one-game playoff victory over Boston after the Red Sox and Indians ended the regular season tied. The Indians then overpowered the Boston Braves in six games in the World Series. "It was like living a dream," Dudley recalled. "Talk about being at the right place at the right time. It was so hard to believe—the crowds flocking to the ballpark each day, the pressure, the Red Sox and Yankees nipping at our heels."[7]

Dudley married Angelyn Hendrick in 1950, and they were married for forty-nine years. They had two children, Douglas and Barbara.

The Indians competed for the first ten years of Dudley's tenure, winning the pennant again in 1954. A winning, competitive team naturally breeds interest, and Dudley turned into a favorite of the Indians faithful as more fans tuned in to listen to the broadcasts. His smooth delivery coupled with his slow, easy rhythm was suitable to the leisurely pace of a baseball game. Dudley believed that his success, and that of other southern-born announcers, came from their voices. "I think our accents appealed to people—they were sort of graceful, they fit in with the game," he said. "Dixie speaking is slow, leisurely, it sort of moves with the weather. And baseball is that kind of game."[8] He was often compared with other broadcasters who were also from the South, among them Lindsey Nelson, Red Barber, Mel Allen, and Ernie Harwell.

Like many announcers at the height of their popularity, the phrases Dudley used to describe the action became everyday lexicon. Dudley would say "the string is out" when the batter had a full count. His homer call was "Going . . . going . . . gone." And his call of a double play usually was "Over to second, one away . . . back to first, it's a double play!"

In 1957 Dudley was joined in the radio booth by Bob Neal. Neal was a stark contrast to Dudley's "aw shucks" style, having once aspired to be an opera singer. He had done play-by-play for the Cleveland Browns in the early 1950s. The pair despised one another, each detesting the other's style and personality. They alternated innings, rarely occupying the booth at the same time. "There was a game when Dudley had a terrible case of the stomach flu," recalled late Cleveland broadcaster Nev Chandler. "Dudley did the first three innings, and then Neal did the middle three. Dudley was in the men's room, very sick. The old broadcaster's code is that you don't leave the booth until your partner comes back. But after the sixth, Neal left. Come the seventh inning, Dudley was still sick. For the first couple of batters in the inning, all you heard was crowd noise, the crack of the bat, and the vendors yelling, 'peanuts, popcorn.' Finally, Dudley dragged himself into the booth and finished the game with no help from Neal."[9]

Cleveland radio personality Pete Franklin recalled, "In my first night at the Stadium, I sat between Jimmy Dudley and Bob Neal, who were doing the radio broadcasts in the 1960s. I had been introduced to them individually and had made small talk before the game. I sat between them for two innings, three innings, then four innings. They never spoke to each other. They would talk to me, and I'd talk to them. But Dudley and Neal wouldn't even look at each other. I felt a chill. They loathed each other."[10]

Neal was moved to TV in 1962, but was reunited with Dudley for three years in 1965. Gabe Paul had come to Cleveland as general manager in 1961. Neal developed a relationship with Paul and used it as leverage to oust Dudley in January 1968. The timing was not lost on Dudley, who realized it would be too late to catch on with another team. "One of Jimmy's mistakes was that he didn't socialize with Gabe Paul, but Bob Neal did," said Cleveland sportswriter Hal Lebovitz.[11]

Dudley caught on with the Seattle Pilots in 1969. He was teamed with Bill Schonely for one year, until the franchise moved to Milwaukee.

Dudley resided in Tucson, Arizona, in the off-season during and after his Major League career. After Seattle, his name was mentioned whenever an opening for a broadcaster appeared. But he never broadcast another Major League game. He did a lot of work for the University of Arizona and the Tucson Toros of the Pacific Coast League, and served as a pitchman for several products in the Cleveland area.

On August 3, 1997, Dudley received the Ford C. Frick Award for his excellent work in broadcasting. "Jimmy Dudley provided tremendous insight to Cleveland Indians baseball for countless listeners," said Baseball Hall of Fame President Donald C. Marr Jr. "Baseball history evolves many wonderful stories. Jimmy's soothing and docile delivery, combined with his keen ability to tell these stories, captivated his listening audience. His name is added to an impressive list of previous recipients of the prestigious Ford C. Frick Award."[12]

Dudley's son, Doug, accepted the award for him. A statement issued for him by the Hall of Fame said, "I'm very honored to be the recipient of this fine award. I'm proud of what I accomplished as a broadcaster and am thrilled to join such a prestigious group of former winners."[13]

Jimmy Dudley died on February 12, 1999, after suffering a stroke. He was survived by his wife, Angie, their two children, and two grandchildren. Many listeners can still hear Jimmy sign off Tribe games with his signature line, "Lotsa good luck, ya heah?"

Chapter 60. Timeline, September 17–September 26

Joseph Wancho

September 17—Detroit—INDIANS CLINCH AL TIE; YANKS WIN—Bobby Avila hits a grand slam in the seventh inning off Ned Garver. Al Rosen strokes a solo homer. Bob Lemon wins his twenty-third game, giving up one earned run in a 6–3 win. The Indians commit four errors.

September 18—Detroit—INDIANS TAKE PENNANT ON 107TH VICTORY—Cleveland clinches the American League flag, ending the Yankees' five-year reign. Dale Mitchell's pinch-hit homer plates two in the seventh inning. Jim Hegan follows with a solo homer. Early Wynn fans six for his twenty-second win, and Ray Narleski registers his twelfth save.

September 19—Detroit—INDIANS WIN 108TH, 4–2: 2,000 WELCOME HEROES—Mike Garcia wins his nineteenth game. Hank Majeski hits a three-run homer in the first inning. The Indians are greeted from Detroit by 2,000 fans at Union Terminal. The Crosstown Parade is expected to draw 250,000.

September 20—Cleveland—DOBY, WERTZ LEAD ATTACK WITH HOMERS—Vic Wertz goes 4 for 4, with two RBIS, two runs scored, and a homer. Larry Doby slugs his thirty-first homer, a three-run shot. Bob Feller wins to improve to 13-3. Indians top the White Sox, 7–4.

September 21—Cleveland—FANS BOO AS INDIANS LOSE TO WHITE SOX, 9–7—The Indians commit five errors, including a passed ball and a wild pitch. Larry Doby smacks his thirty-second home run. Mickey Grasso hits his first home run for the year. Stan Jok and Willard Marshall each knock in two runs for the White Sox. Morrie Martin pitches one inning and wins in relief. The Tribe loss snaps an eleven-game winning streak.

September 22—Cleveland—INDIANS TIE YANKEES' 110-VICTORY MARK—Don Mossi goes nine innings, scattering five hits and fanning three for the win. Al Smith goes 2 for 3, with an RBI, a run scored, a double, and a triple. George Strickland adds an RBI.

September 24—Cleveland—TIGERS SPIKE BID BY TRIBE TO WIN 111TH—Jim Delsing drives in two runs with a homer. Ray Boone hits a solo shot. Al Kaline goes 2 for 3 with an RBI.

September 25—Cleveland—INDIANS WIN 111TH TO SET AL RECORD—Early Wynn records his twenty-third win. The Cleveland offense pounds out fourteen hits, including four doubles (Doby, Avila, Mitchell, Philley). Dale Mitchell and Dave Philley each drive in a pair. The Tribe breaks the record set by the 1927 Yankees for most wins in a season.

September 26—Cleveland—GARCIA'S BID FOR 20TH IS SPIKED, 8–7—The Tigers pound out eighteen hits in a thirteen-inning affair. Jim Delsing goes 4 for 6, with an RBI, two runs, and a homer. Frank House goes 4 for 6, with an RBI, two runs, and a homer. Walt Dropo drives in two. Fred Hatfield homers. Bobby Avila and Dave Pope homer for the Indians. Mike Garcia goes twelve innings, strikes out seven, and gives up six earned runs.

Chapter 61. **1954 World Series**

Jeanne M. Mallett

1954 World Series—Al Lopez and Leo Durocher before Game One of the 1954 World Series. (The Cleveland Press Collection, Cleveland State University Library)

"It's now or never" for the Indians, wrote veteran *Cleveland Plain Dealer* sports editor Gordon Cobbledick at the outset of the 1954 season. He reasoned that although the team had been competitive the previous three seasons, finishing second to the New York Yankees in each of those years, the front office had not significantly improved the club in the off-season. Cleveland's unmatched trio of starting pitchers—Early Wynn, Bob Lemon, and Mike Garcia—were getting older. Cobbledick concluded that the Yankees had weak spots and could be taken for the first time in years. But the Indians could be the ones to take them only if they started thinking like champions who could win the "big one" when it counted. Reluctantly, he picked them to finish second again, as did his colleagues in the Cleveland sportswriting community.

The Indians, however, rose to the challenge. Playing inspired baseball, even while enduring numerous injuries, they not only wrested the American League pennant from the mighty Yankees, they left no doubt who was the better team. They won 111 games to the Yankees' 103, defeating the Yankees in a mid-September doubleheader that sent all of Cleveland into a joyful frenzy of baseball fever for the first time since 1948. The 111 victories also bested the previous one-season record of 110 set by the fabled Murderers' Row, the 1927 New York Yankees. Small wonder, then, that although the Indians had yet to clinch the pennant (they did so the next weekend by defeating the Detroit Tigers), the business office was flooded with mailbags full of orders for World Series tickets; in fact, customers of banks and post offices complained about the long lines of fans getting money orders and certified checks to send along with their ticket applications.

The Indians were installed as 9-to-5 betting favorites over the New York Giants, who won a much closer race with the defending champion Brooklyn Dodgers for the National League crown. Sportswriters around the country picked the Indians by a 2-to-1 ratio. Cobbledick and his Cleveland colleagues all predicted Cleveland in six games. Despite the Giants' better hitting and defense, they generally agreed with Yankees catcher Yogi Berra that the Indians' starting pitching and overall pitching depth would be the determining factor. The Big Three had won 65 games between them—Lemon finished 23-7; Wynn, 23-11; and Garcia, 19-8. The rotation rounded out with Art Houtteman winning 15 games and Bob Feller, at the end of his career, winning 13. The bullpen was anchored by a pair of fine young arms, right-hander Ray Narleski and lefty Don Mossi. "The Indians will get at least two or three runs in every game," Berra said. "And with that pitchin', two or three will be enough."

One of the few to raise a warning voice was Berra's former teammate, Joe DiMaggio, who was writing a syndicated column covering the World Series that was carried in numerous papers including the *Cleveland Press.* Joltin' Joe, now retired as a player, said that the 1954 Giants were a lot better team than the one he and the rest of the Yankees had beaten easily in the 1951 Series. The pitching was better, Mays was "twice the player he was in 1951," and this year "almost any time [Durocher] waved to the bench somebody like Dusty Rhodes or Bobby Hoffman stepped up to the dish and whacked one into the seats." Although DiMaggio did not quote statistics, in fact, the Giants had a record ten pinch-hit home runs in 1954. DiMaggio also made what proved to a prescient observation: "Despite all you hear about 'Chinese home runs' in the Polo Grounds it's a tough park on a hitter unless he pulls the ball right down either foul line. The fences are so short fielders don't have to protect the lines and sort of gang up on you and you have to hit a ball a long way to right-center or left-center to get it in safe. With all that room to roam both at the Polo Grounds and in Cleveland's big Municipal Stadium Mays may have the Indians hitters talking to themselves before the Series ends." As the Series played out, no professional sportswriter's analysis fared as well as the Yankee Clipper's.

The Series featured a number of interesting matchups. The two competing teams knew each other better than any two teams ever to face each other in a World Series. Since 1934 the Indians and Giants had played each other in spring training and preseason barnstorming 263 times. After 1946 they were the first two teams to move their spring training camps to Arizona—the Giants to Phoenix and the Indians to Tucson—and they played each other almost exclusively. And for the first time in twenty-three years, two league batting champions would face off against each other: second baseman Bobby Avila for the Indians and center fielder Willie Mays for the Giants. Finally, the two managers were a study in contrasts. "Señor" Al Lopez, a quiet yet determined man who played by the book, led the Indians. He was universally liked by sportswriters and players alike as a genuinely "nice guy." Opposing him was the flashy, quotable Leo "The Lip" Durocher, a notorious hunch player as a manager, who had famously said, "Nice guys finish last." The stage was set.

Game One—Wednesday, September 29—Polo Grounds—A-Mays-ing Catch and a "Chinese" Home Run

Even without the Yankees' participation, the World Series opened in New York City, lending the proceedings a particularly festive air. The Indians and their wives arrived on a special New York Central train from Cleveland, pulling into Grand Central Terminal in Midtown Manhattan early in the morning of Tuesday, September 28. They were greeted by crowds and by television cameras from Dave Garroway's *Today* show. The police roped off a special aisle so the Indians contingent could move through the crowd to their headquarters, the nearby Biltmore Hotel. Indians players were all business, giving only brief interviews before getting into the hotel, resting, and heading to the Polo Grounds that afternoon for a two-hour drill in unseasonably warm weather. While they knew the Giants team well from their numerous spring-training meetings each year, the Polo Grounds was a different story. The Indians had to accustom themselves quickly to what was a quirky old ballpark, with short right- and left-field foul lines, 258 feet and 280 feet respectively, and a deep center field ranging from 425 feet in left-center to 475 feet in center, and then to 450 feet in right-center.

On Wednesday, the Polo Grounds gates opened at 9 a.m. to accommodate the more than 2,000 fans already waiting for game-day sales of 3,800 bleacher seats at $2.10 apiece and 4,009 standing-room tickets at $4.20. Outside the 155th Street subway stop, scalpers were asking $100 for $10 box-seat tickets. By game time at 1 p.m., a National League record crowd of 52,751 fans had passed through the turnstiles. Among them were Mrs. John McGraw, widow of the legendary Giants manager, who had attended every Giants World Series game since 1905,

and celebrities Tallulah Bankhead, Sammy Davis Jr., Jeff Chandler, and Spencer Tracy, who escorted Giants manager Durocher's wife, actress Laraine Day. Crooner Perry Como led the crowd in singing the National Anthem, and twelve-year-old Jimmy Barbeiri, the captain of the Little League champion Schenectady, New York, team, threw out the first ball, a strike right to the mitt of Giants catcher Wes Westrum.

At game time the temperature was only in the mid-seventies, but the strong sun and high humidity made the conditions uncomfortably hot and humid. Both managers had waited until late the day before to name their starting pitchers. In the end both chose veteran hurlers. Thirty-four-year-old Bob Lemon, a converted infielder and one of the few remaining members of the Indians' 1948 World Series Championship team, took the mound for the Tribe. And, unlike in his two previous World Series appearances, Durocher did not play a hunch for his opening game starter, naming instead Sal "The Barber" Maglie, the thirty-seven-year-old curveballer who won only fourteen games during the season but won several key games, including the pennant clincher. Durocher did not play hunches with his starting lineup for the opener either, disappointing some who had predicted he would start a part-time player, Dusty Rhodes, over Monte Irvin in left field. Rhodes had proved to be a much better hitter during the season than the aging Irvin (.341 batting average for Rhodes in 164 at bats versus .262 for Irvin in 432 at bats), but he was an erratic fielder.

Despite their veteran status, both pitchers struggled in the early innings. In the first inning Maglie's lack of control got him in early trouble. After throwing three wide pitches to Al Smith, Cleveland's leadoff hitter, Maglie hit Smith in the side with the fourth pitch. Maglie threw yet another ball to the next hitter, American League batting champion Bobby Avila, before throwing a strike, which elicited loud cheers from the crowd. But Avila stroked the next pitch into right field for a single. Smith raced to third when right fielder Don Mueller booted the ball. Then Maglie righted himself, getting the dangerous Larry Doby to foul out to third and then Al Rosen, swinging at the first pitch, to pop out to first baseman Whitey Lockman. Maglie had got by two-thirds of the dangerous middle of the Indians' lineup, and an anxious crowd calmed. Then lefty-slugging first baseman Vic Wertz stepped to the plate. After taking a ball, Wertz lined a deep drive over Mueller's head in right-center. The ball caromed off the wall and bounced past the Giants' bullpen before center fielder Willie Mays ran it down. Wertz ended up with a triple, scoring both Smith and Avila. With the Indians suddenly leading, 2–0, Don Liddle hurriedly started warming up in the Giants' bullpen. But Maglie got the next batter, right fielder Dave Philley, to line out to Mueller for the third out.

Lemon also got in trouble in the bottom of the first, walking shortstop Alvin Dark with one out, then giving up a single to Mueller. With runners on first and third, though, Lemon got National League batting champion Willie Mays to pop up to shortstop and third baseman Hank Thompson to ground out to first.

The second time through the Giants' lineup, Lemon could not escape. In the third, lead-off man Lockman singled to right and advanced to third when Dark lined a single past the mound into center field. Mueller grounded into a force at second, but Lockman scored the first run for the Giants. Mays walked and Thompson singled to drive in Mueller and tie the score at 2–2. With only one out and runners on first and third, it was the Indians' turn to get the bullpen up as Art Houtteman started warming. But Lemon, like Maglie, recovered. He fanned left fielder Irvin and got second baseman Davey Williams to ground out to short.

Both pitchers steadied in the middle innings. Maglie gave up a single to Wertz in the top of the fourth. The Giants got two singles off Lemon in the bottom of the inning. Otherwise, both veterans justified their managers' faith in them.

Maglie got into trouble in the sixth but was bailed out by sterling infield play by third baseman Thompson. Wertz singled for his third hit of the day and ended up on second when right fielder Mueller threw wildly to first in a vain attempt to get Wertz there. After an infield out put Wertz at third with one down, Maglie got shortstop George Strickland to pop out. Then catcher Jim Hegan hit a hard smash over the bag at third. Thompson knocked the ball down in foul territory and fired to first to retire the slow-footed Hegan.

In the eighth the Indians finally succeeded in knocking Maglie out of the game. But once again, sterling defense—this time a play that would live on in World Series lore—kept the Indians from taking the lead. Maglie opened the inning by walking Larry Doby. Third baseman Al Rosen, who had been held hitless, singled off shortstop Dark's bare hand. Maglie's day was done. Durocher brought in the diminutive Don Liddle, who had been warming up on and off since the first inning, to face Vic Wertz. Wertz hit a towering 450-foot drive to deep center field that sailed over Mays's head. But Mays turned and raced after it, catching it with his back to the plate. Holding out his gloved hand to keep from crashing into the wall, Mays turned and fired the ball to the infield to keep the runners from advancing. Wertz later said, "I never hit a ball harder in my life, . . . I thought Mays had given up. . . . Next thing I knew he had it in the end zone." Mays had, in fact, slowed down when he started chasing it because he wanted to "judge it right." Mays added, "You can't catch a ball going full speed. After I saw where it was going, and timed it, I went for it." Went for it, caught it, and broke the hearts of Indians fans everywhere because, as both managers later agreed, Mays's miraculous catch was the real turning point, although there was more drama still to play out in this close, hard-fought game.

After Mays's catch, Liddle, who had come so close to disaster, was lifted for Marv Grissom, a veteran hurler who mixed screwballs and fastballs to keep the Tribe hitters off-balance the rest of the way. Lopez, who had already sent up Hank Majeski to pinch-hit for Dave Philley, immediately countered by putting in lefty swinger Dale Mitchell to face the right-handed Grissom. When Mitchell drew a walk, loading the bases with only one out, the Indians still had a chance to break the game open. Lopez sent in Dave Pope, another lefty, to bat for the light-hitting Strickland. But Grissom reached back into his bag of tricks and struck out a surprised Pope. The threat ended with catcher Jim Hegan flying out.

In the last of the eighth, the Giants mounted their first threat against Lemon since the third. Thompson walked and advanced to third on a sacrifice and a wild pitch. But catcher Wes Westrum flied to Doby in center, ending the threat.

In the top of the ninth, the Giants unexpectedly gave the Indians an opportunity to score when Monte Irvin, normally a sure-handed fielder, dropped Avila's pop fly for a two-base error. The crafty Grissom, however, intentionally walked Doby and got Rosen to fly to left, where Irvin redeemed himself by catching the ball to end the ninth.

In the top of the tenth, Wertz came up again and again clubbed the ball, this time doubling to center, his fourth hit. When Lopez replaced him with pinch runner Rudy Regalado, the New York crowd gave Wertz a well-deserved ovation. Sam Dente, who had replaced Strickland at shortstop, sacrificed, sending Regalado to third. Grissom walked Pope, putting two on with only one out. The threat fell apart when Grissom struck out pinch hitter Bill Glynn, and Lemon, trying to win the game himself, lined out to the first baseman.

By contrast with the Giants' pitchers, Lemon had handled the Giants with little trouble since they last scored in the third. As he faced them in the bottom of the tenth, he still seemed in command, opening the frame with a strikeout of Mueller. He then walked Mays. With second-string catcher Mickey Grasso now behind the plate for Cleveland, Durocher called for a steal with Hank Thompson at the plate, which Mays neatly executed, beating Grasso's poor throw. The steal changed the Indians' strategy and Thompson was given an intentional walk. The strategy might have worked if the next hitter, Monte Irvin, who had been ineffective all day, had come to bat. The aging Irvin was good for at least one out and was a good candidate to hit into a double play. But Irvin never came to bat.

Durocher, finally playing a hunch, pinch-hit for Irvin with Jim "Dusty" Rhodes, who had hit .341 in part-time duty during the season and had two of the Giants' record ten pinch-hit home runs. Rhodes came to bat intending to take the first pitch. But the high curve Lemon threw him was "too good." So he swung at it and connected. Coming off the bat, the ball seemed like an ordinary pop fly. But it hugged the right-field foul line, staying just fair as the wind pushed it toward the right-field stands. Right fielder Pope thought until the last moment that he would catch it. He backed against the wall and leaped as the ball came down. But the ball came down instead in the stands, bouncing back onto the field after it hit a fan trying to catch it. The ball had traveled all of 270 feet. As soon as umpire Larry Napp signaled home run, Lemon disgustedly threw his glove in the air and the Giants began their celebration.

Game Two—Thursday, September 30—Polo Grounds—Here Comes That Man Again

Before Game Two, Dusty Rhodes proudly waved a telegram from the owner of a local Chinese restaurant who did not seem to mind the designation of Rhodes's winning hit as a "Chinese" home run, which was understood in baseball lingo as a cheap hit. The wire read: "In honor of your game-winning blow, we invite you to restore your energy with our homer-producing Chinese food." There was no word on whether Dusty immediately ordered take-out or not. But once again he was a key factor as the game developed.

The heartbreaking extra-inning loss in Game One did not discourage Indians fans. The Indians had suffered a 1–0 loss in the first game of the 1948 World Series but eventually prevailed. And this time Indians fans knew they had another ace on the hill, burly Early Wynn, like Lemon a twenty-three-game winner in 1954. He faced the Giants' young phenom, lefty Johnny Antonelli, who had won twenty-one games. In contrast to Game One, the sky was overcast and threatening rain. The 49,099 fans who crowded into the Polo Grounds hardly noticed the oppressive humidity as they saw another tight, tension-filled game.

The Indians again took a first-inning lead as lead-off batter Al Smith powered the first pitch he saw onto the roof of the left-field stands. Antonelli then got two quick outs when Avila grounded out and Doby took a called third strike. But Al Rosen and Wertz drew walks. Right fielder Wally Westlake followed with a sharp single past the mound to center. Rosen, slowed by a leg injury, was held at third as Mays fired the ball home. When Strickland popped up to first, the threat was ended.

Early Wynn nursed the one-run lead, pitching a perfect game through the first four innings. The Indians kept the heat on Antonelli but couldn't push another run across. Catcher Jim Hegan opened the second inning with a double down the left-field line and was sacrificed to third by Wynn. Hegan was stranded, however, when Smith struck out and Avila fouled out. In the third, the Indians were at Antonelli again as Wertz singled and Westlake walked. Again both runners were stranded when Strickland bounced into a force for the third out. In the fourth, a dazzling defensive play by Hank Thompson snuffed out another scoring chance as Al Smith walked with two out and Bobby Avila followed with a sharp grounder past third that looked like a sure double. Instead, Thompson snagged it and threw to first for the out. In the fifth, Rosen singled but was left at first.

In the bottom of the fifth, Wynn suddenly lost control. He walked Mays on five pitches. Then Thompson singled to right for the Giants' first hit. Monte Irvin was up next and, although it was still early in the game, Durocher played a hunch again

and brought in Game One hero Dusty Rhodes to pinch-hit. Wynn had a 1-2 count on Rhodes when he served up a curve that Rhodes promptly popped into short center for a single, scoring Mays with the tying run. *Plain Dealer* reporter Harry Jones noted later that the hit was a soft fly that Doby might have caught if he had started in faster. Instead he reached the ball just after it dropped safely and threw to third in a futile attempt to get Thompson. The throw arrived late while Rhodes moved to second. With two men in scoring position and none out, Wynn struck out Davey Williams, but after giving catcher Westrum three balls, he intentionally walked him, loading the bases for the young pitcher Antonelli. Antonelli hit a grounder to Avila that might have been a double play except that after Westrum was forced at second, Strickland's relay to first was too late to catch Antonelli. Thompson scored, giving the Giants a 2–1 lead.

Wynn, attempting to help his own cause, doubled off the left-field wall in the top of the sixth but was left stranded. In the seventh, Avila led off with a walk and advanced on a grounder but was trapped between second and third when Rosen tapped a grounder to the mound. Wertz then walked but Westlake grounded to Dark to end that rally. In the bottom of the seventh, Dusty Rhodes, who had stayed in the game replacing Irvin in left field, added insurance for a Giants victory by belting a home run off the roof of the right-field stands.

With Antonelli still pitching in the ninth, the Indians had one last chance to rally from the 3–1 deficit. Smith led off with a single off Antonelli's shin. Avila singled to left with Smith stopping at second. Doby, after failing to sacrifice, struck out for the third time. Rudy Regalado forced Avila at second. The dangerous Vic Wertz, batting .625 in the two Series games thus far, came to the plate. Antonelli pitched him carefully and Wertz responded. He fouled off several 3-2 pitches before finally hitting a fly ball to Rhodes in deep left field, ending the threat and the game.

For the second game in a row, Indians pitching had been stellar, as predicted, but Indians hitters had wasted chance after chance on the base paths, unlike their opportunistic play in winning 111 games during the season. For the second day in a row, the Tribe had stranded thirteen runners. To manager Lopez the story of Game Two was obvious: "We didn't hit when it counted and they did."

As the Indians headed home to play the third game at Municipal Stadium, they were now the underdogs. While oddsmakers made the Indians 7-to-5 favorites to win the third game, the Giants were named 2-to-1 favorites to win the Series. And 10-to-1 to sweep in four games.

Game Three—Friday, October 1—Municipal Stadium—The Colossus of Rhodes

Even before the first pitch of Game Three, the Giants scored another victory—beating the Indians home to Cleveland by about 11 hours. After Thursday's victory, the Giants made the short trip to LaGuardia Airport, hopped a Capital Airlines charter flight to Cleveland, and arrived at 8 p.m., still in time for a late dinner and a full night's sleep at the Hotel Manger. The Indians returned by train, arriving at 6:40 a.m., just hours before the Friday afternoon game. While the Indians surely had the opportunity for a good night's sleep in the lush sleeper cars of the special train chartered for them, their early arrival on game day and the limited time left before getting to the park may have played a part in their listless play that afternoon.

A crowd of 71,555 hopeful but anxious Indians fans packed spacious Municipal Stadium to cheer the team to a victory. In the pregame ceremonies, fans warmed up their vocal cords cheering for comedian and singer Danny Kaye, who sang the National Anthem, and for a white-haired Tris Speaker, who, although he had been hospitalized after a heart attack in July, delivered a strong first pitch to Jim Hegan.

The cheers faded as the game began. The gloomy skies and oppressively humid weather seemed to suck the life out of both the Indians and their fans. The Tribe's hitting woes continued as they were held to only four hits by Giants starter Ruben Gomez and the knuckleballing reliever Hoyt Wilhelm. And for the first time, the Indians' pitching failed as well. In contrast to the first two games, the Giants struck first. Lead-off hitter Whitey Lockman lined Mike Garcia's first pitch into right field for a single. Garcia bore down, striking out Alvin Dark and getting Don Mueller to ground to Avila for a force of Lockman at second. But shortstop Strickland, trying for a double play, threw wildly to first and Mueller ended up at second. The next hitter, Willie Mays, singled to right for his first hit of the Series. Mueller raced home from second to give the Giants a 1-0 lead. Garcia then walked Hank Thompson but got Monte Irvin, starting once more in left, to foul out to Hegan.

Defense let the Indians down again in the third when the Giants, sparked once more by super pinch hitter Rhodes, scored three runs and sent Garcia to an early shower. First Dark singled to center. Then, as Hank Majeski, starting in place of the injured Al Rosen at third, came in expecting a bunt, Don Mueller lined a hit past him into left field, putting runners on first and third. Cleveland caught a break when Mays grounded to Majeski and Dark was run down between third and home. But the Giants' captain avoided the tag long enough for Mueller to reach third and Mays second. Garcia, following the standard playbook, walked Thompson to get to Irvin, who had no hits with two strikeouts in the Series so far. But, of course, Garcia and Lopez had to know by now that Irvin would never come to bat in that situation, even though it was only the third inning. For the third straight day over the public address system came the words by now feared by every Cleveland fan: "For New York, Rhodes now batting for Irvin." Dusty immediately justified that fear by driving Garcia's first pitch between Avila and Wertz into right field for a solid single, scoring Mueller and Mays. The Giants took further advantage of the reeling Indians when the next batter, Davey Williams, perfectly executed the squeeze play, bunting the ball slowly toward the mound as Thompson raced in from third. Garcia fielded the ball but, having no play at home, turned quickly and threw wildly to first, allowing Williams to reach safely. Garcia managed to get out of further trouble. But by the end of the third, the Giants were leading 4–0, and Garcia was lifted for a pinch hitter in the bottom of the third.

Art Houtteman got the Giants out in the fourth. In the fifth, however, Thompson legged out a double to center and came home on a single to left by Westrum. In the sixth, the Giants got what turned out to be their final run, off Ray Narleski, when Lockman walked, Dark sacrificed him to second, and Mays singled him home.

The Indians could get nothing going against Ruben Gomez, who stifled them on four hits. The crowd had nothing to cheer about until their chief tormenter Rhodes came to the plate in the bottom of the seventh and Narleski struck him out on three pitches, Rhodes swinging mightily past each one. The crowd erupted and that seemed to bring some life to the Indians as well. In the bottom of the seventh, Vic Wertz, the Tribe's one consistent hitter during the Series, crushed a ball into the stands in right-center 375 feet away. Gomez responded by quickly setting down the next three batters. In the eighth, however, Bill Glynn, batting for Hegan, hit a sinking liner close to the foul line in right field that Don Mueller got his glove on but could not hold. Glynn raced to second for a double and advanced to third on pinch hitter Dale Mitchell's groundout. Then the Giants gave the Indians another rare gift with a defensive lapse. Al Smith topped a grounder to shortstop. Dark fielded it but threw wildly to first, allowing Glynn to score and Smith to get to second. Bobby Avila walked. At that point Durocher brought in his ace reliever Hoyt Wilhelm, who calmly set down five Indians in a row to finish the eighth and close the door in the ninth.

With the once-favored Indians facing elimination with one more loss, the huge crowd filed out dejected. A fan spotted comedian Bob Hope, one of a number of celebrities at the game, and shouted, "You'd better sell all your stock in the Indians." Hope, himself a former Clevelander, retorted jokingly, "Communist!" Fans within earshot laughed heartily even as their hearts were breaking for their team.

Game Four—Saturday, October 2—Municipal Stadium—Cleveland's Last Stand

The 78,102 fans who crowded into Municipal Stadium were greeted with a perfect early-autumn afternoon. The stifling humidity of the previous days had given way to warm but refreshing weather. Fans thought the clear blue sky overhead signaled a change in Cleveland's fortunes as well. The huge crowd waited quietly as Hollywood heartthrob Jeff Chandler sang the National Anthem. They cheered loudly as the lineups were announced. Manager Al Lopez had pulled out all the stops, bringing slugger Al Rosen back to play third and replacing Strickland at short with Sam Dente, a better hitter. He also brought back Game One starter Bob Lemon on two days' rest. Both Lopez and the competitive Lemon felt this was the right choice. Lemon had worked effectively on two days' rest more than once during the season. To face him, Durocher chose Don Liddle, whose appearance in Game One had been memorable only because his pitch provided Willie Mays the opportunity to make a miraculous catch of Wertz's 450-foot drive. Indians fans suddenly had reason to hope.

Hope was short-lived as Cleveland's weak defense undercut Lemon's efforts. In the second, Thompson walked. Monte Irvin, who had thus far served mostly as a decoy for the pinch-hitting heroics of Rhodes, slammed a double to left-center, sending Thompson to third. With both runners going, Davey Williams lined a drive directly to Wertz at first, seemingly an easy chance for a double play. Irvin was caught off second but Wertz had to delay a throw because no Indian was covering the bag. Shortstop Dente raced to get there ahead of the returning Irvin. When Wertz finally threw the ball, he rushed it and the ball sailed into left field for an error, allowing Thompson to score and Irvin to advance to third. Next, Wes Westrum hit a short fly to right. Westlake waited under it, readying himself to catch it and make the throw to the plate. But he dropped the ball for another error, allowing Irvin to score easily. Lopez protested to umpire Charlie Berry that Westlake had caught the ball and held it long enough for at least one out to be declared, but to no avail. Lemon assured that no further damage was done as he struck out pitcher Liddle, and Westrum was caught stealing with Lockman at bat.

The Giants got another run in the third as, after singles by Dark and Mueller, Mays hit a chopper that bounced over Rosen's head and rolled unattended into left while Dark scored. With Mays at second and Mueller at third, Lemon limited the damage by giving Thompson an intentional walk to load the bases. Durocher then surprised everyone by allowing Irvin to bat a second time instead of bringing in Rhodes. This time Durocher's hunch did not pay off as Lemon fanned Irvin, then coaxed Williams to ground into a force out. Still, the Giants were ahead, 3–0, and the Indians were not mounting any attack against Liddle, who had allowed only one hit, a double by Vic Wertz in the bottom of the third.

In the fifth, the Giants put the game away, routing Lemon and his successor, Hal Newhouser, with four runs. After Dark and Mueller opened the inning with singles and Lemon walked Mays to load the bases, Lopez came to the mound and took the ball from the pitcher. The crowd gave the courageous warrior a heartfelt ovation as he left. The lefty Newhouser, the one-time Detroit Tigers ace and star of the 1945 World Series, came in to relieve but could not get anyone out. He walked Thompson to force in a run. Then Irvin lined a single to left that drove in two more. Lopez then brought in

Ray Narleski, who managed to quell the uprising, although not before another run scored on a sacrifice fly by Westrum. The Giants led, 7–0.

With an unhappy end to a great season seemingly imminent, the Indians battled back in the bottom of the fifth to the delight of their fans. Once again their rally was helped by unexpected lapses in the Giants' generally superior defensive play. With two outs, Sam Dente grounded to first. Lockman scooped it up and tossed to pitcher Liddle covering the bag. But Liddle missed the bag; Dente was safe and the inning continued. Next, shortstop Davey Williams muffed an easy ground ball by Hegan. Hank Majeski pinch-hit for Narleski and hit a towering home run to left, clearing the wire barrier at 350 feet. The huge crowd burst into cheers. Although the home run was only the second hit off Liddle, it scored three runs. The Indians were back in it.

In the seventh, Cleveland fans got even more excited as Indians batters knocked Liddle out of the game. Wertz opened with a single, his eighth hit of the Series. After the next two batters went out, Hegan singled and Regalado, batting for pitcher Don Mossi, singled to drive in Wertz. Giants 7, Indians 4.

Durocher brought in Hoyt Wilhelm, who had stifled the Indians in Game Three. Wilhelm immediately snuffed out the rally by getting pinch hitter Dave Pope to ground the ball back to the mound for the third out. This time, however, Wilhelm was not invincible. He opened the Indians' eighth by striking out Avila on a knuckler that had so much action on it that catcher Westrum missed it as well and Avila ended up on first. After Doby flied out, Rosen singled, putting two men on with one out. Durocher brought in Johnny Antonelli, the Game Two starter and winner, who quickly struck out both Wertz and Westlake to end the threat. Antonelli remained on the mound for the ninth, giving up an opening walk to Dente before getting Hegan on a pop foul to first and striking out pinch hitter Dave Philley. Suddenly, Dale Mitchell, another pinch hitter, was the Indians' last hope. Antonelli got him to swing at an outside pitch that Mitchell hit for a short foul near third base. Hank Thompson raced over, grabbed it, and kept running to the Giants' celebration developing around Antonelli on the mound. In deference to their worthy opponents, the Giants' players just hugged each other and quickly left the field, saving the more raucous celebrating for the clubhouse and the party later that night at the Biltmore in New York. On his third try, Durocher finally had a world championship ring.

For the Indians and their fans it seemed particularly cruel that a fine Saturday afternoon and a Saturday evening when the bars would normally be full with partiers were ruined. No one was in the mood to have any sort of party. In the stores, bars, and even the public library—wherever televisions had been set up and crowds gathered—the gloom spread as the final game unfolded. Men stood silently at the bar from the fifth inning through the ninth. At one bar a sign announcing "Open Sunday, Oct. 3," no doubt in anticipation of a fifth game, was unceremoniously ripped down as the final out was recorded. By 4:30 p.m. bar owners and their patrons were crafting funeral wreaths around team pictures for their windows.

Postmortem

For the tenth time in World Series history, the Series had ended in a four-game sweep. The Indians, who had gone in as heavy favorites, got behind and could never regain their footing. Sixteen records were broken and fifteen were tied in the short Series. For the Indians the records were ones of futility—most players left on base in a four-game series, 37; most players used in a four-game series, 24. The Giants' Hank Thompson received the most bases on balls for a four-game series, 7, while his teammate Wes Westrum recorded the most sacrifices, 3. And, of course, Dusty Rhodes equaled the record for most successful pinch hits, 3, every one a critical blow.

Why did the Indians, who had won a record 111

games in the regular season, collapse so completely in the World Series? There were many theories. To the superstitious the answer was obvious: The Indians' special train to New York to open the Series left on Track 13. It arrived on Track 26 (13 x 2). The Indians left 13 runners on base in each of the first two games. The unlucky number had in fact been hanging over the Indians' heads since spring training when the Giants won their exhibition series 13 games to 8. The misogynists claimed that Lopez's allowing the Indian wives to accompany the players to New York had done them in. Other fans claimed the team was too old. The young guys should have been given more of a chance. *New York Times* columnist Arthur Daley opined that, in retrospect, one could see that the Indians' record season was deceptive because the American League on balance was much weaker than the National League. Only the top three teams, the Indians, Yankees, and White Sox, were truly competitive. *Cleveland Press* sports editor Franklin Lewis laid the blame on the key injuries that hobbled Indians stars Rosen and Doby. The *Plain Dealer*'s Gordon Cobbledick noted that the Indians' superior pitching had crumbled at key moments.

Manager Lopez offered no excuses. He gave the Giants' defense special credit for killing a number of Tribe rallies. He admitted he did not know at first that Rosen and Doby were hurt as badly as they were. But the basic cause for the stunning loss was obvious to Lopez. "They were a hot ballclub and we were cold," he said. "We didn't hit—at least when it counted."

After praising his players' effort and willingness to do whatever was expected of them, winning manager Leo Durocher was diplomatic and gracious in his assessment. "I never thought we could do it in four straight," he said. "Frankly, I wasn't even sure beforehand that we could do it at all. We got all the breaks. That helped." On that point, desolate Indians fans would agree. It was left to GM Hank Greenberg to provide the perfect coda: "We had a great season. It just lasted four games too long."

Chapter 62. **A Day in the Grandstand**

Matthew Silverman

On September 29, 1954, the opening game of the World Series was played at New York's Polo Grounds. Among the 52,751 in the stands for the contest between the Cleveland Indians and the New York Giants was a thirty-one-year-old writer named Arnold Hano, who crafted a memorable narrative of the game from the center-field bleachers. *A Day in the Bleachers*, published the following year, became a classic of baseball observation and a sort of extended blog entry nearly half a century before that writing form became commonplace.

Also in the stands that Wednesday afternoon at the Polo Grounds was a fifteen-year-old who was missing school to sit in the grandstand. Ted Feeney, of Kingston, New York, about a hundred miles north of New York City, was sitting with his older brother in the lower grandstand just four rows from the field and a few feet from the right-field foul pole.

One thing neither Hano nor Feeney nor anyone else watching that day could know was that this game, an epic World Series game between a superb New York team that wasn't the Yankees and a record-setting American League club that was also not the Yankees, marked the end of an era. The next day would be the last of forty-two World Series games played in the Polo Grounds between the time the ballpark was rebuilt in concrete and steel in 1911 and the time when the team left New York, along with the Brooklyn Dodgers, after the 1957 season. And as for the Indians, fresh off a 111-victory season, they would not see another World Series for forty-one years.

It was a perfect Indian summer afternoon, though it had a far-from-perfect conclusion for the Indians.

Back when every World Series game still began in mid-afternoon, this game would remain frozen in the memories of most who watched it. There was certainly enough to remember.

"In 1954 I was going on fifteen years of age and I was happy to be there with my brother, who was ten years older than I was," Ted Feeney recalled. "My brother was a lawyer and he was just getting ready to go in the army. We sat in right field, right in the first tier. I looked down and I could see both bullpens. We got there early and saw Sal Maglie warming up and we watched the other players take batting practice. We were in the lower deck. We had a good look."

It was a classic pitching matchup, with Maglie facing future Hall of Famer Bob Lemon. Early Wynn, who would also wind up in Cooperstown, and Lemon had each won twenty-three games in '54. Lemon, a year younger, had an ERA (2.72) that was one-hundredth of a point lower than Wynn's. Mike Garcia just missed twenty wins, and the legendary Bob Feller couldn't even crack Cleveland's postseason rotation despite a 13-3 record at age thirty-five. The Indians had dominated the American League and set a league mark by winning 111 games. They had to be nearly perfect to knock off the 103-win Yankees, who had won five straight pennants and would win the next four after 1954. The 97-win Giants were almost as happy as Cleveland's supporters to have the Yankees out of the World Series. The Yankees had beaten the Giants in four straight World Series dating back to 1923, the year the Yanks ceased sharing the Polo Grounds with the Giants. The Yankees had even managed to throw cold water on the Miracle of Coogan's Bluff by beating the Giants in the 1951 World Series after Bobby Thomson's remarkable home run that clinched the pennant at the Polo Grounds in the last inning of a three-game playoff with the rival Dodgers. Feeney recalled that moment vividly, watching it on the family's new television.

"I was only twelve years old at the time, in my little den coming home from school, with my cousin," Feeney said of the fateful afternoon of October 3, 1951. "I was on my knees almost crying because they were losing. We were there praying. When he hit that home run I just went crazy and ran down the street to jump on the Dodgers fans."

Feeney planned to go to the '51 World Series with his brother, but the game he was going to was rained out and he didn't get another chance. Now, three years later, he was inside the Polo Grounds, along with a packed house at Coogan's Bluff. Only 34,320 had been at the Polo Grounds for the Thomson game. "No one wanted to miss it this time," he said.

And after all the buildup and wait, it seemed as though it could be over early. Vic Wertz laced a two-out double off Maglie to knock in two runs in the first inning. "I was depressed because there was trouble in the air, I thought it was going to be a rout," Feeney recalled. "You're young then and you're really into the game and you say, 'We've got to stop this stuff.'"

Maglie stopped the Indians from that point on, and the Giants managed to tie the game with a pair of runs in the third inning on a groundout by Don Mueller and a single by Hank Thompson (the "other" Thomson, the one with no "p" in his name, had been sent to the Milwaukee Braves the previous winter). The 2–2 tie held for most of the tense afternoon. Maglie had been able to minimize trouble after the first inning because the Indians' lineup dropped off precipitously after Wertz's fifth spot in the order. The pitcher, Lemon, who came up to the Major Leagues as an outfielder, had two home runs and a .214 average that was a point higher than that of his shortstop, George Strickland; right fielder Dave Philley (.226) and catcher Jim Hegan (.234) also didn't create a lot of fear among opposing pitchers. The first part of the Indians lineup, however, was a different matter. The lineup started with productive lead-off man Al Smith, followed by .341 hitter Bobby Avila; then came future Hall of Famer Larry Doby, the league leader in home runs (32) and RBIS (126), who was followed by the previous year's MVP, Al Rosen. Feeney, and the Giants fans around him, fretted whenever the Cleveland lineup flipped over. "I always worried about Rosen coming up," Feeney said. "He was a dangerous hitter. Him and Doby."

In the eighth inning, for the first time since the opening inning, the heart of the Cleveland order was due up. Doby drew Maglie's second walk of the day. He took off for second as Rosen hit a hard ground ball that seemed ticketed for the outfield, but Giants shortstop Alvin Dark used his bare hand to keep the ball in the infield and prevent Doby from advancing to third base.

Two men on, nobody out, just like the first inning—though now the game was at its crux. With Wertz, already 3 for 3, at the plate, Giants manager Leo Durocher decided to try to prevent a recurrence of the first-inning trouble. He made the signal for Don Liddle.

"I'm sweating," Feeney recalled.

Liddle was a left-hander, therefore they were playing the percentages. . . . Maglie I loved, I thought he was a real money pitcher with the curveball and he had tremendous control over it. I thought they may have brought Marv Grissom in to pitch, but it was a righty-lefty situation and it was a different ball game altogether. They went with the percentage and then all of a sudden . . .

When Wertz hit that ball I was shocked. I saw that ball go out there and just said, "Oh my God, this is going to go in the bleachers." I saw the ball out and I saw Mays just running backwards, away from us. And I could not believe . . . out of nowhere, he caught the ball. And then I just saw this whirling dervish, all of a sudden like a bullet (the ball) coming in from the outfield. I was stunned. I was absolutely stunned by that play. I don't know how he ever caught it. There he is running backwards and then he just reaches out his arm. Everything happened so quickly.

The ball was in what you would call deep, deep right-center. It had passed the 440 sign in the bullpen, we know that. So he was probably 460 to 470 feet from home plate when he caught it. It seemed like a long way, I'll tell you.

It was a shot, I'm not going to go "Shot around the World," but it was a shot. And I think the throw was just as important. Because he made the whirl on it, the Indians runners—I wasn't looking at them at that time because I was following where Mays was going—Doby tagged up and went to third. It was first and third. Any other Major League ballpark, they would have been circling the bases. That was it for Liddle.

Durocher came back out and removed the lefty after his one memorable pitch. Now the Giants brought in Grissom. The crowd was still buzzing from the Mays catch.

"You just took a deep breath after the play was over with," Feeney recalled. "And thank God they brought in another pitcher because it gave you time to sort of regroup and think about what really went on. You say to yourself, 'Holy mackerel, Did that really happen?' Then we got down to basics again."

The basics were men on the corners. The bases were soon loaded on a walk to lefty-swinging pinch hitter Dale Mitchell. Another pinch hitter, left-hander Dave Pope, came up with the sacks full. Grissom struck him out looking as the crowd roared. Jim Hegan then hit a high fly down the line in left that seemed perilously close to the overhang that had turned countless pop-ups into home runs. Left fielder Monte Irvin went back to the wall, and as *A Day in the Bleachers* author Hano noted from

his perch on the left-center-field side of the bleachers, "Irvin suddenly stepped away from the fence to gather in the ball. The little breeze—so soft for so long—had developed a backbone, and Hegan's fly ball was ever so slightly pushed by it, away from the beckoning overhang."

The Giants had escaped. The Indians had come perilously close to breaking the game open, but with the horseshoe-shaped dimensions of the Polo Grounds, the Tribe had been pushed aside again. Nine Indians had been left on base so far, six of them in scoring position.

The Giants got a runner into scoring position with one out in the bottom of the eighth, and Lemon wild-pitched him to third with two outs. Wes Westrum had shaken his light-hitting tag for a day (his batting average that season was .187) and collected two singles and a line drive at the center fielder his first three times up against Lemon. With the pitcher on deck, the Indians took their chances with Westrum and he hit the ball hard again—but once more it was right to Doby. The score remained tied.

Irvin, whose catch had ended the Indians' rally in the eighth, gave the Indians hope when he dropped a fly ball with two out and none on in the ninth. After an intentional walk to Doby, Rosen hit a fly to left-center—the fifth straight ball directed toward Irvin. The left fielder caught it with his back to the wall, and another Cleveland rally was snuffed.

After the Giants were retired in the ninth, the Indians continued their siege on the Polo Grounds' outfield in the tenth. Wertz scorched a double to left-center that could have gone for a triple, but the slow-footed Wertz, who had undoubtedly seen enough of Mays's defensive skills, halted at second when Willie quickly got the ball in to the infield. It was Wertz's fourth hit—the only time he'd been retired was on his best-hit ball of the day. Now Wertz was gone from the field, replaced by runner Rudy Regalado. After a sacrifice and an intentional walk, Hegan, who had narrowly missed a grand slam his previous time up against Grissom, was called back by manager Lopez. Lefty-swinging Bill Glynn, who would bat just once more in the Major Leagues (and get a double in Game Three), was struck out by Grissom in yet another crucial moment in the World Series opener.

Lopez used eleven different players in the five through eight spots in Cleveland's batting order, yet he sent his pitcher to bat with the go-ahead run on third in the tenth inning. Lemon, far from your typical weak-hitting pitcher, hit the ball hard but right at Whitey Lockman at first base to end the inning. The Indians were 1 for 16 with men in scoring position, stranding thirteen men on base—eight of them in scoring position.

Lemon fanned Don Mueller to start the bottom of the tenth, but Mays followed with a walk and stole second. After an intentional walk to Hank Thompson, Dusty Rhodes was sent to bat for future Hall of Famer Irvin—the first change of the day to Durocher's batting order besides the pitching substitutions in the eighth inning.

"Dusty Rhodes pinch-hits and hits a ball right over the top of us," Feeney recalled, looking up as he spoke. "Right field, upper deck, where the overhang is. We saw the ball coming out, sailing toward us, and we were up on our feet. And you couldn't see, with the overhang, the ball where it dropped or bounced off the overhang, but it was a home run. It was a high fly, what they used to call a Chinese home run at the Polo Grounds. It was only 257 down the line. Heck, you can play slow-pitch softball at 200 feet down the line. Dusty became a hero in that Series."

James Lamar Rhodes homered the next day off the bench as well and wound up knocking in seven runs in just seven plate appearances. But when people talk about New York's stunning sweep of the Indians in 1954, the discussion invariably comes back to Willie Mays and "The Catch."

"Let's face it," said Feeney, "I'm a Giants fan and I have to say that under the circumstances, the size of the ballpark, how far he had to go to get it, and the throw—it was the greatest catch I've ever seen in my life. He had great speed, Mays, but he also had great baseball instincts—an innate knowledge of where to position himself on hitters."

It was also the only World Series game he ever saw his beloved Giants play at the Polo Grounds. "Three years later," he said, his voice trailing off, recalling how long he had left to root for his team in New York. Feeney attended Fordham University in the Bronx, a stone's throw from the Polo Grounds—yet his Giants were gone by his sophomore year.

I have an indelible picture of the Polo Grounds in my mind and where I was the first time I went to a game. Against Boston. I was in left field. That ballpark I always was in awe of. Maybe it was because I was a Giants fan. I went to the Polo Grounds first, but then I went to Yankee Stadium. We sat in the first row in right field next to the field. And back then the wall at Yankee Stadium came about to my leg. The players were right there, you could BS with them. It was a whole different atmosphere. But I wasn't a Yankees fan, so I always rooted against the Yankees when I went to those games.

The Polo Grounds, it was a mystique in those years, and the mystique always stayed with me. Baseball has changed and I just wonder if fans think the same way as the Giants fans did in '54, '51, or before they left.

Feeney went on to Albany Law School, formed a law practice, and became a judge in his hometown of Kingston, where in 2011 he still served on the bench. When the Giants changed coasts he was heartbroken, but he remained tuned into Giants baseball despite their removal from New York and the late start times. Fifty-six years after he sat in the crowded grandstand at the Polo Grounds and watched Willie Mays steal a game and maybe even a World Series from Vic Wertz and the Indians, Feeney finally saw the Giants win another title, beating the Texas Rangers—a franchise that did not even exist when he saw the 1954 World Series.

Through McCovey and Marichal, Clark and Williams, Bonds Junior and Senior, all the way to Lincecum and Cain. It's fans like Feeney that the Giants honored when the team brought its 2010 World Series trophy to New York for a few days in the snowy January of 2011, inviting Giants fans to view the prize so long in coming. And it also allowed these expatriate fans a chance to talk about their team and meet players in the flesh rather than following the club through drooping eyelids on ESPN or in road grays once a year at the Mets' Citi Field. These fans have proved one thing: You can take the Giants out of New York, but you can't take the Giants fan out of New Yorkers who have been holding on tight for more than half a century. They have never let go of their team. And it appears they never will.

Notes and References

1. Hank Greenberg

1. Greenberg, *Hank Greenberg*, 17. Hereafter cited as *Greenberg*.

2. *Greenberg*, 23.

3. Ross, "Greenberg & Bobo."

4. *Greenberg*, 120.

5. Pluto, *Sixty-One*, 109.

6. *Greenberg*, 66.

7. *Greenberg*, 128.

8. *Greenberg*, 155.

9. *Greenberg*, 216.

10. *Greenberg*, 216.

Cramer, Richard Ben. *Joe DiMaggio: The Hero's Life.* New York: Simon & Schuster, 2000.

Dewey, Donald, and Nicholas Acocella. *Encyclopedia of Major League Baseball Teams.* New York: Harper Collins, 1993.

Greenberg, Hank. *Hank Greenberg: The Story of My Life.* Edited and with an introduction by Ira Berkow. New York: Times Books, 1989.

Horvitz, Peter S., and Joachim Horvitz. *The Big Book of Jewish Baseball.* New York: SPI Books, 2001.

James, Bill. *The Bill James Guide to Baseball Managers: From 1870 to Today.* New York: Scribner, 1997.

———. *The New Bill James Historical Baseball Abstract.* New York: Free Press, 2001.

———. *The Politics of Glory.* New York: Macmillan, 1994.

Leavy, Jane. *Koufax: A Lefty's Legacy.* New York: Harper Collins, 2002.

Levine, Peter. *Ellis Island to Ebbets Field.* Oxford: Oxford University Press, 1992.

Nemec, David, and Saul Wisnia. *Baseball: More Than One Hundred Fifty Years.* Lincolnwood IL: Publications International, 1997.

Pluto, Terry, with Tony Kubek. *Sixty-One.* New York: Macmillan, 1987.

Rader, Benjamin G. *Baseball: A History of America's Game.* Urbana and Chicago: University of Illinois Press, 1992.

Ribalow, Harold. *The Jew in American Sports.* New York: Bloch, 1948.

Seidel, Michael. *Ted Williams: A Baseball Life.* Chicago: Contemporary Books, 1991.

Stroh, Guy W. *American Ethical Thought.* Chicago: Nelson Hall, 1979.

Wallace, Joseph, ed. *The Autobiography of Baseball: The Inside Story from the Stars Who Played the Game.* New York: Henry Abrams, 1998.

Ward, Geoffrey C., and Ken Burns. *Baseball: An Illustrated History.* New York: Knopf, 1994.

White, Edward G. *Creating the National Pastime.* Princeton NJ: Princeton University Press, 1996.

Will, George. *Bunts.* New York: Scribner's, 1998.

Ross, Mike. "Hank Greenberg & Bobo." *National Pastime: A Review of Baseball History* 22 (2002): 124–28.

Hank Greenberg obituary. *New York Times*, September 5, 1986.

Interview with Russell Turkel, resident of Beaumont, Texas.

Hank Greenberg's files at the National Baseball Hall of Fame Library, Cooperstown NY.

2. Al Lopez

1. Niebuhr, "Hall's 'Senor' Citizen," par. 16.

2. Niebuhr, "Hall's 'Senor' Citizen," par. 16.

3. McEwen, "El Senor Gave So Much," par. 31.

4. Goldstein, "Al Lopez," par. 11.

5. Niebuhr, "Hall's 'Senor' Citizen," par. 15.

6. Niebuhr, "Hall's 'Senor' Citizen," par. 15.

7. Niebuhr, "Hall's 'Senor' Citizen," par. 18.

8. McEwen, "El Senor Gave So Much," par. 25.

9. Madden, "Reminiscing with Al Lopez," par. 2.

10. Daley, "Two Managers."

11. Madden, "Reminiscing with Al Lopez," par. 3.

12. Niebuhr, "Hall's 'Senor' Citizen," par. 19.

13. Baseball-Reference.com.

14. Johnson and Wolff, *Encyclopedia of Minor League Baseball*, 253.

15. Retrosheet.org.

16. *Operation White Sox*, 67.

17. Retrosheet.org.

18. *Exciting Story of the White Sox*, 65.

19. Retrosheet.org.

20. Daley, "Two Managers," 39.

21. Daley, "Two Managers," 39.

22. Madden, "Reminiscing with Al Lopez," par. 11.

23. Dewey and Acocella, *Total Ballclubs*, 110.

24. Dewey and Acocella, *Total Ballclubs*, 110.

25. Dewey and Acocella, *Total Ballclubs*, 110.

26. Retrosheet.org.

27. Daley, "Two Managers," 39.

28. Kuenster, "Oldest Hall of Fame Member," par. 31.

29. Niebuhr, "Hall's 'Senor' Citizen," par. 34.

30. Hamilton and Schlossberg, *Making Airwaves*, 56.

31. *Operation White Sox*, 67.

32. *Operation White Sox*, 67.

33. Niebuhr, "Hall's 'Senor' Citizen," par. 14.

34. Dewey and Acocella, *Total Ballclubs*, 125.

35. Goldstein, "Al Lopez," par. 14.

36. Dewey and Acocella, *Total Ballclubs*, 67.

37. Goldstein, "Al Lopez," par. 15.

38. Rosenthal, *Baseball's Best Managers*, 148.

39. Niebuhr, "Hall's 'Senor' Citizen," par. 4.

40. Baseball-Reference.com.

41. Rosenthal, *Baseball's Best Managers*, 146.

42. Rosenthal, *Baseball's Best Managers*, 152.

43. Schneider, *Cleveland Indians Encyclopedia*, 513.

44. Weiss and Wright, "Team #85," par. 6.

45. Weiss and Wright, "Team #85," pars. 9, 12.

46. Weiss and Wright, "Team #85," par. 8.

47. Schneider, *Indians Encyclopedia*, 513.

48. Schneider, *Indians Encyclopedia*, 513.

49. Schneider, *Indians Encyclopedia*, 514.

50. Schneider, *Indians Encyclopedia*, 514.

51. Rosenthal, *Baseball's Best Managers*, 150.

52. Schneider, *Indians Encyclopedia*, 512.

53. Schneider, *Indians Encyclopedia*, 514–15.

54. Schneider, *Indians Encyclopedia*, 67.

55. Schneider, *Indians Encyclopedia*, 69.

56. Schneider, *Indians Encyclopedia*, 513.

57. Schneider, *Indians Encyclopedia*, 513.

58. Schneider, *Indians Encyclopedia*, 471.

59. Schneider, *Indians Encyclopedia*, 469.

60. Arsenault, "Our Roots Run Deep," 93.

61. McEwen, "El Senor Gave So Much," par. 26.

62. Kay, "Al Lopez," pars. 13–16.

63. Schneider, *Indians Encyclopedia*, 517.

64. Rosenthal, *Baseball's Best Managers*, 152.

65. Gutteridge et al., *Don Gutteridge*, 175.

66. Gutteridge et al., *Don Gutteridge*, 174.

67. Gutteridge et al., *Don Gutteridge*, 175.

68. *Operation White Sox*, 35.

69. *Operation White Sox*, 35.

70. Gutteridge et al., *Don Gutteridge*, 175.

71. Goldstein, "Al Lopez," par. 4.

72. Goldstein, "Al Lopez," par. 9.

73. Hamilton and Schlossberg, *Making Airwaves*, 65.

74. Hamilton and Schlossberg, *Making Airwaves*, 56.

75. Hamilton and Schlossberg, *Making Airwaves*, 55–56.

76. Baseball-Reference.com.

77. Dewey and Acocella, *Total Ballclubs*, 171–72.

78. Dewey and Acocella, *Total Ballclubs*, 172.

79. Rosenthal, *Baseball's Best Managers*, 155.

80. Dewey and Acocella, *Total Ballclubs*, 180.

81. Rosenthal, *Baseball's Best Managers*, 155.

82. Rosenthal, *Baseball's Best Managers*, 155.

83. Rosenthal, *Baseball's Best Managers*, 155.

84. Bodley, "Lopez—The Senor," pars. 9–10.

85. Bodley, "Lopez—The Senor," par. 12.

86. "Garter on the Sox," par. 2.

87. "Garter on the Sox," par. 2.

88. "Garter on the Sox," par. 2.

89. Baseball-Reference.com.

90. Helpingstine, *Chicago White Sox*, 53–54.

91. Bodley, "Lopez—The Senor," par. 23.

92. Gutteridge et al., *Don Gutteridge*, 182.

93. Gutteridge et al., *Don Gutteridge*, 183.

94. "Son, Grandson, Great Grandson," par. 4.

95. McEwen, "El Senor Gave So Much," par. 20.

96. Bodley, "Lopez—The Senor," par. 5.

97. Bodley, "Lopez—The Senor," par. 1.

98. Goldstein, "Al Lopez," par. 2.

99. Niebuhr, "Hall's 'Senor' Citizen," par. 37.

100. Murr, "Broussard's Homer," par. 9.

101. "Son, Grandson, Great Grandson," par. 2.

Dewey, Donald, and Nicholas Acocella. *Total Ballclubs: The Ultimate Book of Baseball Teams.* Toronto: Sport Media Publishing Inc., 2005.

The Exciting Story of the White Sox. Chicago: Chicago White Sox, 1965.

Gutteridge, Don, Ronnie Joyner, and Bill Bozman. *Don Gutteridge in Words and Pictures.* Dunkirk MD: Pepperpot Productions, Inc., 2002.

Hamilton, Milo, and Dan Schlossberg. *Making Airwaves: 60 Years at Milo's Microphone.* Champaign IL: Sports Publishing LLC, 2006.

Helpingstine, Dan. *Chicago White Sox: 1959 and Beyond.* Jefferson SC: Arcadia Publishing, 2004.

Johnson, Lloyd, and Miles Wolff. *The Encyclopedia of Minor League Baseball*, 2nd ed. Durham NC: Baseball America, 1997.

Operation White Sox. Chicago: The Chicago White Sox, 1964.

Rosenthal, Harold. *Baseball's Best Managers.* New York: Bartholomew House, 1961.

Schneider, Russell. *The Cleveland Indians Encyclopedia.* Champaign IL: Sports Publishing LLC, 2001.

Arsenault, Raymond. "Our Roots Run Deep." *Tampa Bay Devil Rays Magazine* 1, no. 1 (March/April 1998): 86–94.

Arthur Daley. "The Two Managers." *New York Times*, September 26, 1954.

Bodley, Hal. "Lopez—The Senor—Has Wonderful Memories of '59 Series." *USA Today*, October 18, 2005: 23 pars. http://www.mywire.com/pubs/USA TODAY/2005/10/18/1053598?&pb=222. Accessed October 7, 2007.

Goldstein, Richard. "Al Lopez, a Hall of Fame Manager, Is Dead at 97." *New York Times*, October 31, 2005: 25 pars. http://www.nytimes.com. Accessed October 7, 2007.

Kay, Jennifer. "Al Lopez, Who Led ChiSox to '59 Series, Dies at 97." *USA Today*, October 30, 2005: 28 pars.

http://www.usatoday.com/sports/baseball/2005-10-30-allopezobit_x.htm. Accessed October 8, 2007.

Kuenster, John. "Oldest Hall of Fame Member Revives Some Baseball Memories." *Baseball Digest*, July 2003: 36 pars. http://findarticles/com/p/articles/mi_m0FCI/is_7_62/ai_10220515/print. Accessed October 7, 2007.

Madden, Bill. "Reminiscing with Al Lopez." *Baseball Digest*, August 2004: 19 pars. http://findarticles.com/p/articles/mi_m0FCI/is_8_63/ai_n618382/print. Accessed October 7, 2007.

McEwen, Tom. "El Senor Gave So Much of His Big Heart Away." *Tampa Bay Online*, October 31, 2005: 40 pars. http://sports.tbo.com/sports/MGBK537BGFE.html. Accessed October 7, 2007.

Murr, Chuck. "Broussard's Homer Helps Top Tribe, 3–1." *Indians Ink*, July 30, 2006: 21 pars. http://indians.scout.com/2/550918.html. Accessed October 13, 2007.

Niebuhr, Keith. "He's the Hall's 'Senor' Citizen." *St. Petersburg Times*, July 25, 2005: 38 pars. http://www.sptimes.com. Accessed October 8, 2007.

Weiss, Bill, and Marshall Wright. "Team #85: 1948 Indianapolis Indians" (2001): 15 pars. http://web.minorleaguebaseball.com/milb.history/top100.jspidx=85. Accessed October 7, 2007.

"The Garter on the Sox." *Time*, May 28, 1965: 8 pars. http://www.time.com/printout/0,8816,941345,00.html. Accessed October 7, 2007.

"Son, Grandson, Great Grandson of Al Lopez to Throw Out First Pitch At Rays' Home Opener." *Devil Rays Homepage*, March 7, 2006: 5 pars. www.devilrays.com. Accessed October 7, 2007.

"Un-Covering the Past—Hall of Fame Manager Al Lopez." *Baseball Digest*, May 2001: 11 pars. http://findarticles.com/p/articles/mi_m0FCI/is_5_60/ai_7263728/print. Accessed October 7, 2007.

Baseball-Reference.com.

Retrosheet.org.

3. Tony Cuccinello

Nash, Bruce, and Allan Zullo. *The Baseball Hall of Shame.* New York: Pocket Books: 1985.

Westcott, Rich. "Tony Cuccinello—A Great Way to Spend a Lifetime." In *Diamond Greats, Profiles and Interviews with 65 of Baseball's History Makers.* Westport CT: Meckler Books, 1988, 94.

Carmichael, John P. "Lollar Play Not Series Key—Lopez." *Baseball Digest* 19 (February 1960): 71.

Chastain, Bill. "This Was the Closest Race Ever for a Batting Title." *Baseball Digest* 52 (December 1993): 63.

Oates, Bob. "It Took Five Perfect Plays to Get Lollar at Plate!" *Baseball Digest* 19 (February 1960): 69.

Daniel, Dan. "Over the Fence: Two Big Breaks Influenced Outcome of Series." *The Sporting News*, October 21, 1959, 10.

Holmes, T. "Carey Experiments with Dodger Infield." *The Sporting News*, March 31, 1932, 1.

Spoelstra, Watson. "Relaxed McAuliffe Gave Tigers Their Flag Spark." *The Sporting News*, October 5, 1968, 33.

"'Dodgers Reeled Off Perfect Play to Nail Lollar'—Lopez." *The Sporting News*, January 20, 1960, 4.

"Majors' All-Stars Meet in 'Game of the Century.'" *The Sporting News*, July 6, 1933, 1.

The Sporting News, October 21, 1959, 12.

New York Times, September 23, 1995.

Baseball-Reference.com.

Retrosheet.org.

SABR Home Run Log, www.sabr.org.

http://web.minorleaguebaseball.com/milb/history/top_about.jsp. Accessed September 16, 2007.

4. Mel Harder

1. Connolly, "How Harder Held Dimag."
2. Goldstein, "Mel Harder."
3. Goldstein, "Mel Harder."
4. Cleveland Indians press release, October 21, 2002.

Allen, Maury. *Baseball's 100*. New York: A&W Visual Library, 1981.

Blake, Mike. *Baseball Chronicles*. Cincinnati: Betterway Books, 1994.

Boston, Talmage. *1939: Baseball's Pivotal Year*. Fort Worth TX: Summit Group, 1994.

Debs, Victor, Jr. *Missed It by That Much*. Jefferson NC: McFarland, 1998.

Dewey, Donald, and Nicholas Acocella. *Encyclopedia of Major League Baseball Teams*. New York: Harper Collins, 1993.

Feller, Bob, with Bill Gilbert. *Now Pitching Bob Feller*. New York: Carol Publishing Group, 1990.

Freese, Mel R. *Charmed Circle*. Jefferson NC: McFarland, 1997.

James, Bill. *The New Bill James Historical Baseball Abstract*. New York: Free Press, 2001.

Kelley, Brent. *The Case for Those Overlooked by the Baseball Hall of Fame*. Jefferson NC: McFarland, 1992.

———. *The Early All-Stars*. Jefferson NC: McFarland, 1997.

———. *In the Shadow of the Babe*. Jefferson NC: McFarland, 1995.

———. *100 Greatest Pitchers*. New York: Crescent Books, 1988.

Kerrane, Kevin. *The Hurlers*. Alexandria VA: Redefinition, 1989.

McCaffrey, Eugene V., and Roger McCaffrey. *A Players' Choice*. New York: Facts on File Publishing, 1987.

Mead, William B. *Baseball Goes to War*. New York: Farragut Publishing, 1984.

Pluto, Terry. *The Curse of Rocky Colavito*. New York: Simon & Schuster, 1994.

———. *Our Tribe*. New York: Simon & Schuster, 1999.

Quigley, Martin. *The Crooked Pitch*. New York: Algonquin Press, 1984.

Connolly, Will. "How Harder Held Dimag to .180." *Baseball Digest*, July 1952. Reprinted in *Baseball Digest*, September 1989, 87-88.

Goldstein, Richard. "Mel Harder, Indians Pitcher and Longtime Coach in Majors." [Obituary]. *New York Times*, October 21, 2002.

Baseball Digest, May 1969 and July 1984.

5. Red Kress

1. *The Sporting News*, March 21, 1956.
2. *The Sporting News*, March 21, 1956.
3. *St. Louis Post Dispatch*, March 25, 1932.

Neft, David S., Richard M. Cohen, and Michael L. Neft. *Sports Encyclopedia: Baseball*. New York: St. Martin's Press, 2000.

Macmillan Baseball Encyclopedia and *Total Baseball*, various editions.

Newspapers from Oakland, St. Louis, Chicago, Los Angeles, Cleveland, Detroit, Minneapolis, Lakeland (Florida), Tucson, and Long Beach, and *The Sporting News*.

Baseball-Reference.com.

Thanks to SABR member Bill Staples for articles about Kress in California winter ball.

Red Kress's file at the National Baseball Hall of Fame Library, Cooperstown NY.
The Sporting News, Reach, and *Who's Who* guides and Cleveland Indians yearbooks.

6. Bill Lobe

1. Hal Lebovitz, "Houtteman Hoots at Hard-Luck Label," *The Sporting News,* June 2, 1954, 5.

2. http://www.baseballinwartime.com/player_bio graphies/lobe_bill.htm, June 19, 2007.

3. Hal Lebovitz, "Grips, Twist and Release Explained by Tribe Coach," *The Sporting News,* April 30, 1952, 3.

4. J. G. Taylor Spink, "Once a Jockey, Now a Big Bear," *The Sporting News,* August 13, 1952, 4.

Cleveland Plain Dealer.
The Sporting News.

Baseball-Reference.com.
http://baseballinwartime.blogspot.com/p/baseball-in-wartime-website.html.

9. Bob Feller

1. Sickels, *Bob Feller—Ace,* 236.

2. Sickels, *Bob Feller—Ace,* 239.

3. Feller, *Now Pitching,* 198.

4. Feller, *Now Pitching,* 201. When asked years later why he had not pitched Feller in the 1954 Series, Lopez responded, "He wasn't that good of a pitcher anymore" (Singletary, *Al Lopez,* 171).

5. Feller, *Now Pitching,* 198.

6. Deford, "Robert Can Still Bring It," 63. Another early example of a father raising a son to be a star athlete is Colonel Robert Jones, who cultivated his son Bobby from an early age to be a champion golfer (Rice, "Regular Fellers," 18).

7. Honig, *When the Grass Was Real,* 261.

8. Sickels, *Bob Feller—Ace,* 11.

9. Feller's dad was quoted as saying, "I don't want him to be a farmer" (Feller, *Strikeout Story,* 4; Daly, *Times at Bat,* 202). The arc lights were used about fifteen years before power lines came to the farm. When Feller was fourteen or fifteen, he threw his father a fastball in the barn when he was expecting a curve. The result was three broken ribs for his father (Honig, *When the Grass Was Real,* 263; Vincent, *Only Game in Town,* 37).

10. Feller, *Strikeout Story,* 9.

11. Feller, *Strikeout Story,* 11–13; Sickels, *Bob Feller—Ace,* 15–17; Feller, *Little Blue Book of Baseball,* 7. In 1946 after Feller's second Major League no-hitter, sportswriters asked him who was the greatest figure in his baseball career. "My father" was Feller's response (Daley, *Times at Bat,* 202–3).

12. Feller, *Now Pitching,* 36; Sickels, *Bob Feller—Ace,* 18–20; Bob Feller, "Bob Feller and American Legion Baseball," *American Legion Magazine,* June 1963, 14–15, 45–46.

13. David Pietrusza, Matthew Silverman, and Michael Gershman, eds., *Baseball: The Biographical Encyclopedia,* 346.

14. Sickels, *Bob Feller—Ace,* 22.

15. Sickels, *Bob Feller—Ace,* 24–26.

16. Rust, *Legends,* 38–40.

17. Both are today in the Bob Feller Museum in Van Meter.

18. Sickels, *Bob Feller—Ace,* 30–31.

19. The game was played during the All-Star break. The Cardinals' thirty-eight-year-old manager, Frankie Frisch, reportedly took himself out of the game after watching Feller warm up, saying, "They're not gonna get the old Flash out there against that kid" (Meany and Holmes, *Baseball's Best,* 38; Meany, *Baseball's Greatest Pitchers,* 53). For other versions of the Frisch story, see Broeg, *Super Stars of Baseball,* 74; and Bartell, *Rowdy Richard,* 190–91.

20. Feller, *Strikeout Story,* 24.

21. Feller, *Strikeout Story,* 25. In his first at bat, Durocher supposedly took two strikes, dropped his bat, and turned toward the dugout. The umpire said, "You've still got a strike left." "You can have it," Durocher said, "I don't want it" (Feller, "Baseball a Game?" 38).

22. Feller, *Strikeout Story,* 27; Daly, *Times at Bat,* 201.

23. Sickels, *Bob Feller—Ace,* 38.

24. It was an appearance Feller wanted to forget. He did not mention it in either of his autobiographies. See Sickels, *Bob Feller—Ace,* 39.

25. Feller, *Strikeout Story,* 40–42.

26. Adding to his record-setting performance was the fact that his father was in the stands that day. See Feller, *Strikeout Story*, 54–58.

27. Gay, *Satch, Dizzy & Rapid Robert*, 163–67. Hall of Fame pitcher Robin Roberts remembered that Feller came to Springfield, Illinois, that year to throw out the first pitch for the Illinois State Amateur Baseball Championship. Roberts, who was nine years old, managed to get a Feller autograph but lost it before he got home (Roberts, *My Life in Baseball*, 5).

28. Feller, *Now Pitching*, 41. Although Feller would have been the subject of a huge bidding war if declared a free agent, he was comfortable with the Cleveland organization and very much wanted to stay there. Sickels, *Bob Feller—Ace*, 51–52; Lewis, *Cleveland Indians*, 195–97; Spink, *Judge Landis*, 193–95.

29. During the face-to-face meeting, Bill Feller had threatened a lawsuit if Judge Landis declared his son a free agent (Pietrusza, *Judge and Jury*, 354; Marshall, *Baseball's Pivotal Era*, 5–6). Landis required Cleveland to pay the Des Moines franchise $7,500 in damages (Sickels, *Bob Feller—Ace*, 57; Fitzgerald, "Feller Incorporated," 62).

30. Feller's high school principal arranged for a tutor and allowed him to graduate with his class if he "could pass the usual tests" (Feller, *Strikeout Story*, 61).

31. Broeg, "No Fireball's Any Swifter," 18; Ed Fitzgerald, "Feller Incorporated," 63.

32. Sickels, *Bob Feller—Ace*, 67–71.

33. Gay, *Satch, Dizzy & Rapid Robert*, 170–78. The Indians did send trainer Lefty Weisman along to watch over their prized property.

34. Sickels, *Bob Feller—Ace*, 75.

35. Feller initially had trouble holding runners on base with his high leg kick. He was also tipping when he was going to throw to first base with a runner on. Ben Chapman reportedly told Feller he could steal second base on him anytime he wanted and, after doing so, told him how he was tipping his pickoff move (Karst and Jones, *Who's Who*, 299–300).

36. They are listed in MacFarlane, *Daguerreotypes*, 92.

37. By his own estimation, Feller threw 136 pitches in his one-hitter, striking out and walking six. He also got two base hits and drove in two runs (Feller, *Now Pitching*, 68–69).

38. Feller, *Now Pitching*, 78.

39. Greenberg did touch Feller for a double while twice striking out (Feller, *Now Pitching*, 83–85; *Strikeout Story*, 143–47; Greenberg and Berkow, *Story of My Life*, 106–22).

40. Feller's wildness in his early years was legendary. In one oft-told incident, Lefty Gomez was batting against Feller late in the second game of a doubleheader at Yankee Stadium. The afternoon shadows were long and when Gomez stepped into the batter's box, he promptly pulled a cigarette lighter out of his pocket, flicked up a light, and held it in front of his face. The umpire was not pleased and said, "C'mon Lefty, are you trying to make a joke out of the game? You can see Feller just fine." The quick-witted Lefty responded, "Hell, I can see him. I just want to make sure that wild man out there can see me" (Werber and Rogers, *Memories of a Ballplayer*, 99; Auker, *Sleeper Cars and Flannel Uniforms*, 197; Daley, *Times at Bat*, 128).

41. Daley, *Times at Bat*, 148.

42. The Detroit game was the first game of the season. The actual Opening Day in St. Louis, which Feller was to start, was rained out (Sickels, *Bob Feller—Ace*, 84).

43. Mrs. Feller required some stitches but was not seriously injured (Boston, *1939*, 140; Sickels, *Bob Feller—Ace*, 84; Smith, *Baseball's Famous Pitchers*, 284–85).

44. The trade of Averill, who had been openly critical of manager Oscar Vitt, to the Tigers was very unpopular in Cleveland (Feller, *Strikeout Story*, 157–59; Sickels, *Bob Feller—Ace*, 85).

45. Feller, *Strikeout Story*, 159–61; Vincent et al., *Mid-Summer Classic*, 39–43. When Feller struck out Stan Hack in the ninth inning to end the game, 63,000 Yankee Stadium fans gave him a rousing standing ovation (Fitzgerald, "Feller Incorporated," 63).

46. Lefty Gomez told the story of batting against Feller and taking the first two pitches for strikes on fastballs he could barely see. When the umpire called strike three on the third pitch, Lefty turned and said, "C'mon. That one sounded a bit low" (Fitzgerald, "Feller Incorporated," 64).

47. Feller also tied for the most shutouts with four and was third with a 2.85 earned-run average. He would finish third in the voting for the Most Valuable Player (Sickels, *Bob Feller—Ace*, 87).

48. Commissioner Landis had set forth an edict lim-

iting postseason barnstorming tours to ten days, thus limiting Feller's West Coast excursion (Gay, *Satch, Dizzy & Rapid Robert*, 178–80; Barthel, *Baseball Barnstorming*, 132, 142).

49. Klima, *Pitched Battle*, 63–67; Westcott and Lewis, *No-Hitters*, 142–44.

50. The Cleveland fans largely took the side of management and several times threw diapers and baby bottles onto the field during games (Sickels, *Bob Feller—Ace*, 92–98; Phillips, *Crybaby Indians*; Johnson, "Crybabies of 1940," 37).

51. Feller had pitched on short rest several times during September and at one point threw twenty-seven innings in eight days (Sickels, *Bob Feller—Ace*, 99–100).

52. Giebel never won another Major League game (Sickels, *Bob Feller—Ace*, 100–101; Lieb, *Detroit Tigers*, 244; Schoor, *Bob Feller*, 132; Kelley, *Pastime in Turbulence*, 41–50).

53. He also tied for the lead in shutouts with four and reduced his walks to 118 to avoid the league lead in that category for the first time since he became a full-time starter.

54. Feller teamed with Earle Mack and Johnny Mize and played games in Little Falls, Billings, Missoula, and Great Falls, Montana, and in Fargo, North Dakota (Barthel, *Baseball Barnstorming*, 144).

55. Feller promptly picked Frey off first (Vincent et al., *Mid-Summer Classic*, 50–55).

56. Feller also led in hits allowed (284) and walks (194).

57. Sickels, *Bob Feller—Ace*, 115–16; Bloomfield, *Duty, Honor, Victory*, 288–89. Feller was already wrestling with whether to enlist or not even before Pearl Harbor (Vaccaro, *1941*, 270; Feller, *Strikeout Story*, 218).

58. Other professional baseball players on the team included Ace Parker, Sam Chapman, Fred Hutchinson, Jack Conway, Vinnie Smith, and Max Wilson (Feller, *Strikeout Story*, 221).

59. In one game against Wilson, North Carolina, a Class C team in the Bi-State League, Feller struck out twenty-one batters (Feller, *Strikeout Story*, 221).

60. Feller requested assignment to the battleship *Iowa*, but apparently there was not room there for everyone from the Hawkeye State (Feller, *Strikeout Story*, 222).

61. Former Indians outfielder Soup Campbell was best man, and teammates Lou Boudreau and Rollie Hemsley also attended the wedding. The newlyweds managed a three-day honeymoon in New York City before Feller returned to active duty (Sickels, *Bob Feller—Ace*, 120–22).

62. There Feller recalled playing softball in Iceland at two in the morning with the sun still up. He also helped a woman stack her peat moss and milk her cows in exchange for a quart of fresh milk (Mead, *Even the Browns*, 193).

63. Feller took the lead in constructing a more proper baseball field than the primitive one they found. Led by his pitching, the *Alabama*'s squad won the Third Fleet championship (Sickels, *Bob Feller—Ace*, 123).

64. Sickels, *Bob Feller—Ace*, 125.

65. Feller, *Strikeout Story*, 213.

66. Feller had by now been married almost two years and had spent just five nights with his wife, Virginia. She immediately flew out from Norfolk to reunite with her husband. See his *Strikeout Story*, 228; Anton and Nowlin, *When Baseball Went to War*, 105–9; Anton, *No Greater Love*, 116–33.

67. Although the roster changed continually, the club was stocked with big leaguers like Ken Keltner, Dick Wakefield, Clyde Shoun, Walker Cooper, Denny Galehouse, and Johnny Gorsica (Anton, *No Greater Love*, 230; Sickels, *Bob Feller—Ace*, 128).

68. Sickels, *Bob Feller—Ace*, 129.

69. Feller, *Strikeout Story*, 230-31. According to Feller, although he had enough points, an admiral at Great Lakes was dragging his heels about his discharge. So Feller called the secretary of the Navy and was discharged the next morning, along with nineteen others who had enough points (Mead, *Even the Browns*, 225–26).

70. In pregame ceremonies, Cleveland great Tris Speaker presented Feller with a new Jeep for use back in Iowa. Feller in turn contributed $1,000 to the Press Memorial Fountain Fund (Sickels, *Bob Feller—Ace*, 133). Cy Young was also present for the occasion (Feller, *Strikeout Story*, 232).

71. Feller had pitched an exhibition game in Cleveland for an all-star service team against the American League All-Stars on June 7, losing 5–0 (Feller, *Strikeout Story*, 231–32).

72. Feller, *Strikeout Story*, 234–35; Sickels, *Bob Feller—Ace*, 134.

73. Feller believed he had lost about $250,000 due to the war. "The trick," he told his wife, "was to make it up"

(Schoor, *Bob Feller*, 141). Commissioner Happy Chandler waived the ten-day postseason barnstorming limit to allow ballplayers returning from the service a chance to earn extra money (Feller, *Strikeout Story*, 236). Paige and Feller pitched before a crowd of 20,000 in St. Louis and 23,000 in Wrigley Field, Los Angeles, where 10,000 fans were reportedly turned away (Gay, *Satch, Dizzy & Rapid Robert*, 205; Barthel, *Baseball Barnstorming*, 146).

74. Feller, *Strikeout Story*, 237.

75. Feller recruited former Major Leaguers such as Dizzy Dean, Bill Dickey, and Lou Fonseca as well as current stars like Joe DiMaggio, Lou Boudreau, Spud Chandler, Eddie Miller, Charlie Keller, Hugh Mulcahy, Rollie Hemsley, and Tommy Bridges to act as coaches (Fitzgerald, "Feller Incorporated," 65; Sickels, *Bob Feller—Ace*, 137–39; Marshall, *Baseball's Pivotal Era*, 84).

76. Feller, *Strikeout Story*, 238; Marshall, *Baseball's Pivotal Era*, 49.

77. The game went into the ninth inning a scoreless tie until Frankie Hayes homered off Floyd Bevens for the only run of the game. Feller threw 133 pitches in the game, which ended with Snuffy Stirnweiss on third base for the Yankees in the bottom of the ninth (Feller, *Strikeout Story*, 241–44; Sickels, *Bob Feller—Ace*, 140–41; Feller, *Now Pitching*, 130–32; Westcott and Lewis, *No-Hitters*, 154–55; Don Schiffer, *My Greatest Baseball Game*, 75–79; Feller, "My Greatest Game," 85–87).

78. Feller started the All-Star Game for the American League, which was held at Fenway Park. He pitched three shutout innings, allowing two hits and striking out three, and was the winning pitcher in a 12–0 American League victory (Vincent et. al., *Midsummer Classic*, 76–82).

79. Feller, *Strikeout Story*, 245.

80. Feller, *Strikeout Story*, 250; Sickels, *Bob Feller—Ace*, 142; Turner, *When the Boys Came Back* 186–89; Feller, *Now Pitching*, 133–35.

81. Feller, *Strikeout Story*, 253–55. Research later revealed that Waddell had struck out 349 rather than 343 batters, snatching the record back (Sickels, *Bob Feller—Ace*, 145; Turner, *When the Boys Came Back,* 204). It has since been broken by Sandy Koufax and Nolan Ryan.

82. The next winningest Indians pitcher was Allie Reynolds with eleven victories.

83. Surprisingly, Feller probably would not have won the American League Cy Young Award had it existed. Hal Newhouser finished 26-9 for the second-place Tigers and led the league with a 1.94 earned run average.

84. Feller's club included Stan Musial, Phil Rizzuto, Ken Keltner, Jeff Heath, Charlie Keller, Johnny Sain, Bobo Newsom, and Spud Chandler among others. Paige's team had Monte Irvin, Max Manning, Buck O'Neil, Sam Jethroe, Hilton Smith, Willard Brown, and Quincy Trouppe (Sickels, *Bob Feller—Ace*, 149–57; Gay, *Satch, Dizzy & Rapid Robert*, 219–45; Barthel, *Baseball Barnstorming*, 146–52; Feller, *Now Pitching*, 136–44; Tye, *Satchel*, 170–75).

85. Feller's total 1947 income including barnstorming and endorsements may have exceeded $150,000, although high postwar tax rates cut into that amount by as much as two-thirds. See Sickels, *Bob Feller—Ace*, 163; Hawkins, "Feller's $150,000 Pitch," 25, 148, 170. For Bill Veeck's account of his salary negotiations with Feller, see Veeck, *Veeck as in Wreck*, 133.

86. In 1947 Billy Goodman, who would win the 1950 American League batting title, was a rookie. He was sent up to hit against Feller and told to make Feller throw him a strike. Goodman later said, "I did better than that. I made him throw me three strikes. I went back and sat down and said to myself, 'Man, you're in the wrong league.' I had never seen anything like that." Robert W. Creamer, *Baseball in '41*, 167.

87. The 1947 version of the "Bob Feller All-Stars" included Andy Pafko, Ralph Kiner, Ferris Fain, Ken Keltner, Eddie Lopat, Ewell Blackwell, Jeff Heath, Jim Hegan, and Bill McCahan. It included several games in Mexico but overall was not a financial success (Sickels, *Bob Feller—Ace*, 177–81; Gay, *Satch, Dizzy & Rapid Robert*, 246–60; Barthel, *Baseball Barnstorming*, 152–55).

88. Feller was nonetheless selected for the All-Star team. He elected not to participate, drawing a firestorm of controversy (Sickels, *Bob Feller—Ace*, 193–94; Feller, *Now Pitching*, 152–53). American League All-Star manager Bucky Harris was particularly vocal, saying that if he had his way, Feller would never be asked to another All-Star Game (Graham, *Baseball Extra*, 143–44). For Feller's side of the story, see Feller, "When the Crowd Boos!," 1.

89. Kaiser, *Epic Season*, 229–30; Schneider, *Boys of Summer of '48*, 62.

90. Parker, *Win or Go Home*, 39–75.

91. Feller, *Now Pitching*, 163–67; Robinson, *Lucky Me*, 65; Reichler, *Baseball's Great Moments*, 32–34; Schneider, *Boys of Summer of '48*, 63.

92. Feller, *Now Pitching*, 170–71; Robinson, *Lucky Me*, 67.

93. Bob Lemon finished 1948 with a 20-14 record and a 2.82 earned run average while Gene Bearden went 20-7 with a 2.43 ERA to lead the league.

94. Sickels, *Bob Feller—Ace*, 205.

95. Feller did participate in a brief, unsuccessful barnstorming tour of the West Coast after the 1949 season (Sickels, *Bob Feller—Ace*, 212; Gay, *Satch, Dizzy & Rapid Robert*, 273–74). The average attendance was about 3,000, but a game in Tijuana, Mexico, attracted a reported 125 fans (Barthel, *Baseball Barnstorming*, 158).

96. In 247 innings, he recorded 119 strikeouts but walked 103.

97. The Tigers' run was aided by Feller's throwing error in the fourth inning. That tied the score, 1–1, where it remained until Luke Easter singled in a go-ahead run in the eighth. Afterward Stengel was quoted as saying, "How did I know the guy would pitch a no-hitter? I'm better off dead." See Sickels, *Bob Feller—Ace*, 218–20; Westcott and Lewis, *No-Hitters*, 167–69.

98. In honor of his great season, the Cleveland sportswriters named Feller "Man of the Year" (Sickels, *Bob Feller—Ace*, 222).

99. Sickels, *Bob Feller—Ace*, 231.

100. He often pitched on Sundays, to maximize his still considerable drawing power (Feller, *Now Pitching*, 210).

101. Sickels, *Bob Feller—Ace*, 247.

102. Sickels, *Bob Feller—Ace*, 248.

103. Feller, *Now Pitching*, 206–8, 215–17.

104. For example, Feller spoke at the author's Little League banquet in Casper, Wyoming, in the summer of 1959 and gave an autographed postcard-sized photo to every Little Leaguer in attendance.

105. Wallace took Feller to task since he had been one of baseball's highest-paid players for many years, but Feller stuck to his guns, noting that the reserve clause very negatively affected the average ballplayer, who averaged only four-plus years in the big leagues (Sickels, *Bob Feller—Ace*, 252–54).

106. In later years, he had a sports radio show in Cleveland and also did some cable-television broadcasting for the Indians (Feller, *Now Pitching*, 211).

107. Sickels, *Bob Feller—Ace*, 255–56. Feller was elected with Jackie Robinson. They were the first first-ballot inductees since the inaugural Hall of Fame elections in 1939. Feller was the first pitcher elected on the first ballot since Walter Johnson. For Feller's view of the Hall of Fame in 1962, the year before he was elected, see Bob Feller, as told to Edward Linn, "The Trouble with the Hall of Fame."

108. Pietrusza et al., *Baseball*, 348.

109. Feller was a lifetime .151 hitter with eight career home runs. One was a pop fly that just fell into the right-field pavilion in Sportsman's Park in St. Louis against Elden Auker. Auker later reported that every time he saw Feller, "that home run gets a little longer" (Auker, *Sleeper Cars*, 120).

110. Creamer, *Baseball in '41*, 167.

Anton, Todd. *No Greater Love: Life Stories of the Men Who Saved Baseball.* Burlington MA: Rounder Books, 2007.

——— , and Bill Nowlin, eds. *When Baseball Went to War.* Chicago: Triumph Books, 2008.

Auker, Elden, with Tom Keegan. *Sleeper Cars and Flannel Uniforms.* Chicago: Triumph Books, 2001.

Bartell, Dick "Rowdy Richard," with Norman L. Macht. *Rowdy Richard: A Firsthand Account of the National Baseball Wars of the 1930s and the Men Who Fought Them.* Berkeley CA: North Atlantic Books, 1987.

Barthel, Thomas. *Baseball Barnstorming and Exhibition Games, 1901–1962.* Jefferson NC: McFarland, 2007.

Berkow, Ira. *The Corporal Was a Pitcher: The Courage of Lou Brissie.* Chicago: Triumph Books, 2009.

Bloomfield, Gary. *Duty, Honor, Victory: America's Athletes in World War II.* Guilford CT: Lyons Press, 2003.

Boston, Talmage. *1939: Baseball's Pivotal Year.* Fort Worth: Summit Group, 1994.

Boudreau, Lou, with Ed Fitzgerald. *Player-Manager.* Boston: Little, Brown, 1949.

——— , with Russell Schneider. *Lou Boudreau: Covering All the Bases.* Champaign IL: Sagamore Publishing, 1993.

Broeg, Bob. *Super Stars of Baseball.* St. Louis: The Sporting News Publishing, 1971.

Bryson, Bill. "Iowa's Favorite Son." In *Best of Baseball*, ed. Sidney Offit. New York: G. P. Putnam's Sons, 1956.

Connor, Anthony J. *Baseball for the Love of It: Hall of Famers Tell It Like It Was.* New York: Macmillan, 1982.

Creamer, Robert W. *Baseball in '41.* New York: Viking Press, 1991.

Crissey, Harrington E., Jr. *Athletes Away.* Philadelphia: Self-published, 1984.

Daly, Arthur. *Times at Bat: A Half Century of Baseball.* New York: Random House, 1950.

Dickson, Paul. *Bill Veeck: Baseball's Greatest Maverick.* New York: Walker Publishing, 2012.

DiMaggio, Joe. *Lucky to Be a Yankee.* New York: Rudolph Field, 1946.

Fehler, Gene. *When Baseball Was Still King: Major League Players Remember the 1950s.* Jefferson NC: McFarland, 2012.

Feller, Bob. *Strikeout Story.* New York: A. S. Barnes, 1947.

——— , with Bill Gilbert. *Now Pitching—Bob Feller.* New York: Birch Lane Press, 1990.

——— , with Burton Rocks. *Bob Feller's Little Blue Book of Baseball Wisdom.* Chicago: Triumph Books, 2009.

——— . *Bob Feller's Little Black Book of Baseball Wisdom.* New York: McGraw-Hill, 2001.

Gay, Timothy M. *Satch, Dizzy & Rapid Robert: The Wild Saga of Interracial Baseball before Jackie Robinson.* New York: Simon & Schuster, 2010.

Goldstein, Richard. *Spartan Seasons: How Baseball Survived the Second World War.* New York: Macmillan, 1980.

Graham, Frank. *Baseball Extra.* New York: A. S. Barnes, 1954.

Greenberg, Hank. *The Story of My Life.* Ed. Ira Berkow. New York: Times Books, 1989.

Halberstam, David. *The Summer of '49.* New York: William Morrow, 1989.

——— . *The Teammates—Portrait of a Friendship.* New York: Hyperion, 2003.

Haupert, Michael J. "Bob Feller, Ace Negotiator." In *Batting Four Thousand: Baseball in the Western Reserve*, ed. Brad Sullivan, 7–12. Cleveland: Society for American Baseball Research, 2008.

Honig, Donald. *Baseball When the Grass Was Real.* New York: Coward, McCann & Geoghegan, 1975.

Johnson, William H. "The Crybabies of 1940." In *Batting Four Thousand: Baseball in the Western Reserve*, ed. Brad Sullivan, 37–42. Cleveland: Society for American Baseball Research, 2008.

Kaiser, David. *Epic Season: The 1948 American League Pennant Race.* Amherst MA: University of Massachusetts Press, 1998.

Karst, Gene, and Martin L. Jones Jr. *Who's Who in Professional Baseball.* New Rochelle NY: Arlington House, 1973.

Katz, Lawrence S. *Baseball in 1939: The Watershed Season of the National Pastime.* Jefferson NC: McFarland, 1994.

Kelley, Brent. *The Early All-Stars: Conversations with Standout Baseball Players of the 1930s and 1940s.* Jefferson NC: McFarland, 1997.

——— . *The Pastime in Turbulence—Interviews with Baseball Players of the 1940s.* Jefferson NC: McFarland, 2001.

Klima, John. *Pitched Battle: 35 of Baseball's Greatest Duels from the Mound.* Jefferson NC: McFarland, 2002.

Lebovitz, Hal. "Mr. Robert, Master Herbie." In *Batting Four Thousand: Baseball in the Western Reserve*, ed. Brad Sullivan, 55–56. Cleveland: Society for American Baseball Research, 2008.

Lewis, Franklin. *The Cleveland Indians.* New York: G. P. Putman's Sons, 1949.

Lieb, Frederick G. *The Detroit Tigers.* New York: G. P. Putnam's Sons, 1946.

MacFarlane, Paul, ed. *Daguerreotypes: The Complete Major and Minor League Records of Baseball's Immortals.* St. Louis: The Sporting News Publishing, 1981.

Markoe, Arnold, ed. *The Scribner Encyclopedia of American Lives—Sports Figures*, vol. 1, *A–K.* New York: Charles Scribner's Sons, 2002.

Marshall, William. *Baseball's Pivotal Era, 1945–1951.* Lexington: University Press of Kentucky, 1999.

McKelvey, Richard G. *Mexican Raiders in the Major Leagues: The Pasquel Brothers vs. Organized Baseball, 1946.* Jefferson NC: McFarland, 2006.

Mead, William B. *Even the Browns: The Zany, True Story of Baseball in the Early Forties.* Chicago: Contemporary Books, 1978.

Meany, Tom. *Baseball's Greatest Pitchers.* New York: A. S. Barnes, 1951.

———, and Tommy Holmes. *Baseball's Best: The All-Time Major League Baseball Team.* New York: Franklin Watts, 1964.

Moore, Joseph Thomas. *Larry Doby: The Struggle of the American League's First Black Player.* Mineola NY: Dover Publications, 2011.

Oakley, J. Ronald. *Baseball's Last Golden Age: The National Pastime in a Time of Glory and Change.* Jefferson NC: McFarland, 1994.

Parker, Gary R. *Win or Go Home: Sudden Death Baseball.* Jefferson NC: MacFarland, 2002.

Peary, Danny, ed. *We Played the Game: 65 Players Remember Baseball's Greatest Era, 1947–1964.* New York: Hyperion, 1994.

Phillips, John. *The Crybaby Indians of 1940.* Cabin John MD: Capital Publishing, 1990.

Pietrusza, David. *Judge and Jury: The Life and Times of Judge Kenesaw Mountain Landis.* South Bend IN: Diamond Communications, 1998.

———, Matthew Silverman, and Michael Gershman, eds. *Baseball: The Biographical Encyclopedia.* New York: Total/Sports Illustrated, 2000.

Pluto, Terry. *Our Tribe: A Baseball Memoir.* New York: Simon & Schuster, 1999.

Porter, David L. *Biographical Dictionary of American Sports: Baseball, Revised and Expanded Edition, A–F.* Westport CT: Greenwood Press, 2000).

Powers, Jimmy. *Baseball Personalities.* New York: Rudolph Field, 1949.

Reichler, Joseph. *Baseball's Great Moments*, 3rd ed. New York: Bonanza Books, 1983.

Roberts, Robin, with C. Paul Rogers III. *My Life in Baseball.* Chicago: Triumph Books, 2003.

Robinson, Eddie, with C. Paul Rogers III. *Lucky Me: My Sixty-Five Years in Baseball.* Dallas: SMU Press, 2011.

Rust, Art, Jr., with Mike Marley. *Legends: Conversations with Baseball Greats.* New York: McGraw-Hill, 1989.

Schiffer, Don. *My Greatest Baseball Game.* New York: A. S. Barnes, 1950.

Schneider, Russell. *The Boys of the Summer of '48.* Champaign IL: Sports Publishing, 1998.

———. *The Cleveland Indians Encyclopedia.* New York: Sports Publishing, 2001.

Schoor, Gene. *Bob Feller: Hall of Fame Strikeout Star.* Garden City NY: Doubleday, 1962.

Sickels, John. *Bob Feller: Ace of the Greatest Generation.* Dulles VA: Brassey's, 2004.

Singletary, Wes. *Al Lopez: The Life of Baseball's El Senor.* Jefferson NC: McFarland, 1999.

Smith, Ira. *Baseball's Famous Pitchers.* New York: A. S. Barnes, 1954.

Spink, J. Taylor. *Judge Landis and 25 Years of Baseball.* St. Louis: The Sporting News Publishing, 1974.

Szalontai, James D. *Teenager on First, Geezer at Bat, 4-F on Deck: Major League Baseball in 1945.* Jefferson NC: McFarland, 2009.

Thorn, John, and John Holway. *The Pitcher.* New York: Prentice-Hall Press, 1987.

Turner, Frederick. *When the Boys Came Back: Baseball and 1946.* New York: Henry Holt, 1996.

Tye, Larry. *Satchel: The Life and Times of an American Legend.* New York: Random House, 2009.

Vaccaro, Mike. *1941: The Greatest Year in Sports.* New York: Doubleday, 2007.

Van Blair, Rick. *Dugout to Foxhole: Interviews with Baseball Players Whose Careers Were Affected by World War II.* Jefferson NC: McFarland, 1994.

Veeck, Bill, with Ed Linn. *Veeck as in Wreck.* New York: G. P. Putnam's Sons, 1962.

Vincent, David, Lyle Spatz, and David W. Smith. *The Midsummer Classic—The Complete History of Baseball's All-Star Game.* Lincoln: University of Nebraska Press, 2001.

Vincent, Fay. *The Only Game in Town: Baseball Stars of the 1930s and 1940s Talk About the Game They Love.* New York: Simon & Schuster, 2006.

Werber, Bill, and C. Paul Rogers III. *Memories of a Ballplayer: Bill Werber and Baseball in the 1930s.* Cleveland: Society for American Baseball Research, 2001.

Westcott, Rich. *Diamond Greats: Profiles and Interviews with 65 of Baseball's History Makers.* Westport CT: Meckler Books, 1988.

———, and Allen Lewis. *No-Hitters: The 225 Games, 1893–1999.* Jefferson NC: McFarland, 2000.

Wilson, Nick. *Voices from the Pastime.* Jefferson NC: McFarland, 2000.

Addie, Bob. "Indians Almost Axed Feller!" *Baseball Digest*, July 1954.

Bloodgood, Clifford. "All-Star Double Feature." *Baseball Magazine*, September 1942.

———. "Has Another Walter Johnson Come Along?" *Baseball Magazine*, March 1937.

Burr, Harold C. "Indians Cross the Border." *Baseball Magazine*, December 1939.

Calhoun, Ralph. "Can Feller Come Back?" *Baseball Digest*, August 1945.

Cannon, Jimmy. "Feller's Legend Bows to Materialism." *Baseball Digest*, 1947.

Cobbledick, Gordon. "Is It True About Bob Feller?" *Sport*, June 1948.

Deford, Frank. "Robert Can Still Bring It." *Sports Illustrated*, August 8, 2005.

Dempsey, Jack. "Why Bob Feller Is a Champion." *Liberty*, August 9, 1941.

Feller, Bob. "Bob Feller and American Legion Baseball." *American Legion*, June 1963.

———. "The Pitcher and the Preacher." *Guideposts*, 1949.

———, as told to Ed Fitzgerald. "Who Says I'm Finished?" *Sport*, April 1949.

———, as told to Ed McAuley. "My Greatest Game—Feller." *Baseball Digest*, January 1951.

———, as told to Ken W. Purdy. "Baseball a Game? What a Laugh!" *Look*, February 11, 1956.

———. "I'll Never Quit Baseball." *Look*, March 20, 1956.

Feller, Bob, et al. "The Players Report Their Doings." *Baseball Magazine*, January 1938.

Feller, Virginia, as told to Hal Lebovitz. "He's My Feller!" *Baseball Digest*, May 1952.

Fitzgerald, Ed. "Feller Incorporated." *Sport*, June 1947.

Flaherty, Vincent X. "Feller Goes to Sea." *Baseball Digest*, March 1943.

Gibbons, Frank. "Determined Mr. Feller." *Baseball Digest*, September 1951.

Hayes, Gayle. "Fanning with Feller." *Baseball Magazine*, December 1938.

Holtzman, Jerome. "An American Hero." *Baseball Digest*, December 2000.

Kirksey, George. "When a Feller Needs a Fella." *Baseball Magazine*, June 1938.

Lebovitz, Hal. "Bob Feller's Disappointment." *Sport*, October 1959.

Mansch, Larry. "Hitting Bob Feller." *The National Pastime* 17 (1997).

McAuley, Ed. "Feller's a Whiz Promoting Two." *Baseball Digest*, September, 1946.

Nason, Jerry. "Feller Slides—Halfway." *Baseball Digest*, July 1948.

Povich, Shirley. "A Chat with Mr. Feller." *Baseball Digest*, August 1946.

Rice, Grantland. "Reg-lar Fellers." *Sport*, September 1946.

Broeg, Bob. "No Fireball's Any Swifter Than Feller's." *The Sporting News*, July 3, 1971.

Feller, Bob. "When the Crowd Boos!" *American Weekly*, July 6, 1952.

———, as told to Edward Linn. "The Trouble with the Hall of Fame." *Saturday Evening Post*, January 27, 1962.

Hawkins, Burton. "Bob Feller's $150,000 Pitch." *Saturday Evening Post*, April 19, 1947.

Stockton, J. Roy. "Bob Feller—Storybook Ball Player." *Saturday Evening Post*, February 20, 1937.

10. Dave Hoskins

1. The state senate tabled the bill a few days later. A similar ban on racially mixed athletic contests was enacted in 1956 but declared unconstitutional. *Dorsey v. State Athletic Commission*, 168 F. Supp. 149 (E.D. La. 1958), affirmed, 359 U.S. 533 (1959).

2. Jones, "Hoskins Reveals Three Threats," 15.

3. Mintline, "The Mint Line." The U.S. Census from 1930 shows that he was twelve years old on May 15, 1930, the date of its enumeration. Ruchelle Hoskins, his eldest daughter and an invaluable source for this article, confirmed in an interview with the author that her father was born in 1917. She also confirmed his middle name, Will, which appears on his death certificate and in an obituary published by the *Flint Journal* on April 4, 1970.

4. Some sources state that Hoskins was a four-sport star at Flint's Northern High School, but "he does not appear in the school's annuals" (Miller, "Dave Hoskins," 328).

5. Wendell Smith, another widely read sportswriter, selected Hoskins, Jackie Robinson, and Sam Jethroe to participate in tryouts that the Red Sox and Braves had agreed, under pressure, to hold for black players in spring 1945. However, Grays owner Cumberland Posey refused permission for Hoskins to attend.

6. Lebovitz, "Hats Off," 17.

7. Jones, "Hoskins Reveals Three Threats," 15.

8. Jones, "Hoskins Reveals Three Threats," 15.

9. Wilonsky, "Bush League of Their Own."

10. Rives, "Had Tougher Time in '48," 4.

11. Lebovitz, "Axe-Swinging Only Sad Note," 21.

Adelson, Bruce. *Brushing Back Jim Crow: The Integration of Minor League Baseball in the American South.* Charlottesville: University Press of Virginia, 1999.

Lacy, Sam. "Will Our Boys Make Big League Grade?" *Negro Pictorial Yearbook* (1945). Reprinted in Dean A. Sullivan, ed., *Middle Innings: A Documentary History of Baseball, 1900–1948.* Lincoln: University of Nebraska Press, 188, 190.

Lanctot, Neil. *Negro League Baseball: The Rise and Ruin of a Black Institution.* Philadelphia: University of Pennsylvania Press, 2004.

Miller, Michael C. "Dave Hoskins." In *African-American National Biography*, vol. 4, ed. Henry Louis Gates and Evelyn Brooks Higginbotham. New York: Oxford University Press, 2008.

Moffi, Larry, and Jonathan Kronstadt. *Crossing the Line: Black Major Leaguers, 1947–1950.* Iowa City: University of Iowa Press, 1994.

Pollock, Alan J. *Barnstorming to Heaven: Syd Pollock and His Great Black Teams.* Tuscaloosa: University of Alabama Press, 2006.

Tygiel, Jules. *Baseball's Great Experiment: Jackie Robinson and His Legacy.* New York: Oxford University Press, 1983.

Wright, Marshall D. *The Texas League in Baseball, 1888–1958.* Jefferson NC: McFarland, 2004.

Bowman, Larry. "Breaking Barriers: David Hoskins and the Integration of the Texas League." *Legacies: A History Journal for Dallas and North Central Texas* (Spring 1991): 14–19.

Scully, Gerald W. "Economic Discrimination in Professional Sports." *Journal of Law and Contemporary Problems* 38, no. 1 (1973): 67.

Jones, Harry. "Hoskins Reveals Three Threats against Life Same Day in '52." *The Sporting News*, March 4, 1953.

Lebovitz, Hal. "Axe-Swinging Only Sad Note in Sunny Outlook for Injuns." *The Sporting News*, April 6, 1955, 21.

———. "Hats Off . . . Dave Hoskins." *The Sporting News*, May 20, 1953, 17.

Mintline, Doug. "The Mint Line." *Flint Journal*, April 3, 1970.

Rives, Bill. "Had Tougher Time in '48 in Central, Says Hoskins." *The Sporting News*, May 14, 1952, 4.

Austin American-Statesman, June 30, 2004.

Baltimore Afro-American, September 20, 1949; September 27, 1949; October 9, 1954.

Charleston (WV) Daily Mail, May 13, 1949.

Cleveland Plain Dealer, February 12, 1954; February 27, 1954; March 5, 1954; October 8, 1954; March 3, 1955; March 29, 1955; April 5, 1970.

Dallas Morning News, January 27, 1952; June 10, 1952; January 1, 1953; May 21, 2000.

Dallas Observer, May 21, 1998.

Jet, August 7, 1952; September 11, 1952.

Milwaukee Journal, July 13, 1948.

News-Palladium (Benton Harbor MI), June 3, 1949.

Spokane (WA) Spokesman-Review, January 1, 1953.

The Sporting News, May 4, 1949; August 10, 1949; February 6, 1952; May 14, 1952; June 11, 1952; July 23, 1952; September 25, 1952; January 14, 1953; March 4, 1953; May 20, 1953; September 16, 1953; November 4, 1953; December 30, 1953; April 6, 1955; April 18, 1970.

Washington Afro-American, September 13, 1949; September 23, 1952.

Winona (MN) Republican-Herald, September 10, 1949.

Death certificate of David Will Hoskins, Michigan Department of Public Health (April 7, 1970).

McNary, Kyle. "Dave Hoskins." Pitch Black Baseball Negro Leaguer of the Month (August 2005). http://www.pitchblackbaseball.com/nlotmdavehoskins.html. Accessed October 16, 2012.

Wilonsky, Robert. "A Bush League of Their Own." *Dallas Observer*, May 21, 1988. http://www.dallasobserver.com/1998-05-21/news/a-bush-league-of-their-own. Accessed October 16, 2012.

"Dave Hoskins, 1987 Greater Flint Afro-American Hall of Fame Inductee." http://www.fpl.info/hallfame/87/hoskins87.shtml. Accessed October 16, 2012.

Baseball-Reference.com.

Pat Doyle, Professional Baseball Player Database (Version 4.1, 2001).

Retrosheet.org.

11. Don Mossi

James, Bill. *The New Bill James Historical Baseball Abstract.* New York: Free Press, 2001.

Neft, David, Richard Cohen, and Michael Neft. *The Sports Encyclopedia: Baseball.* New York: St. Martin's Press.

Shatzkin, Mike, and Jim Charlton. *The Ballplayers.* New York: Arbor House, 1990.

The Sporting News Baseball Guide.

The Sporting News Baseball Register.

Thorn, John. *The Relief Pitcher: Baseball's New Hero.* New York: Penguin Group, 1985.

Dell Sports Baseball Stars.

Sport.

Sport World.

Chicago Sun-Times.

Cleveland Plain Dealer.

New York Times.

Seattle Post-Intelligencer.

The Sporting News.

Washington Post.

Baseball-Almanac.com.

Baseball-Reference.com.

Interview with Don Mossi by James Floto and Randy Rosenblatt, 1995.

12. Hank Majeski

1. Baumgartner, "Meet Majeski," 74.
2. Rumill, "Majestic Majeski," 43.
3. Rumill, "Majestic Majeski," 43.
4. Rumill, "Majestic Majeski," 43.
5. Klapach interview.
6. Levinson interview.
7. DeRenzo interview.

Thorn, John, et al., eds. *Total Baseball*, 8th ed. Munster IN: Sports Media Publishing, 2004.

Baumgartner, Stan. "Meet Majeski—Houdini of the Hot Corner." *Sport Life* (1949): 10–11, 73–74.

Rumill, Ed. "Majestic Majeski." *Baseball Digest*, July 1948, 42–44.

Hank Majeski's obituary. *New York Times*, August 14, 1991. http://www.nytimes.com.

Baseball-Almanac.com.

Baseball-Reference.com.

Carmine DeRenzo, telephone interview, December 27, 2010.

Bill Klapach, telephone interview, December 29, 2010.

Bert Levinson, telephone interview, December 27, 2010.

13. Dale Mitchell

1. Mitchell file.
2. Mitchell Jr. interview.
3. Mitchell file.
4. Mitchell file.
5. Mitchell file.
6. Mitchell file.
7. Mitchell file.
8. Mitchell file.
9. Mitchell file.
10. Mitchell file.

Cleveland Plain Dealer, 1946.

Interview with Dale Mitchell Jr., December 2010.

Dale Mitchell's file at the National Baseball Hall of Fame Library, Cooperstown NY.

Washita County Historical Society, Cordell, Oklahoma.

14. Mike Garcia

1. *The Sporting News*, August 22, 1951, 3.
2. *The Sporting News*, August 13, 1952, 4.
3. Donald Honig, *The Man in the Dugout* (Chicago: Follett, 1977), 196.
4. Russell Schneider, *The Cleveland Indians Encyclopedia*, 2nd ed. (Champaign IL: Sports Publishing, 2001), 482.
5. *The Sporting News*, August 19, 1953, 12.
6. Schneider, *Indians Encyclopedia*, 165.
7. Honig, *Man in the Dugout*, 195.
8. Associated Press, *New York World-Telegram & Sun*, February 15, 1948, page unknown. Clipping in Mike Garcia's file at the National Baseball Hall of Fame Library, Cooperstown NY.
9. *The Sporting News*, May 13, 1959, 17.
10. *Cleveland Plain Dealer*, March 13, 1983. Clipping in Garcia's HOF file.

11. Bill James, *The New Bill James Historical Baseball Abstract* (New York: Free Press, 2001), 916.

16. Larry Doby

1. Kevin Kernan, "Larry Is the Stuff of Legends: Struggles of Doby a Lesson for Any Time," *New York Post*, July 28, 2002, 97.

2. Kernan, "Stuff of Legends."

3. Joseph Thomas Moore, *Pride against Prejudice: The Biography of Larry Doby* (Westport CT: Praeger Publishers, 1988), 7.

4. Moore, *Pride*, 6.

5. Moore, *Pride*, 9.

6. David L. Porter, ed., "Doby, Lawrence Eugene 'Larry,'" in *Biographical Dictionary of American Sports* (Westport CT: Greenwood Press, 1987), 151–52.

7. Moore, *Pride*, 12.

8. Moore, *Pride*, 12–17.

9. Moore, *Pride*, 16.

10. Moore, *Pride*, 19–20.

11. Moore, *Pride*, 23.

12. Dave Anderson, "A Pioneer's Hall of Fame Wife," *New York Times*, July 26, 2001, D2.

13. Moore, *Pride*, 24–25.

14. Moore, *Pride*, 25.

15. Moore, *Pride*, 29.

16. Anderson, "Hall of Fame Wife."

17. Anderson, "Hall of Fame Wife."

18. Dave Hutchinson, "Doby Relives Past, the Good and the Bad: Indians Retire His Number Today." No publication given. Clipping from Larry Doby's file at the National Baseball Hall of Fame Library, Cooperstown NY.

19. Moore, *Pride*, 41–45.

20. Moore, *Pride*, 47.

21. Jerome Holtzman, "Doby's Rightful Recognition," *Chicago Tribune*, March 4, 1998, available at https://chicago.tribune.com/sports/whitesox/article0,1051,ART-4566,00.html.

22. Sam Goldaper and Jack Cavanaugh, "Sports World Specials; Honors for Doby," *New York Times*, July 6, 1987.

23. Hutchinson, "Doby Relives Past."

24. Daniel, "Mick Thought Homer Cleared Stadium," July 24, 1957. No publication given. Clipping from Doby's HOF file.

25. United Press, "Carrasquel, Busby Acquisitions 'Round 1' for Trading Tribe." Clipping from Doby's HOF file.

26. "Doby Now Tonic to Old Foe: Ex-Indian Esteemed by Chicago Pilot," May 5, 1956. No author or publication given. Clipping from Doby's HOF file.

27. "Doby Connects: Jersey Vet 'Finds Range' for Chisox," June 23, 1956. Clipping from Doby's HOF file.

28. "Police Grab Martin After Fighting Doby: Drysdale and Logan Swap Punches in Brooklyn Free-for-All," June 13, 1957. Clipping from Doby's HOF file.

29. "Chisox Fans Sour on Doby; Forced Deal with Baltimore," December 11, 1957. Clipping from Doby's HOF file.

30. "Chisox Fans Sour on Doby."

31. "Doby to Enter Johns Hopkins, Career in Danger," August 25, 1959. Clipping from Doby's HOF file.

32. Porter, *Biographical Dictionary*.

33. Bob Decker, "Doby's Next Goal—Manage in Majors," *Newark Star-Ledger*, January 24, 1971, section 5, 6.

34. Decker, "Doby's Next Goal."

35. Hutchinson, "Doby Relives Past."

36. Tom Melody, "Doby's Dream Now a Nightmare," *Akron Beacon Journal*, August 21, 1978.

37. Hutchinson, "Doby Relives Past."

38. Hutchinson, "Doby Relives Past."

39. American League press release, "Doby Named Special Assistant to the American League President," April 17, 1995.

40. "Doby among 3 Named to Baseball World Board," *Cooperstown Crier*, July 8, 1999. No author or page number given. Clipping from Doby's HOF file.

41. Kernan, "Stuff of Legends."

42. Associated Press, "Finally a Hankering to Honor Doby: Aaron Says Thanks to Barrier-Breaker on 50th Anniversary of His AL Debut," *Newark Star Ledger*, July 6, 1997, section 5, 8.

43. Jerome Holtzman, "Doby's Rightful Recognition," *Chicago Tribune*, March 4, 1998, available at https://chicago.tribune.com/sports/whitesox/article0,1051,ART-4566,00.html.

44. Holtzman, "Doby's Rightful Recognition."

45. Anderson, "Hall of Fame Wife."

46. Steve Politi, "Doby Recalled as a Hall of Famer in Life," *Newark Star Ledger*, June 24, 2003, 53.

47. Baseball Hall of Fame press release, "Postal Service to Unveil New Stamps Depicting Hall of Fame Legends on Friday in Cooperstown," July 16, 2012. Clipping from Doby's HOF file.

17. George Strickland

1. Hogan, "Local Player Strickland Dies," quoting New Orleans sportswriter Peter Barrouquere.

2. Information provided by John T. Strickland, his son.

3. Rick Bradley interview, February 1993.

4. Cohen, "What's What," 108.

5. *New Orleans Times-Picayune*, undated.

6. *Christian Science Monitor*, March 26, 1948.

7. *New Orleans Times-Picayune*, July 18, 1943, 19.

8. *New Orleans Times-Picayune*, undated.

9. Peary, *We Played the Game*, 128.

10. Peary, *We Played the Game*, 128.

11. Nichols, "Timely Tips."

12. Rick Bradley interview.

O'Toole, Andrew. *Branch Rickey in Pittsburgh: Baseball's Trailblazing General Manager for the Pirates, 1950–1955*. Jefferson NC: McFarland, 2000, 178.

Peary, Danny, ed. *We Played the Game*. New York: Hyperion Books, 1994.

Gibbons, Frank. "Playmaker Strickland Bargain of Year; 10-G Prize Keys Indians Infield." *Baseball Digest*, September 1953, 5–8.

Lebovitz, Hal. "Strickland Fooled Them All." *Sport*, September 1954, 64–66.

Cohen, Nate. "What's What: When Strickland Was Called 'Baby.'" *New Orleans Times-Picayune*, April 12, 1964.

Hart, Carol. "Jays Place Five on All-Legion Ball Team." *New Orleans Times-Picayune*, July 18, 1943, 19.

Hogan, Nakia. "Local Player Strickland Dies." *New Orleans Times-Picayune*, February 23, 2010.

Nichols, Max. "Timely Tips from Battling Billy." *The Sporting News*, March 28, 1962, 17.

Summers, Waddel. "Stars Abounded on 1941–42 Peters Baseball Team." *New Orleans Times-Picayune*, June 26, 1965.

Christian Science Monitor.

New Orleans Times-Picayune.

Baseball-Reference.com.

Retrosheet.org.

E-mail correspondence with George Strickland's son, John Thomas Strickland, March–October 2010.

Interview with George Strickland, conducted by SABR member Rick Bradley, February 1993.

Written correspondence with George Strickland by the author, November 2009.

George Strickland's clippings file at the National Baseball Hall of Fame Library, Cooperstown NY.

18. Cleveland Stadium (1932–96)

1. *Cleveland Plain Dealer*, August 1, 1932.

2. *Plain Dealer*, August 1, 1932.

3. *Plain Dealer*, August 1, 1932.

4. National Register of Historic Places Inventory—nomination form, October 1985.

5. National Register, nomination form.

6. *Cleveland Plain Dealer*, January 20, 1980.

7. *Plain Dealer*, January 20, 1980.

19. Jim Hegan

1. Hal Lebovitz, "Trade Will Help Cavaliers—If Turpin Has Heart," *Cleveland Plain Dealer*, June 20, 1984.

2. Interview with Mike Hegan, August 12, 2009.

3. Thanks to Mike Hegan for supplying much of the information regarding Jim's family background.

4. All additional quotations from Mike Hegan come from the 2009 interview.

5. Hal Lebovitz, "Hegan Has Gone, but Leaves Us Memories of a Truly Class Act," *Cleveland Plain Dealer*, June 19, 1984, 1-D.

6. Lebovitz, "Hegan Has Gone," 1-D.

7. *Cleveland Plain Dealer*, September 10, 1941.

8. Lebovitz, "Hegan Has Gone," 3-D.

9. Associated Press, "Veeck Contemplates Few Changes in Indians' Squad for 1949 Season," *New York Times*, October 15, 1948, 29.

10. Mike Petraglia, "No-Hitter a Record Fourth for Varitek," available at http://mlb.mlb.com/news/article.jsp?ymd=20080519&content_id=2733852&vkey=news_mlb&fext=.jsp&c_id=mlb.

11. Joe Wancho, "Mike Hegan," Baseball Biography Project, available at http://bioproj.sabr.org/bioproj.cfm?a=v&v=l&bid=1681&pid=6068.

12. Louis Effrat, "Cleveland Contends Wind Contributed to Downfall at Two Important Points," *New York Times*, September 30, 1954, 41.

13. Lebovitz, "Hegan Has Gone," 3-D.

14. Lebovitz, "Hegan Has Gone," 1-D.

15. Bob Dolgan, *Heroes, Scamps and Good Guys* (Cleveland: Gray & Company, 2003), 35.

16. Al Doyle, "Sustaining a Long Career: Despite Weak Hitting Abilities, Some Catchers Make an Impact in the Major Leagues Strictly on Their Defensive Expertise," *Baseball Digest*, October 1996, 57.

17. John Drebinger, "Fisher in 7-Hitter," *New York Times*, September 4, 1960, 129.

18. http://mlb.mlb.com/nyy/history/coaches.jsp.

19. http://mlb.mlb.com/mlb/history/all_star_event.jsp?story=16.

20. Lebovitz, "Hegan Has Gone," 3-D.

21. Lebovitz, "Hegan Has Gone," 1-D.

22. Dolgan, *Heroes, Scamps and Good Guys*, 34.

21. Dave Philley

1. Tom Walts, *Paris (TX) News*, June 20, 1990.

2. Art Morrow, *The Sporting News*, May 27, 1953.

3. BaseballHistorian.com.

4. *The Sporting News*, May 27, 1953.

5. *The Sporting News*, May 27, 1953.

6. Bill Thompson, *Paris News*, February 21, 1954.

7. Thompson, *Paris News*, April 7, 1954.

8. Thompson, *Paris News*, October 10, 1954.

9. *Salisbury (MD) Times*, April 24, 1956.

10. Thompson, *Paris News*, October 1, 1958.

11. *Paris News*, March 8, 1959.

12. Tom Walts, *Paris News*, June 20, 1990.

New York Times.
Paris (TX) News.
Salisbury (MD) Times.
The Sporting News.
Washington Post.

Astroland.net.
Baseball-Almanac.com.
Baseball-Reference.com.

22. Bob Lemon

1. Feller, *Strikeout Story*, 241.

2. Schneider, *Tales from the Tribe Dugout*, 102.

3. *The Sporting News*, August 18, 1954.

4. *The Sporting News*, September 29, 1954.

5. *The Sporting News*, December 15, 1954.

6. *The Sporting News*, August 15, 1956.

7. *The Sporting News*, August 21, 1957.

8. *The Sporting News*, May 7, 1958.

9. HOF induction speech.

10. *New York Times*, January 13, 2000.

11. *The Sporting News*, June 30, 1979.

12. *The Sporting News*, September 26, 1981.

13. *New York Times*, September 7, 1981.

14. *New York Times*, September 7, 1981.

The Bill James Historical Baseball Abstract.
Feller, Bob, *Strikeout Story*. New York: A. S. Barnes, 1947.
McAuley, Ed. *Bob Lemon, the Work Horse*. New York: A. S. Barnes, 1951.
Schneider, Russell. *Tales from the Tribe Dugout*. Champaign IL: Sports Publishing, 2002.

"Hall of Fame Pitcher Bob Lemon Takes It Easier Now." *Los Angeles Times*, April 21, 1988.
Cleveland Plain Dealer and *Cleveland Press*, 1946–58.
New York Times, various issues, 1978–82.
The Sporting News, various issues, 1942–82.

Baseball-Reference.com.
Internet Movie Database.
Retrosheet.org.
Wikipedia.org.

Bob Lemon's induction speech, National Baseball Hall of Fame, August 9, 1976.

23. Rudy Regalado

1. Unless otherwise indicated, all quotes are from telephone interviews with Regalado.

2. *Cleveland Press*, April 28, 1954.

3. "Batting Around," February 25, 1954, 21.

4. Cobbledick, "Regalado Could Be Spark."

5. Gibbons, "Rudy Makes Varsity."

6. Cobbledick, "Indians Management."

7. "Batting Around," April 12, 1954, 29.

8. Darvas, "Regalado Rigoletto" (cartoon).

9. *Cleveland News*, May 20, 1954.

10. "Rosabell Wins," 29.

11. www.baseball-reference.com/bullpen/Mexican _Pacific_Coast_League (accessed April 14, 2011). Additional information and statistics on Culiacan via e-mail from Jesus Alberto Rubio and Alfonso Araujo, April 17, 2011.

12. Bailey, *Junior World Series*.

13. Regalado interview, February 5, 2011; Clavin and Peary, *Roger Maris*, 83.

14. E-mail from Alberto Rondon, April 13, 2011, with information supplied by Jorge Figueredo; all Venezuelan statistics from *Enciclopedia del Béisbol en Venezuela, 1895–2006* (Caracas, Venezuela: Impresión Arte CA, 2007).

15. "Venezuelan Vitamins," 25.

16. Seattle Mariners press release, September 16, 2010.

Bailey, Bob. *History of the Junior World Series*. Lanham MD: Scarecrow Press, 2004.

Clavin, Tom, and Danny Peary. *Roger Maris: Baseball's Reluctant Hero*. New York: Touchstone/Simon & Schuster, 2010.

Thorn, John, Pete Palmer, and Michael Gershman, eds. *Total Baseball*, 7th ed. New York: Total Sports Publishing, 2001.

Cobbledick, Gordon. "Indians Management Appears Determined to Prove Regalado Isn't Big League." *Cleveland Plain Dealer*, April 1, 1954, 27.

——— . "Regalado Could Be Spark That Tribe Lacks." *Cleveland Plain Dealer,* March 31, 1954.

Darvas, Lou. "Regalado Rigoletto" [cartoon]. *Cleveland Press*, April 12, 1954.

Gibbons, Frank. "Rudy Makes Varsity—as Utility Player." *Cleveland Press*, April 6, 1954.

"Batting Around." *Cleveland Plain Dealer.*

"Rosabell Wins Winter Loop Race." *The Sporting News*, December 29, 1954, 29.

"Venezuelan Vitamins." *The Sporting News*, February 11, 1959, 25.

Cleveland Plain Dealer.

Cleveland News.

Cleveland Press.

New York Times.

The Sporting News.

Baseball-Reference.com.

Retrosheet.org.

San Diego History Center, www.sandiegohistory.org.

Rudy Regalado, telephone interviews, February 5 and April 13, 2011.

24. Ray Narleski

1. *Cleveland Plain Dealer*, July 5, 1954.

2. *Cleveland Plain Dealer*, July 5, 1954.

3. *The Sporting News*, March 11, 1959, 16.

4. Birdie Tebbetts and James Morrison, *Birdie: Confessions of a Baseball Nomad* (Chicago: Triumph Books, 2002), 130–31.

5. Russell Schneider, *Whatever Happened to "Super Joe"?* (Chicago: Gray & Company, 2006), 143–47.

6. *Baseball Digest*, October 1955, 73–86.

7. *Baseball Digest*, October 1955, 73–86.

8. *Baseball Digest*, October 1955, 73–86.

9. *The Sporting News*, October 3, 1955, 8.

10. *The Sporting News*, August 14, 1957, 25.

11. National Baseball Hall of Fame Archives, Cooperstown NY.

12. *Cleveland Plain Dealer*, November 21, 1958.

13. *The Sporting News*, January 21, 1959, 3.

14. Schneider, *Whatever Happened to "Super Joe"?*, 147.

26. Sam Dente

1. *Mansfield (OH) News Journal*, July 2, 1967.

2. *The Sporting News*, July 4, 1961.

3. *The Sporting News*, August 25, 1954.

4. 1930 U.S. Census.

5. *Trenton (NJ) Evening Times*, November 16, 1939.

6. *Brooklyn Eagle*, August 14, 1947.

7. *New York World-Telegram*, June 25, 1941.

8. *Newark Star-Ledger*, April 17, 2007.

9. Undated newspaper article from Sam Dente's file at the National Baseball Hall of Fame Library, Cooperstown, NY.

10. Fred Bendel, "'No Hit' Dente Hit at Short." *Baseball Digest*, March 1951, 91–92.

11. Bendel, "'No Hit' Dente."

12. *The Sporting News*, January 3, 1951.

13. *The Sporting News*, February 4, 1943.

14. U.S. World War II Enlistment Records, 1938–46.

15. *Red Bank (NJ) Register*, April 3, 1973.

16. *The Sporting News*, March 30, 1949.

17. *Lowell (MA) Sun*, March 7, 1947.

18. *Binghamton (NY) Press*, November 12, 1946.

19. *New Orleans Times-Picayune*, September 25, 1946.

20. *The Sporting News*, December 25, 1946.

21. *The Sporting News*, December 4, 1946.

22. *Cleveland Plain Dealer*, July 14, 1947.

23. *Lowell Sun*, March 14, 1947.

24. *The Sporting News*, March 19, 1947.

25. *The Sporting News*, March 26, 1947.

26. *The Sporting News*, April 16, 1947.

27. *Lowell Sun*, April 18, 1947.

28. *The Sporting News*, July 16, 1947.

29. *The Sporting News*, July 23, 1947.

30. Undated newspaper article from Dente's HOF file.

31. *The Sporting News*, August 6, 1947.

32. Undated newspaper article from Dente's HOF file.

33. *The Sporting News*, August 13, 1947.

34. *Trenton Evening Times*, March 17, 1948.

35. *The Sporting News*, March 31, 1948.

36. *The Sporting News*, June 2, 1948.

37. Eric Stone, *Wrong Side of the Wall: The Life of Blackie Schwamb, the Greatest Prison Baseball Player of All Time* (Guilford CT: Lyons Press, 2004), 121.

38. The number of people on the parade route varies in sources from 5,000 to 10,000 people. See Tom Deveaux, *The Washington Senators, 1901–1971* (Jefferson NC: McFarland, 2005), 174; *The Sporting News*, October 19, 1949.

39. Bob McConnell and David Vincent, *SABR Presents the Home Run Encyclopedia* (New York: Macmillan, 1996), 450.

40. *The Sporting News*, July 6, 1949.

41. *The Sporting News*, September 14, 1949.

42. *The Sporting News*, August 31, 1949.

43. *Cleveland Plain Dealer*, September 30, 1949.

44. *Brooklyn Eagle*, September 29, 1949.

45. *The Sporting News*, November 23, 1949.

46. *Dallas Morning News*, January 13, 1950.

47. *The Sporting News*, March 28, 1951.

48. *The Sporting News*, January 31, 1951.

49. *Amsterdam (NY) Evening Recorder*, March 26, 1951.

50. *The Sporting News*, June 6, 1951.

51. *The Sporting News*, July 30, 1952.

52. *Springfield (MA) Union*, November 28, 1951.

53. *The Sporting News*, February 27, 1952.

54. *Springfield Union*, March 11, 1952.

55. *The Sporting News*, April 23, 1952.

56. *The Sporting News*, December 24, 1952.

57. *The Sporting News*, November 19, 1952.

58. *Cleveland Plain Dealer*, May 6, 1953.

59. *The Sporting News*, June 24, 1953.

60. *Logansport (IN) Press*, September 22, 1953.

61. *Nashua (NH) Telegraph*, October 28, 1953.

62. *Rockford (IL) Register-Star News*, October 28, 1953.

63. *Amsterdam Recorder*, March 22, 1954.

64. *Cleveland Plain Dealer*, April 2, 1954.

65. *Kalispell (MT) Daily Interlake*, June 11, 1954.

66. *Augusta (GA) Chronicle*, June 14, 1954.

67. *Lima (OH) News*, July 15, 1954.

68. *Cleveland Plain Dealer*, July 16, 1954.

69. Undated newspaper article from Dente's HOF file.

70. *Corpus Christi (TX) Caller-Times*, July 25, 1954.

71. *Lima News*, July 28, 1954.

72. *Cleveland Plain Dealer*, August 7, 1954.

73. *Brooklyn Eagle*, September 1, 1954.

74. *Cleveland Plain Dealer*, September 10, 1954.

75. *Corpus Christi Caller-Times*, September 10, 1954.

76. *The Sporting News*, September 29, 1954.

77. Hank Greenberg, "How We Got Into the Series," *Life*, September 27, 1954, 138–52.

78. *Brooklyn Eagle*, November 9, 1954.

79. *Cleveland Plain Dealer*, January 24, 1955.

80. *Cleveland Plain Dealer*, March 28, 1955.

81. *The Sporting News*, June 15, 1955.

82. *Oil City (PA) Derrick*, June 16, 1955.

83. *Racine (WI) Journal-Times*, June 16, 1955.

84. *Sandusky (OH) Register*, October 17, 1955.

85. *The Sporting News*, November 23, 1955.

86. *Red Bank (NJ) Register*, May 24, 1956.

87. *Red Bank Register*, May 24, 1956.

88. *Cleveland Plain Dealer*, April 16, 1970.

89. *The Sporting News*, December 14, 1955.

90. *Racine Sunday Bulletin*, November 13, 1955.

91. *Abilene (TX) Reporter-News*, February 16, 1956.

92. *The Sporting News*, February 29, 1956.

93. *Kalispell Daily Interlake*, March 20, 1956.

94. *Red Bank Register*, April 3, 1973.

95. *Red Bank Register*, April 3, 1973.

96. *Cleveland Plain Dealer*, August 23, 1956.

97. *The Sporting News*, September 5, 1956.

98. *Red Bank Register*, April 3, 1973.

99. *Connellsville (PA) Daily Courier*, January 22, 1959.

100. *Hagerstown (MA) Daily Mail*, August 7, 1967.

101. *Red Bank Register*, May 24, 1956.

102. *Sandusky Register*, February 7, 1969.

103. *Newark Star-Ledger*, April 17, 2007.

104. *Cleveland Plain Dealer*, April 16, 1970.

27. 1954 Cleveland Indians by the Numbers

Schneider, Russell. *The Cleveland Indians Encyclopedia*, 3rd ed. Champaign IL: Sports Publishing, 2004.

Society for American Baseball Research. *The SABR Baseball List and Record Book*. New York: Scribner, 2007.

Sugar, Burt Randolph, ed. *The Baseball Maniac's Almanac*, 3rd ed. New York: Skyhorse Publishing, 2012.

Baseball-Almanac.com.

baseballlibrary.com/chronology.

Baseball-Reference.com.

Retrosheet.org.

thisgreatgame.com/1954.html.

28. Jim Dyck

1. Various newspaper clippings for this biography are courtesy of Bill Francis, at the Baseball Hall of Fame, Cooperstown NY. Thanks also to Joan Mamanakis, director of the Cheney (Washington) Historical Museum, for her guidance on questions of research.

2. Thanks are due Jim Dyck Jr., who through e-mails and a lengthy phone interview on January 3, 2011, provided a great deal of information and insight into his father's career and life.

3. "Second Wreck Victim of Year," *Jefferson City (MO) Post-Tribune*, August 28, 1936.

4. Father's and sons' talent in local sports is reflected in various issues of the *Jefferson City Post-Tribune* from the late 1930s and early 1940s.

5. Jimmy Dyck's player file at the National Baseball Hall of Fame Library, Cooperstown NY.

6. "Jimmy Dyck Signs Contract to Play for Yankee Farm Club," *Jefferson City Post-Tribune*, September 18, 1940.

7. Minor League information from http://www.baseball-reference.com/minors/player.cgi?id=dyck—001jam.

8. James Dyck Jr. e-mail, January 1, 2011.

9. James Dyck Jr. e-mail, December 30, 2010.

10. Dyck Jr. e-mail, December 30, 2010.

11. "Venezuelan Cops Roughed U.S. Players, Says Hurler," *The Sporting News*, December 13, 1950.

12. "Dyck Gem in Browns' 'Jim-Dandy' Garden," *The Sporting News*, May 21, 1952.

13. "Coleman Joins Return Parade of Old Brownies," *The Sporting News*, August 4, 1952.

14. "Car, Gifts for Jim Dyck—Jim Dykes Wins Twin Bill," *The Sporting News*, September 24, 1952.

15. "Rookie Award to Courtney Lauded by Manager Marion," *The Sporting News*, October 1, 1952.

16. "Veeck Serves Contracts at Lunch; Seven Wield Pen at Mass Signing," *The Sporting News*, January 14, 1953.

17. "Veeck Beams Over Gains; Stresses Star Young Trio," *The Sporting News*, October 8, 1952.

18. "Bill Veeck Claiming Post-Season Title for Adding Players," *The Sporting News*, November 12, 1952.

19. "Bobo Holloman Scheduled to Face A's Again Tuesday," *Hartford Courant*, May 8, 1953; "Holloman, Facing Axe, Hurls No-Hitter," *The Sporting News*, May 13, 1953.

20. "New Third Sacker Ready for Browns–It's Mr. Shortstop!" *The Sporting News*, June 17, 1953.

21. "Brownies Homer Binge Knots Two Major Marks," *The Sporting News*, July 29, 1953.

22. Phone interview with Jim Dyck Jr., January 3, 2011.

23. "Oriole Ducat Sale Given New Speed by Spieler Dykes," *The Sporting News*, January 20, 1954.

24. "Feller Beats Drums against Dyck Deal," *The Sporting News*, July 13, 1955.

25. "Triandos Betters Orioles' Home Record With Nine," *The Sporting News*, July 27, 1955.

26. "In the Clutch," *Jefferson City Post-Tribune*, May 22, 1956.

27. "In the Clutch."

28. "Redlegs Finally Send Dyck to Minor Leagues," *Hartford Courant*, July 26, 1956.

29. E-mail from Jim Dyck Jr., January 1, 2011.

30. Dyck Jr. phone interview, January 3, 2011.

29. Bob Chakales

Thanks to Bob Chakales and James Chakales, and to Debbie Matson of the Boston Red Sox.

1. Communications with Bob and James Chakales via telephone and e-mail, July 2009.

2. E-mail communication from James Chakales, July 17, 2009.

3. Hal Lebovitz, "'Shackles' Binds Tribe Foes," *Baseball Digest*, August 1951.

4. *Christian Science Monitor*, June 14, 1944.

5. *Washington Post*, March 16, 1945.

6. Diamantis Zervos, *Baseball's Golden Greeks: The First Forty Years, 1934–1974* (Canton MA: Aegean Books International), 94.

7. Interview with James Chakales, July 17, 2009.

8. Lebovitz, "'Shackles' Binds." Lebovitz seemed fascinated with Bob's regional accent, but Chakales had better communication skills than Lebovitz attributed to him—and he even worked for a while as a temporary sports columnist in Richmond when the regular writer, Lawrence Leonard, was on vacation or sick.

9. Zervos, *Baseball's Golden Greeks.*

10. *The Sporting News*, September 8, 1948.

11. Zervos, *Baseball's Golden Greeks.*

12. Hal Lebovitz, "'Shackles' Binds."

13. *The Sporting News*, April 4, 1951.

14. *The Sporting News*, March 19, 1952.

15. *The Sporting News*, June 25, 1952.

16. *The Sporting News*, December 31, 1952.

17. *The Sporting News*, March 17, 1954.

18. See David Nemec et al., *The Baseball Chronicles* (Lincolnwood IL: Publications International, 1992), 288.

19. Communication from James Chakales, July 17, 2009.

20. Zervos, *Baseball's Golden Greeks,* 97–98.

21. E-mail from James Chakales, August 10, 2009.

22. *New York Times*, June 8, 1955.

23. *Washington Post*, February 25, 1956.

24. *Washington Post*, March 4, 1956.

25. *Christian Science Monitor*, May 7, 1957.

31. Al Rosen

Horvitz, Peter S., and Joachim Horvitz. *The Big Book of Jewish Baseball.* New York: SPI Books, 2001.

Neft, David S., Richard M. Cohen, and Michael L. Neft. *The Sports Encyclopedia: Baseball.* New York: St. Martin's Press, 2000.

Ribalow, Harold U., and Meir Ribalow. *Jewish Baseball Stars.* New York: Hippocrene Books, Inc., 1984.

BaseballLibrary.com.

Baseball-Reference.com.

Files of the National Baseball Hall of Fame Library, Cooperstown NY.

32. Wally Westlake

1. Westlake interview, February 22, 2006.

2. *Los Angeles Times*, April 5, 1942.

3. Westlake interview, February 22, 2006.

4. Povich, "This Morning," April 30, 1947.

5. Daniel, "Dan's Dope," October 6, 1947.

6. *New York Times*, June 15, 1949.

7. Williams, "Busy Baseball Traders."

8. Westlake interview, February 22, 2006.

9. Lebovitz, "Relief Hurler Next ."

10. *Chicago Daily Tribune*, August 28, 1953.

11. Veeck, *Veeck as in Wreck*, 178.

12. Lebovitz, "Flickers Helped Westlake."

13. Lebovitz, "Flickers Helped Westlake."

14. Lebovitz, "Flickers Helped Westlake."

15. Westlake interview, February 22, 2006.

16. Westlake interview, February 22, 2006.

17. Westlake interview, February 22, 2006.

18. Westlake interview, February 22, 2006.

19. Westlake interview, February 22, 2006.

20. Westlake interview, February 22, 2006.

Gillette, Gary, and Pete Palmer, eds. *The 2006 ESPN Baseball Encyclopedia.* New York: Sterling Publishing, 2006.

Johnson, Lloyd, and Miles Wolff, eds. *The Encyclopedia of Minor League Baseball*, 2nd ed. Durham NC: Baseball America, 1997.

O'Toole, Andrew. *Branch Rickey in Pittsburgh.* Jefferson NC: McFarland, 2000.

Veeck, Bill, with Ed Linn. *Veeck as in Wreck: The Autobiography of Bill Veeck.* Chicago: University of Chicago Press, 2001. Originally published New York: Putnam, 1962.

Daniel, Dan. "Dan's Dope." *New York World Telegram*, October 6, 1947.

Lebovitz, Hal. "Flickers Helped Westlake Lick Swat Sag." *The Sporting News*, July 7, 1954.

———. "Relief Hurler Next on Tribe Shopping List." *Cleveland News*, August 1, 1952.

Povich, Shirley. "This Morning" (column). *Washington Post*, April 30, 1947.

Williams, Joe. "Busy Baseball Traders Can't Always Be Right." *New York World Telegram*, June 19, 1951.

Chicago Daily Tribune, August 28, 1953.

Los Angeles Times box scores.

Los Angeles Times, April 5, 1942.

New York Times box scores.

New York Times, June 15, 1949.

The Sporting News, July 7, 1954.

Baseball-Almanac.com.

BaseballLibrary.com.

Baseball-Reference.com.

Retrosheet.org.

Wally Westlake's file at the National Baseball Hall of Fame Library, Cooperstown NY.

33. Dick Tomanek

1. *Reading (PA) Eagle*, February 18, 1954, 17.
2. *Milwaukee Journal*, February 8, 1954, 15.
3. *Milwaukee Journal*, April 19, 1954, 2.
4. *Portsmouth (OH) Times*, May 22, 1958, 38.
5. *Portsmouth (OH) Times*.
6. *Portsmouth (OH) Times*.
7. *Portsmouth (OH) Times*.
8. *St. Joseph (MO) News-Press*, July 10, 1959, 16.
9. Tomanek declined to be interviewed for this biography.

34. Dave Pope

1. Brent P. Kelley, *The Negro Leagues Revisited: Conversations with 66 More Baseball Heroes* (Jefferson NC: McFarland, 2000), 211.
2. Kelley, *Negro Leagues Revisited*, 210.
3. Bill Young, "Ray Brown in Canada: His Forgotten Years," *The National Pastime* (SABR-Quebec, 2007).
4. Christian Trudeau, "First Season for a Young Pitcher, Last Season for a Small City," SABR-Quebec, 2006.

5. SABR-Quebec.
6. Christian Trudeau, "La Provinciale: Une Ligue de Haut Caliber," in *Disorganized Baseball: The Provincial League from Laroque to the Expos* (Merritt Clifton, 1982).
7. Kelley, *Negro Leagues Revisited*, 213.
8. Richard Ian Kimball, "Beyond the 'Great Experiment': Integrated Baseball Comes to Indianapolis," *Journal of Sport History* 26, no. 1 (Spring 1999): 151.
9. *Spokane Spokesman-Review*, July 2, 1952.
10. Kelley, *Negro Leagues Revisited*, 210.
11. Kelley, *Negro Leagues Revisited*, 210.
12. *The Sporting News*, November 3, 1955.
13. Kelley, *Negro Leagues Revisited*, 214.
14. Kelley, *Negro Leagues Revisited*, 212.
15. Kelley, *Negro Leagues Revisited*, 210.
16. Kelley, *Negro Leagues Revisited*, 213.

36. Luke Easter

1. Goodrich, "King of Swat?"
2. Swaine, *Black Stars*, 77.
3. *Sports Illustrated*, April 9, 1979; Cattau, "Maybe There Really Is."
4. All listed as survivors on the program from Easter's memorial service.
5. Cattau, "Maybe There Really Is."
6. Cattau, "Maybe There Really Is."
7. Swaine (*Black Stars*), who denies that Jethroe was driving with Easter at the time (p. 68), has his dates confused.
8. Cattau ("Maybe There Really Is"), who interviewed several of Easter's family members, claims that he worked in Portland, Oregon, in a shipyard for the duration of the war. It is clear at any rate that he played no baseball between 1942 and 1945.
9. Goodrich, "King of Swat?"
10. Goodrich ("King of Swat?") tells an apocryphal-sounding tale in which Easter is first turned down by Taylor, who dismisses him as "too big and too awkward." Easter then earns a spot on a semipro team by convincing the desperate, short-handed manager that he's actually "a better pitcher than a first baseman," pitches against and defeats Taylor's Giants in an exhibition, and hits three home runs instead of the two he had promised.
11. Cattau, "Maybe There Really Is."

12. Robinson and Bauer, *Catching Dreams.*

13. O'Neil et al., *I Was Right on Time.*

14. Virgil's obituary from May 1, 2001, lists a stepson, Terry Sr., who was named as a son in Luke's obituary. Her obituary also mentions son Gerald Sr., not named in Luke's obituary. Gerald is, however, mentioned in Cattau's article ("Maybe There Really Is") as Luke's son, so this may have been an accidental omission.

15. *The Sporting News*, March 30, 1949.

16. Doyle, *Myth, Legend, Superstar.*

17. Baseball Think Factory; Bjarkman, *Baseball with a Latin Beat*; Peary, *We Played the Game*, 348.

18. Buck Leonard reports, "We sold Easter to the Cleveland Indians for $10,000. They were going to pay another $5,000 if he went to the majors. But when he went to the majors, Luke wanted the other $5,000 himself. He had an argument with the Homestead Grays' management. At that time Rufus Jackson was dead and his wife was in charge. Luke said he wasn't going if he didn't get the $5,000, but they got together on something and Luke went" (Holway, *Voices,* 271).

19. Swaine, *Black Stars*, 79.

20. *The Sporting News*, March 30, 1949.

21. Goodrich, "King of Swat?"

22. *The Sporting News*, August 24, 1949.

23. Cattau, "Maybe There Really Is."

24. Goodrich, "King of Swat?"

25. Schneider, *Tribe Dugout,* 51.

26. Cattau, "Maybe There Really Is."

27. Cattau, "Maybe There Really Is."

28. Overfeld, *100 Seasons*, 150.

29. Swaine, *Black Stars*, 82.

30. Overfeld, *100 Seasons*, 151.

31. *Sports Illustrated*, July 15, 1957.

32. Cattau, "Maybe There Really Is."

33. Mandelaro and Pitoniak, *Silver Seasons*, 114.

34. Mandelaro and Pitoniak, *Silver Seasons*, 114.

35. *Sports Illustrated*, July 14, 1960.

36. Mandelaro and Pitoniak, *Silver Seasons*, 114; Swaine, *Black Stars*, 83.

37. In fact, it is not entirely clear whether Luke spent 1965–66 in Rochester or in Cleveland. His obituary from the March 30, 1979, *New York Times* mentions that he had worked at his job in Cleveland for "about fifteen years," that is, since 1964. The obituary from his memorial service, however, says that he returned to Cleveland in 1966.

38. Robinson and Bauer, *Catching Dreams,* 188. This may be the Majestic Hotel, which stood at East 55th and Central Avenue. Joe Mosbrook describes it as "Cleveland's primary African-American hotel" ("Jazzed in Cleveland"). The Majestic had featured a jazz room since 1931.

39. Cattau, "Maybe There Really Is."

40. Cattau, "Maybe There Really Is."

41. Obituary from memorial services.

42. Virgil Easter's obituary. When she died at the age of 77, Virgil had eight grandchildren and a great-grandchild.

43. Moore, *Pride*, 92.

44. Nelson, *Story of California Baseball*, 240.

45. Cattau, "Maybe There Really Is."

46. Goodrich, "King of Swat?"

47. Goodrich, "King of Swat?"; Peary, *We Played the Game*, 199.

48. Peary, *We Played the Game*, 101.

49. Overfeld, *100 Seasons*, 150.

50. Cattau, "Maybe There Really Is."

Bjarkman, Peter C. *Baseball with a Latin Beat.* Jefferson NC: McFarland, 1994.

Holway, John. *Voices from the Great Black Baseball Leagues.* New York: Dodd, Mead, 1975.

Kelley, Brent. *Voices from the Negro Leagues.* Jefferson NC: McFarland, 1998.

Mandelaro, Jim, and Scott Pitoniak. *Silver Seasons: The Story of the Rochester Red Wings.* Syracuse: Syracuse University Press, 1996.

Moore, Joseph Thomas. *Pride against Prejudice: The Biography of Larry Doby.* New York: Praeger Press, 1988.

Nelson, Kevin. *The Story of California Baseball.* San Francisco: California Historical Society Press, 2004.

O'Neil, Buck, Steve Wulf, and David Conrads. *I Was Right on Time.* New York: Simon & Schuster, 1997.

Overfeld, Joe. *The 100 Seasons of Buffalo Baseball.* Kenmore NY: Partner's Press, 1985.

Peary, Danny, ed. *We Played the Game.* New York: Hyperion Press, 1994.

Robinson, Frazier, and Paul Bauer. *Catching Dreams: My Life in the Negro Baseball Leagues.* Syracuse: Syracuse University Press, 1999.

Schneider, Russell. *Tales from the Tribe Dugout.* Champaign IL: Sports Publishing, 2002.

Swaine, Rick. *The Black Stars Who Made Baseball Whole.* Jefferson NC: McFarland, 2006.

Cattau, Danniel. "So, Maybe There Really Is Such a Thing as 'the Natural.'" *Smithsonian* 22, no. 4 (1991): 117–28.

Doyle, Pat. "Luke Easter: Myth, Legend, Superstar." *Baseball Almanac*, September 2003.

Goodrich, James. "Luke Easter, King of Swat?" *Negro Digest* 8, no. 10 (1950): 3–9.

Sports Illustrated, July 15, 1957, 22–24.

Sports Illustrated, April 9, 1979, 18.

Obituary of Luke Easter, March 30, 1979, *New York Times.*

Obituary of Virgil Easter, May 1, 2001, *Cleveland Plain-Dealer.*

The Sporting News, March 30, 1949.

The Sporting News, August 24, 1949.

The Sporting News, September 14, 1960.

The Sporting News, March 1, 1969.

The Sporting News, October 4, 1969.

Mosbrook, Joe. "Jazzed in Cleveland." Pt. 49, January 3, 2000. www.cleveland.oh.uRs/wmv_news/jazz49.htm.

Obituary from Luke Easter's memorial service, Mt. Sinai Baptist Church, April 3, 1979, online at www.redwingsbaseball.com.

Baseball-Almanac.com.

BaseballThinkFactory.org.

Buffalo Bisons, www.bisons.com.

Rochester Red Wings, www.redwingsbaseball.com.

National Archives, Washington DC.

37. Early Wynn

1. Kahn, "Early Wynn."
2. *The Sporting News*, June 15, 1963, 7.
3. Smith, *Red Smith on Baseball*, 325.
4. Kahn, *Season in the Sun,* 108.
5. Wynn, "Four Sides."
6. Dickson, *Baseball's Greatest Quotations*, 606.
7. *The Sporting News*, October 7, 1959, 4.
8. Singletary, "Senor."
9. *The Sporting News*, February 5, 1972, 32.

Appel, Marty, and Burt Goldblatt. *Baseball's Best: The Hall of Fame Gallery.* New York: McGraw-Hill, 1980.

Dickson, Paul. *Baseball's Greatest Quotations*, rev. ed. New York: Harper Collins, 2008.

Kahn, Roger. *A Season in the Sun* (Lincoln: University of Nebraska Press, 2000).

Smith, Red. *Red Smith on Baseball.* New York: Ivan R. Dee, 2000.

Kahn, Roger. "Early Wynn: The Story of a Hard Loser." *Sport*, March 1956, 53–62.

Singletary, Wes. "Senor: The Managerial Career of Al Lopez." *Sunland Tribune (Journal of the Tampa Historical Society)* 19 (November 1993): 57–66.

Wynn, Early. "The Four Sides of the Beanball Argument: The Pitcher's Side." *Sport*, January 1956.

New York Times, April 6, 1999.

The Sporting News, May 14, 1942; October 7, 1959; June 15, 1963; February 5, 1972.

38. Hal Naragon

The author would also like to thank Lynn O'Neil and Rebecca Larson-Troyer of the Barberton Public Library Local History Room for assistance with finding yearbooks and other early material regarding Hal Naragon.

1. Interview with the author.
2. Interview with the author.
3. "Baseball 1944," *Barberton High School Yearbook* (Barberton OH, 1945), 77.
4. Interview with the author.
5. Phyllis Taylor, *100 Years of Magic: The Story of Barberton, Ohio, 1891–1991* (Akron: Summit County Historical Press, 1991).
6. *A Bicentennial Remembrance: Barberton Ohio the Magic City* (Akron: Beaumarc Publications, 1975), 147.
7. "B.H.S. Baseball Team Captures Three Contests," *Barberton Herald*, April 18, 1947.
8. Interview with the author.
9. "Hat Naragon Booked as Harrisburg Catcher," *Barberton Herald*, April 30, 1948.
10. "Harold Naragon Begins New Baseball Season at Harrisburg," *Barberton Herald*, April 29, 1949.
11. Interview with the author.

12. Interview with the author.

13. Interview with the author.

14. Harry Jones, "Naragon's Triple in 10th Wins," *Cleveland Plain Dealer*, August 26, 1954, 1.

15. Interview with the author.

16. Interview with the author.

17. Interview with the author.

18. Interview with the author.

19. Interview with the author.

20. "Kaat's Meow," *Sports Illustrated*, October 17, 1966, 24–25.

21. Watson Spoelstra, "Sain's Advice Huge Plus for Tiger Hurlers," *The Sporting News*, September 7, 1968, 9.

22. Watson Spoelstra, "Sain, Naragon Give Tigers Early Line on '69," *The Sporting News*, November 2, 1968, 29.

23. Max Nichols, "Dropped by Twins, Sain and Naragon Join Tigers," *The Sporting News*, October 15, 1966.

24. Interview with the author.

25. Interview with the author.

26. Interview with the author.

27. Watson Spoelstra, "Price Is Right as No. 2 Backstop, Bengals Learn," *The Sporting News*, June 22, 1968, 9.

28. Interview with the author.

39. 1954 All-Star Game

1. *The Sporting News*, July 14, 1954, 10.

2. Al Rosen quoted in *The Sporting News*, July 7, 1954, 11.

3. Casey Stengel and Al Rosen quoted in *Cleveland Plain Dealer*, July 14, 1954. See also Rosen's quotes in *Cleveland Press*, July 14, 1954.

4. The record has since been tied by Willie McCovey (Giants, 1969) and Gary Carter (Expos, 1981). See Baseball-Reference.com.

5. David Vincent, Lyle Spatz, and David W. Smith, *The Midsummer Classic: The Complete History of Baseball's All-Star Game* (Lincoln: University of Nebraska Press, 2001), 132.

6. Leo Durocher quoted in *Cleveland Plain Dealer*, July 14, 1954.

7. Bill Stewart quoted in *Cleveland Plain Dealer*, July 14, 1954.

8. Alvin Dark's quote and Red Schoendienst's comments in *Cleveland Plain Dealer*, July 14, 1954.

9. Leo Durocher quoted in *The Sporting News*, July 21, 1954, 10.

10. Arch Ward quoted in *Cleveland Plain Dealer*, July 14, 1954.

11. Vincent et al., *Midsummer Classic*, 133.

12. Ed McAuley's comments appear in the column "Ed McAuley," *Cleveland News*, July 15, 1954. See also Francis Kinlaw, "Plenty of Stars, but Few Victory Cigars," *Monumental Baseball: The National Pastime in the National Capital Region*, Society for American Baseball Research (SABR), 2009 Convention Publication, 85.

13. *The Sporting News*, July 21, 1954, 8.

14. Casey Stengel quoted in *The Sporting News*, July 21, 1954.

15. Al Lopez quoted in *Cleveland News*, July 14, 1954.

16. *Cleveland Plain Dealer*, July 14, 1954.

41. Al Smith

1. Hines, *Sports Collectors Digest*, 188.

2. Hines, *Sports Collectors Digest*, 188.

3. Quote taken from article in Al Smith's file at the National Baseball Hall of Fame Library, Cooperstown NY; publication and author unknown.

4. Veeck, *Veeck as in Wreck*, 348.

5. Goldstein, "Al Smith Obituary."

6. Goldstein, "Al Smith Obituary."

7. Goldstein, "Al Smith Obituary."

8. Vanderberg, *'59 Summer of the Sox*.

9. Lindberg, *White Sox Encyclopedia*.

10. O'Conner, "Obituary."

Lindberg, Richard. *The White Sox Encyclopedia*. Philadelphia: Temple University Press, 1997.

Vanderberg, Bob. *'59 Summer of the Sox: The Year the World Series Came to Chicago*. Champaign IL: Sports Publishing, 1999.

Veeck, Bill, with Ed Linn. *Veeck as in Wreck*. Evanston IL: University of Chicago Press, 1962.

Conklin, Mike. "A Wet Sox Memoir." *Chicago Tribune*, April 14, 2000.

Goldstein, Richard. "Al Smith Obituary." *New York Times*, January 6, 2003.Peticca, Mike. Obituary. *Cleveland Plains Dealer*, January 4, 2002.

Enright, James. *Chicago American*, January 30, 1962.

Hines, Rick. *Sports Collectors Digest*, June 21, 1991.

Marazzi, Rich. *Sports Collectors Digest*, September 27, 1996.

Munzel, Edgar. *Chicago Daily News*, December 25, 1957, and March 30, 1963.

O'Conner, Patrick. "Obituary: Al Smith Former Outfielder/Third Baseman Passes Away." www.mlb.com, January 3, 2002.

42. Vic Wertz

Thanks to granddaughter Rachel Wertz, great-nephew Rick Murphy, and baseball historian Dennis Dillon.

1. Charles Adams III, *Baseball in Reading* (Mount Pleasant SC: Arcadia Publishing, 2003), 51.

2. Lyall Smith, "Wertz Is a Workhorse," *Sport*, September 1950, 22.

3. Smith, "Wertz Is a Workhorse," 22.

4. Smith, "Wertz Is a Workhorse," 22.

5. Jack Newcombe, in Ray Robinson, ed., *Baseball Stars of 1958* (Utica NY: Pyramid, 1958).

6. Arno Goethel, "Wertz to Retire," *The Sporting News*, October 5, 1963, 30, 38.

7. Newcombe, *Baseball Stars of 1958*.

8. Newcombe, *Baseball Stars of 1958*.

9. "Marion Tags Wertz Slugger With Browns," United Press, August 15, 1952.

10. Tommy Devine, "Wertz Lives Anew," *Baseball Digest*, November 1954.

11. Devine, "Wertz Lives Anew."

12. Arthur Daley, "The Man Who Licked Polio," *New York Times*, January 19, 1956.

13. Herbert Kamm, "Vic Wertz Still Slugging Despite Polio and Other Injuries," *Pittsburgh Press*, April 3, 1959.

14. Chris Stern, *Where Have They Gone* (New York: Tempo Books, 1979).

15. *USA Today*, July 8, 1983.

43. Hal Newhouser

1. Quote attributed to Wish Egan, source unknown.

2. "Transformation to Pitcher," *New York Times*, June 11, 1989.

3. Buster Olney, "The Pride of Kalamazoo," *New York Times*, April 4, 1999.

4. Milton Gross, "The Truth About Newhouser," *Sport*, August 1948.

Goldstein, Richard. *Spartan Seasons*. New York: Macmillan, 1980.

James, Bill. *The New Bill James Historical Baseball Abstract*. New York: Free Press, 2001.

Jordan, David. *A Tiger in His Time*. Dallas: Taylor Publishing, 1990.

Meany, Tom. *Baseball's Greatest Pitchers*. New York: A. S. Barnes, 1951.

Neft, David, Richard Goldstein, and Michael Neft. *The Sports Encyclopedia: Baseball*. New York: St. Martin's, 2007.

Newhouser, Hal. *Pitching to Win*. Chicago: Ziff-Davis, 1948.

Shatzkin, Mike, and Jim Charlton, *The Ballplayers*. New York: Arbor House, 1990.

The Sporting News Baseball Guide.

The Sporting News Baseball Register.

Amman, Larry. "Newhouser and Trout in 1944: 56 Wins and a Near Miss." *Baseball Research Journal* 12 (1983): 18–23.

44. Bill Glynn

1. Hal Lebovitz, *Cleveland News*, July 6, 1954, 4-D.

2. Hulme Kinnebrew, "Phillies Beat Tigers 10–8, Cusick Hurt." *Americus (GA) Times Recorder*, date unknown, in Glynn's file at the HOF Archives.

3. Hal Lebovitz, "Indians Get Early Chance to Test Improved Bench," *The Sporting News*, April 29, 1953, 11.

4. Hal Lebovitz, "Luke's Homers Add Up to Plenty of Singles," *Cleveland News*, August 15, 1953, 9.

5. Harry Jones, "Indians Trade Chakales for Wertz," *Cleveland Plain Dealer*, June 2, 1954, 1D

6. "Glynn Returns to First Base Tonight," *Cleveland Plain Dealer*, July 2, 1954.

Americus (GA) Times Recorder.

Cleveland News.

Cleveland Plain Dealer.

Cleveland Press.

The Sporting News.

Baseball-Reference.com.

Retrosheet.org.

Bill Glynn's file at the National Baseball Hall of Fame Archives, Cooperstown NY.

46. José G. Santiago Guzmán

Crescioni, José A. *El Beisbol Profesional Boricua.* Self-published, 1997.

Monserrate, Joaquín. "Tite y Pantalones: Los Dos Colosos del Sur." *El Nuevo Dia*, November 5, 2000, 166.

Baseball-Reference.com.

Interviews with José G. Santiago by author, 2011.
Interview with Minnie Minoso by author, February 2011.

47. Bob Kennedy

I wish to thank my wife, Diane, for editorial skill and David Ehlert for biographical research.

Baseball Encyclopedia, 8th ed. New York: Macmillan, 1990.
Chadwick, Bruce, and David M. Spindel. *Chicago Cubs: Memories and Memorabilia of the Wrigley Wonders.* New York: Abbeville Press, 1994.
Schneider, Russell. *Tales from the Tribe Dugout*, Champaign IL: Sports Publishing, 2002.

Treder, Steve. "Bob Kennedy (Parts 1 and 2)." *The Hard Ball Times*, July 15 and 22, 2008. Downloaded December 27, 2010: http://www.hardballtimes.com/main/printarticle/bob-kennedy-part-1/ and http://www.hardballtimes.com/main/printarticle/bob-kennedy-part-2/.
———. "The THT Interview: Terry Kennedy." *The Hard Ball Times*, November 25, 2008. Downloaded January 22, 2011: http://www.hardballtimes.com/main/article/the-tht-interview-terry-kennedy/.

48. Mickey Grasso

1. Gary Bedingfield, "Behind the Wire: Baseball Players Who Were POWs in World War II," www.baseballinwartime.com/pow.htm.
2. Burton Hawkins, *The Sporting News*, March 11, 1953.
3. Shirley Povich, *Washington Post*, March 20, 1950.
4. Shirley Povich, *Washington Post*, January 22, 1954.
5. Bob Addie, *Washington Post*, February 25, 1961.
6. Bob Addie, *Washington Post*, January 12, 1962.
7. Shirley Povich, *Washington Post*, March 2, 1953.
8. Herb Heft, *Washington Post*, August 30, 1953.
9. Povich, *Washington Post*, January 22, 1954.
10. Povich, *Washington Post*, January 22, 1954.
11. Herb Heft, *The Sporting News*, February 10, 1954.
12. Bob Addie, *Washington Post*, April 11, 1954.

Wolter, Tim. *POW Baseball in World War II.* Jefferson NC: McFarland, 2002.

New York Times.
Pacific Stars & Stripes.
The Sporting News.
Washington Post.

U.S. Census, 1930.

Baseball-Almanac.com.
BaseballLibrary.com.
Baseball-Reference.com.
BaseballinWartime.com.

49. Bobby Avila

1. Callum Hughson, "Beto 'Bobby Avila' Bio," *Mop-Up Duty*, http://mopupduty.com/beto-bobby-avila/ (August 10, 2010), 1.
2. Callum Hughson, "Beto 'Bobby Avila' Bio," *Mop-Up Duty*, 5.
3. Baseball-Reference.com, Avila Statistics and History, 11 yrs, http:www.baseball-reference.com/players/a/avilabo0l.html.
4. J. G. Taylor Spink, "Mays and Avila No. 1 Players of '54," *The Sporting News*, October 13, 1954, 1.
5. Baseball-Reference.com, Bobby Avila, Birthplace.
6. Hal Lebovitz, "Cleveland's Bobby Avila, A Real Good Hitter," *Baseball Digest* 5 (June 1953): 5–13.
7. Rich Westcott, *Splendor on the Diamond* (Gainesville: University of Florida Press, 2000); Bobby Avila, 119.
8. Baseball-Reference.com, Bobby Avila, Minors Batting, 1948.
9. Lebovitz, "Cleveland's Bobby Avila."
10. Lebovitz, "Cleveland's Bobby Avila."
11. Bill James, *The New Bill James Historical Baseball Abstract* (New York: Free Press, 2001), 508.
12. Lebovitz, "Cleveland's Bobby Avila."
13. Baseball-Reference.com, Bobby Avila, Standard Batting, 1949.
14. James, *Historical Baseball Abstract*, 508.
15. Baseball-Reference.com, Standard Batting, 1950.

16. Baseball-Reference.com, Standard Batting, 1951.

17. Baseball-Reference.com, Bobby Avila, June 20, 1951, Play-by-Play.

18. Lebovitz, "Cleveland's Bobby Avila."

19. Baseball-Reference.com, Standard Batting, 1952.

20. John Phillips, *The Story of Bobby Avila* (Kathleen GA: Capital Publishing, 2006), 5.

21. Lebovitz, "Cleveland's Bobby Avila."

22. Ray Gillespie, "Mexican Kids Idolize Avila as Hero, Want to Play Ball in US," *The Sporting News*, March 14, 1951, 18.

23. Baseball-Reference.com, Standard Batting, 1953.

24. Baseball-Reference.com, Standard Fielding, 1953.

25. John Phillips, *The Story of Bobby Avila*, 5.

26. Bill James, *Historical Baseball Abstract*, 509.

27. Rich Westcott, *Splendor on the Diamond*, 121.

28. Hal Lebovitz, "Injury Jinx Chips Two High Men Off Tribe's Totem Pole," *The Sporting News*, June 16, 1964, 3–4.

29. Westcott, *Splendor on the Diamond*, 121.

30. "Good Judgment Shown in Avila Penalty," *The Sporting News*, June 16, 1954, 12.

31. J. G. Taylor Spink, "Mays and Avila No.1 Players of '54," *The Sporting News*, October 13, 1954, 1.

32. Westcott, *Splendor on the Diamond*, 122.

33. Baseball-Reference.com, Standard Batting, 1954.

34. "Avila Unanimous Selection as 'Cleveland Man of the Year,'" *The Sporting News*, November 3, 1954, 20.

35. Hal Lebovitz, "Avila Toasts His Greatest Year in Milk," *The Sporting News*, September 29, 1954, 12.

36. Frederick Lieb, "Giants' Sweep Rivaled Game's Greatest Upsets," *The Sporting News,* October 13, 1954, 9.

37. Dade Hayes, "'54 Series Rears Its Ugly Head," *Chronicle-Telegram* (Cleveland OH), October 2, 1954, B2.

38. "Mexico Gives Bobby Avila 900-Mile Motorbike Escort," *The Sporting News*, October 13, 1954, 26.

39. Jorge Alarcon, "Avila Makes Pilot Bow at Mexico City," *The Sporting News*, December 15, 1954, 25.

40. "Avila's Surrender Brings Last '55 Holdout Into Fold," *The Sporting News*, March 28, 1955, 25.

41. Hal Lebovitz, "War Clubs Silent, So Tribe Chief AL Props Defenses," *The Sporting News*, July 6, 1955, 4.

42. Hal Lebovitz, "Hit-Hungry Injuns Get Chance to Feast at Boston Tea Party," *The Sporting News*, May 25, 1955, 7.

43. "Major Flashes, American League," *The Sporting News*, August 3, 1955, 21; Hal Lebovitz, "Avila Filling Bill as Senor Al's Hot Temale Thumper," September 21, 1955, 4.

44. Baseball-Reference.com, Standard Batting, 1955.

45. Miguel Calzadilla, "Mexico Red Have Major Glow, Inking Lemon, Wynn, Rivera," *The Sporting News*, October 19, 1955, 24.

46. Franklin Lewis, "Avila Late Again—Hank in Huff Over 'Holdouts,'" *The Sporting News*, March 21, 1956, 6.

47. Hal Lebovitz, "Avila Speaks for Specs as Hitting Help," *The Sporting News*, August 14, 1957, 20.

48. Hal Lebovitz, "Land Labels Keystone Combine Cornerstone in Indian Buildup," *The Sporting News*, November 20, 1957, 4.

49. Baseball-Reference.com, Bobby Avila, Standard Fielding, 1958.

50. Westcott, *Splendor on the Diamond*, 123.

51. Roberto Hernandez, "Slumping Chili's Streak Toward Top Under Avila," *The Sporting News*, January 20, 1960, 29; Roberto Hernandez, "Chili's Red Hot, Boot Squawking Parrots," *The Sporting News*, January 20, 1960, 29.

52. "Avila Will Play in Native Mexico," *Stevens Point Wisconsin Daily Journal*, April 19, 1960, 10.

53. Hughson, "Beto 'Bobby' Avila Bio," 5.

54. Baseball-Reference.com, Bobby Avila, Statistic and History, Standard Batting, 11 seasons.

55. Robert Hernandez, "Avila Named President of New Circuit," *The Sporting News*, October 26, 1960, 36.

56. Baseball-Reference.com, Salon de la Fama members BR Bullpen, Beto Avila (accessed December 6, 2010).

57. Hughson, "Beto 'Bobby' Avila Bio," 5.

58. Westcott, *Splendor on the Diamond*, 118.

59. Hughson, "Beto 'Bobby' Avila Bio," 5.

60. Westcott, *Splendor on the Diamond*, 120.

50. Joe Ginsberg

1. Horvitz and Horvitz, *Big Book of Jewish Baseball*, 69.

2. Telephone interview with Joe Ginsberg, July 5, 2010.

3. *The Sporting News*, October 26, 1944.

4. *The Sporting News*, September 14, 1944.

5. *The Sporting News*, January 3, 1946.

6. Telephone interview with Ginsberg.

7. *The Sporting News*, January 17, 1946.

8. *The Sporting News*, June 2, 1948.

9. *The Sporting News*, September 15, 1948.

10. *The Sporting News*, September 15, 1948; *Holland (MI) Evening Sentinel*, September 25, 1948.

11. *Toledo Blade*, April 4, 1951.

12. *The Sporting News*, April 2, 1952.

13. Telephone interview with Ginsberg.

14. *Oakland Tribune*, April 6, 1955.

15. *USA Today*, July 8, 2007.

Boxerman, Burton, and Benita W. Boxerman. *Jews and Baseball: The Post-Greenberg Years*. Jefferson NC: McFarland, 2010.

Horvitz, Peter S., and Joachim Horvitz. *The Big Book of Jewish Baseball: An Illustrated Encyclopedia and Anecdotal History*. New York: SPI Books, 2001.

James, Bill. *The New Bill James Historical Baseball Abstract*. New York: Free Press, 2001.

Peary, Danny, ed. *We Played the Game*. New York: Black Dog and Leventhal, 1994.

Rolfe, Red, with William M. Anderson, ed. *The View from the Dugout, the Journals of Red Rolfe*. Ann Arbor: University of Michigan Press, 2010.

Oakland Tribune.
The Sporting News.
Toledo Blade.
USA Today.

Baseball-Reference.com.
Retrosheet.org.

Telephone interview with Joe Ginsberg, July 5, 2010.

Joe Ginsberg's player file at the National Baseball Hall of Fame Library, Cooperstown NY.

52. Cleveland Indians World Championships

1. Wiley, George. *The 1920 Cleveland Indians*. Indiana PA: Copies-Now, 1993, 6.

2. "Red Sox, Redbirds Rated Flag Redhots," *The Sporting News*, April 21, 1948, 3.

53. Rocky Nelson

1. *Los Angeles Times*, July 25, 1963.

2. *The Sporting News*, November 18, 1953

3. *Youngstown Vindicator*, February 25, 1954.

4. *Youngstown Vindicator*, March 29, 1954.

5. *Youngstown Vindicator*, March 15, 1954.

6. *The Sporting News*, May 19, 1954.

7. Terrell, "Million and One Alibis," *Sports Illustrated*, August 18, 1958.

8. Terrell, "Million and One Alibis."

9. Terrell, "Million and One Alibis."

10. Terrell, "Million and One Alibis."

McAuley, Ed. "The Eternal Door-Knocker." *Baseball Digest*, March 1959.

Terrell, Roy. "The Man with a Million and One Alibis." *Sports Illustrated*, August 18, 1958.

Los Angeles Times, July 25, 1963.

The Sporting News, November 18, 1953; February 3, 1954; April 14, 1954; May 19, 1954.

Youngstown Vindicator, February 25, March 15, and March 29, 1954.

Steve Treder. "Rocky Nelson." *Hardball Times*, April 5, 2006, http://www.thehardballtimes.com.

54. Art Houtteman

1. Smith, "Art Houtteman," 27.

2. *The Sporting News*, September 3, 1947, 14.

3. *The Sporting News*, August 28, 1948, 11.

4. *The Sporting News*, September 8, 1948, 6.

5. *The Sporting News*, September 14, 1949, 10.

6. *The Sporting News*, February 8, 1950, 14.

7. *The Sporting News*, January 15, 1952, 7.

8. Fehler, *Tales*, 84, 105.

9. *The Sporting News*, December 31, 1952, 20.

10. *The Sporting News*, June 2, 1954, 5.

11. *The Sporting News*, May 29, 1957, 18.

Fehler, Gene. *Tales from Baseball's Golden Age*. Champaign IL: Sports Publishing, 2000.

Smith, Lyall. "Art Houtteman, The Comeback Kid." *Sport*, July 1950, 24–30.

Lustig, Dennis. "Where Are They Now?" *Detroit News*, June 20, 1973.

Sipple, George. "Former Tiger Whiz Kid Houtteman Dies." *Detroit Free Press*, May 8, 2003, 5C.

U.S. Census, 1920.

Art Houtteman's file at the National Baseball Hall of Fame Library, Cooperstown NY, contains unidentified (some undated) clippings from Detroit papers, the *New York World-Telegram and Sun, Baseball Digest,* and the Associated Press.

55. Bob Hooper

1. Lebovitz, "Hooper's Pitching Lifts Tribe's Hopes."
2. Gibbons, "Bullpen Bonfire."
3. U.S. Census, 1940.
4. Shearon, *Canada's Baseball Legends,* 129–31.
5. Shearon, *Canada's Baseball Legends,* 129–31.
6. Shearon, *Canada's Baseball Legends,* 129–31.
7. Earl Lawson, "Bob Hooper Purchased from Cleveland Indians," April 14, 1955, clipping in Hooper's HOF player's file.

Shearon, Jim. *Canada's Baseball Legends.* Kanata, Ontario: Malin Head Press, 1994.

Gibbons, Frank. "Bullpen Bonfire Kept Cooper Hot." *Cleveland Press,* April 17, 1953.
Lebovitz, Hal. "Hooper's Pitching Lifts Tribe's Hopes for Stronger Bullpen." *Cleveland News,* April 17, 1953.

Cleveland News.
Cleveland Press.
The Sporting News.

Baseball-Reference.com.
Retrosheet.org.

Bob Hooper's player file at the National Baseball Hall of Fame Library, Cooperstown NY.

57. Ken Coleman

Material, including quotes, is derived from Curt Smith's books *Voices of The Game* (New York: Simon & Schuster, 1992), *Of Mikes and Men* (South Bend IN: Diamond Communications, 1998), *Voices of Summer* (New York: Carroll & Graf, 2005), *The Voice* (Guilford CT: Lyons Press, 2007), *A Talk in the Park* (Dulles VA: Potomac Books, 2011), and *Mercy! A Celebration of Fenway Park's Centennial Told Through Red Sox Radio and TV* (Dulles VA: Potomac Books, 2012).

58. Jim Britt

1. Audiotapes from the John Miley Collection of Jim Britt's Sports Roundup, 1950.
2. Wells Twombly, "Those '48 Braves Were the Greatest," *The Sporting News,* July 11, 1970.
3. Curt Smith, *Voices of the Game* (Lanham MD: Diamond Communications, 1987), 81.
4. Letter from Jim Britt to the author, January 1952.
5. From Hadley's nightly sports show as recalled by the author.
6. www.narragansettbeer.com/history.
7. From Hadley's play-by-play announcing as recalled by the author.
8. Smith, *Voices of the Game,* 82.
9. Smith, *Voices of the Game,* 82.
10. Ray Fitzgerald, "Voice from Hub's Past Is Stilled," *Boston Globe,* January 1981.
11. Ted Patterson, *The Golden Voices of Baseball* (Champaign IL: Sports Publishing, 2002), 74.

59. Jimmy Dudley

1. Russell Schneider, "The Best Team, the Best Group of Guys," *Cleveland Plain Dealer,* July 15, 1984, 11-B.
2. Schneider, "Best Team."
3. Schneider, "Best Team."
4. Schneider, "Best Team."
5. Curt Smith, *Voices of the Game* (Dallas: Taylor Trade Publishing, 1987), 165.
6. Smith, *Voices of the Game,* 165.
7. Smith, *Voices of the Game,* 165.
8. Smith, *Voices of the Game,* 165.
9. Terry Pluto, *The Curse of Rocky Colavito* (New York: Simon & Schuster, 1994), 182–83.
10. Pluto, *Curse of Rocky Colavito,* 182–83.
11. Terry Pluto, *Akron Beacon Journal,* August 3, 1997, C7.
12. Baseball Hall of Fame news release, February 13, 1997
13. Hall of Fame news release.

61. 1954 World Series

Bartlett, John. *Familiar Quotations,* 14th ed. Edited by Emily Morison Beck. Boston: Little, Brown, 1968.
Reichler, Joe. *Inside the Majors.* New York: Hart Publications, 1952.

The 1993 Indians Game Face Magazine, Final Series at Cleveland Stadium Commemorative Issue. Cleveland: Cleveland Indians Baseball Company, October 1993.

Associated Press. "Maglie Can't Shake First-Inning Troubles." *Cleveland Plain Dealer,* September 30, 1954.

———. "Tribe Now 9–5 Favorites and 6–5 in Opener." *Cleveland Plain Dealer,* September 28, 1954.

Cobbledick, Gordon. "Cobbledick Picks Indians Second to Yanks, but Says Champs Face Problems." *Cleveland Plain Dealer,* April 11, 1954.

———. "Indians' Flop Rivals A's 4-Game Defeat; Can Only Say It Was Inexpressibly Sad." *Cleveland Plain Dealer,* October 3, 1954.

———. "Pitching Will Subdue Giants; Tribe Needs Only Two or Three Runs to Win Games." *Cleveland Plain Dealer,* September 29, 1954.

Cordtz, Dan. "Durocher Declares He Was Saving Rhodes." *Cleveland Plain Dealer,* September 30, 1954.

———. "Lopez Offers No Alibis, Takes Sweep in Stride." *Cleveland Plain Dealer,* October 3, 1954.

———. "Lopez Says Not Even Mays Could Have Caught Rhodes' Blooper." *Cleveland Plain Dealer,* October 1, 1954.

———. "Never Hit Ball Harder, Wertz Says of Longest Series 'Out.'" *Cleveland Plain Dealer,* September 30, 1954.

Daley, Arthur. "Does This Explain It?" *New York Times,* October 4, 1954.

DiMaggio, Joe. "These Giants Top '51 Club." *Cleveland Press,* September 29, 1954.

Drebinger, John. "Durocher Scotches Rumors He Intends to Quit Giants; Will Return in '55." *New York Times,* October 4, 1954.

———. "Giants Crush Indians, 6–2, For 3–0 World Series Lead." *New York Times,* October 2, 1954.

———. "Giants Defeat Indians, 7–4, and Sweep World Series." *New York Times,* October 3, 1954.

———. "Giants, Paced by Rhodes, Again Defeat Indians, 3–1." *New York Times,* October 1, 1954.

———. "Giants Win in 10th from Indians, 5–2, on Rhodes' Homer." *New York Times,* October 1, 1954.

———. "Indians Favored Over Giants in World Series." *New York Times,* September 26, 1954.

Hand, Jack. "Indians Remain 17–10 Favorites." *Cleveland Plain Dealer,* September 29, 1954.

International News Service. "Clubhouse Quotes at a Glance." *Cleveland Plain Dealer,* September 30, 1954.

———. "Clubhouse Quotes at a Glance." *Cleveland Plain Dealer,* October 3, 1954.

Jones, Harry. "Giants Today; Comeback Here." *Cleveland Plain Dealer,* October 1, 1954.

———. "Flag Is Immediate Goal for Indians." *Cleveland Plain Dealer,* September 16, 1954.

———. "Giants Whip Indians, 5–2." *Cleveland Plain Dealer,* September 30, 1954.

———. "Indians in Six Games, Jones Predicts." *Cleveland Plain Dealer,* September 28, 1954.

———. "78,102 See Giants Sweep, 7–4." *Cleveland Plain Dealer,* October 3, 1954.

Lewis, Franklin. "Tribe Futile Because of Cripples—Lewis." *Cleveland Press,* October 4, 1954.

Mellow, Jan. "Tribe Loss Plunges City's Stores and Bars in Gloom." *Cleveland Plain Dealer,* October 3, 1954.

Sheehan, Joseph M. "'Chinese' Homer: How It All Began." *New York Times,* October 1, 1954.

Silverman, Alvin. "Notables Steal Show at Series." *Cleveland Plain Dealer,* October 2, 1954.

———. "13 is No Magic Number for Vanishing Indians." *Cleveland Plain Dealer,* October 1, 1954.

United Press. "Experts Pick Tribe." *Cleveland Press,* September 29, 1954.

"Giants to Beat Indians Home." *Cleveland Plain Dealer,* September 30, 1954.

"Sixteen Records Are Broken and Fifteen Tied during the 1954 World Series." *New York Times,* October 3, 1954.

"300 Watch Giants Reach Cleveland." *New York Times,* October 1, 1954.

Baseball-Almanac.com.

Contributors

MARK ARMOUR is the author of *Joe Cronin: A Life in Baseball*, the coauthor of *Paths to Glory*, the founder and director of SABR's Baseball Biography Project, and a contributor to many baseball journals and websites. He writes about baseball from his home in Oregon's Willamette Valley.

THOMAS AYERS is a diehard Blue Jays fan who was born and raised in Toronto, where unfortunately he was slightly too young to truly appreciate the team's success in the early 1990s. He is a graduate of Queen's University, the London School of Economics, and the University of Toronto. A SABR member since 2005, he has written several biographies for the Bio Project.

RICK BALAZS is an attorney and CPA based in Columbus, Ohio. He grew up in Greater Cleveland and is an avid Indians fan. He holds an accounting degree from Case Western Reserve University, a master's in accounting from Ohio State, and a law degree from the University of Virginia.

JON BARNES is a public relations professional based in Cleveland, Ohio, and a former business journalist. While growing up in Kansas City, Jon became a fan of Bob Lemon for the managerial job he did with the Royals in 1971, giving Kansas City its first Major League Baseball team with a winning record.

RALPH BERGER owns a bachelor of arts degree from the University of Pennsylvania and a master's degree in public administration from Temple University. He has written forty-eight online bios for the SABR Bio Project. He lives in Huntingdon Valley, Pennsylvania, with his wife, Reina. Ralph has traveled extensively in Europe and has been a diehard Phillies fan for seventy years.

MORT BLOOMBERG was born and raised on Boston's North Shore. He is a cofounder of the Boston Braves Historical Association. Mort has been a SABR member since 1976 and years ago earned a BA from Clark and a PhD in psychology from SUNY at Buffalo. Over the past fifteen years, he has had a variety of jobs in pro baseball. Now living in Tempe, Arizona, where he is an adviser to ballplayers, the "ham" in him awakens each spring training when he becomes one of the Milwaukee Brewers Racing Sausages.

DAVID BOHMER is a native of Cleveland, Ohio, and continues to be an avid fan of the Indians. For the past nineteen years, he has been Director of the Pulliam Center for Contemporary Media and Media Fellows at DePauw University. For over a decade he has taught a course at DePauw on baseball as history and hopes to continue work on a book about nine greats who never played.

PHILIP A. COLA is Vice President, Research and Technology at University Hospitals Case Medical Center and Adjunct Assistant Professor at the Case Western Reserve University (CWRU) School of Medicine. He is a doctoral candidate at the Weatherhead School of Management, CWRU.

TRACY J. R. COLLINS lives in Mt. Pleasant, Michigan, where she teaches at Central Michigan University. When she is not teaching, she likes to travel, read, play softball, and play catch in her backyard with her husband and daughter.

WARREN CORBETT is the author of *The Wizard of Waxahachie: Paul Richards and the End of Baseball as We Knew It* and has contributed to six other baseball books.

GREG ERION and his wife, Barbara, live in South San Francisco, California. Retired from the railroad industry, he currently teaches U.S. history part time at Skyline College. Greg has contributed several articles to the ongoing SABR Biography Project and is currently working on a book about the 1959 season.

EDWIN FERNÁNDEZ was born in New York City and grew up in San Juan, Puerto Rico. A banker and a computer professional in his other life, he is now a baseball historian and a sportswriter, former president of the Sports Journalists Association in Puerto Rico, and coauthor of *JONRON*, a book on the Latin and Caribbean players in the Major Leagues. At present, he is a member of the International Press Association (AIPS) Board of Directors and member of the Selection Committee of the Latino Baseball Hall of Fame. He joined SABR in 1999 and is a former chairman of the Latino Baseball Committee and founder of the Puerto Rico Chapter.

DAN FIELDS is a manuscript editor at the *New England Journal of Medicine*. He loves baseball trivia, and he regularly attends Boston Red Sox and Pawtucket (Rhode Island) Red Sox games with his teenage son. Dan lives in Framingham, Massachusetts.

DAVID L. FLEITZ is a SABR member and systems analyst who lives in Pleasant Ridge, Michigan. His eighth book, Napoleon Lajoie: King of Ballplayers, will be published in 2013 by McFarland and Company.

TOM HEINLEIN grew up in Connecticut and has moved around during adulthood, first to Baltimore and then to Europe for ten years before moving back to the United States in 2001 to the Boston area, where he resides today with his wife and two sons. Tom follows the local team, the Red Sox. Currently a marketing manager at an engineering firm and managing editor for a quarterly association journal, he has served in various writing and editorial roles during his career.

An English teacher at Saint Ignatius High School in Cleveland where he taught a course titled "Baseball Literature" for twenty years, MARK HODERMARSKY has written or edited five sports books, including Baseball's Greatest Writers (2003). He annually reviews baseball books for the *Cleveland Plain Dealer*.

RICK HUHN and his wife, Marcia, live in Westerville, Ohio, not far from the retirement home of the famed baseball writer Hugh Fullerton. The retired attorney is the author of *The Sizzler: George Sisler, Baseball's Forgotten Great*, as well as *Eddie Collins: A Baseball Biography*. A SABR member since 2003, Rick is an organizer and one of the coordinators for the Hank Gowdy Columbus (Ohio) Chapter of the organization.

BOB HURTE lives in the small hamlet of Stewartsville, New Jersey. He has been a SABR member since 1998. He is active in the Bio Project and has written over a dozen bios. Aside from contributing player's bios, he has had articles published on Seamheads.com and the *NJ Baseball Magazine*. His father's favorite player was Wally Westlake, and he considers Wally a good friend. They chat on the phone at least once a month! One of the best memories he has of his dad was arranging a birthday call from Wally on his seventy-fifth birthday!

STEVE JOHNSON is a graduate of Eastern Kentucky University. He is a retired school band director, having served twenty-nine years in that capacity. He has volunteered at the Baseball Hall of Fame library and has done some research for the Cleveland Indians. Johnson has spent many years researching the career of player/umpire Charlie Berry, a friend of his father.

MAXWELL KATES is a chartered accountant with a midsize Toronto firm. He has lectured at the 2004 Limmud Conference at York University and the 2006 SABR Convention in Seattle. The Director of Marketing for the Hanlan's Point Chapter, his work has appeared in four issues of The National Pastime and several SABR Bio Projects.

LEONARD LEVIN is a retired newspaper editor and a longtime (and sometimes long-suffering) fan of the Boston Red Sox. While employed at the Providence Journal, he often wrote historical baseball pieces for the sports section. Nowadays he confines himself to editing for SABR book and biography projects. His wife is a college professor and they have two daughters.

GARY LIVACARI, a lifelong White Sox and Cubs fan, is a practicing dentist in his "day job." He also fancies himself as a freelance writer and amateur baseball historian with a special ongoing interest in the Deadball Era. He has contributed to baseball publications, most recently The Elysian Fields Quarterly. He and his wife, Nancy, and their two children reside in Park Ridge, Illinois.

SCOTT LONGERT is the author of Addie Joss: King of the Pitchers (Society for American Baseball Research, 1998) and The Best They Could Be: The Cleveland Indians, 1916–1920 (Potomac Books, 2013). He has written for The National Pastime and The Baseball Research Journal.

JEANNE M. MALLETT, an attorney and writer now living in Washington DC, was born and raised in northern Ohio. Thanks to her father, she is a lifelong baseball fan who appreciates the glory and tragedy of America's grand game, especially for Cleveland fans. Not allowed to play Major League Baseball, she often writes about it. This is her fourth baseball-themed publication.

BARB MANTEGANI is a SABR member by heart and a Mayo Smith Society member by marriage, maintaining dual citizenship to both Red Sox and Tigers Nations. She has contributed to two other bio book projects. A tax attorney in real life, she conducts a series of clinics each year to help impoverished Americans fill out their tax forms.

MEL MARMER lives in Philadelphia and works for Weavers Way Co-op. He is a graphic designer who draws chalkboard art signs. He has been a SABR member for nine years and is currently editing a book for SABR about the 1964 Philadelphia Phillies.

RICHARD MARSH has been a SABR member since 2001. He is a lifelong Cleveland Indians fan, residing on the city's west side. Richard works as a teacher in the Cleveland city school district. His favorite Tribe memory is when he saw a Bubba Phillips home run in 1962 lead Cleveland to a win over New York.

JOHN MCMURRAY is Chair of the Society for American Baseball Research's Deadball Era Committee. He contributed to SABR's book Deadball Stars of the American League and is a past chair of SABR's Ritter Award subcommittee, which annually presents an award to the best book on Deadball Era baseball published during the year prior. He has contributed many interview-based player profiles to Baseball Digest in recent years.

JACK MORRIS is a corporate librarian for an environmental engineering company. He lives in East Coventry, Pennsylvania, with his wife and two daughters. He has contributed biographies to several books including The Team That Forever Changed Baseball and America (1947 Brooklyn Dodgers) and Bridging Two Dynasties (1947 New York Yankees). He is not the Jack Morris of World Series fame, though occasionally he wishes he was.

JUSTIN MURPHY is a reporter for the Democrat and Chronicle newspaper in Rochester, New York, his hometown, where a giant stuffed Luke Easter races Cal Ripken Jr. and Joe Altobelli in between innings at Triple-A Red Wings games. He has also contributed biographies to SABR books on the 1959 Chicago White Sox and the 1964 St. Louis Cardinals.

BILL NOWLIN is cofounder of Rounder Records, and author or editor of more than thirty-five books on baseball, most of them about the Boston Red Sox. He has been vice president of SABR for quite a few years now and is an active contributor to BioProject, as well as coeditor of *Can He Play? A Look at Baseball Scouts and Their Profession* and *Red Sox Baseball in the Days of Ike and Elvis*.

CHRIS RAINEY began his SABR career in 1976 when he helped Gene Murdock transcribe audiotapes. He is now retired from thirty-five years as a teacher and coach. He spends his retirement time spoiling his wonderful wife and writing for SABR's BIO Project.

C. PAUL ROGERS III is the coauthor of four baseball books including *The Whiz Kids and the 1950 Pennant* (Temple University Press, 1996), with boyhood hero Robin Roberts, and most recently *Lucky Me: My 65 Years in Baseball* (SMU Press, 2011), with Eddie Robinson (Eddie was the first baseman for the 1948 Indians, the last time the Tribe won the World Series). Paul is president of the Hall-Ruggles (Dallas–Fort Worth) Chapter of SABR, but his real job is as a law professor at Southern Methodist University, where he served as dean of the law school for nine long years.

MATTHEW SILVERMAN is the author of the 2013 book *Swinging '73*. He has also written *New York Mets: The Complete Illustrated History, Mets Essential, 100 Things Mets Fans Should Know and Do before They Die*, and *Best Mets: Fifty Years of Highs and Lows from New York's Most Agonizingly Amazin' Team*. He blogs regularly at metsilverman .com.

CURT SMITH has written fifteen books, many of them on broadcasting, including the classic *Voices of the Game, Pull Up a Chair, A Talk in the Park*, and *Mercy!* A former Gannett writer, *Saturday Evening Post* senior editor, and speechwriter to President George H. W. Bush, Smith is a GateHouse Media columnist, Associated Press award-winning commentator, and Senior Lecturer of English at the University of Rochester. Bob Costas says, "Curt Smith stands up for the beauty of words."

JOHN STAHL lives in suburban Washington DC with his wife, Pam. They have two grown children and two grandchildren. He has written ten SABR individual player biographies. Nine of the biographies appear in four published SABR Team books.

MARK STEWART has authored more than two hundred nonfiction sports books for children and adults, including a 2012 title on the Cleveland Indians for the school and library market. Pieces from his Cleveland Indians memorabilia collection are featured on the Team Spirit "Extra Innings" page: www.teamspiritextras.com.

CORT VITTY is a native of New Jersey and a graduate of Seton Hall University. A lifelong fan of the New York Yankees, he's a SABR member (Bob David's Chapter) since 1999. Vitty's work appeared in *The National Pastime* and *Go-Go to Glory— The 1959 White Sox*. Web articles appear at Seamheads.com and PhiladelphiaAthletics.org. In addition to the Mickey Grasso and Dave Philley essays in this publication, Vitty also authored SABR biographies of Buzz Arlett, Lu Blue, Goose Goslin, Babe Phelps, and Harry "Suitcase" Simpson. Vitty resides in Maryland with his wife, Mary Anne.

JOSEPH WANCHO lives in Westlake, Ohio, and has been a SABR member since 2005. He is a twenty-year veteran at AT&T, serving in different managerial capacities. He serves as the chair on SABR's Minor League Research Committee and